A Life in the
Twentieth Century

Books by Arthur M. Schlesinger, Jr.

ARTHUR M. SCHLESINGER, JR.

A Life

IN THE

Twentieth Century

Innocent Beginnings, 1917–1950

Houghton Mifflin Company

Boston   New York

2000

For information about permission to reproduce selections
from this book, write to Permissions, Houghton Mifflin Company,
215 Park Avenue South, New York, New York 10003.

Visit our Web site: www.houghtonmifflinbooks.com.

Library of Congress Cataloging-in-Publication Data
Schlesinger, Arthur Meier, date.
A life in the twentieth century : innocent beginnings,
1917–1950 / Arthur M. Schlesinger, Jr.
p. cm.
Includes index.
ISBN 0-395-70752-8
1. Schlesinger, Arthur Meier, 1917– 2. Historians —
United States — Biography. I. Title.
E175.5.S38 A3 2000
973.91'092—dc21
[B]   00-061322

Printed in the United States of America

Book design by David Ford

QUM 10 9 8 7 6 5 4 3 2 1

The author is grateful for permission to quote from the following works: "Poor Little Rich Girl" by Noel Coward. © 1925 (renewed) Warner Bros., Inc. All rights reserved. Used by permission of Warner Bros. Publications U.S., Inc., Miami, FL 33014. "Remember My Forgotten Man" by Al Dubin and Harry Warren. © 1933 (renewed) Warner Bros., Inc. All rights reserved. Used by permission of Warner Bros. Publications U.S., Inc., Miami, FL 33014. Three lines from "Where Are the War Poets?" by C. Day Lewis. From *C. Day Lewis: The Complete Poems*, published by Sinclair-Stevenson (1992). Copyright © 1992 in this edition. Reprinted by permission of The Random House Archive & Library and the Estate of C. Day Lewis. "Autumn Journal" by Louis MacNeice, from *Collected Poems*, edited by E. R. Dodds (London: Faber & Faber, 1966). Reprinted by permission of David Hingham Associates. "I'll Be Seeing You." Lyric by Irving Kahal. Music by Sammy Fain. Copyright © 1938 (renewed 1966). All rights in the United States for the extended term administered by Fred Ahlert Music Corporation on behalf of The New Irving Kahal Music Company. All rights in the United States for the extended term administered by Fain Music Company on behalf of Sammy Fain. For the World excluding the United States and excluding 50% of the British Reversionary Territories, Copyright © 1938 (renewed) by Williamson Music. All rights reserved. Reprinted by permission. All rights relating to the interest of Irving Kahal in Canada and the reversionary territories are controlled by Bienstock Publishing Company on behalf of Redwood Music, Ltd. Used by permission. All rights reserved. "The Dying Scholar's Confession" by Geoffrey Strickland. Reprinted by permission of the family of Geoffrey Strickland. This poem first appeared in the *London Review of Books*, vol. 8, no. 3 (www.lrb.co.uk). All rights reserved. "The Second Coming" by W. B. Yeats, from *The Collected Poems of W. B. Yeats*, revised second edition, edited by Richard J. Finneran. Copyright © 1924 by Macmillan Publishing Company, renewed 1952 by Bertha Georgie Yeats. Reprinted with the permission of Scribner, a division of Simon & Schuster, and A. P. Watt, Ltd. on behalf of Michael B. Yeats.

*To my children — and to children the
world over — in the hope that they will do better
with their century than we did with ours.*

The Moving Finger writes; and having writ,
Moves on; nor all thy Piety nor Wit
Shall lure it back to cancel half a Line,
Nor all thy Tears wash out a Word of it.

— OMAR KHAYYÁM

Acknowledgments

I am deeply grateful to four people who cast vigilant eyes on most or all of the manuscript: Roy and Jennifer Jenkins, Barbara Wendell Kerr and Alexandra Emmet Schlesinger. I have much benefited from consultation on particular points with Kate and Hermann Field, Fritz Stern, Carl Schorske, Stuart Hughes, Franklin Ford, Allen Weinstein and John Haynes. William vanden Heuvel has been an inexhaustible source of wise counsel on a variety of matters. I owe much to the thoughtful intervention of Jean Stein and Torsten Wiesel, who, after a fire drove us out of our New York City brownstone, made available an office at Rockefeller University, where the first half of this book was written. I am indebted to Marian Cannon Schlesinger for digging out letters I wrote when overseas during the war. I am also indebted to Megan Desnoyers and Will Johnson, custodians of my papers at the John F. Kennedy Library, for their unstinting assistance. On the Houghton Mifflin front I owe much to Wendy Strothman for astute editorial suggestions, to Eric Chinski for thoughtful editorial management, to Luise Erdmann for exemplary copy editing and to Gordon Brumm for the index.

And to Alexandra, my wife, for her patience, forbearance and support during the throes of composition, my thanks and my love.

ARTHUR M. SCHLESINGER, JR.

Contents

Foreword

I NEVER EXPECTED to write a memoir. But age puts one in a contemplative mood, and the onset of the millennium induces reconsiderations of a traumatic century. I have lived through interesting times and had the luck of knowing some interesting people. And I concluded that if I were ever to do a memoir, I had better do it while I can still remember anything.

This volume covers the first half of the twentieth century — initially through the eyes of my parents, for I didn't make the scene till the century was seventeen years old; thereafter through my own eyes and memories. Of course, little is more treacherous than memory. Can one always distinguish between what one personally remembers and what one is later told? or is led to imagine? Jean Negulesco, the painter and film director, called his memoir *Things I Did . . . and Things I Think I Did.* The generic title for all memoirs should be *Things I Remember . . . and Things I Think I Remember.*

The past is, alas, beyond retrieval. Wordsworth had it right in the Tintern Abbey poem: "I cannot paint / What then I was." And what one becomes reconstructs what one was. Stephen Dedalus muses on June 16, 1904, to the Quaker librarian: "In the future, the sister of the past, I may see myself as I sit here now but by reflection from that which I shall be." One can only draw so much from the murky wells of memory. Autobiography in the end is an interrogation of the past by the present.

It is not always clear, moreover, which counts more in later life — the reality or the recollection. In 1850 Charles Francis Adams took his twelve-year-old son by railway coach and steamboat from Boston to Washington. Sixty years later, in the greatest of American autobiographies, Henry Adams described the journey — at least, he quickly added, the journey as he remembered it: "The actual journey may have been quite different, but the actual journey has no interest for education. The memory was all that mattered." This remains the autobiographer's dilemma.

As a historian, I well know the fallibility of memory. I remember lunching one day with Dean Acheson when he was writing his superb memoir, *Present at the Creation*. He seemed more than usually wrathful. "I had a most disconcerting morning," he said, calling urgently for a dry martini. "I was writing about the decision in 1941 to freeze Japanese assets in the United States" — the decision that, we now know, led the Japanese to attack Pearl Harbor. "I have the most vivid memory of the meeting in President Roosevelt's office. The President was sitting at his desk; Cordell Hull [the secretary of state] was sitting opposite him; I was in a chair by the Secretary's side. I can close my eyes and see the scene," he said, closing his eyes. "But my damned secretary, Miss Evans, checked the record and found that Mr. Hull had the flu and was off in White Sulphur Springs recuperating. He wasn't at the meeting at all. I can't believe it."

Free-wheeling raconteurs — and Acheson was one of the best — improve their tales until telling reorganizes reality. Conscientious memoirists — and Acheson was one of the best — check the record. As a historian, I felt a professional obligation to supplement and rectify memory by recourse to documents. I have tried in effect to write a biography of myself as if I were writing a biography of someone else.

I have diaries and *aides-mémoires* kept intermittently over the long years (how I wish I had kept them more faithfully). My mother, Elizabeth Bancroft Schlesinger, preserved letters and memorabilia going back to my childhood. Both my mother and Marian Cannon Schlesinger, my first wife, saved letters written from overseas during the Second World War. A succession of expert secretaries — Julie Jeppson Ludwig at Harvard in the 1950s, Gretchen Stewart in Washington and New York in the 1960s, Dianne Sikorski, Mary Chifriller, Julia Galea, in later years — maintained orderly files, most of which are now in the John F. Kennedy Library in Boston. I have benefited from the cooperation of other libraries holding papers of people with whom I corresponded. Since I have written about some events in other connections, I have not hesitated on occasion to recycle past recollections for this memoir.

And as a historian I am tempted to widen the focus and interweave the life with the times in some reasonable, melodious and candid balance. Some may find the division into decades arbitrary; indeed, I find such division hard to justify on theoretical grounds. Yet, practically speaking, who can deny that the Twenties in the United States were different from the Thirties or the Fifties from the Sixties? Decades, like generations, often have, or acquire, identities of their own.

For the author, the great enticement of memoirs, I suppose, is the voyage of self-discovery. After all, as Gibbon said in his autobiography, "No one is so well qualified as myself to describe the series of my thoughts and actions." The voyage, however, never reaches its destination. In the end, no one can really know oneself — or anyone else either.

Still, as Mark Twain once wrote to William Dean Howells, "An autobiography is the truest of all books, for while it inevitably consists mainly of extinctions of the truth, shirkings of the truth, partial revealments of the truth, with hardly an instance of plain straight truth, the remorseless truth *is* there, between the lines."

ARTHUR M. SCHLESINGER, JR.

1

Backdrop

MY EARLIEST MEMORIES are of a place where I never lived. Xenia, Ohio, in the 1920s was a town of ten thousand people in rolling green country along the Little Miami River some sixty miles southwest of Columbus, the state capital. My father was born in Xenia, and each summer my parents took my younger brother and me to visit our grandparents there.

The town was founded in 1803 a few months after Ohio became a state. Some wanted to name the settlement for George Washington; others proposed naming it for Mad Anthony Wayne, the local hero who had recently beaten the Indians at the battle of Fallen Timbers in northern Ohio. The debate grew heated. Finally a scholarly looking man stepped forward and said, "In view of the kind and hospitable manner in which I have been treated whilst a stranger to most of you, allow me to suggest the name of *Xenia*, taken from the Greek and signifying hospitality." Xenia won by a single vote. Or so the story goes.

My grandfather arrived in Xenia in 1872. He was born in 1846 in Koenigswalde in East Prussia. In 1860, not yet fourteen, he made the great transatlantic journey west to join an older brother in Newark, New Jersey. His brother was in the leather business, and my grandfather made knapsacks for Union soldiers during the Civil War. After the war, venturing still farther west, he clerked in a store in Springfield, Ohio, before moving to Xenia, a few miles away.

There he fell in love with Katharine Feurle, an Austrian girl from the village of Kennelbach in the Tyrol. In the 1850s her parents had settled in Xenia. Her father ran a tavern for German-speaking travelers, complete with a grapevine-covered beer garden. Kate Feurle's family was Roman Catholic, Bernhard Schlesinger's Jewish; the young people resolved whatever religious dilemma there may have been by turning Protestant and joining the German Reformed Church. There they were married in 1873. He was twenty-seven; she was twenty-three. They had two daughters and two sons before my father was born fifteen years later.

My grandfather died in June 1920, when he was seventy-four years old and I was nearly three. I have no memory of him except faded photographs revealing a bulky, elderly man with a kind face and a discreet mustache. My father described him as courteous, reticent and undemonstrative, the final arbiter in family discussions, terminating an argument by saying very firmly "*Genug*" — that is, "enough" — but seldom speaking otherwise. Generally a tolerant man and himself fond of cigars, he abominated cigarettes and, with a certain prescience, brusquely rebuffed cigarette smokers who asked for a light.

Both grandparents had come to America as children, and acculturation was rapid. Except for the occasional *genug*, little German was spoken in the house; my father certainly acquired no fluency in the language. Bernhard Schlesinger made a modest living as an insurance agent. He was an ardent Democrat. My father was born on February 27, 1888, when Grover Cleveland was preparing to run for a second term, and my grandfather wanted to name the new baby Grover Cleveland Schlesinger. Luckily, my father's sisters intervened and killed the idea, thereby perhaps sparing me the ungainly name of Grover Cleveland Schlesinger, Jr.

My grandfather, largely self-educated, had a profound faith in public education. Regularly elected to the Xenia School Board for more than forty years, often at the head of the ticket, he served for many years as its secretary. The Schlesinger family library — three or four hundred volumes — was one of the largest in Xenia. The daughters, Olga and Marion, were both schoolteachers. In occasional years when the insurance business was bad and their father could not afford the tuition, Olga and Marion helped send their three younger brothers through Ohio State University.

Of the brothers, Hugo, ten years older than my father, became a lawyer. He was by all accounts a bright and attractive young fellow with wide interests, and my father adored him. He entered politics, a Democrat of course, and in 1918 was elected prosecuting attorney of Franklin County, in which Columbus was located. People spoke of Hugo Schlesinger as on his way to the governorship when he suddenly died after an operation in 1920, at the age of forty-two. The next brother, my uncle George, was a jovial man, a civil engineer by profession, who served as Ohio's highway commissioner in the 1920s. His belief in the virtue of brick roads led him to Washington in the 1930s as executive director of the National Paving Brick Association.

Though their political paths diverged, my father was fond of him. He died in 1939 at fifty-five.

*   *   *

My father greatly enjoyed his boyhood. Xenia at the turn of the century was a pleasant community, its streets shaded by elm and maple trees and its houses surrounded by green lawns. It was both a market town and a center for the twine and cordage industry. There were good public schools, thirty thousand volumes in the handsome Carnegie Library, three newspapers, several theaters and a brick opera house with stone trim, a mansard roof and four square towers. Helen Hooven Santmyer's *Ohio Town* (which my father persuaded the Ohio State University Press to publish in 1962) charmingly recalls the Xenia of this era.

Twenty years later Helen Santmyer published a best-selling novel about Xenia, ". . . *And Ladies of the Club*," which redressed the vote of 1803 and changed the town's name to Waynesville, after Mad Anthony. In the novel, Bernhard Schlesinger is very likely the model for Herman Lichtenstein, who becomes president of the school board and wins the battle for a public library; as one character says, "He *believes* in books." Lichtenstein is a bulky man with "a child-like candor, an open friendliness, in the broad face, the clear blue eyes." He is "an insurance agent and a notary public, by which means he earned a sufficient living for his family, if not quite a comfortable one." The Lichtensteins are "scraping by on nothing a year" but "seemed to enjoy life as much as anyone and more than most." Though "partly Jewish," Herman is a Lutheran. Unlike my Democratic grandfather, however, Lichtenstein is a socialist. His oldest son, Rudy, like Hugo Schlesinger, is a lawyer who runs for county prosecutor. His second son, Max, like George Schlesinger, becomes rich and conservative. His youngest son, Franz, like my father when young, is a radical. A Waynesville Anglo-Saxon reflects on the German Americans: "No doubt about it: in their case, the second-generation Americans would achieve professional standing, and some of them very high professional stature."

My father used to regale his children with tales of life in Xenia, some of which he reprinted in his memoir, *In Retrospect: The History of a Historian*. His maternal grandmother had closed down the tavern after her husband's death, and my father and his chums used to play among the tables and benches of the old beer garden. On rainy days they would retreat to the attic with its stacks of *Harper's Weekly*s and

other magazines of Civil War vintage, which, my father guiltily recalled, "to my grief in later years, we used as ammunition in our own
pitched battles."

He told us many stories. When a distillery burst into fire in August
1904 at Trebein, a few miles away, in order to save the building fire-
men diverted stores of raw alcohol into the Miami River. The next
morning, all of Xenia was on hand with bucket and basket to scoop
up the helplessly drunken fish. "This is one fish story I can vouch for,"
he would say.

He fished and swam on summer days and took bobsleigh rides in
winter moonlight. He learned to play the piano by ear but could
never read music and regularly attended the German Reformed Sunday school but did not join the church. He was in the crowd that
greeted William Jennings Bryan at the railroad station in the 1896
campaign; in a small boy's excitement, he got in line again and shook
Bryan's hand a second time. He went to dances in winter at the
Knights of Pythias hall and in summer by swaying trolley to the pavil-
ion by the lake in Neff Park, nine miles away, where a young black fellow and his sister played two-steps on piano and drum.

He saw *Uncle Tom's Cabin* and other popular dramas as an unpaid
usher at the Xenia opera house and, developing an appetite for better fare, went sixteen miles to Dayton by interurban trolley to see New
York stars like Julia Marlowe and George M. Cohan from the topmost
gallery of the Victoria Theater. He attended Buffalo Bill's Wild West
Show when it came to Xenia and, at the age of thirteen, was taken to
the Pan-American Exposition in Buffalo. Shortly afterward, President
McKinley visited the Exposition and Czolgosz shot him. My father
heard the news at a Xenia lawn party. It seemed incredible. The kids
laughed and said the president must have been shot with a camera.
(The Brownie box camera had recently gone on sale; it cost a dollar.)
And my father read, read, read — 598 books, according to the list he
compiled at the age of fourteen.

He was president of his class at Central High School, delivering an
address of welcome, as the *Xenia Gazette* noted on one occasion, "in
his usual easy and pleasing manner." He graduated at the head of the
class with an average of 97.218 (subtractions for poor deportment
brought his record down a point). And he entertained the graduat-
ing class, according to the *Gazette,* "at the spacious home of his parents." Long streamers wound about the hall and the several porches,
one of which held a punch bowl in a bower of yellow and white.

His "remarkable ability as an orator" (again, the *Gazette*) was displayed in his valedictory address, "The Approach of the Dawn." Inspired by Edward Bellamy's *Looking Backward*, he said that uncontrolled competition might be the life of trade but was the death of many who depended on trade; competition brought wages down, exploited women and children and produced shoddy goods. Public ownership of the railroads and other utilities would hasten the dawn of the ideal social state.

His more conservative father, whose political creed consisted largely of an almost religious belief in low tariffs, must have disapproved, "but, characteristically," my father recalled, "he did not say so."

*   *   *

The next year my father went on to Ohio State as a member of the Class of 1910. His sisters were paying for brother George's senior year and had nothing left for the youngest brother. But he had saved enough money as Xenia's sales agent for the *Cincinnati Times-Star* to pay for freshman year. When George graduated, the youngest brother received the sisterly subsidy.

Ohio State was then a smallish institution, far from the behemoth it is today. Excelling as usual in his studies, my father made Phi Beta Kappa and graduated *summa cum laude*. His main extracurricular activity was the *Ohio State Lantern,* the undergraduate weekly. The editorship had been controlled by four fraternities, rotating the post from one to another. Though my father had followed his older brothers into Phi Delta Theta, he was not a passionate Greek. (For an only somewhat heightened account of fraternity high jinks in these years, see George Fitch's once popular Siwash stories; compare and contrast with John Landis's *Animal House.*) His record won him the editorship out of rotation. But when, at the end of his term, he backed a non-fraternity man for the job, the Greeks regained control and the meritorious candidate lost.

Many years later, my father read in a newspaper that Phi Delta Theta's constitution excluded Jews and blacks and that the national convention had reaffirmed the ban over the protests of student delegates. Hitherto unaware of the restrictive clause, he wrote to the alumni president, condemning the ban and submitting his resignation. The president replied that the rules did not permit resignation; he would have to be expelled. "So, to our mutual gratification," my father said, "I returned to the ranks of the unanointed nearly half a century after my initiation."

His fondness for the theater often took him to downtown Columbus, a mile away, to see David Warfield in Belasco's *The Music Master,* Maude Adams in Barrie's *What Every Woman Knows* and, to my father's particular joy, Bert Williams, the celebrated black entertainer. With less regularity he went to hear Washington Gladden at the First Congregational Church, attracted by Gladden's moral force as a preacher of the Social Gospel. "With his great, flowing white beard and noble forehead he looked not unlike Michelangelo's conception of God."

As a land-grant college, Ohio State required two years of military training. Students who failed were obliged to repeat the ROTC course. This penalty, my father said, sufficed to make him a model cadet. James Thurber, '18, "a more rebellious soul," flunked the course and had to keep on drilling throughout his undergraduate life — but thereby gained material for one of his funniest Columbus sketches.

This was the height of the Progressive era. The 1908 election pitted Bryan against William Howard Taft. My father, as he had a dozen years before, thrilled to Bryan's rich, organ-like tones — "the most eloquent, though hardly the profoundest, political orator I have ever heard." President Theodore Roosevelt, who came to Columbus on behalf of Taft, his (rather temporary) protégé, made a less favorable impression. He spoke, my father recalled, in a rasping voice, often rising to the falsetto, and relied excessively on arm-pumping gestures and toothy smiles.

* * *

In his junior year my father met Elizabeth Harriet Bancroft. She was a pretty coed returning to college after two years spent teaching in a one-room country school in order to earn the money to complete her education. Their paths often crossed as they made their way to class. She thought it foolish to continue passing without speaking and, in the manner of a Shavian young woman, finally addressed him. He responded with enthusiasm, much taken by her chestnut brown eyes, alert mind and zest for life. But she had many admirers. He sought to outmaneuver his rivals by making her society editor of the *Lantern.*

Elizabeth Bancroft was born in Columbus in 1886 and was thus two years older than my father. Her own father was a newspaperman named Arthur Bancroft. His family had come from New England in the nineteenth century and old England on the ship *Francis* in 1634. My great-great-great-grandfather David Bancroft lived in Worcester, Massachusetts, where the famed George Bancroft was born, and family tradition has presumed a blood relationship with America's first major historian.

Undated newspaper cuttings in my mother's papers report the expulsion from the Democratic party about 1886 of a certain R. J. Bancroft by a rump group at the end of the Democratic Primary Convention in Batavia, Ohio. "As soon as the hundreds of Democrats on the streets heard of this outrage," said the *Cincinnati Evening Post,* "a burst of indignation followed, and is to-day spreading over the county." Bancroft was described as "the brains of the reform movement," also as a writer of "literary and historical articles for pay." This controversial Bancroft must have been my mother's grandfather.

Arthur Bancroft was evidently a charming man whose irregular newspaperman's habits, especially with regard to hours and to drink, displeased a severe and strong-minded wife. After three children were born, the marriage broke up, leaving my mother faint but abiding memories of a much loved father. In her papers I find a yellowed sheet in his handwriting. He had scrawled an unattributed quotation: "Nothing is so contagious as enthusiasm. It is the real allegory of the tale of Orpheus. It moves stones, charms brutes. Enthusiasm is the genius of sincerity, and truth accomplishes no victory without it." My mother's note to me on the sheet: "Just to show you my father's writing, darling."

My grandmother did not believe in enthusiasm. A formidable, imperious and selfish figure, Clara Bancroft organized a divorce in an age when divorces were traumatic and then, a sternly liberated woman, found employment for herself in the Veterans Bureau, first in Columbus, later in Washington. Clara, my mother's younger sister, showed a certain talent as a painter, and a watercolor sketch of a Venetian canal used to hang in my parents' house. She died in 1903 at the age of fourteen. My mother's brother, Will Bancroft, a tall, slim, blond, urbane man, went on to become a prosperous paper manufacturer in Dayton, Ohio.

In Washington Grandmother Bancroft had a circle of admiring friends. I hold before me a postcard photograph of what appears to be Wilson's second inauguration. A circle is drawn in pencil around a face in the crowd directly behind Wilson. On the back in my grandmother's forceful writing is a message to her sister, Mrs. J. Upton Gribben of Columbus: "If you will get a strong magnifying glass you will see, where the pencil mark is, a face that is a bit like your own. I had a purple veil on."

She somehow acquired a quasi-aristocratic manner. In later years I occasionally visited her in her stiff, claustrophobic apartment at the Ontario, where General Douglas MacArthur (and his mother) had resided during the Great War (as it was known before 1939). I remember her introducing me once to Dr. Joel Boone, an assistant White House physician, a tiny man who had done his best to rescue Warren G. Harding from the misdiagnoses of Harding's pal Dr. Charles Sawyer. During the Second World War she expressed indignation that my younger brother, Tom, should have to serve as "a common foot soldier." She lacked the power to hurt me, and I rather fancied her as a character. But she retained an awful desire to dominate my mother and a capacity to wound her. Telephone conversations with her could reduce my emotional mother to tears and drive my reserved father to anger.

My mother was a liberated woman too, but of a gentler mold. By the time of her graduation from college in 1910 she and my father had reached what was called an understanding. Long engagements were standard in those remote days. The two were, in a way, contrasting figures. My mother was spontaneous and demonstrative. My father was contained, almost to the point, some thought, of austerity. My mother relied on intuition, my father on reason. My mother's forte was enthusiasm, my father's was judgment. My mother overflowed with vulnerabilities; my father had iron self-control. I think I inherited my passion from my mother, my discipline from my father. But their opposite qualities complemented each other. In spite of temperamental differences, they had a strong and loving partnership.

I also owe to my mother something that has proved invaluable all my life: the ability to read fast.

*   *   *

When my father went to Ohio State, his ambition was to become a newspaperman. Besides working as the local agent for the *Cincinnati Times-Star,* he had written for the *Xenia Gazette* and for the Springfield paper. He liked to write, and the dashing example of the popular foreign correspondent Richard Harding Davis filled journalism with excitement and glamour. But Ohio State offered no courses in journalism. My father instead turned to history. He found therein his lifetime vocation.

His voracious reading had prepared him for history. The top author (49 titles) in his fourteen-year-old's list of 598 books was G. A.

Henty, the once famed Victorian writer of historical stories for boys. In the British Army and later as a war correspondent, Henty had seen the Crimean War, Garibaldi and the Risorgimento, the Austro-Italian War, Lord Napier's Abyssinian campaign, the Franco-Prussian War, the Paris Commune, the Ashanti Wars (where he traveled with H. M. Stanley) and the brutal Serbo-Turkish War of 1876.

In his forties Henty turned to writing historical novels. Choosing a *mise-en-scène*, he would read ten relevant books obtained from the London Library and then dictate his stories, sometimes completing a tale of 140,000 words in twenty days (and in his rush sometimes lifting paragraphs from his sources). His *oeuvre* consists of more than a hundred books. His publisher estimated that they sold well over a million copies.

Every Henty book opened with a letter addressed to "My Dear Lads," sketching the historical background of the tale to follow. His heroes were boys of sixteen or so, brave, "manly," and, if at all possible, English, "with a full share of that energy and pluck which," as he wrote in the introduction to *The Lion of St. Mark's*, "more than any other qualities, have made the British empire the greatest the world ever saw."

Though an old-fashioned imperialist, Henty strove for accuracy, certainly in his battle scenes, and, though a hurdy-gurdy writer, he spun a good tale, "it being my object now, as always," he wrote in the introduction to *With Lee in Virginia*, "to amuse as well as to give instruction in the facts of history." His grasp reached from ancient Egypt through the Middle Ages and Renaissance to the Boxer Rebellion. "A man seldom knows just what causes him to choose his life career," my father later wrote, "but I do not doubt that in my case the love of Henty was a formative influence."

His own father also influenced the way my father began to think about history. Once, as a small child, he returned from school and said (as he recalled) with a quaver in his voice, "Daddy, the boys at school say I am not as good an American as they are. They say I can't be because you were born in Europe and their folks have been here hundreds of years." His father laughed reassuringly. "You tell them, son," he said, ". . . that their parents had no choice about coming, but I came because I wanted to — because I thought the United States the best country on earth." My father thereafter began to think of immigrants not as a chosen people but as a choosing people; and he began to appreciate how enormous a decision it was to quit one's native soil for a land of strange ways, alien speech and uncertain fortune.

Their small Ohio town contained not only Anglo-Saxons but large and visible contingents of Germans and Irish. So many blacks lived in Xenia's East End that a local joke described Xenia as the place where the Underground Railroad had broken down. Yet the textbooks my father read in the Xenia schools portrayed Great Britain as the one and only mother country. His father, an admirer of Carl Schurz, observed ironically, "Apparently the only Germans worth mentioning were the Hessians who had fought on the wrong side in the War for Independence."

What was it, my father wondered, that turned diverse peoples flowing in from the corners of the earth into Americans? And he was further puzzled that his schoolbooks omitted any account of the way the American people lived — how they worked, played, loved, ventured, suffered, died. "Though my thoughts were immature and unformulated," he later said, "I could not help feeling there was something wanting in a history that skipped so much that seemed to me so important."

My father was thus responsive early on to the triple challenge of broadening American history beyond its Anglo-Saxon base, of understanding how multifarious newcomers were transformed into Americans and of recovering the past in its social and cultural totality. But American history as taught at Ohio State was strictly Anglo-Saxon, and its coverage was strictly politics, war and diplomacy. He felt frustrated by a conception of history that ruled out the social and cultural factors so potent in the life of a nation, nor could he understand why American history and American literature, two subjects close to his heart, were taught as though they had no connection with each other.

By the time he graduated, he had decided on history as his life's work. With Elizabeth Bancroft's encouragement and strong support from the faculty, he applied for scholarships at Harvard and Columbia. "Mr. Schlesinger has made," Professor G. W. Knight wrote to Professor William A. Dunning of the Columbia history department, ". . . the best record ever made by an undergraduate here. . . . He is clean morally, physically and mentally and is by instinct a gentleman." He won both fellowships and, encouraged by his professors and tempted by New York City, chose Columbia. Had he turned down Columbia, the scholarship would have gone to the alternate, an English applicant named Lewis B. Namier, later to become the great scholar of eighteenth-century Britain.

*　　*　　*

While Elizabeth Bancroft went north to teach history at a high school in Kalamazoo, Michigan, my father spent two exciting years in New York City. They wrote each other constantly and copiously, letters filled with poignant devotion of the sort later to be rendered obsolete by long-distance telephone.

I found reading his letters, carefully preserved by my mother, rather a strange experience. Children rarely associate parents with sexual passion, even though we must know that, without such passion, we wouldn't be here to tell the tale. My father, as noted, was a reserved man. It is startling to read in letter after letter: "I wish we could get married at once and do away with all the waiting. . . . I wish you were here so I could crush you close to me and kiss you and love you as you want to be loved. . . . I hunger for your lips and to take you in my arms. . . . If I could draw you close to me and kiss your dear, wondrous lips I should be absolutely happy." At times he became philosophical: "Love is the principal thing in life — not because it is a thing apart from life, but because it is *the way* of living life. It is the clarifying lens thro' which we see life." One spring Elizabeth came east for a romantic interlude. After she left, he wrote, "I feel as lost and helpless as if an arm or leg had been amputated."

Apart from the agony of separation, the young man from the provinces was thrilled by the great bustling city. He explored it by foot, subway, bus, trolley, horsecar and the elevated railway. A particular friend in Columbia's Livingston Hall was Thomas Reed Powell, a lawyer seeking a degree in political science, later to be the resident constitutional expert and acerbic wit at the Harvard Law School. The young fellows dined at Italian restaurants for twenty-five or thirty-five cents, saw E. H. Sothern and Julia Marlowe in *Macbeth* and *The Taming of the Shrew*, watched Al Jolson and Frank Tinney perform at the Winter Garden and Frank Crumit (an Ohio boy) and Julia Sanderson in musical comedy. They bought season tickets to the opera, where they heard Geraldine Farrar in *La Bohème* and *Madame Butterfly* and Caruso in anything — "he sings," my father wrote to Elizabeth, "with the joy and ease of a bird." He formed an abiding love for Puccini and Wagner (the latter not to be inherited by his son).

With a presidential election impending, 1912 was a grand political year, filled with strong personalities and hot issues. My father, remembering Edward Bellamy, was still interested in socialism, viewing it as an extension of the self-government principle to the economy. He spent an evening with Morris Hillquit, the city's leading Socialist, and another with Upton Sinclair of *The Jungle* and the Helicon Hall community. Sampling other radical sects, he heard Emma Goldman speak at an anarchist rally on the anniversary of Czolgosz's execution. Goldman, he wrote to Elizabeth disapprovingly, eulogized McKinley's murderer. He became ironic: "I had never before realized what a heroic figure he was. She also defended the McNamaras in the Los Angeles dynamite case."

But socialism was a sideshow, even with the appealing Eugene Debs as the Socialist candidate. My father waited for two hours to hear Fighting Bob La Follette, the Progressive Republican from Wisconsin, at an overcrowded Carnegie Hall and was turned away with thousands of others. Later, Theodore Roosevelt led the Progressive bolt from the Grand Old Party and William Howard Taft. My father held Taft in low regard. When a pension bill came to the White House, "I hope he vetoes it," he wrote to Elizabeth, "because I should like to approve of one of his acts while president." But he did not think much better of TR.

His heart remained with Bryan. In the spring the veteran leader spoke at the Columbia chapel, his topic "The Real Issue of 1912." "I couldn't miss him," my father reported, "altho' I have heard him 8 or 10 times. . . . A person could not have a higher ideal than to live a life such as he has, — one of purity, unselfishness, wholehearted devotion to the cause of the people. I hope I may contribute my mite some day." He soon joined the crowd in Times Square watching bulletins from the Democratic convention in Baltimore flash on the *Times* board. "I *couldn't* leave," he wrote to Elizabeth, "until the convention adjourned." When Wilson passed the five hundred mark, "there was a great cheer. I have never read anything so thrilling and so stimulating as Bryan's part" in Wilson's nomination.

Back in Columbus in November my father cast his first presidential vote. As election night returns indicated a Wilson victory, he wrote to Elizabeth in Kalamazoo that the crowds were blowing horns and yelling; "it would be a great night to be on Broadway." He added: "I am inclined to think that this may be my last Dem. national vote, and that next time I shall either be voting Progressive (if anyone but Roosevelt is nominated) or Socialist."

My mother had her own agenda. An enthusiastic suffragist, she prodded him into watching the great women's rights parade on Fifth Avenue in the spring of 1912. He conceded that it was "an impressive spectacle," women walking four and sometimes eight abreast with bands and banners and flags and mottoes in a procession that took an hour and a half to pass. One motto read: "Men bear arms, and women bear men." "I wonder how many women in the parade had borne men," he wrote sarcastically to Elizabeth. Female suffrage did not seem to him an issue of consequence. "What a shame it was to expend such an immense amount of energy on a cause that just pricks the surface of the great social questions. I hope equal suffrage comes quickly so that people may devote their attention to the *real* issues."

He was among the unconverted. "I don't object to your being a suffragette," he told Elizabeth loftily, "as long as you aren't too militant." Of course in time women were bound to get the vote. "Still I think a woman should remain womanly in her struggle for suffrage." Nor would the vote make much difference. "I don't anticipate any better political conditions from a feminine addition to the vote than we have under the present regime." Obviously his consciousness badly needed raising. On the other hand, his last point was not without merit, considering that the first president elected after the enfranchisement of women was Warren G. Harding.

* * *

Nineteen twelve was the exciting year of Wilson's New Freedom and of Roosevelt's New Nationalism. It was also the year of James Harvey Robinson's *The New History,* and for a Columbia graduate student impatient with the old history this book by one of his professors was just as exciting.

"History," as Robinson defined it, "includes every trace and vestige of everything man has done or thought since he appeared on the earth. . . . Its sources of information extend from the rude flint hatchets of Chelles to this morning's newspaper." To write the New History, Robinson continued, historians must draw on "the new allies of history" — anthropology, economics, sociology, political science, geography, psychology. Robinson's lectures were the high point of my father's Columbia years, and the New History formulated notions that had long been churning in his mind, reinforcing his conception of history as "the product of a complexity of forces, governmental and personal . . . social, economic, geographical and religious" (to quote from the preface to his Ph.D. dissertation).

Next to Robinson, my father was most impressed by Charles A. Beard, with his bravado style and his bold emphasis on the impact of economic forces on politics. Beard's iconoclastic — and, to the establishment, shocking — *An Economic Interpretation of the Constitution* came out in 1913. My father hoped to write his dissertation with Beard, but his fellowship required him to work with the colonial historian Herbert L. Osgood.

Osgood, whom my father used to describe as the dullest lecturer and the most thorough scholar he had ever met, represented the orthodox institutional approach to history. However, he directed his students to primary sources, which was stimulating, and he permitted my father to examine a colonial class — the merchants — rather than a colonial institution. My father's dissertation topic — the role of the merchants in the movement for American independence — thus enabled him to combine the research methods of Osgood with the analytic insights of Beard.

In the autumn of 1912, he returned to Ohio State as an instructor in history and political science on a salary of $900 a year. Over the next summers he conducted massive research for his dissertation in archives from Boston to Charleston. In the winters, during intervals permitted by a thirteen-hours-a-week teaching schedule, he wrote chapter after chapter. Both Osgood and Beard applauded the result, and Beard suggested the title: "The Colonial Merchants and the American Revolution."

"Don't say a word in title or text about 'economic interpretation' or 'aspects,'" Beard warned him. ". . . Just gives the mob a chance to yell and to kill you. I know from experience. Fools who never read it will damn it." In another letter he added: "Don't mention my name in your preface. It is a red rag to the historical bull and furthermore might interfere with my doing the review up in proper style." To this my father acceded with reluctance, replying, "I am more indebted to you intellectually than to any man alive." Beard soon proposed that they collaborate on an American history textbook — a project that never materialized but suggests the early affinity between the two historians.

Colonial Merchants was published in 1918. Beard, handsomely fulfilling his promise, called it in the *New Republic* "the most significant contribution that has ever been made to the history of the American Revolution," and the American Historical Association awarded it the Justin Winsor Prize. The book established my father as a comer in the profession. At one AHA convention in these years, he had the singular pleasure of introducing Beard and the other influential American historian of the time, Frederick Jackson Turner, to each other; they had never met before.

*   *   *

The New History did not appeal to Ohio State's traditionalist department. My father had to wait for seven years before he lectured on social history. Finally, in the summer session of 1919, he was allowed to offer a course entitled "Some Revisions of American History."

Despite such frustrations, he enjoyed his new life. When early on his salary was raised to $1200, marriage became at last an economic possibility. On September 5, 1914, Elizabeth Bancroft and Arthur Schlesinger were wed in the study of a Congregational minister; they honeymooned in Atlantic City. When they returned at the start of the new academic year, my father had less than a dollar in his pocket. In time, they settled in a house at 398 West Ninth Avenue in Columbus.

My father liked his colleagues, especially the political scientist Francis W. Coker and the historian Homer C. Hockett, with whom he later wrote a highly successful college textbook along the lines he had once contemplated with Beard. Ludwig Lewisohn in the German department brought a disorderly but engaging flavor of Bohemia into bourgeois Columbus. Lewisohn's memoir, *Up Stream,* later denounced the city and the university in unbridled terms.

My father was an effective but tough instructor. Stories abounded regarding his classroom technique. During one final examination, the *Lantern* reported in 1916, a student asked whether he could answer part A of one question and part B of another. "This is no à la carte exam" was the crisp reply. The *Lantern* headlined the item "Table d'Hôte."

Among his students, my father found particular pleasure in two free spirits, James Thurber and Elliott Nugent. In a 1959 interview Thurber said, "I remember, on the last day of a history class at Ohio State in 1914, after the bell had rung, Professor Arthur Schlesinger, Sr. — the old man — saying, 'Mr. Spencer, who is President of the United States?' Mr. Spencer said, 'Woodrow Wilson.' Professor Schlesinger said, 'Thank you! I was determined that you get one question right this year.'" Thus reminded of his errant past, my father deplored the tendency of young instructors to indulge in sarcasm.

After my parents moved on to Harvard, both Thurber and Nugent paid calls when they passed through Boston. I have only dim recollections of Thurber, but I well recall his wife, Althea. She resembled the overpowering women in her husband's drawings and would complain to my parents, before and after their divorce in 1935, about Jim's bad temper and his drinking as if his old professor might still have some influence on him.

Nugent was a more frequent visitor. He was an engaging man of diffident charm, and I owe to him the weakness for people of the theater that I have had ever since. I had no idea, however, when he politely sipped tea with my parents, of the inner torments that would drive him, like Thurber, to drink and, in time, to acute depression, to insulin shock treatments, and to confinement in mental hospitals — wryly described in his 1965 autobiography, *Events Leading Up to the Comedy.*

Nugent was a delightful actor in both theater and film; he was especially memorable playing opposite Margaret Sullavan in John Van Druten's *The Voice of the Turtle* on Broadway. He was also a film director, most successful in handling lighthearted comedy with players like Harold Lloyd, Bing Crosby, Bob Hope and Danny Kaye. His version of *The Great Gatsby* with Alan Ladd and Betty Field had an interesting feel for the Fitzgeraldian Twenties. He also wrote a novel, *Of Cheat and Charmer,* and co-authored several plays.

And most famously, of course, Nugent and Thurber together wrote their half-nostalgic, half-satiric valentine to Ohio State, *The Male Animal.* The types are familiar — the idealistic English professor who insists on reading a Bartolomeo Vanzetti statement to his class as an example of beautiful writing by an uneducated man; the red-hunting trustee who regards this act as subversive; the star halfback returning as a revered alumnus for the homecoming game; the professor's wife who was once courted by and is still attracted to the halfback; the radical student determined to expose assaults on academic freedom. Nugent himself played the professor on the stage and directed Henry Fonda in the movie. *The Male Animal* is stereotypical in characterization, but it has witty lines and ingenious situations and remains a winning picture of life in a midwestern state university.

*　　*　　*

My father kept up his interest in politics. Wilson turned out to be more of a fighter and reformer than he had expected, but he still flirted with democratic socialism. Those Socialist missionaries John Spargo and Rose Pastor Stokes stayed with the young Schlesingers when they carried the gospel to Ohio State's Intercollegiate Socialist Society. (Democratic socialism was even then an unstable compromise. In another decade Spargo was a Republican, Stokes a Communist.)

War broke out in Europe five weeks before my parents were married. My father grew increasingly impatient with Wilson's neutrality policy but was even more dismayed by the rush of pro-German support to Charles Evans Hughes, the Republican candidate in 1916. Despite the Democratic "he kept us out of war" campaign, my father voted for Wilson a second time. My grandfather, with a sentimental attachment to the *Vaterland,* was for a time among the pro-Germans, but when the United States entered the war in April 1917, he stood with the land of his children against the land of his forefathers, saying, with customary economy, "It is now our fight."

One student, Thelma Paquette Pryce, recalled that my father would begin his lectures each morning with a résumé of the news from Europe: "We could tell by his face when we walked in whether the Allies were winning." He proposed to Governor James M. Cox that a concerted effort be made to document Ohio's participation in the war. In February 1918 Cox appointed him chairman of the Ohio Historical Commission, and he set up county branches to collect printed, manuscript and pictorial materials that would otherwise be lost to posterity.

In June 1918 he returned to Central High School in Xenia to give a commencement address, "The Old Order Changeth." According to a religious cult, he said, the war meant the end of the world. At first, he continued, he had smiled at "this strange conceit until I began to think that, after all, these people were, in a sense, right. The world as we have known it is coming to an end." The war was creating the opportunity for a brave new world. It will be "a world of women as well as men"; marriage was beginning to raise his consciousness. Organized labor will eliminate autocracy from industry. Public ownership will increasingly replace private profit. The republic would breathe a new spirit of internationalism on behalf of world democracy.

He was now sharply critical of the Socialist party for its opposition to the war. It had tarred itself, he wrote, with "copperheadism" and, in addition, was "medieval" in its discipline. He congratulated John Spargo for leaving it. "The times call imperiously," he added, "for the marshaling of the liberals of the country for the purpose of making the war an instrument for the purpose of social justice and public ownership."

But he was also disturbed by the angry emotions let loose by war — the attack on the German language (Henry Reuss, a distinguished congressman, once told me that in the anti-German zeal of the day Schlesingerville, in Washington County, Wisconsin, became — and remains to this day — Slinger) and more particularly Attorney General A. Mitchell Palmer and his Red Scare. The crusade for democracy abroad threatened to be undercut by the assault on democracy at home. "I believe," he wrote, "that the liberal forces of the country are ripe for the formation of a party which, holding the Socialist commonwealth as its goal, would bring an enlightened and fearless opportunism to the solution of public questions and which will permit and encourage freedom of opinion and speech within its own ranks. Many of us are awaiting an opportunity to cooperate with such a movement."

In October 1918, Spargo invited my father to a meeting of disaffected liberals in Chicago seeking a new political alignment. The resulting Committee of Forty-Eight (for the forty-eight states then in the Union) proposed a new Radical party to stand midway between the Wilson Democrats and the Socialists. In the spring of 1919 my father actively promoted the idea in speeches to church and labor groups in Ohio.

He was not universally applauded. "The effrontery of it!" wrote one Columbus newspaper. "A member of the faculty of Ohio State University uttering Bolshevik propaganda in the pulpit of an Episcopal church in Columbus on Sunday!" The *Columbus Labor News,* noting that the university was a state institution, hoped to hear "of this un-American being summarily fired."

The authorities took no action, but the speeches upset Ohio State's president. Then, in the midst of the clamor, the University of Iowa offered my father the chairmanship of the history department with a salary increase to $3500 and the assurance that he could teach any courses he chose. Ohio State, perhaps relieved to get rid of a potential problem, gave him high recommendations. "It did not mar my pleasure in accepting," he later wrote, "to suspect I was being kicked upstairs." And in the longer run the failure of the Committee of Forty-Eight left my father with an abiding skepticism about third parties.

In the meantime, my parents had started a family. Their first child, Katharine, was born on September 27, 1915. To their everlasting sorrow, she died of an intestinal ailment ten months later. It was a terrible blow for the young couple. Many years later Saul Benison, interviewing my father for the Columbia Oral History Research Office, asked about Katharine's death and mentioned a moving letter of condolence from Washington Gladden. My father, Benison recalls, looked puzzled, asked for the letter, read it, was silent for a long moment, then said, "I've driven all of that out of my mind."

I was born on October 15, 1917, and named Arthur Bancroft Schlesinger. The headline in that day's *Ohio State Journal* was: WILSON

CALLS ON NATION TO AID NEW LOAN . . . MUST WIN WAR. . . . Asserts All Persons Should Show the Enemy Countries America Means to Be Victorious. In the *New York Times* (which in 1917 cost one cent in the city and three cents elsewhere), John Philip Sousa led the Navy band in a concert at the Hippodrome and Theda Bara opened in *Cleopatra* ("With Much Rolling of the Eyes She Portrays 'the Siren of All Ages'"). In the *New York Sun,* Harry Lauder entertained the troops on Governors Island, Saks advertised a sale of men's hats at $1.95 and men's shoes at $5.95, Thurlow Weed's grandson denounced the direct primary, and Morris Hillquit assailed the attorney general's ban of the Socialist paper *The Call* at an overflow mass meeting in Madison Square Garden, after which thousands marched up Fifth Avenue shouting, "Down with capitalism! Down with the plutocrats! Down with Morgan and Rockefeller!" In Paris, Mata Hari was executed as a German spy. The brave new postwar world had mixed auguries.

PART I

The Twenties

2

East from Iowa

I HAVE NO CHILDHOOD MEMORIES of Columbus, a city I left at the age of two. I do remember Iowa City, where I lived between the ages of two and six. Once the capital of Iowa Territory, Iowa City lost out to Des Moines when the territory became a state. By the time the Schlesingers arrived, Iowa City had settled into an agreeable midwestern university town. It had about the population of Xenia, and it looked rather like Xenia, with its frame houses, green lawns, white picket fences and drowsy streets shaded by elm and oak.

In 1980, when I was doing research at the Herbert Hoover Library nearby in West Branch, I drove over to Iowa City on a mild April evening. Iowa City was half a dozen times larger and far more bustling than the quiet little town I had known sixty years earlier. As I strolled about, my memory was jogged by the gray stone building in the middle of the university campus, a quasi-classical structure of the 1840s with Doric columns by the entrance and Corinthian columns supporting the dome. It had been the capitol in Iowa City's days of territorial glory; subsequently the university had taken it over. I suddenly remembered how often I had walked by it so many years before, holding tightly to my father's hand.

Returning to my rented car, I found myself mysteriously propelled, without asking directions, to 427 South Johnson Street, where we lived in the early 1920s. The rickety house had long since been torn down, and an apartment building now stood in its place. I thought for a moment of our beloved collie, Max, run over by a careless motorist on South Johnson Street, and of his successor, a small brown dog of indeterminate breed named Brownie. I thought of the time I was tangled up in Max's leash, tripped, fell, bit through my tongue (which in those days was generally sticking out of my mouth), bled copiously and was rushed to the hospital where the tongue was efficiently sewn up with, I was told, kangaroo fiber.

The university ran an experimental 'preschool laboratory' for the Iowa Child Welfare Research Station under the direction of Bird T.

Baldwin. According to a monograph published seventy years later (Hamilton Cravens, *Before Head Start: The Iowa Station and America's Children*), it was the first institute in the world "whose sole purpose was to conduct original scientific research on the development of normal children." I survived the experience without undue damage.

My parents had no automobile, but friends did, and one day — or do I imagine this? — I was being driven along the Mississippi River when before my dazzled eyes there suddenly appeared *two* gleaming, white and gold paddlewheel steamboats, one after the other. Whether this really happened or not, I certainly loved to make drawings of two steamboats in the preschool laboratory. As Henry Adams said, the memory is all that matters.

*   *   *

But my vivid memory is not of Iowa City but of Xenia, no doubt because Xenia was where the Schlesingers came from and where we continued to go each summer. My grandmother's two sisters lived in Xenia — her brother John, a professional gambler and a friend of Whitelaw Reid, another local boy who became publisher of the *New York Tribune,* had departed for more exotic places — and so did a dozen cousins of my father's generation and as many of mine. Holidays produced convivial family reunions. The Arthur Schlesingers could not make Xenia for Christmas and New Year's Eve, but our summer visits were generally timed to coincide with the Fourth of July.

The great day would begin with a salvo of firecrackers and the bang of 'torpedoes,' small round objects encased in tissue paper with caps that blasted off when thrown down hard on the sidewalk. In those dissolute times, fireworks, except for the most obviously lethal (like four-inch salutes), could be bought anywhere. Today in my state of New York lighting a sparkler — a sparkler? — is, George Plimpton, New York City's unpaid commissioner of fireworks, tells me, a punishable offense. I suppose the abolition of individual fireworks is sensible. But what fun July 4 was for small boys seventy-five years ago!

At noon came the parade, rendered notable for me by the appearance of Civil War veterans, members of the Grand Army of the Republic, shuffling proudly along in the procession. After all, we were much closer then to Appomattox — only sixty years away — than to the day, seventy-five years later, on which I write these words. A Union soldier who, like Stephen Crane's Henry Fleming, might have been eighteen at the Battle of Chancellorsville would have been only seventy-eight in 1923. Indeed, as late as 1982 the Veterans Administration was still sending out pension checks to fifty Civil War widows. In July 1997 two Civil War widows laid roses on the tomb of an unknown soldier killed at Gettysburg. Never forget the brevity of American history.

In Xenia the grand climax of the glorious Fourth came after sunset. The Schlesinger house stood high above South Detroit Street, its wide green lawn rolling down to a steep stone parapet overlooking the street. Tables were set out on the lawn; older folk sat about in chairs; kids chased fireflies ("lightning bugs," we called them) or squatted on the stone wall waiting for the fireworks. When darkness fell, my uncles and cousins put on the big show — Roman candles, pinwheels, sky rockets, bombs bursting in air. When the pyrotechnics finished, saucers of ice cream were offered to young and old. It was a noble occasion.

My grandmother was a small, faded, gentle lady, lacking her husband's intellectual bent, my father thought, and given to worrying over trifles. He felt closer to Elizabeth Bauser, the housekeeper, who had come from the neighboring village of Old Town at the age of eleven to help out when Olga was born and had never left. By the time I knew her, Lizzie was a sharp, wrinkled, resourceful and humorous woman in her sixties who did most of the work in the house. I would watch with astonishment when she beheaded a chicken, the decapitated creature then running around the yard in circles till it dropped. Lizzie had long since become a member de facto of the family, eating with us at the dinner table and joining the talk in the living room afterward. Though she outlived my grandmother by twenty years, the family tie endured, and Lizzie quite rightly lies today in the Schlesinger lot in the Xenia cemetery.

*　*　*

These were the years when the Ku Klux Klan invaded the north on its mission to save the republic from Catholics, Jews, blacks, Bolsheviks, foreigners and associated menaces. Ohio was less hospitable than Indiana, where the Klan came close to taking over the state; but one day Lizzie darkly informed me that the man who lived across the alley behind the Schlesinger house was a Klansman. I was not at all sure what the Klan was but gathered it was something sinister, and I used to peer anxiously down the alley, expecting the worst.

My grandmother, much agitated when our shoemaker joined the Klan, went at once to inform him that he could expect no more business from her. As my cousin Cecilia Baldner Taylor remembers the story, Grandmother then rushed over to tell her sister Rosina Bloom of this outrage but found only Rosina's son Karl at home. When she announced that she, the family joiner, would never join the Klan, my jovial uncle Karl replied, "Aunt Kate, having been born in Austria, baptized a Catholic, and married to a Prussian Jew, I think your chances of joining the KKK are very slight."

The circus came to Xenia in the summer, complete with the old-fashioned sideshow — the sword swallower, the fire eater, the snake charmer, the living skeleton, the tattooed man, the bearded lady, the alligator girl, giants and midgets, assorted freaks and other politically incorrect phenomena. Tod Browning's film of 1932, *Freaks,* gives the flavor. I have no doubt that the abolition of freak shows is a gain for civilization, but I am bound to confess that the small boy found the sideshow fascinating. In Xenia, too, I saw my first opera. It was *Faust,* and, as I remember, I saw it not in the opera house but in some sort of outdoor staging.

My father's sister Marion was teaching in Dayton, where she had married a high school administrator named Samuel Heitz. One day in July 1925 Aunt Marion and Uncle Sam took me for an automobile trip to see the Great Serpent Mound on Brush Creek in Adams County. I was liable to carsickness and threw up repeatedly during the ride. But the mystery of the Moundbuilders overcame nausea. I gazed awestruck at the great mound, a twisting earthen snake rising nearly ninety feet into the air, built by ancestors of the Indians centuries before Columbus. "It was covered with grass," I wrote excitedly to my parents. "*It belonged to Harvard but the state of Ohio bought it.*" This was roughly true. Frederic Putnam, an early American anthropologist, bought the site for Harvard's Peabody Museum to protect it from erosion and vandalism; later, Harvard donated it to the state of Ohio. "It used to be higher," I continued, "but the rain and wind tore it down. . . . Maybe they prayed to it — know [sic] one knows."

Who had built the Serpent Mound? Where had they come from? What had happened to them? I heard the range of speculations: perhaps the Mound Builders had been driven north from Mexico; perhaps they were intrepid Celtic or even Phoenician voyagers; perhaps, religious people said, they were the Lost Tribes of Israel. In any event, the magic of history was working its enchantments.

My grandmother died in December 1927, and our visits to Xenia became infrequent. Half a century later, after Xenia had been celebrated by Helen Hooven Santmyer and devastated by the tornado of 1974, I returned and took a fresh look at the Schlesinger homestead on South Detroit Street, now an apartment house. Xenia had changed a good deal less than Iowa City. The Schlesinger relatives had mostly died or left for more stimulating places, but the quiet midwestern town was still there, almost a historical artifact.

No doubt Xenia had its dark side, the side explored in the anti–small town literature of the Twenties, Winesburg and Spoon River and Gopher Prairie, but I was too young to detect coercive pressures and broken lives. When I think of Xenia, I recall rather that most evocative of American sounds, so rarely heard anymore — the sound of the train whistle, conjuring up in its lonesome wail feelings of distance, of longing, of regret, of the journey home.

The committee of historians that prepared my father's Harvard obituary called the Xenia of his youth a pure expression of what midwestern writers liked to idealize as "the valley of democracy." This still seemed roughly true in the 1920s. Xenia taught me much about the benign aspects of middle-class, middle western America, and I count myself lucky for this early immersion in Norman Rockwell–Andy Hardy country.

*   *   *

My father's translation to Iowa City was a consequence of the drive by Walter A. Jessup, the University of Iowa's new and ambitious president, to build a first-class institution. To do this, Jessup needed the support of the conservative state legislature, and he rather skillfully navigated the tricky waters between academic freedom in Iowa City and legislative primitivism in Des Moines.

Thus when one lawmaker complained about my father's association with the Committee of Forty-Eight, Jessup was relieved to learn that my father had dropped out. When my father edited a booklet for the history department called "Great Charters of Americanism" and dared include the Covenant of the League of Nations, Iowa isolationists — and they were much in the majority — raised a storm of protest. In retrospect, my father agreed that inclusion was premature since the Senate in Washington was still arguing about America's membership in the League. Jessup suspended distribution of the pamphlet but refused to delete the Covenant until the Senate itself had voted it down.

Upton Sinclair, collecting material for his book *The Goose-Step*, about the domination of American universities by capitalists and religious zealots, asked my father about Jessup. My father replied, "Since his main job is to get funds from the state legislature, he does not propose to allow the indiscretions of a professor to damage the cause of the University. . . . He would even protect a professor from outside criticism, up to a certain point. But if appropriations are involved, then his allegiance is to the appropriation. But in justice to the president I must add that no alleged radical has been dismissed from the faculty."

Jessup had indeed assembled a lively young faculty, most of whom in time were lured away by more established institutions. The most challenging intellect my father encountered was the economist Frank Knight, now mainly remembered, alas, as a founder of the Chicago school of laissez-faire doctrinaires but with a far more original and unfettered mind than his epigones. Other friends were the Shakespearean scholar Hardin Craig, later of Stanford, and Herbert F. Goodrich, later dean of the University of Pennsylvania Law School and a distinguished federal judge. And he recruited for the history department bright younger scholars like Raymond J. Sontag, later of the University of California, and Ralph E. Turner, later of Yale.

The faculty, to my parents' surprise, gave elaborate black-tie parties. This was the first year of prohibition, but Iowa had long been a dry state, so no one seemed to miss drinks before dinner. Eminent foreign visitors were made much of. One of them, A. Percival Newton of the University of London, incensed the locals by his rudeness. At a dinner party my parents gave in his honor, Newton declined to shake hands with the guests, informing them that this was not the English custom. He regarded himself as a social lion, and my father was reminded of the remark of a Boston hostess about a more eminent English scholar, E. A. Freeman, that the lion was in truth the king of beasts.

The genial historian J. Holland Rose of Cambridge University made a far better impression. He stayed in our jerry-built house, and my parents discovered with chagrin that he had stuffed the rattling window frames with newspapers in order to get to sleep. He did not complain. One morning my father (as I remember him telling the story) found Rose looking at newspaper reports of the Scopes case in Dayton, Tennessee, where Clarence Darrow and William Jennings Bryan were debating Darwin versus creationism. Rose read aloud in an incredulous voice an account of Bryan holding forth before the jury with his thumbs in his suspenders. "How could this be?" he asked. A perplexing conversation followed until it emerged that what the British call suspenders are what Americans call garters — devices used in those ancient days to hold up one's socks.

But this episode could not have happened in Iowa City. The "monkey trial" took place in 1925, by which time the Schlesingers had gone east. I must misremember: probably the incident happened in Cambridge and to some other visiting English scholar. But the story is too good to be omitted.

The university had its share of eccentrics — the little chemistry professor who was dominated by a large masculine wife and, after her death, proceeded to marry a deaf-and-dumb woman; the absentminded psychology professor who, taking off his clothes to put on his dinner jacket, put his pajamas on instead and went off to bed. One of the older members of the history department used to threaten to kill himself when his wishes were denied "until," my father recalled, "at last I suggested he do as he thought best."

My parents made warm friends in the town as well. My father was even elected to the Iowa City Lions Club, a booster organization straight out of Sinclair Lewis, and he used to entertain his children (my brother, Thomas Bancroft, was born in Iowa City in 1922) and later his grandchildren by emitting the Lions roar that traditionally opened the weekly luncheons.

*   *   *

Free at last to promote the New History, my father offered a course called "New Viewpoints in American History" and, after that course became a book, another, "The Social and Cultural History of the United States" — the first of its sort in any university. He delivered papers at conventions of the American Historical Association. One on the American Revolution impressed a promising Harvard historian of his own age. The paper, Samuel Eliot Morison later wrote, "showed so much original thought, expressed with such verve and humor, that I promptly introduced myself, and in the few uninterrupted conversations possible in that session, we became friends."

In April 1922 Macmillan published *New Viewpoints in American History.* Years later a considerate friend sent me a copy he had picked up in a secondhand bookstore — worn and annotated with a bookplate displaying a clipper ship in full sail and bearing the inscription "Ex Libris Samuel Eliot Morison."

New Viewpoints employed a literary technique underused in American historiography. Morison had pasted in the back of his copy a review written for the *Political Science Quarterly* by David Saville Muzzey, a senior historian of the day. "In one form of historical writing," Muzzey wrote, "we [Americans] have been sadly deficient. The interpretative essay, dealing in suggestive summary with persistent influences or changing ideals through successive generations, has found few authors in our country to set beside the name of the Guizots, the Actons and the Freytags of Europe." Muzzey concluded that "these illuminating essays . . . will bear reading and re-reading before either the charm of their presentation or the profit of their contents is exhausted."

The book's longest essay was "The Role of Women in American History." My mother had raised my father's consciousness considerably since his dismissive remarks a decade before about the women's suffrage parade on Fifth Avenue (which is why the Women's Archives my father helped found at Radcliffe College in 1944 is now properly called the Arthur and Elizabeth Schlesinger Library on the History of Women in America). "If the silence of historians is taken to mean anything," the essay began, "it would appear that one-half of our population have been negligible factors in our country's history." But that silence meant little, my father observed, for "all of our great historians have been men and were likely therefore to be influenced by a *sex* interpretation of history all the more potent because unconscious."

The piece emphasized the bitter quest of American women for freedom and equality — a novel point for a male historian to make in 1922. It ended with the optimistic prediction that women were on the threshold of a new era. They would no longer figure in the American story, my father thought, only as "represented by men to whom they 'belong' in some relation. They are directly responsible for their choices and decisions and are placed in a position to increase immeasurably their contributions to American development." Of all the new viewpoints of 1922, the triumph of women and their history would, I believe, have pleased him most.

"The Influence of Immigration on American History" expressed an older preoccupation. "Whatever of history may be made in the future," he wrote, ". . . will not be the result primarily of an 'Anglo-Saxon heritage' but will be the product of the interaction of these more recent racial elements upon each other and their joint reaction to the American scene." Here again he helped legitimate a rich new field of scholarship. Colleagues like Marcus Lee Hansen, whose manuscripts on the history of immigration my father prepared for publication after their author's premature death, and students like

Oscar Handlin, in books of their own, vindicated the significance he gave to what later generations called multiculturalism as a primary force in the remaking of American nationality.

The United States had been from birth a multicultural society, and my father and his generation saw multiculturalism as a stage in the absorption of newcomers into an American nationality and culture that they remolded as they entered. Acculturation seemed to them both inevitable and desirable. They believed in *unum* as well as *pluribus*. By the Nineties, however, multiculturalism, at least in some hands, developed an ideology and mystique of its own. Ideologues saw ethnicity as *the* defining experience for Americans. Division into ethnic communities, they believed, established the basic structure of American society and the basic meaning of American history. They favored the retention and promotion of ancestral cultures and the perpetuation of separate ethnic and racial communities. Multiculturalism in this militant version rejected the concept of a common culture and of a single American nationality.

My father's perception was very different. He demanded recognition for the role of non-Anglo-Saxons in forging the national identity. But he also gave equal time to the process by which newcomers transcended their origins, became Americans and in the process enriched and modified the Anglo-Saxon heritage. This was the view set forth in his 1942 presidential address to the American Historical Association, entitled, after Hector St. John de Crèvecoeur's celebrated question (celebrated at least among American historians), "What Then Is the American, This New Man?"

A Frenchman who had come to the American colonies in the 1750s, married an American woman and settled on a farm in upstate New York, Crèvecoeur published his *Letters from an American Farmer* during the Revolution. Herein he gave the classic answer to his own question: "*He* is an American who, leaving behind him all his ancient prejudices and manners, receives new ones from the new mode of life he has embraced, the new government he obeys, and the new rank he holds. . . . Here individuals of all nations are melted into a new race of men, whose labours and posterity will one day cause great changes in the world." The American identity, as my father saw it, was forever in the making, but he had no doubt that there was an American identity.

His essay hardly mentioned black Americans. My father soon came to notice this omission himself. A decade later he was a member of the board of editors of the *Journal of Negro History* as well as the last white member of the council of the Association for the Study of Negro Life and History and an "ardent supporter" (as the *Journal* put it after his death) of its director, the black historian Carter G. Woodson. He welcomed young black historians like John Hope Franklin and Alrutheus A. Taylor to Harvard; Franklin in later years recalled him as his mentor. Still, for all his support of black Americans in their struggle for equal rights, that struggle was never a major theme in my father's historical work.

A similar gap between public and scholarly concerns occurred with the American Indians. He expended much time and concern as a member of the Commission on the Rights, Liberties and Responsibilities of the American Indian set up by the Fund for the Republic in 1957; but the red man (and woman) entered little into his historical writing.

*   *   *

Seventy years after *New Viewpoints,* I tried to strike the same balance between multiculturalism and acculturation in a controversial tract entitled *The Disuniting of America.* This was not the only case in which I found myself reprising themes from *New Viewpoints.* The literary form that my father used and Muzzey praised — interpretative essays musing on central aspects of the national experience — is one to which I naturally turn, as in *The Cycles of American History.* The cyclical hypothesis itself I inherited from my father, though his analysis of the recurrent rhythms of American politics was only foreshadowed in *New Viewpoints.* While he noted there that "epochs of radicalism and conservatism have followed each other in alternating order," the hypothesis awaited his influential *Yale Review* essay of 1939, "Tides of American Politics," for its mature formulation.

The cyclical perspective rests on generational analysis, an approach to history whose vogue I attributed in *Cycles* to the transatlantic sages Ortega y Gasset and Karl Mannheim, altogether forgetting that my father had discussed it in *New Viewpoints.* I was surprised, too, on rereading *New Viewpoints,* to discover that the idea of the accelerating pace of social change, the mounting velocity of history — an idea that I thought I had picked up from Henry Adams and that is fundamental to an understanding of modernity — is there in the essay "The Foundations of the Modern Era."

And of course a major thesis of *The Age of Jackson* — that Jacksonian democracy, traditionally regarded as a breakout from the wild frontier, had vital eastern origins — was elegantly set forth in his essay

"The Significance of Jacksonian Democracy." "The revolt of [urban] labor against . . . hard conditions of life," my father wrote, "formed an integral part of the democratic upheaval of Jackson's time," and he described too the interplay between political and literary ferment in that turbulent age.

His advocacy of social and cultural history did not lead him to minimize the role of politics. In "The State Rights Fetish" he demonstrated that state rights doctrine had been historically a convenient political weapon rather than an immaculate constitutional principle. Our most notable leaders, he showed, had flipflopped on state rights without compunction or a backward look.

So at the Constitutional Convention James Madison proposed a national veto on state legislation. A decade later, he joined with Jefferson in the Kentucky and Virginia Resolutions defending state nullification of federal law. Federalists responded in the 1790s with a righteous denunciation of the state rights heresy. Fifteen years later, after Mr. Jefferson's embargo and Mr. Madison's war, Federalist leaders themselves unfurled the state rights banner at the Hartford Convention. Daniel Webster began as a state righter and, when New England shifted its economic base from trade to industry, became the great advocate of nationalism. John C. Calhoun began as a nationalist and, when South Carolina grew dependent on exports and slavery, became the great theologian of state rights. In the twentieth century, Democrats and Republicans have traded places on state rights as the changing interests of their constituents dictated.

"The group advocating state rights at any period," my father concluded, "has sought its shelter in much the same spirit that a western pioneer seeks his storm-cellar when a tornado is raging." Political parties in his view were destined by their nature to revise their principles in order to keep their constituents. "American parties," he later wrote, "have been symbolized by such animals as the elephant and the donkey, but not by the leopard, which never changes its spots."

To take a less cosmic question, the decline in voter turnout in presidential elections, a phenomenon much discussed today and one I considered at length in *Cycles,* was identified long before in *New Viewpoints.* "This tendency," my father wrote, "has been most marked since the McKinley-Bryan campaign of 1896; and its lowest point was reached in the last presidential election (1920) when about half of the citizens entitled to vote went to the polls." In 1924 he co-authored a piece for the *New Republic* entitled "The Vanishing Voter." I found that, like my father before me, though with some difference in argument, I ascribe the decline to the decay of the political party as an agency of voter mobilization.

New Viewpoints offered clues to his own creed. "The thinking conservative," he wrote in one passage,

> finds his chief allies in the self-complacency of comfortable mediocrity, in the apathy and stupidity of the toil-worn multitudes, and in the aggressive self-interest of the privileged classes. All those who dread uncertainty either because of timidity or from conventional-mindedness or for fear of material loss are enlisted under the conservative standard.
>
> The honest radical draws much of his support from self-seeking demagogues and reckless experimenters, from people who want the world changed because they cannot get along in it as it is, from *poseurs* and *dilettanti,* and from malcontents who love disturbance for its own sake. The two schools have more in common than either would admit; both have their doctrinaires and dogmatists; both tend toward a stiffening of intellectual creeds.

Reading these words, Sam Morison took up his pencil, drew a black line down the margin of the page and wrote "*très bien.*" In 1923 Morison, soon to depart for Oxford as the first Harmsworth Professor of American History (hence his famous *Oxford History of the United States*), urged Harvard to invite my father to take his place for a year as visiting professor. Frederick Jackson Turner and Edward Channing, the senior American historians, backed the proposal. So, after five years in Iowa City, the Schlesinger family set out for what we all supposed would be a year in Cambridge, Massachusetts.

In May 1924 the Iowa City Lions Club sent out an invitation: "COME OUT AND HEAR ART ROAR. . . . No other club has Art's talent in this line. . . . Art will be back in a year."

*　　*　　*

I was on the brink of my seventh birthday when we settled in a rented house on Hilliard Street, near Harvard Square. But our future changed almost at once. Soon after the autumn term began, Columbia offered my father James Harvey Robinson's old chair at what in those days was the munificent salary of $6000. At the request of the Harvard history department, President A. Lawrence Lowell matched Columbia's offer and proposed a permanent appointment. Walter Jessup of Iowa then came east to raise the Columbia-Harvard bid by $500.

My father had much loyalty to and affection for Columbia. But he liked his Harvard colleagues and students, was promised a free hand in developing social and cultural history and thought Cambridge a better place than Manhattan to raise a family. Disquieting rumors, however, had reached the middle west that the great Turner, who had gone to Harvard from Wisconsin in 1910, had been snubbed by his New England colleagues, especially by the crusty Edward Channing, and that he regretted ever having left Madison.

It is true that Channing, who was still turning out volume after volume of his *History of the United States,* once said, "Turner is a dear fellow, but he has no idea of the value of time. He has never written any big books." (Actually, Turner's small essays have had far greater impact than Channing's big books.) But Turner, who had just retired, assured my father that the rumors were all wrong: he liked Channing, and he liked Harvard. His successor in western history was to be his protégé Frederick Merk, another middle westerner, who provided further reassurance. My father chose Harvard and never regretted it.

From Hilliard Street we moved to houses first on Avon Street and then on Avon Hill Street, where the steep hill offered fine sledding in winter. In 1927 my parents bought for $6000 a lot on a pastoral lane north of Harvard's Botanical Garden in an area just opened for residential housing. The new street was named Gray Gardens after Asa Gray, the nineteenth-century Harvard botanist. In collaboration with my mother, the architectural firm of Putnam & Cox drew up plans, and the house was built in the same year at a cost of $20,000.

Nineteen Gray Gardens East was a pleasant brick house in the colonial Georgian style. It was a lively neighborhood. Fred Merk in his bachelor days came to live on the third floor. Next door lived Alfred Baker Lewis, a millionaire Socialist and perennial candidate for senator. Down the street lived Eleanor Thomas Metcalf, Herman Melville's granddaughter and the mother of my contemporary Paul Metcalf, whose avant-garde writings and shoulder-length hair won him a reputation of his own. ("Because of my relation to him," Paul Metcalf wrote, "Melville was the monkey on my back . . . and I could never come to terms with myself until relieved of him.") Around the corner lived William L. Langer, the sardonic diplomatic historian, with his brilliant bluestocking wife, the philosopher Suzanne Langer. A block down Garden Street lived Harlow Shapley, the astronomer and, like my parents, a midwesterner.

Our living room soon became the setting for famed Sunday-afternoon teas. My parents invited graduate students and bright undergraduates to meet Harvard professors, foreign visitors like D. W. Brogan, Harold Laski and C. K. Webster and, after the establishment of the Nieman Fellowships in 1939, newspapermen (and women) enjoying a year in Cambridge. When I became a professor myself, I marveled at my parents' readiness thus to surrender every Sunday afternoon — I could never have done it. But many people have since told me that my parents' teas provided about the only human contact with professors they had in their years at Harvard.

My father worked in his book-lined study in the back of the house overlooking the garden, wearing a green eyeshade of the kind familiar in the newspaper offices of his youth and generally smoking a pipe. When he needed a change, he liked to join my mother in gardening, an interest inherited by Tom but not at all by me. He was old-fashioned in certain habits: he carried a gold Elgin pocket watch on a chain from which his Phi Beta Kappa key dangled; and to the end of his life he applied lather to his face with a brush and shaved with a straight razor stropped on a band of leather — a morning ceremony that Tom and I used to watch with fascination.

He still played the piano (and still could not read music). My parents' pleasure in opera found new sustenance in Boston. Wagner was all too often on our Victrola (so named after RCA Victor). He also loved hearing Ruth Etting sing "Shine On Harvest Moon." They were fond of the legitimate theater and musical comedy, adored Marx Brothers movies and relaxed after a busy day by listening to "Amos 'n' Andy" at seven o'clock every night, much as their son viewed *Sergeant Bilko* in the Fifties, *All in the Family* in the Seventies and *Seinfeld* in the Nineties. In later years "Amos 'n' Andy" was condemned for racial stereotyping. It was in fact a good-natured show with engaging characters and conceits — the Fresh Air Taxi Company and the Mystic Knights of the Sea, the Kingfish and Madame Queen and "I's regusted." In 1997, dining with Henry Louis Gates, Jr., Stanley Crouch and the *New York Times* columnist Bob Herbert, I was cheered to learn that many black Americans also enjoyed "Amos 'n' Andy."

My father was given, regrettably, to puns and, more forgivably, to limericks. A favorite verse felicitously combined both addictions:

> The Reverend Henry Ward Beecher
> Called the hen a most elegant creature.
> The hen just for that
> Laid an egg in his hat
> And thus did the hen reward Beecher.

He also used to recite what was alleged to be Woodrow Wilson's favorite limerick:

> In beauty I'm not a great star.
> There are others more handsome by far.
>   But my face I don't mind it
>   For I am behind it.
> It's those in front that I jar.

*   *   *

The Harvard history department, contrary to rumor, turned out to be most congenial. The redoubtable Channing proved a kindly and amusing man. I remember meeting him from time to time — very short and peppery, scant white hair, his face a bright pink, friendly to little boys. Albert Bushnell Hart, with his impressive white beard, had retired but was in evidence around Widener Library; a considerable historical entrepreneur in his day, he was sadly slipping into senility.

Sam Morison received his appointment as full professor the same day as my father and thereafter referred to him as his "academic twin." Though Sam had a somewhat deserved reputation for frostiness, he arranged, on his return from Oxford the next year, for my father's entry into the venerable Massachusetts historical societies and, with his charming wife, Bessie, welcomed the young midwestern couple to their house on Brimmer Street, at the foot of Boston's Beacon Hill.

My parents soon acquired friends beyond the department. They were much stimulated by Bernard DeVoto, the irreverent historian, critic and novelist, who had come east from Utah via Northwestern. They found the philosopher Ralph Barton Perry, brother-in-law of Bernard Berenson and biographer of William James, politically and intellectually sympathetic. My father's interest in public affairs brought him particular friends in the Law School — the brilliant and effervescent Felix Frankfurter, the dour and trenchant James M. Landis and an old friend from Columbia, the jovially caustic Reed Powell.

The free-drinking habits of Cambridge rather shocked my parents, coming as they did from bone-dry Iowa. They had favored the Eighteenth Amendment and were in any case law-abiding by nature. But booze appeared wherever they went in the Boston area. To be polite, they would accept the proffered cocktail, but for a time declined to serve liquor themselves. Finally they abandoned the high ground.

When Benny DeVoto offered to bring back contraband for the Schlesingers on his regular sorties across the Vermont border into Canada, my father succumbed. My own first notion of DeVoto, as I watched him in our driveway unloading bottles from the trunk of his car, was that he must be the family bootlegger.

* * *

My father, a fugitive from the heartland, had what can only be described as a passion for the sea. After a seaside excursion in his New York days, he had written to Elizabeth Bancroft in Kalamazoo, "The ocean was beautiful — some day we *must* spend a summer along the ocean." Our first summer in Cambridge, we took a cottage on Horseneck Beach, near New Bedford. Inspired by *Treasure Island,* I packed a miscellany of items into a wooden crate and buried it, with appropriate private ceremony, in the dunes. In later years we would spend a month each summer on Cape Cod, generally in Chatham.

Unaware of the lethal effects of ultraviolet rays, my father worshiped the sun, but his hours lying on the sun-soaked beach seemed to do him no harm. He loved the surf, the dunes, the tang of the sea air, the soaring gulls, the shimmering inland ponds and the trim Cape villages, still relatively uncorrupted in the Twenties. So did his two sons, obedient always, though, to the prevalent parental injunction: Don't go into the water until two hours after eating lest you get cramps and drown.

Back in Cambridge, my father occasionally took us to Revere Beach, but carsickness handicapped me for long expeditions. "All my precautions of giving Arthur soda mint pills in advance and having him chew gum," my father wrote to my mother in the summer of 1926, "proved of no avail. Therefore, we stopped along the street, and while a group of young fellows yelled, 'Atta-boy!' Arthur surrendered his dinner."

The L Street Beach in Boston, for men only, was closer, and we sometimes went there on warmish spring or autumn days. At Revere Beach men wore, not trunks, but respectable bathing suits that covered the chest. As late as 1939, the Gallup poll reported that a third of respondents thought it indecent for men to appear topless, and the sight of men clad only in jockstraps — the L Street Brownies, as for some reason they were known — was a surprise. On New Year's Day the tougher Brownies would intrepidly plunge into the freezing ocean. My father's winter exercise was a locally invented game called fistball, which faculty members played once a week at the close of the day in a gymnasium near the Law School — an occasion that from time to time his sons were privileged to attend.

I do not recall his participating much in sports with his sons, except for swimming. Nor, though Tom and I were baseball addicts, do I recall his taking us to Braves Field or Fenway Park. He did, however, like football. On crisp, smoky fall days (householders were then permitted to burn their fallen leaves, giving the autumnal air a wonderful aroma), we would join the crowd streaming over the bridge across the Charles River to the stadium on Soldiers Field and then streaming back in the dusk to Harvard Square. There we would stop by Leavitt & Pierce, the tobacconist, where the results of games elsewhere were chalked up on a blackboard. We retained a family interest in the fortunes of Ohio State and Iowa in the Big Ten.

*   *   *

My parents liked Boston. My father's reserve, sober judgment and laconic humor fitted in easily with the old Yankee style, and my mother's zest for life appealed to Yankee women like Bessie Morison, too long repressed by Yankee men. The smug conservatism of old Harvard grads on the North Shore was depressing, and in certain moods my father agreed with Frankfurter, who in March 1931 wrote him that Boston was "fundamentally an arid soil — hostile to variety and color, to richness and esprit. . . . The civilization here is thin and self-defensive, because it lacks passion, and its ruling traditions educate to stifle the exercise of passion."

But the old Yankee stock also had bred individualists and reformers, and this strain greatly attracted my parents, as indeed it did Frankfurter, whose hero was Justice Oliver Wendell Holmes. Even Sam Morison, for all his patrician hauteur, was a pretty reliable and outspoken liberal and took pride in his abolitionist heritage.

In the autumn of 1924 my father expounded an early version of his cyclical theory of American politics before an audience in Nantucket. Reviewing the regular alternation of liberal and conservative phases through American history, he observed that, if the rhythm held, Coolidge-style conservatism could be expected to last until 1932. This prediction provoked an anguished and audible "My God!" from a member of the audience. The complainant turned out to be David K. Niles, the director of the Ford Hall Forum, a Boston institution where lecturers discussed political and social issues and in which my father was soon involved.

Dave Niles, though born in Boston, was hardly an old Yankee. He came from a Russian-Jewish family; his original name was Neyhus. In 1924 he was running the speakers' bureau for the new Progressive ticket of Robert M. La Follette, Sr., and Burton K. Wheeler. Round-faced and balding, with heavy, horn-rimmed glasses, he was soft-spoken, somewhat mysterious, a staunch liberal and a tireless advocate for the rights of minorities, blacks as well as Jews. In later years Harry Hopkins brought him to Washington, where in time he joined Roosevelt's White House and ended as one of President Truman's special assistants.

Ford Hall in the Twenties was militant in its campaign against the local censorship imposed by an odd alliance between Yankee neo-Puritans and Irish Catholics. The "banned in Boston" label on a book assured good sales in the rest of the country. Among the beneficiaries were Dreiser, Hemingway, Dos Passos, Sherwood Anderson, Sinclair Lewis and Upton Sinclair (who said, "Boston is our advertising department").

On one occasion in 1929, Boston's flamboyant mayor James M. Curley forbade Margaret Sanger to speak about birth control. The sale of condoms was illegal in Massachusetts. Even the word was unknown in polite society, and impolite society, first looking to the right and left, would whisper to the drugstore clerk the key word: "safes" or "rubbers." Mrs. Sanger, after being ceremoniously gagged, handed her speech to my father, who read it aloud to the audience. The next day the *Boston Transcript* denounced Ford Hall for "wasteful clowning," and an officer of the Veterans of Foreign Wars proposed that the participants in the evening be deported.

On another occasion, the old (and bearded) Socialist Morris Hillquit had to cancel at the last moment, so my father took his place. After the lecture began, a woman rushed in, looked up at the speaker and cried out, "My God, Morris, how you have changed!" In that night's lecture, "Conservatism and Radicalism in American History," my father further developed his cyclical hypothesis. Radicals, he said, were optimists; conservatives, pessimists. Newpapers reported that the audience particularly enjoyed it when he called a pessimist the wife of an optimist and the electoral college "the only college without a college yell."

Liberal Boston and liberal Cambridge offered an environment into which my parents happily fitted and from which they drew continuing sustenance. It was this environment that shaped the outlook of their children.

3

Midwesterners in Cambridge

MY FORMAL EDUCATION now began. Most faculty parents sent their children to private schools, especially to the modishly progressive Shady Hill School. My parents, with their robust midwestern commitment to public education, sent me to the Peabody School on Linnaean Street, a few blocks from our house.

The instruction at Peabody was not at all bad. I remember with particular gratitude Miss Trefethen, my gifted and imaginative fifth-grade teacher. I was pushed rapidly ahead, skipping the second and fourth grades. This meant that from the age of nine I was younger by two years and therefore smaller and less socially adept than my classmates. Also, as one condemned to eyeglasses by myopia and astigmatism, I was a "four-eyes," in the school slang of the period.

Fashions in pedagogy later turned against skipping on the theory, apparently, that social adjustment is more important for the young than intellectual stimulus. It is true enough that skipping two grades denied me any future in sports. But, in retrospect, I have no doubt that athletic deprivation was a small price to escape the boredom and stultification that could so easily have resulted from being held back.

*   *   *

In the meantime, my father was settling into Harvard. He seems to have made a strong early impression as a fair-minded and judicious counselor. Someone recently gave me a copy of a letter Felix Frankfurter sent to Grenville Clark, an eminent lawyer and a member of Harvard's ruling body, the Corporation. The Corporation was beginning its search for a successor to President Lowell, and Clark had asked Frankfurter to recommend faculty members whom he should consult. Frankfurter supplied three names — my father (first), the psychologist Harry Murray and the legal scholar Henry Hart. Arthur Schlesinger, he told Clark, was "excelled by no one in the disinterestedness and objectivity of his judgment."

These qualities were one reason for his growing influence in the Harvard community — though Benny DeVoto, in a disgruntled mood, put it differently. "The meek and mild Arthur Schlesinger," he wrote to a friend, "has a tremendous drive for power and he dominates every committee he gets on." The diplomatic historian Richard W. Leopold would have disagreed, writing in his reminiscences of the Harvard history department, "Schlesinger rarely sought to impose his views on others." In any event, my father commanded faculty confidence and was regularly appointed to committees considering major academic issues, such as the reform of the tenure system (the controversial Walsh-Sweezy case of 1937), Harvard's program "General Education in a Free Society" and the search for a new president of Radcliffe.

His major undergraduate course was American Social and Intellectual History (History 63, later History 163) and he was a good and popular lecturer. David Riesman '31, wrote him about History 63, "I had more real kick out of it than any other course I have taken." Denis Brogan, who came from Oxford in 1925 to study American history, was impressed by "the lucidity and force of his lectures."

My father's primary interest, however, lay in graduate seminars, where both his technical proficiency and his moral force placed an imprint on several generations of historians. Brogan attended the seminar and soon discovered that "underneath Arthur Schlesinger's prim or grim manner was a highly ironical mind." He would listen to seminar papers with great care and slowly dissect them, sometimes, Brogan observed, to the serious discomfiture of the victims, "but no doubt it was good for them." "I was always a bit afraid of Mr. Schlesinger," the historian Henry F. May, one of his Ph.D.'s, has written, "and had to stop, pull myself together, and swallow hard before I knocked on the door of his office. . . . A truly kind man, he was unable to unbend."

Where more exciting teachers produced students who imitated their ideas and methods, Schlesinger's gift, May decided, was for gently guiding students to topics that suited their interests and abilities and then leaving them alone: "No one in the country had as many students who turned out to be creative scholars, and each was entirely different: there was no Schlesinger pattern." "His reputation as a teacher," wrote Carl Bridenbaugh, another of his Ph.D.'s, "and his phenomenal success in placing his Ph.D.'s in positions best suited for them attracted a larger number of able and intellectually venturesome students to his classes than ever worked with any other professor of American history."

As a native of Ohio and a graduate of Ohio State, Paul H. Buck attracted my father's special solicitude. He was plainly a promising young scholar, and the history department soon appointed him to join my father and Merk in the survey course in American history. Meanwhile Buck labored away on his dissertation, a study of the reconciliation between the north and the white south after the Civil War. Time passed, and the evident reluctance of so manifestly able a man to finish his manuscript worried his elder colleagues. My father, deciding that Paul had to be shocked into action, told him brusquely to renounce perfectionism and hand in a chapter a week. He did so, and his book *The Road to Reunion, 1865–1900* won the Pulitzer Prize in 1938.

Buck went on to become provost of Harvard and de facto president when James B. Conant was away during the Second World War. The Schlesinger seminar, Buck said, provided "more than exposure to instruction from a master craftsman. . . . He probed gently yet skillfully until he found what was good in the individual and then gave it nurture. At times his exterior seemed chilled by a rigid insistence upon professional ethics and scholarly integrity. But he won followers to his high standard not with a rod but with the warmth he brought to human relationships."

*   *   *

My father's mission remained the New History. He liked the lapidary words of Mr. Dooley:

> I know histhry isn't thrue, Hinnissy, because it ain't like what I see ivry day in Halsted Sthreet. If any wan comes along with a histhry iv Greece or Rome that'll show me th' people fightin', gettin' dhrunk, gettin' married, owin' th' grocery man an' bein' without hard-coal, I'll believe they was a Greece or Rome, but not befure. . . . Histhry is a postmortem examination. It tells ye what a counthry died iv. But I'd like to know what it lived iv.

In this spirit my father, a month after *New Viewpoints* appeared in 1922, proposed to Macmillan a multivolume collaborative history of the American people. *A History of American Life*, co-edited with an old Columbia friend and fellow historian, Dixon Ryan Fox, was to absorb an inordinate amount of his time and energy for the next twenty years. Though Schlesinger and Fox signed up established scholars to write the books, the editors soon found that too often they had to check, revise and in some cases rewrite the generally tardy submissions. "What the hell's the matter with American historians anyway?" asked Carl Becker, Cornell's scintillating intellectual historian who read the manuscripts as consulting editor. A truthful title page for the volumes, Becker proposed, would read: "Ghosted by Arthur M. Schlesinger and Dixon Ryan Fox for the Following Eminent American Historians."

Charles Beard counseled my father against editing in 1927: "What a waste of your time. Break away as soon as you can. . . . Break away, my dear boy, and think for yourself as hard as you can, trying to divine the center and drift of things. Pardon, I did not intend to preach." Becker repeated the warning in 1943: "I swear, my dear Arthur, if you don't from now on become entirely selfish (professionally) and devote yourself and your talents to the writing of the three or four books which you might have written if you hadn't spent the time correcting other people's grammar and literary construction — why I will condemn you to the lowest depths of hell." My father must have mourned the books he failed to write, for he used to caution me in somber terms against ever taking on any large editorial project.

But he was a man with a mission. The academy still was ruled by J. R. Seeley's famed dictum: "History is past politics." Their objective, Schlesinger and Fox told their publisher, was "to free American history from its traditional servitude to party struggles, war and diplomacy and to show that it properly included all the varied interests of the people." The *Saturday Evening Post,* they contended, had as real a place in history as the *Atlantic Monthly,* ragtime as choral music, the chautauqua as the great university.

Social history, my father said in a note I found in his papers after his death, assumes that "politics has seldom or for long been the major concern of society. Other goals — bread-winning, mating, personal immortality, self-improvement, personal power, the betterment of the community, the love of beauty — these and like interests have day in and day out absorbed man's energies and thought. An understanding of the molding forces should go far to answer the question: why we behave like Americans." Why leave to novelists and journalists the story of how the great anonymous majority works, plays, loves, ventures, endures, dies? Why let only the poet write: "I am the man, I suffer'd, I was there"?

This was still heresy within the guild. The front-page review of the first four volumes of *A History of American Life* in the *New York Times*

Book Review in January 1928 was couched in part as a colloquy between a "traditional" and a "social" historian. "I abhor your ways," the traditionalist tells the upstart. "You are the bad boy of the profession." But Schlesinger and Fox were undaunted, and seventeen years later, in January 1945, a front-page review of the entire series in the *Times Book Review* measured their success. "So secure is the position of social history today," Carl Bridenbaugh wrote, "that it may seem strange that even historians once met the new history with scorn. . . . Much of the renewed interest in the American past today is directly traceable to the 'History of American Life.'"

By mid-century, social history and its offshoots — intellectual history, women's history, urban history, labor history, ethnic history, black history, the history of immigration, of education, of science and technology, of law — were becoming routine in academic curricula; and political, diplomatic and constitutional history was increasingly seen as animated by social, economic, psychological and ideological interests.

* * *

If social history triumphed, *A History of American Life* did not. By the Seventies and Eighties, a new generation of social historians dismissed the Schlesinger-Fox series as superficial and anecdotal, lacking big theories, deep structures, conceptual frameworks. A "new" social history now appeared, more quantitative in its approach, more sophisticated in its computerized statistics, more aggressive in its "from the bottom up" ideology, more pretentious in its vocabulary, more righteous in its moral fervor.

The "new" social historians sometimes wrote as if they had just invented social history. But in the end they suffered the same fate for which they had disdained *A History of American Life*. They too failed to come up with the analytic synthesis that would absorb chaotic social data in a "deep," all-embracing conceptual structure. As some among them finally admitted, "Coherence, purpose, and direction all floundered in the churning waters" (Alice Kessler-Harris). The dream of integrated social history remains a dream, a faint glimmer in the far distance, quite possibly a will-o'-the-wisp.

Perhaps that is why Mark Carnes's excellent one-volume condensation and bibliographical updating of *A History of American Life,* published by Scribner in 1996, had a modest success. "In rescuing this enormous work from oblivion," said the historian John Higham, "Mark C. Carnes has discerned its inner coherence and its stunning relevance to what historians today are doing." And in 1999 the Ohio State University Press reissued my father's volume in the series, *The Rise of the City*.

*   *   *

The "new" social history also regarded political, diplomatic and military history with a snootiness that my father definitely did not share. While he rejected Seeley's definition of history as *only* past politics, he never for a moment succumbed to the opposite fallacy — that politics is only froth on the waves of history. Some of his most influential writing dealt with persisting problems of the presidency, political parties, foreign relations and the martial spirit — in other words, with the state, diplomacy and war. Half the essays in *New Viewpoints* and in his 1949 collection, *Paths to the Present*, address political and constitutional questions.

It can be said, I think, that the "new" social history, in belittling the event-making individual and assuming the omnipotence of social forces, does as much damage to the past as traditional history did in omitting those quotidian experiences that hurry us all from the womb to the tomb. The *longues durées* of Fernand Braudel have considerable explanatory power on one level of historical understanding, but the much-scorned *histoire événementielle* remains the history people live and the history they most need to know. "Social science," Braudel has written, "has almost what amounts to a horror of the event." Maybe so; but to adopt that view is to take the history out of history.

Contemporary conceptions of social history, pressed too far, render history static and change a mystery, whereas history, if anything, is forever in motion, and change is its essence. Pressed too far, the "new" social history abolishes narrative, which is the expressive form for the portrayal of change. The more technical social historians even scorn readability and write in a dialect of their own. But what is history without readers?

When historians lose interest in communication, when they refuse a lay audience, they discard history's social function. For history is to a nation as memory is to the individual. Individuals deprived of memory are disoriented and lost, not knowing where they have been or where they are going. So too a nation, denied a conception of its past, will be disabled in dealing with its future. How ironic, then, when history is denied by historians themselves.

I venture to surmise that my father would not have disagreed with these observations. *"Nothing stands still,"* he once noted, underlining those three blunt words (later used as the title of his posthumous book of essays). I am confident that, like other social historians (Lawrence Stone, for example, in his valuable essay "The Revival of Narrative"), he would have believed that the recoil against the history of events can go too far and that the "new" social history, paradoxically, runs the risk of severing history's lifeline to society.

* * *

No doubt my father's refusal to exclude politics from history resulted from the role politics continued to play in his own life. He never thought that his commitment as a scholar abrogated his conscience as a citizen, though he did see scholarship and citizenship as somewhat separate responsibilities. As a scholar, he believed (another scribbled note found in his papers) that "historians should not study the past with a determination to find ideas and events which are peculiarly significant for the present. This tends to distort the actual historical process." At the same time, he believed that historians as citizens could and should bring history to bear on dilemmas of the present.

He also enjoyed politics. In 1920, fulfilling an old ambition to see a nominating convention in action, he attended the Republican convention in Chicago, heard Henry Cabot Lodge deliver a poisonous personal attack on the ailing Wilson, and deplored the result when Harry Daugherty's smoke-filled room produced Warren G. Harding. In the election he enthusiastically supported his friend Governor Cox of Ohio. "The fact that someone named Franklin D. Roosevelt shared the ticket," he later wrote, "made no impression on me one way or the other."

But in the 1920s cultural warfare was more intense than political combat. It was an era of contradictions — the decade at once of fundamentalists and flappers, prohibitionists and bootleggers, a book on Main Street and a boom on Wall Street, disenchantment with war and enchantment with business. Two contrasting symbols were Calvin Coolidge, the dried-up Yankee who succeeded to the presidency after Harding's death in 1923, and H. L. Mencken, the joyously satirical editor of the *American Mercury.* My parents were great fans of Mencken.

One basic cultural clash was between rural America and the expanding and noisy city. The agrarians had their last great national triumph when they forced prohibition on a hapless nation in 1919. The next year the census showed that, for the first time, more Americans lived in towns and cities than in the countryside. Rural America began to dig in for a rearguard stand to save morality, patriotism, prohibition, white supremacy and the old-time religion ("traditional values," later generations would say) from Catholics, radicals, wets, atheists, labor organizers, pacifists, Negroes and foreigners. The Ku Klux Klan in Xenia, the monkey trial in Tennessee (the courtroom filled, Mencken wrote, with "gaping primates"), were harbingers of things to come.

In 1924 country and city battled at the Democratic convention. W. G. McAdoo, backed by Bryan and the agrarian wing of the party, fought it out with Governor Alfred E. Smith of New York, a slangy son of the polyglot city, an Irish Catholic and a wet. The convention took place in New York City — for Bryan "the enemy's country," for Al Smith, home. A resolution to condemn the Klan by name failed, after furious debate, by a single vote. Then came the presidential nomination. We heard it all — "Alabama casts twenty-four votes for Oscar W. Underwood" — over earphones on our rudimentary Crossley Pup radio, a small black box from which rose a faintly gleaming silver tube. Exhausted by 103 angry ballots, the delegates finally turned to the upright and respectable John W. Davis.

Davis's conservatism drove many liberals to the La Follette candidacy on the Progressive ticket. But my father's skepticism about third parties and his sense of Davis as a Wilsonian internationalist kept him from what would have seemed his more natural vote. Davis lost badly. Silent Cal reigned in the White House, and cultural warfare intensified.

Mencken's journalism and Sinclair Lewis's novels portrayed a land in which freedom of thought was under siege by the community's insistence on orthodoxy and conformity (which is why the "communitarianism" in vogue in the Nineties turns off people who remember the Twenties). My father, too, worried about the future of individual liberty in a nation that seemed increasingly dominated by predatory businessmen and fanatical fundamentalists. In June 1926 Ohio State University invited him back to Columbus to give the commencement address. Noting that this year marked the 150th anniversary of the Declaration of Independence, he asked how well the republic had lived up to the principles on which it was founded.

Political democracy, my father argued in "The New Tyranny," had encouraged the mischievous idea that majority rule applies to social and moral as well as legislative questions. Therefore those who disagree with the majority on any question can rightfully be suppressed. "Out of the very womb of triumphant democracy . . . was born an evil principle that robbed the individual of much of the freedom which the law intended to give him." This new doctrine threatened "to erect a real tyranny of the intellect amidst the freest political institutions the world has ever known."

The new doctrine, he continued, had been latterly reinforced by the power of large organizations. Standardization was now a principle of American society: "The typical American today may be pictured as a man wearing a Knox hat, an Arrow collar, a Manhattan shirt, a Hart, Schaffner and Marx suit, and a pair of Walkover shoes, seated in a Ford car with a *Saturday Evening Post* under his arm on his way to the monthly meeting of the National Association for the Banishment of Privacy from the American Home." The forces making for the suppression of individuality — the fundamentalists, the superpatriots, the large corporations — were growing stronger. "We are in danger of becoming a nation of parrots." In this sesquicentennial year of independence the republic was, he thought, confronted by a strange paradox: "America has achieved the greatest measure of political freedom known to history, but Americans individually have never before possessed so little intellectual and spiritual freedom."

*   *   *

This address caused a certain furor in Columbus, but nothing to what awaited him in Chicago. For the cultural conflict between city and countryside was matched in intensity by the conflict within the city between cosmopolitans and nativists. Paradoxically, the cosmopolitans were often old Americans secure in their sense of belonging, while the nativists were often new Americans eager to prove their patriotism. "Before I was here a month," as Mr. Dooley phrased the latter sentiment, "I felt enough like a native born American to burn a witch."

The cosmopolitans, in addition, were often Anglophiles, while the nativists, though marginally concerned about bearded Bolsheviki lurking in dark corners, saw suave, perfidious Britishers as the immediate threat. Irish Catholics had hated England since Cromwell's massacre at Drogheda in 1649. German Americans blamed England for what was now the widely regretted American entry into the Great

War. Never again, isolationists said, would wily British propagandists beguile Americans into "pulling England's chestnuts out of the fire." Even Yankees of the Henry Cabot Lodge school had regarded England as the enemy since the Boston Tea Party in 1773.

In 1921, the Hearst press found "the spirit of Benedict Arnold reincarnated" in "Anglicized School Histories." Patriotic societies and veterans' groups joined the cry against British propaganda. Mayor John F. Hylan of New York directed David Hirshfield, his commissioner of accounts, to investigate pro-British textbooks in the public schools. "It is amazing," Hylan said, "to think that any publication intended for the use of school children, should refer to our early patriots as 'hot-headed mobs,' 'smugglers,' and 'pirates.'" Our children "must not be inoculated with the poisonous virus of foreign propaganda."

After eighteen months' study, Hirshfield called for the ban of eight texts. The offending books, he suggested, were part of Cecil Rhodes's plot, already manifest in the Rhodes scholarships, to reclaim the United States "as an integral part of the British Empire." American historians, it was charged, were selling out to British gold. The theory soon spread across the country. "We demand," resolved the Veterans of Foreign Wars in its annual national encampment, "that the treason texts be thrown out of the public schools in every State." "We would be unworthy sons," said the New Jersey Knights of Pythias, ". . . if we have not the spirit and strength to retain in ink what they wrote in blood."

It was not just Anglophobia. A more comprehensible motive was the feeling that school textbooks systematically ignored the role of non-Anglo-Saxons in American history. The Hearst press saw a plot "to envelop America of today in the myth of Anglo-Saxon origin and kinship." Hirshfield and his allies, the *New York Times* reported, wanted "recognition in schoolbook histories for American heroes of Jewish, Dutch, Swedish, Irish and African descent." The Knights of Columbus, representing Irish as well as (by its name) Italian interests, declared: "The achievements of many different races — Irish, German, Italian, French, Scandinavian, Slavik [sic], Polish, Spanish, etc. . . . are treated with contempt to the glory of England — the age-long, implacable foe of America."

The assault on American history was thus conducted by multiculturalists *avant la lettre*. By the Nineties, when multiculturalism had materialized as a word and a movement, its champions were left-wing ideologues. Their precursors, these premature multiculturalists of the Twenties, were right-wing demagogues. Ideologues and demagogues united in calling for repression and censorship.

* * *

The cultural wars reached their climax in Chicago. This was the Chicago of the Twenties, immortalized by Ben Hecht and Charles MacArthur in *The Front Page,* so brilliantly filmed by Lewis Milestone in 1931 — a roaring, brawling town run by pompous politicians, crooked municipal officials and cynical newspapermen. The Hecht-MacArthur mayor, seeking reelection on the promise to "Reform the Reds with a Rope," was inspired by Chicago's mighty windbag William Hale Thompson.

In 1927 Big Bill, running for mayor, appealed to German, Irish, Italian and Polish voters by denouncing "pro-English" textbooks for ignoring those real heroes of the War for Independence — the Poles Pulaski and Kosciusko, the Germans von Steuben and de Kalb, the Dutchman Schuyler, the Irishmen Montgomery, Sullivan and Wayne. The villains responsible for these dastardly omissions were the devilish British and their American bootlickers. He would, Big Bill promised, "biff King George on the snoot" should the British monarch dare show his face in the Windy City. (This led to a Gluyas Williams cartoon in the comic magazine *Life* portraying mass lamentation in the royal drawing room: "TRAGEDY IN BUCKINGHAM PALACE: King George V learns that he must cancel his plans for spending the winter in Chicago.")

My father's chapter "The American Revolution" in *New Viewpoints* began ironically: "The representatives of George V rendered homage a few years ago at the tomb of the great disloyalist and rebel of a former century, George Washington. . . ." Irony is often dangerous; and Big Bill, informed that *New Viewpoints* was on a University of Chicago reading list, castigated the "infamous book" and its infamous author for this blasphemous characterization of the sainted Father of His Country. Reading the offending passage aloud to a *Boston Herald* reporter, he shouted, "From cover to cover this book would nauseate half a patriot. Whose account of the revolution should we accept, that of our ancestors who fought in it, or that put out by the British ruling classes?"

Once elected mayor, Big Bill kept up the attack. "I will not rest," he cried, "until I have purged this entire city of the poison that is being injected into the heart of American youth to eulogize England." He suspended the superintendent of schools as a "stool pigeon for King George" and put him on trial before the school board. Charles Edward Russell, the old muckraker and Socialist, told the board, "The world is threatened now with the greatest menace — the advance of the Anglo-Saxon." The English Speaking Union, Russell said, was "the most dangerous organization in the world."

New Viewpoints was a particular target. Chicago's Republican congressman, John J. Gorman, said that it "teems with un-American and unpatriotic statements" and demanded a congressional investigation. One of Big Bill's henchmen, a Damon Runyon type called U. J. (Sport) Herrmann, tried to remove *New Viewpoints* from the public library. Frustrated there, Sport bought a copy of the "treason-tainted" volume and burned it publicly in a patriotic bonfire. An applauding Chicago schoolteacher said, "Schlesinger should be in a cell in federal prison." My father, asked for comment, said, "I do not like to take part in a sham battle staged by pothouse patriots."

All this caused much merriment in the press, in Chicago and beyond. It was rumored that Mother Goose was next on Big Bill's hit list because "Sing a Song of Sixpence" was full of monarchical references and "pocket full of rye" might suggest to simple minds a defiance of Prohibition. A cartoon showed a cop stopping a truck and asking the driver what was inside. "Only booze," the driver said. "Drive on, brother," said the cop. "I thought it was history books." Big Bill reminded some of the Minneapolis mayor who ordered the Bible removed from the public library because it referred to Saint Paul and made no mention of Minneapolis. "It is not a laughing matter," William Randolph Hearst indignantly responded, "to have British propagandists . . . invade our schools and mold the impressionable minds of our young Americans."

At Harvard, Edward Channing kidded my father about Bill Thompson, calling him a natural product of the uncouth midwest. My father pointed out that Big Bill had been born in Boston. As for the superpatriots "who want everything but the hurrahs left out of the history books," my father commented in *Publishers Weekly*, ". . . deep down in their hearts [they] suspect that our country's history contains things so discreditable that it is not well for young ears to hear them. . . . If I thought as ill of my country's history as those who would falsify it for young minds, I would flee these shores without further ado and adopt another country and allegiance."

*   *   *

The cultural warfare came to a more somber climax that same year in Boston in the case that, as my father wrote without undue hyperbole, "created an atmosphere of popular tension, dread and crisis without parallel in Massachusetts annals since the exiling of Roger Williams and Anne Hutchinson and the witch persecutions of the seventeenth century."

In 1921 Nicola Sacco and Bartolomeo Vanzetti had been convicted and sentenced to death for killing two men in a payroll robbery in South Braintree. As foreigners, draft dodgers, anarchists and atheists, Sacco and Vanzetti were natural objects of disgust for one-hundred-percent Americans. The trial judge called them "anarchistic bastards." The foreman of the jury opined that, regardless of the evidence, "They ought to hang anyway." The evidence against them was scant, and the undisguised prejudices in the judicial proceedings would seem to call for a new trial. The campaign on their behalf had now dragged on for six years.

My father's new best friend, Felix Frankfurter, was active in the call for a new trial, and he soon enlisted my father. The immediate issue, as my father saw it, was not whether the two men were innocent or guilty. It was the less complicated question: Had they had a fair trial? On this point the answer seemed quite clear.

Another vivid personality now entered the lives of the Schlesingers when Gardner (Pat) Jackson, a *Boston Globe* reporter, became executive secretary of the Sacco-Vanzetti Defense Committee. Pat Jackson was a Coloradan, the son of a wealthy banker and railroad man. His father's first wife had been Helen Hunt Jackson, whose books of the 1880s, *A Century of Dishonor* and *Ramona,* had drawn national attention to the miserable treatment of American Indians. After her death, W. S. Jackson married her niece, who was Pat's mother.

A humanitarian crusader by birthright, Pat came east to Amherst College, where he combined undergraduate high spirits with attempts to organize Polish farmworkers in the Connecticut Valley. At Amherst he was somehow close both to Alexander Meiklejohn, the reformist president, and to Meiklejohn's deadly enemy, Robert Frost, the censorious poet. Throughout his life Pat attached himself to powerful figures — Franklin D. Roosevelt, Brandeis, Frankfurter, Gutzon Borglum, Henry A. Wallace, John L. Lewis, Lee Pressman, James G. Patton, John F. Kennedy, John Dos Passos, Edmund Wilson, Isaiah Berlin — who, for their part, were beguiled by his exuberance, charm and need for hero worship.

He had left Amherst for the Army and in 1920 joined the *Globe,* where he made a name for himself as a lively and idiosyncratic reporter. When Daniel C. Marsh became president of Boston University in 1925, Pat sent in a story in which Marsh, who believed in phrenology, explained his own character in terms of the bumps on his head. When the story failed to appear, Pat complained to Larry Winship, the editor. "Come off it," Winship said. "We knew you must have been drunk." The story finally ran, bumps and all.

Pat was a stocky, rumpled crusader, impulsive, generous, humorous, vulnerable, disorderly, romantic, brave, whose hero worship rather regularly crumbled into disillusion. He was the ready friend of people in trouble. If a telephone call came from someone in distress, he would say, not "What is the problem?" but "Where are you? I'll be there." If he could get no one to work with him in combatting the indignities of the world, he would cheerfully set out to do it by himself. Because he cared so deeply about people and injustice, he forgot things other people cared about, like power, success, prestige, money. He gave not only time but cash to the Sacco-Vanzetti defense — nearly half a million in end-of-the-century dollars. They would later say about Pat Jackson in New Deal Washington, "The underdog has him on a leash."

Not devoid of human frailties, in particular a weakness for drink, he found it natural to distinguish between the sin and the sinner. His forbearing and forgiving wife Dorothy — "Dode" — represented the stability principle in his life. A vegetarian herself, she was admired for the opulent roasts and joints she served at the Jackson table. Pat's everlasting strength was his conviction that people mattered more than dogma and sympathy more than righteousness, this and a rare humor and modesty about himself and, above all, a gusto for life.

He swept into my parents' lives like a whirlwind. Pat and my father could hardly have been more dissimilar in temperament, but they shared the same liberal ideals, and they took to each other at once, Pat envying my father's self-discipline, my father admiring Pat's passion. As Pat told the Columbia University Oral History people, it "hit me right off the bat . . . that we were going to be bosom pals from the very start." He became in some respects my father's closest friend.

* * *

In the summer of 1927 the Sacco-Vanzetti case was rushing toward its bitter dénouement. Yankee justice had no concern for a couple of anarchistic wops. Motions had been denied, appeals exhausted. There would be no new trial.

But Pat Jackson and the Defense Committee had made Sacco and Vanzetti a national, indeed an international, issue. Writers, artists and assorted radicals flocked to Boston for a final protest as the day of execution — August 22 — drew near. An atmosphere of hysteria hung over the sweltering city. John Dos Passos stormed into my father's Widener study, offering to find a horse and colonial costume and ride, like Paul Revere, through every Middlesex village and farm shouting "Save Sacco and Vanzetti!" — a venture from which he was only with difficulty dissuaded.

On the night of the execution, the Charlestown prison was armed and garrisoned as if it were under siege, its walls lined with searchlights and machine guns. Policemen guarded public buildings and patrolled the streets, arresting 156 "Death Watch" pickets in front of the State House. The mood in Boston that wild night was later wonderfully rendered by Benny DeVoto in *We Accept with Pleasure,* his best novel. The memory lingered when Jim Thurber and Elliott Nugent made the reading of Vanzetti's last letter the crisis of *The Male Animal.*

The execution of Sacco and Vanzetti had sharp political repercussions. Cultural conflict was transmuted into class conflict. "America our nation," wrote Dos Passos, "has been beaten by strangers who have turned our language inside out who have taken the clean words our fathers spoke and made them slimy and foul." "Don't you see the glory of this case," said a character in Upton Sinclair's novel *Boston.* "It kills off the liberals!" "All right," said Dos Passos, "we are two nations."

In the summer that Sacco and Vanzetti died, I was nine years old and at a boys' camp in New Hampshire, reading newspapers primarily for the baseball scores, yet dimly aware that something awful was happening to two men who had never received a fair trial. I still remember my inexpressible shock when I heard one of my camp counselors, holding up the great black headline splashed across the front page of the *Boston Herald,* say happily to another, "Thank God — at last they got those sons of bitches."

*   *   *

Public school exposed me to another dimension of cultural conflict — that between Yankees and Irish in Massachusetts. It is hard in post-Kennedy America to remember the abhorrence with which the old Yankees once viewed the Irish. It was in its own way as intense as the prejudice against blacks. W.E.B. Du Bois, the great black scholar, recalled in his memoirs that, when he grew up in Great Barrington in western Massachusetts, "the racial angle was more clearly defined against the Irish than against me."

Irish-Yankee feuding reached a new high in 1928 when the Democrats dared run Al Smith for president. My father worked with Dave Niles in backing Smith through the Massachusetts Independent Voters Association. Only some forty members of the Harvard faculty, a beleaguered minority (though it included Frankfurter, Morison, Ralph Barton Perry, F. W. Taussig, L. J. Henderson and James B. Conant), signed a statement in support of Smith. Respectable people were fervently for Herbert Hoover. The kids I met in summer play groups and at dancing class — my parents' two concessions to private education — looked with incredulity on anyone whose parents were for Al Smith.

Except for other faculty children whose midwestern parents sent them to public schools, like my good friend Willis Shapley, most of my regular playmates were Irish boys — Bob Toomey, Jim Conlan, Al Maguire, Leonard Mahoney, Harry Gallagher. Toomey, who went on to an eminent career as a hospital administrator in South Carolina, continues to this day to keep the Peabody Class of 1929 in touch with one another by annual Christmas letters.

By the 1920s Irish politicians ran Cambridge, including the school committee. They did not, in the manner of future ethnic minorities, seek to impose a Gaelocentric curriculum and glorify their particular ancestors; but they did regard the schools as repositories for ill-qualified friends and relatives. The Cambridge schools, despite a few first-rate Irish teachers, were in deplorable condition. My mother, a natural reformer, joined the League of Women Voters and agitated for better public schools. But proper Cantabrigians, with their own children in private schools, were not to be bothered about public education.

My mother labored on nevertheless. I remember her returning so often in a state of high exasperation from meetings of the school committee, of which she was a close observer, and the library board, of which she was a member. When a Cambridge mayor replaced her on the library board in 1939, she reviewed the appointments made during her term and said that the library had become "a nice quiet little pond where almost any politician can cast his line and pull out a job for someone."

After reading the powerful pacifist tract *Testament of Youth* by Vera Brittain (whose daughter, Shirley Williams, later became my good friend), my mother also became active in the Women's International

League for Peace and Freedom. From its viewpoint, her elder son's enthusiasm for toy soldiers was gravely suspect. I used to play elaborate war games with Willis Shapley, Leonard Mahoney and Harry Gallagher. We deployed our troops on a terrain with simulated rivers, forests and hills and subjected them to cannon fire by rolling marbles across the floor. My mother worried for a while that this might turn me into a militarist. My father worried less. In fact, playing with toy soldiers had no perceptible effect on my political views.

I was also an avid stamp collector. My father arranged for me to go to the basement of Widener Library, where I spent happy hours searching through piles of discarded envelopes for stamps from abroad. Even H. L. Mencken was recruited in the cause. In 1931 he came to Boston with Alfred A. Knopf, his publisher. Knopf delighted my parents, great fans of Mencken and the *Mercury*, by inviting them to dinner with him — "a very pleasant evening," Mencken wrote in his diary, "and they stayed until nearly one o'clock." Knopf in his diary noted that my mother "fell, as all women do, for Henry, whom she expected to see eat human flesh raw. But we had a very pleasant evening."

Afterward Mencken wrote to Knopf, "Do you recall me promising to send postage stamps to the young son of someone we met in Boston? I recall the promise, but can't remember to whom it was made." Knopf reminded him, and in due course a package of stamps arrived. I sent a dutiful letter of thanks. "I was very glad," I wrote, "to add your autograph to my collection which has among its members Owen Wister, Senator D. I. Walsh, 'Al' Smith, Steffanson, Presidents McKinley and Harding, Helen Keller, James J. Davis, 'Old Bob' La Follette and others." (Where is my autograph collection now?)

*   *   *

Rereading the letter to Mencken, I notice that, while the stationery is imprinted "Arthur B. Schlesinger," the signature is "Arthur M. Schlesinger, Jr."; so it must have been about this time that I changed my middle name. Whatever the name, confusion would have been inevitable once I entered my father's profession. Perhaps the "Jr." lessened it marginally. There are a few of us who out of filial piety and/or because we are in the same line of work have kept "Jr." as part of our names, even unto old age — Adolf A. Berle, Jr., Douglas Fairbanks, Jr., Martin Luther King, Jr., Kurt Vonnegut, Jr., Franklin D. Roosevelt, Jr., Albert Gore, Jr., Maury Maverick, Jr., George Stevens, Jr., Henry Louis Gates, Jr., William F. Buckley, Jr., Robert F. Kennedy, Jr.

I should add that Henry Cabot Lodge, Jr., does not count. His father was George Cabot Lodge, and his real name was Henry Cabot Lodge II, but lest this might seem repulsively aristocratic on the Massachusetts ballot, Cabot changed it to "Jr." The Wagner dynasty in New York had a revolving "Jr." Robert F. Wagner, Jr., son of the great senator, dropped his "Jr." after he became mayor of New York City, or rather transferred it to his own son, Robert III, a most promising public servant before his untimely death.

On coming to Cambridge, my parents shifted their tenuous religious allegiance from the Congregationalists to the Unitarians. I was sent to the Unitarian Sunday school, which in those days specialized in comparative religion. I learned a good deal about Buddhism, Confucianism and Islam, not much about Christianity.

I also joined Troop 6 of the Boy Scouts, which met in the basement of the church. My scouting career was inglorious. With great effort I mastered the square knot but was unable to solve enough other knots to rise from lowly tenderfoot status. I have always lacked manual dexterity. At "sloid," as the compulsory carpentry class at Peabody School was known, it took me most of the year to plane a board accurately enough to be allowed to advance to more complicated woodworking. I finally produced a large wooden box in which I stored duplicate stamps.

During a couple of summers I was sent off to camp in New Hampshire. The camps had Indian names — Wonalancet and Pemigewasset — and enthusiastic counselors. Wonalancet, where I went in 1927, was on Crystal Lake, in the White Mountains — a camp (I note in a brochure that somehow survived) for "Christian boys of good character," a stipulation that people did not particularly notice in the Twenties. Pemigewasset, which suffered me in 1930, was run by people from Oberlin and was presumably more enlightened. The camp's report to my parents said of me: "His friends respect his judgment and actions. He is liked by boys of all ages. Emotionally he is a little high-strung."

I neither especially liked or disliked camp and learned little except swimming and interminable verses of campfire songs like "The Wreck of the Old 97" and "Abdul Abulbul Amir (and Ivan Skavinsky Skivar)":

> The sons of the prophet were brave men and bold
> And quite unaccustomed to fear,

But the bravest by far in the ranks of the Shah
Was Abdul Abulbul Amir,

If you wanted a man to encourage the van
Or to harass the foe in the rear,
Or to storm a redoubt you had only to shout
For Abdul Abulbul Amir.

The heroes were plenty and well known to fame
In the troops that served for the Czar,
But the bravest of all was the man by the name
Of Ivan Skavinsky Skivar.

He could imitate Irving, play poker and pool,
And strum on a Spanish guitar.
In fact, quite the cream of the Muscovite team
Was Ivan Skavinsky Skivar.

And so on. It sounded great around the campfire.

Other summers, in the weeks we were not on the Cape, were passed agreeably in Cambridge. There were still horse-drawn wagons — above all, the ice wagon that clattered down the street and provided a cool refuge for small boys, who hoisted themselves onto the wagon's back. Mothers put signs marked ICE in the window, and with giant tongs the iceman would deposit the glistening blocks in the kitchen ice box.

The drugstore was a particular center of social life. Most drugstores in those happy days had a long, flat, marble-like counter known as a soda fountain, from which was dispensed a thrilling variety of frozen concoctions — ice cream sodas, sundaes, frappes (as milkshakes were known in New England), banana splits — and soft drinks — root beer, birch beer, lemon and lime, sarsaparilla, Moxie and Coca-Cola. The last two were then regarded as rivals, at least in New England; Moxie is now almost extinct save in its native state of Maine, Coke the world champion.

*   *   *

My childhood was, in recollection, a generally sunny time. I don't remember (or have repressed?) bad moments. There was an innocence about growing up in those days. I was a little scared of the tough Italian boys roaming on Huron Avenue, just north of Gray Gardens East. Walking to the drugstore on the corner of Huron and Concord avenues was an adventure. But one risked only taunts, threats, occasionally being surrounded or chased, once or twice even hit — but no knives, no guns, no mayhem in the contemporary style.

Though I played mainly with my Irish pals, I was also exposed to Yankee society through the summer play groups and Miss Keeler's dancing class. The dancing classes were held at the Hotel Commander, where I looked with distant admiration at pretty Jane Holcombe, the daughter of Arthur N. Holcombe, the political scientist. I doggedly executed the steps as directed by Miss Keeler (not, alas, Ruby), but it was only some years later that I experienced the revelation that the steps were to be performed in rhythm with the music.

I generally escaped children's diseases except for chicken pox. Summers were haunted by the specter of infantile paralysis, as polio was then known, and children were forbidden swimming pools and crowded places. Tom came down one spring with scarlet fever, and our house was put under quarantine. My parents sent me to stay with Paul and Sally Buck. I well remember the pleasures of that fortnight, ranging from the delight of escorting Sally Buck to Braves Field on ladies' day to the discovery of an unexpurgated edition of *Gulliver's Travels* in the Buck bookcase. I was transfixed by Gulliver's adventures on the nipples of the gigantic Brobdingnagian women.

Neither of my parents was a very strict disciplinarian. My father administered occasional spankings when Tom and I were very young, but his heart did not seem to be in it. My mother, no doubt misled by the manuals of the day, insisted for a time that we had to eat our vegetables whether we liked them or not, and in my case served me uneaten cauliflower meal after meal until I forced it down or surreptitiously disposed of it. The result was to leave me with an unconquerable aversion to cauliflower, much like George Bush's to broccoli (and I could not stand broccoli either). My parents generally preferred subtler methods. On the Fourth of July, for example, we would be offered the choice of a dollar to buy fireworks or two dollars if we abstained.

*   *   *

My mother was the heart of the household. My parents were rarely apart, and when they were, they kept in daily touch. Thus a letter from my father to my mother in August 1926: "I love you dearly, desperately, eternally." A devoted wife, she was also a concerned and imaginative mother, lively and curious and kind. She loved flowers and gardens and good food and music and Emily Dickinson and beautiful things and communicated that love to her family. She began to find time for her own research in women's history, publishing articles about such nineteenth-century liberated women as "Fanny Fern" (Sara Willis Parton, the sister of the critic Nathaniel P. Willis and the wife of the biographer James Parton), "Jenny June" (Jane Cunningham Croly, the mother of Herbert Croly of *The Promise of American Life*), Abigail May Alcott (Louisa's mother), Eliza Follen and others.

In the spring of 1929 my mother took me on a grand trip to New York and Washington. We traveled from Boston by night boat and stayed at the Hotel Bristol on West Forty-eighth Street. On our first morning in the big city, I climbed to the top of the Statue of Liberty. We went on to the Woolworth Building, then the tallest in the world. "He confided to me on the elevator," my mother wrote to my father, "'This is one of the things I've dreamed about doing.'" My mother showed me the city — Broadway, Wall Street, the Metropolitan Museum (I loved the armor), the Museum of Natural History, Grant's Tomb, F.A.O. Schwarz, Roxy's theater — and I recorded it all in my first diary.

We spent a weekend with the Dixon Ryan Foxes in Scarsdale, then went on to Washington, where Uncle George Schlesinger drove us around town and to Mount Vernon; thence to my grandmother Bancroft, who took me to the Capitol, where I heard Senator Tom Heflin of Alabama shout an hour-and-a-half tirade against the pope and his minions. I paid my first visit to the White House and saw the Blue and Green rooms. The whole trip was an exciting introduction to the larger world.

As long as I can remember, my mother kept two slim, leather-covered volumes by her bedside — the *Discourses* of Epictetus and the *Meditations* of Marcus Aurelius. I have wondered at her fondness for the Stoic philosophers. No doubt a woman so sensitive, even perhaps so vulnerable, found consolation in the Stoics' emphasis on mastering passions and transcending emotions. Epictetus and Marcus Aurelius, slave and emperor, agreed in their acceptance of the limits of life and in their recognition of individual responsibility for virtue and happiness. Perhaps this wisdom helped in producing the serenity of her old age so marvelously caught in Gardner Cox's portrait, now in the Schlesinger Library.

4

Life of a Reader

I PARTICULARLY REMEMBER my mother sitting in her chair reading aloud to her children. She was a splendid reader, spirited and expressive, and Tom and I insisted that she keep on reading to us long after we were able to read to ourselves. She was also an astute skipper. I recall her amusement at my indignation when I discovered that, in books like *Ivanhoe* and Parkman's *Conspiracy of Pontiac,* she was unscrupulously omitting passages she found static or boring.

Of all childhood pastimes, reading was my passion. Now that television has replaced the book in the life of the young, mine may have been the last generation to grow up in the high noon of the print culture. Perhaps it may be of historical interest to recall the profound excitement, the abiding fulfillment, books provided in those ancient and no doubt unimaginable days.

My mother gave me an appetite for books as well as a capacity to read them quickly. "Perhaps it is only in childhood that books have any deep influence on our lives," Graham Greene has well said. ". . . In childhood all books are books of divination, telling us about the future. . . . What do we ever get nowadays from reading to equal the excitement and the revelation of those first fourteen years?" To which I would add that most people will have done most of the reading they will ever do by the age of twenty-five and must live off those books for the rest of their lives.

My mother began with fairy tales, the Brothers Grimm and Hans Christian Andersen; with Greek and Roman mythology, especially as marvelously rendered by Hawthorne in *The Wonder Book* and *Tanglewood Tales;* and with the wondrous *Arabian Nights.* When I began to read for myself, a six-volume series called *My Book House* came into my life, an entrancing and resplendently illustrated anthology of historical adventure, fairy tale, poetry, mythology, something for every mood and moment.

I fear that such an initiation into a larger world would be much condemned today. For these were all tales filled with cruelty and violence, mutilation and murder, magic and fantasy, streaked by what is now seen as classism, sexism, racism and superstition. Approved children's books today are by contrast didactic in intent, dealing with prosaic, everyday events and intended to improve relations among classes, sexes and races. Such books, it is argued, lead children to face reality rather than to flee into fantasy.

Is this really so? Bruno Bettelheim may have lied about his life and mistreated children in his experimental school, and his *The Uses of Enchantment* certainly overdoes psychoanalytic jargon, but the book seems to me broadly right in seeing fairy tales and myths as symbolic reenactments of deep psychological and social dilemmas. In this sense, the classic fantasies may well be more realistic than the contemporary morality tales. Too many modern stories, Bettelheim observes, "peg the child's imagination to the level he has already reached." Moreover, the propaganda effect of morality tales is surely exaggerated. Social attitudes — courtesy, tolerance, curiosity, partnership, egalitarianism — are communicated more powerfully by the way parents behave in their own lives than by the books they give their children.

There is nothing new about the contemporary insistence on morality tales. Since the invention of type, most children's books have been designed to make children behave better. Yet good-behavior tales do not survive, and gods and goddesses, dragons and ogres, are with us still. Hawthorne in his day felt the pressures of moralistic didacticism. "These old legends, so brimming over with everything that is most abhorrent to our Christianized moral sense," he wrote ironically in his introduction to *Tanglewood Tales*, ". . . How were they to be purified? How was the blessed sunshine to be thrown into them?" Purification and sunshine, he said, were to be dismissed. "The author has not always thought it necessary to write downward in order to meet the comprehension of children. . . . Children possess an unestimated sensibility to whatever is deep or high, in imagination or feeling."

Childhood is finite. So is the number of books one can read. Why spend time on a modern morality tale in which the girl plays doctor and the boy plays nurse and their patient is the black child down the block when you can read about Huck and Tom and Nigger Jim? The serious point of children's books is not to improve behavior but to expand imagination. Great children's literature creates new worlds that children enter with delight and perhaps with apprehension and from which they return with understandings that their own experience could not have produced and that give their lives new meaning.

The classical tales have populated the common imagination of the West. They are voyages of discovery. They introduce children to the existential mysteries — the anxiety of loneliness, the terror of rejection, the need for comradeship, the quest for fulfillment, the struggle against fate, victory, love, death. "Small children," Henry James observed in his preface to *What Maisie Knew,* "have many more perceptions than they have terms to translate them." The classical tales tell children what they unconsciously know — that human nature is not innately good, that conflict is real, that life is harsh before it is happy — and thereby reassure them about their own fears and their own sense of self.

*   *   *

So I devoured the classics. But there were also home-grown fairy tales, and the best of them took place in the Land of Oz. I read all fourteen of L. Frank Baum's Oz books and most of the continuation of the series by Ruth Plumly Thompson. In those days educators and librarians looked down on the Oz stories. But the capacity to create lasting characters should never be underrated, and Baum had that gift. Who can forget Dorothy and Toto, the Cowardly Lion and the Scarecrow and the Tin Man, the Good Witch and the Wicked Witch and the Wonderful Wizard? Baum could also construct agreeable plots and write serviceable plain English: recall the bleak description of a Kansas farm in the opening paragraphs of *The Wonderful Wizard.*

He had started out in the theater, even trying his hand at musical comedy, and his cheerful and eccentric characterizations were redolent of American vaudeville. Indeed, he promptly made a musical out of the *Wizard,* with those popular vaudevillians (and great favorites of my father) Fred Stone and Dave Montgomery as the Tin Woodman and the Scarecrow. When Bert Lahr played the Cowardly Lion, Ray Bolger the Scarecrow and Jack Haley the Tin Woodman in Victor Fleming's inspired movie version of 1939, these splendid latter-day vaudevillians were continuators of a grand tradition.

It was the movie and the Harold Arlen–Yip Harburg score that made the Oz books at last respectable. Salman Rushdie saw the film in Bombay's Metro Cinema at the age of ten; "it made a writer of me." Gore Vidal confessed, "With *The Emerald City,* I became addicted to reading." Scholars got to work on Baum, and in 1964 Henry M. Littlefield proposed an ingenious reading of *The Wonderful Wizard* as a parable of the campaign of 1896, when Bryan spoke out for free silver and pleaded not to crucify mankind upon a cross of gold. After all,

Dorothy wore magic Silver Shoes when she set forth on the Yellow Brick Road. What could be clearer than that? The Cowardly Lion, Littlefield suggested, was Bryan; the Scarecrow, the farmer; the Woodman, the worker; the Wicked Witch of the East, the banker; the humbug Wizard, McKinley; the Emerald City, Washington, D.C.; Oz itself, the abbreviation for an ounce (of gold).

Maybe, but if so, a triumph of the unconscious; for Baum does not seem to have been very political. He even wrote a pro-McKinley poem in '96; he also marched in a Bryan torchlight procession. No one knows how he voted. Littlefield himself later agreed that there was "no basis in fact to consider Baum a supporter of turn-of-the-century Populist ideology." Probably Baum regarded all politicians as humbugs like the Wizard. As he himself put it, he wrote "solely to pleasure children of today." In that he certainly succeeded; and his fantasy created, as Marius Bewley has said, a great good place, "a specifically American fairyland." "Toto," said Dorothy, "I have a feeling we're not in Kansas anymore." •

*　　*　　*

From L. Frank Baum it was a natural progression to Mark Twain. My father bought the red-bound Harper's set with the titles in gold and inside a printed inscription in the author's handwriting: "This is the authorized Uniform Edition of all my books." When we spent our summer at Horseneck Beach, he brought a new volume each weekend. I read all of them, or nearly all — I bogged down when Mark Twain wrote about Joan of Arc and Christian Science. But I loved his essays and his casuals, and later, after Benny DeVoto began to publish the darker writings that Mark Twain himself suppressed, I sympathized with the old man's despairing reactions to the anarchy of the universe.

I read and reread *Tom Sawyer* and *Huckleberry Finn;* and, with my weakness for sequels, went on to read *Tom Sawyer Abroad* and *Tom Sawyer, Detective*. What a marvel *Huck Finn* remains for every age! No book evokes more vividly the terrors and joys of childhood, or has a more exact sense of the rhythms of the American language, or uses more effectively an artless vernacular to convey the subtlest perceptions, or covers a wider range of American emotion and experience.

The scene that sticks forever in memory comes when Huck, obedient to conventional morality, decides that the "plain hand of Providence" requires him to write a letter telling Miss Watson where she can find her runaway slave, Nigger Jim. Huck feels suddenly virtuous, "all washed clean of sin." He trembles to imagine how close he had come to "being lost and going to hell." Then he begins to think of Jim and the rush of the surging river and the storytelling and the singing and the companionship. He takes up the letter of betrayal, holds it in his hand. "I was a-trembling because I'd got to decide, forever, betwixt two things, and I knowed it. I studied a minute, sort of holding my breath, and then says to myself, 'All right, then, I'll go to hell' — and tore it up." What an affirmation of humanity against the absolutes!

Perhaps this scene is why Louisa May Alcott, who ironically had her own dark side, said, "If Mr. Clemens cannot think of anything better to tell our pure-minded lads and lasses, he had best stop writing for them." The Concord Public Library banned the book — an action imitated in our own day by the New Trier High School Board of Education in Illinois and by other multicultural busybodies across the land.

There were other enjoyably subversive chronicles of boyhood, subversive because told from the boy's viewpoint. William Dean Howells praised Thomas Bailey Aldrich's *The Story of a Bad Boy* (1870) because it was written "with so great a desire to show what a boy's life is, and so little purpose of teaching what it should be." Aldrich ended, however, as one of the literary grandees of his day. There was the more slapstick *Peck's Bad Boy* (1883), whose author, George Washington Peck, later went straight like Aldrich and became governor of Wisconsin. There were Booth Tarkington's Penrod and Sam books, which I read with pleasure, oblivious to genteel anti-black and anti-Semitic undertones. English writers tended to propagate an adult view of boyhood. Still, Thomas Hughes's *Tom Brown's School Days* was a favorite; Kipling's *Stalky & Co.*, with its smug bullies, less so. There was more the American flavor of a child's revenge against the grownup world in F. Anstey's delightful *Vice Versa,* in which a magic lamp enables a schoolboy to exchange bodies with his authoritarian father.

I greatly liked *Two Little Savages,* written and illustrated by the Canadian Ernest Thompson Seton. It is the story of two white boys, Yan and Sam, whose dream is to live like Indians. The book is, among other things, an engaging how-to-do-it manual in which the reader follows Yan and Sam in learning how to build a tipi, how to feather an arrow, how to put on war paint, how to make a drum, how to construct a dam. I never succeeded in doing any of these things, but I greatly enjoyed thinking I might.

I read simplified children's versions of *Gulliver's Travels* and *Robin-*

son Crusoe. I have reported on the erotic delights of the unexpurgated *Gulliver,* but it was some years before I discovered how long the un-abridged *Crusoe* was and that Defoe had produced a sequel (which I then read, too). I remember liking *Swiss Family Robinson* as a child. But when I later read Johann Wyss's rip-off of *Crusoe* to my own children, the Robinson family seemed to me a pack of bloodthirsty Calvinists who spent an inordinate amount of time (a) in praying and (b) in massacring inoffensive animals. Nor was Wyss, even though the author of the Swiss national anthem, near Defoe's class as a writer.

I find a letter (typed) to my mother in the summer of 1926, when I was eight years old. She was on a trip and had asked me to send the names of books I might want. "Here are some," I replied. "'20,000 Leagues under the Sea,' 'The Freshman,' 'Moby Dick,' 'A Diary of Adam' and 'A Diary of Eve.'" The last two, I guess, are Mark Twain. I have no idea about *The Freshman;* perhaps it was a novelization of the Harold Lloyd movie of the year before.

That summer the director of the Yale University Press gave us a set of *The Pageant of America,* illustrated volumes dealing with themes in American history. I replied (in a letter the director sent my father after the publication of *The Age of Jackson*): "I liked the one on Indians and adventures best. I liked the ones on literature and slaves second best. I liked the one on machinery third best."

* * *

As I grew older, I began to turn to historical novels. I suppose the historian's basic impulse is to find out what the past was really like. Whether by nature or nurture, I have always had this impulse. I cannot walk down Fifth Avenue without wondering how the street and the people on it would have looked a hundred years ago.

My father had preserved his store of Henty books, and I soon became as absorbed in Henty as he had been. But my case was more peculiar. After all, Henty, who died in 1902, was still producing when my father was a boy. When I started reading him, he had been dead for a quarter of a century, and he carried the stigmata of a Victorian imperialist in a time of debunking and disillusion. Yet such knowledge as I have about ancient Egypt (*The Cat of Bubastes*), the Venetian republic (*The Lion of St. Mark's*), India (half a dozen Henty books), the rise of the Dutch republic (*By Pike and Dyke*), the struggle for Chilean independence (*With Cochrane the Dauntless*), the Franco-Prussian War (*The Young Franc-Tireurs*), the Boxer Rebellion (*With the Allies to Pekin*) and much else came initially from Henty.

He also provoked thought about history. A sturdy Tory, Henty wrote about the American Revolution from the viewpoint of the Loyalists (*True to the Old Flag*) and the Civil War from the viewpoint of the Confederates (*With Lee in Virginia*). One received a new slant on what had seemed historical verities, nor was one corrupted thereby. And even Henty had his subtexts. *With Lee in Virginia* overtly supported the slave system, but his rebellious slaves were as brave and manly as his Confederate heroes.

Another interesting point: the critic George Steiner has pointed out that the great British nineteenth-century novelists ignored the British nineteenth-century wars. Stendhal wrote about the Napoleonic wars; so did Tolstoy. Except for Waterloo's cameo appearance in *Vanity Fair,* nineteenth-century war hardly existed in the serious English novel. Jane Austen, Dickens, the Brontës, George Eliot, Trollope — no battle scenes. As the Henty scholar Dennis Butts observes, if you want to find out what it was like to be in the Crimean War, you have to turn to G. A. Henty.

Through the years I have collected the names of people who have declared a debt to Henty: the Rabelaisian novelist Henry Miller ("my favorite author. . . . I must have read every blessed one before I was fourteen. Today . . . I can pick up any book of his and get the same fascinating pleasure I did as a boy"); the non-Rabelaisian novelist Graham Greene ("I particularly liked the dull historical parts"); the conservative billionaire J. Paul Getty, who read Henty all his life; the iconoclastic radical historian A.J.P. Taylor ("They were my favourites. . . . He taught me more history than anyone else"); General George C. Marshall (who visited Tunisia in 1943 and told General Eisenhower, as they inspected the ruins, that he knew about Hannibal from Henty's *The Young Carthaginian*); Admiral Elmo Zumwalt ("they taught me more about history than more academic texts, and were key in motivating me for a life of adventure"); the conservative senator Richard B. Russell ("He was sort of an old-time royalist, but he really knew how to advance his heroes quickly"); the liberal senator Ernest Gruening; the actor Elliott Nugent; the historian Samuel Eliot Morison and the historian and Socialist Kenneth Wiggins Porter; Harold Gray, the reactionary begetter of Daddy Warbucks and Little Orphan Annie; my English contemporary and friend, the historian and founder of the Liberal Democrats, Roy Jenkins.

Not that Henty can be revived today. In the fast-forwarding tempo of modern life, he is a lost cause. Or perhaps I am wrong? *The Economist* on December 11, 1999, reports that Henty's books are being reissued by the Lost Classics Book Company of Lake Wales, Florida, and PrestonSpeed Books in Mill Hall, Pennsylvania, and that a complete edition is available on CD-ROM.

Anyway, thanks for the memory.

* * *

Henty led on to more polished and sophisticated books. Scott and Cooper, for all their stilted manner and occasional *longueurs,* cast their spell. I was fond of Captain Maryatt's *Mr. Midshipman Easy* and its nautical slapstick. And Conan Doyle: not just the great Sherlock Holmes but Doyle's historical novels as well, *The White Company* and *The Exploits of Brigadier Gerard.* The American Howard Pyle enchanted not only by his writing but by his wonderful illustrations as he retold the tales of King Arthur and Robin Hood or created historical stories of his own, *Men of Iron* and *Otto of the Silver Hand* — not to forget *Howard Pyle's Book of Pirates.* N. C. Wyeth studied with Pyle, and his illustrations of *The Last of the Mohicans, Treasure Island, The Boy's King Arthur* and *The Mysterious Island* marvelously enhanced the suspense and wonder produced by the narrative. (In later years N. C. Wyeth's painter grandson, Jamie, became a friend.)

Then there were those mythical Balkan kingdoms with their imagined histories, their dashing heroes and villains and their romantic derring-do. The model and by far the best was Ruritania, as suavely portrayed in Anthony Hope's *The Prisoner of Zenda* and its sequel, *Rupert of Hentzau.* (John Cromwell's 1937 movie of *Zenda* was one of the few wholly satisfying translations of a novel into film. Douglas Fairbanks, Jr., who stole the show as the charmingly villainous Rupert of Hentzau, once told me that he had hoped for the lead; but the double role of Rudolf Rassendyl and the king went instead to Ronald Colman, and he was offered Rupert. Disappointed, he was about to turn it down when his father said, "Take it, take it. No one ever loses as Rupert of Hentzau.")

I even read Hope's much inferior American imitator George Barr McCutcheon and the road company Ruritania he called Graustark. Also several steps down from Hope but still entertaining, despite their Wardour Street dialogue, were the swashbuckling Regency romances of the British writer Jeffrey Farnol, *The Broad Highway* and *The Amateur Gentleman,* and the Anglo-Italian Rafael Sabatini's *The Sea Hawk, Captain Blood* and *Scaramouche.* (Norman Mailer was another Farnol-Sabatini fan.) My enjoyment of Baroness Orczy's *The Scarlet Pimpernel* did not turn me into a counter-revolutionary any more than

Henty and P. C. Wren's Foreign Legion tales, *Beau Geste, Beau Sabreur* and *Beau Ideal,* turned me into an imperialist.

Even poetry had its historical impact — Scott's *Lady of the Lake,* Macaulay's *Lays of Ancient Rome,* Tennyson's *Idylls of the King.* In 1932 my mother gave me for Christmas the Cambridge edition of the *Collected Poetry of Lord Byron,* and I became a permanent fan. I could go on this way for a while, but let me mention three writers who made a particular impression.

Who remembers H. Rider Haggard now? Film versions of *King Solomon's Mines* and *She* occasionally show up on late-night television, but (except for Helen Gahagan's *She*) they betray the originals. Haggard, who had served in the British Civil Service in Africa as a young man, did for southern Africa what Kipling did for India, creating a British myth of an exotic culture. The Allan Quatermain stories have a hypnotic force with their evocation of the great, trackless veldt, the snow-capped mountains beyond, the discovery of ancient kingdoms, the mystic appearance of Ayesha in her "awful loveliness," the sublimely beautiful She-who-must-be-obeyed. Haggard was an English gentleman and a believer in the *mission civilisatrice.* But he was not a racist. "I could never discern," he wrote, "a superiority so great in ourselves as to authorise us, by divine right as it were, to destroy the coloured man and take his lands. It is difficult to see why a Zulu, for instance, has not as much right to live in his own way as a Boer or an Englishman."

He glorified the Zulus, much preferred them to the Boers, and gave them some of his best lines. Umbopa meditates beautifully on life and death in *King Solomon's Mines:*

> Out of the dark we came, into the dark we go. Like a storm-driven bird at night we fly out of the Nowhere; for a moment our wings are seen in the light of the fire, and, lo! we are gone again into the Nowhere. Life is nothing. Life is all. It is the hand with which we hold off death. It is the glow-worm that shines in the night-time and is black in the morning; it is the white breath of the oxen in winter; it is the little shadow that runs across the grass and loses itself at sunset.

A better writer and even more gripping storyteller was Robert Louis Stevenson. Strangely underrated today, or so it seems to me, Stevenson produced at least two masterpieces: *Treasure Island,* the perfect boys' book, *The Strange Case of Dr. Jekyll and Mr. Hyde,* the perfect horror story — not to mention *Kidnapped* and *The Master of Ballantrae* and *The New Arabian Nights.* And he died at forty-four! Had Stevenson lived as long as Somerset Maugham, who vied with him both as storyteller and South Seas traveler, he would have died, not in 1894, but in 1941. What would he have written in the twentieth century? He very likely would have moved more along the darker lines so keenly foreshadowed in his unfinished *Weir of Hermiston*. I find in Stevenson an insight into human ambiguities that foretells the literary modernism to come.

But of all writers in the historical vein, the supreme was the great Dumas. His capacity to merge historical data with swiftly paced narration was unparalleled; he had a vivid sense of scene, and he imprinted his characters with lighthearted gallantry or darkhearted villainy. His output was prodigious: 301 volumes in his collected works. Though he ran a sort of literary factory — "I have collaborators," he said grandly, "the way Napoleon had generals" — he gave most of his books a distinctive personal touch that his collaborators never achieved on their own.

I could never decide which was my favorite — *The Three Musketeers* or *The Count of Monte Cristo*. Heaven alone knows how many times I read and reread those glorious works. And of course I read the sequels. The later volumes in the D'Artagnan saga — *Twenty Years After, The Vicomte de Bragelonne, Louise de la Valliere, The Man in the Iron Mask* — are in a class with the original. Widener Library's rich Dumas collection also provided me with the deservedly less well known sequels to *Monte Cristo* — *Edmond Dantes, The Son of Monte Cristo* and other inferior products of the Dumas factory. But D'Artagnan, Athos, Porthos, Aramis, Dantes, the Abbé Faria, Mercedes, Danglars, de Villefort — these were favorite companions of my boyhood, and they gave a panorama of French history from St. Bartholomew's Eve to Napoleon.

*   *   *

If Dumas opened up the possibilities of the past, so another nineteenth-century French writer opened up the possibilities of the future. Jules Verne, a quarter century younger, was in fact a Dumas protégé, and he collaborated on occasion with Dumas *fils,* the author of *La Dame aux Camélias,* who once generously said that, from a literary viewpoint, Verne was a truer son of his father. Verne occasionally wrote stirring adventure tales in the Dumas vein if not in the Dumas class, like *Michael Strogoff* (which Turgenev read in manuscript to check the Russian atmosphere). But his genius lay in what William James called a "sense of futurity."

He wrote at least sixty-five books and, unlike Dumas, wrote them all himself. His style was often pedantic in its insistence on technical detail, but it was redeemed by Gallic vivacity, by a certain innocent charm and by the power of his imagination of the future. He wonderfully took his readers where no man had gone before. We circumnavigated the globe in eighty days, penetrated to the center of the earth, went by rocket to the moon, traveled in Captain Nemo's *Nautilus* twenty thousand leagues under the sea — Captain Nemo, the anarchist, as dedicated to revenge as Edmond Dantes — and thence to the Mysterious Island.

• *From the Earth to the Moon* displayed a particular prescience. Though Verne had not at that point — 1865 — visited the United States, he made his astronauts American, for Americans, he said, were "the first mechanicians in the world, engineers — just as the Italians are musicians and the Germans metaphysicians — by right of birth." He launched his rocket with a crew of three from Florida in a place only about 140 miles west of Cape Canaveral, where *Apollo 11* took off with its crew of three 104 years later. Verne's craft took 97 hours and 13 minutes to reach the moon; *Apollo 11* took 100 hours and 46 minutes. His astronauts, like their real-life successors, went through the experience of weightlessness. Both spaceships returned to earth in about the same place in the Pacific. "It cannot be a mere matter of coincidence," the astronaut Frank Borman wrote to the grandson of Jules Verne. "Our space vehicle was launched from Florida . . . ; it had the same weight and the same height, and it splashed down in the Pacific a mere two and a half miles from the point mentioned in the novel." •

Verne sometimes got things wrong: the shock of blastoff, for example, would have crushed the occupants of his capsule. But he did his best to make his fantasies correspond to the available scientific knowledge. He thought it a low trick to transgress the laws of physics and mechanics. Herein Verne differed from his great successor H. G. Wells. "His stories," Verne said of Wells, "do not repose on very scientific bases. . . . I make use of physics. He invents. I go to the moon in a cannon-ball, discharged from a cannon. Here there is no invention. He goes to Mars in an airship, which he constructs of a metal which does away with the law of gravitation. . . . Show me this metal. Let him produce it."

Wells agreed: Verne "dealt almost always with actual possibilities. . . . [My stories] are all fantasies; they do not aim to project a serious possibility; they aim indeed only at the same amount of conviction as one gets in a good gripping dream." But Wells was a far better writer, and his stories reached into the unconscious, as Verne's rarely did. There was one other salient difference. Though Verne had his dystopian moments of doubt (as in the recently discovered *Paris in the 20th Century*), he generally bathed the future in amiability and eccentricity, presenting a moral extension of Victorian life fused with a quite modern delight in the potential of technology.

For Wells, the future was filled with foreboding. His reputation as a utopian comes from his manifestos, not from his tales. In *The Time Machine* the world in another thirty million years has become an "abominable desolation," inhabited by green liverworts and lichens; "the sky was absolutely black." The Time Traveller grieved to think "how brief the dream of the human intellect had been. It had committed suicide." *The Invisible Man* described the awful consequences of careless scientific experimentation. *The Island of Dr. Moreau* warned against the scientist who tries to play God. *The First Men in the Moon* envisaged what his son Anthony West (in later years to become my brother-in-law by marriage) called "the worst conceivable kind of slave state." *The Sleeper Awakes* conveyed another picture of a grim and degenerate future. *The War of the Worlds* and *The Food of the Gods* were filled with calamities. In *The World Set Free* he even predicted nuclear war, beginning in 1956; by 1959, two hundred "atomic bombs" have destroyed the great cities of the world. *The Shape of Things to Come*, especially William Cameron Menzies's grandiose film version, mingled Wells the pessimist with Wells the utopian; the passages of disaster, however, are what linger in the mind.

Dr. Edward Teller, who evidently inspired the mad scientist in Stanley Kubrick's *Dr. Strangelove*, once observed that he used to read science fiction — "my favorite author was Jules Verne" — but he reads it no longer. "When I was young, science fiction said, 'How wonderful.' Today, science fiction says, 'How horrible.' . . . We are afraid of the power which man now holds in his hands."

*　　*　　*

Wells popularized one new character of particular fascination for the historian: the time traveler. After all, what are historians but time travelers? What historian does not long to climb into a time machine, whirl back to his period and find out what the past was *really* like?

American writers have played effectively with time. Mark Twain's *Connecticut Yankee* is a classic of time travel; so is Henry James's *The Sense of the Past*, better known in John Balderston's dramatization as *Berkeley Square;* so is Edward Bellamy's *Looking Backward*. Nicholas

Meyer made an engaging movie, *Time after Time*, in which Jack the Ripper escapes on Wells's own time machine from Victorian London into contemporary San Francisco, to be pursued there by Wells himself. Jack Finney's *Time and Again* carries a man back from contemporary New York to the New York of the 1880s, filling the historian with envy.

An earlier writer, Frank R. Stockton, was an amiable fabulist with a puckish imagination, remembered (if remembered at all) for the story "The Lady or the Tiger." This tantalizing tale tells of a young man in a barbaric kingdom who commits the grave offense of winning the love of the king's daughter. The king decrees a punishment: the young man must enter a great arena and open one of two doors. Behind one door is a beautiful maiden of the court. If he opens her door, he must marry her at once. Behind the other door is a ferocious tiger.

The young man strides into the arena and looks up at his beloved. The princess covertly signals him to open the door on the right. This he unhesitatingly does. But will the barbaric princess yield her lover to a beautiful maiden of whom she is already fiercely jealous? or will she consign him to the tiger? "And so I leave it with all of you," Stockton concluded. "Which came out of the open door — the lady or the tiger?"

This became a great conversation piece in literary circles in the 1880s. Robert Browning, for example, wrote that he had "no hesitation in supposing that such a princess under such circumstances would direct her lover to the tiger's door." Stockton himself would only say, "If you decide which it was — the lady, or the tiger — you find out what kind of a person you are yourself."

Stockton wrote two Verne-like novels I found enjoyable. *The Great War Syndicate* tells of a naval war between the United States and Great Britain. The American government subcontracts the conduct of the war to a group of capitalists employing new, quasi-scientific methods. They build Repellers, steel-plated ships with powerful projectile launchers, and Crabs, heavily armored boats designed to rip off the rudders and propellors of the British dreadnaughts. The syndicate wins the war expeditiously, and the result is the formation of an Anglo-American War Syndicate to keep the world's peace.

Better was *The Great Stone of Sardis*. Here Stockton in 1897 envisions the world of 1947. Progress has stagnated; "it had become fashionable to be unprogressive." But an inventor, possibly based on Stockton's New Jersey neighbor Thomas A. Edison, is among those determined "to shake themselves free of the drowsiness of their years of inaction." Stockton's themes — reaching the North Pole, descending into the depths of the earth — and his inventions — Artesian rays, projectiles, explosives — as well as the ingenuous naiveté of the characterizations are all reminiscent of Verne.

In time, though not for Teller's reasons, I gave up science fiction. There were a few exceptions, especially Ray Bradbury's *The Martian Chronicles* (later I met Ray Bradbury and discovered that this enthusiast for intergalactic travel hated flying on airplanes). And I fell into the habit of watching Gene Roddenberry's *Star Trek* series with my children. But the impact of Verne and Wells on one's imagination and expectation remains.

For me, the most exciting event of the twentieth century was the landing of men on the moon. And I surmise as a historian that if historians five hundred years from now remember our century for anything, it will be as the century when man first burst terrestrial bonds and began the exploration of space, the ultimate frontier.

*　　*　　*

Happily undistracted by television, one read incessantly in the early years of the century. The *Saturday Evening Post* arrived each week, and I faithfully followed the Earthworm tractor saga in which William Hazlett Upson recounted the humorous misadventures of a traveling salesman; followed too the affectionate but condescending 'darky' stories of Octavus Roy Cohen; read romantic stories gorgeously adorned by John La Gatta's tall, silken, sophisticated women. I relished the comic magazines *Judge* and *Life* with witty drawings by John Held, Jr. (who became a friend in later years, a quirky, roly-poly man in blazing tweed jackets). I liked *Popular Mechanics* and its monthly display of gimmicks of the future; also the advertisements in which heavily muscled men — Charles Atlas and Lionel Strongfort and Earle Liederman — promised to turn ninety-seven-pound weaklings into stalwart defenders of a girlfriend's honor.

A man named Emanuel Haldeman-Julius lived in Girard, Kansas. Like Stephen Girard, for whom the town was named (I assume) and who forbade men of the cloth to enter the grounds of the college he endowed in Philadelphia, Haldeman-Julius was of an iconoclastic disposition and had a particular dislike for priests. In the 1920s he began to publish the Little Blue Books, so called because of their size (three and a half by five inches) and the color of their covers. They sold at first for a quarter, then for a nickel, began with the *Rubáiyat* and the

Ballad of Reading Gaol and soon expanded into free thought, self-improvement, humor and sex. In the end he published more than 500 million Little Blue Books, of which I acquired a couple of dozen, mostly of an anticlerical vein. Haldeman-Julius, a colorful figure, drowned in his swimming pool in 1951, shortly after his conviction for income tax evasion.

I found much enjoyment in the catalogue issued by the Johnson Smith Company of Racine, Wisconsin, with its fascinating offering of magic tricks, puzzles, trick spectacles, Chinese linking rings, stink sprays, disappearing ink, itching powder, how-to-pickpocket manuals and other childhood necessities. Johnson Smith also advertised dubious books — William Morgan on the secrets of freemasonry; Maria Monk's *Awful Disclosures* on the vile goings-on in a Montreal nunnery. In recent years, the catalogues that arrive in the junk mail from a Johnson Smith Company of Mount Clemens, Michigan, later of Bradenton, Florida, are pallid imitations of the gaudy original.

Then each year I immersed myself in the new *World Almanac.* With a precision of memory that has, alas, latterly escaped me, I used to bore my parents' Sunday afternoon teas by asking those present the population of the world's major cities — and then implacably telling them. I was equally in insufferable command of baseball batting averages.

A special pleasure was to accompany my father on his periodic tours of Boston's secondhand bookshops. I grew to love those dark, musty caverns with books piled everywhere, generally arranged in a semblance of order but with unexpected treasures to be found on unexpected shelves. I haunted the ten-cent and twenty-five-cent cases, and I still have a recurrent dream of wandering about a maze of streets in central Boston, going from one secondhand bookshop to the next, clutching great finds.

Having noted what I did read, I perhaps should confess what I failed to read. I did not read Horatio Alger or Zane Grey or Edgar Rice Burroughs or A. A. Milne or the products of Edward Stratemeyer's factory — the Rover Boys and the Tom Swift books.

*   *   *

What I did read inspired me to try my hand at writing. Juvenilia carefully preserved by my mother show an early preoccupation with history. I wrote stories about pirates in the Spanish Main and desperadoes in the American west; also "Alice's Adventures in Cambridge," with President Lowell cast as the Red King, the historian Charles H.

Haskins as the Duke and Albert Bushnell Hart as the Messenger; also, more ambitiously, at least so far as titles were concerned, "A History of the United States" and "The Age of Discovery, 1000–1780."

In a later notebook, I find thirteen chapters of a story, obviously modeled on *Treasure Island,* about a boy cast among pirates. Then, fascinated by knights of fact and fiction, I imagined a series of knightly jousts on the lines of a tennis tournament and wrote it up as a sporting event with Bertrand Du Guesclin beating Allenstadt of the Teutonic Knights in one semifinal and Edward the Black Prince beating Ivanhoe in the other. The Black Prince won the finals.

One lived in a pageant of historical dreams. Here is a letter to my father I wrote at the age of eight while staying with friends at Squam Lake in New Hampshire and reading Henty's *Under Drake's Flag:* "Every morning before breakfast Ed and I go out in the canoe. . . . Ed and I pretend we're Francis Drake and his men. We have a rock which we call 'Panama.' Cotton's Cove is the 'Pacific Ocean.' Ed's house is 'Valparaiso.' We have a wharf where we captured two galleons and defeated one galley."

I even began a parody encyclopedia, as if written by historians of the remote future garbling their accounts of notables of the past. This suggests an early skepticism about the capacity of historians to get the past right:

HOOVER, HULBERT C. or K. General. Little known about him, supposed to be a friend of Uriah Z. Graunt, the famous poet.

ROGERS, WILL. Tragedian. Was popular in the reign of Gruffer Clevelandt. He is said to have composed "Poor Richard's Almanac," the jazz music of the time. Appeared first on stage at Walshington, C.D.

SMITHE, ALBROD E. or G. Famous orator. Born in Alaska in the 23rd century. . . . Spoke at the death of Jam I of England and at the coronation of Lewis IXX of Frenchland.

ROOSEVELT, THEODORA. A speaker in the birth control campaign of 1727. . . . Led the Tough Riders in the War of Spinach Succession.

HASTY, WARREN. Criminal. Born in Injia (possibly part of Siam) at the time of the great flood. Son of Noah and called his father a drunken galoot and his father changed him into the Wandering Jew. He was elected Shah of Injia, where he murdered one Robber Clive.

I particularly like the entry on DOWES, CHARLES (Charles G. Dawes was Coolidge's vice president), described as a twelfth-century poet and author of "Pair of Dice Lost and Regained."

St. Nicholas, a favorite children's magazine of the period, invited contributions. I made the St. Nicholas League along with more talented children — Ring Lardner, Henry R. Luce, Samuel Eliot Morison, E. E. Cummings, Montgomery Clift, Eudora Welty, Edna St. Vincent Millay, Scott Fitzgerald, Harrison Salisbury — and was even asked to review a book called *The Last Wanigan*. I can find no evidence that the review was ever published. *St. Nicholas* barely survived the depression and folded in 1943.

*   *   *

In June 1929 I graduated from Peabody School. On October 15 I had my twelfth birthday. Fourteen days later Wall Street laid its famous egg, and the economy began to crumble into depression. I was not especially aware at first of ominous developments. My father was not in the stock market. His job was secure, and academic salaries, modest during the boom, now held stable as prices fell. Only in the winter of 1930–31 did one begin to notice the shuffling lines of the unemployed and sense an enveloping pall of gloom.

From Peabody I moved on to the Cambridge High and Latin School. There I had one or two fine teachers, especially Miss Hagerty in Latin. But some of my teachers were disasters. The parental faith in public education fell under increasing strain. One day in my sophomore year I came home and reported that my civics teacher had informed the class that the inhabitants of Albania were called Albinos and had white hair and pink eyes. That finished it so far as my father was concerned. He forthwith called his friend Corning Benton, the treasurer of Phillips Exeter Academy, and entered me as an upper middler for the autumn of 1931.

PART II

The Thirties

5

Prep School

IN SEPTEMBER 1931 I traveled forty miles north from Cambridge to boarding school. The pleasant town of Exeter, first settled in 1638, lay just across the state line in southeastern New Hampshire. Phillips Exeter Academy was founded in 1781, during the War for Independence, by John Phillips, a local merchant who three years before had joined with his nephew Samuel to found Phillips Academy in Andover, Massachusetts. The oldest American preparatory schools, Andover and Exeter were traditional rivals. By the twentieth century they had higher academic and lower social pretensions than the so-called St. Grottlesex schools of the late nineteenth century — Groton, St. Paul's, St. Mark's, Middlesex.

In 1931 Exeter was a big, impersonal school with a first-class faculty and a highly competitive student body of nearly seven hundred boys. Tuition was $350 a year plus another $300 or so for room and board at $9 a week. I was two years younger than the rest of my class, shy, stammering, bespectacled and with a case of acne that, if not so disfiguring as the psoriasis that John Updike recalls so feelingly from his own boyhood, still was demoralizing, especially when I was in the company of girls.

I cannot truthfully say that my two years at Exeter were the happiest of my life, but this was not Exeter's fault. Adolescence is an unhappy time. I would have moped and maundered wherever I might have been. Indeed, the freedom and impersonality of Exeter in those days offered an excellent environment for boys caught in a low gear of incertitude and discontent. Social relations were easy and casual. You had friends when you wanted them, and you could be left alone when you wanted to be left alone.

As a late entrant, I was assigned not to a dormitory but to a rooming house just off the campus. My roommate was John Aloysius O'Keefe, a bright, stubborn boy from Swampscott, Massachusetts, whose devotion was divided equally between the Roman Catholic church and astrophysics, to which he later made notable contributions as a government space scientist; the O'Keefe Asteroid was named for him. We spent the first term arguing fiercely but amiably about religion and playing a popular board game of the period, halfway between checkers and chess, called Camelot.

Camelot! During the Christmas vacation in 1931, John invited me to dinner at his parents' house. His father, Edward S. O'Keefe, was a leading doctor, and his mother, a charming and intelligent woman, had gone a quarter century earlier to a convent in the Netherlands, where her best friend was another girl from Boston named Rose Fitzgerald. Rose Fitzgerald soon thereafter married Joseph P. Kennedy and rapidly had a number of children.

One of them, Rosemary, seemed a little backward compared to the rest of the spirited Kennedy brood. Medical knowledge of retardation was then primitive, and Rose Kennedy and Ruth O'Keefe thought it might be a good idea for Rosemary to spend the winter with the O'Keefes, where Dr. O'Keefe could observe her professionally and the two lively O'Keefe girls, Mary and Frances, could become her friends.

So at dinner in Swampscott in December 1931 I had my first encounter with the Kennedy family. Rosemary seemed a pleasant but slow girl, rather nonplussed by the animated talk swirling around her. I saw her next a couple of years later at a dance to which John O'Keefe invited me when we were both at Harvard. Rosemary, I noted, was a sturdy, obstinate young woman who insisted on leading her partners.

I did not see her again for more than half a century. In the Eighties and Nineties, she often spent Thanksgiving in Bridgehampton on Long Island with her sister Jean Kennedy Smith. Jean and Stephen Smith were dear friends, and my wife Alexandra Emmet and I spent many holidays with them. Rosemary, lobotomized a dozen years after I had first met her and living thereafter in a Catholic retreat in Wisconsin, was now a crotchety old woman, escorted by nuns and treated with affectionate consideration by her family. Her personal tragedy was terrible, but it yielded immense dividends in the crusade the Kennedys, especially Jean Smith and her sister Eunice Kennedy Shriver, later led on behalf of the handicapped and the retarded.

*   *   *

Between Camelot, religious disputation and 'heeling' for the student paper, the *Exonian,* my studies went by the board. Then the first-term grades arrived: D's in Latin, French and English; a C in mathematics. For one who had pulled down A's without effort in public school, the shock was salutary. I now set to work — never worked so hard in my life. In my second term I received a B and three C's; in my third term, three B's and a C. Whatever defects Exeter may have had, the standards were high, and the intellectual training was superb. After Exeter, Harvard was a breeze.

The oil millionaire Edward Harkness, though a St. Paul's graduate himself, had given Phillips Exeter in 1930 $6 million — a prodigious gift; nearly $70 million in twenty-first century dollars — for the development of new educational methods. The Harkness Plan, instituted in 1932, represented a considerable innovation. Instead of a master lecturing from a platform to thirty or so students sitting at desks below, a dozen students sat with the master around a table and were encouraged to talk back to him. Education became not a recitation but an exchange. I found the result most enlivening.

Harkness also provided for new faculty, and among those arriving in my senior year, two young instructors had a particular impact, William Gurdon Saltonstall in history and Robert Cunningham in English. Both were young, enthusiastic and stimulating. Bill Saltonstall was a dedicated sailor and hockey player, but he and his delightful wife, Katharyn, also had time for shy and bookish students. They invited me to dinner, and their friendship increased one's own social confidence. In 1946 Bill became the school's principal, serving until 1963, when President Kennedy asked him to run the Peace Corps in Nigeria. Bob Cunningham first roused my interest in poetry. He left Exeter after a time and had a rather erratic career, but, with the circularity of life, I met him again many years later when he married a cousin of my friend Barbara Wendell Kerr.

The principal in my Exeter years was Lewis Perry, one of a generation of legendary headmasters — Endicott Peabody at Groton, Frank Boyden at Deerfield, Alfred Stearns at Andover, Samuel Drury at St. Paul's. Actually, Dr. Perry was a rather remote figure. He often spoke at daily chapel, but he had little direct contact with the students, at least not with me. He used occasionally to call a few students by name to "remain after chapel." Once (as Bill Saltonstall recalled in his memoir *Lewis Perry of Exeter*) he asked a brilliant student, "Are you getting any B's?" The straight-A student said he was not. "Well," said Perry, "I'll be seeing you again next term and hope by then you'll be getting a B." The next term, Dr. Perry asked the same question: "Are you getting any B's?" "Yes," the boy said. "One." "Good," said Perry. "Keep it up." Perry was not especially popular in my day. It was only when I came to see something of him in a later time that I discovered a man of considerable urbanity and wit.

Two masters whom I never had in class exerted much influence on other students and on me. One was the dean E. S. Wells Kerr, a humane and sagacious educational administrator who combined short-term gruffness with long-term patience and whose intimate knowledge of the students compensated for Dr. Perry's remoteness. Another was Henry Darcy Curwen, an imperious teacher of English, tall, erect, with a clipped mustache, looking like a Bengal lancer, much given to salty quotations from Dr. Johnson. Darcy Curwen's sarcastic humor ("Have you miserable bipeds done your homework?" was a typical greeting to his class) could not conceal the real concern he felt for his flock.

One duty he assumed with particular pleasure was choosing the movies to be shown every Saturday night in the gymnasium. The student crowd was often unruly in its reactions, but Darcy had excellent and eclectic taste and showed us everything from Laurel and Hardy to Greta Garbo. My own seduction by movies began in the Exeter gym, and my weekly letters home were too often capsule film reviews. Thus Ernst Lubitsch's *Trouble in Paradise:* ". . . the nearest approach to pure art the movies have yet made. The grace and adeptness, facility and symmetry of direction was [sic, alas] marvelous, a wonderful piece of work." Grammar aside, I will still endorse the opinion.

* * *

The students were mostly good, solid, middle-class boys. Some came from private schools, many from public schools; a number were on scholarship or earned money by waiting on table, a job that brought no social stigma. We were instructed to say "Hi" to other students whether we knew them or not. I fell into the habit, and nearly seventy years later I still find myself saying "Hi," if now only to people I know (or think I know). Also, Dr. Perry, having been told by a doctor that hats in freezing weather would prevent mastoids, required all students to wear hats outside in winter term. (Bill Saltonstall lifted that ban when he became principal.) We were expected to tip our hats when we passed a master.

Discipline was fairly strict. Upperclassmen could smoke in common rooms, but drink was forbidden. One spring afternoon a couple of seniors bicycled over to Hampton Beach, eleven miles away, and drank some 3.2 percent beer; they were, if I recall correctly, expelled shortly before graduation. Drugs were of course unknown.

There was much clandestine reading of books frowned on by the authorities. Adolescent boys were inevitably preoccupied with sex, and bawdy novels passed from hand to hand until they were dog-eared. Favored authors were Tiffany Thayer (*Thirteen Men* and *Thirteen Women*) and Thorne Smith (whose *Topper* inspired the popular Topper movie series with Constance Bennett and Cary Grant). How ribald and (in the term of the time) risqué these books seemed in 1932! How tame they seem today!

We were prurient little boys who used to gaze admiringly out the windows of Abbot Hall when the luscious wives of Dexter Butterfield, a mathematics master, and Percy Rogers, a French master, passed below. Robert Anderson '35, whose play *Tea and Sympathy* turned on a master's wife going rather far to reassure a student doubtful of his masculinity, once told Mrs. Rogers that people thought she was the original of Laura Reynolds. Mrs. Rogers frowned and said, "She was naughty. Couldn't she just have held his hand?"

We kept applauding a lady singer in one of the occasional concerts in the chapel because, when she bowed low in grateful response, we had an uninterrupted glimpse of her cleavage. And we believed that our food in dining hall was sprinkled with saltpeter to reduce our nascent lust. My classmates imported girls for dances, but I was too shy and too pimply to follow their example.

Dr. Perry liked the existing composition of the student body. "I am sure that a colored boy is hurt rather than helped by his entrance into Exeter," he wrote to a friend in 1938, and he quietly limited the number of Jews. "He invariably treated individual blacks and other minority members with utmost courtesy," Bill Saltonstall later wrote, "but at the same time he thought the school 'had to be careful in regard to Jews.'" Perry also resisted the abolition of fraternities. Saltonstall later ended both quotas and fraternities.

* * *

John O'Keefe and I remained good friends, but in my senior year I decided for various reasons to room by myself in Abbot Hall. By now I had made the *Exonian*, where I displayed a facility for the lowly chore of headline-writing. I joined the Herodotan Society, a club for embryonic historians, and the Golden Branch Debating Society. Athletics were part of the required program. In fall and spring I played tennis in a desultory way, and in winter I went gloomily out for track (and made the squad).

Both daily chapel and Sunday church were compulsory — an ordinance that irritated many students and that in my case transformed indifference to religion into active hostility. "Compulsory church," I wrote to my grandmother Bancroft, "is an invention of the devil. Certainly it is bringing more souls to his side." I found spiritual consolation rather in long, blissful hours of undisturbed reading — Byron, Thackeray, Conrad, Maugham, Galsworthy, Hemingway, Huxley — in deep leather chairs in the Davis Library.

I was a Thackeray fan, preferring his parlor cynicism to what seemed to me the jocosity and sentimentality of Dickens, a writer whom at that point I rather disdained. My mother was dismayed to learn that I had been reading Huxley's daring (then) *Point Counter Point*. "You must realize that I am growing up," I replied. "Besides it was in the Davis Library which is supposedly run for students and is carefully expurgated. I can't understand how *Point Counter Point* stayed after they did away with *An American Tragedy*, but it did. I advise you not to read it for it will probably injure your sensibilities."

I was then much under the spell of the Twenties and, indeed, have remained so in some respects ever since. Years later, in Edmund Wilson's journal of the Sixties, I read, with a shock of recognition, a confession dropped along the way. "I find I am a man of the Twenties," Wilson wrote. "I am still expecting something exciting: drinks, animated conversation, gaiety, brilliant writing, uninhibited exchange of ideas." That is how the Twenties appeared to me.

We were too young to patronize speakeasies and dance the Charleston; but, against the grim backdrop of depression, the Twenties shone for the generation of the Thirties with romantic glamour as a bright interlude of carefree conviviality and reckless creativity. Modernism had arrived in America — Hemingway, Fitzgerald, Faulkner, Dos Passos, Cummings, Stevens. Popular culture had come into its own, Gilbert Seldes having legitimated movies, vaudeville, jazz and the comic strip in his beguiling *The Seven Lively Arts* (1924). New magazines — the *New Yorker, Time* and especially the *American Mercury* — transmitted the pulsations of the Jazz Age. Looking back from the Thirties, our own gray decade, we envied that lively time of cultural guerrilla warfare against a smug, stifling and now thoroughly discredited business civilization.

The romance of the Twenties abided, the romance and the mystery. Noel Coward:

> The craze for pleasure
> Steadily grows,
> Cocktails and laughter,
> But what comes after?
> Nobody knows.

*   *   *

Mencken was my particular hero. A small green book is still on my shelves with its inscription in my mother's handwriting: "Arthur M. Schlesinger, Jr. Christmas 1932." It is the first volume of Mencken's *Prejudices,* published in 1919 and reprinted by Knopf in 1932 as a Borzoi Pocket Book (pocket books had hard covers then).

The book dazzled me: the superb clarity of style, the exuberant iconoclasm, the liberated and liberating tone, the rollicking satirical wit; most of all, I suppose, the air of worldliness and cosmopolitanism. Easy allusions to Nietzsche and Shaw, Bach and Wagner, Ibsen and Sudermann, Thorstein Veblen and James G. Huneker, along with contempt for the *booboisie,* made one feel part of a wonderfully sophisticated club.

I never had the good luck to meet Mencken, but, after the dinner with Knopf, my father and he kept up an intermittent correspondence. Thus in 1936 my father, noting that Mencken in *The American Language* had found no record of the use of the word "bum" before the Civil War, pointed out that in 1771 the *Massachusetts Spy* had written of "the united resolves of all the lawyers and bums in North Carolina." Mencken replied that he would send the news to the brethren at the University of Chicago working on the *Dictionary of American English:* "They will denounce you for upsetting their doctrine but they'll immortalize you in their learned work." In another dispatch Mencken wrote: "I am still hoping to see you in Baltimore. The whole town is gradually falling to pieces, but a number of meritorious saloons still survive."

My affection for Mencken outlasted even his virulent attacks on Franklin D. Roosevelt and the New Deal and his sour dissent from the Second World War. One could understand the resentment of the great cultural heretic of the Twenties when he was suddenly confronted and confounded by the harsh political antagonisms of the Thirties. Mencken was a libertarian, not a democrat. He had never taken democracy seriously except as a cultural threat, and he had always regarded democratic leaders, whether Bryan or TR or Wilson or FDR, as bamboozlers of the *Boobus Americanus*. But to his fans he redeemed himself in the Thirties by *The American Language* and in the Forties by his three marvelous volumes of (not very reliable) autobiography.

In recent years, Mencken's reputation has suffered from the multicultural rage over ethnic and racial cracks. One cannot doubt that, like Theodore Dreiser, T. S. Eliot, Thomas Wolfe and other writers of the day, Mencken was given to random slurs about Jews. But this never prevented enduring friendships with Alfred Knopf, George Jean Nathan and Felix Frankfurter. While he occasionally professed a belief in the biological inferiority of black people, this never stopped him from publishing black writers in the *Mercury* and inviting them to his home. By Ann Douglas's count in her book on the Twenties, Mencken ran fifty-four articles by and about blacks between 1925 and 1933 and was tireless in his efforts to bring black talent to the notice of white publishers. In 1935 he testified before Congress for an anti-lynching bill: "No government pretending to be civilized can go on condoning such atrocities. Either it must make every possible effort to put them down or it must suffer the scorn and contempt of Christendom."

He had a shrewd understanding of race relations. Few white men, he wrote, can fool the black man; "the white man, even in the South, knows next to nothing of the inner life of the Negro. . . . What the average Southerner believes about the Negroes who surround him is chiefly nonsense." America needed, Mencken thought, a portrait of the Negro by one who sees from within. "The Negro author who makes such a book will dignify American literature and accomplish more for his race than a thousand propagandists and theorists. He will force the understanding that now seems so hopeless." An interesting anticipation of Ralph Ellison and *Invisible Man!* Mencken's last published column denounced segregation in a Maryland park.

Mencken was in fact an equal opportunity ethnic calumniator. His passing cracks about Jews and blacks were nothing compared to his loathing for those purest of Anglo-Saxons, the hillbillies of the south. "Here in Baltimore," he wrote to my father in 1943,

> I live in a slum that is now crowded with war-working immigrants from the Appalachian Chain. I thought I was familiar with these anthropoids but I must now report that they are much worse than I ever suspected. Some of

them are really caricatures of Homo sapiens. The birth-rate among them is enormous. In their native wilds there is some compensation in the high infant death-rate, but here in Baltimore their young are coopered and fostered at the public expense. . . . In all the world I have never seen a more wretched class of white men, not even in Southeastern Europe.

Times and fashions change, and much of what seemed high-spirited in the Twenties seems mean-spirited in the year 2000. Reading Mencken's diaries left me with the opposite of the impression his *Prejudices* had made on me at Exeter. The diaries reveal not a paragon of worldliness and sophistication but a rather provincial, naive and, indeed, innocent fellow. Still he had been a great figure in the intellectual life of America. Walter Lippmann in 1926 called him "the most powerful personal influence on this whole generation of educated people." His hyperbole was a potent instrument of cultural liberation, for me and for many others. The swashbuckling vigor of his style will, I believe, keep him alive for a long time to come.

This style certainly had an immediate impact. I find an Exeter theme that I entitled "Highbrow: A Term of Respect." The word, I said, was commonly a "term of envy . . . applied by yokels, 100% Americans, Hoover Republicans, and other dull fellows to those whose perceptions were keener than their own." Such persons think highbrows get more pleasure out of a sense of superiority to others than out of things they honestly like. "This, of course, is so much poppycock and buncombe. Do you get more pleasure out of reading Conrad than Zane Grey because the *hoi polloi* does not understand Conrad or because of the intrinsic fineness in his writing? . . . The Babbitts, down at their own level, revelling in Tiffany Thayer, Cecil B. DeMille and James Montgomery Flagg, are jealous of those who prefer W. Somerset Maugham, Ernst Lubitsch and Winslow Homer." And so on. The Mencken influence is obvious.

My father wrote indulgently, "I liked your essay . . . and know that you must have had fun writing it. There is always a little thrill one gets from saying things well." This last sentence for some reason has lingered in my mind ever since. It remains true.

*   *   *

During the depression, only the affluent could afford boarding school, so Exeter's students were therefore mostly from Republican families. In the autumn of my senior year came the 1932 election, pitting President Herbert Hoover against Governor Franklin D. Roosevelt. "The school," I informed my parents, "is filled with the most conservative, illiberal, intolerant, narrow-minded bunch of fellows which were ever brought together. There are about 125 people who are not dead dry conservatives and don't think that Socialists and Reds should be shot at sight. . . . Most think that all Jews are inferior and poisonous to touch and taste, Hoover is the greatest man of the century, Cal Coolidge and Dawes being close seconds, . . . that Roosevelt is controlled by Tammany, Hearst, Garner, Gene Tunney, and Marion Davies."

I was among a tiny band committed to the cause of FDR. In a theme entitled "Why Hoover Should Not Be Elected" (B+), I concluded, "Republican propaganda has tried to show Hoover as a demi-god and Roosevelt as a demagogue. According to all indications, however, the people refuse to be fooled." On a fine October morning, FDR drove through Exeter. He was scheduled to come at nine-forty, but, like all politicians, he was running late, and I reluctantly went off to a ten o'clock class without seeing him. That evening I spoke for FDR at a Golden Branch debate. One opponent said, "Washington freed the country; Lincoln the slaves; Hoover the workingman." "Yeah," I wrote home. "Hoover freed the workingman from his home and possessions."

The majority of the school remained automatically and unshakably conservative. Among the small minority of liberals, many dismissed Roosevelt as timid and mediocre. My friend John L. (Jock) Saltonstall, Jr., a Brahmin rebel, led the Norman Thomas campaign and outorganized the Democrats. In the campus straw poll, Hoover received 494 votes as against 84 for Thomas and 80 for Roosevelt. (William Z. Foster, the Communist, and William D. Upshaw, the Prohibitionist, each received a single vote.)

In the letter home reporting this vote, I predicted that "Frank will win by 8,000,000 votes in the country" (the actual margin was seven million). Four months later I sat with a small group around a radio in the Phillips Hall common room, hearing Roosevelt say that the only thing we had to fear was fear itself. It was a thrilling moment for some of us, but not many Exonians appeared to care.

It was also a chastening moment for me. My aunt Marion in Dayton had sent me a Christmas check for $25, a princely sum for a kid in those days (about $275 now). In the indolence of youth, I had not yet troubled to cash it. When Roosevelt closed the banks, the Dayton bank never reopened. It was a useful lesson against procrastination.

Exeter in my day lacked a powerful tradition of concern with public affairs. I don't know why this should have been. Many masters had an avid interest in politics, and morning chapel rang with exhortations to students about their public responsibilities. Dr. Perry actually endorsed Roosevelt in the election. But there seemed something about the Exeter ethos that resisted national politics. The school turned out civic-minded businessmen who worked hard for good local government and the Community Fund. It turned out scholars and teachers and writers. It turned out scientists, doctors and engineers. But it turned out surprisingly few political leaders and public servants.

Compared to Groton (Franklin D. Roosevelt, Averell Harriman, Dean Acheson, Sumner Welles, Francis Biddle, Bronson Cutting, Joseph C. Grew or, in my own generation, Douglas Dillon, Joseph and Stewart Alsop, FDR Jr., McGeorge and William Bundy, Richard Bissell, Jonathan Bingham, Bill Blair, Frank Keppel), Exeter's representation in public leadership in the twentieth century was negligible. Groton was a much smaller school with much richer and more snobbish boys, yet its role in the days of FDR and, later, John F. Kennedy was far greater than Exeter's.

Perhaps the Exeter ethos was inclined to take social values as they were because the school's aim was to train middle-class boys to be decent citizens in society as it is, whereas the best of the church schools tried to train upper-class boys to meet their responsibilities to the less fortunate as Christian gentlemen. This is not to overlook the fact that many graduates of the church schools were very often selfish, mean, pompous, obtuse, reactionary, even crooked (Richard Whitney, for example) and that, as Harriman used to say, to do good thereafter it helped to have been unhappy at Groton.

Still, for all the indifference to public affairs, one cherished the physical loveliness of Exeter, the wide green playing fields and the red brick pseudo-Georgian buildings, the brilliance of the New Hampshire autumn heavy with the smell of burning leaves, the stillness of the campus in winter buried deep in snow, the sudden, glorious fragrance of spring. If I did not precisely enjoy the academy, it was an indispensable part of my education.

And, after a slow start, I had a strong finish. As my friend Nathaniel G. Benchley, the son of Robert Benchley, wrote in Darcy Curwen's compilation *Exeter Remembered,* there was "the Prize Day when what seemed like three-quarters of the prizes were won by Arthur M.

Schlesinger, Jr., who wore a path up and down the aisle. I think I remember Dr. Perry saying, after giving him one prize, 'You might as well stay up here, Arthur; you're getting the next one, too.'"

Dr. Perry's account of me in the "Principal's Report" to the Harvard admissions office was, I fear, more generous than accurate. "A tall, slender, stalk of a boy with a face illumined by intelligence and adolescent joys. . . . Earnest and devoted to his studies, with genuine intellectual interests going beyond the limits of the class-room. He is really concerned about the affairs of the world outside the school. He has an attractive personality and many friends." I was not, alas, very tall and can only hope that the rest of the report was more reliable.

6

Round the World

I WAS FIFTEEN YEARS OLD when I graduated from Exeter in 1933, and my parents thought I was a little young to go on to Harvard. Also, my father was scheduled to give the Commonwealth Lectures at the University of London in February–March 1934. Neither of my parents had ever been outside North America, and in a triumphant burst of imagination they decided to travel westward around the world to London, taking Tom and me with them.

My father, though hardly nature's big spender, decided to do it in style. Elaborate arrangements were made through Thomas Cook & Son. The timing of our route across the bristling world, it turned out, was lucky. The Japanese, after transforming Manchuria into Manchukuo the year before, had suspended their encroachments on China. French Indochina and British India were tranquil, at least on the surface. In Europe we were to miss the violent episodes of 1934, going through Paris a day after the Stavisky riots, leaving Austria a fortnight before Chancellor Dollfuss's assassination, arriving in Germany a fortnight after the purge of Ernst Roehm.

Encouraged by my parents, I kept a journal of the trip, a habit I have continued intermittently ever since (too intermittently, I discover as I labor now to recapture the past). The volume covering the journey from Boston across Asia to the Mediterranean contained, according to my computation at the time, some sixty thousand words. It also contained the stern admonition: "This book is not intended to be read by any one save its author."

Nor was it; and the author, rereading it in 1937 from the superior vantage point of a third-year man at college, found it "pretty bare bones: dry and detailed descriptions of places visited with here and there a tart impertinence in the way of criticism and very rarely an outburst of emotion which seems ridiculous next to the placidity of most of the entries. I wish now I had written more freely on people and less conscientiously on places." Reading it again after more than sixty years, I find it an affecting portrait of an earlier self, ingenuous, eager, hopeful, with an eye out for pretty girls and with, occasionally, some redeeming twists of mind and phrase.

* * *

On September 1, 1933, the Schlesinger family embarked on its great adventure. We left by train for Montreal, where we picked up the Canadian Pacific railroad, spending three days at Lake Louise before crossing the majestic Canadian Rockies and going on to Vancouver to board the *Empress of Japan.* "The girls seemed to improve the further West we got," I wrote about the journey across Canada.

The *Empress of Japan* thrilled. We traveled first class in an age when ocean liners still drew firm barriers between the classes. The experience, I regret to say, instilled a taste for luxury that I was never thereafter quite able to shake. "A floating palace," I exulted in my journal. ". . . Our staterooms are splendid." The glorious voyage from Vancouver to Yokohama took two enchanted weeks, including a day's stopover in Honolulu.

Kathleen Norris, an immensely popular women's novelist, was a fellow passenger, along with her husband of the purple waistcoats, Charles G. Norris, a more serious if less successful novelist and the kid brother of that really strong novelist Frank Norris. Another passenger was the Japanese novelist and politician Yusuke Tsurumi, a smooth and smiling man, fluent in English. Charles Beard had given my father a letter of introduction to him, and he at once befriended my parents.

More important to me, indeed the source of the seaborne enchantment, was a pretty young woman from Johannesburg. She was married to a South African businessman who spent most of the trip in his cabin drinking milk for his stomach ulcers. "I hesitate, from the apprehension of ridicule," wrote Gibbon in his *Autobiography,* "when I approach the delicate subject of my early love." I hesitate too, but, according to my journal: "My chief companion in promenades and opponent in pingpong is the most charming woman I have ever met. . . . Between us we have entered almost all the tournaments to be held on the ship."

Ocean travel, with its abstraction from quotidian realities, invites rapid intimacy and a free exchange of confidences. Moreover, my acne, still an embarrassment, had the happy effect of making me compensate by becoming as lively as I could in conversation, as adolescent fat boys often divert attention from their blubber by cracking jokes. Ann B.'s sweet acceptance of my company did wonders for my morale; and, since she was an attractive blonde, I naturally fell in love with her. When we parted in Yokohama — I quote my journal — "I stammered around, was on the verge of tears (imagine!) and then had to rush away. . . . My future biographers shall have to enter it as my first affaire d'amour." Not much of an affair, though.

*   *   *

The Thomas Cook courier met us at the dock, a suave, efficient and cynical gentleman, a slave to cigarettes, dressed like a dandy and crammed full of information about Japanese art and history. Mr. Koshino accompanied us everywhere during our fortnight in Japan. There is little more boring than someone else's travelogue; so I shall not go on about exquisite Nara and exquisite Nikko and exquisite Kyoto — except to wonder whether the price of such highly controlled exquisiteness was psychic repression that could be relieved only by outbursts of violence. I remember crowds gathering admiringly around a huge figure of King Kong erected outside the Tokyo cinema where the wondrous film was playing. One surmised that the Japanese identified with the great ape as a fellow victim of Western imperialism.

In Tokyo we stayed at Frank Lloyd Wright's Imperial Hotel, with its crenellated walls and its presumably earthquake-proof structure. One evening, while Tom and I had sukiyaki at the hotel, our parents dined with Prince and Princess Konoye at Yusuke Tsurumi's house. Eight years later, Konoye as prime minister would seek a meeting with Roosevelt in an effort to avert war, but the price of peace would have been American acquiescence in the Japanese conquest of China, and this price FDR refused to pay. Tsurumi also arranged for my father to meet Prime Minister Saito and leading members of his cabinet.

Toward the end of the Thirties, Tsurumi visited my parents in Cambridge and confided his son Shunsuke, later a professor of philosophy in Japan, to my father's care while studying in America. But the elder Tsurumi took my parents aback with his mounting admiration for Hitler. After Pearl Harbor, he delivered radio broadcasts calling Americans "barbaric" and "brutal" and at the same time weaklings who couldn't put up a fight. My father expected him to side with his country but not to go out of his way to defame a people whom he had known so well. After the war, Tsurumi tried on his visits to America to see my father, but my father said, "I had no heart for renewing our relations."

Militarism seemed to hover over Japan in 1933. In the Osaka sta-

tion, we saw railroad cars crowded with soldiers bound for Manchukuo. "I have seen more soldiers in two weeks in Japan," I noted,
"than in fifteen years in America." But these were days of Western
condescension toward the Japanese. No one took them very seriously
as a military or economic threat. They were believed to produce bungled imitations of Western goods and technologies. According to one
story, they made ersatz Scotch whisky and marked it Queen William.
A retired U.S. Army captain told us that they named a town Sweden so
that the factories could produce matches labeled "Made in Sweden."
Their shipbuilders stole Western blueprints, we were told, and then
built ships that sank on launching. The Japanese were supposed to
have a certain pigmentation or slant of the eye that handicapped
them in landing airplanes. This myth of Japanese technological incompetence perished rather rapidly eight years later.

We ended at Kobe, where we were to embark for China and where I
had my last meeting with Ann B. Her husband genially invited me to
dine with them and served me my first champagne. "I like it very
much, a great deal better than sake." There was much gaiety, and I returned to our hotel tipsy. The next morning Ann brought me a pile of
*New Yorker*s to read on the boat. She gave me a number to call in London, but, when I arrived at the end of January, she had left for South
Africa a fortnight before. I never saw her again.

"She will always be an ideal to me, and I never even really kissed
her," I wrote despondently. ". . . *Thus endeth the first lesson.*" (Later I
scribbled in the margin: "*Note* — respect this paragraph; it was written at the time!") For a while we kept up a correspondence. Thirty
years later, after I joined John F. Kennedy's White House, I received
in that once familiar handwriting an affectionate letter of congratulation.

*   *   *

We embarked in the rain on the *Choan Maru* of the O.S.K. line. The
four-day voyage was altogether unpleasant. The cabins were grim.
The library was unreadable. The food was inedible ("when I think of
the food I used to revile last year at Exeter!"). The weather was rough,
and heavy seas delayed us long enough to miss the tide for Tangku
and lose a day in China. (A week later a typhoon sank a thousand-
ton boat with an almost complete loss of life.) The Yellow Sea was
definitely yellow.

Finally we disembarked at four-thirty in the morning to catch the train to Peiping, as it was then styled. We passed in the silent darkness an encampment of Chinese soldiers surrounded by barbed wire, sandbags and sentries. Tientsin, an hour's ride, was the first stop. After Tientsin my father managed to get us a compartment. We reached Peiping in midmorning, were met by the man from Thomas Cook & Son and went to the Grand Hotel de Pekin.

I had my sixteenth birthday in Peiping and spent most of it in the marvelous Forbidden City. Again I will spare the reader sightseeing minutiae except to remark on the state of dilapidation into which the glories of Peiping had fallen by 1933. The city was filled with beggars, ruthlessly accosting foreigners. The priests and acolytes in the Lama Temple were unkempt and odorous, giggling and laughing during their prayers. From time to time we rode in rickshaws. "Logic is on the side of rickshaws. The boys are cheerful, they are used to the work, and the more of it they have, the more money they make and the better they live. Still I do not like being pulled about by a fellow human being."

Troubles and fears abounded. The Ming tombs, we were told, could not be visited: bandits. Happily, the Great Wall was approved. The train took four and a quarter hours to traverse fifty-five miles. An earlier train had killed a man who had been gathering coal along the tracks. Now he lay on the ground covered by a blanket. His daughters were kneeling beside him, sobbing and screaming. The passengers took up a collection for them. Then a grizzled old hag pulled up the grieving daughters and made them bow to the passengers. "It was a little too crude for me."

We went on to the Wall in sedan chairs, carried jerkily by four bearers. It was a brilliant autumn day, and we were mesmerized by the sight of the Wall as it curled along the hills and across the countryside against an intense blue sky. There were few people, and we strolled along almost by ourselves, meditating on the majesty of history.

One day a Harvard graduate student named John King Fairbank and his bright, pretty wife came by the hotel to see us. He seemed to know a lot about China. We spent a day at Yenching University in the outskirts — handsome buildings in the Chinese manner, with red columns and tiled roofs. A big tea was given for my parents in the American-style house of a Chinese professor, then dinner in the Chinese-style house of an American professor. "I had a lot of fun at the tea. I am now becoming an excellent conversationalist. I mentally set down a group of questions, to which I added and from which I subtracted at intervals during the tea, about the universities of Peiping, about this, about that, about everything. I enjoyed myself immensely." Did others enjoy me all that much? "There was a very pretty girl named Boyden from Vassar." I met her again when she married Robert K. Lamb, my economics instructor at Harvard.

The ride back to the city was interesting, if grim. There were many soldiers along the road. We were stopped twice, once with leveled rifles. I saw more soldiers in two days in China than in two weeks in Japan. A week after we left Peiping a rabble of rebellious troops advanced to within twenty miles of the city. But usually the soldiers were loafing around railroad stations and other public places. It was much like Josef von Sternberg's vivid movie *Shanghai Express,* which had come out the year before. When the Schlesingers boarded the Shanghai Express, traveling first-class deluxe in a wagon-lit, it was a great disappointment not to find Marlene Dietrich ("It took more than one man to change my name to Shanghai Lily"), although the pretty girl in the next compartment wore enticing pajamas.

We went on to Nanking and the lovely lakes of Hangchow before returning to Shanghai. Here we stayed at the grand old Astor House, walked along the handsome, bustling Bund and inspected the bazaars in the native quarter, where I was impressed by a man selling little boxes with crickets inside. The bearded, turbaned Sikh policemen looked like maharajahs. The Eurasian ladies on parade along the Bund were bewitching. Shanghai was energy, vitality, speed, sophistication, cosmopolitanism. In contrast, Peiping had seemed a dying, or at least a decadent, city.

On to Hong Kong and thence to Manila on the *Empress of Canada* ("there is no one goodlooking enough to excite interest"). Dave Niles had sent word of our arrival to Frank Murphy, the governor general, later governor of Michigan and a justice of the Supreme Court. His military aide met the ship, and an official car took us on a tour of the city. That night over dinner at the governor general's palace Murphy, "a youngish man with red hair and bushy red eyebrows," held forth in slow, low, measured tones. Franklin Roosevelt, he said, was "the greatest politician the U.S. has ever produced," but Father Coughlin (the incendiary radio priest from Royal Oak, Michigan, whom Murphy knew well) was "next to FDR the most powerful man in the United States." If Roosevelt failed, Coughlin "could be dictator in two weeks."

Back to Hong Kong, in those days a charming, old-fashioned British treaty port before developers made it look like Houston; then by evening river steamer to Canton, a filthy city, its river filled with houseboats inhabited by a quarter million people; then an aborted try for Macao, the ship, battered by the edge of a typhoon, having to turn back to Hong Kong. On November 7 we boarded the *Athos II* (a happy touch, that, for a Dumas fan) of Messageries-Maritimes bound for Saigon.

It had been an engrossing month in China, and as we left I set down my political observations. In Peiping the fear, I thought, was of the Japanese, and people seemed to be reconciled to the inevitability (in their eyes) of Japanese occupation. The spirit had drained from them. In central and south China the fear was of communism. "Several interior provinces are reputed to be in the hands of the Reds. The Chinese army is at present trying to subdue the communists; but we were told in Shanghai that unless something is done about the farmers China will soon become communistic." Nothing was done about the farmers, and, when I next went to Shanghai, fifty-four years later, the prophecy of 1933 had long since been fulfilled.

*   *   *

We were in Saigon for Armistice Day. It had been fifteen years since the end of the Great War, and the city was bedecked with flags. I marveled at the Vietnamese soldiers in the Armistice Day parade, some carrying paper figures lit from the inside by candles, proudly celebrating their part in a war they had fought on the other side of the world over issues of no concern to them. "More stir is made about the holiday in this remote French colony," I wrote, "than in the United States."

We set out by automobile to Phnom Penh; thence to Angkor. The magnificent ruins of the once great Khmer city-state were only gradually being recaptured from the jungle. One remembers extraordinary friezes and carvings in crumbling sandstone, yellow-robed priests mumbling in the temples, skittering monkeys and parakeets protesting the human invasion with shrill yells. Some temples — Pra Khan, for example — were still overgrown with weeds and moss.

The stench of bats in Angkor Wat was oppressive. After sundown, thousands streamed in a straight line from one of the towers, flying toward the jungle in a column half a mile long. A madman lived near the temple's altar, claiming to be king of Angkor; every night he donned ludicrous robes and crown and stood outside the door of the Hôtel des Ruines begging for alms. "He manages in some way to invest his crazy garments with a certain dignity."

We spent three fascinated days in Angkor; thence to Siam, as it was then known, where senior Army officers had recently attempted a coup. Professor Francis B. Sayre, Woodrow Wilson's son-in-law, had given my father a letter of introduction to Prince Damrong, who was away when we reached Bangkok but whose son called on us *in loco parentis*. At dinner the young man said that more than six hundred people, including his brother, had been imprisoned without charges on suspicion of sympathy for the failed coup. Why had it taken place? The manager of the largest movie palace in Bangkok, owned by the king of Siam, told us that no one, not even the rebels themselves, knew what the coup was all about. The mysterious East.

Bangkok was a riot of brilliant color. The bespangled temples glittered in the sun as we went by motorboat through the *klongs* and inspected the floating markets and houses. Today, I understand (I have never been back), those wonderfully picturesque canals are mostly filled in. So vivid were the porcelain and glass temples that they seemed like "delicate toys," I wrote, "not like buildings made to withstand age and the vicissitudes of weather."

Bangkok was populated by a prodigal variety of Buddhas, in gold, in jade, in bronze, sleeping and awake, haggard after the wilderness, serene in meditation. I was dazzled by the Grand Palace and the "splendor and magnificence which never in my palmiest of dreams have I imagined." Bangkok, I concluded, "I unhesitatingly place with Nikko and Peiping as the high points of our trip."

The next stop was the island of Penang in the Straits Settlements and the oddly named but lovely Eastern and Oriental Hotel. We were now in Somerset Maugham country — the clipped British accents of the younger sons of the upper class, cricket on the lawn, fans spinning placidly on the ceilings, gin slings in the bar (not for me, though). There we took the boat to Rangoon, with its Reclining Buddha and the Shwe Dagon Pagoda, its women with golden rings in their noses and its streets splotched with the blood-red spit of betel nut.

*   *   *

We continued by boat to Calcutta. A Kansas missionary was aboard, "very prohibitionistic," with a pretty thirteen-year-old daughter who was forbidden to dance, play cards or date. The father made one think of Maugham's Reverend Davidson. The daughter, I decided, "was at the dangerous age — did not know what was troubling her — and tried to work it off in exercise." On the last night under a full moon "she blossomed out a new personality, vivid and very attractive."

A Cook's bearer met us in Calcutta to chaperone us through India. It was now December, and Darjeeling, our first destination, was seven thousand feet in the sky and briskly cold. At two-thirty the next morning groaning rickshaw boys took us to watch a lurid red sun rise over the Himalayas. The snows of Mount Kanchenjunga, the world's third highest peak (28,208 feet), were bathed in rose, soon turning to gold. Mount Everest, alas, was enveloped in clouds and remained invisible.

Then Benares: pilgrims bathing in the sacred Ganges (but not so many as expected); magicians; snake charmers; lepers with white splotches on face, hands and feet; clamorous beggars; ghats, where the dead were cremated. Benares reinforced my prejudice against religion and initiated, I am ashamed to say, a prejudice against Indians. "When I see these crippled and deformed beggars approaching, I feel a great desire to kick them instead of pity. Dad suggests that this feeling may be caused by the (even in the east) abnormal filth of Benares. I hope he is right, for I do not like to feel this way." But Agra, with its red sandstone Fort, the gleaming Taj Mahal, the shining white marble mosques, the wonderful deserted Mogul city of Fatehpur-Sikri, improved my state of mind. "India, a great disappointment up to Agra, has triumphantly reinstated itself."

Delhi, Jaipur, Udaipur, Bombay: the anomalies of India multiplied — beautiful palaces with pornographic frescoes, intelligent professors, pertinacious beggars, crowded bazaars, insistent shopkeepers, hideous Hindu idols, obsequious Indians, arrogant Britishers. When my mother asked a British official how to say "thank you" in Hindustani, he refused to tell her; "no white person ever thanks an Indian for anything."

After three weeks in India, I brashly decided that the Indians were not ready for self-government. "With all due respect to Mr. Gandhi, whom I formerly admired and to a certain extent supported, I think he is crazy. . . . Self-government would be impossible, with the eternal religious brawls and the caste system of the Hindus."

It seems likely that old Gandhi was less crazy than young Schlesinger. India, despite religious brawls and the caste system, has made a go of self-government. And self-government has transformed the Indians. In 1933 white people encountered darting looks of sheer hatred from scorned and humiliated natives, an upsetting experience for innocent Americans. When I returned to India thirty years later, I was struck by the way that independence had revived Indian pride and dignity. There were no more looks of hatred; only a robust sense of equality. And an astonishing residue of Englishness: as Malcolm Muggeridge once said, the only real, old-fashioned, *pukka sahib* Englishmen left are Indians.

*   *   *

Christmas 1933 found the Schlesingers on a P&O steamer bound for the Suez Canal, Aden and Port Said. Thence to Cairo, the Pyramids, the Sphinx and the great museum; to Assuan, where our guide claimed to have guided Theodore Roosevelt in 1909; to Luxor, the Temple of Karnak, the tomb of Tutankhamen (one room only open to visitors) and the Colossi of Memnon. I enjoyed Egypt.

We left Alexandria on a miserable Romanian boat for Piraeus and Athens. The Acropolis temples were still accessible to the wandering tourist; today, fences around the Parthenon prevent entry. In those unpolluted times we had a marvelous view all the way to the Bay of Salamis in one direction and the mountains on the other. On another fine day we drove along the Eleusinian Way to Corinth and Mycenae, admiring the luminous waters sparkling in the sunlight and the snow-covered mountains to the north.

We sailed on an Italian boat from Piraeus to Naples, where we stopped for the marvels of Pompeii; then on to Marseilles, where I was delighted to see Edmond Dantes's Château d'If in the harbor. Onshore, posters mounted by the Croix du Feu, a cryptofascist organization of war veterans, assailed the Stavisky scandals, the "parliamentary vermin," and the "bandits of the Senate." An overnight train took us to Paris a day after an angry mob rioted against Stavisky; thence Boulogne, the Channel, a day before a severe storm disabled two ships, Folkestone, London. It was now January 30, 1934.

*   *   *

London provided time to digest the exotic diet of places, colors and creeds we had consumed in five rich months. As for Britain, none of us had been there before, but reading had given us a sense of recognition, almost of coming home. My mother was an admirer of D. H. Lawrence and Katherine Mansfield and soon developed a passion for Trollope. Conan Doyle had prepared me for London. In 1934 people still burned soft coal and generated thick Sherlock Holmes fogs. I had also read extensively in Galsworthy (the entire *Forsyte Saga*), Arnold Bennett, John Buchan and even a trilogy by a forgotten English writer, Ernest Raymond's *Once in England*. I wrote in my journal, "I looked forward to seeing England more than any other country."

We settled in Carlton Mansions, a pension on Bedford Place between Bloomsbury and Russell squares, around the corner from the British Museum and not far from the University of London. Corrupted by our previous Cook's luxury, I wrote snippily in my journal, "A pension is a place with all the bad points and none of the good points of a hotel." But we grew fond of Miss Mullin, the genial proprietress, and decided not to take a furnished flat.

Bedford Place was within strolling distance of the bookshops on Charing Cross Road and the theaters on Shaftesbury Avenue. On our first Sunday we walked a little farther, to Hyde Park, to hear the orators. This became a weekly expedition. Our particular favorite was an Ulster Irishman named Bonar Thompson, who wore a large black hat, denounced work, talked satirically about anything else that came to mind and bantered with the delighted audience. "On the London buses," he would say, "a notice says *Spitting Prohibited: Penalty 40/*. In the British Museum a notice says *Spitting Prohibited: Penalty 20/*. What's the moral? If you must spit, spit in the British Museum." He quoted Shaw and Mencken, G. K. Chesterton and Groucho Marx, William Butler Yeats and Sean O'Casey, and reveled in the cadences of language and the follies of humankind. His autobiography, *Hyde Park Orator*, was a dyspeptic book for which his friend O'Casey wrote a disapproving foreword. But his Hyde Park performances were great fun. Michael Foot called him "the best one-man act London ever saw in his own time."

My father's Commonwealth Lectures were a notable success. While my parents saw the Laskis and other academic friends, I walked all over London, visited museums and galleries, frequented second-hand bookshops and saw sixteen plays by mid-April (mostly from the gallery): among them, Fred Astaire in *Gay Divorce;* Gertrude Lawrence in *Nymph Errant;* Jack Buchanan in *Mr. Whittington;* O'Casey's *Within the Gates;* Elisabeth Bergner in *Escape Me Never;* Noel Coward's *Conversation Piece,* in which he co-starred with Yvonne Printemps; Edmund Gwenn in Priestley's *Laburnum Grove;* George Robey and Lili Damita in *Here's How;* John Gielgud and Gwen Frangcon-Davies in *Richard of Bordeaux;* Celia Johnson in *The Wind and the Rain;* Edith Evans and Cedric Hardwicke in *The Late Christopher Bean;* Peggy Ashcroft, Lupino Lane and Ernest Thesiger in *The Golden Toy;* Ina Claire in S. N. Behrman's *Biography;* Adele Dixon, Charlotte Greenwood and Stanley Holloway in the Jerome Kern–Oscar Hammerstein operetta *Three Sisters* (far from Chekhov). Fancying a future as a drama critic, I filled a notebook with reviews.

*   *   *

On a sullen afternoon in late February 1934 the Communists organized a demonstration denouncing an unemployment bill they portrayed as the entering wedge for fascism. The Hunger March ended with speeches in Hyde Park. Fog made London dark as night, and the drizzle of rain added to the gloom. Policemen in ponchos were everywhere. There were, the *Times* reported, fifty thousand people in the Park. I was one of them.

Among the more rational speakers were Aneurin Bevan and John Strachey, later to become my friends. But Communists dominated the scene. Bill Gallacher told how the Russian Revolution had killed off the tsar and tsarina and all the dukes (pronounced *jukes*) and duchesses and the financiers who battened off the working class; revolution, he observed, was what Britain needed today. Another speaker denounced Franklin D. Roosevelt, calling his Civilian Conservation Corps fascist and comparing the CCC camps to the Hitler Jugend. My journal: "Rarely have I heard so much slop in one afternoon. . . . the vilest and most complete bilge that has come my way for a long time. I don't know which infuriates me more: to hear a conservative talking about a communist or a communist discussing a conservative."

Days passed, the fogs lifted, spring arrived in a burst of fragrance. One Saturday Diana Laski, Harold's daughter, invited me to go on a hike in the country. "My paradisical solitude was thus disturbed," I wrote, but felt I should go anyway. Diana and her friends were "pseudo-sophisticated, smoking and making supposedly witty allusions. It is a kind of group which I find, to my shame, I can fit into easily."

Soon the Schlesingers set out to see the rest of Britain. My parents were faithful and well-organized tourists. Making their first journey abroad, they were determined to see the things they had heard about all their lives and hopeful that their sons would share their enthusiasms, which, being both acquiescent and interested, Tom and I more or less did most of the time.

We went to lovely Cambridge, Lincoln, York, then to Edinburgh, where my father lectured at the university; on to the Lake District (it was now May), Stratford-on-Avon, Oxford (which I compared unfavorably to Cambridge). It was a delightful journey except for the food, which, outside London and private houses, was deplorable. "If that is tea," as the American tourist said after tasting a steaming cup of an indeterminate brown liquid, "bring me coffee. If that is coffee, bring me tea." The remarkable improvement in British cooking since the war contradicts the decline-of-England literature.

*　*　*

At the end of May we proceeded to Paris, staying at a small hotel on the rue Molière by the Comédie-Française and near the Bibliothèque Nationale. One attraction of the Hôtel Félix for Americans was that the actor Otis Skinner (*Kismet*) habitually stayed there, as did his daughter Cornelia (*Our Hearts Were Young and Gay*). They were not there, however, in June 1934, but Skinner memorabilia abounded. I quickly succumbed to the magic of Paris. The old Boston wit Tom Appleton had it right: "Good Americans, when they die, go to Paris."

As usual, we saw all the sights, including a gorgeous Fête de la Nuit in Versailles. And we took in two wonderfully enjoyable operettas. Max Reinhardt had brought his production of *La Chauve-Souris* (Johann Strauss's *Die Fledermaus*) to Paris. The stage not only revolved but moved up and down, so we could see guests enter an anteroom for a reception, then, by means of the sinking stage, ascend to the next floor, where, by means of the revolving stage, they pass onto the terrace and into a ballroom. Erik Charrell's *L'Auberge du Cheval Blanc* (*White Horse Inn*) was even more spectacular, "about the best produced musical show I have seen." Ferryboats, tourist buses, trains, sailboats, presented no obstacles, and Ralph Benatzky's stirring score cheered French audiences much as it cheered New York audiences the next year (and, when I went to see it again, gave me my first sight of beautiful Kitty Carlisle, later to become a dear friend).

There followed a week in Switzerland among the Alps, which, I chauvinistically noted, "did not compare in ruggedness and grandeur to the Canadian Rockies." Italy came next — Milan, Genoa, Pisa, Florence and, above all, Venice, then and thereafter my favorite city next to Paris. On to Vienna, where we stood transfixed before the fascinating Brueghels in the Kunsthistorisches Museum — Pieter Brueghel and sons, the first great social historians. We enjoyed the Prater and Heuriger wine and music in Grinzing and even came upon a pleasant little square called Schlesingerplatz.

On to Prague and then (it is now mid-July 1934) into Nazi Germany. On the train to Dresden, an attractive German girl, returning from three months abroad and speaking excellent English, astonished us by her irreverence toward *der Führer,* telling Hitler jokes and denouncing Nazi practices. "She spoke with complete and very surprising freedom and indifference to Hitler." I was surprised, too, to find the London papers and Paris editions of the *New York Herald Tribune* and the *Chicago Tribune* on the newsstands. *Unter Weg,* the translation of FDR's *On Our Way,* was in the bookstores.

From the pre–Bomber Harris glories of Dresden, we moved on to Nuremberg, where the windows were filled with photographs of Hitler kissing little girls or meditating before a fireplace with a large dog sprawled by his side. The gate to the holy ground around the church of Saint Catherine (see the first act of *Die Meistersinger*) bore the notice "Juden, kein Eintritt" — the first sign of that sort we had seen. I went to the movies; a favorite actress, Lilian Harvey, was in *Ein Blonder Traum.* The newsreel showed Rudolf Hess, "a tough-looking, square-jawed chap," addressing Nazi "Frontkämpfer" in Prussia; the front-line fighters on the screen roared their approval, but the Nuremberg audience sat on their hands.

On to medieval Rothenburg, Munich, Heidelberg, Wiesbaden and, by Rhine steamer, Cologne. The Rhine trip was a disappointment; the rock of the Lorelei seemed quite ordinary; "for lovely scenery, I prefer the Albany–New York trip on the Hudson." But my political sensibility was suspended. "I found Germany very pleasant," I am ashamed to see that I wrote in my journal. "There were absolutely no traces of tension, fear, mass-hysteria or anything similar." I had expected much worse.

Thence to Brussels and back to London and Carlton Mansions toward the end of July. The rest of the family then left for a fortnight's holiday on the Isle of Wight; I persuaded my father and mother to let me stay on in London. Years later, when my own sixteen-year-old children demanded independence from close parental supervision, I tried to remember the admirable willingness of my own parents to leave me on my own in a big city. So for two weeks I wandered through the town, returned to bookshops and the theater (in Vincent Lawrence's *Sour Grapes* I saw Constance Cummings, the beautiful American actress whom I had admired since I first saw her in Harold Lloyd's brilliant *Movie Crazy*) and in general consolidated my affection for London and the English.

On August 22, 1934, the Schlesinger family boarded the White Star's *Georgic* in Liverpool and, after an uneventful voyage, arrived a week later in Boston. Harvard loomed ahead. "Well," I wrote in the last line of my travel journal, "the party's over." And what a grand party it had been! For a naive and impressionable boy, a trip around the world was the best possible education. It widened horizons, polished manners, stimulated curiosity, strengthened self-reliance and, along the way, provided an introduction to the political disquietudes of the twentieth century.

7

Harvard College: What I Did

IN SEPTEMBER 1934, a fortnight after returning from the great adventure, I entered Harvard College in the Class of 1938. Tuition was $400 a year. Room and board added another $700. (Sixty years later the total was $34,350.) Freshmen lived in dormitories in Harvard Yard. My room was on the second floor of Thayer Hall, a nondescript structure in the center of the Yard. We ate at the Harvard Union in what Henry James called a "great, grave, noble hall," baronial, oak-paneled and spacious, built by McKim, Mead & White in the first decade of the century and chopped up unfeelingly into administrative offices in the century's last decade.

My roommate in Thayer 7 turned out to be a decent, reticent, forbearing young man from Chicago, Edward T. James, later known for his work on the *Dictionary of American Biography* and *Notable American Women*, and we roomed together throughout our college years. The Thayer Hall fellows were a good robust lot, many from the middle west, most from public schools. Robert Wernick, a bright Boston Latin boy, became in later life a talented and versatile contributor to magazines; John Andrew Moore, a dry, thoughtful, quizzical Missourian, became a professor of Greek at Amherst. Our bull sessions surveyed politics, religion and (above all) sex from a diversity of viewpoints. We argued a lot, naifs all (though some, like me, more naive than others), pretending to know more than we did while covertly seeking tips from the rest, particularly about dealing with girls.

* * *

Let me recall superficialities of life in the Thirties. Daily routines were more complicated then. When we went to bed at night, we had to wind our watches; the battery-powered watch was still to come. When we dressed in the morning, some began by putting on BVDs, a form of one-piece underwear now extinct; the more advanced turned to shorts and undershirts, though, after seeing Clark Gable in *It Happened One Night* in 1934, most of us discarded the undershirt, never to be worn again (at least in my case — the undershirt, a useless and ig-noble item, had a mysterious revival toward the end of the century).

When we bought a suit, two pairs of pants came with the jacket and vest. After putting on pants (no khakis or jeans), we had to button our flies; the zipper did not appear till the late Thirties (and at first did not always work, thereby sometimes causing acute embarrassment on dates). Garters still held up socks, and we had to lace our shoes; the loafer or moccasin was not yet acceptable. The fashion at Harvard was to wear black and white saddle shoes of the kind known in England, as I later discovered when I mistakenly wore them there, as "co-respondent" shoes; that is, shoes favored by professional co-respondents in divorce cases, like the Erik Rhodes character in the Fred Astaire–Ginger Rogers movie *The Gay Divorcee* (so called before the same-sexers kidnapped the word 'gay').

It was in these years that I went over to the bow tie. Many men I admired wore bow ties — Franklin Roosevelt, Winston Churchill, Harry Truman, Humphrey Bogart, Groucho Marx. Bow ties are not only neat and suggestive of insouciance; they have in addition one inestimable advantage, especially for sloppy eaters. It is impossible, or at least it requires extreme agility, to spill anything on a bow tie. A spill on a four-in-hand tie ruins it forever; dry cleaning never restores a tie to its primal innocence. The same spill falling on a shirtfront is easily erased by dipping a napkin in a glass of water and wiping the spot away.

There is also an instructive story told to me by Charles E. Bohlen about Hervé Alphand, a memorable French ambassador to the United States. One day, when Bohlen was counselor of the State Department, Alphand stormed into his office to make a formal protest about something or other (he was an epigrammatic diplomat, but rather given to protests). Sitting down by Bohlen's desk, he leaned over in order to bang the desk and thereby emphasize his grievance. As he leaned, he glanced down and saw that his fly was open. Without stopping his flow of speech, he zipped his fly. A moment later, having completed his protest, he straightened up — and discovered that he had zipped his tie in his fly. This could never happen to a bow tie wearer.

*   *   *

When we wanted sandwiches, we had to use a knife to slice the bread; sliced bread was still in the future. When we went outdoors, we put on hats — gray felt in winter, soft panama in summer. Hatless John Kennedy killed the hat craze in 1960, much to the chagrin of his powerful supporter in New York, Alex Rose, the head of the Hatters Union and boss of the Liberal party. On cold days in the year 2000 I wear a cap; in the Thirties the cap was strictly a proletarian taste. The Russian fur hat, now so fashionable, was as little known in the America of the Thirties as vodka.

When we had writing to do, we filled fountain pens from inkwells; the ball-point pen was still to come. The word processor was beyond imagining, even by Verne or Wells. In those days before computers, as Nardi Reeder Campion, Wellesley '38 and the witty wife of my Harvard classmate Tom Campion, puts it, "a chip meant a piece of wood, hardware meant hardware, and software wasn't even a word."

Telephone calls cost a nickel. (A depression joke: President Hoover asked Andrew Mellon, his secretary of the treasury, for the loan of a nickel to call a friend. Mellon replied, "Here's a dime, call up all your friends.") If we had letters to mail, we used a two-cent stamp, which we had to lick before affixing to the envelope. There were two mail deliveries a day in residential areas, more in business districts. A letter posted in Boston before five in the afternoon was delivered in New York before nine the next morning. If the message was urgent, we paid ten cents for special delivery. If the urgency was extreme, Western Union or Postal Telegraph would deliver messages to the door at all hours of day and night.

When it rained, we carried only black umbrellas. When we traveled, redcaps were available to carry excess luggage; suitcases in those days had no wheels. When we were sick, doctors paid house calls. There was no penicillin for them to prescribe. People smoked all the time. Movie houses had balconies.

Newspapers cost two cents, and there were still afternoon papers. On Sunday the *New York Times* cost ten cents. Novels cost two dollars and a half; nonfiction, three dollars; afternoon movies a quarter; plays in the evening up to $4.40. A haircut was fifty cents; cigarettes, fifteen cents a pack. Five-and-ten-cent stores — Woolworth's or Kresge's — sold things for five and ten cents. Those of us whose pecuniary reflexes were formed in the Thirties are perennially outraged by the prices demanded in the twenty-first century. "I simply cannot afford to live, it daily seems to me," writes John Updike, "as I size up 1999 prices in the dollars of 1939."

For more expensive purchases, we used cash or charge accounts. Although Edward Bellamy had invented the credit card half a century before in *Looking Backward,* capitalism would not catch up with his socialism in this respect till the Fifties. We had no television, no air conditioning, no electric blankets. Women did not wear pants. Thank heavens.

When we drove, we shifted gears and lowered windows by hand. Automobiles had a choke and running boards but no seat belts or directional signals; you stuck out an arm to alert the car behind you to a slowdown or a turn. Flashy people had cars with rumble seats. Flashier ones had convertibles. Gasoline cost eleven cents a gallon, and station attendants rushed to fill the tank, check oil and water, wipe the windshield — and provide *free road maps*. Burma-Shave, a popular shaving cream, entertained us on country roads with catchy jingles:

Pity all	He had the ring
The mighty Caesars	He had the flat
They pulled	But she felt his chin
Each whisker out	And that
With tweezers	Was that
BURMA-SHAVE	BURMA-SHAVE

Our drinking tastes tended toward sweetness: old-fashioneds (bourbon or rye with sugar, bitters and fruit), Manhattans (gin and sweet vermouth), Stingers (brandy and crème de menthe), Tom Collinses (gin, lime juice and sugar) and the Sloe Gin Fizz, the last of which was supposed to reduce the most obdurate female to acquiescence. Ed James and I used to serve a drink made of gin, grapefruit juice and grenadine — it sounds horrid in retrospect. Drugs? We had heard of marijuana as an addiction of jazz musicians and had listened to Cab Calloway singing "Reefer Man" and "Minnie the Moocher," but a sensational (and terrible) film of 1936, *Reefer Madness*, warned us where reefers led. Nardi Campion again: for the Thirties, "grass was something you mowed, Coke was something you drank, and pot was something you cooked in." She adds: "Closets were for clothes, not for coming out of."

Manners were more formal. Older men, even close and devoted friends, often addressed each other by last names. Few men, except for Grover Cleveland Alexander and the House of David baseball team, wore beards. Long hair, crew cuts, sideburns, were little seen. Social kissing between men and women, now so common, was rare, at least in academic circles. In 2000 cheek-kissing, devoid of romantic or sexual implication, often takes place after the first meeting; there has even arisen the tiresome fad of double-kissing — both cheeks. In the

Thirties the double kiss was regarded as a comic French eccentricity. Divorce, in Boston anyway, was still a scandal. When Charles P. Curtis was divorced, he resigned from the Harvard Corporation; when Kenneth Murdock was divorced, he resigned as master of Leverett House.

"Swell," a beatific Twenties word denoting special enthusiasm (equivalent, for example, to "terrific" in the Sixties), lingered a bit in the Thirties, especially in Hollywood musicals ("Go out there and be so swell you'll make me hate you," Bebe Daniels, the star, to Ruby Keeler, her replacement, in *42nd Street*). The Thirties came up with no beatific word of its own, not being a notably beatific decade.

And no one in the Thirties ever said, "Have a nice day."

*　*　*

At the end of freshman year, we had to choose not only a field of concentration but also a place to live. Harvard had recently entered a new era in living arrangements. Edward Harkness, the philanthropist who, though a St. Paul's man, had changed Exeter, now, though a Yale man, was changing Harvard. He had a romantic view of the colleges of Oxford and Cambridge; and when Yale initially turned down his offer to establish a college system in New Haven, President Lowell persuaded Harkness to transfer his vision and $10 million to Cambridge.

Under the House plan, as it was called, undergraduates spent their last three years not in traditional dormitories but in Houses equipped with masters, resident tutors, common rooms, libraries and dining halls, each House a community to itself. The sensitive, Dos Passos–like Harvard novel by George Weller '29, *Not to Eat, Not for Love* — still the best college novel I know — came out in 1933, and we all read it with fascination. But the first of the new Houses had opened the year after Weller's graduation, and the Harvard College he so poignantly portrayed already seemed another age. (Weller became a foreign correspondent and was the first American reporter to write from Hiroshima. I knew him after the war as one of Harvard's first Nieman Fellows — journalists awarded a year's fellowship — and then as a stocky, tough, experienced, rather cynical foreign correspondent working for the United Press in Rome.)

Ed James and I decided on Adams House. This was partly because Adams was the only one with its own swimming pool and its own kitchen, the latter supposed to guarantee superior food. Also, my father was a fellow of the House, and consequently I had had some acquaintance with it.

The master was my father's good friend James Phinney Baxter, Harvard's splendid diplomatic historian who became president of Williams in our junior year. Jim Baxter — Phinney, old friends called him — was a hearty, shrewd, rubicund, twinkling man who liked undergraduates, entertained them with an abundance of stories and radiated a refreshing Yankee downrightness amid the preciosities of Harvard intellectualism. Raphael Demos, an engaging and tolerant Greek philosopher, took over as master in our senior year, and S. Everett Gleason, a medieval historian of much wit and charm, became senior tutor. Their sons, John Demos and Abbott Gleason, later became able historians in their own right.

Unlike the tidy neo-Georgian houses so recently erected along the Charles River, Adams House was an amalgam of old and new. Westmorley and Randolph, the two old halls, were part of the luxurious Gold Coast, privately built years before for rich undergraduates who disdained monastic college dormitories. This explained the swimming pool. C entry, where Ed James and I lived, was a new structure between Westmorley and Randolph and connecting them through a network of tunnels. C entry contained a hospitable common room in red, blue and gold, an excellent library and a men's room proudly described as the largest north of Radio City. Soon to hang in the Adams House common room was a portrait of John Reed '10, the author of *Ten Days That Shook the World,* who was subsequently buried in the walls of the Kremlin. This was presented in 1935 by Corliss Lamont '24 and other Harvard graduates wishing amid the ruins of capitalism to honor Reed for his "courage, idealism, and independent mind."

Ed James and I occupied an airy suite on the top floor of C entry. We each had a bedroom and shared a capacious living room and a narrow balcony looking toward the Yard. Daily "biddie" service rescued rooms from undergraduate clutter. The dining hall lived up to its reputation. Even in the depression, Harvard Houses had table service with printed menus. Students wore jackets and neckties. We had hardly anticipated how comely some of the waitresses would be. I longed to summon up the courage to ask Nadine or Jean for a date. One of our friends fell into a tortured affair with a less attractive waitress. (Coming back after the war was a great letdown: waitresses gone; menus gone; jackets and ties gone; students lining up as if in an Army mess to receive food shoveled into indented trays; four or five students now occupying Adams C-57.)

For some reason I abandoned journal-keeping in my freshman year. Then, for some reason, I resumed it as a sophomore, keeping a record faithfully for the next two years and fitfully as a senior. The journal, I regret to say, gives far less space to professors, books and lectures than to parties, movies, plays, late-night bull sessions, random adventures and girls (as young women were known in the benighted Thirties). In my sophomore year, I would even summarize the day's activities in five categories: Weather, Work, Smoking, Liquor and Love. I am glad to see that Work made the cut.

*   *   *

The Class of 1938 was not a distinguished class. This was not clear to us at the time. How excitedly we talked in those bull sessions, and how seriously we took those talks — and ourselves! One is educated as much, it is said, by contemporaries as by teachers. Yet probably the most lasting education comes from recollections of one's own folly.

We sometimes wondered whether we were not like the famous Class of 1910 — T. S. Eliot, Walter Lippmann, John Reed, Heywood Broun, Hamilton Fish. In fact, the nearest thing to the Harvard Class of 1910 in these years must have been the Yale Class of 1936 — John Hersey, Brendan Gill, Walt Rostow, August Heckscher, Stewart Alsop, Jonathan Bingham, Dillon Ripley, Chester Kerr, David Dellinger.

We fell far short of that. The best-known member of our class in later years was probably the vivid journalist Theodore H. White. Recalling Harvard in his fine memoir, *In Search of History,* Teddy White divided our class into three categories — white men, gray men and meatballs. The white men were prep school, "white shoe" boys and included such sons of the famous as John Roosevelt from the White House, Benjamin Welles, whose father, Sumner, was soon to be undersecretary of state, Kenneth MacLeish, the poet's son, Randolph Hearst, son of the wicked publisher, Joseph P. Kennedy, Jr., Marshall Field, Jr. The gray men in Teddy's taxonomy were middle-class public school boys like Caspar Weinberger, who later served as Ronald Reagan's secretary of defense (and as hopelessly impervious a conservative in Harvard College as he was half a century later in the Pentagon), and John King, who became governor of New Hampshire. Teddy placed himself among the meatballs — scholarship boys and day students, mostly lower-class Irish, Jewish or Italian.

As for me, Teddy wrote that Schlesinger "defied categorization. Definitely no meatball, Schlesinger lacked then either the wealth or the savoir-faire of the white men. Indeed, Schlesinger . . . was one who could apparently mingle with both white men *and* meatballs. In his

youth, Schlesinger was a boy of extraordinary sweetness and generosity, one of the few on campus who would be friendly to a Jewish meatball." How could one not be friendly to dear Teddy White, himself the
most loyal and sentimental of old friends? In the interests of full disclosure, I must add that in the same paragraph Teddy went on to note
that in later years Schlesinger "developed a certainty about affairs, a
public tartness of manner associated with the general liberal rigidity
of the late Sixties that offended many."

That tartness offended many in the Thirties too. In my freshman
year, the *Herald* printed a letter of protest I had written about something or other. Felix Frankfurter sent a note of congratulations on the
letter but added that I could have made my point "in language more
effective because less polemic, and less animadverting upon people
who don't share your views. Perhaps a year's experience in England
[he had just been Eastman professor at Oxford] has made me realize
more than ever how persuasive understatement and impersonality in
argument are."

It took a while, far too long a while, before I appreciated the wisdom of Frankfurter's advice. The certainty and tartness that Teddy
White attributed to me in the Sixties were well advanced in the Thirties. Pat Jackson in his Columbia Oral History (1959) recalled a dinner when my mother suddenly stopped in the midst of making a
point and said to me, "Why are you shaking your head? Can't I say
what I believe?" I replied, "No, mother, not when you don't know
what you are talking about." I fear something like that may well have
taken place. "I talked with his father about this a good deal," Pat continued. "His father has been very frank with me about his distress over
manifestations of arrogance."

It was not so much arrogance, I think, as cockiness, but, whatever it
may have been, it was not attractive.

* * *

The exciting undergraduate in Adams House, at least for the young
intellectuals, was Chadbourne Gilpatric '37, a philosophy student of
flashing charm and audacity. In later years I much enjoyed working
with his older brother Roswell when he was deputy secretary of defense in the Kennedy administration (the circularity of life). For a
sophomore like me (the magic diminished a bit in time), Gil seemed
a fascinating combination of deep thinker, man about town and intrepid adventurer.

I also learned much from two foreign students assigned to Adams

House while they pursued postgraduate study in economics: Robert Triffin of Belgium and Shigeto Tsuru of Japan. They were a little older and combined intellectual cosmopolitanism with a genuine zest for things American. Triffin was a man of keen intelligence and altogether delightful wry humor. When he became an American citizen, I had the honor of standing up with him before the authorities. Later he worked with the Marshall Plan and devised ingenious schemes for the reconstruction of the European monetary system. Eventually, after teaching at Yale, he returned to Belgium and ended as a baron. Tsuru, with whom I had many a struggle on the squash court, had, I thought, the most subtle and rigorously logical mind I knew. Marxism was part of his analytical arsenal, but he could take it or leave it alone. In time he became the elder statesman of the economics profession in Japan.

Gilpatric was the energizer of the group. Living as he did by a gospel of spontaneity, he would burst into our rooms and say, "Let's get out of here," and off we would go, whether to the Wellesley campus to call on tolerant girls; or to seedy bars in Scollay Square in Boston to pick up babes and sample the low-life dives, watching Sally Keith, the queen of the tassels, at the Crawford House or Ann Corio in burlesque at the Old Howard; or to Revere Beach and the great roller-coaster; or for weekends to small towns in New Hampshire or the Berkshires.

Once we went with Triffin and a Belgian friend of his to inspect the foliage in western Massachusetts on a brilliant October day. We spent the night in Monterey at the bed-and-breakfast house of an old man — Princeton '79 — who regaled us with anecdotes about his classmate "Tommy" Wilson (who dropped his first name before he became president of the United States) and reminiscences of the Bad Lands in the 1880s. What seemed even then the remote past still had its eyewitnesses, if sometimes of doubtful reliability. On another occasion I went with Ed James and John O'Keefe on a jaunt to Cape Cod. There another old fellow entertained us with stories of Grover Cleveland and his friend Joseph Jefferson, the actor (Rip Van Winkle was his famous part), getting tipsy and chasing each other around the Sandwich railroad station. Grover Cleveland?

I was not high on Boston's social lists, but I received occasional invitations to coming-out parties, where, still younger than my classmates and still embarrassed by acne, I would huddle on the sidelines with other bashful stags, risk an occasional dance, drink too much champagne and, sometimes, throw up vigorously on my return to Adams

House. Yet, whenever I hear Cole Porter's "Just One of Those Things," I remember it with a certain nostalgia as the tune of the season at those parties.

Athletics were on the far edge of life. Football on crisp autumn afternoons remained the chief attraction. When the aging Babe Ruth (i.e., thirty-nine years old) joined the Boston Braves in 1935, I saw him hit a home run. Hockey was the preferred winter sport; in New England in those remote days basketball was regarded as primarily a pastime for girls. The Charles River sometimes froze over, and little was more delicious than skating along the glistening ice on a moonlit night. My own sport, then as now, was tennis.

Gilpatric was an avid sailor, and, visiting him in the summer at Somesville on Mount Desert Island off the Maine coast, I received my initiation in cruising. As evening fell on the first night, we reached Great Cranberry Island. Directed to cast off the anchor, I distinguished myself by failing to note that the anchor line was not secured to the boat. Gil, not unnaturally, was furious. We spent the next couple of hours grappling before the anchor was recovered. I noted then (and with other skippers later) how, once in command of a sailboat, the most courteous fellows on land turn into raging martinets.

*   *   *

That summer of 1935 was the last totally relaxed time. Thereafter summer jobs were on the agenda, and in 1936 my father prevailed on a friend from Ohio, now an executive on William Randolph Hearst's tabloid *Boston Daily Record*, to take me on as an office messenger for $10.50 a week (about $120 today). The job was humble, and I was too absentminded to do it well. Still, the world of business was new to me, and any association with a newspaper, even the advertising side, was of interest.

Hearst was then at the height of his crusade to rouse America to the dangers of communism. His targeting was not always accurate. In November 1934, when New York University refused his demand that it fire those dangerous subversives Professors Sidney Hook and James Burnham, Hearst asked whether NYU was to be classified hereafter "as an active center of treasonable plotting for the overthrow of the American Government." He was not disturbed by fascism. "When you hear a prominent American called a 'Fascist,'" he said in October 1935, "you can usually make up your mind that the man is simply a LOYAL CITIZEN WHO STANDS FOR AMERICANISM."

Hearst was abominated in liberal and academic circles, and yet I cannot recall any qualms about taking a job on one of his terrible papers. My uncle Will Bancroft, the paper manufacturer from Ohio, an agreeable and tolerant man whom I liked very much, visited us that summer. One night he asked me, "How do you feel about accepting money from Hearst and then speaking about him the way you do? Don't you think that your loyalty, as well as your services, is involved in the job?" Loyalty, Uncle Will argued, was essential both for business efficiency and for personal success. I replied that in my view the worker had no obligation to his employer beyond that of performing faithfully the job for which he was hired. I stand by this answer, but it was an ethical problem that had not occurred to me and a useful by-product of my exposure to the ethos of business.

My life as a messenger thrust me into association with people of a new sort. "They seem to have no ideas, no interests," I wrote rather snottily in my journal; "the talk is devoted almost exclusively to kidding and to shop talk. They are not interested in sports, or in politics, or in the movies, or in girls. . . . But they remain very companionable." Companionability triumphed over all. When I departed two months later, to genial handshaking all around, I had learned a good deal about Boston and about newspapers and about people. My fellow messengers, I felt, had been condemned by circumstances to mediocrity, whatever their innate abilities might be; this hardly seemed a fair way to run a society.

The next summer, after my junior year, the intercession of Dave Niles brought me a National Youth Administration job in the Charlestown Prison, a forbidding, gloomy, gray structure erected in the early nineteenth century and not much improved since. My assignment was to write up case histories for prisoners about to appear before the parole board, for which I received $85 a month. My boss was an intelligent and conscientious man named Richard Winslow, whom, in the circularity of life, I would encounter again a quarter century later when he was chief administrative officer of the United States Mission to the United Nations and I was President Kennedy's liaison with our ambassador to the U.N. Adlai Stevenson.

We wrote our case histories out of court records, social workers' reports and prison interviews and assessments. It was good training for an embryonic historian. We were understaffed and had to work hard to keep up with the flow. I noted, "I rather like this sense of several balls in the air at once." The work was also an education in the agonies and cruelties of life — child abuse, rape, incest, men driven by dark psychic compulsions and obsessions. I learned a lot about human nature in the Charlestown Prison.

*   *   *

My chief extracurricular interest at college was the *Harvard Advocate*. Founded in 1866, seven years before the *Crimson*, it had established its identity as the undergraduate literary magazine in the 1880s. Here Theodore Roosevelt '80, Edwin Arlington Robinson '95, Wallace Stevens '01, Van Wyck Brooks '08, T. S. Eliot '10, Conrad Aiken '11, E. E. Cummings '15, James Agee '32 and others had published their early work.

The *Advocate* offices were on the third floor of a dingy frame building at 40 Bow Street, across the street from Adams House. One climbed musty stairs to arrive at last at a tangle of small rooms, "five mystical chambers," as Norman Mailer '43 later described them, "full of broken-down furniture, and the incomparable odor that rises from old beer stains in the carpet, and syrup-crusted empty Coke bottles in the corners."

The dominating presence when I went out for the *Advocate* was James Laughlin IV '36, the handsome, rangy, debonair heir of Jones & Laughlin steel money. I had mixed feelings about Laughlin — "utterly charming and utterly unreliable; both adjectives are inescapable," I wrote in my journal. ". . . He is a shrewd politician who has devoted most of his great diplomatic talent to one end — obtaining what he wants."

After taking six months off from Harvard to work with Ezra Pound in Rapallo, Jay Laughlin had returned from Italy the champion of literary modernism. Pound, he later said, changed the shape of his mind; but he meant poetry, not Pound's fascist politics. "I think anti-Semitism is contemptible and despicable," Laughlin once wrote to his master, "and I will not put my hand to it."

Laughlin found in John Slocum '36, the *Advocate*'s president, a staunch ally in the cause of literary modernism. The local police were less enthusiastic. Massachusetts was still a citadel of censorship. When the September 1935 *Advocate* ran "Glittering Pie," procured by Laughlin from Henry Miller in Paris, along with Jay's own story "A Natural History," the cops seized the issue, and the district attorney denounced "the grotesque brainchildren of these college boys" as "obscene and degrading." He demanded that the Harvard authorities maintain "rigid supervision over the childish efforts of those em-

bryonic authors [Miller was nearly fifty] who seem to think it a mark
of distinction to dish up dirt." Threatening to jail the authors, "suffering from allusions [sic] of grandeur," he forced the resignation of six
editors, including Slocum and Gerard Piel '37, the business manager.
I do not recall that the Harvard authorities protested this miserable
assault on the freedom of expression.

When Jay had shown his poetry to Pound, Pound observed, "Jaz,
you're never going to be any good as a poet." After musing that Jay
might better devote his talents to assassinating Henry Seidel Canby,
the editor of the *Saturday Review of Literature,* Pound said, "You'd
better become a publisher. You've probably got enough brains for
that." Laughlin followed this advice, and his New Directions became
one of the most creative of American publishing houses.

I saw little of Laughlin in the years after Harvard. But John Slocum,
a collector of James Joyce manuscripts, remained a good friend during his years abroad with the United States Information Agency and
in his retirement at Newport. Gerry Piel became the influential editor and publisher of *Scientific American.*

I began as the *Advocate*'s drama critic. Later I wrote about jazz, politics and Harvard. The piece on Harvard argued that the old Harvard
of clubmen, gentleman's C's and acute social stratification was fading
away. The invasion of middle westerners, public school graduates and
the newer immigrants, I contended, was destroying the homogeneity
that had spawned the old-style Harvard man, the Harvard man you
could always tell, though you couldn't tell him much. The House
plan in particular, I suggested, had probably ended any really useful
role for the final clubs by providing facilities that beat the clubs in
comfort, convenience and general amplitude. "With a wave of Harkness's wand, their chief excuse for existence — the pleasant living
they provided — vanished." The clubs, I predicted, would now retreat to the margins of undergraduate life. The Houses, based on the
cross-section principle, and President Conant, with his emphasis on
scholarly rather than social distinction, would make Harvard a more
democratic institution than ever before. (I forgot the power of snobbery.)

The piece went to the printers during the summer, while the senior
Advocate editors were away. They were mostly clubmen themselves
and not at all happy when they returned and read the proofs. They
looked at me, I recorded, "with mingled horror and incredulity," as if
I had been exposed as a traitor in their midst. One said, "How could
you have written it? . . . If it had been anyone else in college. . . ." Now

was the time, I thought fleetingly, to stand up and fight. "And what did I do?" I quote my journal. "I turned on the charm and polish; and, without retracting or qualifying a statement in the article, I restored myself to their good graces with all the ease of an accomplished double-dealer. I seem to hunt with the hounds and run with the hares without any strain of conscience or intellect. . . . A savage, bitter, knock-down drag-out contest might do me good."

*   *   *

The *Advocate* specialized in parties for visiting literary celebrities. In the winter of 1934–35 Gertrude Stein, Radcliffe '97, returned to the United States for the first time in thirty years. She had hoped to lecture at her alma mater, but the Radcliffe board of trustees declined to pay her honorarium of $100. The Harvard English department showed no interest in sponsoring her. Then Ada Comstock, the president of Radcliffe, found someone who would guarantee the fee, and Miss Stein lectured to an overflow house. The *Advocate* gave her a reception. I remember a smallish, stocky woman, gray hair cut short, surrounded by eager questioners to whom she returned crisp answers. The wispy Miss Alice B. Toklas was silent at her side.

Walter Lippmann '10 dropped by the *Advocate* in January 1936. Reading his omniscient columns in the *New York Herald Tribune,* I had expected someone cocksure and pretentious but found him "pleasant and unassuming . . . mild-mannered and giving the impression of being humble in opinion and reflective in thought . . . nowhere dogmatic . . . often confessed ignorance." This was three months after Mussolini had ordered the invasion of Ethiopia, and Lippmann told us that the Italians were beaten and might face a disaster as great as Adowa. He still seemed sympathetic to Roosevelt and the New Deal but was going west to see Governor Alfred M. Landon of Kansas, the likely Republican candidate. (In the fall Lippmann endorsed Landon, a decision that came after much tribulation and attracted much attention. Twenty years later, when Governor Landon opened his papers to me in Topeka, I asked him over luncheon one day about the Lippmann endorsement. "Lippmann," he said. "Walter Lippmann? Did he come out for me?")

Sean O'Casey spoke — "an extraordinary spectacle. I have never seen a notable make such an ass of himself. O'Casey does not hesitate to lie and make dirty personal remarks about contemporary playwrights and critics." Unfortunately I did not record the specifics. The great poet Robert Frost was another eminent figure to arouse my pre-

sumptuous disapproval — "full of a petty malice and a petty conceit
. . . a tendency to make spiteful remarks about other people and to
regard himself with considerable solemnity and self-satisfaction. . . .
I grew so disgusted that I left as soon as I decently could."

The Signet Society was another refuge for undergraduates of a literary bent. Founded in 1870, it had occupied a house on the corner
of Dunster and Mount Auburn streets since 1902. In the Thirties it
served the best luncheons in Cambridge, prided itself, sometimes
justifiably, on the quality of its table talk and gave parties for visiting
dignitaries, like a surprisingly mute H. G. Wells in November 1937.

I was chosen in the first sophomore seven; some of the others were
Ben Welles, later foreign correspondent for the *New York Times* and a
lifelong friend; Francis Keppel, later Kennedy's commissioner of education; Hans Zinsser, who became like his father an eminent doctor;
and Alfonso Ossorio, the surrealist painter. Initiation was an ordeal.
The candidates, frozen with nervousness, dazzled by a bright light in
a darkened room, had to provide witty answers to stupefying questions issuing out of the shadows, several in the unmistakable octoge-
narian voice of A. Lawrence Lowell. Later I discovered that this was a
feat of mimicry performed by George Lee Haskins '35, subsequently
a noted legal historian.

Lowell was in fact a devotee of the Signet. Once I heard him remi-
nisce about the election of 1860 — 1860! — and the discomfort he
felt (he was then on the brink of his fourth birthday) because his father was for Lincoln and his playmates' fathers were all for Bell and
Everett — a bracing reminder of the brevity of American history.

*　　*　　*

Rereading my journal, I am struck, in contrast to, say, the preoccupation with girls, by the lack of preoccupation with politics. I watched
the political scene with interest but, sure that the republic was in
good hands, I was not moved to political activism.

Like my parents, I was an ardent New Dealer. I was thrilled when
Franklin D. Roosevelt '04 spoke at the Harvard Tercentenary in 1936,
and I was among the few undergraduates to cheer FDR when he
drove through Harvard Square during the presidential campaign
later that year amid a chorus of boos from students whose rich fathers
hated the president as a traitor to his class. (Even before he was
elected, Harvard students had regarded Roosevelt with suspicion. In
1932 the undergraduate straw poll went 3–1 for Hoover, a Stanford
graduate, against the Harvard man. Norman Thomas, a Princeton

graduate, beat FDR in five of the seven Houses; the *Crimson* headlined the story: HOOVER SWEEPS UNIVERSITY IN GREATEST REPUBLICAN LANDSLIDE ON RECORD.)

Now that Ronald Reagan (who, after all, voted four times for Roosevelt) and even Newt Gingrich have freely acknowledged FDR as the greatest president of the century, it is hard to recall how hysterically he was reviled in the Thirties by those who saw their power and income threatened by his New Deal. A gentle version was Peter Arno's famous *New Yorker* cartoon portraying a group of wealthy idlers in dinner jackets and furs calling to similarly garbed friends in a brownstone window: "Come along. We're going to the Translux [a newsreel theater] to hiss Roosevelt." More to the point was the book by Marquis Childs of the *St. Louis Post-Dispatch* entitled starkly: *They Hate Roosevelt.*

The battles of the Thirties shaped my politics, giving me a lasting, if at times disappointed, loyalty to the Democratic party and a profound impression of the political shortsightedness and stupidity (as well as the greed) of American business leadership. Little had changed since the elder Henry Cabot Lodge observed to Theodore Roosevelt in 1902, "The businessman dealing with a large political question is really a painful sight. It does seem to me that businessmen, with a few exceptions, are worse when they come to deal with politics than men of any other class."

That was supremely true in the Thirties. Consider the vicious business resistance in those years to reforms that were saving the system by which they benefited — not to mention the squalid relish with which they invented and circulated lies about Roosevelt and his wife. It was FDR's ironical achievement to rescue capitalism from the capitalists.

FDR regarded the haters with evident contempt. In his climactic campaign speech in 1936 at Madison Square Garden, he condemned "government by organized money" as just as dangerous as "government by organized mob." Never before in history, he continued, had organized money been so united against one candidate. "They are unanimous in their hate for me — and I welcome their hatred." Wild applause. "I should like to have it said of my first Administration that in it the forces of selfishness and of lust for power met their match." Over the cheers of the audience, he went on: "I should like to have it said —"; but the mounting roar of anticipation promised to drown out his words. He paused and cried, "Wait a moment!"; then, "I should like to have it said of my second Administration that in it these forces have met their master." The crowd's roar was like thunder. This was the atmosphere of the time.

I had no doubt that FDR and the New Dealers could work things out and do so within the system. I still subscribe to the dictum of Orestes A. Brownson, the subject of my senior honors essay: "The men of wealth, the business men, manufacturers and merchants, bankers and brokers, are the men who exert the worst influence on government in every country. . . . They act on the beautiful maxim, 'Let the government take care of the rich, and the rich will take care of the poor,' instead of the far safer maxim, 'Let government take care of the weak, the strong can take care of themselves.'" FDR summed it up in January 1937 in his Second Inaugural: "The test of our progress is not whether we add more to the abundance of those who have much; it is whether we provide enough for those who have too little." I remain to this day a New Dealer, unreconstructed and unrepentant.

*   *   *

As an undergraduate, however, I was opposed for a season to undue political activism. When a group was formed in 1935 to repeal a teacher's oath imposed by the Massachusetts legislature, I wrote priggishly in my journal, "I shall never consider it my duty to fight vigorously for a program merely because I believe in the program; it will take some further inducements to lure me from my ivory tower. Those who want the barricades can have them; but I don't, and I admit no mystical obligations which drive me there."

I recall the spring of 1935. It is eleven o'clock on a dewy April morning. The island of grass behind Memorial Hall is covered with people. A speaking stand has been set up. A fellow holds forth with gestures and shrill intonations; he is saying something that he feels, or thinks he feels, perfervidly. Others sit on the platform, waiting their turn to denounce the idea of war. Young men and women in the crowd listen intently. This is the once famous peace strike of 1935; 175,000 students on a score of campuses are gathering in similar meetings to affirm the virtues of pacificism. Some, imitating their contemporaries at Oxford, swear an oath never "in any circumstances" to fight for their country.

I watched the great peace strike with skepticism and applauded when young Princetonians, as usual more frivolous than the rest, established the Veterans of Future Wars, demanding immediate payment of their bonuses while they were still alive to enjoy them. On the campuses of women's colleges the Association of Future Gold Star Mothers soon arose to call for free trips to Europe so that they could inspect the future graves of their future sons. I thought all this appropriate commentary.

The peace strike seemed to me misdirected and silly — what was the point of striking against universities, which were hardly the cause of war? And students who took the Oxford oath went on in the same breath to advocate collective security. This was quite a contradiction. How could collective security work without military enforcement?

After Mussolini invaded Ethiopia, I heard Sir Norman Angell, who a quarter century before had pronounced war "the Great Illusion," speak at Ford Hall Forum. "Everyone, except sentimentalists and pacifists, grants that the USA can't hope to stay out of another world war," I noted in my journal, "and that economic sanctions, to be effective, must imply military sanctions (if, indeed, there be a real difference between starving the enemy and shooting him). Why not, then, serve the cause of world peace and make the League of Nations effective in that cause by crushing Italy at the outset? I could think of no immediate answer except the purely selfish one of staying out for 4 or 5 years in the hope that the other nations will settle it." That turned out to be quite a contradiction too.

The ivory tower mood persisted. When Harvard students organized a chapter of the American Student Union in 1936: "I am not joining because of a firm conviction that any spare time I have in college should be spent in enlarging my intellectual horizons rather than in messing about with pseudo-political organizations that will never do anything very effective."

My ivory tower, however, was subject to moments of unease. One day in 1937 I fell to talking with a couple of striking seamen, who gave a graphic account of conditions on board the American merchant marine. "This episode made me feel acutely uncomfortable because of the contrast between, on the one hand, the very evident courage of these men and their very real devotion to a cause whose success would help many besides themselves, and, on the other, my own (unspoken) wish that they had not intruded their gallantry and their suffering into my orbit. My discomfort was heightened, of course, by my knowledge that in the evening I would go out and spend (quite unnecessarily) enough money to give a dozen sailors a place to sleep." Such intrusions of conscience, along with a growing belief in the value of new experience, eventually led me to join the Harvard Student Union in my senior year, if as a very passive member.

*   *   *

The American Student Union was a by-product of the reversal in the Communist line decreed by the Comintern's Seventh World Congress in the summer of 1935. Revolutionary extremism gave way to the concept, more useful to a Soviet Union threatened by Hitler's Germany, of a united front of all antifascist forces. Roosevelt, denounced by American Communists shortly before as a "social fascist," was now a leader to be wooed. "Communism," declared Earl Browder, the boss of the American Communist party, "is twentieth century Americanism." The ASU, dominated by an inner core of members of the Young Communist League, represented the popular front on the campus.

I was quite unimpressed by the ASU organ, the *Student Advocate*, especially by the hopeless jargon and sloganized polemics of the party hacks. "One of the chief things I have against Communists," I wrote to Ed James in the summer of 1935, "is that they do not know how to argue in a quiet, restrained and intelligent manner and in name-calling they are less urbane, and thus less effective, than the capitalists." As for the *Student Advocate*, "Wechsler," I noted in my journal, "is the only one on the staff who can write English which is at once forceful and good." And in commenting on a later issue, "No one on the staff, with the striking exception of Wechsler, the editor, can write." I could not have anticipated that James Wechsler, then a YCL leader, would in another decade become one of my dearest friends and a staunch partner in the anti-Stalinist cause.

So far as I was concerned, the New Deal was the main event, Marxism a sideshow, irrelevant to the American future. At the same time, I certainly had an analytical, if not a political, interest in Marxism. How could one not when the Great Depression might well be verifying Marx's prediction that laissez-faire capitalism would be destroyed by its own contradictions? And Marx, after all, was not only an influential but a weighty and illuminating social thinker, whatever crimes were subsequently committed in his name.

Henry Adams had written that education for modernity would have to deal with Karl Marx much more than with John Stuart Mill, and one recalled Adams's lament that as a Harvard undergraduate he had never "heard the name Karl Marx mentioned, or the title of 'Capital.'" (The latter would have been quite a feat since the first volume of *Das Kapital* was not published till nine years after Adams graduated.) There was plenty of mention of Marx in my Harvard, though more from an intellectual than from an evangelical viewpoint.

In my capacity as the *Advocate*'s drama critic, I saw a number of 'proletarian' plays, especially Clifford Odets's electrifying excursion into agitprop *Waiting for Lefty*. I interviewed people involved in the Theatre Union and other left-wing drama groups and wrote a piece for the May Day issue in 1935 called "The New Theatre." "The spread of play-producing associations imbued with Marxist ideology," I said, "is a significant indication of the force and vitality of the New Theatre. . . . The bourgeois theatre must face the situation squarely." I concluded more realistically, however, that "the amazing thing about capitalism is the tenacity of its hold on humanity." My enthusiasm for proletarian drama seems to have faded by December of the same year when, discussing left-wing playwrights in "Criticism and the American Theatre," I observed that, until George Sklar, Paul Peters and Albert Maltz "are convinced that plays are something more than staged sermons, they must expect to remain shrill propagandists."

Later I rejoiced in Orestes Brownson's discovery of class war and published a paper in the *Sewanee Review* in 1939 entitled "Orestes Brownson: An American Marxist Before Marx." The piece applauded Brownson's social analysis, but a secondary point was to kid the radicals by showing that, like the conservatives they scorned, they always used the same old arguments. "On both sides the arguments were probably invented in the critical Neanderthal days when conservatives and radicals battled over the infamous suggestion that huts were preferable to caves. . . . Radicalism, like capitalism, has its folklore." (The last was an allusion to Thurman Arnold's then influential book *The Folklore of Capitalism.*)

I never felt much sympathy for the Soviet Union. In 1929 I had eagerly followed, week after week, a serialized novel in *Liberty* magazine called *The Red Napoleon*. The author was the colorful foreign correspondent Floyd Gibbons, who had lost an eye at Belleau Wood and was famed for the white patch he wore thereafter as well as for his staccato radio delivery of more than two hundred words a minute. The Red Napoleon was Karakhan, a Soviet marshal who at some future point would launch a war against the West — a story rendered more arresting by simulated newspaper headlines and fake photographs depicting Karakhan's advance across Europe.

The pleasure with which I followed the weekly installments suggests a predisposition to distrust Communism that must have come from my parents. Sturdy liberals, they were on principle hostile to dogma and dictators, nor were they impressed by American Communists. I find, for example, a letter my mother wrote in 1930 to the *Boston Herald* questioning the space devoted to the activities of the Communist party, "this small and ineffective group of our citizens." (Felix Frankfurter wrote her, "I am very glad you wrote what you did to the Herald, though it does no good except to relieve your feelings and mine.")

* * *

In general, Communism was not at all the consuming issue at Harvard that it was at Columbia and City College as reported by Jimmy Wechsler (in *The Age of Suspicion*) and Alfred Kazin (in *Starting Out in the Thirties*) or at Cambridge (England) as recorded by Noel Annan (*Our Age*). There were no furious sectarian battles among Trotskyites and Lovestoneites and Schachtmanites, nor do I recall great arguments about the purges or the Moscow trials or the gulags in Siberia.

The Harvard Student Union had in my senior year around five hundred members, about a quarter of the undergraduate body. A secret Communist cell did its best to control policy. The politics of the popular front gave party members cover, and, with one or two exceptions, they did not identify themselves. The YCL's underground branch was rumored, I am sure incorrectly, to have nearly a hundred members, including, one was told darkly, people whom you would never suspect.

The Harvard Teachers Union confronted the same problem of secret Communist manipulation. Formed after the teacher's oath fight of 1935, the Union attracted some of the bright stars among the younger faculty. The majority were New Deal liberals or Norman Thomas Socialists, but, as Harry Levin of the English department rather bitterly recalled, a smaller group "caucused secretly and voted according to the Communist Party line." This cell, however, had only about fifteen members, nearly all nontenured, out of a faculty of nearly two thousand.

Though there were avowed Communists around — the literary critic Granville Hicks was a tutor in Adams House in 1938–39 — secrecy was deemed vital to the party operation. The historian Richard Schlatter, who had returned from Oxford a party member, thus was ordered to conceal an important part of his life even from his best friends. F. O. Matthiessen, an influential teacher of American literature and himself something of a fellow traveler, knew that Dick

Schlatter was a Communist because he had asked him and received a truthful reply; but Perry Miller, the intellectual historian of Puritanism and an anti-Stalinist, never knew until Schlatter confessed it before the House Un-American Activities Committee a dozen years later and was, Schlatter recalled, "deeply offended."

Secrecy, deceit and manipulation were the hallmarks of Communists and their fellow travelers when I first encountered them — this and a conviction that protection of the Soviet Union was the supreme duty. There were two main Stalinist types in academic circles: the dogmatists, who believed that Marx and Lenin had discovered the iron laws of history and economics and that these laws would govern the future; and the idealists, who believed that people could find some better way of living together than the dog-eat-dog competition of capitalism, that the cooperative commonwealth was not an impossible dream. A new social structure, in their view, could transform human nature, and the Soviet Union alone was showing the way.

The dogmatists were hopeless. Looking back at the idealists, I guess that, in my irritation over their slavish defense of everything Stalin did, I did not do justice to the generosity of spirit that animated people like Matthiessen and Schlatter. Their faith in the possibility of a redemptive new society, moreover, was accompanied — and strengthened — by the conviction that the Soviet Union was the only reliable bulwark against Hitler. Given this brave effort by a backward country to oppose fascism and seek a better world, why not subdue doubts — as some fellow travelers and even some party members certainly did — and give Stalin unconditional support? Why give aid and comfort to reactionary red-baiters like William Randolph Hearst? It was a contest, as Arthur Koestler said, between those who were right for the wrong reasons and those who were wrong for the right reasons.

In conceding that some American Communists were, in their way, idealists, I must point out that the CPUSA was a revolving door — perhaps a quarter million Americans passed through the party between 1919 and 1960 — and that the principled among them departed for the same reason that they had entered: because they remained faithful to ideals of democracy and justice that they found had no standing or sustenance within either the American party or the Soviet Union.

Nor can one take seriously the claim advanced by both obsessive anti-Communists and pro-Communist revisionist historians that the CPUSA exerted great influence on the United States in the Thirties. Sidney Hook, who played an honorable role in the Thirties and

Forties in exposing the maneuvers and lies of the Stalinists, wrote in his memoirs that Communist popular front organizations "dominated the cultural, literary, and in part the academic landscape."

It is true that fellow travelers had a certain power in secondary areas like book reviewing and publishing and that they often used this power to vilify writers who dared criticize the party line. A notable example was James T. Farrell. In a time when the left was exalting proletarian literature, Jim Farrell's *Studs Lonigan* could be considered the truest example of the genre. But when, in *A Note on Literary Criticism*, Farrell dared in 1936 to challenge the mechanical, party line application of Marxist criticism, the Stalinists mounted a brutal campaign against him.

But these were highly marginal operations, far from Sidney Hook's theory of the CPUSA's domination of the intellectual landscape. In the spring of 1939 Hook and John Dewey issued a statement in the name of the Committee for Cultural Freedom condemning "the totalitarian idea" as "enthroned in Germany, Italy, Russia, Japan, and Spain" and condemning also those who "exalt one brand of servitude over another." In early August a fellow-traveling group calling itself the Committee of 400 issued a counterstatement condemning "the fantastic falsehood that the USSR and the totalitarian states are basically alike" and condemning also the Committee for Cultural Freedom as "Fascists and allies of Fascists."

The *Daily Worker* named only 167 signers of the Committee of 400 manifesto; a comparison of the two lists shows that Hook's committee attracted incomparably more distinguished people (Carl Becker, Elmer Davis, Walter B. Cannon, Norman Thomas, Sidney Howard, John Dos Passos, Ralph Barton Perry, William Carlos Williams, Dorothy Thompson and my father among them) than the collection of (mostly) hacks and dupes who signed the pro-Soviet statement. Five of those who signed Hook's statement had been among the fifty-two writers who endorsed William Z. Foster, the CPUSA presidential candidate, in 1932 — which suggests the way the tide was flowing; and it was flowing hard before the Stalin-Hitler pact of late August 1939.

Far from dominating the intellectual landscape, the CPUSA exerted negligible influence on anything serious, with the possible exception of the struggle for racial justice. The New Deal, the labor movement, foreign policy, literature and the arts: all would have evolved in much the same way had the CPUSA never existed. What the CPUSA did succeed in doing was to compromise and to betray American radicalism and to demonstrate beyond argument that liberalism and Communism had nothing in common in their means or in their ends.

*   *   *

Watching the next highly politicized college generation in the Sixties, one was struck by the contrast with the Thirties. In my student days, agitation turned on national and international issues. The most revolutionary radicals obediently wore the jackets and ties required in the dining hall and observed without protest parietal rules of an absurdity that would be incomprehensible today ("A student living in a House must obtain special permission from the Master or the Senior Tutor to receive women guests in his room. . . . Such permission will be granted only when a chaperon is to be present"). Nor did they think of demanding student participation in the governance of their institution. Even those YCLers who met secretly and conspiratorially to overthrow the capitalist system never dreamed of doing anything to revolutionize their immediate environment.

It is often said that undergraduate politics trains the leaders of the future, that the voices of student protest will be spokesmen of their generation for years to come. This rarely happens. Few from the radical student movement of the Thirties had any public influence in later years, and most of these — Edward R. Murrow, Eric Sevareid, Jimmy Wechsler, Joseph P. Lash, Theodore Draper (none Harvard men) — as commentators rather than players. I have no idea what became of the conspicuous student radicals of my day at Harvard.

One almost detects a tendency among those who engage too fiercely in protest when young to succumb to premature fatigue or disillusion and to withdraw from public concerns thereafter. Perhaps it may be that there is some rhythm of life by which people exhaust themselves too quickly, become disenchanted too soon, and that mature political commitment depends on wider and richer interests in one's youth. Certainly the one man in my Harvard years who had the greatest public impact in later life — John F. Kennedy '40 — was uninvolved in political action as an undergraduate.

In retrospect, it was probably a lucky instinct that led me to eschew political activism at Harvard College and to concentrate instead on enlarging intellectual horizons.

8

Harvard College: What I Enjoyed

CONFIDENT THAT FDR had matters in hand, I did not worry all that much about politics. Other things filled the interstices of life in the Thirties — especially theater, jazz, above all the movies. Literature was not so important, unlike the Twenties, when novels and short stories were a source of constant excitement, at least for the reading class.

People in that golden decade (as we in the Thirties regarded it) were dazzled month after month by the new Hemingway, Dreiser, Fitzgerald, Cather, Wharton, Faulkner, Sinclair Lewis, Sherwood Anderson. The fiction of the Thirties generated no comparable excitement. Of course one did not altogether give up reading new fiction. James T. Farrell's passionately gritty *Studs Lonigan* impressed me a lot; so did John O'Hara's acidly observed, class-obsessed short stories; so did Fitzgerald's unfashionable *Tender Is the Night* and, in a different mode, John Steinbeck's *In Dubious Battle* and *The Grapes of Wrath*.

Especially electrifying was John Dos Passos's *U.S.A.*, the panoramic trilogy published from 1930 to 1936. Dos Passos amazed us by the scope of his ambition — "the slice of a continent," he called his book — and by the modernist experimentation that mingled realistic narrative with Joycean "camera eyes," social history "newsreels," mordant biographical profiles and urgent political radicalism. *U.S.A.* was made to order for the social turbulence of the depression years. Today, alas, it seems clinical in its characterizations and dated in its emotions.

Except for Jim Farrell, Dos Passos was the only one of these novelists I knew personally. Pat Jackson brought us together in the Fifties, by which time Dos had moved far to the political right. He was nevertheless a sweet man, benign in manner, interested in history and in friendly discussion. As a man of the right, he oddly retained some of the positions he had earlier taken as a man of the left. From whatever perspective, America was an imperialist state. "One ought, I think," he wrote me in 1958, "to recognize that we are really an expanding power unit, and that all our idealism is eyewash." He was basically a gentle anarchist in revolt against a mechanized, bureaucratized, de-humanized society.

I did not share the enthusiasm of many of my coevals for Thomas Wolfe's *Look Homeward, Angel* (actually published in the Twenties) and *Of Time and the River.* Wolfe's narcissistic lyricism seemed over the top. Bernard DeVoto's exercise in demolition, cruelly entitled "Genius Is Not Enough," expressed, and no doubt shaped, my view of Wolfe. Though Faulkner wrote some of his best novels in the Thirties — *Light in August* in 1932, *Absalom, Absalom* in 1936, *The Wild Palms* in 1939, *The Hamlet* in 1940 — I somehow was oblivious until Richard Rovere and Malcolm Cowley forced him on one's consciousness in the Forties. As for the proletarian literature of the early depression, this was too schematic and agitprop to have artistic vitality or even political plausibility.

In the main, we fiction readers of the Thirties lived off those wonderful books of the Twenties: *The Great Gatsby, An American Tragedy, The Sound and the Fury, A Lost Lady, The Age of Innocence, The Sun Also Rises, Main Street, Babbitt, Winesburg, Ohio.* Of those once dazzling writers, Fitzgerald, Faulkner and, to some degree, Dreiser survive; Hemingway hangs on, barely; Wharton has had a revival, and Cather is still there in a minor key; Dos Passos, Sinclair Lewis and Sherwood Anderson are forgotten.

*   *   *

Nor were the Thirties a decade of drama. But the plays interested me rather more than the novels. In those days before previews, Broadway shows opened 'out of town,' often in New Haven, then on to Boston for further polishing. I was a regular at the Colonial and Shubert theaters and at the smaller, handsome Wilbur.

And Broadway itself was not too far away. The New York, New Haven and Hartford Railroad carried us from South Station to Grand Central Station, anticipation mounting from the moment the train made its initial Manhattan stop at 125th Street. But the night boat was the favored way to go to New York — casting off in Boston Harbor, passing through the Cape Cod Canal at dusk, an abundant dinner, a dance band in the evening, awakening to see New York Harbor and the Statue of Liberty. From such a pleasant boat Starr Faithfull threw herself overboard in 1931 after years of sexual abuse by a family friend, Mayor Andrew J. Peters of Boston; she became Gloria Wandrous in O'Hara's *Butterfield 8,* named after the fashionable Manhattan telephone exchange (latterly demoted to an uninteresting

288). The Boston–New York boat service was suspended during the war and, alas, never resumed.

I used to stay for $7.50 a night in one of the eccentrically shaped rooms of the Royalton Hotel on West Forty-fourth, a humble alternative to the famed Algonquin across the street. Actors out of work in those days would move from the Algonquin to the Royalton; employed, they would move back to the Algonquin. (In the Nineties the Royalton went glossy and swank, and the balance of trade was reversed.) George Jean Nathan maintained a suite at the Royalton, and, with lingering thoughts of becoming a drama critic, I always hoped to run into him in the elevator. The only time I did I was too shy to utter a word.

New York even in the grim depression was a friendly city. Curtain time was at the civilized hour of eight-thirty for straight plays, eight-forty for musicals, thereby facilitating a leisurely dinner in advance. One night after the theater, my journal reminds me, I wandered around Times Square and Forty-second Street — then so colorful at night; in the Eighties so squalid and almost sinister; by 2000 reclaimed and almost genial — stopped at a bar and had a couple of beers. When I gave the bartender a quarter, he affably pushed back fifteen cents — beer was a nickel a glass — and gave me a third glass "on the house."

It was a rich theatrical decade. I saw several Hamlets: Leslie Howard, pale and pensive; the vigorous Maurice Evans; the stentorian Walter Hampden; most notable of all, John Gielgud (with Judith Anderson as the queen; Nathan unkindly said that they should have exchanged roles). That fine actor Walter Huston was a disappointment in *Othello,* too prosaic for Shakespeare. I was thrilled by Orson Welles's WPA production of Marlowe's *Doctor Faustus* and by his own performance, at the age of twenty-three (two years older than I), in the title role. I saw Alla Nazimova in Ibsen and shuddered at the tigerish joy with which she burned the only copy of Lovborg's manuscript in *Hedda Gabler.* (How would Ibsen have found the dramatic equivalent of this terrible scene had he lived in the age of the copying machine?) I admired Katharine Cornell in *St. Joan* and *Candida.*

There was a steady stream of new American plays. I was transfixed by Humphrey Bogart's performance as the killer Duke Mantee in Robert E. Sherwood's *The Petrified Forest,* though I found the play contrived and pretentious. Lillian Hellman's *The Children's Hour* and Sidney Kingsley's *Dead End* were crisper and better. The Group Theater did not open its plays in Boston and, save *Waiting for Lefty,* I saw none of the Odets dramas. Among American plays I particularly enjoyed the high comedies of Philip Barry and of S. N. Behrman, especially Behrman's *Biography* and *End of Summer* as played by the delectable Ina Claire.

And I lost no opportunity to see George M. Cohan in his gentle comedies of illusion. With his strong, quizzical stage presence, he commanded the audience to the extent that, when other characters were talking, we kept our eyes fixed on Cohan listening. Perhaps Cohan when young had been the peppy, nervy, hyperactive figure so brilliantly invented by James Cagney in *Yankee Doodle Dandy*, but the Cohan I saw was distinguished by the power of his serenity. He was wonderful as the father in Eugene O'Neill's *Ah, Wilderness!* — that sunny New London play of which the dark and terrible *Long Day's Journey into Night* is the obverse.

DeVoto, who detested O'Neill, had given me a prejudice against him. But *Long Day's Journey* is surely the great American play; and, after seeing *Mourning Becomes Electra* and *Strange Interlude* in later years, I understood how much more penetrating a dramatist O'Neill is than it seemed proper to say in the Thirties, at least in Benny's hearing.

* * *

In recollection, the high point of the American theater in the Thirties was the musical. It was the glorious era of Jerome Kern, Irving Berlin, George and Ira Gershwin, Cole Porter, Richard Rodgers and Lorenz Hart, Harold Arlen. I saw my first musical in the autumn of 1931 on a visit to New York with my mother. It was the Jerome Kern–Otto Harbach *The Cat and the Fiddle* — a melodious operetta rather in the continental vein. I was an instant convert to musical shows.

The revue — a show that blithely strung together skits, songs, dances and gorgeous chorus girls — had been a favorite art form in the Twenties (*Ziegfeld Follies, George White's Scandals*, the *Earl Carroll Vanities*, the *Little Shows, Charlot's Revues, The Band Wagon*). I saw the last of the authentic *Ziegfeld Follies* at the Boston Opera House in 1936, with comedy by Fanny Brice, Vernon Duke's songs sung by Josephine Baker, dances staged by George Balanchine and Bob Hope pleading with Eve Arden, "I Can't Get Started with You."

George S. Kaufman, Morrie Ryskind and the Gershwins gave the musical comedy a political edge in *Strike Up the Band* (1930) and *Of Thee I Sing* (1931). These were book shows (and I did not see them until their revival many years later), but revues (which I did see) soon went political too. The Irving Berlin–Moss Hart *As Thousands Cheer*

(1933) was inspired by newspaper headlines of the day. In an un-
forgettable scene, played under the headline UNKNOWN NEGRO
LYNCHED BY FRENZIED MOB, Ethel Waters wonders in Berlin's moving song "Supper Time" how to tell her children about their father's
awful fate.

The respectable Theatre Guild even put on a bitter left-wing revue,
Parade, with Jimmy Savo. In a skit about the San Francisco general
strike, a pompous one-hundred-percent American shouts at the strikers to go back to where they came from. The strikers shout back: "But
we come from San Francisco." Later the International Ladies' Garment Workers' Union presented a more genial revue, *Pins and Nee-
dles*, featuring clever songs by Harold Rome, especially "Sing Me a
Song of Social Significance," "One Big Union for Two," a romantic
number, and a frenzied dance "Doing the Reactionary" ("Close your
eyes to where you're bound"). Rome followed this with *Sing Out the
News* and his great hit saluting the birth of a black child: "He can't be
a dud or a stick in the mud / He's Franklin D. Roosevelt Jones."

George M. Cohan himself played FDR in *I'd Rather Be Right*, with
book by Kaufman and Moss Hart and music by Rodgers and Lorenz
Hart. The show had great fun with the cabinet, the Supreme Court,
Alf Landon and Walter Lippmann, and Cohan, though he apparently
loathed Roosevelt and disliked the subtleties of the score, did an effective professional job. In his excellent chronicle *American Musical
Theatre* (very helpful in documenting one's recollections), Gerald
Bordman writes, "Behind the scenes Cohan referred to his song writers as Gilbert and Sullivan — and he didn't mean the comparison to
be complimentary."

The depression placed a premium on comedy. Ed Wynn was a great
figure, with his weird costumes, his silly inventions — an eleven-foot
pole, for example, for people he wouldn't touch with a ten-foot pole
— his endearing lisp and his high-pitched laugh. I greatly enjoyed
Hooray for What (1937), a book show, antiwar and antidictator, in
which Wynn invents a gas to kill appleworms. When it turns out to kill
humans too, the great powers at the League of Nations try to steal the
formula. Harold Arlen wrote the music, Yip Harburg the lyrics. And
we listened faithfully to Ed Wynn as the Texaco Fire Chief on radio.

Then there was the marvelous English comedienne Beatrice Lillie.
It was in *At Home Abroad*, a 1935 revue directed by Vincent Minnelli,
that she famously negotiated with Reginald Gardner the purchase
of "two dozen double damask dinner napkins." The next year Lillie
and the great Bert Lahr worked together in *The Show Is On*, another

Minnelli revue, in which Lahr wickedly parodied Nelson Eddy in "The Woodman's Song."

The age of the revue was, alas, nearing its end. By the Fifties television put on its own revues — most notably Sid Caesar's often brilliant *Your Show of Shows*. Revue, moreover, was an art form hard to translate into film, and it eventually disappeared when film sales became an essential part of the producer's budget.

Cole Porter contributed mostly to book shows, and they generally opened in Boston; so I saw *Anything Goes* in 1934, my first sighting of the marvelous Ethel Merman, *Jubilee* in 1935 ("Just One of Those Things" and "Begin the Beguine") and *Red, Hot and Blue!* in 1936, with Merman again, Jimmy Durante and Bob Hope ("It's De-Lovely"). No one sang more ardently, lucidly, vigorously, humorously and passionately than Ethel Merman. Every syllable was distinct in the farthest reaches of the theater, all without benefit of microphone. The *Earl Carroll Vanities* of 1940 was the first musical to be miked, a horrible innovation denounced at the time by Brooks Atkinson in the *Times* and Richard Watts, Jr., in the *Herald Tribune* but surviving to deafen audiences and to dominate and almost to doom musical comedy.

If the plays of the Thirties are extinct and the musicals mostly forgotten, the songs magnificently endure. "Happy Days Are Here Again" (Jack Yellen and Milton Ager) still brings memories of the election of FDR: "The skies above are clear again / Let us sing a song of cheer again." "Who's Afraid of the Big Bad Wolf?" from Disney's *Three Little Pigs* acquired new resonance later in the decade when isolationists, like the carefree little pigs, declined to be alarmed by the big bad wolf in Berlin.

Bing Crosby was the male voice of the Thirties, as Frank Sinatra was of the Forties, Elvis Presley of the Fifties, Bob Dylan of the Sixties, Bruce Springsteen of the Seventies. Crosby and Sinatra together sang Cole Porter's "Well, Did You Evah . . . What a Swell Party It Is" in the 1956 movie *High Society*, and, to the cheers of the Thirties generation, the film critic Andrew Sarris, a man of the Forties generation, awarded the palm to Crosby.

• "Strange how potent cheap music is," said Elyot in *Private Lives*. Nothing, at least for my generation, recalls the past more affectingly than the songs of our youth. In the years since, the country has been washed over by new tides of popular music: folk, country-and-western, gospel, rock, reggae, rap, heavy metal, grunge, heaven knows what. Perhaps they are equally evocative for the young, but they do little for my generation, nor can I believe that they will still be played sixty years after, as the elegant, passionate, silvery songs of the Thirties are still played today — "Night and Day," "Stormy Weather," "Stardust," so many others. Louis MacNeice:

> The same tunes hang on pegs in the cloakrooms of the mind
> That fitted us ten or twenty or thirty years ago
> On occasions of love or grief. ✤

*   *   *

The Twenties have gone into history as the Jazz Age, but my impression is that the young of the Twenties did not take jazz into their hearts as we did in the Thirties. They danced the Charleston and listened to Paul Whiteman and his orchestra, but they did not gather in darkened, smoky rooms to hear clarinets or trumpets soar into brilliant contrapuntal improvisations and then gracefully recede into the massed harmony of the band. "A band swings," said John Hammond, the grand impresario of jazz, "when its collective improvisation is rhythmically integrated." (Not everyone around in those days swung. There is the priceless entry in H. R. Haldeman's White House diary about a dinner planned in 1969 for Duke Ellington's birthday. President Nixon told Haldeman to invite "all the jazz greats, like Guy Lombardo." Haldeman philosophical comment: "— oh well!" Lombardo, billed as playing "the sweetest music this side of heaven," was of course the antithesis of jazz.)

The roots of jazz were in the small backroom ensembles of New Orleans, Memphis, Chicago and Kansas City, but the big bands of the Thirties relied less on inspiration and more on orchestration. It was 1935 when Benny Goodman made his triumphal way east from the Palomar Ballroom in Los Angeles bearing the gospel of swing. In February 1936 Fletcher Henderson, the great jazz arranger, brought his own band to Adams House for an evening of rhythmic scintillation, reaching a mad, uproarious climax with his rendition of "Christopher Columbus." A poor businessman, Henderson failed as a bandleader but prospered thereafter as an arranger for Goodman. In the spring of 1937 Adams House brought in another of the great bands — Artie Shaw, in person, wielding his wondrous clarinet. The music went 'round and 'round, as a popular song of the day had it, and it came out everywhere.

In the evening we could go to clubs in Boston like the Savoy Cafe and hear top black jazz artists. On trips to New York we would visit

Tommy Dorsey at the Commodore and Goodman at the Manhattan Room of the Hotel Pennsylvania. The grand moment with Goodman came when the lights dimmed and the quartet — Goodman at clarinet, Teddy Wilson at piano, Lionel Hampton on vibraphone, Gene Krupa on drums — took the floor, and people listened with hushed intensity.

John Hammond, born in marble halls on East Ninety-first Street, his mother a Vanderbilt, was the great jazz talent scout. He discovered and promoted bandleaders like Goodman, Henderson, Count Basie, Fats Waller, and singers from Bessie Smith and Billie Holiday to (many years later) Bob Dylan and Bruce Springsteen. He was a crusader for racial justice in an age when even jazz was segregated. Active on the board of the National Association for the Advancement of Colored People, he vigorously supported black bands and vigorously agitated for the integration of white bands. Benny Goodman, who married Hammond's sister Alice, was the first well-known white bandleader to recruit black musicians.

In later years, relations between Goodman and Hammond became strained. I came to know them both — indeed, spoke at Hammond's memorial service and wrote Goodman's memorial for the Century Association Yearbook. Benny, as I used to see him toward the end of his life, was a pleasant, courteous, disciplined man, definite but tactful in his opinions, with an ironic turn of humor and quiet but rather remote dignity. John Hammond, with his effervescent charm, enthusiastic manner, crewcut hair, bright tweed or madras jackets, was a joyous, jaunty figure to the end of his gallant life. Every day was a new adventure for him, "setting out," as he wrote, "to discover the world all over again." He always expected to hear "a voice or a sound I have never heard before, with something to say which has never been said before." His wonderful instinct for creativity in others made him a vast creative force himself.

How to explain my generation's rage for jazz? David W. Stowe in his perceptive study *Swing Changes: Big-Band Jazz in New Deal America* contends persuasively that swing, as the popular cultural form embodying individual freedom, ethnic and regional inclusiveness and collective creative energy, was the musical expression of the New Deal.

*   *   *

Though we who came of age in the Thirties adored jazz, we were most of all, as Roger Angell (b. 1920) of the *New Yorker* put it, "the Movie Generation." Nadine Gordimer (b. 1923) writes, "I belong to the first generation for whom film has been an art form, along with literature, music, painting, and sculpture, rather than a technical discovery." My enthusiasm for Gore Vidal (b. 1925) remains under control, but the first sentence of his delightful book *Screening History* strikes a responsive chord: "It occurs to me that the only thing I ever really liked to do was go to the movies."

Film, moreover, is not only the distinctive art of the twentieth century, it is *the* American art — the only art to which the United States has made a major difference. Strike the American contributions to music, painting, sculpture, drama, even to poetry, the novel and architecture, and the world's achievement is only marginally diminished. But film without the American contribution is inconceivable. "The movies and America," said Federico Fellini at the 1993 Academy Awards, "are almost the same thing."

It took time for American intellectuals to appreciate the upstart art. For movies came out of hole-in-the-wall storefronts in the downmarket sections of the great anonymous cities. There were few livelier and more inquisitive American minds in the early twentieth century than Henry James, Henry Adams and Theodore Roosevelt; yet, though they died respectively in 1916, 1918 and 1919, well into the age of cinema, I cannot find a reference in their volumes of published correspondence to ever having seen a movie. (Woodrow Wilson saw at least one movie — D. W. Griffith's *The Birth of a Nation* — which he reportedly said was "like writing history with lightning.") In the Twenties Gilbert Seldes in *The Seven Lively Arts* (1924) argued that movies should be taken seriously, but it was not till the Thirties that the movies really came into their own.

My passion for reading did not decline then, but in that decade moviegoing, I believe, seized me and my contemporaries with singular intensity. I still have the notebook listing, with capsule reviews and letter grades, the 482 movies I saw between June 1, 1931 (Josef von Sternberg's *Dishonored* with Marlene Dietrich, B+) and sometime in 1936 (Robert Z. Leonard's and P. G. Wodehouse's *Piccadilly Jim* with Robert Montgomery, B−). The title of the next to last flick in this compilation predicted the nation's dreary destiny: a film with Mary Astor and Lyle Talbot, rated by me D+. It was called *Trapped by Television*.

*   *   *

Movies quite overpowered my interest in the stage. My first contribution to the *Harvard Advocate* argued that, contrary to a piece by St. John Ervine, the drama critic of the *Observer* of London, film was a more compelling art than the theater. (I sent the article to Ervine, who replied politely that he had read it "with much interest, if with little agreement" — a formula I have used myself many times since.)

In the era of the silent film, my parents took me to Charlie Chaplin, to Harold Lloyd, to historical films like James Cruze's *Old Ironsides* and John Ford's *The Iron Horse*, to the adventures of Douglas Fairbanks (*Robin Hood, The Thief of Bagdad, The Three Musketeers, The Black Pirate*) and to a series of (to me) less than gripping animal documentaries, like Ernest Schoedsack's *Grass* and *Chang* and Martin Johnson's *Simba*.

Came the talkies. The University Theater in Harvard Square was a constant refuge. So was George Kraska's Fine Arts Theater, near Symphony Hall in Boston. Here one saw the great UFA movies from Germany — von Sternberg's *The Blue Angel*, Fritz Lang's *Metropolis* and *Die Frau im Mond* (*By Rocket to the Moon*), both feeding my fascination with the future, and his powerful and scary *M*, with Peter Lorre as the child murderer. Here too one saw lighthearted German musicals like Erik Charrell's *Congress Dances* and William Thiele's *Die Drei von der Tankstelle*, where I acquired an early enthusiasm for the ravishing Lilian Harvey, English by birth but a great favorite in pre-Hitler Germany.

Seeing such films again sixty years later on television via American Movie Classics or Turner Classic Movies, one marvels at the boldness of pace, the crispness and speed of dialogue, the intensity of black-and-white cinematography, the ingenious verisimilitude of studio sets and the surprisingly high quality of products rolling off studio assembly lines.* These films, most of them as alive today as they were when they were made, recall the zest, creativity and provocation generated by the Hollywood of my youth. For the young intellectuals of the

* Let me recall some of the Hollywood productions of my youth. Take 1933, for example: Garbo in Rouben Mamoulian's *Queen Christina; King Kong; 42nd Street;* the Marx Brothers in Leo McCarey's *Duck Soup;* Victor Fleming's *Blonde Bombshell* with Jean Harlow; Frank Lloyd's *Cavalcade;* Mae West in Lowell Sherman's *She Done Him Wrong;* Lubitsch's *Design for Living.* In 1934: Howard Hawks's *Twentieth Century;* Bette Davis and Leslie Howard in *Of Human Bondage;* Powell and Loy in *The Thin Man;* Astaire and Rogers in *The Gay Divorcee;* Chevalier in Lubitsch's *The Merry Widow;* James Whale's *Bride of Frankenstein;* the Hecht-MacArthur shocker with Claude Rains *Crime Without Passion;* King Vidor's *Our Daily Bread;* Capra's *It Happened One Night.* In 1935: John Ford's *The Informer;* Garbo in *Anna Karenina;* the Marx Brothers in *A Night at the Opera;* Astaire and Rogers in *Top Hat;* Lloyd's *Mutiny on the Bounty* with Laughton and Gable; Hepburn in George Stevens's *Alice Adams;* Noel Coward in the Hecht-MacArthur *The Scoundrel;* Laughton in McCarey's *Ruggles of Red Gap;* Henry Hathaway's *Lives of a Bengal Lancer.* Could Hollywood sixty years later offer comparable lists?

Thirties, film replaced the novels and short stories that had so moved young intellectuals in the Twenties.

* * *

It was not that Hollywood necessarily made its best pictures in the Thirties. The great silent movies still astonish, and plenty of fine movies have been made in the years since. But in the Thirties film had a vital connection with the American psyche — more, I think, than it ever had before; more certainly than it has had since.

In those happy years before television, film monopolized public attention as it never will again. Hollywood owned the nation. In 1936 69 percent of the population went to the movies at least once each week — a figure that understates the consumption since most movie houses showed double features, two movies for the price of one (a quarter in the afternoon, seventy-five cents or a buck in the evening).

More than this, movies had a new role, I believe, in the nation's psychic economy. The Thirties represented America's first great crisis of confidence since the Civil War. For most of American history, the republic had lived free of doubt about the future. Rivers could always be forded, mountains climbed, wilderness domesticated, Indians subdued. The national belief was in the omnipotence of the happy ending.

Then came the Great Depression. Abruptly the party was over, the American dream exposed as mirage. The birthrate registered with precision the decline of faith in the future. Population increase in the Thirties was only half what it had been in the Twenties. Doubt, disillusion, despair, created psychological needs that movies seemed to fill. It was more than the need for distraction and escape. It was the need for reassurance and hope. With the republic struck down by circumstances beyond individual control, people longed for some vindication of individual identity, for restoration of the sense of individual potency.

To console an age in which the individual felt helpless in a malevolent world, Hollywood in the first years of the depression offered a gallery of strong men who, when they could not order their environment, could at least take revenge on it. The gangster film of the early Thirties became the protracted parable of man's relationship to a hostile society. The gangster was the man who rejected the social order — who, almost alone in the stricken country, lived in luxury, drove swift and silent cars, ignored hiring line and breadline and saw himself as the master of his destiny. He was the free man who, by carrying freedom to evil excess, wrought his own destruction; yet the symbolism of self-determination remained compelling. Who in the Movie Generation could forget Edward G. Robinson crying, "Mother of God, is this the end of Rico?" in Mervin LeRoy's expressionist *Little Caesar* (1930); or James Cagney smashing the grapefruit in Mae Clarke's face in William Wellman's *The Public Enemy* (1931); or Paul Muni lusting after his sister in Howard Hawks's *Scarface* (1932), with George Raft balefully flipping his coin in the corner.

Then came 1933. In Washington, a strong president showed that the nation did not have to lie down and take it. The combination of the Great Depression and the New Deal gave Hollywood an eager audience, at once demoralized by the downfall of the system, exhilarated by the promise of action and responsive to images of purpose and freedom. As FDR and the New Deal showed that good guys could be strong too, the gangster genre lost its original function. By 1935 Cagney, no longer the public enemy, had become a G-man. Robinson parodied his earlier roles marvelously in Lloyd Bacon's *A Slight Case of Murder* (1938); by 1939 he became a G-man himself in Anatole Litwak's *Confessions of a Nazi Spy*. I saw that film in London, where a morose English audience watched gloomily as Nazi spies worked their will in the United States. When, after half an hour or so of unrelieved Nazi chicanery, the film cut to the FBI in Washington and revealed Agent Edward G. Robinson as the man in charge of the case, the audience broke into grateful applause. Cagney by 1941 was portraying the flag-waving George M. Cohan in Michael Curtiz's *Yankee Doodle Dandy*. Muni, latterly transmuted in his billing into *Mr.* Paul Muni, moved on from Scarface to noble historical figures — Pasteur, Zola, Juárez.

The symbolism of self-determination found benign incarnation in the private detective. The passage from gangster to private eye was conducted by that most sardonic and evocative of Hollywood actors, Humphrey Bogart. Bogart began his serious film career when Leslie Howard insisted that he repeat his stage role as Duke Mantee in Archie Mayo's film of *The Petrified Forest* (1936). Five years later, in the Raoul Walsh–John Huston *High Sierra*, he provided an almost elegiac rendition of the gangster's last stand.

As social stresses relaxed, it was increasingly possible, even desirable, to be at once alienated and a good guy. Dashiell Hammett and Raymond Chandler had already created in pulp magazines the pro-law hero to replace the gangster antihero. Their private eyes, Sam Spade and Philip Marlowe, had the loneliness, the toughness and the disdain of the gangster, but they had a sense of honor that kept them honest in a corrupt world. Unlike the power-mad mobster who wanted it all, they had a realistic sense of limits, without hope and without illusion, always faithful in the mean streets to their personal code. In John Huston's version of Hammett's *The Maltese Falcon* (1941), in Howard Hawks's version of Chandler's *The Big Sleep* (1946) and of course in Michael Curtiz's *Casablanca* (1942), Bogart became a mythic figure, with harrowed and brooding face, sharp, expressionless eyes, twisted mouth and weary walk, mingling cynicism and duty as the moral man in an immoral society and eventually finding, in movies and in life, the perfect mate in the spirited and beautiful Lauren Bacall.

* * *

The change from the Twenties to the Thirties was also manifest in comedy. In the complacent optimism of the New Era, comedy sprang from frustration, timidity, defeat. Characteristic figures were Little Men pushed around by Big Men — Chaplin, Lloyd, Keaton, Laurel and Hardy, forever beset, forever buffeted, retaining shreds of dignity in the face of overwhelming tribulation.

The Thirties saw a shift from this comedy of pathos to the comedy of aggression. The great comedians were now impatient, domineering figures, openly derisive of the folkways to which Chaplin, Lloyd and Keaton had tried so timorously to conform. The comedians of the Twenties made valiant efforts at survival. I admired Chaplin's brilliant films of the Thirties — *City Lights, Modern Times, The Great Dictator;* in the last, Chaplin's concluding speech, deemed maudlin at the time, plays much better in the nuclear age.

Harold Lloyd's *Movie Crazy* (1932) is one of the funniest movies ever made. Lloyd is as usual an eager, naive, unconquerably optimistic young man, in this case aspiring to become a film star. Given a screen test, he manages to spoil one take after another, each in a different way — a hilarious sequence. Putting on a magician's tailcoat by mistake at an elaborate Hollywood party, he suddenly exudes doves, rabbits and white mice while he nervously dances on with the producer's wife. The Lloyd estate unfortunately released his movies to Time-Life Films, which reedited some, badly, and buried others; so *Movie Crazy* is not even to be seen on television in 2000.

Lloyd's disappearance is a cultural loss. When asked to pick films revealing the real America, Gabriel García Márquez, no fan of the United States, chose Lloyd for his spirit of "idealistic liberalism," noting the "historic irony that this idealism has not found its way into the American political reality." Orson Welles told Peter Bogdanovich that Lloyd was "the most underrated of them all. The intellectuals don't like the Harold Lloyd *character* — that middle-class, middle-American, all-American college boy . . . they miss that incredible technical brilliance."

But Chaplin, Lloyd and Keaton were obsolescent types in the shift to the comedy of aggression. No one could ever call Groucho Marx or W. C. Fields a Little Man. They had sharpened their acts in the Twenties, but the special needs of the Thirties gave them new centrality. The Marx Brothers, in their classic Paramount period in the early Thirties, represented the polar opposite of the comedy of the Twenties. Whatever existed was there not for deference but for deconstruction. Society matrons were to be assaulted, blondes to be chased, top hats to be knocked off, social conventions to be punned and pummeled out of existence. They had the imagination of anarchy. "Whatever it is," said Groucho, "I'm against it." The surrealism of *Duck Soup* (1933) carried the demonic Marxian logic almost beyond the point of no return.

The great Fields, equally immersed in the destructive element, played the cunning *contra mundum* rogue, capable of loathing every wife, kicking every child, humiliating every banker, exploiting every weakness and overcoming every crisis. It was Leo Rosten who said so unforgettably of Fields, "Anyone who hates babies and dogs can't be all bad." The title of Fields's 1941 film *Never Give a Sucker an Even Break* epitomized the new mood in film comedy. Preston Sturges, the Mencken of the movies, refined and polished the comedy of aggression in a series of brilliant films in the early Forties.

There came as well the rise of the independent woman. My early favorite was Ann Harding, an ash blonde who played humorous, self-reliant upper-class girls determined to affirm an identity and therefore made to order for the sophisticated comedies of Philip Barry, as in *Holiday* (1930) and *The Animal Kingdom* (1932). Unfortunately she was derailed into mawkish soap operas about suffering ladies, even into the old English tear-jerker *East Lynne,* and in time Katharine Hepburn succeeded her as the perfect Barry heroine. Ann Harding is forgotten today, but I was delighted many years later when Laurence Olivier, who played opposite her in *Westward Passage* (1932), told me how much he appreciated her kindness to him as an unknown English import in one of his first Hollywood roles.

Independence often had a satiric edge. The wisecracking female had been a familiar type (Joan Blondell, Glenda Farrell, Eve Arden) but mostly as the heroine's friend. Now she became the heroine herself, not only beautiful and seductive but funny. Jean Harlow, who began in Howard Hughes's *Hell's Angels* (1930) as the embodiment of single-minded sexuality, developed in films like George Cukor's *Dinner at Eight* (1933) into an astute and fetching comedienne. We saw her ripened talent in *Bombshell,* one of the best of Hollywood self-satires.

Harlow died in 1937. Her merger of humor and sex acquired new finesse in the hands of Carole Lombard, beautiful, alert, deft, romantic, with her weakness for romance always tripped up by her instinct for absurdity. Lombard held her own against some of the best male performers of the time — William Powell, John Barrymore, Jack Benny, Fred MacMurray — and illuminated a remarkable series of films — Hawks's *Twentieth Century,* Gregory La Cava's *My Man Godfrey,* Wellman's *Nothing Sacred,* Wesley Ruggles's *True Confession,* Lubitsch's *To Be or Not to Be.* Like Harlow, Lombard died prematurely. In later years, the tradition was charmingly sustained by Marilyn Monroe. Why did so many of these satiric beauties, from Harlow, Lombard and Thelma Todd (a great foil for Groucho) to Monroe, Judy Holliday and Kay Kendall, die young, at the top of their careers?

The satiric woman cheered everybody with her affirmation both of identity and of competence. In Mae West the satiric woman satirized herself. Myrna Loy, Katharine Hepburn, Jean Arthur, Margaret Sullavan and (by 1944) Lauren Bacall carried the type from farce into drama and furthered the impression that the liberated female could cope with anything.

*   *   *

We went to the movies for entertainment, of course, but almost as much for instruction in techniques of self-presentation. The movies supplied our models and shaped our dreams. Young men sauntered insolently down the street like James Cagney, wisecracked like William Powell, cursed (expletives deleted by censors) like Humphrey Bogart and wooed like Clark Gable. Young women sighed like Garbo and laughed like Carole Lombard and kidded like Myrna Loy and looked (or tried to look) like Hedy Lamarr. I cherished actors like Gary Cooper, Bogart, Cagney, Edward G. Robinson and Walter Huston, but they were beyond personal emulation. The style to which I vainly aspired was the witty, urbane, nonchalant, unruffled type —

Powell, especially as Hammett's Nick Charles, Fred Astaire, Robert Montgomery, Rex Harrison.

I remember movies of the Thirties better than I remember movies I saw last week. The magical Garbo haunts one still — "What one sees in other women when drunk," said Kenneth Tynan, "one sees in Garbo sober" — and I could watch *Grand Hotel* (1932) a dozen more times. I was — still am — a great admirer of Lewis Milestone's movie *The Front Page* (1931), where the speed and bite of the Hecht-MacArthur dialogue are joined to reckless fluency in camera movement and virtuosity of performance, especially by Adolphe Menjou.

We rejoiced at the discovery of an English director named Alfred Hitchcock as his films began to cross the Atlantic: *The Man Who Knew Too Much, The Thirty-Nine Steps,* a movie that for once greatly improved the novel from which it was drawn, and best of all *The Woman Alone* (as it was called in the United States; *Sabotage* in Britain), based on Conrad's *The Secret Agent.* The very name of Hitchcock's studio, Gaumont-British, had a pleasurably exotic ring. We rejoiced even more when Hitchcock soon crossed the Atlantic himself.

I had a special enthusiasm for Lubitsch movies: for *To Be or Not to Be,* that superbly audacious black comedy; for the enchanting *Ninotchka;* for *The Shop Around the Corner,* that delectable Viennese pastry; most of all, for *Trouble in Paradise,* a small but perfect movie, glittering like a diamond. Lubitsch's elegant, witty, high-polish comedies drew their art from his subtle mastery of intimation, nuance, gesture and timing and from the choreographic precision with which he managed his actors. The shot of Herbert Marshall thoughtfully eyeing Kay Francis's bed in *Trouble in Paradise* is a good deal more seductive than the familiar Nineties scene of two naked bodies pulsating on a bed locked in steamy embrace.

And there were the screwball comedies, cynical, fast, colloquial, disrespectful, disenchanted and unrepentant. Wellman's *Nothing Sacred* (1937) summed up the genre in its slashing cinematic attack as well as in its title. I liked Milestone's disillusioned *The Captain Hates the Sea* (1934), with its implied parable of a society adrift, and Wesley Ruggles's *True Confession* (1937), a black farce in which society rewards a woman who confesses to a murder she has not committed but spurns her when she tells the truth. Screwball had an evident muckraking impulse and loved to use the indignities of slapstick to illustrate the precariousness of social pretension. It was not, however, populist; it derided the mob as enthusiastically as it did the elite and had no patience with Capra-esque sentimentality. (Before Capra went gooey, he made a couple of fine, hard-edged films — *Platinum Blonde* and *The Bitter Tea of General Yen.*) Screwballism was incipient hysteria in a lunatic world in which only cynics could survive.

* * *

I had particular affection for the vernacular movies turned out in these years by Warner Brothers — gritty, racy, unsentimental, fast-moving films recording the idiom, the daily routines, the texture, the dilemmas, values, hopes of working-class and lower-middle-class America. The Warner Brothers stars — Paul Muni, Bette Davis, James Cagney, Edward G. Robinson, Humphrey Bogart, John Garfield, Ann Sheridan, Pat O'Brien, Claude Rains — and the 'stock company' — Frank McHugh, Joan Blondell, Glenda Farrell, Guy Kibbee, Aline McMahon, Ned Sparks, Allen Jenkins, Hugh Herbert, Alan Hale — appeared in a variety of entertainments, from Busby Berkeley musicals to Michael Curtiz costume melodramas; but one remembers particularly the hard-hitting movies dramatizing social problems and aspirations in the Great Depression.

Mervin LeRoy's *I Am a Fugitive from a Chain Gang* sensitively caught the despair of 1932. An unemployed war veteran marginally implicated in a robbery is condemned to a Georgia chain gang. He escapes, changes his name and attains respectability. Betrayed and returned to the chain gang, he escapes again. In the movie's last scene it is night, and the fugitive seeks out the woman he loves. When a sound causes him to take sudden flight, she calls desperately after him, "How do you live?" He whispers back, out of the dark, "I steal," and his footsteps fade away.

LeRoy later dealt memorably with lynching in *They Won't Forget* (1937). Other Warner films took up sharecropping (Curtiz's *Cabin in the Cotton*, 1932), labor organization (falteringly in Curtiz's *Black Fury*, 1935; forthrightly in Bacon's *Racket Busters*, 1938), depression kids (Wellman's *Wild Boys of the Road*, 1933), juvenile delinquents (Archie Mayo's *Mayor of Hell*, 1933), Indians (Alan Crossland's *Massacre*, 1934), Chicanos (Mayo's *Bordertown*, 1935) home-grown fascists (Mayo's *The Black Legion*, 1937). The Warners even turned Robin Hood into a sort of popular front leader delivering Saxon peasants from Norman exploiters in Curtiz's (and Errol Flynn's, and Erich Wolfgang Korngold's) glorious *Adventures of Robin Hood* (1938).

Poverty and despair driving decent people to a life of crime was a favorite Warner theme, concisely summarized in the title of Busby

Berkeley's nonmusical *They Made Me a Criminal* (1939). The American process of justice and punishment was subjected to skeptical analysis from the environment that breeds crime to the last mile before execution. Some situations were repeated so often that they became formulas: the unemployed veteran or slum-bred youth driven to crime by poverty; the innocent bystander tumbled into jail by purely circumstantial evidence; the brutal prisons and sadistic guards; the convict on parole balked by a hostile society in his efforts to go straight. Hollywood made movies inspired by the Sacco-Vanzetti case (*Winterset*), by the Leo Frank case (*They Won't Forget*), by lynchings (Fritz Lang's *Fury;* Wellman's *The Ox-Bow Incident*), by political frame-ups.

Warner Brothers movies also dramatized the humdrum struggles of daily life for shopgirls, truck drivers, factory workers, white-collar employees and small businessmen, including adequate versions of Lewis's *Babbitt* and *Main Street* (*I Married a Doctor*). The Warners presented a world of stress, anxiety, scrabbling for survival, ambition unfulfilled, hope betrayed; life was a struggle, often a racket, always an existence of quiet or, more often, noisy desperation, redeemed only by the modest joys of a raise or a love affair. The aggregate effect was to question the verities of American society.

It is true that many social films of the Thirties pulled their punches at the end. *Black Fury,* under pressure from the Hays Office (where Will Hays, Harding's postmaster general, reigned as 'czar' of the industry), changed the script to blame the strike not on miserable working conditions but on the dirty deeds of outside agitators. In LeRoy's *Oil for the Lamps of China* (1935), after an impassioned account of the callousness with which Standard Oil used its employees, the hero suddenly receives a long-merited promotion through the intervention of a corporate official hitherto unseen.

My interest in movies led me to the Museum of Modern Art in New York, where Richard Griffith, the film curator, persuaded me that pulling punches didn't matter all that much. When movies had something dangerous to say, he pointed out, a perfunctory happy ending in the last five minutes could not entirely erase ninety minutes of detailed and bitter indictment. What lingered was not the final twist but the bill of charges that went before. Indeed, the contrived happy ending in a sense legalized a film's darker message.

Years later, over dinner on Martha's Vineyard, I asked James Cagney and Frank McHugh how they accounted for the colloquial verve and social thrust at the Warner studio in the Thirties. Some of the best screenwriters, they said, were newspapermen who had lost their jobs in the depression and now transferred to screenplays their cynical knowledge of crooked politicians, city halls, courthouses, jails and other seedy standbys of urban life.

And the brothers Warner, as FDR devotees, gave the muckrakers their head. They even put an ad in the *New York Times:* "Warner Brothers have consistently demonstrated their belief that the screen is not merely a medium of entertainment. It is an institution significant socially and responsible morally. Its obligation is to inform, to interpret, to lead and — most important of all — to establish an enduring record of our forward marching civilization."

The Warner subtext in the Thirties was the song Harry Warren and Al Dubin wrote for LeRoy's *Gold Diggers of 1933.* Joan Blondell sang it in a slit skirt, standing by a lamppost, as a line of soldiers returning proudly from the Great War before cheering crowds is transmuted, under the magic wand of Busby Berkeley, into a shuffling breadline of the unemployed:

> Remember my forgotten man,
> You put a rifle in his hand.
> You sent him far away,
> You shouted hip hooray,
> But look at him today.

*   *   *

The Warner movies gave me a certain admiration for the studio system. Curtiz's *Casablanca* was the supreme triumph of that system — a movie as freshly full of spirit, wit, romance and effrontery today as it was sixty years ago. *Casablanca* showed how brilliantly professional a Hollywood studio could be even when it wasn't trying to make a film for the ages.

My general impression was that, given the dependence of Hollywood on money, banks, corporations and censors, the film industry was surprisingly critical in its inventory of American civilization. The older generation of intellectuals, with a few exceptions like Gilbert Seldes, did not share this regard for Hollywood. Charles and Mary Beard in *America in Midpassage,* their 1939 sequel to *The Rise of American Civilization,* devoted thirty caustic pages to the movies. Frederick Lewis Allen, whose *Only Yesterday,* a shrewd and thoughtful account of the Twenties, had delighted us all, had a piece in the January 1940 *Harper's* condemning American movies for their evasion of the "ugly and heart-rending facts of American life." Allen found "hardly a glimpse of the real America" in the movies of the Thirties. Looking back at these films in the 1970s, Allen said, people would have no idea of "the ordeal which the United States went through in the nineteen-thirties." Hollywood, in the Beard-Allen account, "took one to a never-never land of adventure and romance," glossed over injustice and inequality, portrayed depression-ravaged America as a rich and smiling land, attacked radicals and beat the patriotic drum for war.

Speaking, I suppose, for the Movie Generation, I rushed to Hollywood's defense. "The theory has become pretty firmly fixed in the credo of the American intellectual," I wrote in a piece I submitted to *Harper's*, "that the movies are essentially an instrument for evading social reality." One doubted that the Beards or Frederick Lewis Allen had gone to many movies. Of a list of thirteen described by the Beards as "war pictures," three were in fact football films, one was a musical, one a strong antiwar film and only two or three contained the militaristic propaganda ascribed to the whole lot. As for Allen, he conceded that literature and drama were no more faithful than film to social realities — "no book on the economic conditions of America got to the top of the best-seller list" — but displayed no comparable indignation over this fact.

My article doesn't read too badly after half a century, though Fred Allen, who was also an editor of *Harper's*, turned it down with a kindly letter. "I confess that I think you caught me in too broad a generalization," he wrote, but my piece, he said, seemed too specialized for publication.

*   *   *

My regard for the studio system extended to a defense of "block-booking" — that is, the insistence of studios that exhibitors rent all the films in a given "block." Reformers wanted to outlaw block-booking on the ground that the practice compelled local exhibitors to show inferior or immoral movies.

Ford's *The Grapes of Wrath* was under attack by the Catholic Church, the *Motion Picture Herald* and other guardians of the public morals, as *Blockade* and *Of Mice and Men* had been in the recent past. Block-booking, it seemed to me, guaranteed the showing of such movies, and its abolition would only transfer the power of choice to local exhibitors who were generally less enlightened even than the studios and far more at the mercy of pressure groups. "I can conceive of few measures more likely to destroy the chances of an intelligent and progressive screen," I wrote to one reformer, "than this. . . . With all its bad effects, block-booking has also been a device to force exhibitors to show unusual films which depart from their (ordinarily childish) notions of what film entertainment should be."

Both sides overstated the case. The Supreme Court disposed of block-booking in 1948, without either the benefit predicted by the reformers or the disaster predicted by me.

*   *   *

Censorship was much on our minds in the Thirties. The talkies had facilitated dialogue and situations that neo-Puritans thought morally corrupting and conservatives thought politically dangerous. In an effort to discourage censorship by cities and states, in 1930 the Hays Office adopted a Production Code, drafted by Father Daniel Lord, a Jesuit priest, and Martin Quigley, publisher of the *Motion Picture Herald* and a prominent Catholic layman.

The Code at first had little success in enforcing "morality" in moviemaking. Hollywood continued to produce movies that, if tame by the standards of 2000, were mettlesome, insolent, free-spoken and sexually realistic. In 1934 the Catholic hierarchy came to morality's rescue. The American bishops set up the Legion of Decency to blacklist films they considered indecent and to prod the Hays Office into more militant enforcement.

This time the cure worked, and a new Production Code Administration imposed a set of detailed and often idiotic restrictions in the name of "correct thinking." The Code declared: "No picture shall be produced which will lower the moral standards of those who see it." Consequent restrictions ranged from the prohibition of words like "broad" and "chippie" (applied to a woman) to the abolition of double beds, even for married couples. "Immoral" situations were generously defined. Had Aeschylus and Shakespeare been compelled to observe the Production Code, the world would have been denied dramatic masterpieces of western civilization. The Code would have censored the Bible itself. A famous instance involving a lesser work was the struggle required in 1939 before Clark Gable was permitted to say to Vivien Leigh in *Gone With the Wind:* "Frankly, my dear, I don't give a damn."

For many years, the Code was applied in a literal and mechanical way with grotesque results. In the Fifties a newspaper column of mine attacking the Legion of Decency led to a correspondence, at first acrimonious, then friendly, with Martin Quigley. While Quigley insisted that the moral principles governing his Code should be kept inviolate, he added, to my surprise, "I agree with your judgment that there is in what is commonly referred to as 'The Production Code' much 'niggling detail'. . . . It is my belief that when you refer to some of this as 'niggling' you are being over-generous. Some of these provisions are now and always have been absurd and ridiculous." Quigley wanted, for example, to delete the miscegenation ban imposed by Will Hays, a Presbyterian elder.

With movies today featuring profanity, sex and violence unimaginable to the Thirties, the old Code restrictions seem equally unimaginable to the twenty-first century. In retrospect, I am impelled to confess that, abhorrent and antiartistic as the Code was, it nevertheless had some beneficial artistic consequences. As my friend Philip Dunne, a screenwriter and director, the son of Mr. Dooley and the most stalwart and principled of Hollywood liberals, put it,

> In a strange way the Code forced writers not only to be cleaner but also to be cleverer. Explicit sex, gory violence . . . demand no mental exertion on the part of the writer. Most good writing (and good direction, for that matter) is adroit indirection. . . . In the proper dramatic context, a touch of the hand, a simple look, could be far more erotic than any of today's explicit tumbles in the hay.

One thinks of the 'Lubitsch touch.' Phil Dunne added: "But don't get me wrong. I still hate censorship."

The Code of the Thirties was an early manifestation of the mania for 'political correctness' that was to infect the country in the Nineties. In the tolerant days of my youth, the comedian Eddie Cantor could cheerfully go on in blackface and describe himself as the coon from Kuhn Loeb and Company — a harmless joke that in later days would offend two minority groups, or at least their self-anointed spokesmen. It is ironic that political correctness, like multiculturalism, having begun as a weapon of the right, should end as a weapon of the left. Repression from either extreme creates odious precedents. As Louis Menand has said, "The censor always rings twice."

* * *

Movies are of particular interest to the historian because of the visual documentation even fiction movies offer of the past. If only we had had a Warner Brothers in the age of Pericles, or of Charlemagne, or of Napoleon! But movies also confront historians with difficult challenges in the reading of evidence.

From birth, film has been a hermaphrodite: half art, half industry. It has engaged the talent of people who might otherwise have been writers of plays, composers of sonatas, painters of pictures. And it has absorbed the energies of people who might otherwise have been garment manufacturers, Wall Street speculators, Main Street merchants or con men. It has represented an improbable and unstable coalition of aesthetics and greed.

In this partnership, greed has generally had the upper hand. Making movies requires heavy financial investment and therefore demands a mass audience for survival. Moreover, the production of a movie is itself a mass undertaking, involving directors, writers, producers, actors, cinematographers and a horde of other technicians (watch the credits unroll), the artifact finally delivered by assembly line to a vast and anonymous audience. "To practice his art," Orson Welles once said, "a poet needs a pen and a painter a brush. But a film-maker needs an army." More than any other art, film depends on collective initiative and collective response.

The writer and director John Sayles compares getting a story from script to screen with getting a bill through Congress: "Someone authors the bill with a certain intention, but to pass it deals must be struck, amendments made, riders attached, until the bill may be so watered down or altered that its purpose has disappeared entirely." Created by a crowd for a crowd, movies inescapably bear the imprint of the society that makes them. What Taine said about books applies equally, or even more, to films: they do not drop from the sky like meteorites. But where is the key that will enable the scholar to unlock the historical riches that movies secrete?

This question began to interest American historians in the Seventies. The Warner movies of the Thirties, for example, are a treasure house for the social historian, with their panorama of life, work, love and death in the great city. And persisting images, genres, styles and myths may disclose deeper concerns. "What films reflect," wrote Siegfried Kracauer, "are not so much explicit credos as psychological dispositions — those deep layers of collective mentality which extend more or less below the dimensions of consciousness."

Yet these deep layers are precisely those most difficult to define and verify. Kracauer's own *From Caligari to Hitler* (1947), the most ambitious attempt to use films as a historical source, discovered "a secret history" in the German movies of the Twenties, among them Fritz Lang's *Dr. Mabuse* films and his *Die Nibelungen* and *Metropolis,* and sought to show how their mysticism and paranoia foretold the rise of Nazism. I remember the excitement with which I read Kracauer's book. Later I mentioned *From Caligari to Hitler* to Fritz Lang when we became friends in the Sixties. Lang flew into a rage and denounced the book as the triumph of hindsight. Then I began to wonder whether, for all its suggestive analysis, Kracauer's book should not have been called *From Hitler to Caligari,* for did it not reason back from the outcome to the omens? If the Weimar Republic had succeeded, might not someone have examined a different lot of films and demonstrated how the German cinema had foretold the victory of democracy?

Film is a duplicitous art. Its manifest content often heads in one direction, its latent content in another. Left-wing critics condemn Hollywood movies as dedicated to the reinforcement of bourgeois privilege. Certainly Hollywood has done its share to strengthen capitalism, chauvinism, hedonism, sexism, racism and so on. But often the explicit moral, as Dick Griffith used to argue, is at war with the implicit message.

Movies are at once unifying and disruptive — another example of duplicity. Film provides a common dream life, a common fund of reference and fantasy, for a society riven by economic disparities and ethnic discriminations. At the same time, film gives the injured and insulted a disquieting sense of the abundance and fulfillment available to the privileged. One may guess that the movies generate as much discontent as they do acquiescence.

And film fans, supposedly sitting passively in the darkened theater, are in fact active collaborators. "The audience," Sam Spiegel, the last of the great producers, used to say, "is the co-author." Those who make up the audience seize from the movie what they need for their individual purposes of tutelage and fantasy, and they respond to each movie not as an isolated event but as reverberant with memories of other films, with the private lives of stars, with their own private lives.

Or at least so it was in the Thirties, when movies were at the operative center of our lives. Woody Allen was born in 1935; but his faith in the redemptive power of Thirties movies and music qualifies him for honorary membership in the Movie Generation. Woody's distraught Manhattanites, as they wobble on the edge of breakdown, are forever saved from the abyss by watching *Duck Soup* (as in *Manhattan*) or Fred and Ginger (as in *Purple Rose of Cairo*).

In the Thirties, movies really counted. The love that cinema then inspired, Susan Sontag wrote at the end of the century, was born of the conviction that "cinema was an art unlike any other: quintessentially modern; distinctively accessible; poetic and mysterious and erotic and moral — all at the same time. . . . It was both the book of art and the book of life." But the love of cinema, she feels, has waned; the age of cinema is over.

Trapped by Television.

9

Harvard College: What I Learned

COLLEGE IN THE END is about education in the formal sense. Exeter had given me such a rough time in the classroom that the transition to Harvard was easy.

In freshman year, I took biology to fulfill the college's science requirement and received my only B in a full course. I had no reason thereafter to doubt my incompetence in science. William Ernest Hocking, with his earnestly benevolent metaphysical idealism, and the brilliant logician C. I. Lewis lectured to freshmen in Philosophy B; I recall nothing of the wisdom they dispensed. In History 1 Roger Bigelow "Frisky" Merriman, a renowned performer on the platform as well as the distinguished historian of the Spanish Empire, entertained the freshmen with his flamboyant ride through European history. (I won History 1's Le Baron Russell Briggs Prize, a leatherbound copy of Jowett's translation of Thucydides, for a paper called, improbably, "The Gradual Secularization of the Papacy from the Pontificate of Gregory VII to the Council of Trent.")

The freshman course I remember best and from which I learned most was given by a young instructor in economics, Robert K. Lamb, who combined Marx with Harvard's Joseph A. Schumpeter in unorthodox but rather fascinating doses. He was radical in his ideas, expressing depression-generated doubts about the survivability of capitalism, but conservative in his dress, wearing natty three-piece suits. "I discover that if I buy my suits at Brooks Brothers and look like a banker," Bob Lamb confided to me one day, "it is much easier to get Harvard students to believe what I am telling them."

*　*　*

Sophomore year required a vital decision: the choice of a field of concentration (Harvard's term for what other institutions called a major). I had no hesitation in choosing History and Literature, a field I assumed to be in its early glory. The intellectual excitement generated in the Thirties by History and Lit, especially the American pro-

157

gram, gave students the illusion that they were present at a creation. Many years later, invited to speak at History and Lit's seventy-fifth anniversary, I discovered that the field had already been around for a considerable time.

I am not clear why it was founded in 1906. Henry James had visited Harvard the year before and, after ironic expressions of admiration for the "new and strange architectures looming through the dark," found one thing missing — the sense of "direct literary consecration" he remembered from the Harvard of his youth; "the light of literary desire is not perceptibly in her." Perhaps these Jamesian vibrations reached the ear of Barrett Wendell, a professor in the genteel tradition but still one of the first rash enough to suggest, in his *Literary History of America*, that America had a literature (even though he described his own book as "Tory, pro-slavery, and imperialistic"). Wendell called colleagues together, and History and Lit was born.

By the time I entered the program thirty years later, History and Lit was at the height of its influence. The number of students accepted each year was limited, and this, combined with the pleasure that both faculty and students found in their work and in one another, gave the program a we-happy-few atmosphere that was sometimes exasperating. Still, the professors were learned and stimulating, and the attempt to work out connections between literature and history made great sense to me. As Whitman said, the poet fails "if he be not himself the age transfigured." I never for a moment regretted my choice.

* * *

The 'progressive historians' of the Twenties — Frederick Jackson Turner, Charles A. Beard and Vernon Louis Parrington — still dominated the study of American civilization in the Thirties. Turner's *The Frontier in American History* (1920), Beard's *The Rise of American Civilization* (1927), written in collaboration with his wife, Mary, and Parrington's *Main Currents in American Thought* (1927–30) constituted what later generations would stigmatize as the canon. (The associated assumption that canons are engraved in stone founders on the fact that today these books, once so mightily influential, are little read, and their authors are largely forgotten.)

Though Turner's frontier thesis loomed over historical discussion in the Thirties, it was of less interest to the depression-tossed young than the Beard-Parrington contention that the key to American history was the conflict between capitalism and democracy. Beard wrote political and economic history, Parrington literary and intellectual history, but their readings of the American past vigorously reinforced each other. *The Rise of American Civilization* and the first volume of *Main Currents in American Thought* actually came out the same year and competed for the Pulitzer Prize in history. Parrington won the prize, but the Beards sold more books.

The Rise marked a considerable stylistic departure from the dry and clinical tone of *An Economic Interpretation of the Constitution*. The Beards now achieved what Sir Walter Scott called the Big Bow-Wow strain. They rendered American history in majestic rolling periods as grand melodrama driven by the rise of capitalism. The Civil War emerged as the decisive moment when industrialists and bankers, clawing their way to power, destroyed their main rival, the planting aristocracy of the south, thereby producing the "Second American Revolution" and assuring capitalism's triumph.

Depression gave the economic interpretation new power. "Along with many other professional historians of my generation, strange as it seems to me now," my contemporary and friend Richard Hofstadter wrote in 1968, "I took up American history under the inspiration" of the Beards, adding that when he read *The Rise of American Civilization* for the first time, in 1934, "all American history seemed to dance to Beard's tune." I would not have disagreed. When the historian Merle Curti interrogated scholars about Beard in 1948, I replied that I thought his "broad influence . . . valuable and liberating. He has done more than any other single historian to free American history from what seem to me the simplicities of Turnerism." Yet the imposing Beardian edifice is today in ruins, undermined by simplicities of its own.

Parrington's fall has been, if possible, even more complete. *Main Currents in American Thought* was a fluent and energetic work enlivened by memorable phrases and flashes of wit. Its theory of American literature as a struggle between democratic realism and aristocratic escapism struck a chord in the rebellious Twenties and instantly synchronized with the politics of the Thirties. Beard himself saluted *Main Currents*, and in my own generation, Daniel Aaron recalls wryly "how refreshing and liberating it was to read *Main Currents* in the '30s, how bold in conception and broad in scope we found it. . . . It lifted American history and literature into the open air." Lionel Trilling's astute deflationary essay in 1940 conceded to Parrington "an influence on our conception of American culture which is not equaled by that of any other writer of the last two decades." As late as 1950 a poll of historians on the best book in the American field in the preceding thirty years had Parrington beating both Turner and the Beards.

But, like *The Rise of American Civilization, Main Currents* impoverished the rich and complex American past. Parrington reduced Jonathan Edwards, Poe, Hawthorne, Melville, Henry James to marginal figures, practitioners of *belles lettres,* not illuminators of the American experience. Harold Laski said in 1937 that Beard and Parrington "opened windows for me into the significance of the American tradition as no other books since Tocqueville." But Tocqueville abides and prospers. Beard and Parrington have vanished, like the works of Ozymandias, king of kings:

> Nothing beside remains. Round the decay
> Of that colossal wreck, boundless and bare,
> The lone and level sands stretch far away.

*　*　*

Even Harvard History and Literature tutors paid homage to Beard and Parrington — ironically so because their own scholarly work was quietly subverting the Beard-Parrington orthodoxy.

In the Twenties, writers and intellectuals, scorning their American present, had joined Parrington and the Beards in debunking the American past. Van Wyck Brooks's *The Ordeal of Mark Twain* portrayed a promising artist crippled by American gentility and materialism. Sinclair Lewis mocked middle-class complacencies. Dos Passos's cinematically vivid *U.S.A.* dramatized the republic's takeover by monopoly capitalism. The cynicism of Mencken hovered over all.

The Thirties were a time of enthusiastic rediscovery of American possibility. FDR's New Deal was giving the American present new purpose and dignity. The rise of fascism and communism in Europe made American democracy look a little better. Intellectuals discovered new values in the American past. Brooks portrayed American culture in *The Flowering of New England* (1936) and the succeeding volumes of his *Makers and Finders* series as rich, abundant and eminently usable. Sinclair Lewis in *It Can't Happen Here* and *The Prodigal Parents* exalted the middle-class America he had once scorned. The title of Dos Passos's book of 1941, *The Ground We Stand On,* made the point. "In times of change and danger," Dos Passos wrote, "when there is a quicksand of fear under men's reasoning, a sense of continuity with generations gone before can stretch like a lifeline across the scary present." On every side there was an evident desire to repossess the national past in all its solidity: even Mencken celebrated the American language.

I was extraordinarily lucky in my tutors — Perry Miller in my sophomore year, F. O. Matthiessen in my junior year, then back to Miller senior year for my honors essay. Miller and Matthiessen were close if sometimes prickly friends but very contrasting teachers. Miller, the historian of ideas, was forceful, brusque, cantankerous, always happy to shake up and shock his students. Matty, the literary critic, was courteous, intense, sensitive, soft-spoken, intellectually insinuating rather than contentious. Perry was a robust atheist, Matty a devout Anglican; Perry a New Dealer, Matty a Stalinist fellow traveler. Perry was, in addition, a dedicated heterosexual, Matty a devoted homosexual; but in my prolonged innocence I was aware of neither proclivity. Both were generous in expending time and concern, and I learned more than I can say in rugged, shouting arguments with Miller at Leverett House and in taut, quiet sessions with Matthiessen in his darkened (as I recall it) Eliot House study.

*   *   *

Miller was twenty-nine years old when I became his tutee in the autumn of 1935. According to the story he so often told — he was given to self-dramatization — he had dropped out of college and, too young for the great adventure of the (first) world war, had set out on adventures of his own. He often referred to a mysterious early career as hobo, actor and seaman on tramp steamers; this gave him a Hemingway flavor in the eyes of the young. His quest ended on the edge of a jungle on the banks of the Congo, where, while supervising the unloading of drums of case oil, he had a vision — "a sudden epiphany (if the word be not too strong) on the pressing necessity for expounding my America to the twentieth century." His search now was for "the innermost propulsion of the United States," and he decided to start at the beginning with the first articulate body of expression he could find. Puritanism became his key to American self-understanding.

Puritans were not in favor in the Twenties. Mencken had defined Puritanism as "the haunting fear that someone, somewhere might be happy," and the fashion was to blame the Puritans for everything that had gone wrong in American culture. Scholars warned Miller that there was little left to say about Puritanism. Miller, along with his Harvard colleagues Samuel Eliot Morison and Kenneth B. Murdock, was to show how mistaken this assumption was. When I became his tutee, he had already written *Orthodoxy in Massachusetts* and was hard at work on the first volume of his great work *The New England Mind.*

He was a tall, bulky man, pink-faced, hair already turning gray, metal-rimmed spectacles, hearty, approachable, irreverent and alternating unpredictably between kindness and gruffness. For all his solicitude for the Puritans, he remained, by Edmund Wilson's definition, a man of the Twenties. Academic history since the Twenties, Miller once wrote, should aim "to systematize and regularize the impact of the jazz age." He loved what one of his finest students, Edmund S. Morgan, called "the he-man pose." A Newport matron who sat next to him at dinner before he spoke at the John Carter Brown Library thought his lecture brilliant, then added, "But why does he keep insisting that he is really a stevedore?" He was a heavy drinker. His candid, affectionate and long-suffering wife, Betty, put up with a lot. One sometimes felt that Perry had never quite grown up.

But as a scholar and teacher, he was a man of rigorous standards. My first tutorial assignment was to read a sermon of the seventeenth-century Puritan divine Thomas Hooker. This was probably a sort of Miller test, for he quoted Hooker in the opening pages of *The New England Mind* as a link to Saint Augustine in the shared sense of human sinfulness and the hunger for redemption. I obviously failed the test, as I learned from the merciless cross-examination the next week when I submitted my report. I noted the next spring in my journal, "Luckily my memory of Perry Miller's onslaught on me in our first tutorial conference last October is revived every time I see him and makes for excessive intellectual humility." Miller early taught me that glibness was not enough, a valuable lesson if one I imperfectly absorbed.

His interest was the history of ideas rather than intellectual history in the broader sense of the interplay between thought and the external environment. As he himself wrote, he "deliberately avoided giving more than passing notice to the social or economic influences." His passion was ideas themselves — in their power, their danger, their autonomy and their intricate interconnectedness. His skill, especially as a lecturer, was to charge the drama of ideas with intellectual excitement. His purpose was the vindication of mind as the determining fact in human history.

I gained from him insights into the dark power of the Augustinian strain in Christianity, the anguished awareness of human finitude, failure, guilt, corruptibility, the precariousness of existence and the challenge of moral responsibility. Miller was an atheist who believed in original sin, and he admired the Puritans because, driven as they were by Augustinian forebodings, they were nevertheless possessed by a great and revolutionary idea — that "no force but the will of man can bring order out of the chaos of human depravity." He made us understand that, underneath their arcane theological formulations, their struggles were also our struggles. As I wrote to a girlfriend in February 1937, Miller led me to discover in myself "a singular, and quite unexpected, fondness for the doctrine of original sin."

Puritan anguish had an obvious counterpart in neo-orthodox theology — it was from Miller that I first heard about Reinhold Niebuhr — and in the angst of the twentieth century. Miller, as in his biography of Jonathan Edwards, may even have read the modern consciousness back too much into the past. Was he also reading his own personal angst back into the past? For this magistral organizer of ideas was a tormented organizer of life, given to explosions of rage, sexual forays, existential dread, and the self-destruction of alcoholism.

Yet, against inner demons, he pressed on in his great work on the life of the mind in America. He left a formidable structure of interpretation; and, though he was a self-styled "lone wolf historian" who could not care less about founding a school, a host of scholars acknowledged their indebtedness to him, many in a special issue of *The Harvard Review* in 1964, "Perry Miller and the American Mind," edited by my son Stephen (again, the circularity of life). The historiography of American Puritanism became a series of glosses on Perry Miller — glosses and then critiques; for the revisionist, or parricidal, impulse that led Miller's generation to overthrow Beard and Parrington led a younger generation to seek to overthrow Miller.

Still, to Edmund Morgan in 1964 he was "the best historical mind of his generation, perhaps of his century"; to Kenneth Lynn in 1983, "America's most eminent historian since Henry Adams"; to Joyce Appleby, Lynn Hunt and Margaret Jacob in their book of 1994, *Telling the Truth About History,* "probably this century's greatest historian." He was certainly one of the greatest teachers of history. And underneath the bluntness and irascibility he was also in unexpected ways a sweet and considerate man.

*   *   *

Miller and Matthiessen were vital collaborators in History and Lit and each admired much in the other; but each also had — and not seldom used — a considerable capacity to irritate the other. Kenneth

Lynn found in Miller's library two of Matty's books: one was inscribed: "Perry — You alleged that you wanted to look up a sentence in this book. Perhaps you can use the rest for kindling"; the other, Matty's masterwork, his great study *American Renaissance,* bore another acid inscription: "For Perry and Betty with much gratitude, though the former has latterly indicated that he finds little value in the method employed in these pages."

Matty was Perry's senior by three years. He came from a wealthy family and was, along with Henry R. Luce and Max Lerner, a member of the Yale class of 1923, where he made Skull and Bones, an association he treasured for the rest of his life. After two years as a Rhodes Scholar at New College, he took a Ph.D. at Harvard. Joining the faculty in 1929, he shifted his major interest from Elizabethan to American literature.

A short, bald man with rimless glasses, lacking Miller's dramatic flair on the podium, Matty was an uneven lecturer. He seemed to think his points through afresh as he talked, with results that were sometimes inspired, sometimes disorganized and confusing. But he was a superb tutor. Because I was temperamentally more akin to Miller, I perhaps learned even more from Matthiessen.

We began tentatively enough. "I think he will do admirably in developing my faculties for literary criticism," I wrote in my journal after my first tutorial, "but I miss with him the sense of understanding that I have with Miller. I talked a little about myself, at his request, and somehow, I think, he misunderstood almost everything I said. . . . Still I like the man." After three conferences: "He is not, I think, an easy talker. He is not, I think, a man of much conviction. [How wrong I was; I mistook diffidence for lack of conviction.] He is not, I think, a man of much understanding (of me, anyway; I always rather feel he misses my points). On the other hand, he is a man of ideas and knowledge. . . . On the whole he has been highly satisfactory so far."

Matty introduced me to poetry — at least to poetry more complicated than *The Lady of the Lake* or *Idylls of the King.* He began by making me read *The Waste Land.* In a juvenile fit of inverse snobbery, I put another jacket on the book lest people think I was succumbing to aesthetic chic. We went over the poem line by line, uncovering deeper resonances and implications. It was a revelation for me.

He was working on the book that became *American Renaissance,* and we read Whitman with similar intensity, another revelation. When Matty's book was published, he sent a copy with the inscription: "For Arthur, to whom I am indebted . . . for a remark about one of Whitman's poems (p. 577), which I stole intact from an examination blue-book." Naturally I turned at once to page 577. There, in a discussion of "On the Beach at Night," he had carefully marked two lines, evidently taken from the bluebook: "the quiet suggestion of illimitability, which is beyond the understanding but within the perception of the small girl." Matty had every right to appropriate those words, since I could never have conceived them had he not taught me how to read poetry. I wrote him about the passage, "If I was its father, you certainly were its grandfather." And his honesty about it was impressive — and typical. Had he simply appropriated the lines, I never would have recognized them. Who can remember what one writes in an examination?

I was quite unaware of his homosexuality. I do remember his once saying rather emphatically to me in tutorial, "The object of love is not important; what matters is the quality of the emotion"; but I cannot remember what occasioned this remark. His affair with the painter Russell Cheney had begun in 1924 and was documented in 1978 when Louis Hyde published a selection of their letters in *Rat and the Devil*, their pet names when they weren't calling each other "dear feller." The letters, if embarrassing in their endearments, are enormously admirable and touching in the determination of the writers to follow their bliss in a day when such bliss was forbidden. "Can't you hear the hell-hounds of society baying full pursuit behind us?" Matty wrote to his lover. ". . . We have a marriage that was never seen on land or sea."

But in my invincible innocence, none of this occurred to me. Even a few years later, when Matty and Cheney moved into their flat in Louisburg Square, on Beacon Hill in Boston, I did think it odd that after dinner they put on heavy leather gloves and had mock fights with their cats, but my sense of their oddity went no further. Homosexuality was not much of an issue for us. As undergraduates, we sometimes idly speculated about the habits of other undergraduates — could so-and-so be a "homo"? But we were not really clear what homosexuality involved nor how widespread the inclination might be. Nor were our elders. I remember my father's rather startled bemusement when his friend Stewart Mitchell, the director of the Massachusetts Historical Society and author of a solid, conventional biography of Horatio Seymour, came to him one day and confessed to homosexual relations with his chauffeur. In later years Lionel Trilling told me that, when he wrote his admirable study of E. M. Forster in the early 1940s, he did not know that Forster was homosexual.

This seemed a marked contrast to the situation in England. As my contemporary and friend Noel Annan wrote in *Our Age*, his scintillating survey of the intellectual and political life of his British generation, "Our Age is remarkable for being a generation which made homosexuality a cult"; and he devoted four chapters to the subject. So too the journalist Peregrine Worsthorne in his memoir *Tricks of Memory* gave several pages to a discussion of his wavering attitude toward homosexuality at Cambridge.

No doubt the absence of any American equivalent of fagging in the British public school is part of the explanation; but the American assumptions of the time simply ignored homosexuality. Few novelists dealt with it. I remember the shock when Sinclair Lewis introduced lesbianism into *Ann Vickers*. In the Thirties same-sex love, even Matty's and Cheney's, dared not speak its name. Now, as has been frequently observed, it won't shut up.

* * *

Matty's politics were less concealed. He really believed that the Bolshevik Revolution was, as he wrote as late as 1948, "the most progressive event of our century, the necessary successor to the French Revolution and the American Revolution" — a belief that survived Stalin, the purges, the trials, the pact with Hitler and the gulags. Only his conviction of original sin, he once told Dan Aaron, kept him from joining the Communist party. But he joined a multitude of front organizations, and he continued to regard Stalin's Soviet Union as the hope of the world.

One wondered: How could so devout a Christian cherish communism? How could a critic so sensitively attuned to aesthetic criteria put up with a vulgar creed that reduced literature and art to socialist realism? I never asked him those questions; I can only suppose that the intensity of his need to believe in an equalitarian society — a need perhaps induced by the guilt of inherited wealth — overpowered spiritual and aesthetic misgivings.

I met Harry Bridges in Matty's Eliot House rooms one evening. They were a contrast — the guileless and hopeful literary scholar deferring to the hard-bitten, saturnine, hawk-eyed, cigarette-smoking leader of the west coast longshoremen, an intrepid organizer and a secret Communist, throwing out sharp, laconic remarks in his Australian cockney accent.

I was not aware how deep our political disagreements were until the fall and winter of 1939. Stalin had made his deal with Hitler;

Great Britain was mired in the ambiguities of the phony war. I remarked to Matty one day that Winston Churchill was the only hope. He fixed me with an icy stare and said with great intensity, "Winston Churchill is the epitome of everything I have hated all my life." As late as March 1941, three months before Hitler invaded the Soviet Union, Matty opposed American intervention at a rally in Boston's Symphony Hall organized by American Peace Mobilization, a Communist front.

Yet his allegiance was sentimental, not intellectual. *American Renaissance,* finally published that same year, was far more influenced by Eliot than Marx. It took off from the appearance within the years 1850–55 of *Representative Men, The Scarlet Letter, Moby-Dick, Walden* and *Leaves of Grass* — an extraordinary burst of concentrated artistic creativity. Matthiessen used these works to explore the inner meaning of American life. He admired, he claimed, Parrington's "elucidation of our liberal tradition"; but he declined to apply political criteria to literature. Unlike Parrington, he valued literary forms and understood how forms reveal tensions and illuminate emotions. Using Eliot's organic theory of literature, he showed how great works in producing new orientations absorb the past and foreshadow the future.

He was too good a Christian to deny the tragic dimension. Parrington had no use for original sin, but man, in Matthiessen's view, was "radically imperfect." Yet, pitiful as man might be in his finite weakness, Matty believed him "still capable of apprehending perfection, and of becoming transfigured by that vision." The common denominator of his five writers, he said, was "their devotion to the possibilities of democracy."

This premise gave his writers an affirmative and redemptive cast. It is hard to see the skeptical Hawthorne, the disenchanted Whitman of *Democratic Vistas,* the despairing Melville, as great champions of democratic possibilities. Still, when *American Renaissance* was published in 1941, democracy's back was against the wall, hardly more than a dozen democratic states were left in the world, and the democratic cause needed all the blessing it could get.

American Renaissance, with its rich diversity of reference and its complex interconnections, opened many new doors to the study of American culture — the relationship of American literature to oratory, for example, to frontier tall tales, to open-air painting, to architecture, to opera, to photography, to allegory and myth, to Dante, Shakespeare, Milton, Donne, Coleridge.

Like *The New England Mind,* it later became the target of parricidal impulses, and its indifference to 'literary theory' no doubt strikes the neostructuralist generation as hopelessly old-fashioned. The political correctness cops point out inanely that Matthiessen ended up "with a list that was entirely male; and it apparently did not even enter his mind that the list was defective because it was wholly white" (I quote Professor William E. Cain). But what American female and nonwhite writers of the age could reasonably be classed with Emerson, Thoreau, Melville, Hawthorne and Whitman? As a writer and as a teacher, Matty immeasurably enriched my understanding of America.

*   *   *

A third member of the faculty who had a great impact on me was Bernard DeVoto, our family bootlegger. A round-faced, generous-hearted, affectionate, testy, pugnacious, insecure, driven man, a failed novelist, an embryonic historian, a lusty polemicist and a professional westerner, he had somehow been invited by the English department to give a couple of courses — one in contemporary literature, the other in composition. The first was lively, opinionated and idiosyncratic; the second was for me a seismic experience.

Benny was thirty-eight years old when I took his composition course in my sophomore year. Born in Utah of a Catholic father and a Mormon mother, he had been suspended in his own family between two contradictory revelations, each authoritatively certified as divine. This bred a profound mistrust of revelation in general. "I early acquired," he later wrote, "a notion that all gospels were false, and all my experience since then has confirmed it." He saw himself as "a pluralist, a relativist, an empiricist. . . . We must avoid certainty, unity, vision and the loaded dice." Alas, certainty was something he rarely avoided himself.

He stormed east from Utah, graduated from Harvard in 1920 and soon was teaching at Northwestern in Illinois. There he spotted a very pretty, bright and sassy young freshman seated with other coeds in the front row of his class — the "chorus line," Benny called it. In those pre–sexual harassment days, he was able to date and soon to marry Avis MacVickar. Benny and Avis created an oasis of advanced thinking in sedate Evanston. George W. Ball, one of Benny's students, later told Wallace Stegner, Benny's biographer, "I shall always be grateful to Benny for teaching me to look down at the bastards surrounding me with a sense of great disdain. . . . No doubt it made me insufferable, but it was helpful at the time." It also helped later when

George Ball became one of the few American diplomats capable of writing lucid, graceful and witty English.

Benny published a couple of anti-Utah, anti-Mormon novels and contributed Menckenesque pieces to the *American Mercury*. In 1927 the DeVotos moved to Cambridge. By the time I knew them, they seemed an emblematic Twenties couple — irreverent, profane, chronically nonconformist, endlessly entertaining, Avis particularly maintaining a delightful individuality in the face of a husband who held definite opinions about everything. For his part, Benny was given to shocking Cambridge gentility by putting on what Stegner called his "western wild man" act.

He was a great teacher. George Homans, the literate sociologist, and Joseph Alsop, the literate columnist, were two of his Harvard students. I began by writing dramatic criticism. George Jean Nathan, the dominant theater critic of the day, was my model — a bad model because, like Mencken, he had a baroque style that worked for him but for no one else. DeVoto soon disabused me of my ambition to become a drama critic. I often thank him when I sit through (or walk out of) our contemporary theater.

"Verbs and nouns are the guts of a sentence," he told his class. "Adjectives and adverbs are the water. A writer is as strong as his verbs. . . . Write for the reader, never for yourself." He handed back an early paper of mine with the comment: "Your principal trouble remains the vague phrase accepted without scrutiny. Don't think in phrases. Turn ideas into component words." He read one's false starts with meticulous care, exposed pretentiousness and phoniness with a pitiless eye, scrawled scathing but unanswerable comments in the margin and goaded his students to think through what they were trying to say and to say it plainly, concisely and concretely. By December 1935 I reported in my journal that DeVoto had "improved (or at least changed) my style about 100%."

And, though he loved living in Cambridge, he persuaded us that the nation stretched far beyond New England into the magnificent, wild, disorderly, troubled land across the wide Missouri, filled with beauty and surprise and possibility but betrayed by its own inhabitants, a region at war with itself. His passion for the west deepened his insights into the frontier as human experience and forever stirred him to excesses of celebration and disgust.

The reading public saw DeVoto as an irascible and truculent figure, given to hyperbolic utterance on everything under the sun. In 1938

Edmund Wilson, not without a talent for irascibility himself, wrote a piece for the *New Republic* asking what in the world DeVoto was always so angry about. Actually, in private relations Benny was a man of exceptional kindness, sensitivity and generosity.

However, he certainly could be irascible and truculent. In the early Thirties and for some time thereafter, his *bête noire* was what he called with scorn "the literary mind." *Mark Twain's America,* his book of 1932, had combined a rich understanding of Mark Twain in the context of western folklore with a cruel attack on Van Wyck Brooks's *The Ordeal of Mark Twain* as a horrid example of the incorrigible preference of literary intellectuals for generalizations over facts. The demolition of the Brooks thesis was total, as even Brooks himself tacitly conceded, but the abusive tone denied DeVoto the approval that his cogent argument should have won him.

The Pareto flu hit Harvard in the early Thirties and provided DeVoto with sociological justification for his abhorrence of the literary mind. The local Pareto proselytizer was the biochemist L. J. Henderson, a man of powerful and stern intelligence noted for his pioneering inquiries into the physiology of blood (and also for his pink whiskers). In the Twenties Henderson had encountered the writings of the Italian economist and sociologist Vilfredo Pareto and, seeing a similarity between dynamic physical and social equilibriums, moved on from natural to social science. Henderson probably put Benny on to Pareto, and in 1932 Benny attended L.J.'s Pareto seminar. It was a brilliant group — the historian Crane Brinton, the economist Joseph Schumpeter, three promising young sociologists, George Homans, Talcott Parsons and Robert K. Merton, the questing doctor Hans Zinsser and the questing lawyer Charles P. Curtis. Curtis and Homans soon produced *An Introduction to Pareto* in 1934, and Henderson himself published *Pareto's General Sociology* the next year.

Pareto's scheme emphasized the superiority of persisting nonlogical sentiments — "residues" — to rationalizations — "derivations" — in the shaping of society. Pareto's contempt for ideology gave DeVoto what seemed for a season a perfect ally in his battle against literary intellectuals mesmerized by abstractions. In a piece in the *Saturday Review of Literature* in 1933, he hailed Pareto as the prophet of a new revelation. But in time the elaborate Paretian machinery began to weary DeVoto. By 1937 he confessed disarmingly, "I am not much of a Paretian" and asked his readers to forget his *Saturday Review* piece — "one of my unfortunate attempts to annoy certain literary people."

But Pareto hovered over his courses in 1935, and I perforce imbibed a little Paretian skepticism myself; no harm done, I think.

Benny hoped for a permanent appointment at Harvard. But James B. Conant, who succeeded Lowell as president in 1933, was inexperienced in his job and awkward in his personal relations. When Conant's elevation was announced, the ordinarily benign philosopher Alfred North Whitehead criticized the Harvard Corporation for choosing a chemist as president. "But Charles W. Eliot was a chemist," someone objected, "and a fine president." "I know," said Whitehead, "but Eliot was a *bad* chemist."

Conant, his budget shrunk by the depression, did not consider teaching composition a scholarly endeavor essential to a great university. In 1936 Benny was offered the editorship of the *Saturday Review of Literature* in New York City. He hoped this might stimulate Harvard to make a better offer. Conant said that he could continue as a lecturer without tenure, but that would be as far as he could hope to go. "In view of this fact," Conant wrote him, "I feel that I must urge you strongly to accept the position which you said had been offered to you." "Which you *said* had been offered to you" — this understandably enraged Benny. But he was trapped, and he and Avis went off disconsolately to Manhattan.

* * *

I took many more courses in history than in English. These were the great days of the Harvard history department. The historians espoused a variety of viewpoints, political as well as historiographical, but they esteemed one another and achieved a remarkable degree of affectionate collegiality (in marked contrast to the snake pit into which the department degenerated in later years). The Harvard historians of the Thirties really did represent, as Fred Merk wrote to the young diplomatic historian Richard Leopold, "not merely high scholarship but high character and personality." Leopold replied that their qualities came out "not only in their scholarship and teaching but in their character and democratic manner. . . . There is no department in any university in which a junior feels more at ease and more that he is genuinely contributing to the work of the group."

Sam Morison lectured in colonial history. He was a stylish figure, both in his way of writing history, where we all admired his urbane and colloquial prose, and, more eccentrically, in his way of being a historian. He would sometimes arrive on the lecture platform in riding boots and habit, a boutonniere on his jacket, and then proceed in a crisp, elegant manner to hold forth on the Puritans. He gave me my second and last Harvard B in the first half of his colonial history course. With great effort, I made an A in the second half.

In personal relations Morison was a shy man who concealed shyness by an aloof and imperious manner. "He went out of his way to do the friendly thing," Edmund Morgan recalled, "and it scared the pants off you. Even before he became an admiral, you felt as though he were one and you were a midshipman." Still, Dick Leopold records that he went on a first-name basis with Morison in 1948 and with Fred Merk in 1949 but not till 1959 with my father.

Merk, who succeeded Turner as the historian of the frontier, was an unassuming, almost ascetic, man but radiant with integrity and the most compelling lecturer among the American historians. One gained from him a sense of what fastidious, scrupulous, passionate scholarship was all about. In southern history Paul Buck's gentle and judicious manner masked firm convictions, a subtle and steely intelligence and a strong will. I learned much too from Charles H. Taylor's thoughtful and superbly organized course in medieval history and from Crane Brinton's exasperatingly casual lectures on European intellectual history — casual at least in presentation but with a surprising cumulative effect in inculcating a set of attitudes toward history.

*   *   *

My father continued to give his popular course on American social and intellectual history, but, working away in his study with that familiar green eyeshade, he was still mired in editing, often rewriting, volumes of the *History of American Life*. The burden increased after Dixon Ryan Fox, his co-editor, became president of Union College in 1934 and had less time for editorial duties.

My father's own volume, *The Rise of the City, 1878–1898,* came out in 1933 and set forth his influential urban interpretation of American development, designed to balance Turner's frontier interpretation. The theme, in the author's words, was "the clash between the two cultures: one static, individualistic, agricultural, the other dynamic, collectivistic, urban." The book, much praised in reviews by Felix Frankfurter and Benny DeVoto, led, however, to a distressing argument with his old teacher and friend Charles A. Beard.

Beard was then in the throes of his murky struggle with the philosophy of history — the struggle that produced later that year his provocative presidential address to the American Historical Association "Written History as an Act of Faith." "Does the world move, and, if so, in what direction?" Beard wanted history to tell him. ". . . Does it move backward toward some old arrangement, let us say, of 1928, 1896, 1815, 1789, or 1295? Or does it move forward to some other arrangement which can only be dimly divined — a capitalist dictatorship, a proletarian dictatorship, or a collectivist democracy? The last of these is my own guess."

Demanding answers to such metahistorical riddles, Beard reviewed *The Rise of the City* for the *American Historical Review* and found it wanting. After agreeable words about the coverage of a tumultuous period, he wrote, "Whether this movement and uproar meant anything then or means anything now, whether it had any center of gravity or was merely chaos floating in chaos, Professor Schlesinger does not venture to say. . . . Apparently he thinks interpretations are wrong, that none is possible, and that impressionistic eclecticism is the only resort of contemporary scholarship."

If Beard really regarded the book as "impressionistic eclecticism," my father wrote him, "I have not made clear to the most acute historical mind in America what I am about." Beard replied that he had meant nothing invidious by the phrase; "for all I know it may be all that anybody can do in history. . . . I do not want the historian to turn moralist and pontificate, but I want him to recognize that at bottom he believes the world is going around in a meaningless circle or is moving toward good or evil." My father politely rejected Beard's proposition that historians should let their guesses about the future determine their interpretation of the past. "I do not propose to be consciously concerned," he wrote to Beard, "with whether the 'damned human race' is growing worse or better." The exchange concluded with warm assurances of mutual regard. Most historians today, I think, would feel that my father had the better of the argument.

*   *   *

I never took a course with the Italian historian Gaetano Salvemini, but I owe to him a long-standing concern with the fate and future of Italian democracy. The Mussolini dictatorship had produced mixed reactions in the United States in the Twenties. Conservatives and business leaders thought Il Duce was bringing order and discipline to an unruly people, and they regarded antifascist Italians as troublemakers and radicals. Liberals condemned Mussolini as a tyrant and praised antifascists as heroes. The Sacco-Vanzetti case had brought my father friends among antifascist Italians, and he knew of Salvemini both as a distinguished historian and as a fiery enemy of fascism. In 1929, as chairman of the history department and with the department's and the dean's approval, my father sent a cable to Salvemini, then in exile in London, inviting him to come to Harvard for a semester as visiting professor.

After the invitation had gone out and before Salvemini had replied, President Lowell told my father that an influential member of the Harvard Corporation strongly objected and that the invitation must be rescinded. My father replied that the department had acted with proper authorization and that the offer could not in honor be withdrawn. Lowell, my father later surmised, may have had doubts about the propriety of his intervention. In any case, he did not pursue the matter.

The exuberant Salvemini, a man of passion, erudition, wit and unconquerable zest for life, quickly captivated Cambridge. Soon the actress Ruth Draper endowed a lectureship for him in the name of her lover, Lauro De Bosis, who had flown to his death after dropping antifascist leaflets on Rome in 1931. Salvemini, who taught at Harvard until he returned to Italy in 1948, was a familiar figure in our household when I was growing up. His wife and five children had been killed in the Messina earthquake of 1903; he had long since parted from his second wife, a Frenchwoman who lived in Paris, and he was a lonely man who enjoyed company.

George La Piana, a specialist in Catholic Church history, was another friend of my parents, and I heard much talk of the hopes Salvemini and La Piana shared for a democratic Italy. Salvemini detested Communists and papists almost as much as Fascists, and he had little use even for Benedetto Croce, whose penchant for rhetoric, he felt, had diverted liberal Italy from the concrete problems of democracy. His presence was both a joy in itself and a constant reminder of the shadows fascism was casting darkly across the world.

* * *

One took only four courses a year, and I missed such famous lecturers as C. H. McIlwain on political thought and W. L. Langer on European diplomatic history. I wish now that I had heard Joseph Schumpeter and Alvin Hansen, but, despite the depression and Bob Lamb, I was not much interested in economics.

I did see a little of the most generally revered man at Harvard in those days, Alfred North Whitehead. Whitehead, I take it, is not much read today and, when read at all, rather as a sage than as a technical philosopher (except for *Principia Mathematica*, his book with Bertrand Russell). But he was a glowing presence in Cambridge in the Thirties.

His book of 1925, *Science and the Modern World*, made a great impression on me. Whitehead, who began as a mathematician and ended as a metaphysician, had written it during his passage from the dry light of logic into the thickets of his philosophy of organism. In the historical sections of the book, he showed how the new scientific outlook had so altered the metaphysical presuppositions and the imaginative contents of the Western mind that old stimuli provoked new responses. His historical inquiry concluded with an account of the predicament in which modern physics had placed science by undermining the old certitudes of scientific materialism.

This was the history of ideas in the grand style, subtle, civilized and richly suggestive. Along the path were strewn marvelous side remarks: for example, "The greatest invention of the nineteenth century was the invention of the method of invention." He usefully identified what he called the Fallacy of Misplaced Concreteness — that is, the fatal error of mistaking ideology for reality. "The intolerant use of abstractions," he wrote, "is the major vice of the intellect." It is also the major vice of politics. The Fallacy of Misplaced Concreteness has underlain the horrible sacrifice of humanity to abstractions that has cursed the twentieth century.

From time to time his able and underrated son, Thomas North Whitehead, a professor at the Harvard Business School, invited students over for an evening with his father and mother. These were taxing but fascinating occasions, greatly relieved by the lively presence of the younger Whitehead's stepdaughter Sheila Dehn, who later married the historian Myron Gilmore. The older Mrs. Whitehead, once beloved by Russell and filled with trenchant reminiscences about "Bertie," was a formidable and quite unpredictable, very British lady. And I was at once awed and beguiled by the old philosopher, so courteous in manner and unaffected in speech, his blue eyes snapping and his imperturbable benevolence concealing a capacity for sharp insight. Perry Miller once told me that Whitehead was another Emerson, "only harder headed and cleverer." Though I doubt that anyone was harder headed and cleverer than Emerson, I can see Miller's point. Whitehead was one of those whose perceptions were far more penetrating than his system.

I attended Whitehead's last lecture in May 1936. He concluded by saying, "Civilizations die of boredom."

*　　*　　*

Boredom arose in my third undergraduate year. I began in the autumn of 1936 — or at least so I recalled in my journal the following May — with "an unprecedented sense of anticipation. I felt overflowing with potency, with a capacity to accomplish things. What things, I did not know; but the conviction that they were around the corner was pretty firm." In the spring I gloomily decided that I had learned nothing, accomplished nothing: "I have exhausted after two years most of what Harvard has to give me at this time." I wished that it were my last year.

The trouble with universities, I noted in my journal, was that they limited the varieties of experience. Yet "the only knowledge worth anything is grounded in experience. . . . The ivory tower is a pretty adequate metaphor. A college professor is rather well insulated from most of the currents which electrify vital life. . . . The range of experience here in Cambridge is too confined to increase my knowledge very much more, except in a purely tape-measure sense. I need a different life, experience of a different character, if I am to grow."

Luckily I was rescued from boredom in my last undergraduate year by a forgotten nineteenth-century American intellectual named Orestes Augustus Brownson. Casting about for a subject for my senior honors essay, I first thought of Brooks Adams, Henry's brilliant and eccentric brother. My father then suggested that I look at the article on Brownson in the *Dictionary of American Biography*. I discovered that Brownson had lived a diverse and controversial life, that his writings, while voluminous, were conveniently available and that he had thus far been overlooked in the new surge of interest in the flowering of New England.

I checked with Perry Miller, who was spending the year in London. He wrote that he was "strongly and emphatically on the side of Brownson." Brownson might not have as first rate a mind as Adams, Perry said, but he was more in the thick of things and through him one could get at a great deal of the thought of the time. (He added disarmingly, "One of the few absolutely definite pleasures about coming back to the mines next year will be being tutored by you again.")

Brownson was one of those figures who had bulked large in his day and then slipped into oblivion. "Riverside Statue Stumps Historians" was a headline in the ordinarily omniscient *New York Times* in July 1937. Someone had found rolling down Riverside Drive in New York City a bronze head of Brownson that a gang of boys had knocked off its pedestal in Riverside Park. "A casual canvass of local historians, literary minds, and young men fresh from study at college," the *Times* reported, "showed that Brownson was unknown to modern minds."

Yet he had cut quite a figure in his day. In the course of a long and stormy life, Brownson took almost every side of every hot question and was a sledgehammer controversialist at every step along his tempestuous path. He began as a Calvinist minister, moved on to Universalism and then Unitarianism, became a preacher to the working classes, met Emerson and joined the Transcendentalist Club, met George Bancroft, President Martin Van Buren's man in Massachusetts, and received a government job, and meanwhile established a hard-hitting but erudite magazine, the *Boston Quarterly Review*.

His 1840 piece "The Laboring Classes" was a thwacking attack on capitalism, a system whose manifest injustices, Brownson wrote, must lead to that "most dreaded of all wars, the war of the poor against the rich, a war which, however long it may be delayed, will come, and come with all its horrors." Our duty, he continued, was "to emancipate the proletaries, as the past has emancipated the slaves." This prediction of class war and proletarian revolution came eight years before *The Communist Manifesto* and was published in the midst of the rancorous "Tippecanoe and Tyler Too" presidential campaign. The Whig press seized on this article by a Democratic officeholder as a revelation of the secret purposes of the Van Buren administration. "Everybody is loud in their denunciation of him," Van Buren's secretary of the treasury wrote to Bancroft. "Why is he kept there? Why?"

Brownson's journey was far from over. From the far left in religion and politics he soon swung to the far right, joining the Catholic Church in 1844 and supporting the presidential hopes of John C. Calhoun. Though he remained a Catholic, he was a restless spirit within the fold, feuding with prelates and Irish Catholics at home and with Cardinal Newman in Britain.

In his day he won both grudging respect for his "transparent and forcible prose" (James Russell Lowell) and condescending amusement over the changeability of his opinions. "No man has ever equalled Mr. Brownson," wrote Dr. James Freeman Clarke, the Unitarian divine, "in the ability with which he has refuted his own arguments." Lowell, while placing him just after Emerson and Bronson Alcott in *A Fable for Critics*, went on:

> He shifts quite about, then proceeds to expound,
> That 'tis merely the earth, not himself, that turns round,
> And wishes it clearly impressed on your mind
> That the weathercock rules and not follows the wind;
> Proving first, then as deftly confuting each side,
> With no doctrine pleased that's not somewhere denied,
> He lays the denier away on the shelf
> And then — down beside him lies gravely himself.

He was a rich subject for a senior thesis. Widener Library, that fabulous aid to scholarship, had the full run of the magazines he edited (and mostly wrote) as well as the devotional labors of his son — a three-volume biography and twenty volumes of his collected writings. Immersion in Brownson became immersion in the theology, philosophy, politics and intellectual ferment of the nineteenth century in America. One also felt the pathos of modernity in this stormy pilgrim, this intellectually displaced person wandering passionately from one system to another until he came to relative rest in the historic certitudes of the Catholic Church. And his life touched contemporary nerves — from the antagonisms of capital and labor to the place of Catholics in American society, from the nature of American culture to the death of God. History and Lit gave the result a *summa*, and Miller and my father encouraged me to turn it into a book.

*   *   *

The test of education, thought Henry Adams, Harvard '58 (1858, that is), is whether students are taught the things they need to know in order to deal with an uncontrollably changing world. In 1904, looking back to what he had been as a Harvard freshman half a century earlier, Adams decided that the boy he was in 1854 stood nearer to the thought of year 1 than to the thought of the twentieth century. "The education he had received," he wrote of himself, "bore little relation to the education he needed." He pronounced Harvard College "a negative force." In 1910 Henry James, after the funeral service for his brother, William, in Harvard's Appleton Chapel, observed dryly that Harvard, "meagre mother, did for him — the best that Harvard can."

In the Thirties Harvard College, for me at least, was, despite *longueurs,* a nourishing mother and a positive force. I felt on the whole happy about the things I had learned. But one could not forget the brevity as well as the velocity of American history. When I graduated in June 1938, I watched the fiftieth reunion class, venerable men, white-haired, leaning on canes, stumbling along, old, they seemed to us, as the hills. After all, they were members of the Harvard Class of 1888.

* * *

To transform the honors essay into a book, I had to inspect the Brownson papers at Notre Dame University. The summer of 1938 was hot in South Bend, Indiana. I stayed in an old-fashioned drummers' hotel, with ghastly rubber plants in the lobby and an icewater tap in the bathroom. The Spanish Civil War was raging, and the Catholic Church, then a monolithically right-wing institution, was militantly pro-Franco. One night I crept off circumspectly to see Henry Fonda and Madeleine Carroll in Walter Wanger's pro-Loyalist movie *Blockade* in an empty theater.

Father Thomas T. McAvoy, the Notre Dame archivist, was most helpful. Research in manuscripts, I discovered, is boundless pleasure. There is nothing like the sense of immediate contact with personality one gets from reading someone's letters, especially when they are written by hand, as they were in the nineteenth century. Time, I find, passes more quickly in archives than almost anywhere else.

In those days one had to take notes laboriously by pencil or pen. Libraries forbade the typewriter lest the clatter disturb other researchers. I came upon much of interest in Brownson's papers and incorporated the new findings in my text.

At Benny DeVoto's suggestion, I sent the manuscript along to his publisher, Little, Brown of Boston. At Benny's recommendation, it was accepted. Having received a Charles and Julia Henry Fellowship for a year of study at Oxford or Cambridge, I was about to depart for England. My overburdened father selflessly undertook to see the book through the press.

His faithful secretary and research assistant, Elizabeth Hoxie, found an excessive number of inaccurate quotations and citations, and my father's paternal regard was sorely tried. "You apparently need," he wrote at one point, "the hard boiled discipline of a seminar." Discovering that I had neglected to consult the papers in New York of Isaac T. Hecker, Brownson's protégé and founder of the Paulist order, he sternly rebuked me: "I do not see how you could have had such a blind spot." (I explained that Father McAvoy had said that there was little of value about Brownson in the Hecker papers.) He concluded, as he wrote me in January 1939, "that the easiest way to be an author is to reside outside the country when the book is going through the press." Having expressed his feelings, he did not dwell on them and moved on to other matters — one reason that he was such a satisfactory father.

A contretemps developed over Little, Brown's hope that the book might be taken by the Catholic Book Club. Father James M. Gillis, editor of the *Catholic World,* thought the manuscript "extraordinarily well done" but "could not approve of the book being chosen for The Catholic Book Club" unless certain phrases were modified or omitted. Some of the objections were doctrinal. Others — references to Brownson's taste for whiskey as an old man and to his daughter calling him "you brutal tyrant" — smacked, Father Gillis thought, of "Lytton Strachey and the modern school that thinks it advisable to snatch up odds and ends of dialogue or incident to give pep to their writing."

The publisher, regarding a life of Orestes Brownson as a chancy proposition and hoping strongly for a book club selection, argued for conciliation. My father showed diplomatic skill in meeting the objections without sacrificing the points. "I particularly hated to supplant your phrase 'with senile cunning' with my phrase 'with offended dignity,'" he wrote. "But 1500 Catholics can't be wrong." The club adopted the book.

Orestes A. Brownson: A Pilgrim's Progress appeared in April 1939. It received kindly reviews. Henry Steele Commager in the *New York Times Book Review* dissented from some of my assessments of Brownson but called the study "masterly" with "technical brilliance — a sure control of materials, an effective handling of background, a skillful use of colors and a certain bravura of execution." The book, he generously said, announced "a new and distinguished talent in the field of historical portraiture." Most thrilling was a handwritten letter from Charles A. Beard himself in which he said he had read the book straight through in one day "and when I laid it down in the evening — Mary Beard my witness — I exclaimed 'Real thinking in American history writing at last, thank God!'"

The other senior honors essay to achieve trade publication in these years was written by a young concentrator in government, two years behind me, whom I knew only by sight in the Yard — *Why England*

Slept by John F. Kennedy '40. His book, published a year after mine, did a good deal better in the bookshops.

* * *

In the meantime, my life had taken a new turn. Like most undergraduates, I was preoccupied with sex. An inordinate amount of time (and, in my journal, space) went to worrying about girls and how to win them. The nature of this concern would prove, I daresay, incomprehensible to later generations, to whom, according to *Harvard Magazine* in 1999, "condoms are distributed like mints during Freshman Week."

In the prim Thirties, Harvard's strict parietal code, especially the third-person-in-a-room rule, threw major obstacles in the way of sexual exploration. We inexperienced young fellows talked among ourselves of 'necking' — physical contact from the neck up — and yearned for 'petting' — physical contact from the neck down. The bolder boasted of 'petting to climax.' We spent more hours figuring how to kiss girls than undergraduates today spend getting them into bed. Whether this represents a gain for progress, I do not know.

I kept falling for a succession of girls, and then, after a few months, would wonder what I had ever seen in them. "It is exceedingly dispiriting," I noted in my journal, "to find that the girl you've had in your mind as the model of her sex turns out to be almost commonplace." This situation was remedied in my senior year when, for the first time, I fell seriously in love. Between them, Orestes Brownson and Marian Cannon rescued my last undergraduate year from doldrums and boredom.

Marian was one of the four daughters of Walter Bradford Cannon, the distinguished physiologist, and Cornelia James Cannon, a novelist and all-purpose reformer. I was introduced to the Cannon household as a sophomore by a cousin whom I had greatly but fleetingly fancied. I met Marian in the spring of my junior year. She was a lively brunette, twenty-four years old (I was nineteen), very intelligent, very pretty, an artist and a writer of children's books, with sparkling dark eyes, definite opinions, snappy comebacks and cosmopolitan experience.

Her older sister Wilma was married to the Sinologist John K. Fairbank. I had encountered the Fairbanks in Peking in 1933 when John was working on his Oxford Ph.D. dissertation on the Chinese Maritime Customs Service. After Marian graduated from Radcliffe in

1934, she accompanied the Fairbanks on a research tour of the treaty ports along the South China coast. They spent the spring of 1935 in Peking. Marian painted with Chinese instructors and became almost engaged, her younger sister Helen told me, to a brilliant young diplomat in the American embassy named John Paton Davies, Jr. On her return to the United States, Marian joined the staff of the Institute of Pacific Relations in New York. Now she had come back to Cambridge to concentrate on painting and to wait for John Davies.

The Cannons lived in a rambling gray frame house on Frisbie Place, behind what was then called the Germanic Museum. Like my parents, they had come from the middle west — in their case, Minnesota — and had remained defiantly faithful to midwestern values, especially plain living and public schools. In the summer they retreated to a farm on a hilltop in Franklin, New Hampshire, where Mrs. Cannon long resisted the introduction of decadent modern conveniences like electricity and plumbing.

The elder Cannons had gone as undergraduates to Harvard and Radcliffe. A member of the class of 1896, Walter Cannon was so impressed by William James that he thought of shifting his field from biology to philosophy. "Don't do it," James said. "You will be filling your belly with east wind," and encouraged him to go on to the Harvard Medical School. There, in his first year, Cannon discovered that the newfangled X-ray could be used to illuminate the workings of the digestive system. It was he who invented the bismuth and barium meals that enable doctors to trace the passage of food through the stomach and intestines.

Dr. Cannon's subsequent experiments on the physiological impact of emotion opened up a new field of investigation. He saw the human organism as an interdependent whole rather than as a collection of specialized parts. His book of 1915, *Bodily Changes in Pain, Hunger, Fear, and Rage,* helped lay the foundations for psychosomatic medicine and incidentally popularized the word "adrenaline." Studies of shell shock conducted in France during the Great War deepened his understanding of the effects of traumatic episodes on the nervous system. In 1926 he coined the term "homeostasis" to describe the self-regulatory processes by which corrective reactions take place in the human body when the stable state is threatened. He elaborated on this idea in 1932 in *The Wisdom of the Body* (a title appropriated sixty-five years later, with due attribution, by Dr. Sherwin Nuland). In a stimulating epilogue, Cannon suggested that comparable homeostasis might regulate the social organism.

He was internationally respected. Ivan Pavlov, the great Russian physiologist, came to Boston for the International Physiological Congress and took a holiday with the Cannons in their New Hampshire *dacha*. Fellow scientists called Cannon "the Claude Bernard of American physiology" and expected him to win a Nobel Prize (which, though several times nominated, he for some reason never did).

In politics, Cannon was rather conservative, mistrustful of the too-smooth FDR and his too-certain New Dealers. In 1936 he voted for Alf Landon. But the Spanish physiologist Juan Negrín was a good friend, and visits to Spain made Cannon an enthusiastic partisan of the republic. After Franco began his revolution in 1936 and Negrín became premier of the republican government in May 1937, Cannon, as chairman of the Medical Bureau to Aid Spanish Democracy, helped send the Loyalists more than a million dollars' ($12 million in fin-de-siècle currency) worth of medicine, hospital equipment and ambulances. This gained him an undeserved reputation as a radical, if not a red, which he endured stoically.

✶   *   *

Though famous in scientific circles, Cannon cut a shy, kindly, diffident, patient figure in his own house, overwhelmed by the seven strong-minded women who surrounded him — his four outspoken and irreverent daughters, his two capable sisters, Ida, a pioneer medical social worker, and Bernice, proprietor of the children's store in Harvard Square, and above all his vital, opinionated, incorrigible wife, Cornelia. The only son, Bradford, later an eminent plastic surgeon, developed a mask of geniality that enabled him to pursue his own interests. The Cannon dinner table was a swirl of spirited female talk, laws laid down, personalities discussed and dismissed, judgments freely rendered, all spiraling up into gales of laughter.

Mrs. Cannon, Radcliffe '99, had attended William James's classes with Gertrude Stein '97, who remained a friend. When she married Walter Cannon in 1901, they spent their honeymoon paddling along the upper Mississippi in a birchbark canoe, then explored what is now Glacier National Park. Informed that the mountain at the top of Lake McDonald was "the worst" in the region and had never been climbed, they decided to climb it, and did so, with considerable difficulty and risk. They were rewarded when the peak was named Cannon Mountain.

In her charming book of 1979, *Snatched from Oblivion*, Marian Cannon Schlesinger draws a vivid portrait of her mother. Cornelia Cannon's energy was boundless, her curiosity tireless, her activity endless. She was short, plump, bustling, brusquely disdainful of frocks and frills, despising all stigmata of worldliness, her hair and dress in shapeless, no-nonsense Boston bluestocking style. She flung herself manically into one agitation after another, writing, speaking, reforming, lobbying, traveling. She preceded my mother as the scourge of the Cambridge School Committee. Her novel *Red Rust,* about the struggle of Swedish wheat farmers in Minnesota against the blight of rust, was a best seller in 1928. She was a birth control zealot at a time and in a place where birth control was illegal. In later years she would travel abroad with a bag full of condoms to distribute along the way. She was an incurable meddler. Reversing Lord Chesterfield, she would cheerfully say, "Whatever is worth doing is worth doing badly."

I fear I never fully appreciated her. I was as opinionated as she was, and, since I took her flip judgments far too seriously, we were in chronic contention. I did not understand that her slaphappy flow was intended mostly to amuse and provoke. "If I had to *prove* every statement I make," she once wrote, "I should be stricken dumb for life!" Nor did she brood over disagreement. "Don't worry about my being 'upset' at your refusal," she told one daughter. ". . . . I shall simply have a dozen more suggestions to take its place. The acceptance of my wild ideas never worries me. All I ask is to retain the freedom to *make* them."

Still, she did her damnedest to form her daughters in her own image. She bred in them a sense of superiority to all other children. The Cannon family was enough: Why go outside it? The Cannon way of life, as John Fairbank warned me one evening in August 1938, was for the Cannons, despite their theoretical "live and let live" talk, the *only* way of life. Part of this was defensive: having been segregated for so long, the girls fell back on the cult of family to escape the insecurity they felt in the world outside. In an age obsessed by the breakdown of family life, it is useful to remember that families can also be too self-contained.

One of Dr. Cannon's close friends was his Harvard Medical School colleague Dr. Harvey Cushing, the famed neurosurgeon. They hiked together and climbed mountains together, and Cannon joined Cushing's Harvard Hospital Unit in France during the Great War. Cushing's three daughters were about the same age as the four Cannon girls. But their mothers had very different aspirations. Mrs. Cannon wanted her daughters to be nonfashionable, sensible, useful women and to marry professors. Mrs. Cushing wanted hers to be fashionable, glamorous, doting women and to marry millionaires. In later years the lovely and perfectly intelligent Cushing girls — Minnie Fosburgh (formerly Mrs. Vincent Astor), Betsey Whitney (Mrs. John Hay Whitney, formerly Mrs. James Roosevelt) and Babe Paley (Mrs. William Paley, formerly Mrs. Stanley Mortimer) — became good friends of mine, and I used to wonder at the widely divergent trajectories of life traced by the daughters of two great doctors who were themselves so intimately allied. Neither trajectory, by the way, was destined to bring great happiness.

* * *

"If I ever fell in love at first sight," I wrote in my journal in May 1937, "it was with Marian Cannon last week." But when I said this to Helen Cannon, she informed me that Marian had gone to meet John Davies, back on home leave, and that they would probably be married in June. In fact, the meeting with Davies resulted in a suspension or termination of their engagement.

I now began a long pursuit. Besides the difference in age, there were other obstacles to overcome. Marian had returned from the "real" world with scorn for academics. June 1937: "she represents the most baffling girl and the most resounding challenge I have yet faced. All my ingenuity barely sufficed to keep her entertained for a couple of hours. Her career has given her such a hard shell that it is damned hard to draw blood. And her prejudice against academic life, of which I seem to her so perfect an example, increases her indifference."

I persisted through the summer and autumn of 1937. She began to soften. In November she invited me for a weekend at the Cannon homestead in Franklin along with the Fairbanks, the historian Myron Gilmore and Barbara Runkle, who later married Sir William Hawthorne, the master of Churchill College in Cambridge. I was suitably abashed by the adult company, with their easy knowledge and easy banter, and felt, I wrote in my journal, "like a bush leaguer given his first trial in the majors." But perseverance began to pay off. By the time of the Yale game, we were discussing the pros and cons of marriage. I was now in so giddy a state that I virtually gave up my journal. "It seemed futile," I wrote, "to try to describe happiness when words were so inadequate and expression served only to cheapen."

Courtship had its vicissitudes. I was immature; she was doubtful; we both had strong egos. We fought, parted and came together again. In early September 1938 I left for England to take up the Henry Fellowship. Marian came down to see me off. We dined at the Canari d'Or, went to the Swing Club on West Fifty-second Street and spent the night warily at the Lexington Hotel — warily because in those puritanical days the house dick was expected to break in on unmarried couples in hotel bedrooms.

The next morning we crossed the Hudson River to Hoboken where I boarded the Dutch liner the *Nieuw Amsterdam* on its maiden voyage. Farewells were painful. "The prospect of not seeing her for ten months, which is precisely the length of time we have really known each other, fills me with horror."

10

The Twilight Year

ASIDE FROM THE PANGS of parting, I embarked with high anticipation. A year in Europe would be an adventure. The Henry Fellowship was named for Sir Charles Henry, a wealthy metal broker who became a backer of Lloyd George and, in consequence, a baronet. Lady
Henry was Julia Lewisohn of New York. Their only son was killed
in the Great War; Sir Charles died soon thereafter; Lady Henry
founded the fellowship in 1930 "in the earnest hope and desire of
cementing the bonds of friendship between the British Empire and
the United States." Britons were offered a year at Harvard or Yale;
Americans, at Oxford or Cambridge.

I chose Cambridge because it attracted fewer Americans than Oxford and would therefore, I thought, give me no choice but to frater-
nize with the natives. After consultation, I chose Peterhouse among
the Cambridge colleges because of its reputation for historical studies. Peterhouse was also the oldest and the smallest college and was
said to have the finest kitchen and wine cellar. The Henry stipend was
then £500 — with the prewar pound pegged at $4.83, a generous
sum. Twenty-four hundred dollars a year in the Thirties was the equivalent of around $27,000 at the end of the century. Long vacations
would provide ample time for exploration of the continent.

* * *

European acrimonies were something that I, like most Americans
in 1938, regarded with detachment. Hitler was on the move: he had
already seized Austria in March 1938, six months earlier, and by September was making passes at Czechoslovakia. Though I fervently
wanted the European democracies to do something to stop Nazi Germany, I remained a stout isolationist and supposed the United States
to be immune from European convulsions.

The *Nieuw Amsterdam* arrived in Plymouth on September 12, 1938,
just as Hitler, in one of his quasi-hysterical speeches, was demanding
self-determination for the Sudetendeutsch, the German-speaking in-

habitants of Czechoslovakia. I went on to London staying, as in 1934, at Carlton Mansions in Bloomsbury. The next night, I joined a thousand people gathering along Whitehall opposite 10 Downing Street, where Neville Chamberlain, the British prime minister, had called a cabinet meeting to discuss the Czech crisis. The crowd was silent, somber and apprehensive. The next morning, as, true to Boy Scout training, I helped a decrepit old man across a street, he told me with great vehemence that it was America's duty to join Britain and France in a short, sharp war to crush Hitler and Mussolini. I noted smugly in my journal, "I shall, for the moment, occupy myself otherwise."

On September 15 Chamberlain flew to Germany. Pursuing his policy of appeasement, a word that had yet to acquire the disastrous connotation it would soon earn, Chamberlain agreed to press the Czech government to yield to Hitler's terms. "It is clear," I wrote on the twenty-first, "that even as an act of expediency [the partition of Czechoslovakia] is stupid and short-sighted, unless it is considered to be directed only to save the interests of Chamberlain and his class. . . . They are more favorable to fascism than communism and probably believe that Germany furnishes the last bulwark against communism in central Europe." This last thought I had from the diplomatic historian C. K. Webster, a friend of my father, who had kindly invited me for tea.

Americans had heard about 'the Cliveden set,' and my journal at this time had its share of Anglophobic comments about the British upper class — "their slick fatuousness in conversation and their self-confident smoothness in manner gained from years of doing the same thing always the same way." On the *Nieuw Amsterdam*, I had prepared myself by reading a book called *With Malice Toward Some*, Margaret Halsey's mischievous account of a year in England, and I used to repeat (boringly) her comment that British conversation was like playing very good tennis without a ball. Still, like most Americans, I had mixed feelings about Britain and was a soft touch, then and ever since, for British high style. After seeing (twice in a week) Herbert Farjeon's witty intimate revue *Nine Sharp*, I announced to myself that "in two hours I was almost reconciled to England."

Soon I went to Oxford to spend a night with Denis and Olwen Brogan. After an excellent dinner, we drank fifty-year-old Madeira till midnight. Brogan, I noted, was so furious about Chamberlain that "he even looked forward to a cabinet headed by Winston Churchill. . . . Churchill, though utterly unprincipled, is at least a man of vigor and intelligence." Churchill then had the reputation of a reckless and unreliable politician; Brogan's were the first favorable words I had ever heard about him. But Brogan was not optimistic about Churchill's prospects. "You have no idea," he told me, "how completely England is in the grip of good form. Truth is actively disliked."

D. W. Brogan, a Scotsman of Irish extraction, knew more about both the United States and France than any other inhabitant of the British Isles. He combined a fantastic memory for detail with a capacity for enlightening generalization. He was generous, learned, pungent, witty, eloquent and highly inventive in denunciation. A passionate liberal democrat, he detested both fascism and communism. In later years he had trouble holding his liquor, but a night befuddled by booze could not stop him from dashing off a brilliant article or book review the next morning. He had been a dear friend of my father, whom he looked on as his American patron (as I tried years later to be for his talented sons), and he became a dear friend and my British patron.

* * *

Chadbourne Gilpatric was now a Rhodes scholar at Balliol, and we had arranged to travel to Ireland in the interval before term began at Oxford and Cambridge. Our journey from Oxford to Holyhead in Wales to catch the boat across the Irish Sea involved changes of trains and much conversation with other travelers stranded in barren, ill-lit stations. War was the universal preoccupation. One woman said to us through clenched teeth, "I think Chamberlain is a swine."

At the Rugby stopover we had time to venture into town, and Gilpatric, with characteristic audacity, knocked on doors to find a house with a radio so we could hear the evening news. The BBC was unrelievedly gloomy. After an official announcement of preparations for hospital care in case of air raids, the man of the house, silent up to that point, muttered dourly, "They'll be making our coffins next."

The anticipation of war in Europe was followed by the report of a hurricane in America killing seven hundred people and devastating the New England coast along which Gil and I had sailed so cheerfully in earlier summers. (Soon a letter from my mother, who had been caught in the storm, described the scene: "It looked as if some giant in great rage had stalked through the countryside pulling up the great beautiful trees with one hand and beating down everything he could with the other.")

The hurricane, the BBC added, was racing across the Atlantic. By two in the morning, when we arrived in Holyhead, the sea was running high, and the wind was stiff and gusty. It was my roughest boat trip since the typhoon off Macao. Most passengers were horribly sick. After five hours of misery on the Irish Sea, we put in at Kingstown, as it was then called, Dun Laoghaire now, and went on to Dublin.

I was enchanted by the elegant if dilapidated squares in Dublin and disappointed by the productions at the Abbey and Gate theaters. On to Killarney, where on September 27 we spent a breathtakingly beautiful day along the Killarney lakes and Dingle Bay. But the ever more grim news from Czechoslovakia dominated our thoughts. That evening we listened to Chamberlain's radio talk about the "quarrel in a faraway country between people of whom we know nothing."

His tone was mournful and fatalistic, as if preparing for the worst. Feeling too far from the action, we cut the trip short and returned to England. I arrived in London on the twenty-ninth as Chamberlain was leaving for Munich. Men were digging trenches in Bloomsbury Square and piling sandbags against basement windows. A notice posted at Carlton Mansions told us where to get gas masks, adding helpfully that there was an air raid shelter at 10 Bedford Place. Underground stations were closed because of "structural alterations" — i.e., turning the tubes into air raid shelters.

I went that evening to see Robert E. Sherwood's antiwar play *Idiot's Delight*. The fast-talking Lee Tracy, a favorite actor of mine, played the sardonic song-and-dance man. Sherwood's lines about the impossibility of war, then its insanity, then its imminence, had frightful relevance, and the air raid that ended the play left the audience, including me, somewhat shattered. As the rattled crowd left the theater, newsboys on the Strand were shouting something — I couldn't quite make it out. At that scary moment, every unintelligible cry became a matter of supreme importance. We clutched for newspapers. Headlines told the story: agreement had been reached at Munich — "for the moment heartening and cause for rejoicing," I wrote later that night, "but on reflection chilling and cause for indignation." The immediate crisis was over. The real crisis waited darkly in the wings.

"I suspect," I wrote home on October 4, "that in six months Germany and Russia will make a non-aggression pact. When Germany prepares to fight again, it will whip Great Britain and France unless the United States steps in. And, if I thought the Chamberlain government was at all representative of the English people, I should hope most strongly that the U.S. keeps out."

*   *   *

After the Munich trauma, I looked to the restorative tranquility of the English countryside. Gil recommended Amberley in Sussex and a pub called the Black Horse. The village was pictorially charming, plausibly medieval (even to the plumbing), with stone houses, thatched roofs and glum and laconic inhabitants. I took long walks across the downs, climbing hills to watch green farms rolling away to the horizon and the sea shining in the distance. I ate (very badly) at the pub, read through a pile of books and at times wandered on the downs at night, where the pale light of a full moon cast sharper shadows than the sun in the morning, giving the silent village a ghostly, flickering charm. I do not recall that I saw the great house of Lady Emmet, though in later years, when the circularity of life involved me with the Emmetry (as Henry James denominated the tribe), I heard a good deal about it.

It was now time to go on to Cambridge. My debut was not propitious. A letter from the authorities at Peterhouse had assigned me to rooms, not in the college itself, but in lodgings in 16 Fitzwilliam Street, around the corner. Staggering under the weight of two heavy suitcases, I presented myself at the Fitzwilliam Street digs. After a long delay, a man answered my ring, expressed respectful surprise that I should have come to Cambridge a day early and inquired whether I had my tutor's permission to be there. I said that I had not asked anyone's permission and that it never occurred to me that a penalty attached to arriving too early — too late, perhaps, but too early?

This was my first brush with the Oxbridge code. Far more rigid in 1938 than in the decadent postwar years, the rules called for the wearing of gowns in dining hall, at lectures and after dark; curfew required the return to one's rooms by midnight, at risk of proctors, reprimands and fines. After the freedom of Harvard, I felt almost as if I were back in boarding school.

As the porter prepared, I thought, to shut the door in my face, I hastily summoned up what capacity I had for indignation and persuasion. Bob Fleet, who turned out to be a genial chap, relented and showed me to my rooms — a large and comfortable downstairs sitting room and an upstairs bedroom. In the midst of the tour of inspection a pleasant-looking young man with glasses, a somewhat saturnine expression and an impressive air of professional efficiency introduced himself. His name, he said, was Charles Wintour, and his was the sitting room next door.

Though he seemed a quintessential Britisher, he had, it turned out, spent the summer in the United States and had actually hitchhiked his way across the continent. He was, he added modestly, editor of *Granta*. This disclosure failed to move me as much as it should have done, since I had never heard of *Granta*, and I asked whether he could show me a copy (of the newspaper? magazine?). He produced a rather slim publication with a light green cover and solicited my frank reaction.

Granta was then an undergraduate weekly, quite different from the pretentious highbrow magazine published under the same name at the end of the century. As I read through my first issue, it seemed to me an unstable combination of the undergraduate journals I had known at the other Cambridge: the *Advocate*, the *Lampoon*, a so-called funny magazine, which indeed the *Granta* had parodied the year before, even touches of the *Crimson*.

I was a brash young man in those days, and I shortly gave my housemate a memorandum setting forth in confident language the manifold shortcomings and defects not only of *Granta*, but, since by then I had examined its two competitors, *Varsity* and *Gownsman*, of British undergraduate journalism in general. Charles Wintour responded with brisk but somewhat enigmatic courtesy and showed the memorandum to his colleagues. Soon I was invited to attend a meeting of the editorial board and challenged to write articles.

Rooming next to Charles was a great stroke of luck — "a man after my own heart," I wrote in my journal; "i.e., inquiring, skeptical, sensitive to relationships among people and politically adept at influencing them, flexible, vigorous." Despite his very British appearance and style, Charles was an Americanophile. He took me under his wing, acted as advance man and publicity agent, opened doors throughout the university, put me on the inside track and was instrumental in making what became for me a memorable year.

In two weeks I wrote to my parents, "I have met more people and gotten involved in more things than would have been likely in two months at Harvard." By November: "I actually know more campus big shots than I ever did at Harvard." Unlike Harvard, notorious for its indifference to foreigners, Cambridge, I thought, was "indecently hospitable." *Granta* introduced me to Eric Hobsbawm, a brilliant Marxist historian; to Ronald Searle, the wonderful cartoonist who, after four years in unimaginably brutal circumstances as a Japanese prisoner of war, became the merry chronicler of St. Trinian's; to Pieter Keuneman, an impressive import from Ceylon, half-Dutch, half-Cingalese, a large, rollicking man who combined Communist politics with a vigorous enjoyment of the pleasures of life.

I spent a good deal of time on *Granta* during the autumn. In an effort to liven up Cambridge journalism, Wintour and I invented a character named A. G. Case (A. Glandular Case in private), who contributed occasional pieces filled with insulting comment about the other undergraduate journals. One day we ran into a columnist from one of our rivals at a crowded sherry party and, pointing vaguely to the far corner of the room, remarked, "Ah, there's A. G. Case." We were rewarded when a social note validated Case's existence in our competitor's next issue.

I wrote about the London theater, undergraduate mores and even tried my hand at poetry. My attempt to render "Good King Wenceslas" as if written by T. S. Eliot was illustrated by Ronald Searle. Conscripted to become *Granta*'s film critic, I engaged in a carefully premeditated controversy with a fellow American who was serving as film critic for the *Gownsman*. That was Herbert Warren Wind, Yale '37, then of Jesus College, in later years to join the *New Yorker* and to become America's best writer on golf and tennis.

At the end of November I wrote home, "I was offered the editorship of the *Granta* for next term this week but turned it down. Next term I intend to work a great deal more." This intention, alas, was not to be fulfilled. As for *Granta*, Eric Hobsbawm became the next editor.

*   *   *

I liked Peterhouse. The college had been founded in 1284, and the great hall, though altered through the years, was six and a half centuries old. In 1588, the year of the Spanish Armada, Peterhouse was already older than Harvard was in 1938. The stately court, with its gabled buildings and oriel windows, completed in the eighteenth century, was filled with history and charm. The college boasted its own Deer Park, a lovely shaded expanse of green. The church of Little St. Mary's on the north side had a monument, erected in 1736, to the Reverend Godfrey Washington, a fellow of Peterhouse; it was claimed that the American flag was borrowed, heraldic eagle and all, from the Washington family's armorial bearings. We dined very well in the hall, and college servants brought around excellent luncheons when we wished to entertain in digs. The wine cellar lived up to advance notices.

In later years Peterhouse became a hotbed of political reaction. When my son Stephen spent a year there in the Sixties, the dominating figure was the right-wing history fellow Maurice Cowling. Indeed, the college swung so far to the right that its master in the Seventies,

Hugh Trevor-Roper, the brilliant and acerbic historian, not at all a man of the left, once told me, "You won't believe it, but the fellows at Peterhouse regard *me* as a dangerous radical." Trevor-Roper had a stormy time at Peterhouse. Someone asked him, "Didn't the fellows know what they were getting when they elected you?" "No, they didn't," said Trevor-Roper, "and that shows what a parochial and provincial lot they are."

That was a very different Peterhouse from the college I knew in the Thirties. Harold Temperley, an influential diplomatic historian, was master. He was hospitable and happy to show off signed portraits of Wilson and Clemenceau and other relics of Versailles, but I did not find him very stimulating. The astute Christian historian and adroit academic intriguer Herbert Butterfield, who as master in the Fifties and Sixties turned the college to the right, was on leave in the autumn term. He was a courteous man whom I did not know well.

I liked the political scientist Ernest Barker. He was a proud and doughty old Yorkshireman, a sturdy Liberal, honest, friendly, open-minded and unpretentious, who invited me to meals, served the best beer I had in England and revealed an unexpected enthusiasm for the writings of Damon Runyon. Barker was beginning his last year, but he very kindly permitted me to read with him.

I had the great luck to have as supervisor Michael M. Postan, the professor of economic history. Munia Postan was nominally a medievalist. He had a lively and wide-ranging mind, penetrating analytic intelligence, a quite un-English interest in social science theory and in historical method, encyclopedic knowledge, scathing wit, boundless enthusiasm and vitality, great charm and a mysterious and variably explained Russian past. He was married to another significant medieval historian, Eileen Power, who taught at the London School of Economics, where she was said to combine the industry of a bee with the grace of a butterfly. A charming woman, ten years older than Postan, she died in 1940, and Munia later married Lady Cynthia Keppel, another charmer. He was a splendid teacher. "A jovial, dynamic person," I noted after our first meeting, "who delighted me from the first by denouncing Laski and exalting in comparison Brogan." Despite my lack of skill (and interest) in economic history, I learned a great deal from him, and we became friends for life.

*　　*　　*

Going to lectures was not especially the Cambridge fashion, but it was my Harvard habit. Postan was a compelling lecturer, and his nine o'clocks in Mill Lane awakened the sleepiest of undergraduates. I also admired I. A. Richards and his course on practical criticism. I liked the dry, ironic tone of his elucidation of poetic ambiguities, and to him I owe the valuable axiom that the origin and value of a proposition are separate and distinct questions.

A virtuous man, Richards observed, may say something foolish; a corrupt man may say something wise: never evaluate a statement by its source. I supposed that Richards had destroyed that fallacy until it was revived in the Nineties under the name of 'perspectivism,' with its claim that the worth of an idea is determined by the identity and interest of the person who presents it.

Ivor and Dorothea Richards had me to tea (with a bevy of Chinese students) later in the year, and we became good friends when they migrated to Harvard after the war. One felt in the end that Richards wasted a sharp and original intelligence on his enthusiasm for Basic English (and mountain climbing); but he was a very nice man and generous to the young.

His great rival at Cambridge, F. R. Leavis, was not a nice man at all. He thumped away fiercely at the podium, promulgated in nasal tones and with quasi-papal infallibility the canon of the English novel (Dickens was out; then Dickens was in, with no explanation) and contemptuously dismissed competing assessments. His passion for close reading was impressive, but his manner was sour and embittered. Some who knew him better considered him paranoid. As a lecturer he put on quite a show, at once engrossing and distasteful.

The venerable American expatriate Gaillard Lapsley, whom F. W. Maitland had brought to Cambridge to teach English constitutional history, a friend of Henry James and Edith Wharton's literary executor, invited me for tea. Fragile in manner and languid in wit, he seemed a minor character in a James short story. He asked me about an American student at King's — "such a nice young man, but not much of a brain. Tell me, what kind of a place is Dartmouth anyway?"

I liked the gentle reasonableness of G. E. Moore but decided once again that my capacity for philosophical analysis was limited. I also attended for a while the lectures of Michael Oakeshott on the theory of the modern state. His assault on rationalism added nothing to what one had already learned from William James and was far more pinched, political and complacent in its tone. In view of Oakeshott's latter-day canonization by right-wing intellectuals, I regret to say that I cannot now remember much of what he talked about. Whatever it was, it evidently did not take. I am fortified in this reaction by the discovery in later years that Isaiah Berlin held Oakeshott in low regard.

The great man at Cambridge, John Maynard Keynes, was disabled that year by a heart attack. I saw him only once, in November at the Arts Theatre, which he had founded, at the opening night of *On the Frontier,* a play by W. H. Auden and Christopher Isherwood. I was thrilled to find myself seated directly behind Isherwood, a small, dark man, and to see sitting across the aisle Auden, tall and blond, furiously smoking Camels (OK in theaters in those dissolute days) and scribbling notes to Isherwood, who couldn't read them in the dark. The play was confused but refreshing, a sophisticated refinement of proletarian agitprop (see A. G. Case's review in *Granta*). Between the acts someone said to me, pointing to a box, "There's Maynard Keynes." I looked up and saw a great pale face staring impassively at the audience below. Keynes is one of the men of the century I would very much like to have known.

* * *

The senior Cambridge historian, the Regius Professor of Modern History, was George Macaulay Trevelyan, of impeccable historical lineage — the son of George Otto Trevelyan and the grandnephew of Thomas Babington Macaulay. He was also the exact contemporary and close friend of Harvard's Roger Bigelow Merriman. In November 1938 Frisky Merriman kindly sent me a letter of introduction to Trevelyan. Busy with *Granta* and dramatics, I put the letter aside. After a while Merriman asked my father whether I had ever received the letter, and my father alerted me. At the end of January 1939 I finally got round to thanking Merriman for his letter and presenting it to Professor Trevelyan. "I am having Schlesinger to lunch next week," Trevelyan wrote to Merriman. ". . . He only presented yours of November 12 yesterday."

I had bungled a marginal role in what became an episode of some minor historical interest. For Merriman, Harvard '96, had been a teacher and remained a friend of Franklin D. Roosevelt '04. As the English historian David Cannadine reconstructed the episode in the June 1999 *New England Quarterly,* Merriman, deeply worried about dictators in Europe and isolationists in America, decided to ask Trevelyan for his assessment of the European situation in the hope that it would impress FDR with the gravity of the impending crisis.

Trevelyan was an attractive man and gave me a most agreeable luncheon, though I was disconcerted by his stalwart support of the Munich agreement. He was, he said, "more grateful to Neville than to any statesman in my lifetime." In his reply to Merriman, Trevelyan · continued his defense of Munich on the ground that a war to save Czechoslovakia could not possibly have been won. But the crisis, he continued, was not over. Hitler and Mussolini were "'rabid' men," bent on aggression. If you don't want Germany to dominate Europe and Japan to dominate Asia, Trevelyan told Merriman, "you had better be reconsidering your isolation policy before you are indeed 'isolated.'"

This was what Merriman had hoped for, and he promptly sent Trevelyan's letter on to FDR. FDR replied with equal promptness. "I wish," he wrote, "the British would stop this 'we who are about to die, salute thee' attitude." Lord Lothian had visited the president a few days before, recanting his belief that Britain could do business with Hitler and telling FDR that the British had been guardians of Anglo-Saxon civilization for a thousand years, "that the scepter or the sword or something like that had dropped from their palsied fingers — that the USA must snatch it up — that FDR alone could save the world — etc, etc."

"I got mad clear through," FDR wrote to Merriman, "and told him that just so long as he or Britishers like him took that attitude of complete despair, the British would not be worth saving." If the British were to take a good stiff grog inducing not only a desire to save civilization but a will to do it, "they will have a lot more support from their American cousins — don't you think so?"

Merriman did think so. He told FDR that he was sending a copy to Trevelyan, "who will doubtless see that it is conveyed to the right quarters." "Well, I'm damned," said Trevelyan when he received FDR's letter, and he sent it on to Lord Halifax, the British foreign secretary. No one can be sure what difference it made, but FDR's words must have strengthened the hands of those convinced that appeasement was a disaster. My inglorious role may actually have improved the timing by delaying the exchange until the failure of Munich was indisputable.

*   *   *

I saw Harold Laski, the flaming radical of the London School of Economics, once or twice at his Sunday-afternoon teas. Forty-five years old, Harold was at the height of his influence. His books were in demand, his articles appeared everywhere, his lectures were enthusiastically applauded, his energy seemed boundless, his influence was global. Anticolonial nationalists in India and Africa in particular looked to him for inspiration. "The center of Nehru's thinking," said John Kenneth Galbraith, "was Laski."

He had many American devotees. As a young instructor at Harvard, Laski had dazzled everyone he met — and he took care to meet everyone of consequence. Among the Americans dazzled, some longer than others, were, in the older generation, Justices Holmes and Brandeis and Herbert Croly of *The Promise of American Life,* and among his contemporaries, Frankfurter, Lippmann, Beard, Roger Baldwin, Edmund Wilson and even, to a moderate degree, my father. Anyone who doubts Laski's youthful brilliance should look at the two sparkling volumes of the Holmes-Laski letters.

Even Joseph P. Kennedy sent Joe Jr. in 1933–34 to study with Laski. "I disagreed with everything he wrote," the elder Kennedy said. "We were black and white." But the boys had heard enough from their father, "and I decided they should be exposed to someone of intelligence and vitality on the other side." When Laski proposed taking Joe with him on a trip to the Soviet Union, his father was delighted. (Young Joe came back "exultant," his mother later said, "in his enthusiasm.")

Harold was a kind man, hospitable to the son of old friends, but, as my gratification over Postan's preference for Brogan over Laski suggests, we really didn't hit it off. Though anticommunist on occasion, Harold seemed unduly soft on the Soviet Union. And though a captivating raconteur, it was sometimes hard to believe the tales he told about himself. Thurman Arnold once observed that Harold was finally getting famous enough to meet the people he had known all his life. What somewhat extenuated Laski's mythomania was that his tales lacked malice and were mostly self-puffery. "He exaggerated about fifty percent," said Rebecca West, "but only in areas where it does no harm."

I last saw Harold when he came to Washington in the autumn of 1946. Jim Rowe, one of FDR's early special assistants, summoned a group of New Dealers to meet with him. Harold lamented the breakdown in relations between the Soviet Union and the Western democracies. The blame, he suggested, rested with the United States. Someone asked what he thought had been the point of no return. "It was," he replied with his usual confidence, "the speech Jimmy Byrnes gave at Stuttgart" — a speech in which the secretary of state had announced American support for a democratic Germany. Someone spoke from the back of the room; it was the familiar quavering voice of Benjamin V. Cohen, a saint among the New Dealers and a man whom Laski greatly admired. "Harold," Ben Cohen said, "Harold, I'm sorry you feel that way, and I think you have it wrong. I should know — Galbraith and I wrote the Stuttgart speech." Laski looked stricken.

Rarely has so vivid a figure faded so fast. He is forgotten today because he left very little to remember. When young, he seemed destined to be a considerable political theorist. But, for all his erudition, he was neither an original nor a penetrating nor even a coherent thinker. He never could reconcile his Holmesian commitment to civil liberties with his Marxist commitment to collectivism. His fatal fluency enabled him to glide over the hard questions. His besetting sin was the substitution of rhetoric for thought.

Laski's personal decline began after the Labour victory in 1945 — ironically, because he had done so much to make that victory possible. His *ex cathedra* pronouncements increasingly irritated the new Labour government. Prime Minister Clement Attlee finally told him: "A period of silence on your part would be welcome." He lost a major libel suit. The Cold War baffled and dispirited him. After the Soviet intervention in Czechoslovakia in 1948, he wrote to Frankfurter, "I have a feeling that I am already a ghost in a play that is over." His last years were forlorn. A broken man, he died in 1950 at the age of fifty-six.

* * *

Though I learned a certain amount, especially from Postan and Richards, formal education did not seem the point of my Cambridge year. Extracurricular pleasures were too enjoyable, and I thought it foolish to deny myself new experience. Early on, a young man knocked on my door and said he was the set designer at the Amateur Dramatic Club. His name was John Dreyfus; later he became a noted book and typographical designer for the Cambridge University Press. The ADC, Dreyfus explained, was a Cambridge institution, founded in 1855 and now with a theater of its own. Charles Wintour had told him of my interest in the drama. Might I care to think about joining?

I thought, why not? When I signed up, I was asked in what category I belonged: actor, set designer, producer (then the British term for director), stagehand. Thinking such self-definition purely nominal, I thought that I might as well seize the top; so I said, "Producer." To my horror, the ADC president soon asked me to produce (i.e., direct) in an evening of one-act 'nursery' plays by which the club tried out new talent. I protested my total inexperience. Accustomed to British self-deprecation, the ADC people took my protest as no more than conventional modesty and disregarded it. I was tempted anyway, so I finally accepted the assignment. The *Varsity Post* reported improbably, "Arthur Schlesinger, who made a name for himself at Harvard University by his dramatic work and producing, is producing a play — 'St. Simeon Stylites.'"

This was a neo-Shavian one-acter by F. Sladen-Smith I had once seen put on at Adams House. Casting was the next step. "Fun for the moment," I wrote in my journal, "but every once in a while I think concretely of what I have to do and wonder why the devil I ever let myself in for it." But I managed to pick actors, plot stage movements and conduct rehearsals. The nursery evening passed without disgrace. The *Granta* reviewer said, "I have nothing but praise for Arthur Schlesinger's production." With a sigh of relief, I decided to retire from the theater.

Then I was invited to co-direct Jean Cocteau's *The Infernal Machine.* Once again I protested; once again I succumbed to temptation. This time I was to work with Donald Beves, a don at King's, ridiculously fingered in later years as the third or fourth man in the Cambridge spy ring and a close associate of George (Dadie) Rylands, the ADC's mentor and a charming Shakespearean scholar. Beves did not show up, however, and I was on my own.

We had a promising weekend of rehearsals in early November, and the play began to take shape. Then the translator suddenly withdrew permission; he was negotiating, he explained, for a commercial production. After a time of consternation, all appeals failing, the ADC gave up and decided instead to put on a Christmas pantomime in the English tradition — a genre that as an American I was quite unqualified to direct. Saved by the bell, relief tinged with regret, I thought that my theatrical career was now really at an end.

I also joined the Cambridge Union and attended debates with some regularity. An impressive figure was Aubrey Eban, born in South Africa and reared in England, who after the war settled in Israel, restored his Anglicized name to Abba and used his intelligence and wit, polished from his years at the Union, to astonish and persuade the diplomatic world. His courage in pressing for reconcilation with the Palestinians, along with his ironical British style, denied him the political success in Israel to which his dedication and talent entitled him.

Debates at the Union operated according to House of Commons rules. Parliamentary courtesies and time limits were strictly observed; reading from a text was deplored. I was a listener until one day in the spring Pieter Keuneman, who was presiding, was prompted by

Charles Wintour to call on me immediately after the designated speakers debating the resolution "That this House is tired of Politics and Politicians." According to the *Gownsman,* "Mr. Schlesinger (Peterhouse) was in a reverie on the front bench when called on unexpectedly, had to be asked to put on his gown and apologised for its appearance. He didn't know there was a debate though he had noticed a gentleman talking to himself. . . . Much the best speech of the evening." "Forced into the limelight by a number of his friends," said *Granta,* Schlesinger "made a brilliant little impromptu speech." The *Varsity* reported that "with his attractive style of dry humour he gave the house some first-class laughs and supported politicians as magnificent circus performers." Flushed with success, I intervened again a couple of weeks later, much less successfully. I should have stopped when ahead, a lesson imperfectly learned.

*   *   *

The harvest of the year lay not in organizations but in friendships. Charles Wintour was the closest, and our camaraderie was consolidated when I introduced him to Eleanor Baker, a friend of mine from Radcliffe, a daughter of Professor Ralph Baker of the Harvard Law School. Nonie Baker was now at Newnham College, one of Cambridge's two institutional concessions to the existence of women. She and Charles hit it off at once, and their courtship zigged and zagged through the twilight year. They were married in 1940 when bombs rained down on London. After the war Charles had a long and distinguished career as editor of the *Evening Standard.* Two of his children followed him in journalism: Patrick as chief political correspondent for the *Guardian,* and Anna, migrating to her mother's homeland, as the smart and stylish editor of the American *Vogue.*

The sherry party was the prevailing social form. I soon discovered that while sherry could not produce the kick of a cocktail, it could, drunk in sufficient quantity, produce just as poisonous a hangover. After my Cambridge year, I rarely raised a glass of sherry again, and I abhor the fashion that spread through America in the Eighties and Nineties of replacing cocktails by white wine. A glass of sauterne is hardly what the organism requires after a hard day.

Still, in Cambridge the sherry party served the social purpose of putting people in circulation, and one got around. Noel Annan of King's I knew only marginally at Cambridge; our friendship flowered in later times. The golden boy at Cambridge was Nigel Bicknell, a very handsome fellow of considerable humor and charm and a good friend. My early weeks were apparently so misspent that, when I finally made an appearance at the University Library in early November, Nigel said to Charles Wintour, "For the first time Arthur looked out of his element."

From time to time I went over to Oxford, usually staying with the Brogans. One night Denis said, "I'm not sure why I'm doing this, but Postan has persuaded me to try it," flourishing a letter he had written, applying for the chair in political science at Cambridge soon to be vacated by Ernest Barker. To his own genuine astonishment, he was soon elected over (as I exultantly wrote to my parents) "a rather vapid fellow named Michael Oakeshott who has been working toward the job for years." Brogan also became a fellow at Peterhouse, where he and Postan, it was said, once amazed the long table by specifying in, say, 1943 what the headlines in the *Times* must have been on the identical date in 1923.

At Oxford sherry parties, Chad Gilpatric introduced me to fellow Rhodes scholars. It was then that I first met Charles Collingwood and Howard K. Smith, who later shone as radio and television commentators, Lane Timmons, who gave me my first copy of Keynes's *General Theory*, became a distinguished diplomat and later in life married the widow of Ernst Lubitch, and Philip Kaiser, who later went from Truman's Department of Labor to serve as ambassador for Kennedy and Carter. Charles Wintour passed me on to English friends at Oxford, especially Woodrow Wyatt, a joyous, jaunty, explosive man, then editing a joint Oxford and Cambridge magazine called *Light and Dark*. In his *Confessions of an Optimist*, he recalls me as "an American with a humorous face and jokes to go with it." Woodrow continued to delight me through his several marriages and his political ramble from the Labour left to the Tory right.

*   *   *

As Christmas 1938 approached, Gilpatric and I accepted an invitation from our Harvard friend Robert Triffin, now back in his native Belgium. I went first by myself to the Netherlands, still in its classic Hans Brinker phase; the hippie-druggie climate into which Amsterdam fell in the Seventies was inconceivable in the Thirties. I enjoyed the canals, the windmills, market day at Delft, with scrubbed white Walt Disney pigs peeking out of carts and country folk riding bicycles in wooden shoes. In the evenings I read, and was much taken by, the Albatross edition of D. H. Lawrence's *Letters*. Lawrence, it then seemed to me, with his sense of life among the ruins, had stabbing insights reminiscent of Emerson and Nietzsche.

After a week among the windmills I proceeded to Brussels, where Gilpatric and Triffin met me at the railroad station. We ate superbly in Brussels and enjoyed the museums and the opera but speculated compulsively about Hitler and his timetable. We spent Christmas Eve in Ghent, ending up at a flashy jazz bar run by a black man from Harlem, with clientele ranging from the haute bourgeoisie to the demi-monde. On Christmas Day we went on to Bruges, a lovely town, white and silent, snow drifting quietly down on gabled housefronts and frozen canals, bells chiming in the distance — a storybook Christmas; and still we talked about the war to come.

Gil and I left for Paris the next day, finding lodgings in a modest hotel along the rue Jacob near St.-Germain-des-Prés, around the corner from those two splendid cafés, Flores and the Deux Magots. Bob Wernick from Harvard was there and introduced us to inexpensive Left Bank bistros and, more lethally, to Pernod. The next fortnight went by in a whirlwind of museums, paintings, movies, cafés, nightclubs — a kaleidoscope of gaiety in the gayest of cities (I use the word in the sense of the Thirties). "It would need Slavko Vorkapich," I wrote in my journal of those spinning Paris days, referring to the Hollywood montage specialist, "to do justice to it." To my parents I wrote enthusiastically, "I am completely sold on Paris and regard the French as — unlike the English — having something to contribute to civilization."

One night we visited the Sphinx, a fashionable bordello on the boulevard Edgar Quinet, where topless girls sauntered in front of a garish Third Empire bar. I admired the effect but dared not go into the backrooms. Arthur Solomon, an American acquaintance from Cambridge, took me to Justin Thannhauser, the art dealer with a superb collection of not yet exhibited Picassos. I saw Maurice Chevalier at the Casino de Paris; his imitation of Hitler brought down the house. Like all good Americans, I went to the Folies-Bergères.

New Year's Eve 1938 was a full and drunken night spent wandering happily from one place to another in Montmartre. In one club Gilpatric noticed a beautiful brunette and sent a note over to her, explaining that we were American students from Oxford and Cambridge, giving his name and hotel and asking whether she would lunch with us. She accepted the invitation a day or two later. She was from Rome, and her name was Tullia Calabi. Luncheon showed her to be not only beautiful but highly intelligent, and she brought up to date the knowledge of Italian affairs I had imbibed from Gaetano Salvemini.

Tullia reappeared in my life the next year when, with her husband, Bruno Zevi, she came to Cambridge, Massachusetts, refugees from fascism, Bruno now at Harvard's School of Design. After the war the Zevis returned to Rome. Bruno became an influential architecture critic and the great champion of organic architecture. Tullia was first a leading Italian journalist and later head of the Jewish community in Italy. Her house in Rome was a salon where for many years I met leading Italian politicians and intellectuals.

In his lament on New Year's Eve 1939, Auden judged the Thirties a low, dishonest decade. So in some, but not all, respects it was. MacNeice's "Autumn Journal" better caught the mood of 1938:

> The New Year comes with bombs, it is too late
> To dose the dead with honourable intentions:
> If you have honour to spare, employ it on the living;
> The dead are dead as 1938. . . .
> To-night we sleep
> On the banks of Rubicon — the die is cast;
> There will be time to audit
> The accounts later, there will be sunlight later
> And the equation will come out at last.

* * *

Marian Cannon remained keenly on my mind. In those remote days before airplanes carried mail across the Atlantic, one read the shipping news to determine the arrival of ocean liners from the United States, bringing, it was to be hoped, letters from loved ones. My spirits rose and fell according to the mail; so did my doubts; so, surely, did hers. A Harvard classmate, now at Oxford, wrote me that an affectionate Wellesley friend could not understand my enthusiasm "on the ground that Marian was lacking in the warmheartedness your emotional make-up demanded of a girl." Could that be so?

By mid-October, my journal recorded an impression that the affair was "crumbling." My dependence on Marian, I thought, was largely because she was the only girl on my mind. "I shall have to remedy *that* state of affairs." In November I went to London for a couple of days. While I was watching Hitchcock's *The Lady Vanishes,* two girls sat down next to me. One was a striking blonde. I examined her closely when her friend asked me for a match to light their cigarettes and decided that she was much too delectable to be allowed to slip away. As I left, I passed her a note saying that I was an American at Cambridge, that she was a beautiful girl and that we must lunch the next day, appending the telephone number of my hotel.

That evening I saw Peggy Ashcroft and Michael Redgrave in Michel Saint Denis's admirable production of Bulgakov's *The White Guard*. The next morning, when I returned to the hotel after a tour of the Charing Cross Road bookshops, a note informed me that Miss Chudleigh had called. We had a cheerful luncheon and, that going well, we had dinner. Yvonne Chudleigh, who came from a military family and modeled for the fun of it, was in retrospect an early version of the Sloane Rangers of the Seventies, lovely and charming but "essentially interested in nothing I am interested in." Still, even this represented a delightful challenge. "I need more often to be thrown with people who do not give a damn about the American elections [which had just taken place, a bad setback for FDR and the New Deal]. . . . It requires me to change my attitudes, manner and premises." We had a good time, and I returned to Cambridge much refreshed.

Also, a series of letters from Marian seemed to suggest a revival of her interest in me. "I think probably I am still in love with her," I confided to my journal. John Fairbank kept me informed of developments at home. Marian was about to leave to spend some months with friends in Guatemala. "She feels," John wrote in late November, "you are losing interest in her and is preparing for the eventual subsidence of the relationship. This is no doubt a 'healthy' situation [presumably improving my bargaining power] unless some Central American thunderbolt turns up."

In the meantime, I found a new distraction in Cambridge. Anne Mortimer Whyte of Girton College was the belle of the university, extremely active, extremely intelligent, bright-eyed and witty. She was sure, Charles Wintour told me, to achieve a double first in history while attending every sherry party in Cambridge. Her father was Sir Frederick Whyte, a handsome and likable man with broad experience: he had been a Liberal member of Parliament, private secretary to Churchill, political adviser to Chiang Kai-shek, president of the Indian Legislative Assembly and was now director general of the English Speaking Union. He would have risen further, but his career was shadowed by a mysterious scandal in China — a dalliance, one heard, with the wife of a European ambassador.

My friendship with Anne ripened in the autumn term. She asked me to the Girton play; I took her to the ADC party; we lunched and dined together; she invited me to her twenty-first birthday dance at her family's house in Great Cumberland Place in London during the Christmas break. "You won't know many people there," she said, "so bring a girl." I brought Yvonne Chudleigh. Resplendent in white tie and tails — de rigueur in prewar days — I went to pick up Yvonne. It was a cold night, and to warm myself while waiting I stood with my back to the gas heater installed in the fireplace. Suddenly I smelled something burning and realized that my coattails were being singed by the flame. So with a charred tailcoat and properly abashed, I took Yvonne on to the Whyte ball. We had a fine time.

I was half in love with Anne through the winter, but thoughts of Marian lingered. I asked her to come over and meet me in Italy during the spring vacation in April and go on to the Dalmatian coast. She declined. Instead I spent a week with the Wintours in Dorset, where Charles's sister was about to marry Eric James, later an eminent educator (and Lord James). Charles's father turned out to be a retired major general with crisp charm along C. Aubrey Smith lines. Driving around Dorset, Charles showed me the Cerne Giant, a nude male figure carved out of a hillside notable for its twenty-six-foot phallus in gigantic erection.

Then Herbert Warren Wind and I started to drive to Italy in his English sports car. "I shall write a diary about the trip," I told my parents, "and call it *Gone With the Wind*." In a snowstorm a few miles from Lausanne, a truck skidded heavily into our car, dislocating the steering mechanism. Leaving the car behind for repairs, we persuaded the insurance company to give us railroad tickets to Florence.

On the night train I shared a compartment with a jolly hooker, who rather upset Herb next door when she exclaimed in the night to some official who wanted to eject me, "*Non, non, il m'a donné le plaisir.*" Such pleasure as I may have given her was entirely conversational. Italy, despite Mussolini, was delectable, though the trains, contrary to the Il Duce fan club, did not run on time.

Venice, magical as ever, was the high point of the Italian trip. When the time came to depart, the gondolier taking us to the railroad station contrived to lose an oar and then to knock himself overboard trying to retrieve it, leaving the gondola to drift in the middle of the Grand Canal with vaporetti rushing madly along in both directions. Herb and I got hold of the remaining oar and managed to propel the boat to shore, where the boatman was sadly cursing to himself.

We left Italy on the day that Mussolini moved into Albania. When we arrived in Lausanne to pick up Herb's car, people said they expected war, but the sense of crisis subsided in twenty-four hours. We drove on to France and the château country, admiring Chenonceaux, sipping *fines* in the cafés of Tours, and finally parting company in Chartres. I rejoined Gilpatric and Wernick in Paris for more bistros and more Pernods.

A foretaste of the future: in London in May, I was introduced to television. The Odeon Theatre showed the fight between the American Henry Armstrong, the world welterweight champion and a great, nonstop boxer, and his English rival Ernie Roderick. The fight was 'live' — i.e., it was going on while we watched it in the cinema. "Our patrons, witnessing this historic event," said the Odeon program, "will no doubt make allowances for the shortcomings of the young art of television." The camera followed the boxers around the ring, and, after technical difficulties at the start, the images were pretty clear. The novelty was exciting. One looked forward to the beneficial effects of television in every house. (One was wrong.)

*   *   *

Hitler hovered over all. His howls on the radio provoked much hilarity, but nervous laughter hardly concealed deep anxiety. If the wishful thinking of the defenders of Munich was trickling away, appeasement was still the policy. When the ADC replaced Cocteau by a Christmas pantomime, it had to submit the new script to the Lord Chamberlain, the official who regulated British stage productions. There were satiric references to a mythical European dictator, and the Lord Chamberlain, fearful of offending the Nazis, demanded the deletion of an uninspired couplet in one of the songs:

> They can't eat their sausages and mash
> Because of one man's small moustache.

I couldn't believe it. If censorship applied to a flip joke in an undergraduate revue, what would the future hold for serious criticism of Nazism? I later learned that Sir Alexander Cadogan, the permanent undersecretary of the Foreign Office, had written the Lord Chamberlain in December 1938 that "all direct references to Germany, to Herr Hitler, or to other prominent personages must be avoided." This idiotic episode symbolized the abjectness of the appeasement policy. "I foresee and foretell," Winston Churchill said, "that the policy of submission [to Germany] will carry with it restrictions upon the freedom of speech and debate in Parliament, on public platforms, and discussions in the Press, for it will be said — indeed I hear it said sometimes now — that we cannot allow the Nazi system of dictatorship to be criticised."

On a Saturday night in London in January 1939 I went to a movie and walked out afterward into Piccádilly Circus. There I ran into a crowd of young fellows shouting "Mosley, Mosley" and "Down with the Jews" and singing a song about "building the Fascist state." These were Blackshirts, followers of Sir Oswald Mosley and his British Union of Fascists, and, as they surged through the Circus, they caught and began to beat people of Jewish appearance.

English fair play thereupon took a curious turn. Bystanders shouted "Form a ring! Form a ring!" so that, in effect, the beatings could be carried on without interference. Eventually the police broke up the riot but arrested more victims than attackers. "The most alarming feature," I wrote home, "was the attitude of the crowd. Some people were terrifically angry and went around swearing to themselves, but most seemed to regard the thing as a spectacle and stood amiably on the sidelines. . . . I have never seen such a mob at work before. My opinion of mankind has somewhat fallen."

* * *

Appeasement was, among other things, a boon for the Communists. With Britain appeasing, France divided and America isolationist, the Soviet Union appeared to be the one stalwart and reliable foe of fascism. By the time I came to Peterhouse, the Cambridge spies — Philby, Maclean, Blunt, Burgess, Cairncross — had long since gone down. But the death in the Spanish Civil War in December 1936 of a much-admired undergraduate, John Cornford, the Communist son of the classicist F. M. Cornford (the author of that incomparable essay on academic politics, *Microcosmographia Academica*), gave Cambridge a Communist martyr whom, with the Spanish republic fighting for its life, we were all bound to respect. This was the atmosphere that had beguiled Michael Straight the year before into his reluctant flirtation with the Soviet espionage apparatus.

Among the *Granta* group, both Eric Hobsbawm and Pieter Keuneman were Communists, Keuneman to the end of his life a leader of the Sri Lankan party. But British Communists, at least in the universities, were very different from the Communists I had known in the United States. Firm in their faith and articulate in its support, they — or at any rate those at Cambridge who had not been recruited by Soviet intelligence — did not pretend to be liberals or social democrats.

They were Leninists, and proud of it. They did not go in for the dissembling and deceit routinely practiced by American Communists.

Incompatibility in ideology did not prevent compatibility in personal relations, at least with Hobsbawm, Keuneman, H. S. Ferns, a Canadian historian at Trinity College, John Alexander, a witty young man from a proper county family, and others. I considered them good friends, and I wholeheartedly endorsed Eric's inscription when he gave me his *Age of Extremes* in 1994: "For Arthur, in memory of 55 years of friendship and disagreement."

Hobsbawm was also a member of the Apostles, the ancient and famed (at least today; I cannot recall having heard of the Apostles at the time) secret society of Cambridge intellectuals given to closed discussion of high thoughts. Once dominated by Maynard Keynes and Lytton Strachey, the Apostles in the Thirties, Noel Annan tells us in *Our Age*, had been taken over by the Communists.

I lunched from time to time with the Marxist economist Maurice Dobb at Trinity. Though a party member, Dobb was a polite and soft-spoken intellectual who had, probably innocently, set Philby on his path to the NKVD and later introduced Burgess to Philby. Yuri Modin, the NKVD controller of the Cambridge agents, has written, "Dobb could scarcely have imagined that he was to be instrumental in creating the most effective spy ring of the twentieth century." I described him to my parents as "a very nice person, thoroughly unmilitant and thoroughly unrecognizable as a Marxist."

The Labour party was a good deal more to my New Deal taste, and I welcomed the invitation from a remarkably able young historian at Pembroke, John Habbakuk, to give a talk on American politics to the Workers Educational Association. Habbakuk, an economic historian who revolutionized the history of English land ownership, went on to Oxford, where he became vice-chancellor (in American terms, CEO). But Labour disappointed in its sodden resistance to rearmament and conscription. The party, I wrote home in April, was "composed of professional idiots." How else would Hitler be stopped?

The Cambridge Union debated the question, L. S. Amery, the Tory imperialist, advocating conscription, B. H. Liddell Hart, the military journalist, opposing. The Union rejected conscription, as did the Oxford Union by an even larger vote, "but I find myself completely in favor of it, and would be if I were English. Charles delivered a very good speech for it at the Union."

For all the belligerence I wished on the British, I still declined to regard Hitler as an American problem. "My old devotion to Roosevelt is rapidly crumbling," I wrote to my family in February 1939. "I think his recent pronouncements on foreign policy are very misguided, even dangerous, and I find myself reluctantly in the same camp with Clark, Johnson, Vandenberg and Nye," naming conspicuous isolationist senators. In April I described FDR's interventionist policy as "all very fine, and ethically inspiring, but it seems to me extremely dangerous. He seems to have delusions of Wilsonian grandeur."

*   *   *

Republican Spain died during the long winter while we "drank for Spain" in a score of Cambridge sherry parties. For us, the Spanish Civil War seemed the clearest and cleanest moral case. We denounced the nonintervention policy adopted by Britain, France and the United States while Germany and Italy openly backed and armed General Franco.

We knew little then about the inner politics of the Spanish republic. George Orwell's *Homage to Catalonia,* a sympathetic portrait of POUM, the semi-Trotskyite revolutionary party crushed by the Stalinists, came out in 1938 and strengthened my anticommunism. I believed, however, and still believe, that Prime Minister Juan Negrin, Dr. Cannon's friend, and the Stalinists were wiser than POUM in arguing that it was better to win the war first before you try to make a revolution. But the Communists' ruthless use of this argument as a pretext to exterminate a rival Marxist sect seemed one more proof of their ideological barbarism. Orwell himself later said that POUM was wrong on strategy but that he thought it imperative to tell the truth about the Stalinists.

Revisionists in recent years take a plague-on-both-your-houses position: if Franco's fascists had not won, they contend, the Communists would have taken over, and the Soviet Union would have had a base on the Atlantic. This does not seem likely. Though there was a strong Soviet influence among the Loyalists, there was also a strong reaction against Stalinist methods. Negrin could not afford to alienate his arms supplier, but he had no illusions about the Communists, and he was sure he could count on the support of the Western democracies if Franco were defeated.

The guilt generated by the abandonment of the republic lingered for a long time. After the war I joined a committee organized by Nancy Macdonald, Dwight's first wife, for aid to Republican exiles in France. For some years I refused to visit Franco's Spain, till it occurred to me that it made little sense to boycott semifascist Spain while visiting communist countries. (When I did go to Spain in the Fifties, I fell into a conversation with a charming young woman in the same compartment on a train. I expressed surprise at her critical remarks about Franco and said, "I had not realized that there is freedom of speech in Spain." She replied, "We have no freedom of speech. But we do have freedom of conversation." A valuable distinction.) And in 1961 when Indalecio Prieto, a robust Loyalist and stout anti-Communist, came to Washington from his Mexican exile, I gave him luncheon at the White House mess in a small effort at symbolic reparation.

*   *   *

Barcelona fell to Franco in January 1939. In February Britain and France recognized the Franco regime. In March the Nazis took over Czechoslovakia. Even Chamberlain acknowledged a shock to confidence. "Czechoslovakia has exploded like a bomb," I wrote home, "and the skies have darkened considerably. . . . Late last night there was a bottle party at the *Granta*. Most of the people there were despairing of England and saw themselves as refugees in the United States or prisoners in concentration camps." My isolationist impulse was not, however, shaken. I objected to FDR's reported statement that America's frontier was on the Rhine. "I am very suspicious of all the arguments about the necessity of fighting Germany in France to avoid fighting it in South America."

My isolationism derived in part from my low opinion of the Chamberlain regime. "The only hope at the moment," I informed my parents in May, "seems to be the speedy elevation of Churchill to the government, but Chamberlain dares not do this. There is no other *man* in England: Cripps is embittered and not very intelligent; the other Socialists are jokes; Sinclair [the Liberal leader] is no leader; Eden is hamstrung by the public school spirit; no one will trust Lloyd George; Hoare is impossible."

In May Winston Churchill came to Cambridge. He spoke in the Corn Exchange, crowded to the rafters, and his words were relayed to the parking space outside by the Red Lion, where I stood with several hundred others. Churchill splendidly denounced the menace of Nazism, calling for conscription, faster rearmament and a Russian alliance. His ringing attack on the government pleased everyone but his sponsors, the Cambridge Conservative Association. "The speech," I noted, "was very impressive and had a statesmanlike character that I did not altogether expect." It was my most thrilling political occasion of the year.

*   *   *

As we watched what appeared to be the dissolution of the West, we began to understand that this was probably the last time for a considerable period that we could expect to live our own lives. It was the long hush, the ominous half-light, the strange silence as before a cyclone strikes. And in the hush and half-light everything became more intense, more hectic, more urgent, larger than life. Never was spring more fragrant. The Backs along the Cam burst into flower. We punted on the river and lunched at the Anchor in Granchester and swam in the pub's pool under the spring sun.

Peterhouse had the custom of putting on Shakespeare in the Deer Park every spring. One day B. L. Hallward, the senior tutor, summoned me and said that, since I was the only ADC professional in the college, he counted on me to direct the play. As before, I resisted; as before, I succumbed. I chose *As You Like It* and for Rosalind — "the most intelligent woman ever represented in literature," according to Harold Bloom, the Yale canonizer — cast Anne Whyte. Charles Wintour was Duke Frederick, and Pieter Keuneman, the Communist, played Charles, a wrestler. Scarlatti provided the background music. My nonexistent theatrical past received new embroidery. The *Varsity* wrote with undergraduate nonchalance that Schlesinger had "acted in stock for a time in the U.S.A."

As You Like It was playing at the Shakespeare Memorial Theatre in Stratford, and one luminous day at the end of May we — Anne Whyte, Nonie Baker, Charles Wintour and I — decided to rush off and see it. We drove through a blazing sunset with the car's top down, dined in Stratford, enjoyed the play, went afterward to a cast party and then set out on the return trip in the light of a full moon. As dawn broke, we reached Cambridge. That careless, glorious, happy excursion lingers in memory as typical of the lunges for happiness in defiance of the war that we all knew was on its way.

When the great day came for our production, however, the skies opened, pouring forth a torrent of drenching rain. The Peterhouse garden was manifestly out. In a frenzy of improvisation, we managed at the last moment to shift play and audience to the Arts Theatre. The happy consequence was the general attribution of the infirmities of the performance to the unplanned change of venue. My reputation as a director emerged intact. "I should like to congratulate you very much on the splendid production of 'As You Like It,'" Mr. Hallward wrote me, "which I and my guests enjoyed very much. It must have been very difficult to transfer it suddenly into the theatre, and the whole production does you all very immense credit."

* * *

My poem in *Granta* in May 1939, "Threnody on Shaftesbury Avenue":

> Oh, sweet Euterpe, hear me ere I leave this gladsome shore.
> I adore you and your country, but your theatre *is* a bore.
> I am getting sick to death of intimate revues.
> I'll not go to any more. I refuse, dear, I refuse
> I'm weary of the coy laments about the lower classes,
> I'm tiring of the winsome lads and not so winsome lasses. . . .
> I don't want to see the girl who tries to thrill the nation
> By putting all she's got upon some stale impersonation.
> Lord, here it comes again — don't shake your head so sadly,
> Beatrice [Lillie] might do it well, but Hermione does it Baddeley.
> Those skits which quiver lightly with laughs so pale and tenuous,
> Those placid, *placid* chorus girls, and dance men ingenuous. . . .

And so on.

The last issue of *Granta* rendered two verdicts on my verdict. The report on the Cambridge Union's year said, "When this droll American goes back to his homeland life will lose much of its beauty." But an anonymous versifier wrote:

> O, intelligent Americans that come to study here
> And intelligently condemn this country in each sphere
> Of its activity. I love your omniscience and wit,
> Your ability to condemn every littlest bit
> Of a complex institution, taking years to understand
> When but newly parted from your greatly cultured land.
> Read Duhamel's "La Vie Future" and perhaps then realise
> That the most intelligent of men cannot thus be wise.
> If you must be destructive, start on your own vanity;
> A little more of Schlesinger, a little less of Deity.

The fellow had a point.

My feelings about England were still mixed. The line I too often took was caustic, probably in overgeneralized reaction to the Chamberlain government. I alleged (and truly felt) a great preference for

France. Yet, underneath, unacknowledged appreciation and affection were growing. When FDR sent Felix Frankfurter to the Supreme Court early in 1939, I apparently expressed my disappointment about the English in my letter of congratulation. "I am sure the Cambridge year will be as unsatisfactory as you indicate," Frankfurter replied, "but somehow or other the byproducts of this year's venture will, I think, have been a very considerable fertilizing contribution to your development." The little justice was everlastingly right.

With war in the back of all minds, the gaiety of May Week (taking place, as always, in June) was never more sustained, more riotous, more enchanted, more desperate — the last fling before Armageddon. The song I associate with that last May Week before the war was "Deep Purple," from a Bing Crosby movie — "When purple shadows fall / On a sleepy garden wall." We danced the night through, my English friends not knowing when they would dance again, the purple shadows fell, and Hitler's clock ticked steadily on.

I wrote home, "This has been one of the happiest years I have ever had, and I shall be very sorry for it to come to an end."

* * *

I had renewed my plea to Marian to join me in Europe. In May she wrote that she had loved me once and conceivably could again but that she did not love me at the moment and therefore saw no point in coming over. I wrote back: OK, we're finished. She cabled a concise and rather humorous request for reinstatement. John Fairbank, my man in Massachusetts, wrote, "Marian has been fluctuating on a ten day cycle with overtones. She would put Sorokin [a Harvard sociologist with his own brand of cycles] in a funk in five days. She doesn't know her own mind five minutes on end. . . . From all this I infer that if *you* know *your* mind, you may get some results. But far be it from me to go on record as prognosticating anything at all. I never even wrote you."

My parents were concerned. A handwritten letter came from my father: "I have hesitated to write you in regard to a matter which you have not chosen to mention, but I think I should do so." He did not know what my relations with Marian now were, but he and my mother were "quite willing for you to take the fateful step if you desire to do so." I replied that my association for the first time in my life with a number of intelligent and attractive girls had not shaken my original allegiance.

Marian finally decided to come and arrived in time for Wimbledon. The day was lustrous, and we wandered among cheerful crowds, rejoicing in the bright green of the grass, the bright red of the cherries on sale at every corner, and the bright beauty of the English girls. We ran into Herb Wind with Leslie Howard's son Ronald, and they gave us their center court tickets. There we saw Queen Mary. But beneath the gaiety there darkly lay forebodings of the war to come.

The first round of the men's doubles pitted two veteran French players, Jean Borotra and Jacques Brugnon, against a German team, Roderick Menzel, who had played for Czechoslovakia until the Nazi takeover three months before, and R. Goepfert. The Germans marched efficiently through the first two sets, winning handily, 6–2, 6–4. Then, as the German team seemed destined for a quick victory, Borotra and Brugnon, drawing on the wiles of years, came back to win the next two sets, 6–3, 6–4.

By now the tension in the stadium was palpable, as if the match were playing out the antagonisms of the impending war. I have been to Wimbledon often since (and to Forest Hills and Longwood), but I have never seen onlookers so desperately engaged as the English crowd that day pleading for the French to win. Every point to the French produced cheers; every point to the Germans, moans of anguish. Then Borotra and Brugnon surged ahead and finally took the last set, 6–2. The crowd went wild. It was as if they willed the result to be the prediction of the war they all knew was coming.

The French team went on to the semifinals, where they lost to Bobby Riggs and Elwood Cooke in four sets. It was Riggs's dazzling debut: he won the men's singles and doubles and the mixed doubles. The next week in Paris I had the luck of seeing legendary players — Bill Tilden, Henri Cochet, Ellsworth Vines and Don Budge — in the world's professional championship at the Stade Roland Garros. Curiously, Jean Borotra ended as Marshal Pétain's minister for sports in the collaborationist regime.

* * *

The reunion with Marian was not an immediate success. "She does seem considerably older than you in her behavior," my frank and discerning friend Charles Wintour wrote after seeing us together. "Whenever there was any kind of a dispute between you, even if her position was weak, she seemed more in control of the situation and was certainly less irascible about it than you. . . . It seems damn priggish advice to tell anyone that they're not old enough to marry." In a

later letter: "Your whole idea of the relationship as a continuous battle is wrecking any chance you have."

"The upshot of it all," I wrote home, "is that we are not going to get
married. Marian feels that we are not temperamentally suited for
each other. I don't know — maybe she's right — but I have never
loved her so much." In fact, she was quite right, but I was in love and
persistent. We went on to Paris where one night, after we had seen
Charles Trenet at the ABC "*théâtre du rire et de la chanson*," she told me,
with fine candor, that during our separation she had been as incon-
stant as I secretly knew I had wished to be. A Central American thunderbolt had turned up after all. I overreacted with an impressive demonstration of total immaturity. But somehow we stuck together.

"I should be the last to urge you to come back," my father wrote,
"until you have had your fill. It may be a long time before you see Europe again." I replied that I had practically no desire to return to Harvard and not much to university life at all. "I should just like to stay on
here in Paris and set up a new lost generation."

I revived my idea about the Dalmatian coast, encouraged by the
discovery that the ticket from Paris to Venice by train and Venice
to Dubrovnik by boat cost a mere $33. The steamer Marian and I
boarded at Venice was filled with German 'tourists,' overbearing, tact-
less and noisy. The food was poor. But the Adriatic sparkled under the
July sun, and the coast delighted with its ever-changing beauties, the
capes and coves and cliffs and inlets, the black rocks jutting out of
the dark blue water and the green hills beyond.

Dubrovnik rose out of the sea like a medieval fantasy. We reveled in
the splendor of the harbor and the fortresses and palaces and ram-
parts and towered churches and shining limestone walls and honey-
colored tiles on the town roofs and curious figures carved in niches in
the walls or on top of pedestals. The Pension Villa Argentina stood
high on a cliff overlooking miles of deep blue water. We swam off the
rocks by the Argentina, and we drank *Kaffee mit Sahne* in the town
square. It was a happy time. It was now August 1939.

We took the boat home, still involved with each other in a sort of
manic-depressive way, still unresolved about the future. On shipboard
I encountered a fellow-traveling dentist who had just visited the Soviet Union. He became furious when I suggested similarities between
communism and fascism, more furious when I renewed my prediction that Hitler and Stalin would sign a pact. We did not speak for the
rest of the trip.

The Pact came on August 24, and Sir Edward Grey's lamps really began to go out all over Europe. The next Friday, September 1, I motored down from Cambridge to spend the Labor Day weekend with Herb Wind in Buzzards Bay, at the near end of Cape Cod, in the baronial mansion of his father, a wealthy shoe manufacturer from Brockton. Soon after my arrival the news came: Hitler had invaded Poland. The Winds, Herb excepted, were not much interested in quarrels in faraway countries between people of whom they knew nothing.

In my frustration I surreptitiously phoned my father and asked him to send me a telegram saying that some drastic event — illness in the family, perhaps — required me to leave at once. The wire duly arrived. I rushed home to hang for hours over the radio and hear the awful bulletins heralding the war that changed our world forever.

PART III

The Forties

11

A Nation Divided

THREE WEEKS AFTER WAR broke out in Europe, I made my debut at a new and peculiar Harvard institution, the Society of Fellows. The Society had been invented half a dozen years earlier by A. Lawrence Lowell and L. J. Henderson as a repudiation of what William James called "the Ph.D. octopus." Neither Lowell nor Henderson had an American Ph.D. (Lowell was an LL.B., Henderson an M.D.), and the Ph.D. system, they believed, was the enemy of intellectual originality and daring. At the older Cambridge G. E. Moore, reporting on Wittgenstein's *Tractatus Logico-Philosophicus*, had said, "This is a work of genius; but it otherwise satisfies the requirements of a Ph.D." American graduate schools, Lowell thought, specialized in the "mass production of mediocrity." He was looking for "an alternative path more suited to the encouragement of the rare and independent genius."

There weren't many rare and independent geniuses about, but the search for alternative paths was laudable. In planning the Society, Lowell, Henderson and Alfred North Whitehead, a partner in the venture, were inspired by European communities of scholars like the Prize Fellows of Trinity (Cambridge), All Souls (Oxford) and the Fondation Thiers (Paris). But the depression made money scarce for educational experiments, even at Harvard. Finally, without explanation, Lowell produced an anonymous gift of a million dollars (over $11 million in the currency of 2000), and the Society opened its doors in 1933. Only after Lowell's death a decade later was he unveiled as the anonymous donor. "There being no visible source of necessary funds," he said, "I gave it myself, in a kind of desperation, although it took nearly all I had."

Henderson was chairman, and the Senior Fellows consisted of half a dozen local eminences, headed by Lowell and Whitehead. The Society offered young scholars — men only, in that benighted age — three-year fellowships to do whatever they wished, except to seek Ph.D.'s. But credentialism was laying its heavy hand on American universities; it proved hard for Junior Fellows to get jobs without doctorates; and in a while the Ph.D. ban fell by the wayside.

I had been nominated for a Junior Fellowship during my absence in England. Perry Miller argued my case successfully before the Senior Fellows. "The chief problem you will have to face," he wrote me, "will be not the bad manners of Professor L. J. Henderson and the ordeal of having to listen at least once a week to Arthur Darby Nock, though these trials will not be of the lightest [Nock, a Senior Fellow and professor of church history, was a kindly Britisher given to arch and interminable monologues on the virtues of P. G. Wodehouse], — but the problem of keeping yourself going for three years on your own steam."

I was assigned a comfortable suite near the swimming pool in Westmorley Hall, the Gold Coast section of Adams House. The Society itself occupied a set of oak-paneled rooms in Eliot House. One room was adorned by a small portrait of the bearded Edward VII bearing a startling resemblance to the bearded Henderson. There the Fellows met every Monday night in term. Sherry, alas, was served before dinner. After a year at Cambridge, my tolerance for sherry was minimal. Excellent claret, laid in by Henderson, a notorious Francophile who venerated Sainte-Beuve as Nock venerated Wodehouse, accompanied excellent dinners prepared in the Society's kitchen. A vital part of the ritual, confided to selected Junior Fellows, was the tossing of green salad in well-burnished wooden bowls.

At their first dinner, new Junior Fellows received silver candlesticks engraved with their names. (Where is mine now?) Henderson would then read a statement drafted by Lowell enjoining the novitiates to "practice the virtues, and avoid the snares, of the scholar," to be courteous to their elders and helpful to their juniors and to seek "knowledge and wisdom, not the reflected glamour of fame. . . . To these things, in joining the Society of Fellows, you dedicate yourself."

Thereafter the Monday dinners were less solemn. The Fellows, Junior as well as Senior, were encouraged to bring (male) guests. Conversation was uninhibited. Henderson was the dominating figure. Perry Miller was right about his bad manners. "His method in discussion," observed the sociologist George Homans, "is feebly imitated by the pile-driver." I can still hear that stentorian voice echoing in one of those silences that suddenly occur in crowded rooms: "Well, Pickman, I suppose that a very stupid man might say that." He regarded history as unscientific and impressionistic: after Thucydides, he would indicate, it had been downhill all the way. One developed nevertheless a grudging affection for old "Pink Whiskers," as L. J. was irreverently known when Senior Fellows were not around.

My father sent an alert to me in England: "Pareto accepted a senatorship from Mussolini. . . . More alarming is the fact that he made a convert of L. J. Henderson." Henderson remained, as Homans said, a "tireless, and to many, a tiresome, proselyte of Pareto." Henderson, Lowell too, were staunch conservatives who detested Roosevelt and the New Deal, but they were intelligent men — indeed, the first intelligent conservatives I had encountered. Dealing with their arguments forced me to reexamine and reformulate my liberalism and give it a more realistic and hard-edged cast.

Whitehead was the wisest of the Senior Fellows, assuaging heated exchanges with casual throwaway lines or making devastating remarks in the most courteous and innocent way. Even Henderson deferred to him. Crane Brinton, a New Dealer at heart, added a useful note of witty skepticism. Sam Morison, another New Dealer, was less regular in attendance but vigorous and to the point when present.

* * *

Among the first group of Junior Fellows in 1933 were Willard Van O. Quine, the great logician, B. F. Skinner, the influential behavioral psychologist, and Garrett Birkhoff, the brilliant mathematician (whose father, George Birkhoff, was also a brilliant mathematician. Someone said to George Birkhoff, "Garrett is certainly a chip off the old block." Birkhoff replied, "Well, I know he's good — but is he really that good?" My father might have said the same about me but didn't).

The terms of the first group had expired by 1939, but they still dropped by for occasional dinners. The senior Junior Fellows when I arrived were George Homans, Harry Levin and David Griggs, all elected in 1934. Homans was an Adams, in lineal descent from the two Adams presidents. He looked a lot like J. Q. Adams and argued like him too. Though a sociologist, he was literate, having been trained by Benny DeVoto to write clear and forceful prose. When his sociological colleagues passed around a jargon-ridden document "Toward a Common Language in the Social Sciences," Homans responded, "Is not English good enough?" In secret he wrote rather touching verse. He was brusque in the Adams manner, noisy, opinionated and pugnacious. Unlike most Adamses, he was also funny and capable of boisterous and drunken gaiety, as when he swung on the chandelier in Sam Morison's house on Brimmer Street (or so Sam claimed; George denied it: "if I had, I should have brought it down"). Every spring he organized a Junior Fellows dance. Homans raised one's spirits and, for all his deeply felt conservatism, I was very fond of him.

Harry Levin was equally intelligent but cautious, formal in dress and manner (no swinging on chandeliers for him), reserved to the point of diffidence, handing down severe judgments in low and cultivated tones. His field was literature, and he seemed to have read everything. His lectures on Shakespeare and on Proust, Joyce and Mann were meticulously prepared and elegantly polished. He threw off epigrams with urbane ease. Underneath the defensive and often mordant wit, he was a kind and affectionate man.

David Griggs, a geologist, was affable on the surface but angry underneath and resentful of what he regarded as Harvard snobbism. He reappeared in my life fifteen years later when he charged that Robert Oppenheimer was a security risk, not to be trusted with atomic secrets. A kindlier scientist among the more recent Junior Fellows was Stanislaw Ulam, a likable and civilized man who in a few years made the crucial breakthrough in the development of the hydrogen bomb. George Lee Haskins, the legal historian and son of the noted medieval historian C. H. Haskins, was a delightful Bostonian in the Homans mold. Paul Samuelson, the economist, was as humane and friendly as he was brilliant. McGeorge Bundy, billed as the brightest man to graduate from Yale since Jonathan Edwards (class of 1720), came on board in 1940 and almost lived up to advance notices. Mac was a great-nephew of Mr. Lowell and by inheritance a Republican, so we had the usual political debates, but we began an enduring friendship.

I learned much in those Monday-evening dinners from the mingling of talents and disciplines around the table. I did have minor social reservations. In the 1950s Brinton, who succeeded Henderson as chairman, circulated a questionnaire to former Junior Fellows. I replied, "I feel strongly that the Society should end its foolish bar against women, either as members or guests. [It finally did, in 1972.] I would also wish that it would end its foolish bar against cocktails. [No action as of 2000.] The present commitment to all-male evenings and to sherry is anachronistic, adolescent and boring." This response, Brinton noted in reporting on the poll, was "not at all typical," but he added that even this dissident (I was not identified) found the Junior Fellowship "a uniquely valuable experience."

* * *

The unique value of the experience was in fact the point that had worried Perry Miller — whether one could keep going for three years on one's own steam. This turned out to be no problem at all.

*My intention was to follow Orestes Brownson with a biography of his friend and my presumed ancestor George Bancroft. I felt an affinity with Bancroft. He had gone to Exeter and Harvard and had thereafter become the first consequential American historian. He was also a Democratic politician, a presidential ghostwriter, a cabinet officer and a diplomat, all of which I dreamily aspired to be. And through all the digressions of politics and the temptations of society, both of which he much enjoyed, he worked steadily away at his monumental *History of the United States from the Discovery of the Continent.*

The first volume was published in 1834. In the same year, the fifth of Jackson's presidency, Bancroft set forth his political credo: "The feud between the capitalist and laborer, the house of Have and the house of Want, is as old as social union, and can never be entirely quieted; but he who will act with moderation, prefer fact to theory, and remember that every thing in this world is relative and not absolute, will see that the violence of the contest may be stilled." Good pragmatic American doctrine.

Appointed Collector of the Port of Boston by Van Buren, Bancroft discharged his duties with brisk efficiency and used federal patronage not only to build a political organization but to provide jobs for literary pals like Hawthorne and Brownson. In spare moments he kept on with the *History;* the third volume came out in 1840. Defeated for governor in 1844 and weary of local political squabbles, he moved on to the national scene. He played a key role in James K. Polk's nomination and was rewarded with the secretaryship of the Navy. He proved a first-class reform secretary, founded the Naval Academy at Annapolis and issued the orders in the Mexican War that led to the annexation of California. But he kept on dividing his life between politics and history. In order to pursue research in British archives, he became Polk's minister to the Court of St. James's.

In the 1850s he concentrated on the *History;* the eighth volume was published in 1860. Thackeray, meeting him in 1852, called him "very ambitious, of a remarkable ability too and a wondrous fluency." He came to admire Lincoln and during the Civil War renewed an old political acquaintance with Andrew Johnson. Bancroft wrote Johnson's first message to Congress, and Johnson named him minister to Prussia. In Berlin Bancroft and Bismarck became fast friends. Bancroft's

German sympathies during the Franco-Prussian War provoked Victor Hugo to blast him in a scathing poem.

Back in the United States, he completed the *History*. All dozen volumes, said J. Franklin Jameson, an elder statesman of the historical profession, continued "to vote for Jackson." Then revising the early volumes to suit changing literary taste, Bancroft slaughtered adjectives and pruned his lush antebellum prose. He never stopped working. At eighty-four, he wrote to Oliver Wendell Holmes, Sr., that he was "yet strong enough to rise in the night, light my own fire and candles, and labor with close application fully fourteen hours consecutively, that is, from five in the morning till eight in the evening, with but one short hour's interruption for breakfast; and otherwise no repast; not so much as a sip of water." What a model for scholars!

Bancroft was one of the last of America's universal men, turning his hand at a variety of trades and pastimes with equable Yankee savvy and success. He was ambitious, incisive and devious. Historian, diplomat, politician, government administrator, parlor radical, bon vivant, he knew statesmen from John Quincy Adams to Bismarck, intellectuals from Goethe and Byron through Emerson and Thoreau to James Russell Lowell and Henry Adams, the last of whom said, with admiring affection, "Old George Bancroft was never more than forty" and asked him to read the manuscript of his history of the Jefferson and Madison administrations. Clover Adams, Henry's wife, before she drank the developing fluid and gave Saint-Gaudens his greatest subject, took a marvelous photograph of Bancroft at work, with his white beard and shrewd, sardonic face. He died in 1891. John Adams was president when he was born, and Theodore Roosevelt attended his memorial service.

His rival was Richard Hildreth, another Exeter and Harvard man but far more austere in both personal and literary style. Hildreth's precise, factual and rather dry six-volume *History of the United States,* published in the 1850s, was generally accounted the Federalist response to Bancroft's Jacksonianism. I chose Hildreth for my paper in Fred Merk's seminar and argued that Hildreth was not philosophically a Federalist at all but rather a pioneer Utilitarian, a follower of Jeremy Bentham. Hildreth favored Hamilton over Jefferson, I proposed, on grounds of practical wisdom, not political ideology. When my paper appeared in the *New England Quarterly,* a Johns Hopkins historian, Donald E. Emerson, who had been working on Hildreth and in 1946 published an excellent biography, sent me a long and exceedingly generous letter — an act of scholarly comity in a field too often riven by competitive jealousies. ⸰

*   *   *

Writing about Brownson, I had been struck by his reading of history as a class struggle. How had it come about that, eight years before Marx and Engels wrote *The Communist Manifesto,* a Jacksonian Democrat in far-off America expressed "Marxist" views in "Marxist" language? I was discovering similar thoughts in Bancroft's letters at the Massachusetts Historical Society and in his public utterances on yellowing pages of century-old Massachusetts newspapers. "It is now for the yeomanry and the mechanics to march at the head of civilization," Bancroft would declare. "The merchants and the lawyers, that is, the moneyed interest, broke up feudalism. The day for the multitude has now dawned." Soon I began to wonder whether the conventional interpretation of Jacksonian democracy was adequate.

That interpretation saw Jackson as a hero of the frontier, his presidency as the surge of the backwoods west into national power. Yet was not someone like Henry Clay of Kentucky quite as representative of the frontier as Andrew Jackson of Tennesee? And Clay, as the champion of the American System of national development, based on the protective tariff, the United States Bank and federal aid for internal improvements ('infrastructure' in the unlovely modern phrase), was Jackson's mortal political antagonist.

My research suggested that eastern intellectuals like Brownson and Bancroft had their own stake in the Jacksonian uprising. If Jacksonianism represented only the eruption of uncouth backwoodsmen onto the national scene, why were so many leading writers and artists of the day ardent Jacksonians — Hawthorne, Fenimore Cooper, William Cullen Bryant, Walt Whitman, Washington Irving, the sculptors Horatio Greenough and Hiram Powers, the actor Edwin Forrest? And if the frontier was the force driving the Jacksonian upheaval, how to account for the obsession in Jacksonian pamphlets and speeches with problems of a capitalist society — with monopoly, with banking, with the business cycle, with the unequal distribution of the fruits of labor, with workingmen, with trade unions, with class conflict? How to account for the hatred the business community showed for Jackson and his works?

All this led me to wonder whether Jacksonian democracy did not have an eastern and intellectual dimension that had not been fully recognized. As I labored away at the Massachusetts Historical Society, the biography of Bancroft began imperceptibly to give way to an exploration of broader Jacksonian terrain.

* * *

That exploration was conducted under the shadow of the war. But the war itself was initially anticlimactic — the "phony war," it was called or, among the more sophisticated, the "*Sitzkrieg.*" Nothing the Chamberlain government was doing changed my low opinion of it. Munia Postan, now working in the Ministry of Economic Warfare, told Charles Wintour in October 1939: "I meet daily numbers of people each of whom is capable of losing the war singlehanded." In the December 1939 issue of the *Harvard Guardian*, I published (under the name A. G. Case) an article entitled "England: Notes on Decline."

It was a quite unfeeling but rather well-written and selectively documented mood piece. A sort of palsy, I contended, had settled over England. In Tory politics "the change from the bluster of Joseph Chamberlain to the quaver of Neville makes the point." Labour had dwindled into a querulous and ineffectual opposition, "sacrificing principle to policy at one moment, policy to principle at the next, and always making the wrong sacrifice at the wrong time." Marxism, I observed, "is the most popular technique for spiritual rejuvenation in England today," and I was not crazy about that. Only Winston Churchill, "a white hope in black sheep's clothing," offered any promise of redemption. Toward the end, perhaps out of guilt over belittling a country that had treated me so generously, I did concede that palsy was not necessarily fatal. "Decline cannot be proven until it has turned into fall," and the war, I speculated, by undermining the old class structure, might still be the saving of England.

The Nazi war remained phony through the winter. We read about the proficiency of the French Army and the impregnability of the Maginot Line and were not greatly worried about Hitler. What appalled was the Soviet invasion of Finland at the end of November 1939. Coming on top of the Stalin-Hitler Pact, the Winter War hardened liberal contempt for the Communists. The CPUSA, after clamoring sanctimoniously for collective security, had whirled smartly about to call, with equal sanctimony, for isolationism. Britain, the comrades and their fellow travelers now told us, was no better than Nazi Germany, and probably worse. If they could help it, the Yanks weren't coming to join what they spurned as an "imperialist war."

* * *

The Communist somersault led to bitter contention within popular front organizations like the American Student Union. ASU leaders who condemned Stalin's alliance with Hitler, notably Joe Lash and Jimmy Wechsler, were now subject to vicious attack by their Stalinist associates. Defenders of the Pact continued, of course, to deny they were members of the Communist party.

In the early winter of 1940 the Dies Committee on Un-American Activities investigated the American Youth Congress; the ASU was its student affiliate. The sympathetic Eleanor Roosevelt, before accompanying Youth Congress leaders to the hearing, told them that she would understand that, growing up in such difficult times, some among them had joined the Communist party, but "I felt it essential that I should know the truth. If we were going to work together, I must know where we really agreed and where we differed. I asked each one in turn to tell me honestly what he believed. In every case they said they had no connection with the Communist party, never belonged to any communist organizations, and had no interest in communist ideas. I decided to accept their word." They were lying through their teeth — and, as Wechsler, who knew them well, later wrote, they seemed "to enjoy the hoax."

At Harvard the Pact and the invasion of Finland tore apart the Student Union at once and the Teachers Union in due course. I was a member of neither, but one heard reverberations of the internal debate all that winter. Secret Communist cells in both organizations enlisted well-intentioned sympathizers who expended much energy in the struggle against aid to Britain — "a struggle" that one of them, the historian Henry F. May, later said, "I now regard as totally and disastrously mistaken." Among the propositions of which May briefly persuaded himself were "that the Soviet-Nazi Pact was a brilliant coup for peace, once one really understood it" and "that in the long run British imperialism and American capitalism were an even more serious menace to the world than Hitler."

The Teachers Union held together till May 1940. Then a stormy meeting, with F. O. Matthiessen in the chair, approved by a single vote a token monetary contribution to the isolationist Harvard Student Union, now under Stalinist control. "Insults," the literary historian Henry Nash Smith recalled, "were uttered and returned with interest." The meeting threatened to break up in disorder. Matty and Perry Miller came to a sharp parting of the ways, the liberals walked out, and the Teachers Union collapsed.

The publication later that year of Arthur Koestler's brilliant tour de force *Darkness at Noon* provided new ammunition for the anti-Stalinists among us. The encounters imagined by Koestler between the cultivated old revolutionary Rubashov, the Bukharin-like character, and the new Soviet man Gletkin, hard and pitiless, confirmed one's sense of what communism had produced and illuminated the confessions in the Moscow trials.

* * *

That winter I occasionally ran into Harry Ferns, the Canadian historian I had known at Cambridge. Harry's communism had survived the Pact and the Winter War, but he was an able scholar and a likable fellow, and we disagreed amicably. A few months later, back in Canada, he came upon a piece of mine containing sideswipes at Marxism and sent me a long polemical rebuttal. My counterrebuttal, equally long, turned on the question of the nature of fascism.

Ferns, as a good Marxist, saw fascism as the creation of monopoly capitalism. I dissented. "I think one can understand world events most usefully today," I wrote, "by regarding fascism as essentially anticapitalistic. It involves a direct and unmistakable transfer of power *from* the capitalistic ruling class *to* a new revolutionary elite." That fact, I continued, was temporarily disguised by the success of fascism in persuading the capitalists to cooperate in their own destruction.

The Nazi rise to power thus enlisted the general consent of the German people, especially the business and military classes. "But the business classes have lost control, just as so often decadent governing groups, which invited barbarians into the empire as a means of bolstering their own rule, found themselves captives of their own protectors. . . . Surely in any case of conflict between the Nazi party and the German business community, there can be no question which would triumph."

I went on to ask Harry Ferns what sort of world he wanted. "Democracy," I said, "is one of the things I want to hold on to, and I see small probability of the continuance of democracy under a communist society." The right of political opposition is the foundation of democracy, but opposition requires a base that is separate from the state. "I can't see that democracy will survive the disappearance of private property. . . . You cannot bring much pressure on the state without leverage; and Communism provides for the automatic liquidation of leverage. Constitutions are of no help, except to impress people like the Webbs." I quoted John Randolph of Roanoke: "You may cover whole skins of parchment with limitations, but power alone can limit power." I have never seen, I concluded, a satisfactory discussion of the problems involved in communism's claim to be democratic while destroying the historical conditions that have undergirded democracy.

"I put the letter aside," Henry Ferns wrote in his 1983 memoir, *Reading from Left to Right.* "I could hardly bear to read it. . . . In my heart of hearts I knew I had no answer." If one admitted that force and political mobilization were autonomous factors in historical development, what value were the Marxist laws of history? "The letter from Schlesinger remained in the back of my mind; remained there, in fact, for twenty years until I found that I could no longer endure the mental confusion and inadequacy of Marxism."

*   *   *

The Stalinists were a small, if rabid, minority, even among the isolationist students. Many, perhaps most, undergraduates were opposed to intervention on quite different grounds. They felt, as most Americans did, that participation in the last war was a hideous mistake. "We are frankly determined to have peace at any price," declared a *Crimson* editorial. "We refuse to fight another balance of power war." In the spring of 1940, hundreds at Harvard signed a petition promising "never under any circumstances to follow in the footsteps of the students of 1917." This provoked an indignant letter from the students of 1917, expressing no regrets and calling on the students of 1940 to follow their example and fight for democracy.

The Soviet-Finnish War came to an end in March. In April the main front suddenly began to show signs of life, or death. The Nazis invaded Norway and Denmark; in May, Belgium and the Netherlands; soon France was staggering under *Blitzkrieg* blows. Chamberlain, thank God, was at last out; Churchill at last was prime minister. Through May we hung on the radio, listening avidly to Edward R. Murrow in London and William Shirer in Berlin, awaiting especially Elmer Davis on CBS at five minutes before 9:00 P.M., summing up the news of the day in blunt, crisp, trustworthy sentences spoken in a gravelly Hoosier accent.

I spent the winter of 1939–40, when not brooding about Marian Cannon or the age of Jackson, in inner turmoil over the war. The isolationism I had brashly expressed in England — partly, I imagine, to prove that I was not to be taken in by British urbanities — seemed increasingly hollow, even false. Forbearing letters from English friends — D. W. Brogan, Charles Wintour, Anne Whyte — were devoid of reproach and increased guilt.

Hitler's spring *Blitzkrieg* shattered my own internal Maginot Line. On May 23, 1940, I made the first entry in my journal for a year. "The invasion of Holland and Belgium," I wrote,

> finally awoke me to Nazism. Hitler is not a mere imperialist conqueror, somewhat nastier and gaudier than the Kaiser, but moved essentially by economic needs and governed by considerations of expediency. His war is not a war for markets and colonies. It is a revolution and a crusade. The analogy is not the first World War. It is the spread of Mohammedanism. Hitler . . . is the prophet of a new religion, and like all prophets is out to convert or destroy. It is democracy or Nazism.

A letter in the same vein to Charles Wintour, now in the British Army but always an editor, provoked an astringent response, applauding my belated conversion but not the prose in which I expressed it: "Hitler may be on a crusade, but that's no reason for your adopting the rhetoric of a Fifth Day Adventist."

*   *   *

I had produced those apocalyptic lines in Independence, Missouri, home town of an obscure back-bench senator up for reelection and fighting for his political life. The name of Harry S. Truman meant little to me, but Independence was where the Santa Fe Trail began, and I was there because of Benny DeVoto. Fed up with New York, that "manic town," Benny had resigned the editorship of the *Saturday Review* and moved back to Cambridge. Now, preparing to write *The Year of Decision, 1846,* he felt an urgent need to refresh his physical sense of the west, to follow the historic trails once again and inspect the weatherbeaten forts and smell the alkali plains and the verdant forests and see the snow melting on the mountains. He invited me to accompany him on the long drive west, an opportunity no young student of American history could resist.

Driving Benny's Buick through the west with this best informed and most zestful of guides resurrected the dusty past. But the insistent present could not be escaped. We lived divided lives on the journey — half absorbed by thoughts of the mountain men who had ventured across hostile country a century before; half absorbed by reports over the car radio of Nazi Panzer divisions striking at the heart of France.

Though Benny, for some reason, had always refused to go to Europe, he was a fervent interventionist. Now I had become one too. But the great American heartland seemed calm, complacent, oblivious. The day after we left Cambridge on May 17, the Germans took Antwerp. On the twentieth, as General Heinz Guderian and his tanks were storming through northern France toward Boulogne and Dunkirk, we passed through Xenia, Ohio, serene as ever, where, after a decade's interval, I had no difficulty in locating the family homestead.

We spent that night with friends of Benny in Oxford, Ohio. Professors from Miami University dropped in after dinner. "I was struck chiefly," I wrote to my parents, "by the placidity with which they viewed the war, quite as if the U.S. had no urgent involvement in its issues and could view any outcome with indifference. . . . DeVoto and I put on a show which made us feel like allied propaganda agents."

In St. Louis, we argued hotly in the editorial chambers of the *Post-Dispatch* with the cartoonist D. R. Fitzpatrick and the editor Irving Dilliard — fine men both and good friends. We told them that they should pay attention to the war in Europe. They said that the Grand Coulee Dam (a mighty public power project in the northwest) was more important to the future of the republic than anything Hitler could do. Our prophecies of disaster provoked Dilliard into writing an editorial, reprinted up and down the Mississippi Valley, accusing FDR of stampeding the nation into war and warning the middle west against panic-spreaders and warmongers from the east. (When I saw Irving Dilliard in London in 1944, he was a major in the United States Army, soon to win a Bronze Star.)

On May 26 we drove through the sullen lands of western Kansas, parched by the sun, enveloped in dust. Crossing into Colorado, I saw a great cloud hanging above the western horizon and predicted a storm. Benny, who knew the territory, said, "No. The Spanish Peaks." The cloud was the eternal snow at the summits. We had reached the Rockies.

Around sunset we approached Trinidad, a bleak mining town. That night Roosevelt was to give a fireside chat on national defense. We parked by the side of the country road in the hope of minimizing static on the car radio. The crimson glow was fading on the Spanish Peaks. Dusk fell. All about seemed dark and silent and limitless. Then the well-remembered voice, at once melodious and urgent, came on the air. Some Mexicans appeared out of an adobe hut, bowing, smiling, apologetic — so Benny described the scene in "The Easy Chair," the monthly column he contributed to *Harper's* — and asked if they might listen too. The grave presidential tones seized us all. No one stirred except to light cigarettes, smoking the car into a gray haze.

"When it was finished," Benny wrote, "one of our guests said, 'I guess maybe America declare war pretty soon now.' We waved goodbye and drove on to Trinidad. I guess maybe."

Two days later, the British began the evacuation from Dunkirk. Benny wrote from New Mexico in June: "We have come twenty-five hundred miles, from Cambridge to Santa Fe. It is a dreamlike time for traveling across America, with the fears loosed from the cave and the whole country roused to dread; and yet as we moved westward we found it progressively less roused, so that we have been bearers of evil tidings, the wave following behind us down the sun's path."

Santa Fe, with its ambling charm, was a delight (when next visited forty years later, it had become a tourist trap). But gloom increased with each broadcast and each newspaper till Benny wanted to cut the trip short and go back east. Avis dissuaded him over the telephone — what could he do in Cambridge to stop Hitler? — so we drove north to Colorado, picking up the Oregon Trail in western Nebraska, inspecting Fort Laramie and Bridger's Fort, heading toward South Pass through a brilliant green valley by a crystal blue stream set within brilliant red cliffs under a brilliant blue sky, finally to Ogden, Utah, where our paths diverged in mid-June, Benny meeting Avis and their son Gordon for a holiday in Jackson Hole.

He had been an ideal companion. For all his public irascibility, Benny was a lovely man, and I learned a great deal in those weeks about America and its west. He loved the west but not the westerners. Nature's great patrimony, he concluded, had become a "plundered province," sold out by its inhabitants in the scramble for fast bucks. This was the western tragedy. Traveling through the west with DeVoto was an exciting experience in education.

* * *

I went on to Cody, Wyoming, to join up with two Harvard historians, Richard Schlatter, a former Rhodes Scholar and later a professor at Rutgers, and Paul Ward, a former Junior Fellow and later president of Sarah Lawrence. Schlatter, though I did not know it then, was a Communist. Ward was a Christian pacifist. Both were opposed to intervention.

Paris fell two days after our rendezvous, but Dick, in the Communist style, waved the news away, claiming to regard the outcome of the war with total indifference. (Later he wrote, "The fall of France was traumatic for me but I still clung, miserably and in violation of my deepest feelings, to the principle of neutrality," following the party line "stupidly, as I think now.") For me, the collapse of my cherished France was deeply depressing. Soon came the plaintive Jerome Kern–Oscar Hammerstein song:

> The last time I saw Paris
> Her streets were young and gay
> No matter what they do to her
> I'll remember her that way.

"England's defeat now seems so inevitable," I wrote home, "or, if it manages to hang on for six months, our entrance. And in any case the kind of world I have been expecting and preparing to live in is gone." Charles Wintour, recently evacuated from France, wrote that he expected an invasion and doubted that he would survive. "I contemplated a letter to everyone I know telling them exactly what I thought of them — all the letters only to be posted when it was known I had been killed."

The fighting fronts were thousands of miles away, but our journey through the west was punctuated by ferocious arguments about the war. We spent three days driving around Yellowstone, and the magnificence was consoling; then we visited the even more glorious Grand Tetons, the peaks thrusting up from the green valleys. Such beauty promised to outlast the thousand-year *Reich*. But the arguments continued.

*   *   *

At Coeur d'Alene, Idaho, I saw my first evangelical camp meeting. It was held in the evening along a black lake, the waters rippling in the mild wind, a half-moon faintly glimmering above. One first heard an indistinct moaning, weird cries rising out of the crowd. The worshipers, to my surprise, were mostly male, though women, it seemed to me, were making the most noise. Some people were hysterical, weeping, shouting, "Jesus, come to me!"; some were rocking back and forth, clasping themselves, their hands working convulsively; some were kneeling or sitting in a cold trance. I wrote to my parents, "I have rarely seen so disgusting a spectacle." It was my first brush with American revivalism.

A woman approached, dark, small, intense, with a charming smile. "I was the biggest chippie in Coeur d'Alene," she said. "Ask anyone in Kellogg or Coeur d'Alene. I had many affairs, with colored men, with men in Spokane not fit to lie with a dog. The Lord got me lower and lower. I married but didn't love my husband. For three years I dreamed every night of another man — a colored man. Then I was saved. Now I think my husband is the most wonderful man in the world. No adulterous thoughts. . . . I'm interested in you. What are you going to do to save your soul? Come to Jesus! I have an intuition that you are a college man. You are an intellectual mess. Face it: aren't you? I was too." I thanked her and said I had to move on. "Come back another night," she said. "Don't come to see me. Come to see Jesus."

The next day, in deference to friends at the *Post-Dispatch,* we visited the Grand Coulee Dam, an impressive structure conferring much social benefit but out of sync, I feared, with the war-torn world. "You get the feeling at Grand Coulee," I wrote to my parents, "of what a great country America could be if it had a decent world to live in." Then we headed south — Rainier, Bonneville Dam, Crater Lake, on to San Francisco, to Los Angeles, where we dined at the Brown Derby and looked in vain for movie stars, to an embryonic Las Vegas, where I won at roulette, to Boulder Dam, to the Grand Canyon, where we rode horses, to Canyon de Chelly, on to Santa Fe again and back to Cambridge early in July. Those weeks in the west were for me a tremendous exposure to the majesty, as well as to the complexities, of my native land.

*　　*　　*

Exasperated by our wrangles over the war, fed up with male company, all three of us — Schlatter, Ward and Schlesinger — on returning to the east promptly proposed to the girls we loved, and all of us were married by the end of August.

John Fairbank had sent Teddy White to China on a traveling fellowship, and Teddy wrote him from Peking in July, "Tell me about Marian Cannon and Arthur Schlesinger. I find Marian well remembered in American diplomatic circles. Her name is usually coupled with that of John Davies, one of the fair-haired boys out here who is at present holding down the post at Hankow and doing a good job." But John Davies was now out of the picture. Marian and I had continued our up-and-down relationship, but we got along well most of the time. I wanted her very much, and my zeal had finally overcome her doubts.

The ceremony took place on the Cannons' hill in Franklin, New Hampshire. There drifted through my mind the parody lyrics irreverently sung by children to the tune of the wedding march:

Here comes the bride
All step aside.
Here comes the groom
Hit him with a broom.

The night before I shared a bedroom with Ralph Barton Perry, the friend and biographer of William James and a kind man whose reflections on marriage (he had been married to Bernard Berenson's sister Rachel) helped soothe my nerves. On a shining August day, a local Unitarian minister with the splendid name of Napoleon Lovely joined Marian and me in holy matrimony. We drove north to Margaree Harbor on Cape Breton Island for our honeymoon.

*   *   *

On our return to Cambridge, we inherited from Harry and Elena Levin an agreeable apartment with high ceilings and a working fireplace on the first floor of a house at 341 Harvard Street. Married life began happily, and new friendships developed.

A couple who entered our lives in these years were Gardner Cox, the painter, a man of great charm and integrity, with rugged features and bushy eyebrows, and his lovely, gamine wife, Phyllis Byrne Cox, one of the most enchanting and exasperating of women. Gardner was doing a portrait of my father, and he would bring Phyllis along to relax his subject during the sittings. My father adored Phyllis, and so did I. She was a gifted pianist, and she was also an impulsive, outspoken and ultimately poignant woman. Reared a Catholic, she had turned sharply against the Church and looked on those who remained in it with incredulity and scorn. She had had a fling in London with Ian Fleming, the creator of James Bond, I learned later, and her sister Helen had caused much scandal by divorcing Hamilton Fish Armstrong, the editor of *Foreign Affairs*, in order to marry his best friend, Walter Lippmann.

The Coxes' rambling house, built originally in 1807 and latterly occupied by the great botanist Asa Gray, was around the corner from Gray Gardens East. They gave excellent parties and provided Cambridge with a captivating taste of upper-class Bohemianism. Gardner went on to become a leading portrait painter — Robert Frost, General Marshall, Dean Acheson, Averell Harriman, Learned Hand, Whitehead, Lippmann, Conant and many others.

We also saw a great deal of John and Wilma Fairbank. At their Thursday-afternoon teas, we used to encounter an exquisite young woman, a Radcliffe sophomore, named Evangeline Bell. We were much taken by Evangeline's wry grace, effortless style and shy and subtle intelligence. Evangeline's father, long dead, was Edward Bell, an American diplomat, and she had spent much of her childhood in Peking. Her uncle Harold, a fussy but friendly bachelor, lived in a house on Beacon Hill, where Evangeline took us from time to time for ornate dinners.

One night in the winter of 1940–41 the Levins asked us to dinner with Edmund Wilson and his wife, Mary McCarthy. I was entranced by Mary — by her beauty, her wit, her cool, measuring mind, her intellectual passion, her eager eyes and her smile so lustrous and penetrating. I was also filled with indignation that this bewitching young woman should be married to a man who, however interesting and distinguished, seemed to me infinitely old. In fact, Mary was then twenty-eight and Edmund forty-five — a smaller gap in age than I presently enjoy in my second marriage.

We must have discussed the war that night. Edmund represented a vanishing species — the crusty old-stock American nationalists who inherited the dislike and distrust of the British Empire bred in their ancestors by the War of Independence and the War of 1812. Dan Aaron once asked Wilson, "Why do you hate the British?" Edmund snorted and replied, "Because of the American Revolution." There were still a few such around, isolationists all — Charles A. Beard, John Dewey, Oswald Garrison Villard, Van Wyck Brooks, Quincy Howe, Alice Roosevelt Longworth, Hamilton Fish, Robert Frost, E. E. Cummings, Edward Hopper, Charles Ives, Frank Lloyd Wright, Robert M. Hutchins, Harlow Shapley, Norman Thomas of the Socialist party and Colonel Robert R. McCormick of the reactionary *Chicago Tribune*. The title of Quincy Howe's tract of 1937 summed up their case: *England Expects Every American to Do His Duty.* Mary, for her part, influenced by Trotskyite friends on the *Partisan Review,* disdained the war as a meaningless clash between rival imperialisms.

I found the Wilsons fascinating. Though in time Mary and Edmund turned against each other, both remained my friends for life. Neither, brilliant as they were in literary, social and moral commentary, had political, far less geopolitical, minds. Edmund was forever a man of the Twenties; Mary was a child of the Twenties, inheriting the rebel spirit, the aesthetic concerns, the satiric bent, the revolt against puritanism, the delight in iconoclasm, the faith in drink and sex and personal freedom — and the indifference to politics. "It was characteristic of the Jazz Age," Scott Fitzgerald wrote in *The Crack-Up,* "that it had no interest in politics at all." (One day in the summer of 1940, I saw a pretty girl rushing across Harvard Yard to make a class. Someone said to me, "That's Scott Fitzgerald's daughter." Twenty years later Scottie Lanahan, as she became, and I were good friends.)

*   *   *

My own understanding of Nazism was greatly sharpened by a growing friendship with Peter Viereck. A year ahead of me at Harvard College, Peter was brilliant, impulsive, voluble and a genuine eccentric. In manner he was at once languid and excitable. In talents he was a potent combination of historian, poet and polemicist.

He was also the son of George Sylvester Viereck, and thereby, we were given to understand, the great-grandson of Kaiser Wilhelm I; the actress Edwina Viereck had been the kaiser's mistress. After the Great War, Peter's father called regularly on Kaiser Wilhelm II in exile at Doorn in the Netherlands. Sometimes he took Peter along. "With a twinkle," Peter wrote me, "the Kaiser called my father 'mon cousin.' . . . Speaking perfect English, the Elba'd emperor talked to me of his interest in *dernier cri* U.S. lit. He did this by mixing up Sinclair Lewis with Upton Sinclair. No wonder he lost a war."

Not at all without flashes of talent, the elder Viereck first attracted attention before the kaiser's war as a writer of erotic verse in the decadent fin-de-siècle style. A clever journalist, he sought out Hitler in 1923 and concluded his interview: "If he lives, Hitler, for better or for worse, is sure to make history." He counted Freud and Bernard Shaw among his friends. But he was best known to my generation as a German propagandist during the First War and as an apologist for Hitler and Nazism in the Second. Though not himself an anti-Semite, he offered sympathetic explanations of Hitler's attitude toward the Jews. Behind the scenes he was, Niel Johnson, his biographer, has written, "Germany's highest paid publicist in America."

For his sons — Peter and George Sylvester, Jr. — this was a torturing predicament. They loved their father, but they hated Nazism. In 1941 Peter published *Metapolitics,* an important and original work tracing the historical roots of Nazi racism and messianism to the excesses of German romanticism, a view rediscovered to much éclat in the Nineties. Wagner was darkly prominent in Peter's analysis, and Thomas Mann, though a fan of Wagner, approved Peter's account and praised him for going back to "the sources of German Nationalism which is the most dangerous in existence, because it is mechanized mysticism."

Peter's father refused for many years to look at *Metapolitics*. Finally, rendered helpless by strokes and cared for by his son, he read the book and said, shortly before his death in 1962, "Peter, you were right." Did he really mean it? Peter could not be sure: "He may have been humoring me, being dependent on me. I simply dunno."

*   *   *

Beneath the din of the increasingly bitter national debate, I labored happily away on the Jacksonian era, exploiting the riches to be found in the endless — and wonderfully accessible — resources of Harvard's Widener Library. But research was an escape. One could never suppress the burning, the implacable, question: What should the republic do about Hitler?

12

On the Brink

WAR HOVERED OVER ALL, and the argument between intervention-ists and isolationists grew each week more savage and despairing. There have been a number of fierce national quarrels in my lifetime — over communism in the later Forties, over McCarthyism in the Fifties, over Vietnam in the Sixties — but none so tore apart families and friendships as the great debate of 1940–41. Though historians have dealt ably with the policy issues, justice has not been done to the searing personal impact in those angry days. Only a couple of short stories by Louis Auchincloss and J. P. Marquand's novel of 1943, *So Little Time*, convey the social flavor of the years between the outbreak of war and Pearl Harbor.

One can guess that the protagonist in *So Little Time*, the play doctor Jeffrey Wilson, like Marquand a veteran of the First World War, expressed the author's concealed forebodings and incertitudes. Marquand's forceful new wife, Adelaide Hooker, had studied in Germany and was an impassioned isolationist. A cool customer, John instinctively sought refuge in irony (we became friends in Cambridge after the war; he was an intelligent, sardonic, touchy man). He detested isolationism but declined to advocate intervention while considering it inevitable. The novel vividly conveys the atmosphere of the time. "You could get away from the war for a little while," Jeffrey Wilson muses, "but not for long, because it was everywhere, even in the sunlight. It lay behind everything you said or did. You could taste it in your food, you could hear it in music." And so it was for many Americans.

* * *

Others wanted to taste and hear the war as little as possible. That traumatic May of 1940, while many of us underwent a conversion to interventionism, many others decided the time had come to stop the drift to war. The America First Committee was born in New Haven, its progenitor a Yale Law School student, the scion of the Quaker Oats fam-

241

ily, named R. Douglas Stuart, Jr. (In 1992, flying back to the United States from Morocco, where we had been marking the fiftieth anniversary of the Casablanca conference, I sat next to an agreeable Chicagoan named Bob Stuart, whom I knew to have been President Reagan's ambassador to Norway. As we chatted away, I idly asked him whether he was by any chance related to the R. Douglas Stuart, Jr., of America First fame. He replied dryly, "That's me.")

In the spring of 1940 Stuart, joined by Gerald Ford, later of the White House, and Potter Stewart, later of the Supreme Court, circulated a petition that concluded starkly: "We demand that Congress refrain from war, even if England is on the verge of defeat." Other Yale students joining the cause included Kingman Brewster, Jr., later president of Yale and ambassador to Great Britain, R. Sargent Shriver, later of the Peace Corps and the War on Poverty, and Jonathan B. Bingham, later a liberal Democratic congressman from New York. Among older adherents were Chester Bowles, William Benton, Philip C. Jessup, Willard Wirtz, Richard M. Bissell, Jr. Among younger adherents was Gore Vidal, who organized the America First cell at Exeter.

Charles A. Lindbergh, in the Twenties the American hero, in the Thirties, after the kidnapping and murder of his infant son, the American martyr, was emerging as America First's most popular figure. In 1998 Vidal called Lindbergh "the best that we are apt to produce in the hero line, American style." Irony? I fear not. In 1940 this best American hero opposed aid to Britain, now standing alone against Hitler, and argued that white people, instead of fighting one another, must unite to resist the onslaught of Asiatic hordes.

His wife's poisonous little best seller *The Wave of the Future* came out in the summer of 1940. The gentle Anne Morrow Lindbergh, lamenting "the beautiful things . . . lost in the dying of an age," saw democracy as finished and totalitarianism, the predestined successor, as a "new, and perhaps even ultimately good, conception of humanity trying to come to birth." She dismissed the evils of Hitlerism and Stalinism as merely "scum on the wave of the future" and concluded that "the wave of the future is coming and there is no fighting it." For a moment she seemed to be right. By the end of 1940, there were only a dozen democracies left on the planet.

Though isolationists were predominantly Republican, conservative and business-minded, the debate cut sharply across party and class lines. The left had its own quota of isolationists: the Stalinists, of course, but the Trotskyites too and half the Socialists. The anti-Stalinist *Partisan Review* declared, "Our entry into the war, under the slogan of 'Stop Hitler!' would actually result in the immediate introduction of totalitarianism over here." John Dewey and William Carlos Williams were among those signing the statement. Later, *PR* ran "10 Propositions on the War," in which Dwight Macdonald and the art critic Clement Greenberg declared, in italics, *"To support the Roosevelt-Churchill war regime clears the road for fascism."*

Many of those from whom one was bitterly divided at the time became friends and allies in later years. Indeed, I myself in retrospect sympathized with part of the isolationist case: that the United States was not commissioned a world savior and should not intervene militarily where vital national interests were not at stake. From time to time in later years I have even found myself described as a neo-isolationist.

But the critical question in 1940 was whether the United States had a vital interest in preventing Hitler's conquest of Europe. On this point I liked to quote Jefferson. "It cannot be to our interest," the France-loving, peace-loving Jefferson observed when Napoleon bestrode the continent, "that all Europe should be reduced to a single monarchy." America would be forever in danger should "the whole force of Europe [be] wielded by a single hand."

My concern was less a Nazi invasion of the Western hemisphere than the political consequences for the United States of a Nazi conquest of Europe. "Hitler's going to win," William Claflin, the treasurer of Harvard, told President Conant. "Let's be friends with him." But my British experience persuaded me that friendship with Hitler would not be all that simple. Hitler was an easily offended man. I remembered the Lord Chamberlain's censorship of an innocuous couplet in an undergraduate show and Churchill's prediction that appeasement would lead to the suppression of all criticism of Hitler and his regime. I was influenced too by the spectacle of Marshal Pétain's France currying Hitler's favor and reduced to servility.

In January 1941 the Harvard Committee against Military Intervention cited Charles A. Beard's contention that America must choose between policing the world and sticking to the Western hemisphere. "If Hitler comes to America," in my paraphrase in a letter to the *Crimson*, "we'll fight him then, so why worry until we see the whites of his eyes." I agreed with "so honored a name" that we should worry about American democracy and reject the role of world policeman, but asked what would happen to American democracy when the Americans who thought we could do business with Hitler came to power, men who sought to repeal the social reforms of the New Deal, and "when every frustrated, unsatisfied hoodlum in America will start buying colored shirts and parading with his local fascist party, when it will be impossible to criticize fascism lest it disturb relations with our good friends and customers beyond the seas. Hitler won't have to invade America until it is so torn by inner conflict that the German army could cross the ocean in canoes."

Most isolationists rejected the argument that our national interest required the preservation of a balance of power in Europe; a few, like Lindbergh, saw Nazi Germany as a necessary force in preserving a balance of power against the Soviet Union. In one way or another, they believed that America could live at peace with a Nazi Europe. The America Firsters were, as their name implied, isolationist for American reasons, not, like the Communists, for Soviet reasons, nor, like a few, very few, for fascist reasons.

But there were those too. In the autumn and and winter of 1940, Marian and I saw something of a brilliant and charming student at the Harvard School of Design named Philip Johnson. I met him because he occasionally took out Rosamond Chapman, a bright, pretty, pert young woman who served as secretary and research assistant for Benny DeVoto and also for Ralph Barton Perry.

Philip, in his early thirties, had had a bizarre political past. He had visited Germany soon after Hitler came to power, was thrilled by the Nazi mass rallies, and on returning to the United States was impressed as well by the intelligent American fascist theoretician Lawrence Dennis. In search of an American political leader he could follow, Philip first chose Huey Long. After Long's assassination in 1935, he moved on to Father Coughlin, the radio priest of Royal Oak, Michigan, whose Sunday-afternoon broadcasts commanded fervent national audiences. In 1939 Philip went back to Germany, this time as a correspondent for Coughlin's paper *Social Justice*.

I was not aware of all this when Rosie Chapman first introduced us. Arguments quickly erupted, but Philip was civilized and amusing, and somehow we preserved the amenities. In later years Philip Johnson, who had long since repented his weird past, was perhaps the most influential American architect of his generation. Meeting again in New York, we became warm friends.

*   *   *

Harvard was in bitter contention. After the fall of France, Conant went on nationwide radio to urge every action possible to ensure the defeat of Hitler — for which he was rewarded with a flood of abusive letters. At the 1940 commencement, the class orator denounced aid to the allies as "fantastic nonsense." When a member of the Class of 1915 told the alumni convocation that "we were not too proud to fight then and we are not too proud to fight now," boos and hisses from more recent graduates drowned him out.

Ralph Barton Perry rallied interventionist members of the faculty in American Defense–Harvard Group to make the case for aid to Britain. I joined Perry's enterprise with enthusiasm. In the September 1940 *Atlantic Monthly* Kingman Brewster, Jr., and Spencer Klaw, editors of the Yale and Harvard student papers, published a manifesto reaffirming student determination not to save Europe from Hitler. American Defense–Harvard Group released my response in a piece called "Arms and the Young Man." Citing my sixteen-thousand-mile auto trip around the country over the summer, I said that "most of the fellows my age with whom I talked had a strong if inarticulate conviction that this man Hitler must somehow be stopped. . . . Only the college boys — and these with surprising unanimity — agreed that they were going to sit this war out."

Undergraduate isolationism, I suggested, represented an intellectual, not a moral, failure, "a skepticism of slogans, not a fundamental cynicism about values . . . a discouragement with means, not a disillusion over ends." The case against war was made, it seemed to me, with genuine moral fervor. "It speaks well for our moral well-being, however dubiously it speaks for our intelligence." When students began to think seriously and practically about the American choices, I thought, they would understand the necessity of rearmament, conscription and all possible aid to Britain.

I was objecting not only to the isolationists but also to the moralistic hectoring of elders like Lewis Mumford, who saw college students as cowards spoiled by luxury and debauched by cynicism. Mumford's book *Faith for Living*, with its high decibel level and its demand that freedoms of speech and assembly be denied to fascist sympathizers, had particularly provoked me. I felt that hysteria discredited the interventionist case.

In October 1940 the *New York Times* printed a long letter from me (in those benign days, the *Times* still ran long letters) arguing that war, for all its horrors, would not turn America into a dictatorship, as the isolationists predicted, and indeed might offer possibilities for social reconstruction along egalitarian lines. This, I added, was not at all to say that war was a spiritual good: "Let us leave that talk to Herr

Goebbels and Mr. Mumford." The single cut the *Times* made in the
letter, perhaps correctly, was the reference to Mumford.

In England, C. Day Lewis, asking "Where Are the War Poets?," put
in incisive verse this mixture of doubt and duty with which many of us
viewed the war:

> It is the logic of our times
> No subject for immortal verse
> That we who lived by honest dreams
> Defend the bad against the worse.

* * *

The debate was beginning to center on the presidential election. The
Republicans, in nominating Wendell Willkie, an ex-Democrat, were
in fact choosing a robust internationalist. But that was not clear at the
time, and it became progressively less clear as, under the pressure of
the campaign, Willkie began to assail Roosevelt as a warmonger. (The
next year, when asked about these speeches, he waved them away as
"campaign oratory.") To some of us Willkie seemed menacing, resem-
bling in bulk and look (we thought) Hermann Goering.

Toward the end of October, John L. Lewis, the head of the Congress of Industrial Organizations (the famous CIO) and the country's
premier labor leader, was to announce his presidential choice in a
long-awaited radio speech. Which way would he go? On the one
hand, Roosevelt had done more for organized labor than any president. On the other, Lewis was an all-out isolationist. The lady or the
tiger?

I listened to the speech with Dick Schlatter and his great friend the
historian Daniel Boorstin. When Lewis declared for Willkie, my indignation knew no bounds. But my two companions seemed strangely
complacent, even pleased, by what seemed to me arrant betrayal. At
that moment it burst upon me that they were very likely members of
the Communist party, as indeed they were. The sensation was not unlike that experienced by viewers of *Invasion of the Body Snatchers* when
they suddenly realize that the bodies of normal American citizens
have been taken over by aliens from outer space.

A few days later, on October 30 at the Boston Garden, I saw FDR indulge in campaign oratory of his own when he promised American
mothers and fathers, "Your boys are not going to be sent into any foreign wars." It was my second and last sighting of the president.

The next week, to our immense relief, he was reelected for his third term — a possibility denied his successors when the Republicans took posthumous revenge after the war and pushed through the Twenty-second Amendment, limiting presidents to two terms. Deservedly, the first two presidents disqualified by that amendment were themselves Republicans, Dwight Eisenhower and Ronald Reagan.

The Schlesingers were not surprised by Roosevelt's victory. In December 1939 my father had predicted in a *Yale Review* article, "Tides of American Politics," that "the revolt against conservatism which began in 1931 will last until 1947 or 1948." Shortly after FDR's third inaugural in 1941, Jim Rowe gave the president my father's article with a cover memorandum reminding FDR of his own observation that the tides between conservative and liberal rule changed about every eight years. "Schlesinger argues the periods of alternation are about fifteen years. . . . I think the third-term election proves Schlesinger right and you wrong." (I might add that my father's article also predicted that, after a conservative interlude, "the next turn of the tide [toward liberalism] will then be due in the neighborhood of 1963.")

*   *   *

Work for American Defense–Harvard Group intensified. Undergraduate opinion was beginning to move, but not fast enough. In May 1941 Stewart Alsop wrote a piece for the *Atlantic* called "Wanted: A Faith to Die For." An interventionist himself, he wondered whether America had a purpose capable of rallying its young to kill and die. He saw no more martial spirit in his coevals "than there is in a turtle." Making the world safe for democracy had worked once, but would not work again: "A kind of democracy that leaves somewhere between nine and sixteen million unemployed for ten years in the richest nation on earth hardly seems worth imposing on the rest of the world." Nevertheless, Alsop soon got himself to England and enlisted in the King's Royal Rifle Corps.

The Harvard Group now began to receive visits from emissaries of the British Information Service in New York — notably John Wheeler-Bennett, the brilliant historian of German militarism, and Aubrey Morgan, who, coincidentally, was married to Anne Morrow Lindbergh's sister. The British agents did their work of pushing America into war with great charm and tact. After the war, Morgan retired with his wife to a farm in Oregon, and I never saw him again, but I often encountered the Wheeler-Bennetts.

One reason for the British visits to Boston was WRUL, the most powerful short-wave radio station in the United States. Its owner, Walter Lemmon, was an internationalist, and it had established on its own a considerable overseas audience. The Harvard Group took responsibility for a program called the Digest of American Editorial Opinion, and we welcomed the opportunity to say things we hoped would inform and cheer the British. I gave over fifty broadcasts, working closely with William R. Tyler, with whom I would work closely again twenty years later when he became assistant secretary of state for Europe in the Kennedy administration.

We did not know it, but the British Security Coordination, an umbrella organization of British intelligence and propaganda agencies under Sir William Stephenson in New York, was moving quietly into WRUL, recruiting staff and subsidizing programs. "By the middle of 1941," according to the BSC's postwar report, "station WRUL was virtually, though quite unconsciously, a subsidiary of BSC, sending out covert British propaganda all over the world."

Like many official reports, the BSC document was perhaps unduly self-congratulatory. Evidently BSC control was not total, for the Harvard program was, after a time, taken off the air. Harlow Shapley was a director of the foundation that operated WRUL, and he had objected especially to me, "on the basis," John M. Potter, the Group's liaison with WRUL and later president of Hobart College, wrote me, "of your youth and inexperience (which, to anyone who has listened to you broadcast, is poppycock) and took the line that 'Young Schlesinger is not yet as good as his father.'. . . It is a pity that Shapley is so extreme an isolationist."

I doubt that the broadcasts did much for British morale, though forty years after, when I was examining British Foreign Office papers at the Public Records Office, I found some of my scripts quoted in Foreign Office memoranda.

*   *   *

My interventionist activism carried me beyond Harvard. At some point in 1940, perhaps at Ford Hall, I met a fiery young Irish-American woman named Frances Sweeney. She had reddish-blonde hair and flashing blue eyes, and she was afraid of nothing. She ran a paper, the *Boston City Reporter,* devoted initially to exposing crooked politicians, mostly as Irish as herself. Her associate in this enterprise was a tall, gaunt, secretive, satirical Greek investigative reporter, Constantine (Gus) Gazulis.

The Massachusetts Irish generally hated Britain, for obvious and understandable historic reasons, and were in consequence passionately, sometimes viciously, isolationist. Too many were imbibing anti-Semitism from Father Coughlin. Fran formed the American Irish Defense Association to oppose and expose isolationism and anti-Semitism. Despite admonitions (as she wrote me) "that more ladylike action is preferred and a reminder that I do have heart trouble," she fearlessly rebuked the formidable Cardinal O'Connell (to his face) for his failure to condemn Coughlin. I greatly liked and admired Fran Sweeney and did what I could to help her (and in 1943 she kindly wrote to Theodore Maynard, the Catholic historian, "When we began this fight up here — Arthur was my mainstay and balance wheel"). In April 1944 Fran died on a Boston street of a heart attack. She was thirty-six years old. A vivid memory.

*   *   *

The war was everywhere. It lay behind everything you said or did. One snowy Sunday morning in the winter of 1940–41 Marian insisted that I accompany her to Memorial Church in Harvard Yard to listen to a professor at the Union Theological Seminary named Reinhold Niebuhr. After Coeur d'Alene, the last thing I felt I needed was a dose of evangelical religion, and I abandoned the Sunday papers and the fireside under protest.

The pews were packed long before the tower bells chimed eleven. A tall, rangy man with a massive bald head came to the pulpit. Establishing instant command over the congregation, he spoke, without notes, in rushes of jagged eloquence. His eyes flashed; his voice rose to a roar and sank to a whisper; outstretched arms gave emphasis to his points; but, underneath the dramatics, the argument was cool, rigorous and powerful. Man was flawed and sinful, he told the hushed but initially dubious audience. Yet even sinful man had the duty of acting against evil in the world. Our sins, real as they were, could not justify our standing apart from the European struggle.

I discovered that Niebuhr, then forty-eight years old, was the son of a pastor of the German Evangelical Synod who had come to the United States after the Civil War. Young Niebuhr's first parish had been in Detroit in 1915. The ministry on the urban frontier, exposing him to poverty, racial tension and savage labor-management conflict, drove him to the left. By 1928, when he departed for New York and the Union Theological Seminary, he was an active Socialist.

Yet, as he moved toward heterodoxy in politics, he contrarily moved toward orthodoxy in theology. Detroit had persuaded him that liberal Christianity, with its sentimental and optimistic view of man, was hopelessly irrelevant to the power realities of industrial capitalism. Christian pacifism seemed equally irrelevant to a world tormented by militaristic dictatorships. When the Socialist leader Norman Thomas, who had himself begun as a liberal Protestant minister, steered the Socialist party toward isolationism, Niebuhr resigned. A more searching conception of human nature was required for a bitterly conflicted world, and this Niebuhr found in the tragic insights of Augustine and Calvin.

The notion of sinful man was uncomfortable for my generation. We had been brought up to believe in human innocence and virtue. The perfectibility of man was less a peculiarly liberal illusion than an all-American conviction. Andrew Carnegie had long since expressed the national faith when, after acclaiming the rise of man from lower to higher forms, he said, "Nor is there any conceivable end to his march to perfection." In 1939 Charles E. Merriam, the renowned political scientist at the University of Chicago, wrote in *The New Democracy and the New Despotism:* "There is a constant trend in human affairs toward the perfectibility of mankind. This was plainly stated at the time of the French Revolution and has been reasserted ever since that time, and with increasing plausibility."

Many American liberals, under the pervasive influence of John Dewey, had a particular weakness for the idea that the troubles of the world were due not to human frailty but to human ignorance and to unjust institutions. Other liberals, under the influence of William James, were more realistic, agreeing, as James had written in *Pragmatism,* that "the trail of the human serpent is thus over everything." Dewey and his followers saw no human serpents. Education of individuals and reform of institutions, they supposed, would remove the obstacles to a better world. The notion of original sin seemed a historical, even a hysterical, curiosity that had gone out with hard-shell Calvinism.

But nothing in the system of human perfectibility had prepared us for Hitler and Stalin. The concentration camps and the gulags were proving human nature capable of infinite depravity. What had happened to man in his march to perfection? Niebuhr's interpretation of man and history came as a vast illumination. His arguments, for which Perry Miller's meditations on Puritanism had predisposed me, had the great merit of accounting both for Hitler and Stalin and for the necessity of standing up to them.

The growing bitterness of the foreign policy debate soon overcame Christian injunctions about turning the other cheek. Friendships fell like leaves in autumn. Let me cite a letter Niebuhr himself wrote in 1941 to Charles Clayton Morrison, the isolationist editor of the *Christian Century* and a friend of many years:

> I note your protestations of friendship but friendship does not exist by fiat but lives in life and deeds. You can get no moral advantage of me by generously claiming to be my friend when I say a friendship is ended. The whole business of covering up ugly realities with words is of no avail. The conflict between you and myself or between your side and mine is, in miniature, as tragic as the world conflict.

*   *   *

In the meantime, my researches in America of a century earlier were carrying me far afield. In May Marian and I set forth, first to New York, where I examined manuscripts and newspapers at the Public Library and the New-York Historical Society. In the evenings we went to the theater, admiring Gene Kelly in *Pal Joey*, Paul Lukas in Lillian Hellman's *Watch on the Rhine* ("immensely moving and exciting," I wrote to my parents) and Victor Moore in *Louisiana Purchase*. Helen Cannon and her new husband, Douglas Bond, a keen young psychoanalyst from Philadelphia, came up one night, and we all saw Orson Welles's *Citizen Kane*. I sat so far from the screen that, with my near-sightedness and too many old-fashioneds at dinner, I had only an imperfect idea of what was going on and had to have crucial details explained to me afterward. Later, of course, I came to admire *Kane* too.

From New York we went on to Washington to look at the papers of Jackson, Martin Van Buren (that most illegible of letter writers), Roger B. Taney and other Jacksonians at the Library of Congress. We found rooms in a boardinghouse at 3021 Q Street in Georgetown. Every weekday morning I disappeared into the cool shadows of the library's manuscript division and immersed myself in the Washington of Andrew Jackson. At four-thirty, when the manuscript division closed, I would come out into the bright sunlight of the Washington of Franklin Roosevelt.

While I was entangled in the nineteenth century, the twentieth century was exploding around me. I remember emerging one afternoon toward the end of May to find newspaper extras announcing that the British had sunk the *Bismarck*, reputedly the most powerful battleship in the world. One could almost touch the wave of elation running through people on the street. It was far from the age of Jackson.

Talk in Washington never ceases to excite — the endless gossip about power, the endless temptations of inside-dopesterism; above all, the size of the stakes, with history always in both foreground and background. Henry James had called Washington "the City of Conversation pure and simple . . . the only specimen, of any such intensity, in the world." In the spring of 1941, with incessant argument about the war, with the struggle to increase defense production against business as usual, with speculation where Hitler might strike next and whether Britain could hold out, Washington was at its most exciting.

Social life was easy. In the Library of Congress I encountered an intelligent and friendly young southern historian, a few years older than I, and had a most enjoyable luncheon with Vann Woodward. Pat Jackson invited Marian and me to dinner with a promising freshman congressman from the state of Washington named Henry (Scoop) Jackson and a leading figure from organized labor (I forget whom) — "appalling stories of Communist influence in the CIO," I wrote home, "concentrated apparently behind Lewis." Marian's friend William S. Youngman, a lawyer working on aid to General Chennault and the Chinese Nationalists, introduced us to an American who had gone down from Cambridge the year before I went there, Michael Straight, "a very alert, nice fellow."

*　　*　　*

One soft spring evening Evangeline Bell, who had left Radcliffe to join Attorney General Francis Biddle's staff at the Department of Justice, took us to dinner at a house called Hockley to meet her friend (and admirer) Ed Prichard. One knew of Prich by reputation. He was a Kentuckian who had graduated from Princeton in 1935 and gone on to Harvard Law School, where he had made a powerful impression. He was Felix Frankfurter's adored protégé, the co-editor at the age of twenty-four with Archibald MacLeish of *Law and Politics: Occasional Papers of Felix Frankfurter.* When Frankfurter went on the Court, Prich was his third law clerk (in those days, justices got along with one clerk per year). Now he was deeply involved in the latest New Deal battle — the struggle against a largely resistant business community to convert the economy to war production.

Prich was one of several New Deal bachelors renting Hockley, an old Virginia mansion on a high bluff in Arlington overlooking the Potomac. We sat on a columned veranda, with a wide lawn before us and the lights of Georgetown in the distance, while Johnson, the Negro (so called then) butler, served mint juleps in silver cups. I had never had a mint julep before. I cannot remember who else were there that night, but, when Prich appeared, he at once took over as the undisputed king of a formidable group of articulate and ambitious lawyers.

The talk was rapid, knowing and droll — talk of the war, of the problems of defense mobilization, of FDR, of Felix and Harry, of Dean and Ben and Tom. I found it all vastly exciting. I do not think it was just the mint juleps. Prich was the dazzling center, exuberant, witty, bursting with legal ideas, political insight, administrative gossip and intrigue. He was enormously fat, enormously well read, enormously funny. He seemed to know everything and everybody, and he mimicked the mighty with immense relish. How I envied the New Dealers with all their opportunities and responsibilities!

Another night Marian and I went to a peace rally. The speakers were Burton K. Wheeler, the fervently isolationist senator from Montana, Norman Thomas and John T. Flynn, a popular economic journalist, now an America First official. Alice Roosevelt Longworth sat on the platform next to Mrs. Robert A. Taft, wife of the Ohio senator. The two ladies — Theodore Roosevelt's daughter and the daughter-in-law of the man TR had chosen as his successor and later attacked as a false friend — chatted affably throughout the evening.

The hall was less crowded than I expected and the audience less hysterical — which I attributed to Washington's lack of the proletarian Coughlinite elements found in industrial cities. But the audience did go wild every time the name of Charles Lindbergh was mentioned, as it was time and time again by Wheeler, by Flynn and even by Norman Thomas. Wheeler gave the most effective speech, I thought; Thomas was too sarcastic; Flynn, who called for a negotiated peace, was a poor speaker.

*   *   *

Back in Cambridge I began to write. I had accumulated several shoeboxes of notes painstakingly inscribed in pen on four-by-six-inch slips. One day I received a charming, handwritten letter from Charles Beard, written from the Curly Horse Ranch in Sonoita, Arizona. My letter thanking him for his kind note about the Brownson book had arrived, and it awakened, he wrote, "memories of many years, your father as a young man full of wisdom beyond his years, and now you whose years of opportunity open before you." Knowing of my Jacksonian labors, he offered me his notes for a book on Jacksonian democracy he had once planned as a sequel to his excellent *Economic Origins of Jeffersonian Democracy* (1915). "I do not presume to think that they will be of much use to you, but with #70 on the horizon I shall never finish the project." The notes did turn out to be of only marginal use, but it was a generous act to a novice in the field.

Then A. Lawrence Lowell, on behalf of the Lowell Institute, invited me to give a series of lectures in October at the Boston Public Library. I had had my first trial as a lecturer that spring when I gave a course on American intellectual history at Radcliffe College. Working out the course was fun, but giving it was not. The twenty or so innocent, harmless and charming young women in the class so terrified me that regularly, before each lecture, I went into the faculty restroom in Longfellow Hall and threw up.

The Lowell Lectures were an entrenched Boston institution, twice a week at eight o'clock, free to all, the lecturer in black tie and dinner jacket. I provided as a title "A Reinterpretation of Jacksonian Democracy." My stage fright was beginning to diminish; at least I no longer threw up before ascending the platform. I also find notations that suggest I or someone counted the audience for each of the six lectures:

"The Background of Jacksonian Democracy" 165
"The War over the United States Bank" 102
"The Rise of the Radicals" 103
"Van Buren and the Struggle for Financial Independence" 76
"The Philosophy of Jacksonian Democracy" 87
"The Biography of a Tradition" 86

The steady decline in attendance was a comment on the awkwardness of the lecturer; also due, I liked to think, to the competition from the Boston theater — Danny Kaye and Eve Arden in *Let's Face It!* with songs by Cole Porter at the Colonial, Taylor Holmes in *The Man Who Came to Dinner* at the Copley, *Rio Rita* at the Opera House.

The outline for a book was now firm. I sketched out my argument:

This book is in part a study of some aspects of the eastern expression of Jacksonian democracy. It is intended to assist in redressing the balance of emphasis, which has generally represented Jacksonian democracy as essentially the product of the western frontier. It does not mean to argue a thesis about whether Jacksonian Democracy was "fundamentally" eastern or western or anything else, but it would suggest that perhaps more things can be understood about it by a class analysis than by a sectional analysis.

The book will deal in particular with the origin and development of the ideas which controlled government policy, the desires and apprehensions which caused some men to formulate them and others to accept them, and the theorists themselves. It will present a view of Jacksonian democracy as being in large part a reasoned reform program, rather than the intemperate and violent thrust of the West into national politics. It will focus particularly on the relationship of Jacksonian democracy toward the emerging economic relationships which came in the wake of the Industrial Revolution. Obviously thought about these relationships was most mature and developed in the East where the Industrial Revolution was most advanced.

This book will seek to examine the ideas, theories and preconceptions which the non-business groups of the day used in their attempt to adjust and moderate a nation increasingly dominated by business — an intellectual history of Jacksonian democracy.

The proposed title was "Jackson and the American Democratic Tradition," and the outline contemplated a work of fifty-eight chapters. I plowed stubbornly on.

*　　*　　*

More than ever the war shadowed all. For months the British had been fighting alone against the fascist states — fighting in Greece, in Norway, in Yugoslavia, in North Africa, in East Africa, in Iraq, in the Atlantic, in the Mediterranean, in the skies over Britain and Germany. How long could a small island sustain so far-flung a war? The question pressed harder every day.

In January 1941 President Roosevelt gave the democratic world its objectives when he proclaimed the Four Freedoms — freedom of speech and expression, freedom of worship, freedom from want, freedom from fear. In March his proposal to lend and lease military aid to Britain, though vociferously opposed in the country by the isolationists (and the Communists), passed Congress by substantial margins. In May FDR proclaimed "an unlimited national emergency" requiring "the strengthening of our defense to the extreme limit of our national power and authority."

Then, on June 22, Hitler's armies invaded the Soviet Union. American diplomats had been warning the Kremlin for weeks that a Nazi attack was imminent. Stalin had dismissed the warnings as a capitalist attempt to divide the dictators. When Hitler struck, I listened on the radio to Churchill's thrilling response. No one, he said, had been a more consistent opponent of communism: "I will unsay no word that I have spoken about it. But all this fades away before the spectacle which is now unfolding. The past, with its crimes, its follies, and its tragedies, flashes away. I see the Russian soldiers standing on the threshold of their native land, guarding the fields which their fathers have tilled from time immemorial. . . ." On went the great, majestic rolling periods: "Behind all this glare, behind all this storm, I see that small group of villainous men who plan, organise, and launch this cataract of horrors upon mankind." Rhetoric, no doubt, but rhetoric rising marvelously to the occasion.

I ran into my friend the Marxist economist Paul Sweezy that day on the steps of Widener Library. "What do you think now?" I asked. Paul replied laconically, "The war has changed its character." Communists and their sympathizers wheeled around once again, destroyed their "Yanks Aren't Coming" pamphlets and posters, shifted the name of their front organization American Peace Mobilization to American People's Mobilization and soon clamored for a second front in Europe. One detested them even more.

Some of those who the year before had denied their party membership to Mrs. Roosevelt came back to her seeking reinstatement. She refused to renew relations. "For years, in this country," she wrote of the Communists on the fourth anniversary of the Nazi attack, in 1945, "they taught the philosophy of the lie. . . . Because I have experienced the deception of the American Communists, I will not trust them."

The debate grew sharper. Aid to the Soviet Union handed the isolationists a new weapon against intervention. "The victory of Communism in the world," said Senator Taft, "would be far more dangerous to the United States than a victory of Fascism." "I would a hundred times rather see my country ally herself with Britain, or even with Germany with all her faults," cried Charles Lindbergh, "than the cruelty, the Godlessness, and the barbarism that exists in Soviet Russia."

In September Lindbergh carried his America First crusade to ominous lengths. Three groups, he charged in a speech in Des Moines, were driving the United States into war: the New Dealers, the British and the Jews. He became specific: "Instead of agitating for war, the Jewish groups in this country should be opposing it in every possible way, for they will be among the first to feel its consequences. . . . Their greatest danger to this country lies in their ownership and influence in our motion pictures, our press, our radio, and our government." I happened, quite by accident, to catch the speech on a car radio — the high-pitched voice, the righteous, messianic tone, the sense conveyed of a man seeing himself as anointed savior of the state: it was all rather scary. Wendell Willkie called it "the most un-American talk made in my lifetime by any person of national reputation."

In a letter to the *New York Herald Tribune*, I asked how a man like Oswald Garrison Villard, the grandson of the great abolitionist William Lloyd Garrison, could possibly stay on the America First Committee after the Lindbergh speech. A few days later a handwritten letter arrived from Villard (whom I did not know). He had in fact long since resigned from the committee, he wrote, "because of one plank in their platform of which you, I am sure, approve" — presumably the plank calling for a strong national defense; Villard was a pacifist. "Lindbergh blundered badly, but is, I am convinced, not anti semitic. Much of what he said about the Jewish situation is true, but had better be left unsaid." So felt many America Firsters.

Opposition to the war did not relent, as we discovered in August when the House of Representatives passed the extension of the draft by a single vote, thereby barely preventing the disintegration of the American armed forces. In Cambridge we watched the outcome with special apprehension. Our congressman, Thomas H. Eliot, formerly Frances Perkins's right-hand man in the Labor Department and later to become chancellor of Washington University in St. Louis, a man we greatly admired, was persuaded by his pacifist wife, Lois, a woman we greatly adored, to vote against the draft extension. Fortunately Tom's vote had not (quite) dissolved the army.

*　　*　　*

Immersed as I was in the age of Jackson, I could not help bringing historical perspectives to bear on the national debate. Soon I found myself drafting an article.

In Britain, I wrote, the shift from Chamberlain to Churchill represented a shift from the plutocracy to the aristocracy as the ruling group. Chamberlain had accurately expressed the sentiments of the business class — the longing for quiet, the hatred of violence, the terror of social upheaval. (This was a reading of the middle class — the "civil society" so revered by pundits in the Nineties — that I had picked up from Georges Sorel and his arresting *Reflections on Violence*. In light of the enthusiasm of the British and French propertied classes for appeasement, Sorel's view made much more sense than the vulgar Marxist idea of a bellicose business community relishing the application of force.)

Chamberlain thought in terms of business deals, not war; of security, not honor; of class, not nation. Churchill, whom the business community had always mistrusted, was a tougher breed. His instincts were those of an imperial aristocracy, bold, vigorous, a bit contemptuous of 'trade,' with power founded not on finance but on land and tradition, devoted to an island and an empire rather than profits, to nation rather than class, and not afraid to fight.

Churchill's side had triumphed in Britain and might save it yet. But the United States had no aristocracy in the British sense. The American plutocracy was prey to the same anxieties and fears as the British, but the Republican party, until Wendell Willkie came along, had no equivalent of the Churchillian Tories, arguing against class for nation. A *Fortune* poll of American business executives had recently shown a large number favoring the appeasement of Hitler because they were confident that they could survive and even prosper doing business with the Nazis.

Now Willkie had appeared, a valiant internationalist (as I had belatedly discovered) determined to persuade the business community that it was as much to their interests as to Franklin Roosevelt's that Nazism be wiped from the earth. But it was easier for British business leaders to swallow Churchill than for American business leaders to swallow FDR. The Republican vote against revision of the neutrality act showed what small effect Willkie's campaign had had on his party. Could the American past throw any light on Willkie's predicament?

I thought it could and proposed a look at the dilemma of the old Whig party, the party of business in antebellum America, confronted by the challenge of slavery. Slavery was as urgent and peremptory a question in the 1850s as Nazism was in the 1940s. Every American had to come to a decision on it. Neutrality was as unreal in 1858 as it was in 1941. Then, as now, those who preached neutrality were practicing appeasement.

How had the Whigs behaved? Many had investments in the south or depended on southern markets or were engaged in profitable activities connected with the cotton trade; many more simply dreaded the notion of war as too rude a shock to the existing order. The Cotton Whigs of the north thus supported concession and compromise. They professed to be "realistic" and believed, in a favorite phrase, in "calculating the value of the Union." They denounced the Declaration of Independence as "empty and glittering generalities," much as their spiritual descendants denounced the Atlantic Charter and the Four Freedoms. They sneered at the members of their own party who believed that all men were created equal as "Conscience Whigs."

William H. Seward of New York was the leader of the Conscience Whigs. He bore about the same relation to Jacksonian democracy as Willkie bore to FDR's New Deal: a steady and effective opponent, but far less angry and embittered than the Daniel Websters or Herbert Hoovers. Like Willkie, Seward realized that the power of the slave system had so grown that any compromise with it — moral or political — would be fatal to American democracy. He was trying to save the Whig party from itself just as Willkie was trying to save the Republican party from itself.

In 1852 the Whig party was one of the two great parties of the nation. By 1856 it was a memory. Because it could not rise to the challenge of slavery, it collapsed. The Conscience Whigs followed Seward into the new Republican party. One wing of the Cotton Whigs joined Buchanan in the appeasement party. Other Whigs followed the last Whig president, Millard Fillmore, into the Know-Nothings, the party of nativism. Today, I thought, appeasement and nativism might well get together. Isolationist Republicans might join a new and more sinister Know-Nothing party under Lindbergh. Could Willkie rescue the Republican party from the Whig fate?

*　*　*

With some trepidation, I sent the piece off to the *Nation*. I then went to Worcester for last-minute research at the American Antiquarian Society. Late one afternoon a call from Marian took me out of the search room. A Mr. Bendiner of the *Nation*, she said, was trying to reach me. I called Robert Bendiner, the managing editor. He said they wanted to publish the piece right away. Soon I received a letter from an assistant editor, a fellow named Richard Rovere, with helpful suggestions.

Not only did the *Nation* print the piece at once under the title "Can Willkie Save the Republican Party?" but they circulated proofs to Republican leaders — to Willkie, Senator Robert A. Taft, Senator Arthur Vandenberg and Governor Harold Stassen of Minnesota, all of whom sent in comments for the next issue.

Taft was, as usual, trenchant and acerbic, observing that "Republicans may well hesitate to take the advice of one who seems to be opposed to every principle for which the Republican Party has ever stood." It was not true, he continued, that conservative Republicans opposed intervention. "The Wall Street bankers, the society group, nine-tenths of the plutocratic newspapers, and most of the party's financial contributors are the ones who favor intervention." It was the average man and woman, the farmer, the workman, the small businessman, who were against going to war.

Republicans, Taft said, had joined in voting countless billions and in granting almost unlimited powers in the cause of national defense. They have only opposed measures of which the logical conclusion was an American expeditionary force. "They do not believe that Hitler presents such a threat to the trade or safety of the United States as requires the sacrifice of several million American boys on the battlefields of the world . . . in an imperialistic war for the domination of Europe, Asia, and Africa, and the supposed 'manifest destiny' of America."

Vandenberg, regretting that he did not have time to analyze the article, left the question of the Republican future for the voters to decide in 1942, saying, "I remember poignantly how often in the twenties I used to bury the Democratic Party and preach its funeral oration." Stassen, a Republican internationalist, disputed the Whig analogy and contended that the foreign policy split was more serious in the Democratic than in the Republican party.

Willkie made the longest and, understandably, the most cordial comment. The Conscience Republicans, he felt, were doing better than the article conceded, but "I thoroughly agree with Mr. Schlesinger, however, that unless the Republican party . . . recognizes that America must assume world leadership not only now but after the war, it will suffer the fate of the Whigs, and suffer it quickly." Subsequently I received a letter from Willkie: "I am of the opinion that you and I are not very far apart in our economic beliefs. I should like some time to have a long discussion with you. You may find yourself coming to New York. If you do, drop me a note. I'd like to have lunch or dinner with you."

Alas, I was too shy ever to take him up on this invitation and thus missed the chance to meet a remarkable American. Later, in a 1944 speech in Ripon, Wisconsin, the supposed birthplace of the Republican party, Willkie discoursed on the Cotton and Conscience Whigs and reminded Republicans of the fate of the Whig party. I came greatly to admire his fight for internationalism abroad and for civil liberties and racial justice at home and mourned his unexpected death in 1944 at the age of fifty-two. Later, talking to some of his close associates, I gained the impression of a man of generous impulse, personal magnetism and political courage but undone by a congenital lack of self-discipline.

*   *   *

My article appeared in the *Nation* of December 6, 1941. The Republican responses appeared in the next week's issue. In the meantime . . .

It was our custom on Sunday afternoons to tune in to the CBS broadcast of the New York Philharmonic Orchestra at three o'clock. On the seventh of December, a crisp winter day, Marian and I returned from luncheon with my parents at Gray Gardens East. As we entered our Harvard Street apartment, the telephone began to ring. In a single gesture I flicked on the radio to Artur Rodzinski at Carnegie Hall and picked up the phone. Radios took a few seconds to warm up in those days. As I heard an agitated Avis DeVoto shout over the phone that something terrible had happened in Pearl Harbor, the radio suddenly blared out the unbelievable news — and an era came to an end.

For my generation, four dates remain indelibly scarred on memory, four occasions when none of us can forget where and how we heard the staggering news: Pearl Harbor, the death of Franklin Roosevelt, the death of John Kennedy, the landing of men on the moon.

13

Washington at War

THE NEXT DAY, huddled around the radio, we heard President Roosevelt condemn the "date which will live in infamy" and, with awful gravity, ask Congress to recognize a state of war between the United States and the Japanese Empire. Japanese planes and ships rushed on to attack Manila, Hong Kong, Singapore, Guam, Wake, Midway. Four days after Pearl Harbor, Germany declared war on the United States. "The forces endeavoring to enslave the entire world," FDR told us, "now are moving toward this hemisphere. . . . Never before has there been a greater challenge to life, liberty, and civilization."

Actually, Hitler's decision made life easier for the president. If FDR wanted to go to war at all in 1941, he wanted to go to war in the Atlantic, not in the Pacific. Germany was his priority. So the charge is absurd that he somehow connived in the Japanese attack. Moreover, if he knew of the impending attack, it would have sufficed to intercept the Japanese task force at sea before it started to sink his beloved Navy. Hitler's declaration rescued Roosevelt from the political storm that would have arisen had he been compelled to ask a Congress raging against Japan to go to war against a nonbelligerent Germany.

* * *

New Year's Eve 1941 was not a happy time. Victory was far from preordained. "We know the end before we consider the beginning," as the British historian Veronica Wedgwood said about the historian's task, "and we can never wholly recapture what it was to know the beginning only."

Moving into 1942, we knew the beginning only. We had no confidence that our side would win the war. The British were overextended more perilously than ever, with the empire itself now staggering under Japanese blows. The Russians, to general astonishment, were still holding out, but no one knew how long that could last. The Americans were untrained and untried. In June 1942 the Princeton Office of Public Opinion Research reported that 39 percent among us thought we were losing the war against only 25 percent who thought we were winning (another 28 percent saw a stalemate).

Compared to the confusions of democracy, Hitler's totalitarian Germany was thought to operate with demonic efficiency. Too many Europeans appeared to be preparing themselves for the reconstitution of a continent under Nazi control. In August 1942 the International Committee of the Red Cross, in the words of its historian Caroline Moorhead, seemed to accept "that at least some aspects of Nazi ideology would be the reality of the new postwar Europe." Democracy, demoralized by depression, unnerved by war, was for the moment a fragile hope.

*　　*　　*

What was one to do? Bad eyesight kept me out of the draft, and my plan was to find a job in Washington. In the meantime, Pearl Harbor overruled Harlow Shapley, and I resumed regular shortwave broadcasts to Britain on station WRUL.

Nine days after Pearl Harbor I received a telegram beginning FULL PARTICIPATION IN WAR MAKES IT IMPERATIVE AMERICAN LIBERALS WORK OUT PROGRAM MOST EFFECTIVE PROSECUTION OF THE WAR FOR DEMOCRATIC ENDS. The wire, a call to a conference in New York later in December, was from the Union for Democratic Action. It was signed by, among others, Reinhold Niebuhr, Walter Reuther of the United Auto Workers, A. Philip Randolph of the Sleeping Car Porters, Herbert Agar, a Pulitzer Prize historian and editor of the *Louisville Courier-Journal,* Bruce Bliven of the *New Republic,* Freda Kirchwey of the *Nation* and my congressman Tom Eliot.

The UDA dated from May 1941, when liberals and labor leaders acted on the need for a progressive interventionist organization. William Allen White's formidable Committee to Defend America by Aiding the Allies recruited conservatives as well as liberals, ignored trade unions and was neutral on domestic issues. Niebuhr became the UDA chairman and James Loeb, a lean, keen and resourceful ex-Socialist, executive secretary.

The UDA supported the New Deal and stoutly opposed communism. Niebuhr, having observed the popular front in the Thirties, had no use for Communists. Loeb had witnessed the Soviet NKVD in cruel action during the Spanish Civil War. Reuther and Randolph had fought Communists in their unions who subordinated labor interests to the zigzags of Soviet foreign policy. When Hitler attacked Soviet Russia, the UDA supported aid to Stalin, but at the same time

Niebuhr called on the membership not to abandon "the process of eliminating Communism from union leadership and from all organizations which stand on the left wing of democracy." All this appealed mightily to me, but I cannot remember whether I attended the New York meeting; probably not, since it took place just before Christmas. The UDA, however, registered on my consciousness and later played a role in my life.

In the meantime, pregnant with a book, I struggled to deliver the manuscript on Jacksonian democracy before I was caught up in the war effort. More important, Marian in the meantime had become pregnant in the literal sense.

*   *   *

I began the search for a job in Washington. My father put me in touch with his friend Waldo G. Leland, the head of the American Council of Learned Societies, and Leland steered me to the Office of Facts and Figures, an agency created in October 1941 and headed by Archibald MacLeish, the poet and Librarian of Congress. OFF's function was to disseminate information about defense policies and activities. MacLeish, an urbane, handsome man filled with charm, was a singular mixture of romantic idealism ("America Was Promises") and high principle with a certain cool ambition. Archie had already recruited a strong group of public-spirited writers opposed, as he said, to "ballyhoo methods" and dedicated to the "strategy of truth."

MacLeish passed me on to Barry Bingham, the editor (and owner) of the *Louisville Courier-Journal,* now in naval uniform and temporarily with OFF. We had a good talk, and he sent me, with a warm recommendation, to Henry F. Pringle, chief of the Writers Bureau. I knew of Pringle by reputation. A journalist in the Twenties, he had specialized in deflationary sketches of prominent figures, many written for the fledgling *New Yorker* and collected in *Big Frogs* (1928). His biography of Theodore Roosevelt, published in 1931, was a brilliant, witty, skeptical account based on thorough and careful research. It won the Pulitzer Prize and set the tone of commentary on TR for a generation or two. "It remains," Professor Ernest May wrote in 1998, "the most enjoyable full-length biography, but it has always suffered from not taking Roosevelt seriously. . . . For Pringle, almost every episode in Roosevelt's life played as *opera bouffe.*" We have come to think better of the first Roosevelt, but Pringle's disenchanted portrait remains to be reckoned with. His less mischievous biography of William Howard Taft (1939) is still, after sixty years, the standard work.

Pringle was forty-five years old when he interviewed me in the spring, a slight, short, balding, businesslike man with a twinkle in his eye. He asked for samples of my prose. "I read your material with interest," he wrote in June, "and I hope we can work something out." But OFF was already on the skids. FDR had not given it any real authority to control government information; the War and Navy Departments in particular ignored it; and MacLeish, as a liberal, an interventionist and a poet, was on all three counts under derisive personal attack from the powerful trio of isolationist papers, the *Chicago Tribune,* the *New York Daily News* and the *Washington Times-Herald.*

In June 1942 Roosevelt, with typical bureaucratic sleight-of-hand, folded OFF into a new agency, the Office of War Information, and appointed Elmer Davis as director. Davis, then fifty-two years old, famed for his incisive and ironic broadcasts, as well as his white hair, black eyebrows, white shirt and black bow tie, was a popular choice. A memorandum he sent around early on suggests his idiosyncratic flavor: "In material issued by the Office of War Information, the phrase World War 1 is not to be used unless referring to the War of the Grand Alliance, nor the phrase World War II unless referring to the War of the Spanish Succession."

The head of the Domestic Branch under Davis was a Willkie Republican, Gardner (Mike) Cowles, Jr., publisher of the *Des Moines Tribune* and *Look,* a picture magazine in competition with Harry Luce's *Life.* Robert E. Sherwood, the playwright and presidential speechwriter, was head of the Overseas Branch. Pringle remained as chief of the Bureau of Publications in the Domestic Branch.

The reorganization, Pringle wrote me, "may mean some delay, although I hope not." In July, through channels I cannot now remember, I received a telegram from the office of the Quartermaster General saying my appointment as associate historian had been approved. I checked with Pringle, who could not, he said, in all conscience tell me to reject the War Department offer, but he still hoped that a place would open up in OWI. Unexcited by the prospect of writing the history of the Quartermaster Corps, I declined the appointment.

It was a restless summer. The Jackson manuscript had grown to more than fifteen hundred pages of typescript. Around the first of August, to Marian's shock and my consternation, we were informed that she was about to give birth to twins. On August 17, 1942, Stephen Cannon and Katharine Bancroft made their debut in this world, two healthy and cunning babies. A week later, word came from Pringle:

"We can offer you a place here as a writer-researcher at $3200, to start at your earliest convenience."

* * *

I arrived in Washington early in September. John and Wilma Fairbank had preceded me, and I found temporary lodging in their house on Thirty-fourth Street in Georgetown. On the eleventh I reported for work in the OWI offices in the new Social Security Building on Independence Avenue and Fourth Street (in the Nineties the home of the Voice of America).

Pringle greeted me amiably and explained the setup. The Bureau of Publications had three divisions: a Book Division under Chester Kerr, later the forceful director of the Yale University Press; a Graphics Division under Francis (Hank) Brennan, the art director of *Fortune* and in later years of *Newsweek;* and his own Writers Division, with Milton MacKaye as his deputy.

MacKaye was an experienced newspaperman who spoke with a stammer but wrote with sardonic fluency. His book on the police scandals in New York City, *The Tin Box Parade,* was both serious and hilarious; it inspired the song "A Little Tin Box" in the Pulitzer Prize musical of 1959, *Fiorello!* Pringle and MacKaye, like MacLeish and Davis, were men of the Twenties. So was Malcolm (Mike) Ross, the recent author of *Death of a Yale Man,* who worked with us until FDR made him chairman of the Fair Employment Practices Commission, the agency established to assure black Americans a better break in the defense industry.

The junior writers had yet to make their names, but Pringle, if I may immodestly say so, had an eye for talent. There were Philip Hamburger, who for the next half century would be a mainstay of the *New Yorker,* and Samuel Lubell, who was soon annexed by Bernard Baruch and later became the most original and influential American psephologist — election analyst — of the mid-century. The desk to which I was assigned had been recently vacated by McGeorge Bundy, who had got into the Army Signal Corps by memorizing the eye chart. At the desk opposite mine was an unassuming but crisp English instructor from the University of Illinois named W. McNeil Lowry. After the war he became a political correspondent for James M. Cox's newspapers. A man of diverse talents, Lowry later organized the Ford Foundation's highly effective program of support for the arts and ended as president of the San Francisco Ballet.

"The writers are men," I wrote home, "and the researchers, who are probably much more competent, are women." Louise Wells Baker, the head of the research staff, had set up the research operation for *Fortune*. Among her recruits were Betty Werlein Carter of New Orleans, married to the courageous liberal editor Hodding Carter, Adrienne Koch, in later years a scholar specializing in Jefferson and Madison, and three bright young Time Inc. veterans, Katharine Douglas from California, Mary Lou Mickey from New York and Barbara Wendell Soule of the North Shore of Boston and Chicago, a granddaughter of Professor Barrett Wendell, who had founded Harvard's History and Literature program.

"Every one," I reported, "seems very nice, friendly and informal. The spirit is extremely good, and they are all devoted to Pringle." The hours were nine to six every day including Saturday, with a tendency, because so much of the work was of emergency character, to slip into the evenings.

*   *   *

The variety was exciting. On my first afternoon Pringle dropped a mass of documents on my desk with a memo scribbled in pencil from Elmer Davis. The material had to do with Nazi atrocities in Slovenia, and I duly turned out an article entitled "Murder of a People."

My next assignment was to write a speech for Frank Walker, Jim Farley's successor as postmaster general. This was my initiation into a long and dubious career as a ghostwriter. David K. Niles, the old Schlesinger friend, now a presidential assisant in the White House, had asked MacLeish to take care of Walker, and Archie passed the job along to Pringle, who passed it on to me. I called on Walker, who apparently had expected MacLeish to write the speech personally. After an uneasy moment, he courteously reconciled himself to an imperfect substitute.

The postmaster general seemed a decent, somewhat bemused man, an experienced politician and probably an able administrator but not very articulate. On the other hand, he was, uncommon among Irish Americans, a strong interventionist. Only the day before, he told me, an old friend had reproached him, "Frank, we shouldn't be in this war; it's none of our business." His speeches — he gave me samples — functioned at a level of floridity which, as his ghostwriter, it was incumbent on me to sustain. I note with interest that I had him call the conflict "the War for Human Rights."

A greater thrill came from occasional White House requests to write low-level messages for FDR's signature. My first success was a presidential endorsement of Universal Bible Sunday — odd in view of my disrespect for organized religion. In my screed FDR eloquently contrasted "the Christian conception of man created in the image of God" with the Nazi conception "created in the image of the beasts of the field" and called the Bible "a book not for a day or a week but for eternity." I was deplorably adept at a ghostwriter's duplicity. Soon I drafted a presidential proclamation for the first anniversary of Pearl Harbor.

In the meantime, I sorely missed Marian and the two babies. Spare moments went to a search for a house — no fun in wartime Washington. A chance meeting at the National Press Club in late October alerted me to an imminent departure. I inspected 5353 Broad Branch Road, near the intersection of Connecticut and Nebraska avenues on the way to Chevy Chase. The house met our requirements (and the rent — $85 a month — was compatible with a salary of $3200 a year).

I rushed back to Cambridge to escort my enlarged family on the hopelessly packed train to Washington. At Union Station a jolly black redcap placed the twins on a baggage cart and, shouting "Make way for two of a kind!" pushed his way through the crowd.

*　　*　　*

Hardly had my family arrived when I found myself on the road. A political storm was brewing about drinking in and around Army camps. Church leaders and dry lobbyists drew a lurid picture of virtuous young draftees led astray by evil companions and turned into drunkards. Dry legislators called for the prohibition of liquor near the camps. Alben Barkley of Kentucky, the Democratic leader in the Senate, warned that, if it came to a vote, the prohibition rider would pass.

This agitation reminded our OWI elders of the disastrous sequence of events a short twenty-five years before. In 1917 Congress, in a moment of excessive wartime concern, had restricted the sale of liquor around the camps. This statute led directly to the Eighteenth Amendment, ratified by three quarters of the states within nine weeks of the Armistice. Could wartime agitation dry up the republic a second time? Pringle and Davis, survivors of the parched Twenties, did not want to repeat what Herbert Hoover had so approvingly called "a great social and economic experiment, noble in motive."

Pringle gave me the job of making a preliminary survey. We talked with Charles P. Taft, the director of Defense Health and Welfare Services. (As we went to see him, Henry remarked that Charlie Taft's older brother, Senator Robert A. Taft of Ohio, had tried to enjoin the publication of Henry's life of their father and that Bob, the conservative, and Charlie, the liberal, were now hardly on speaking terms.) Taft's staff consisted largely of social workers professionally inclined to look on prohibition as a good thing, so their testimony that draftees were not drinking to excess carried weight. I discovered that my Harvard classmate Frank Keppel was secretary of the Joint Army-Navy Committee on Welfare and Recreation. He gave us polls taken by the Army's Special Services Section indicating that the drinking problem was greatly exaggerated.

I recommended that OWI undertake a fact-finding report: "The government clearly cannot take a stand for or against prohibition. But it can properly present the facts about the Army camps." Pringle sent a memorandum to Elmer Davis and Mike Cowles: "We shall be accused, whatever we do, of taking part in a political controversy, and this will be the case however honest, factual, and objective is our report. But here is a subject of such grave import and of such overwhelming importance to the morale of the troops that I think we should face the danger and go ahead." Davis and Cowles agreed. Henry decided that OWI writers should visit Army camps across the country and report on what they saw. Mac Lowry and I were dispatched to camps in the south and middle west.

*   *   *

We left Washington in early November 1942. Our first stop was Fort Bragg, near Fayetteville, North Carolina, a town of 17,000 people surrounded by an encampment of 125,000 recruits. We interviewed the mayor, the editor of the local newspaper, the provost marshal, the chief Army chaplain, the head of the Military Police, merchants and townspeople. Our mission, we discovered not without pleasure, required frequent stops at local bars and night spots.

Except for preachers and prohibitionists, the Fayetteville witnesses felt that the situation was under control. "Agreement is general among all authorities," I reported to Pringle, "that prohibition, by destroying the legal foundations of orderly regulation, would make the liquor problem much worse." The mayor told us, "Dry sentiment gains strength as people turn to religion during the war and the

young men disappear into the Army." He added shrewdly, "The prohibition movement may also be getting support from bootleggers."

Then south to Columbus, Georgia, and Fort Benning. Unlike Fayetteville, the city administration in Columbus, dominated by a racke-
teer with the Faulknerian name of Fate Leebern, gave the military
only the bare minimum of cooperation. Everyone drew the contrast
between Columbus and the Alabama town across the Chattahoochee
River, long considered by those who knew it as irrevocably depraved,
Phenix City.

The extremely high rate of venereal disease caught in the brothels
of Phenix City had led to Army intervention earlier in the year. The
city officials cooperated wholeheartedly, drove out organized prosti-
tution and cleaned up a town hitherto supposed beyond redemption.
One night the editor of the *Columbus Ledger-Enquirer* and a couple of
officers from Fort Benning took us on a tour of the reformed Sodom.

Two honky-tonks had led in venereal infections. Ada Cash's was
now drab and desolate, with a dice table, shabby slot machines and a
deserted bar. A few bored and lonely soldiers were hanging about.
The backroom, formerly equipped with cribs for a quick lay, was now
bare and empty.

Beachy Howard's was livelier. Mrs. Howard, a faded southern lady,
presided benignly over the bar. As she offered us drinks on the house,
she said she had run a bordello for twenty-eight years. In the good old
days before the cleanup, Beachy Howard's had ample facilities in
back. One of our guides, overcome with nostalgia, wistfully recalled
that on payday nights fifty or sixty soldiers stood in line waiting their
turn as if, he said, they were waiting for dinner. Beachy's daughters,
cheap, pretty gals, ran around alluringly with tight sweaters and skirts
above the knee, but the place looked fairly dead.

A law enforcement officer mournfully confirmed the picture of
a purified Phenix City. He said that soldiers often propositioned
Beachy's daughters (one GI is said to have offered $90; $1000 in the
currency of the Nineties), but they got nowhere. The prevailing
mood among the few soldiers in sight was intense, pathetic lonesome-
ness. "Unless this was strictly an Intourist view of Phenix City," I reported to Pringle, "that town is certainly cleaned up." (After the war
came the relapse. Phenix City soon recovered its reputation as the sin
city of Alabama.)

As for Columbus, there seemed little prospect of reform so long as
Fate Leebern ran the city. But none of the people to whom we talked

thought that the problem of drunkenness among the draftees was acute. Prohibition, most said, would make conditions worse.

* * *

Our next stop was the Army Air Force base at Keesler Field, near Biloxi, Mississippi. Mississippi was technically a dry state, but Biloxi had never been dry, not even in the days of the noble experiment. A resort city, it had long catered to Mississippians who wanted to drink, gamble and relax. Few Biloxians complained about drunkenness among the soldiers. An exception was a Baptist minister who solemnly told us that drinking was debilitating our Army and sapping its will to victory: "Already in Biloxi it has provoked soldiers to such crimes as whistling at girls in the street and asking them for dates without introduction."

We moved on to the lower middle west — Fort Riley in Kansas, Fort Crowder in Missouri, Fort Knox in Kentucky — asking the same questions to the same array of witnesses, military and civilian, and hearing the same answers, even from chaplains. Traveling on crowded trains and buses, interviewing by day and writing up notes in tacky hotels by night, Lowry and I managed to cover six camps in sixteen days.

Back in Washington, I reported to Pringle that the chief source of the anecdotal evidence flourished by prohibitionists was drinking on trains. Soldiers at the beginning or end of furloughs, in many cases their last furlough before embarkation, were likely to drink. "Celebration on trains becomes unhappily conspicuous, but they should not be made the basis of unfounded generalizations about the normal conduct of soldiers."

There were, I wrote, three sorts of drinkers in the camps. Draftees who had been habitual drunks in civilian life constituted the great bulk of the offenders. Poolroom tough guys and streetcorner loafers accustomed to getting tight every Saturday night had no intention of changing their ways because they were now in uniform. A second group drank out of loneliness and ennui. Many had never taken a drink before they joined the Army, and inexperience sometimes led to excess. A third group, characteristically paratroopers, airborne troops and the Air Corps, drank as a release from tension. Under strain because of hazardous duties, they were often encouraged by their officers to be reckless and daring.

Drunkenness among the troops, we reported, was nowhere regarded as a problem; prohibition was nowhere regarded as a solution.

As the commandant of Camp Crowder told us, prohibition "would fill every alley with bootleggers." The repeal of local dry laws would actually improve the system of regulation. Beer on the post was desirable because it reduced the stampede into town for a drink. The Military Police were everywhere doing a good job, and the situation was everywhere under control.

Our colleagues who covered other parts of the country reached the same conclusions. The OWI's "Coast to Coast Survey of Drinking Conditions in and around Army Camps" was published to wide acclaim at the end of December 1942. Despite Alben Barkley, the prohibition rider failed in Congress. Little was heard thereafter (or since) about a return to the prohibition of hard liquor. Cigarettes (by the Nineties), yes; booze, no.

* * *

The trip through the south was comparable to the journey with Benny DeVoto around the far west as an education in the mysteries of American life.

Southerners showed little interest in our inquiry into drunkenness among soldiers. But people told us again and again: "If you really want to investigate something, investigate the Nigras." The south, I wrote to my parents, was "highly explosive and bitter — more than I had ever anticipated — on the Negro question." Growing up in a liberal family, I had always been made aware of racial injustice. But the true horror of the black predicament had not burst upon me until I crossed the Mason-Dixon Line.

At Fort Bragg, for example, we interviewed the wife of the Episcopal minister, a charming southern gentlewoman — charming, at least, till she launched into a hysterical tirade on race. The only kind of equality that interested the Negro, she passionately declared, was equality with white women, and she seemed almost to relish the thought of sex-mad, drunken black men aiming at miscegenation and rape. Catching her maid reading a Baltimore colored paper with the headline FBI TO INVESTIGATE LYNCHINGS IN MISSISSIPPI, she had told her that the Nigra boys deserved to be lynched. The maid shut up, but the minister's wife cited her sullen anger as proof of the rebellious spirit of her race.

"The Negroes were better off under slavery," she told us. ". . . Southerners are the only people who understand how to treat the Negro." If this were the case, I asked, why so much discontent among

My father and mother on their honeymoon,
Atlantic City, 1914

Three generations; my grandfather wears a bow tie

Taking a test at
the Pre-School
Laboratory, 1922

At three and a half, listening to my mother read aloud

"I'm an Indian too . . ."
(now politically incorrect), c. 1922

Marian Cannon
Schlesinger and our
twins, Katharine and
Stephen, c. 1944

George Bancroft, putative ancestor and possible
role model, photographed by Mrs. Henry Adams
(who later killed herself by drinking developing fluid)

My father in a contemplative mood, c. 1950

A movic addict with Jean Pierre Aumont, Jean Simmons and my closest (male) friend in Hollywood, Philip Dunne, Harvard '30, son of Mr. Dooley

On the roof of 79 Champs-Élysées, Paris, October 1944

Two Harvard professors, c. 1950

southern Negroes? Her answer was immediate: they had been stirred up by northern agitators. "Everyone in the South," she said venomously, "hates Mrs. Roosevelt." She had no doubt about the existence of "Eleanor Clubs" — secret cells of black women determined to get out of domestic service and meanwhile asking that their weekly wage be raised from three or five to ten dollars. "All of this," I noted, "throws the southern upper classes into fury and provides the main theme of dinner table conversation."

We glimpsed the other side too. In Biloxi a couple of armed Military Police had taken us for a tour of the colored district. We visited the Plantation — "one of the saddest, shabbiest and most desolate dives I have ever seen, filled with hard-faced, silent Negroes, some drinking at a squalid bar, others playing pool and spitting on the floor." Normally the unsanitary conditions would have closed down a place like this, but, if such dives were put off-limits, blacks would have had nowhere at all to go. There and elsewhere I felt that I had never imagined such misery and wretchedness in America.

❊　❖　❊

Falling into the historian's habit, I tried to put race relations in a longer perspective. In a memorandum to Henry Pringle and letters to my father, I suggested that what had so long held the south together was the fairly durable relationship between a majority of the white planter class and a majority of the black population. They were used to each other, and this sense of mutual understanding fostered paternalistic relations between the races. Poor whites, on the other hand, had found in the Negro the group on which they could take out their manifold frustrations and insecurities, hence their bitter anti-Negro feeling.

The striking fact about the south today, I thought, was that the paternalistic relationship seemed to have largely vanished. Occasionally we encountered elderly men still speaking of the Negro in the old way, as an amiable and useful child. But middle-age people and younger seemed to regard the Negro as the enemy, treacherous, savage and biding his time. The whole white south, it appeared, had adopted the poor white view of blacks.

The cause of this change, I thought, was the growing black defiance. Inspired by a decade of democratic enthusiasm, generated first by the New Deal, now by a war fought against the idea of a master race, southern Negroes were beginning to claim their constitutional rights as American citizens. The result frightened the master race in the Jim Crow south. "They feel that not only their social status but their physical security is essentially imperilled, along with the purity of their womanhood and the lives of their children. These fears are probably justified" — so long, that is, as the white south maintained its rigid belief in white supremacy.

Lowry and I were appalled, as I wrote to my father, by "the passionate conviction on the part of many [white] southerners that terrorism and repression are the only policies open to them." Concessions to blacks, we were told, would only lead to further demands, just as appeasement had only increased Hitler's appetite. We heard lynching defended by people who, one felt sure, would have condemned it ten years before. They defended it now on the ground that even when innocent people were lynched, lynching kept the Nigra in his place.

I was also struck by the rise of anti–New Deal sentiment in what was still the solidly Democratic south. Southern Democrats, we were repeatedly told, had supported New Deal measures that they did not much like, and now New Dealers were displaying their gratitude by undermining southern racial arrangements. Yankees were, as ever, hopeless. The economic backwardness of the south was due to northern exploiters and the racial bitterness to northern agitators. The result was to discredit in advance any northern thoughts about race.

My conclusion was grim and contained statements I would soon renounce. But this is how I saw it at the time:

> The tragedy of the situation is that no improvement would be made by giving more power to the Negro. The southern Negro would abuse power even more than the reactionary southern white. The northerner is excluded for reasons given above. The only hope in the situation lies in activity by the southern liberals, and this hope is scant. It is very difficult in the war situation to see any steps which might be taken without antagonizing either the conservative whites or the radical Negroes. The situation just looks bad.

This was not completely the way I saw it. "For the first time," I wrote to my father, "I developed some sympathy with the Negro attitude toward the war. It seems to me almost the literal truth that they could not be worse treated by Hitler than they are by the southerners today." "The consequence," I predicted to Pringle, "will be a shocking explosion along the lines of Nat Turner's Insurrection one of these days."

*　　*　　*

Another southern excursion in January 1943 furthered my education. This trip was to investigate communities reporting a shortage of doctors. About a third of American doctors were already in the services, and more were called up every week. This left many places with limited or no medical attention. I was sent off by myself to inspect a dozen such cities in Florida, Georgia and the Carolinas.

The trip began agreeably. In Miami the writer Philip Wylie, who had just identified the phenomenon of Momism in his rollicking polemic *Generation of Vipers*, took me for a swim; then an entertaining luncheon with the producer and librettist Lawrence Schwab reminiscing about his shows *The New Moon, The Desert Song, Good News*. The American Federation of Labor was meeting in Miami, and in the afternoon I attended President William Green's press conference. He struck me "as a very sincere, honest, winning and befuddled kind of guy." On to Key West, then a colorful fishing village along the lines of Hemingway's *To Have and Have Not*.

Thence to begin a march through Georgia (SHERMAN HAD NOTH-ING ON ME, I wired Pringle). In Atlanta I spent a memorably riotous evening with Hervey Allen, the author of *Anthony Adverse*, a popular picaresque novel of the early Thirties. Allen, who was now regional information director for the War Manpower Commission, brought with him a beauteous and bright reporter from the *Atlanta Journal* named Rebecca Franklin. What made the evening especially memorable was the unexpected kiss I received at the end from Becky Franklin, very consoling for one who continued to doubt his appeal to women.

I pursued my search for doctors into the Carolinas. In exquisite Charleston, W. W. Ball, the crusty Confederate editor of the *News and Courier*, gave me one more dose of white bigotry. I went on to New Bern, North Carolina, where I suddenly felt awful and discovered I had a temperature of 103. Naturally, since I was in New Bern because it had reported a shortage of doctors, I could not find one for myself. Finally a doctor materialized and brought down the fever with heavy doses of sulfathiozole (this was before penicillin). After a few days I returned to Washington, severely weakened but able to offer personal testimony about the doctor shortage.

The trip impressed me with the patriotism of the doctors who enlisted and the patriotism of those who stayed behind and worked to the limits of their endurance. It also impressed me with the complexity of the problem. The doctor shortage, the OWI investigation concluded, had not yet seriously harmed the nation's health, but the maldistribution of doctors was doing great harm in particular localities. Why not then simply move doctors from areas of relative over-supply to areas of acute need?

On closer examination, however, relocation raised new problems. It meant that the practice of a doctor who had left for the war would fall to a relocated doctor. What would happen after the war? What guarantee that the relocated doctor would depart? Would not the doctor who went overseas be out in the cold? For such reasons, medical societies often resisted "outside" doctors, especially when they were European refugees. Meanwhile, the overworked doctors who remained had more patients than they could handle, and especially in rural areas the sick sometimes had no doctors at all.

There were no easy solutions. This, I was beginning to discover, was true of too many problems.

*　　*　　*

Henry Pringle saw a double function for the Bureau of Publications: it should provide honest, objective, factual reports on situations of national concern; and it should explain the purposes of the war and what we were fighting for. Both functions were politically sensitive.

Pearl Harbor had led to a congressional mood of all-out support for the administration. After a year, the frustrations and sacrifices imposed by war were generating a new mood of querulousness and complaint. The midterm elections in November 1942 produced striking Republican gains — forty-seven seats in the House of Representatives and ten in the Senate. A campaign backed by the Union for Democratic Action against prewar isolationists was a bad flop; out of one hundred and fifteen, only five were beaten. We OWI writers, absorbed in our jobs, were slow in seeing that the new Congress might well move against OWI's Domestic Branch as a New Deal propaganda agency.

14

Blowup at OWI

I ENJOYED THE VARIETY of jobs falling to the Bureau of Publications. My ghostwriting career thrived. For FDR's signature I wrote messages to such august bodies as the Foreign Press Association, the American Platform Guild, even in April 1943 to Mrs. Pouch, the president of the Daughters of the American Revolution. I doubt that the President ever saw my words, and my services to him never, alas, rose to a higher level.

I wrote a Polish Constitution Day speech for John McCormack of Massachusetts, the majority leader of the House (and Speaker in the Kennedy years). My draft unguardedly ascribed the Katyn Massacre, then much in the headlines, to the Nazis. McCormack wisely deleted this passage.

*　*　*

My most entertaining speechwriting assignment was for Maury Maverick, a shrewdly intelligent, exuberantly radical and joyously explosive Texan. It was his Maverick grandfather's preference for unbranded cattle that gave rise to 'maverick' as a term for politicians too independent to bear any man's brand. Maury himself was a classic maverick, lower as well as upper case.

He was a decorated veteran of the First World War, a rambunctious liberal congressman in the Thirties, then mayor of San Antonio; now he was in charge of the War Production Board's relations with local government, and soon FDR made him chairman of the Smaller War Plants Corporation. An omnivorous reader, Maury flavored a pungent populist style with scholarship. One reason he looked kindly on me was that in his lively book *In Blood and Ink* he had cited an obscure article of my father's, "Colonial Appeals to the Privy Council." An excellent writer, he had fastidious respect for the English language. A person, he said, "should be held morally responsible for his words just as he is accountable for his other acts." This led him in

1943 to coin the memorable word 'gobbledygook' for the Latinate prose preferred by the bureaucracy.

Maury was perfectly capable of writing his own speeches, but his WPB duties left him no time. He was quite a challenge to a novice speechwriter. He also had the habit, whenever a phrase or idea struck him, of calling me up at once. Since these flashes of inspiration seemed to come very often at two or three in the morning, Maury's phone calls alternated with the cries of the twins to make sleep difficult for a time in the Schlesinger household.

I did four speeches with him in the spring of 1943 — New York, Seattle, Salt Lake City, Denver. He was a stimulating man, lively, humorous, extravagant, and I learned much about Texas and about life from our collaboration.

* * *

Speechwriting was an OWI sideline for which I happened to show a fatal aptitude. Another sideline required me to write captions for a traveling OWI photographic exhibition "This Is Our War." The task involved me with Roy Stryker, who had been head of the Farm Security Administration's superb photography unit, and a madman named Edwin Rosskam — "an ace designer of photographic exhibits," I wrote home, "but otherwise a complete screwball." I found the photographers exceedingly irritating to work with, but I did learn a lot about the art, or hocus-pocus, of writing captions.

Meanwhile, Pringle's division kept on with its central job of explaining war aims and reporting on situations of national concern. The president's January 1941 'annual message' (not yet known as 'state of the union address') had skillfully condensed his war aims into the famous Four Freedoms. MacLeish and Pringle enlisted a formidable team to expatiate on the Freedoms — E. B. White on Freedom of Speech, Reinhold Niebuhr on Freedom of Worship, Malcolm Cowley on Freedom from Want and Max Lerner on Freedom from Fear. White, who was not at all happy with official ways, had the uncongenial job of putting the text into final form. OWI's Four Freedoms pamphlet had a run of 400,000 copies.

Philip Hamburger's *Tale of a City* was a grim presentation of the fate of Warsaw under Nazi occupation. I was assigned to explore the feasibility of a pamphlet along similar lines about the Japanese treatment of foreigners in Shanghai. We dropped this project when I reported that the Japanese treatment of the British and Americans in

Shanghai appeared to compare favorably to our treatment of the Japanese Americans in Los Angeles.

One of my undertakings was a pamphlet about foreign nationality groups in the United States. The idea was to reassure recent immigrants that they were not second-class Americans and to reassure first-class Americans that immigrants contributed positively to the national life. It was also designed to prepare the United States for postwar glory by arguing that "the presence in our land of all peoples living together harmoniously qualifies us peculiarly for world leadership."

I called it, borrowing the phrase from Walt Whitman, "Nation of Nations," and the first epigraph was FDR's famed exhortation to the Daughters of the American Revolution: "Remember, remember always that all of us . . . are descended from immigrants and revolutionists." The second came from Hitler's propagandist, Dr. Joseph Goebbels: "The America of today will never again be a danger to us. Nothing will be easier than to produce a bloody revolution in the U.S. No other country has so many social and racial tensions. We shall be able to play on many strings there."

Admitting that the melting pot was often a "facile and optimistic symbol," I noted that nevertheless the American theory of harmonious diversity was our challenge to the coerced uniformity of fascism. The mass of immigrants had come to our shores as rebels against tyranny and intolerance — in search, in short, of the Four Freedoms. "The issues of this war go to the very roots of their presence in America. . . . Our immigrant stocks contain resources of the greatest importance for winning the war and working out the peace." Oddly, I covered much the same ground half a century later in *The Disuniting of America*.

Another assignment was to work with Charles Taussig, a liberal businessman, on the report of the Anglo-American Caribbean Commission. The job, I wrote home, was "much complicated by the vanities and ambitions" of Taussig, but it was of great value as an introduction to the perplexities of the rest of the Western hemisphere, a part of the world that has fascinated me ever since.

Going around town to consult experts on foreign nationality groups, the Japanese, the Caribbean and other matters taught me a lot not only about the particular topics but about the workings of the national government.

*   *   *

Washington itself was perhaps an even more valuable education. Much of our social life was spent among OWI colleagues. Henry Pringle was married to the writer Helena Huntington Smith, an attractive, intelligent, competitive and sometimes devastatingly frank woman. Larry McMurtry considers *We Pointed Them North*, the book Helena wrote for Teddy Blue, "the single best memoir of the cowboy era." The occasional Pringle parties seemed to me straight out of the Twenties, with drunken hilarity, noisy argument and pervading mutual affection. The last evidently did not apply to Henry and Helena. Perhaps stifled by the company-town aspect of Washington, Helena Pringle wanted to strike out on her own, and their marriage was breaking up. We were all rather surprised when Henry married Kate Douglas in 1944, a well-concealed office romance. Less well concealed was the relationship between Barbara Wendell Soule and Chester Kerr, who were also married in 1944.

Milton MacKaye's wife was Dorothy Cameron Disney, a writer of detective stories who became well known in the Fifties through her monthly column in the *Ladies' Home Journal* called "Can This Marriage Be Saved?" The MacKaye parties too had a strong Twenties flavor. Hodding Carter, the courageous editor who had challenged Huey Long in Louisiana and defended the rights of blacks in Mississippi, was a striking presence in our intramural evenings until he went off to North Africa in 1943.

We enjoyed occasional sallies beyond the Writers Division into the larger City of Conversation. Phyllis Cox had alerted her sister to our arrival, and Helen and Walter Lippmann, surprisingly hospitable to unknown young people, invited us to cocktail parties where we shook hands with, and occasionally talked to, senators, journalists and Supreme Court justices.

Pat Jackson was of course a major resource. As Communists secreted in the government held their regular cell meetings, so Pat convened dinners at regular intervals for what might be called an anticommunist cell. There I met Ernesto Galarza, chief of the labor section of the Pan-American Union, John Edelman of the Textile Workers, Leo Goodman of the Wholesale and Retail Workers, Jim Killen, who later became chief of the labor division in the occupation of Japan, Dick Deverall of the Association of Catholic Trade Unionists and the radical playwright Paul Sifton, among others, for an exchange of information about the latest CP machinations inside the government.

Pat's anticommunist zeal as labor reporter for the New York newspaper *PM* brought frightful revenge. In 1944 he was set upon with brass knuckles, badly beaten and permanently blinded in one eye by Jack Lawrenson, a vice-president of the Communist-controlled National Maritime Union, and other NMU thugs. It took painful months for him to bound back to his normal ebullience.

* * *

One night in the winter of 1943–44 the Jacksons invited us to a dinner that led to one of the abiding friendships of my life. Ed Prichard was there, scintillating as always. He was about to be drafted, all three hundred pounds of him. "They have scraped the bottom of the barrel," he said. "Now they are taking the barrel."

Prich had brought a friend from the British Embassy with whom he was now sharing an apartment. This was the Oxford philosopher Isaiah Berlin, currently writing weekly political summaries for the Foreign Office and the prime minister. Berlin's acute insights into American affairs made his dispatches required reading at the highest level. On one notable occasion Churchill, hearing that Berlin was in London, summoned him to luncheon at 10 Downing Street and asked penetrating questions about American politics. Disappointed by weak and uninformed answers, he complained later, "Berlin writes better than he talks." In fact, he had invited the wrong Berlin — Irving, not Isaiah.

At the Jacksons' that night Prichard and Berlin sat next to each other on a huge sofa, exchanging gossip, witticisms, recondite literary and philosophical allusions and ruminations about the war and the future while the rest of us listened in fascination. Each set the other off as in one of those firework displays where each rocket shoots higher in the sky than the one before and leaves an ever more glittering trail of light and color behind. I thought then I had never heard such conversation. Perhaps I have not heard its equal since.

Isaiah was thirty-four years old, balding, with black hair, alert, snapping eyes and a smile of delighted discovery. He seemed then a man of indeterminate middle age; when I last saw him, a few weeks before his death at eighty-eight in 1997, he still seemed a man of indeterminate middle age. He changed in appearance less than anyone I have ever known.

I still see him that first night on the Jacksons' sofa talking at immense speed in a torrent of words, initially hard to make out until one surrendered to the cascade and let the meaning pour in. His sentences were intricate and erudite but filled with wit, warmth and humanity. He was unassuming and approachable, never pulling intellectual rank. He had an enormous generosity of spirit, an unparalleled sense of fun and an unquenchable pleasure in the vagaries of human experience. And he had the marvelous quality of *intensifying* life so that one perceived more and thought more and understood more.

In 1946, when Harold Laski came to America, I mentioned my new enthusiasm. "Ah, Isaiah Berlin," Harold said. "A brilliant young man. He is the kind of brilliant young man of whom people are saying today, 'What a great book he will write one day.' In a few years, people will say, 'What a great book he must be writing.' When he is old, people will say, 'What a great book he could have written.'" Alas for Harold, his own books are long forgotten, while Isaiah's essays, now collected in a dozen large volumes, will dazzle and enlighten for years to come.

*　*　*

In the course of the year I began another abiding friendship of comparable consequence. I had known of John Kenneth Galbraith as a promising and provocative economist, but we had somehow managed to elude each other. He was at Cambridge University in 1937–38, when I was in my last undergraduate year at Harvard; and I was at Cambridge in 1938–39, when he was at Harvard. When I was back at Harvard in 1939–40, he had moved on to Princeton.

In 1941 Leon Henderson, an enormously capable New Deal economist and head of the Office of Price Administration, appointed Galbraith as his deputy director in charge of price control. OPA was popular (at least according to the polls), and it was impressively successful in checking wartime inflation. But it was also a major irritant for powerful interests, especially businessmen and farmers eager to raise prices on their products. And it was a natural target for the right-wing press, intent as always on crucifying the New Deal bureaucracy.

The Republican gains in the 1942 midterm election portended the liquidation of the New Deal, or at least of vulnerable New Deal agencies. FDR retained nominal control of Congress, but he could no longer count on southern Democrats and confronted a de facto opposition majority on many domestic issues. Henderson and Galbraith were irrepressible men, masterful in their technical knowledge, militant in support of their policies, cheerful at internecine combat, ill equipped temperamentally to mollify opposition and especially deficient in the capacity to resist making wisecracks.

As political pressure intensified after the election, Henderson, a true hero of war mobilization, was forced out. His successor, Prentiss Brown, a well-meaning ex-senator from Michigan, brought in a Detroit advertising executive named Lou Maxon as his deputy. Enjoying his fifteen minutes of fame, Maxon launched a campaign against Galbraith, who was forced out as well in May 1943. "The fight in OPA," I wrote to my parents, "is another example of Roosevelt's retreat all along the line. He has allowed practically all the agencies operating on the home front to fall into Republican hands."

The Galbraith-Schlesinger affinity as embattled New Dealers was confirmed when we discovered that we were both born on October 15, though his debut preceded mine by nine years. At six feet eight, he was also nearly a foot taller. A Canadian by birth, he migrated south, became a citizen in 1937, established credentials as an agricultural economist and soon stood out as an iconoclastic wit in the tradition of Thorstein Veblen, whom he greatly admired. He was a man of true originality of mind and generosity of spirit, and we became friends at once.

Meanwhile, I devoted evenings and weekends to the revision of the now gigantic Jackson manuscript. In January 1943 I sent the typescript, 330,000 words, more than thirteen hundred pages, to my father. He was generous in praise and incisive in criticism. Instructed by his line by-line editing, I spent evenings and weekends squeezing out superfluous language and cutting the manuscript down to publishable size. Looking back, I marvel at the magic energies of youth.

*　　*　　*

The war rumbled on. We call it the Good War at the millennium and smother it in sentiment. Of course, no war is any good, but occasionally a few, like the American Civil War and the Second World War, are necessary. Still, even the few Good Wars can be corrupting as well as murderous.

The Good War myth envisages a blissful time of national unity in support of noble objectives. Most Americans indeed accepted the necessity of the war, but that hardly meant the suppression of baser motives. In Washington we saw the seamy side of the Good War. We saw greedy business executives opposing conversion to defense production, then joining the government to maneuver for postwar advantage. We saw the campaign by dollar-a-year men against 'grade labeling' of canned products — the tactic OPA used to prevent the sale of diluted goods at the same price. We were informed that one in eight business establishments was in violation of the price ceilings. We saw what a little-known senator from Missouri called "rapacity, greed, fraud, and negligence" in the national defense program, and we applauded Harry Truman's committee for its work of investigation and exposure.

The war called for equality of sacrifice. But everywhere one looked was the miasma of 'chiseling,' the term applied to those, and there were plenty of them, who were out to get more than their fair share. The home front was not a pretty sight at a time when young Americans were dying around the world.

*　*　*

Beyond the chiseling at home lay the bitterness of the war abroad. One day I received a call from Nigel Bicknell, the golden boy I had known at Cambridge University the year before the war. I had heard that he joined the Royal Air Force and was one of the Few who gloriously defended England in 1940. I had read about Nigel in Richard Hillary's *Falling Through Space*, the classic account of the Battle of Britain, and a best seller in 1942 (the English title was *The Last Enemy*).

Nigel was briefly in Washington on a mission, he said, and could we have a drink. We arranged to meet at the bar of the Mayflower Hotel. I looked around and could not see the handsome face of my old friend. Then a man appeared, his face somehow familiar but twisted beyond recognition. "I'm Nigel," he said. "I crashed, and they've given me a new face."

*　*　*

I remained in close touch with Peter Viereck, more eager than ever after Pearl Harbor to find a place in the war effort. With his expertise on Nazism, his knowledge of German, French and Russian, his unassailable anti-Nazi credentials, Peter was eminently qualified for a job in OWI or in William L. Langer's Research and Analysis Branch of the Office of Strategic Services. But his father's name and work haunted him. "The reasons why Elmer Davis, Prof. Langer, and the rest are wary of using me," he wrote me, "is because they fear that my appointment would get congressional or journalistic opposition."

His father's troubles certainly did not help. In March 1942 George Sylvester Viereck was indicted for violations of the Foreign Agents Registration Act. Appeals, reversals and retrials followed until he was sentenced in July 1943 to prison, where he remained till 1947. His wife, Gretchen, often in Washington for the trials, phoned us from time to time, knowing Marian and me to be Peter's friends. One never knew how to respond to that lonely, quavering voice, but we did our best to console her. (Afterward the Viereck marriage broke up, and Gretchen Viereck sold most of their property, donating the proceeds to Jewish and Catholic charities.)

Peter continued his struggle to get into the war, asking the authorities for "a fair chance to redeem the honor of my last name, despite all prejudice, by my work against Nazi Germany." Finally he was drafted, served in North Africa and Italy and won two battle stars. In February 1944 his brother George Sylvester Viereck, Jr., was killed fighting the Nazis at Anzio.

* * *

Movies as usual provided a form of solace. I remember four in particular from these years. *Casablanca,* of course, remains the greatest triumph of the Hollywood assembly line. No film half a century later is more quoted or quotable — "I'm shocked, shocked to find that gambling is going on here" and "Round up the usual suspects" and "Of all the gin joints in all the towns in all the world, she walks into mine" and "Play it, Sam. Play 'As Time Goes By'"; but imagine the surprise, the excitement, the glorious delight, in coming on *Casablanca* for the first time. When Humphrey Bogart nodded to Sam and the refugees in Rick's Place drowned out the Horst Wessel Lied by singing "La Marseillaise," the audience, the young Schlesingers among them, cheered and wept and cheered again.

Part of *Casablanca*'s enduring power surely derives from the vivid Europeanness of the production, with its Hungarian director, Michael Curtiz, and so many fugitives from Nazism in the cast — Conrad Veidt, Peter Lorre, Paul Henreid, Marcel Dalio, S. Z. Sakall, Ludwig Stossel, Leonid Kinsky, Helmut Dantine. Part derives from the vivid Americanness of the saturnine, understated Bogart, emotions tightly repressed and cynically expressed. Part derives from the quiet message that there are, after all, things worth fighting for. *Casablanca* was the unforced parable of a nation's journey from cynicism — "I stick my neck out for nobody" — to responsibility.

Casablanca was an immediate hit. The second film I remember best was not. Many at the time were appalled by Ernst Lubitsch's *To Be or Not to Be,* a comedy thriller about the Nazi occupation of Warsaw. After the atrocities recorded in Hamburger's *Tale of a City,* the notion of using Warsaw as a backdrop for laughs was, at the very least, risky. "To say it is callous and macabre," Bosley Crowther wrote in the *New York Times*, "is understating the case. . . . Where is the point of contact between an utterly artificial plot and the anguish of a nation which is one of the great tragedies of our time?" There was a lot of this in the press.

But Lubitsch's exquisite felicity of touch and timing, the deft way Jack Benny and Carole Lombard played off each other, the seamless manner in which farce mingled with melodrama, overcame at least my reservations about taste. Half a century later, *To Be or Not to Be* is indisputably one of the great comedies. Again, memorable lines: Sig Rumann, as Ehrhardt, the Gestapo chief, commenting on the self-styled "great, great Polish actor" played by Benny: "What he did to Shakespeare, we are doing now to Poland" (a line Lubitsch's friends and his wife pleaded with him to cut from the film); again, Benny, disguised as a Nazi agent, to Rumann, "You're quite famous in London. They call you 'Concentration Camp Erhardt,'" to which Erhardt responds affably, "We do the concentrating and the Poles do the camping"; and Rumann, then and later, always smiling with self-satisfaction, "So they call me Concentration Camp Erhardt!"

Such lines are more acceptable today than in 1942, but to an ardent minority they sounded pretty funny then. In the inevitable arguments, I defended Lubitsch on the ground that it was a brilliant film. In his own defense of the film in the *New York Times*, Lubitsch explained why he had not portrayed Nazis in the usual Hollywood fashion — torture chambers, flogging, terror. "My Nazis are different; they passed that stage long ago. Brutality, flogging and torturing have become their daily routine. They talk about it with the same ease as a salesman referring to the sale of a handbag." Had I thought about it more, I would have recognized that Lubitsch, in his portrayal of Nazis as ordinary, dumb jerks doing their job, long preceded Hannah Arendt in understanding the "banality of evil."*

The two other films that left their mark were British. Thorold Dickinson's *Next of Kin* was made for distribution to the British Army. It was a demonstration that careless words dropped by soldiers in commando training could be pieced together by Nazi spies, thereby enabling the Nazis to smash the commando raid. *Next of Kin* gripped

---

* It is interesting that Hitler was evidently a fan of Felix Bressart, the actor in Jack Benny's troupe whose ambition is to deliver Shylock's great speech ("Hath not a Jew eyes? . . ."). According to Konrad Heiden's generally reliable biography, Hitler once said, "Pity that this Bressart is a Jew."

through the crisp, grim, quasi-documentary treatment and the frank talk (forbidden words like "damn" and "hell" figured in the dialogue).

Roy Boulting's *Desert Victory* was a genuine documentary about Montgomery's victories in North Africa. Through brave and resourceful camera work, it placed the audience in the midst of the noise, the smoke, the convulsion of battle. I saw *Desert Victory* with my mother about the time my brother, Tom, was called up for active service. She came out deeply shaken. I suddenly understood that every time a British soldier fell wounded or dead, she shuddered for her younger child's future.

"I have been preparing myself for this for a year," she had written us on New Year's Day 1943.

> I knew after Pearl Harbor that his going was inevitable. I won't let myself think personally about it. I am only one of millions of mothers who love their sons and see them go off to war and my feelings are universal not mine alone. I have accepted what I must face and live with for many future months and perhaps years. Tom said, "Why I thought you would be much more upset about my going." Little does he know the depths of what it means to me and the countless anxieties that clamor for my thoughts.

* * *

The Writers Division was an unusually cohesive group with uncommonly high esprit de corps. Henry Pringle was a father figure for the younger people. He was wise, wry, considerate, protective, with the uncommon gift of phrasing criticism in the most courtly and acceptable way, "a marvelous, even-handed, very intelligent man," Archie MacLeish mused forty years later. We were drawn together by our devotion to Pringle, by the job, as we understood it, of writing honestly about the war and by the fact that we were true believers in FDR's New Deal and his Four Freedoms. We shared MacLeish's conception of OWI as an educational agency providing, as he wrote to the president, "a full knowledge of what we are fighting for."

There were reasons to doubt that many Americans understood the war as more than a response to a dastardly Japanese attack on Pearl Harbor. I became aware of that on my middle western travels to inspect honky-tonks around Army camps. "We arrived," I wrote to my parents, "in the midst of the whining about gas rationing, and it was pretty depressing. The anti-administration feeling is strong and open." The basic trouble, I thought, was that middle westerners were not really sold on the war. They saw it as vengeance against the Japanese, not as vindication of the Four Freedoms.

The lingering feeling that we had been dragged into an unnecessary war seemed to foretell a reversion to isolationism after victory, as had disastrously happened twenty years earlier. An OWI poll in the summer of 1942 reported that a third of Americans would accept a separate peace with Germany. The War Department's Research Branch found a year later that more than a third of a three-thousand-man sample in the armed forces had not even heard of the Four Freedoms; only 13 percent could name some of them.

*   *   *

We OWI writers hoped to fill the war-aims gap. But our own future was clouded. OWI, like the Henderson-Galbraith OPA, was a favored target of the new Congress. The Domestic Branch, especially the Bureau of Publications, was under particular attack as propagandists for Roosevelt and his policies.

Mike Cowles and Milton Eisenhower, the general's brother and now OWI's deputy director for administration, proposed a retreat. OWI, Eisenhower contended, "should be thought of primarily as an *information* agency." MacLeish, trying to hold on to the idealism of the Office of Facts and Figures, replied that this would convert it into "a mere issuing mechanism for the government departments." Frustrated by the minimalist conception of OWI, Archie resigned in January 1943 and returned to the Library of Congress. His resignation, Elmer Davis wrote in a warm letter of thanks for his services, would force the *Washington Times-Herald* to find new targets "among the prose writers" — a prescient observation.

Cowles was already disturbed by the prose writers' reports on controversial situations. Sam Lubell's *Battle Stations: The Story of the Fight to Control Living Costs* was damned on Capitol Hill because it argued for "taking the profit out of war," advocated price control and rationing and recommended anti-inflation measures not yet approved by Congress. *Negroes and the War,* written by the black activist Chandler Owen and edited by Milton MacKaye, was denounced, in the words of one southern congressman, as "an attempt to use the war to force upon the South a philosophy that is alien to us."

I had written a pamphlet, "The Myth of a Postwar Depression," drawing on National Resources Planning Board memoranda to show that after the war Keynesian methods could maintain full employment in a system of free enterprise. "The postwar depression project," I wrote home in January 1943,

> has come to a temporary halt, first because MacLeish's resignation has left the postwar world without very energetic representation in OWI, and then because, with Congress in its present mood, every one is afraid to move until our appropriations are secure. Accordingly I am now doing a pamphlet on the Hull reciprocal trade agreements, though there is even some feeling that we should not come out for them, lest it be interpreted as partisanship.

The pamphlet "For a Greater Foreign Trade" was, I apologized to Pringle, "a rather dull document. In fact, the subject of Trade Agreements seems to be peculiarly unsusceptible to lively treatment." But even a dull document opposing high tariffs promised to provoke further wrath on the Hill. In the meantime, Mac Lowry produced an incendiary report on the food situation, matching the food requirements of our people, our Army and our allies with probable food production in the year ahead. Its tone was tough, and its effect was to justify food rationing. Elmer Davis had approved the report. Then Cowles showed it to Chester LaRoche, chairman of the National Advertising Council. LaRoche's firm, Young & Rubicam, handled the General Foods account.

The fact that LaRoche was Rosalind Russell's brother-in-law, much as we admired her, did not spare him in our eyes. The delivery of a draft government report to men financially interested in information policies based on that report seemed to us a shocking breach of ethics. Then Cowles directed Pringle and Lowry to rewrite the report, muting its hard tone and turning it into an optimistic appeal for sacrifice. They refused. Cowles complained to Davis, who observed that he had never heard of a reputable newspaper that asked an editorial writer to write things he did not believe. But the report was suppressed.

*　　*　　*

In later years Mike Cowles and I became good friends. We did not talk much about OWI, and then only in a glancing way. He was a decent man, and in retrospect I am sure he felt he had the best interests of OWI in mind. At the time I thought him, as I reported to Benny DeVoto (who was a close friend of Davis's), "a weak, amiable guy, who up to now has entered every situation with the backing of the Cowles fortune and an entourage of able assistants." He had, I thought, no real idea what his job was.

Cowles did not like the writers' attitude. We were doubtless an irritating group, accustomed to our independence and resistant to being treated as hirelings. Mike preferred public relations types, trained to please not themselves but the men who paid them. Like OPA, OWI now suffered from a plague of advertising men. Once confined to the Bureau of Campaigns, they began to strike out for more and more power over OWI's Domestic Branch. The assistant directors were William B. Lewis, a smooth operator from Columbia Broadcasting System who had begun with J. Walter Thompson and ended with Kenyon & Eckhardt, and James Allen, a government press agent (also, by odd coincidence, a cousin of Jimmy Wechsler).

Cowles meantime continued to be amiably evasive. When he talked to Pringle, he seemed to agree with Pringle. When he talked to Bill Lewis, he agreed with Lewis. "Mike," I wrote to DeVoto, "is unrestrained by any sense of self-respect, so that he can go back on his word with none of the inhibitions which might discourage more honest people."

The issue seemed clear enough to the writers. The ad men believed that any information campaign likely to affect a vested business interest should first be cleared with that interest. We considered this a sell-out. And there were deeper differences. We had a perhaps naive faith in the ability of the American people to reach sensible conclusions on the basis of sober and uncensored information. The ad men doubted that we had the slightest idea how to reach and persuade Americans.

They cited Norman Corwin's idealistic radio show "This Is War!," which, though carried by the major networks in prime time on Saturday nights, had a disappointingly small audience. "Our whole plan," said Bill Lewis, "is based upon finding ways and means to use the existing large audiences, and not to spend the first vital year of the war in building new audiences which may or may not respond to new ideas." The ad men believed that the way to 'sell' the war was to exploit the well-honed Madison Avenue armory of promotional techniques as if they were selling cigarettes or soft drinks.

Such techniques, Hank Brennan protested, did more toward "spreading the sticky syrup of complacency over the people than almost any other factor." Their approach, as we saw it, was based, in the words of Malcolm Cowley, an OFF veteran, "on distrust and contempt for the people." This was what MacLeish had feared: "ballyhoo methods" as against "the strategy of truth."

In February Lewis and Allen drew up for Cowles a scheme of reorganization arguing the need to "streamline" the agency in preparation for the impending tussle over appropriations. Both Pringle's Writers Division and Hank Brennan's Graphics Division were now to be placed under ad men. The Writers Division, as we saw it, was to become a glorified advertising agency with a cage full of copywriters to leap around as the 'idea' men directed.

Pringle led the fight against the Cowles plan. He was, he said, a writer, not a copywriter. Apparently losing, he submitted his resignation. Davis refused to accept it and instead brought in the publisher Harold Guinzburg of Viking, a man of books and a man of business, well equipped, Elmer thought, to serve as a buffer between writers and advertising executives.

On the evening of April 1, Davis, Cowles, Guinzburg, Pringle and Jimmy Allen met and came to substantial agreement about the future of the Bureau of Publications. On April 6, Lewis in effect vetoed the agreement. The next day Cowles fired Pringle. Guinzburg resigned that afternoon. In the following days most of Henry's gang also decided to resign. Elmer Davis did nothing.

* * *

In retrospect, what could he have done? His main concern in those busy days was to extract information about the war from the War and Navy Departments. The Navy Department and especially Admiral Ernest J. King, the chief of naval operations, were crustily resistant to telling the American people about anything, especially about naval losses. King's idea of war information, Davis once said, "was that there should be just *one* communiqué. Some morning we would announce that the war was over and that we won it."

Compared to his titanic arguments with the Pentagon and also to the challenges of waging psychological warfare abroad, the revolt of writers in the Domestic Branch seemed a minor matter. If it came to a choice between Cowles and Pringle, Davis had to choose Cowles. The resignation of the Republican director of the Domestic Branch would have doomed OWI's domestic budget, still in contention before Congress. FDR, who paid little attention to OWI, would have been displeased at having to take on one more congressional battle over what he would have regarded as an inconsequential dispute.

We writers believed that, if Elmer had been in Henry's place, he would have acted as Henry did. Perhaps; perhaps not. For all his intellectual forthrightness, Elmer was at a psychological impasse. His was an impossible job with ill-defined objectives and without adequate authority to achieve them. He was unaccustomed to bureaucratic infighting and not much good at it. He lacked powerful friends in high places. He had no gift for internal administration. He hated scenes.

He knew little about the Domestic Branch except what Cowles and Lewis told him. When they insisted that they were all in favor of honest information, he took them at their word and permitted himself to regard Pringle's protests as the result of a clash of personalities. Why couldn't the writers, the people in the agency to whom he felt closest, forget their egos and adapt themselves to wartime exigencies?

Pringle and Cowles had agreed to say nothing to the press. Then Ben Gilbert of the *Washington Post* got wind of Pringle's resignation and asked Cowles what had happened. Cowles said that the paper shortage was the cause of the trouble. Actually, the Bureau of Publications used less paper than was required for a couple of issues of Mike's *Look*. Lewis declared that the Bureau was incompetent. Davis told his press conference on April 14 that it was a fight about personalities, not principles.

* * *

I had not decided to resign until that day — two babies made one hesitate before indulging in romantic gestures — but the actions of Lewis and Cowles convinced me that I could not stay on. "I came down to Washington," I wrote to Davis,

> because of my great confidence in you, in Henry Pringle, and in your common determination to carry out the policies you enunciated so ably in your first days in office. It now seems to me that Henry Pringle has become a victim of his loyalty to those policies, while the Domestic Branch has been delivered almost intact into the hands of men for whom putting out the truth is a secondary consideration. . . .
>
> My own contacts with them in OWI have led me to conclude that they regard the plain recital of facts as exhibiting somehow a lack of proper ingenuity, and hardly worth doing. . . . I retain my confidence in you, and I hope that the Domestic Branch may in the long run return to the objectives for which you have always stood.

I went to see Davis on the afternoon of the fourteenth. It was not a happy interview. I asked Elmer how he could believe that Cowles and Lewis were interested in putting out honest information about the war when they could not even put out honest information about the fight in OWI. Elmer just looked terribly sad and mumbled something about maybe they were misquoted. I brought up points from my letter of resignation. He returned gloomy and, to my mind, evasive answers. "But he is such a fine man," I wrote to Benny DeVoto, "and of such obvious personal integrity, that I came out feeling very lousy."

After Cowles and Lewis had given false accounts of why we resigned, we changed our minds about putting out a statement. "There is only one issue," we said, "— the deep and fundamental one of the honest presentation of war information." Domestic information activities were now "dominated by high-pressure promoters who prefer slick salesmanship to honest information." These promoters treat the American people as "stupid and reluctant customers." They are turning the Office of War Information "into an Office of War Ballyhoo."

Hank Brennan and the graphics people, now under the overlordship of the former advertising manager of Coca-Cola, responded to a suggestion of Phil Hamburger's and produced a poster of the Statue of Liberty. The lady held not a torch but four Coca-Cola bottles. The caption: THE WAR THAT REFRESHES: THE FOUR DELICIOUS FREEDOMS.

Though the resignation statement affirmed our confidence in Elmer Davis's personal integrity, he, not unreasonably, got really mad and ordered our names instantly struck from the payroll. We were told to clean out our desks at once; the next day workmen arrived to take the desks away — "the only efficient administrative action," I wrote to my parents, "I have seen at OWI." Chester Kerr, informed that one writer would be assigned to the Book Division, asked for me. But Davis had decided that no one who signed the statement would ever again be employed by OWI: "When people jump out of a ten-story building, they ought to have considered everything in advance." (MacLeish commented, "What does Elmer mean by comparing himself to a ten-story building?") On the other hand, Elmer did write Henry Pringle, "Sorry all this happened. My personal esteem for you remains as high as ever."

* * *

The resignation of the troublemakers did not solve OWI's problems. In June 1943 the House of Representatives voted 218–114 to abolish the entire Domestic Branch. The Senate opposed abolition, and in the end Congress reduced the domestic budget sufficiently, Davis wrote to DeVoto, "to relieve them of the odium of having put us out of business, and carefully not enough to let us accomplish anything much."

For Davis, betrayal by his friends rankled for a time. Two years later, in a final report to the president, he held forth on

the problem of the brilliant and zealous individual who cannot work as part of a team. . . . An information agency, in a war which was in some of its aspects ideological, naturally attracted many free-lance writers and others who had been used to working by themselves and had always jealously cherished their personal integrity and freedom of expression. Such a man is very apt to insist that he must proclaim the truth as he sees it; if you tell him that, so long as he works for the Government he must proclaim the truth as the President and the Secretary of State see it, he may feel that this is an intolerable limitation on his freedom of thought and speech. In that case, he must go.

And so we went, no doubt with lessons learned.

15

Oh So Secret

WHAT NOW? Two war agencies beckoned: the Board of Economic Warfare, known familiarly around town as BEW, and the shadowy Office of Strategic Services (OSS).

With FDR's surrender of OWI and OPA, the BEW was one of the few war agencies still firmly controlled by New Dealers. In 1943 many of us regarded BEW's chairman, Vice President Henry Wallace, as the great liberal hope. I was now offered a job there as executive assistant to Fowler Hamilton, an able, likable and enlightened New York lawyer whom I was to encounter again twenty years later when President Kennedy made him head of the Agency for International Development.

OSS was the secretive new intelligence agency led by the dashing Colonel William J. (Wild Bill) Donovan. Here Harvard professors in its Research and Analysis Branch eased my way. William Langer, the dean of diplomatic historians and now the hard-driving chief of R&A, and Donald McKay, a sober and capable French historian, offered me a job as political analyst on their Current Intelligence Staff.

I thought hard about the choice. I was much attracted by the activism of BEW. People there were rushing around doing things — imposing blockades, buying up scarce metals, blacklisting Axis-controlled firms, plotting to deny the enemy strategic materials. R&A/ OSS would be almost a return to academic life — "depressing," I wrote to my parents, "to be in the middle of a lot of Ph.D.'s once again." But I chose OSS in the end because I felt a good deal more at home with politics than with economics.

*   *   *

FDR had a weakness for colorful Irishmen — Tom Corcoran, Jim Farley (for a while), Joe Kennedy (for a while), Ed Flynn, even Irish Republicans like Pat Hurley and Bill Donovan. The last was an energetic lawyer and, when younger, an aspiring New York politician (beaten by Herbert Lehman in 1932 for the governorship). He had a famous record of bravery in the First World War, a memory renewed in 1940 by the Warner Brothers film *The Fighting 69th*, George Brent playing Donovan.

Irish-American interventionists were in short supply in 1940. Donovan was one of the few, and Roosevelt sent him on confidential missions abroad. His ambitions whetted by friends in British intelligence, who saw him as someone they could do business with, Donovan persuaded FDR in July 1941 to make him Coordinator of Information, an innocuous label for a secret intelligence agency. Eleven months later, the executive order that created OWI also rebaptized COI as the Office of Strategic Services.

OSS was housed mostly in buildings recently vacated by the Public Health Service, at Twenty-third and E streets in Foggy Bottom. Donovan soon had a full hand of clandestine activities — espionage in the Secret Intelligence Branch (SI); covert action, aid to resistance groups, guerrilla warfare, in Secret Operations (SO); psychological warfare in Morale Operations (MO); counterespionage in X-2. R&A was a service branch, providing basic data to the cloak-and-dagger branches and, presumably, to policymakers throughout the national security community.

I began work on May 8, 1943. First impressions of my new life were not encouraging — "a tremendous anti-climax after OWI," I told my parents. The job had its agreeable aspects: people did not seem to work too hard; the material was interesting; there were nice perquisites, such as the screening of new Hollywood releases on Saturday afternoons for those on Colonel Donovan's list (I soon made it).

But it was so terribly remote from the political scene. "For all the deathly secrecy of much of the material," I wrote home, "there is an ivory-tower serenity about the place; no one seems to care very much about what is happening in Congress or OPA or WPB [War Production Board]." I repeated to one of R&A's great minds Leon Henderson's famous crack on being introduced to Lou Maxon after Ken Galbraith's dismissal. "It took me a year and a half to become the greatest son-of-a-bitch in the country," Henderson told Maxon. "You've done it in six weeks." The R&A man said, "Who is Lou Maxon?" An understandable comment perhaps, but it seemed to sum up R&A's isolation from the Washington hurly-burly.

Our little group of OWI resignees lunched once a month on Saturdays with Henry Pringle at Harvey's, that fine old paneled Washington restaurant then in its original location, and commiserated with one another over the frustrations of our new lives. As I wrote home,

"This job will be in no sense a developing experience, as my other one was; it will not make me wiser, or give me new skills, or teach me more about government, or put me in touch with new and different people, or enlarge my range of experience."

*   *   *

I was wrong, but it took a while for new experience to click in. The Current Intelligence Staff was headed by an old friend, Everett Gleason, the medievalist who had been senior tutor at Adams House. Ev Gleason proved an efficient and sardonic administrator intelligently unimpressed by his superiors. After the war he collaborated with Langer in writing the classic history of FDR's foreign policy before Pearl Harbor. Never returning to academic life, Ev ran the secretariat of the National Security Council in the Fifties.

My job was to edit the *PW Weekly*, a classified journal (SECRET) distributed in numbered copies — number one going (so we understood) to the Map Room in the White House. *PW* stood for psychological warfare, the fad of the moment — a weapon of war since cavemen first howled at strangers but now awarded a pretentious name and considered by some as of magical effectiveness. This exaggerated regard was due to the supposed successes of fascist 'fifth columns' employing what Edmond Taylor of the *Chicago Tribune* called in his influential and elegant 1940 book *The Strategy of Terror.*

The *PW Weekly* began each issue with a survey, "The Week in Psychological Warfare," and for a while, until I killed it, ran a section called "Enemy Vulnerabilities," that is, supposed opportunities for PW to work its magic. R&A even had a Rumors Committee, and MO produced a steady flow of campaigns designed to demoralize the foe. The Evil Eye campaign, in the summer of 1943, for example, was intended to persuade "the lower classes of Southern Italy, Sardinia and Sicily . . . that their misfortunes arise from Hitler's having had the Evil Eye."

I was skeptical about the thaumaturgic qualities of psychological warfare. Economists, geographers and topographers, I argued in a memorandum toward the end of my first month, supplied hard information of operational value in winning the war. Movements of ships, trains, raw materials, helped predict military deployments. Knowledge about harbors, beaches, bridges, canals, mountains, was essential for military action.

But psychoanalysis of Nazi propaganda, a current PW enthusiasm, was not likely to furnish clues to German intentions. We had no idea whether the German Propaganda Ministry had advance knowledge of the *Wehrmacht's* military intentions. Perhaps, like OWI, it was kept in the dark. Even if Dr. Goebbels's propagandists knew more about military plans than Elmer Davis's propagandists did, "Can we escape from the fact that Nazi propaganda, in making a point, may choose to make that point directly, or to make the diametrically opposite point, or to make any number of points in between?" There were just too many variables to lay a basis for forecasting the moves of the enemy. As for undermining enemy morale, psychological warfare seemed infinitely less potent than successful military action.

* * *

The *PW Weekly* was compiled from reports produced by R&A's regional divisions. As editor, I steered it away from psychological warfare into political analysis. My routine was to make the rounds of the regional desks every couple of days, chatting with section chiefs, inquiring what studies were in preparation, sometimes suggesting new topics of inquiry, collecting completed studies for the *Weekly,* later condensing and rewriting them. Felix Gilbert, a truly distinguished historian in the German section, recalls in his memoirs: "Arthur M. Schlesinger, Jr., made the various articles readable, and he did so in an admirable way. Once during a half hour while the rest of us were at lunch, he transformed an interesting but complicated, long, and abstract article by Leonard Krieger into a piece that, with none of the ideas lost, was entirely clear and readable." My collaborators in the boiling-down procedure were Richard P. Stebbins, later editor of the Council on Foreign Relations annual *The United States in World Affairs* series, and Maurice Ragsdale, who had learned the arts of condensation on *Reader's Digest;* later came Ray S. Cline, another Harvard historian and Junior Fellow who went on to a lofty career in the Central Intelligence Agency; Leonard Meeker, with whom I would work again when he was the State Department's legal adviser in the Kennedy years; Edward Downes, the music critic; and Sebastian di Grazia, whose book on Machiavelli won the Pulitzer Prize in 1990.

The *Weekly* was dutifully sent to high officials around the government. I have come upon no evidence that it had any influence or even that any top officials found time to read it. Nor could it draw much on the more secret and sensitive sources available within OSS. It did, however, play a useful role in R&A by providing an outlet for the work of the regional desks and thereby sustaining the morale of analysts.

There was an air of unreality about it all. As I wrote to my parents, I had "a mounting suspicion that the whole thing is a gigantic boondoggle" (the word applied by critics of the WPA to what they considered make-work projects). R&A's psychological warfare reports went to a so-called Planning Group of wise men, who then thought up subjects for new reports, which were then duly prepared, submitted and reviewed; but "very rarely in this process is anything outside OSS affected by anything inside it." In OWI I had had, if on a low level, a sense of effectiveness. Someone would make a speech or issue a statement that came from me; one's work had visible consequences. In OSS it was as if one put a message in a bottle and threw it into the sea.

*   *   *

Disagreement among the regional desks reduced R&A's influence. In August 1943 I sent up a memorandum entitled, in deference to the PW craze, "The Need for Intellectual Guidance in Psychological Warfare Research." If R&A was to have any impact on policy, I argued, it must strive for "a greater degree of intellectual unity." Internal inconsistencies and divergences "weaken the impact of R&A conclusions on outside markets."

Of course, I continued, some in OSS claimed that R&A should keep away from policy. R&A's function, the Planning Group thought, was exclusively to present facts, an "altogether neutral" process. This notion, I complained, was "founded on a crude conception of the intellectual processes which go into analysis. . . . Fact, judgment and value are inextricably entangled." The "epistemological naiveté" of this approach was matched by "its practical unworkability." The very act of selecting facts inevitably meant making judgments. And judgments were often in conflict.

Was it in the national interest, for example, to support Mihailovich's Chetniks or Tito's Partisans in Yugoslavia? General de Gaulle or General Giraud in France? Occasionally consensus emerged. R&A thought Winston Churchill quite right in preferring Tito to Mihailovich, Roosevelt and Secretary of State Cordell Hull quite wrong in preferring Giraud to de Gaulle. The "OSS consensus," I wrote to my parents, regarded our snubbing of de Gaulle and his French Committee of National Liberation as "inexcusable." Reading State Department cables every day, I found myself "mildly horrified by how much more deliberately bad their policy is than I had suspected."

But in many cases there was no internal consensus. When regional desks disagreed, little was done to reconcile their judgments. The Central European desk, I observed,

> adopts the Social Democratic, central-core-of-decency theory of the German people, whereas the Low Countries believe that the German people cannot be cleared for a moment of the crimes of Nazism. No steps toward reconciliation.
>
> Scandinavia disapproves of Danish sabotage, while Central Europe is delighted by it and urges it on. Again no steps at reconciliation.

Yet decisions about such matters could not be indefinitely postponed; and, "since most decisions have to be made on imperfect data, the obligation of the expert to participate in making them becomes all the greater." Chronic internal disagreement thwarted any OSS prospects for affecting policy. As I argued in another memorandum, "Only by enforcing agreement upon itself can R&A hope to bring much influence to bear on people outside." This was not a plea for R&A to enter the policy business in a big way. After all, R&A's influence depended on the appearance of objectivity. It was a plea rather for settling internal disputes and for strong analysis implying policy conclusions.

I don't remember that these memoranda wrought any miracles, though I learn from Professor Robin Winks's excellent book on OSS, *Cloak and Gown: Scholars in the Secret War* (1987), that "The Need for Intellectual Guidance" spurred on Sherman Kent, the sharp and profane Yale historian who headed the Europe-Africa Division, to deal further with the problem.

In any case, the rapid movement of events called with mounting urgency for expert appraisals leading to policy recommendations. R&A had more global specialists than any other branch of the American government, and Bill Langer effectively widened the market for R&A assessments. In the end, R&A studies covered most of the planet, clarified political and strategic quandaries and perhaps made a modest contribution to military victory. And the *Weekly* became a livelier and, I believe, more useful journal. The official R&A history attributes its popularity to "Schlesinger's peppy style and all-consuming intellectual appetite."

*   *   *

But the search for "intellectual unity" in R&A still ran into difficulties. Like any faculty, the R&A professors argued interminably among themselves. The *Weekly* had to go to press every seven days, so in cases of disagreement someone had to decide what should be said. A Schlesinger memorandum to Ev Gleason in January 1944: "The qualities of dilatoriness, hypercaution, illiteracy, verbosity, passionate partisanship, special pleading and plain lack of good judgment too often displayed by the divisions cannot be easily harmonized into a coherent, sober and honest whole unless someone outside the divisions is charged with the authority to do so." That someone, I thought, should be the *Weekly*'s editor. And most disagreements among rational people proved in the end to be negotiable.

I encountered only one nonnegotiable case. It had to do with Latin America. The chief of the Latin American division was a former University of Oklahoma professor named Maurice Halperin. I soon noticed in my rounds that Halperin kept the *Daily Worker* on his desk and that his reports regularly followed the Communist party line.

Indeed, as I later discovered, Halperin in 1942, before I joined OSS, had circulated a paper, "Pro-Axis and Anti-Axis Forces in Mexico." Listed in the pro-Axis category were, highlighted by italics, "*a group of foreign Trotskyites*," including rather well-known anti-Nazis like Victor Serge and Gustav Regler. This charge had earlier appeared in the *Daily Worker*, provoking Reinhold Niebuhr, Norman Thomas, Roger Baldwin of the American Civil Liberties Union and Michael Straight to send an open letter to the Mexican president vouching for the anti-Nazi record of the so-called Trotskyites.

Halperin's paper went on to claim that North American Trotskyites had "connections with the Gestapo . . . revealed when the United States Government recently prosecuted the leaders of the group in Minneapolis." Halperin referred to the prosecution under the Smith Act of a Trotskyite faction in the Teamsters Union — a prosecution applauded by American Communists (though a decade later, when the Smith Act was used against them, they characteristically reversed field and whined that the law was unconstitutional). Nor in fact had the prosecution revealed the slightest connection between the Minneapolis Trotskyites and the Gestapo.

Still, Latin America was a marginal area in the global war, and no one paid much attention to reports from R&A's Latin American division. Then in December 1943 a revolution overthrew Enrique Penaranda's conservative, pro–tin mine owners, pro-U.S. government in Bolivia. The *Daily Worker* promptly condemned the revolution as a pro-Nazi putsch: "The events in La Paz are part of a far reaching development — yes, a conspiracy — fanning out from Buenos Aires, the capital bridgehead of the German Nazis, the Italian fascists, and the Spanish Falangists in the Americas." R&A's Latin American division once more parroted the Communist line.

I had heard a very different interpretation from Pat Jackson's friend Ernesto Galarza of the Pan-American Union and from Laurence Duggan of the State Department. The Penaranda regime, in Duggan's words, was "corrupt, thoroughly discredited as a tool of the tin mining interests, and had permitted all sorts of activity beneficial to the Axis." The revolution, Galarza told me, had brought to power the MNR (Movimento Nacionalista Revolucionario), the party of the tin mine workers, led by an intellectual, Victor Paz Estenssoro. Its purpose was domestic reform. They were not Nazis.

The new regime quickly pledged its fidelity to the United Nations and to Bolivia's inter-American commitments, including the supply of strategic materials to the allies. It soon dispatched to Washington a highly intelligent and persuasive envoy (and Dartmouth graduate), Enrique Lozada, to set forth its reform agenda.

In the *PW Weekly* I portrayed the coup as an indigenous explosion against "the domination of the country by the tin interests, the inefficiency and corruption of the Penaranda Government, the food shortages and the uncontrolled inflation." The revolution had taken place exactly one year after a massacre of workers by soldiers at the Catavi mines. Mine owners, I continued, had found it helpful to call labor protests "Nazi-inspired," and "the Communists who are also making this charge, have backed Penaranda, opposed attempts to agitate the Catavi issue and are tending to play a conservative role in South American labor affairs." The United States "must await more conclusive evidence of pro-Nazi leanings than tales from sources close to the mine owners or from Communist organizations."

* * *

All this infuriated Halperin, an overbearing man with the swagger of a bully, and he denounced me to Bill Langer. Hoping to work things out, I went over to Halperin's office. An argument ensued. Halperin later told Professor Don S. Kirschner, the author of a thoughtful and judicious biography, *Cold War Exile: The Unclosed Case of Maurice Halperin* (1995), that Schlesinger appeared "in a rage, like a young child in a tantrum" and that he thereupon grabbed Schlesinger "by the collar, turned him around, and shoved him out." My memory is of a vigorous exchange of words. I am sure I would have recalled physical assault.

I received staunch support from Ev Gleason, who explained to

Langer that the Latin American division from the start had portrayed the new regime as "irrevocably committed to Germany and Argentina" but that Latin American experts outside R&A "argue for the primacy of internal factors in the Bolivian coup" — a point the Current Intelligence Staff felt worth making. Gleason added:

> In defense of the editor of the *PW Weekly* it may be said that however truculent he may appear to Mr. Halperin it is true that his relations with every other division and section chief in R&A have been excellent. He seems to be able to row with most of R&A and come to some kind of compromise. This has been true even of the USSR Division. It is only in the case of the Latin American Division that a complete impasse has been reached.

(I note now that my efficiency rating reports, obtained many years later under the Freedom of Information Act, gave me "outstanding" on everything but "cooperativeness," where I received only an "adequate.")

Langer refused involvement in the Bolivian argument and ruled on orthodox bureaucratic grounds that either I should use reports from the Latin American division or print nothing at all about Latin America. Meanwhile, Halperin would be free to disseminate his views in his division's situation reports. He did so, week after week. In a March 1944 memorandum to Gleason, I wrote, "The Latin American Division has carried on its policy of distortion and suppression in what would appear to be the interests of the Communist Party line to intolerable lengths."

Cordell Hull, for wholly different reasons, also viewed the coup as instigated by Argentina and Germany. He had a long-standing prejudice against Argentinians, and he disliked the more patient line toward Latin America advocated by Sumner Welles, the undersecretary whom he had helped drive from the department a few months before. Against the counsel of Foreign Service experts like Duggan and Philip Bonsal and without consulting Latin American governments, Hull refused to recognize the Paz Estenssorro regime.

After seven months and much Latin American protest Hull gave up, and diplomatic relations were restored. The *PW Weekly*'s assessment of the Bolivian revolution of 1943 was vindicated. Paz Estenssorro later served three times as a reformist president of Bolivia — I had a long and interesting talk with him when President Kennedy sent me on a tour around South America in 1961 — and in the Nineties Enrique Lozada's son was elected president of Bolivia.

Puzzles remain. In the Bolivian argument Laurence Duggan

strongly opposed the Communist line. Yet Soviet intelligence files seem to show that in the Thirties Duggan, despite misgivings over the Moscow trials and other matters, passed State Department documents to Soviet agents and continued with evident reluctance to do so during the war.

I knew Larry Duggan a bit. He was intelligent, moderate and unassuming. He did not give off the effluvia of a fellow traveler. I remain impressed by the confidence of Sumner Welles and Adolf Berle in him — Berle especially, because he was a fierce anticommunist. In December 1948, a few days after an FBI agent questioned him about Alger Hiss, Duggan fell or jumped to his death from his sixteenth-floor office on East Forty-fifth Street in New York. It was a snowy day, and Duggan was wearing one overshoe; the other was found in his office. His death remains a mystery. One wonders what impulses of idealism may have inextricably entangled this decent man with the harsh machinations of Stalinist tyranny.

Halperin joined the faculty of Boston University after the war. In 1951 an ex–Soviet agent named Elizabeth Bentley named him in her book *Out of Bondage* as part of the Soviet spy network in Washington. Bentley was rather free with accusations, but her account of Halperin contained plausible detail. Allen Weinstein and Alexander Vassiliev in *The Haunted Wood*, their study of NKVD records, provide corroboration about Halperin, noting, however, that Moscow "criticized the paucity of information he delivered."

In 1953 the Senate Internal Security Subcommittee summoned Halperin as a witness. He refused to answer questions, invoking the First and Fifth amendments. Later that year, confronted by new inquiries, he abruptly decamped to Mexico City. In 1958, fearing extradition to the United States, he moved on to Moscow. Disenchanted with Soviet communism, he moved on again in 1962 — this time to Fidel Castro's Cuba. Disenchanted once more, he left Cuba in 1968 for Simon Fraser University, in British Columbia, from which refuge he published intelligent critiques of Castro. A turbulent man, Maurice Halperin lived a turbulent life, but in the end he had the honesty and the guts to break with the Communist illusion to which he had sacrificed so much.

*   *   *

How far did Communist penetration of OSS go? The agency was by its nature a high-priority target for Soviet espionage; nor was OSS itself terribly concerned about Communist or fellow-traveling employees.

An intelligence agency had its uses for Communist networks and contacts. Bill Donovan, for example, sent Communist veterans of the Abraham Lincoln Brigade to work with Spanish Civil War comrades organizing Communist resistance groups in Italy. "I'd put Stalin on the OSS payroll," Donovan said, "if I thought it would help us defeat Hitler."

Donovan knew about some OSS Communists but not perhaps about others. Duncan Lee, whom he brought from his own law firm to serve as his personal assistant, was, if Elizabeth Bentley and NKVD documents can be believed, in the espionage network. Lee, like Duggan, apparently came to regret his ensnarement and refused further cooperation, nor was he ever charged with anything.

Actually, Donovan's nonchalance about Communists may have helped more than it hurt. There is no evidence that the information OSS moles gave the Kremlin did much damage to the United States. But the discovery that OSS was not planning subversive operations against the Soviet Union may well have soothed Stalin and reduced any chance of his making a separate peace with Hitler, a prospect that periodically worried Roosevelt and Churchill.

General Donovan (he was promoted in April 1943) was in his eccentric way a remarkable man, a winning combination of charm, audacity, imagination, optimism and energy — above all, energy. He was a disorderly administrator and an impetuous policymaker, racing from here to there, coming up with ideas and initiatives and then cheerfully moving on to something else. "He ran OSS," wrote Stewart Alsop and Thomas Braden, two OSS veterans, "like a country editor." He was exasperating but adorable, and he was generally forgiven and adored.

*   *   *

The Central European section of R&A had the heavy responsibility of reading the mind of the enemy. It was dominated by a group of illustrious German refugee scholars — Franz Neumann, Felix Gilbert, Hajo Holborn, Herbert Marcuse, Otto Kirchheimer — surrounded by an admiring circle of younger historians of American birth, later to make their own mark on the profession — Carl Schorske, Stuart Hughes, Leonard Krieger, Franklin Ford, John Clive, Henry Roberts.

Neumann was the section's accepted leader. He was a man of high intelligence, incisive speech, brusque language, a shining bald head, an elaborate hearing aid and considerable charm. Dogmatic, even peremptory, in manner, he relished argument and listened as well as talked. I liked him very much. He was a Marxist trained in the German juridical-metaphysical style, but he had in the end an Anglo-American empirical cast of mind and did not, like most German scholars, automatically prefer the abstract to the concrete. His (wrongheaded) analysis of Nazi Germany as the by-product of monopoly capitalism, *Behemoth: The Structure and Practice of National Socialism*, came out in 1942 and was the section's bible.

A mystery hangs over him. NKVD documents have been interpreted to allege that Franz Neumann passed OSS reports to Soviet agents. Those of us who worked with him — Schorske, Hughes, Ford, Schlesinger — find this almost inconceivable. Franz was relentlessly critical of the Soviet Union in his conversations with us; his anti-Stalinism seemed an absolute. Yet the biographical profile of "Ruff" in NKVD files clearly matches Neumann's life.

His great friend Herbert Marcuse was another puzzle. I rather liked him without ever really trusting him. He was charming and civilized, but one felt something sinister within, some form of hostility transmuted into a soft reasonableness, an uneasy mixture of defiance and the desire to please. Under the spell of Hegel, Heidegger and the hermetic Frankfurt Institute of Social Research, Marcuse sought to relocate Marxism in metapolitical cultural and psychological contexts. He had the Hegelian penchant for rhetorical abstractions that repel the Anglo-American mind (cf. William James's scathing piece "On Some Hegelisms").

Hajo Holborn and Felix Gilbert were distinguished historians, not Marxists at all but liberal democrats in the school of their teacher Friedrich Meinecke. Both were scholars of acute insight and wide cultivation. Gilbert in particular became a good and lasting friend.

It was a remarkable group, and they did fine work, especially in preparation for the occupation of Germany and for the Nuremberg war crimes trials. A question remains: How did they handle the Holocaust?

*   *   *

In the Eighties and Nineties, a furious controversy erupted over the supposed failure of the American and British governments to do more to save the Jews of Europe. One wonders why this controversy suddenly exploded so many years after the fact. The word 'holocaust' was not even applied to Hitler's extermination of the Jews till the Sixties; it did not acquire a capital letter until the Seventies.

Very likely, as the historian Peter Novick suggests in *The Holocaust in American Life*, it was because the decline of anti-Semitism and the rise of intermarriage in the United States came to be seen in some Jewish circles as a threat to the very survival of an American-Jewish community. Those seeking to repel the menace of assimilation seized on the Holocaust as the last bond holding Jews together and the vital means of restoring a sense of Jewishness. The Holocaust became, in Novick's words, "virtually the only common denominator of American Jewish identity in the late twentieth century."

The controversy turned in part on the extent of knowledge in Washington and London about the Nazi decision, taken in 1941, to change the anti-Semitic policy from expulsion to extermination. I have asked myself and I have asked R&A colleagues when any of us first became aware of a program of mass murder as something qualitatively different from the well-recognized viciousness of the concentration camps. OSS presumably received the best possible intelligence, and German-Jewish refugees would have been the last people inclined to ignore or discount reports of a Final Solution.

Yet my recollection is that, even in the summer of 1944 as we received with horror the mounting flow of information about the camps, most of us were still thinking of an increase in persecution rather than a new and barbaric policy of genocide. This was certainly the line of the *PW Weekly*, and I cannot find R&A colleagues who recall a moment of blazing revelation about the Final Solution. Nor do I recall the question of rescue operations coming up.

In his excellent study *Foreign Intelligence: Research and Analysis in the Office of Strategic Services 1942–1945* (1989), Barry M. Katz writes of the Central European analysts, "Although they had reported regularly on incidences [sic] of official violence and terrorism, on mass deportations, and on the network of Nazi concentration camps, their papers prior to [1945] . . . yield no unambiguous evidence that they had grasped these as elements of a systematic policy of genocide." Neither Felix Gilbert nor Bill Langer even mentioned the Holocaust in their memoirs. "In retrospect," wrote Stuart Hughes in his memoir, "what amazes me is how little heed I had paid to the 'Final Solution.'"

*　*　*

Yet the American and British governments had intimations of the Final Solution as early as August 1942. That November, after the confirmation of dread reports by Undersecretary of State Sumner Welles,

Rabbi Stephen Wise went public in a dramatic press conference. WISE SAYS HITLER HAS ORDERED 4,000,000 JEWS SLAIN IN 1942 was the headline in the next day's *New York Herald Tribune*. On December 17 Roosevelt and Churchill issued a joint statement condemning the "bestial policy of cold-blooded extermination." Edward R. Murrow, broadcasting from London, dismissed the term 'concentration camp' as "obsolete. . . . It is now possible to speak only of 'extermination camp.'" American newspapers carried stories of the Nazi program of mass murder.

Why did R&A analysts not make more of this ghastly development? Some may have been diverted by Franz Neumann and what he called "the spearhead theory of anti-Semitism." Franz saw Hitler's war against the Jews not as an end in itself but as a way of whipping up mass support in order to attain a larger end — "the destruction of free institutions, beliefs, and groups." His "personal conviction," he even wrote in *Behemoth*, was that "the German people are the least anti-Semitic of all." Marxists — Bertolt Brecht was another example — tended to regard anti-Semitism not as an all-devouring Nazi obsession, but rather as a cynical tactic used to steer the masses away from the class war.

Myopia was widespread. Non-Marxists were equally oblivious. OWI's Voice of America employed many European Jews in foreign language broadcasts. Yet VOA's historian, Holly Cowan Shulman, whose father (and my good friend) Lou Cowan ran the Voice in the last years of the war, went through file after file of VOA papers and found no mention of the Holocaust and little about the plight of the European Jews. She was astonished by "the yawning silence with which the Voice of America treated the persecution and ultimate destruction of European Jewry."

Forty years after, she asked the French-Jewish journalist (and Chagall son-in-law) Michel Gordey, of the wartime VOA's French desk, how they all could have ignored the Holocaust. If there had been an OWI directive not to mention the massacre of the Jews, Gordey told her, he would have resigned. "The only conclusion I can draw is that I did not know about the Holocaust."

When Jan Karski came out of Poland and brought Washington the news of the extermination policy, Felix Frankfurter refused to believe it. "I do not mean that you are lying," he told Karski. "I simply said I cannot believe you." "We knew in a general way that Jews were being persecuted," said William J. Casey, the head of SI/OSS in Europe,

". . . but few if any comprehended the appalling magnitude of it. . . . The most devastating experience of the war for most of us was the first visit to a concentration camp." Although the Roosevelt-Churchill declaration of December 17, 1942, was "front-page news," Telford Taylor, an American intelligence officer destined to be a major prosecutor at the Nuremberg trials, later wrote, "[I]t made astonishingly — indeed shamefully — little impact on the public mind. I myself did not become aware of the Holocaust until my exposure to the relevant documents and witnesses at Nuremberg." The correspondent William Shirer had broadcast from Berlin in the Thirties and published his best-selling *Berlin Diary* in 1941. Asked later how he had reacted to reports that a whole people were being systematically obliterated, Shirer replied, "I couldn't believe it. . . . I did not get the story, really, until the war-crimes trial at Nuremberg."

Daniel Lerner, of Russian-Jewish extraction and the chief editor in the Intelligence Branch of the Psychological Warfare Division, in his 1949 book *Sykewar: Psychological Warfare Against Germany, D-Day to VE-Day* is oblivious to the Final Solution. "The full horrors of Auschwitz and Buchenwald," wrote George Ball, co-director of the United States Strategic Bombing Survey, later undersecretary of state, "made a deep impression only after the documented revelations of Nuremberg. It was only then that I became fully and sickeningly aware of the atrocious persecution of Jews and Slavs." "Even we refugees from Germany," wrote Max Frankel of the *New York Times,* "were predisposed to disbelieve the reports of genocide. Did the Nazis persecute the Jews? Yes, of course, we knew that. . . . But gas chambers? Ovens? . . . Unbelievable. Unimaginable." The *Pocket Guide to Germany,* issued by the War Department for the instruction of the army of occupation, did not mention the death camps.

The British were equally unknowing. Brian Urquhart, an intelligence officer advancing with his unit into Germany, later the great international civil servant of his (my) generation, recalled, "The actual extermination of millions of people was simply unimaginable. We were completely unprepared for Belsen." "It took some time," my Cambridge friend Noel Annan, another intelligence officer, has written, ". . . for the enormity of Germany's crimes against the Jews to sink in. In intelligence we knew of the gas ovens, but not of the scale, the thoroughness, the bureaucratic efficiency with which Jews had been hunted down and slaughtered. No one at the end of the war, as I recollect, realised that the figure of Jewish dead ran into millions." Isaiah

Berlin, a Zionist and an intimate friend of the Jewish leaders Chaim Weizmann and Nahum Goldman, writing his weekly political reports in the British Embassy in Washington, told me in later years that he knew nothing about the Holocaust until 1945.

The formidable political philosopher Raymond Aron, a French Jew working for de Gaulle in London, thought that the murder of a whole category of humanity was inconceivable. He was not aware of the Holocaust, he said, until allied armies liberated the death camps in 1945. Even David Ben-Gurion read reports of the Final Solution with disbelief and busied himself not with rescue plans for European Jews but with postwar plans for Palestine. "As far as overall Zionist priorities were concerned," Peter Novick writes, "it is clear that working for the creation of a Jewish state took precedence over working to save Europe's Jews."

*　　*　　*

How does one reconcile two clashing impressions? One is that from late 1942 on everyone, more or less, had heard about the Final Solution. The other is that many people in a position to be informed and with a predilection to care, people who listened to Ed Murrow and read about Rabbi Wise's press conference and the Roosevelt-Churchill statement of December 17, 1942, still did not comprehend the actuality of the Final Solution. How could both things have been true?

In his *Grammar of Assent*, Cardinal Newman distinguishes between notional and real assent. Notional assent is assent to abstractions; real assent is assent to things. Notional assent does not affect conduct; real assent does. This distinction applies, I think, to perceptions of the Holocaust. "To have read about it in the papers," Holly Cowan Shulman writes, "and to incorporate that knowledge into one's being are two different things." Abstract knowledge is not enough.

We now know that the Holocaust was terribly real, and latter-day critics castigate those who failed to see it as terribly real at the time. But knowing how it all came out confers a considerable advantage. At the time, faced by an uneven flow of uncertain and speculative reports, many Americans — many refugees too — were honestly puzzled and, reluctant to accept the most pessimistic possibilities, found persuasive reasons for postponement or denial.

People remembered the phony atrocity stories of the Great War only thirty years before — Germans invading Belgium, children with their hands cut off, mass rapes and executions, all attested by such authorities as Lord Bryce. Later these stories turned out to be inventions of allied propaganda. Recalling this, skeptical newspaper editors rarely put stories about Nazi atrocities on the front page. For most Americans who read about it at the time, the Final Solution commanded notional rather than real assent.

"Perhaps we were so preoccupied with the squalid menace of the war," wrote George Ball, "we did not focus on this unspeakable ghastliness. It may also be that the idea of mass extermination was so far outside the traditional comprehension of most Americans that we instinctively refused to believe its existence."

In the Nineties many Americans condemned their parents and grandparents for standing aside in the Forties when unconfirmable reports came that the Nazis were slaughtering the Jews of Europe. Let them wonder why they themselves flinched from the commitment of American ground forces when ubiquitous television cameras left no doubt at all about slaughter of the innocents in Bosnia, Kosovo, Rwanda, Congo, Liberia, Sierra Leone, East Timor.

Philip Gourevich, author of the heartbreaking book about Rwanda *We Wish to Inform You That Tomorrow We Will Be Killed with Our Families*, recalls standing one morning in front of the Holocaust Museum in Washington reading the *Washington Post*. The front page displayed photographs of bloated Tutsi bodies floating down a river, victims of genocide in Rwanda. "And people are walking by me on the way to work with buttons saying REMEMBER and NEVER AGAIN." Righteousness is easy, also cheap, in retrospect.

*   *   *

The blame-lovers of the Nineties, while inert before the holocausts of their own day, became virulent critics of Franklin D. Roosevelt and accused him of betraying the Jews.

Actually, FDR was probably the most pro-Jewish of all American presidents. No president up to his time had so many Jews in his inner circle or appointed so many to high office. Opponents called it the "Jew Deal." And FDR well knew how strong anti-Semitism was in America during the Great Depression. The Swedish economist Gunnar Myrdal, imported in the late Thirties to study the Negro question, observed in his great work *An American Dilemma* that anti-Semitism in America "probably was somewhat stronger than in Germany before the Nazi regime."

FDR perfectly understood that it would be fatal to let the war against Hitler be defined as a war to save the Jews. He knew that he must emphasize the large and vital interest all Americans had in stopping Hitler. Anti-Semitism actually increased as the war wore on. In 1945 Hadley Cantril's Office of Public Opinion Research at Princeton reported that 64 percent of Americans believed that "Jews have too much power and influence in the United States."

Yet for all that, FDR repeatedly protested the slaughter of the Jews. In his presidency, Gerhard Weinberg, that fine historian of the Second World War, reminds us, "The United States accepted about twice as many Jewish refugees as the rest of the world put together: about 200,000 out of 300,000." FDR's priority quite properly was winning the war, and he had no doubt that this was the best way to save the Jews, and everybody else.

Professor Weinberg, recalling the daily death toll in the extermination camps, asks us to consider "how many Jews would have survived had the war ended even a week or ten days earlier — and, conversely, how many more would have died had the war lasted an additional week or ten days." The number, he concludes, would be greater than the total number of Jews saved by the various rescue efforts of 1944–45. Was winning the war as quickly as possible really such a bad idea?

*   *   *

As 1943 drew to a close, we were starting to feel that it was, as Churchill said, the end of the beginning if not yet the beginning of the end. Midway, Stalingrad, Guadalcanal, El Alamein in 1942, names etched in blood and forever etched in memory; in 1943, the fall of Mussolini, the defeat of the U-boat in the Atlantic, Flying Fortresses over Germany — all surely meant that the balance of the war had turned. Two thirds of Americans, according to a Gallup Poll in August 1943, expected the war against Germany to end in 1944 (more than a third, however, believed that the war with Japan would still be going on in 1946).

In the Schlesinger family, it was the first sentient Christmas for the twins, now fifteen months old and learning to walk, and their present-opening enthusiasm lived up to parental anticipations. We had saved enough ration stamps to have roast beef for luncheon. Logs blazed in the fireplace in the afternoon. Across the country Irving Berlin's (and Bing Crosby's) "White Christmas," that cry of longing for the innocent past, was winning its place in the canon of carols.

I cannot forbear quoting a Christmas verse my father wrote that December for my mother:

> What a time to make a rhyme!
> War is raging all the time;
> Railroad men are soon to strike;
> It's much colder than we like;
> Meat is scarce or can't be got;
> Oil's too short to keep us hot;
> And to thicken shades of gray,
> Art and Tom are both away.
> But for me there's Christmas cheer
> Because, my darling, YOU are here.

16

London 1944

"ARTHUR SCHLESINGER," Ev Gleason wrote to Bill Langer in November 1943, "has recently expressed a strong desire to see service in one of the R&A outposts, preferably London, in the not too far distant future. . . . Needless to say it would be a great hardship to lose Schlesinger, who virtually gets out the *PW Weekly* singlehanded. On the other hand, he has been at the job for a considerable time and I expect that if he continues at it for many more months he will begin to feel somewhat stale."

I was already beginning to feel somewhat stale. And I was desperate to get overseas. One wanted a larger share, in Justice Holmes's great phrase, of the "passion and action" of one's time. I agitated all that winter for a London assignment. Langer readily agreed. So too did Crane Brinton, now R&A chief in London, who asked in early 1944 "that Arthur Schlesinger be assigned to London at the earliest possible date and that he be entrusted here with the completion of the weekly summary." It would expedite matters, I was informed, if I, like other R&A colleagues, were to be commissioned as a naval officer.

*   *   *

I had already been through government security investigations. Some months after I joined OWI, the Civil Service Commission got round to interrogating people who had known me in Cambridge. Nothing derogatory turned up. The Commission made its routine check with other security agencies. The Federal Bureau of Investigation (FBI) reported that "the Bureau had no identity [sic] on the Subject"; the Office of Naval Intelligence (ONI) reported "no record." The Army's Military Intelligence Division (MID), however, said: "Information has been received that one ARTHUR M. SCHLESINGER was a Communist in New England in 1941. Identity with Subject has not been established. Evaluation of Source — reliable; Evaluation of Information

— reliable." The Civil Service Commission, no doubt because it knew the military, was evidently untroubled by the MID bulletin.

Finally, on June 14, 1943, the Commission, noting that I was "under investigation for the position of Junior Defense Information Writer, Office of War Information" — a position from which I had in fact resigned two months before — called me in for interrogation under oath. The examiner prefaced every question with the ritualistic phrase "information has reached the Civil Service Commission that one Arthur M. Schlesinger is associated with" followed by the name of some presumably incriminating petition or organization — a statement calling for the abolition of Martin Dies's House Un-American Activities Committee, for example, or a letterhead in defense of Loyalist Spain.

It soon appeared that I had inherited my father's roster of liberal causes. Why should security people in a liberal administration have regarded liberal causes with such apparent suspicion? To do FDR's Civil Service Commission justice, its official report, which I obtained many years later through the Freedom of Information Act, concludes with a scribbled note by the examiner: "The investigation established conclusively that the appointee is sound with reference to his loyalty to the Government," adding that Schlesinger was unmistakably "anti-Communistic."

* * *

That sufficed for OWI and for OSS. The Navy proved another matter. At OSS's behest, I applied for a commission on December 23, 1943, and underwent the normal gamut of interviews and physical examinations. On January 15, 1944, I was summoned for a new interview.

Two lieutenants confronted me. Questions had arisen, they gravely said, as a result of the preliminary investigation. What about my articles in the *Nation* (the piece about Wendell Willkie) and the *New Republic* (which had bought but never published a piece about a noxious isolationist *Boston Herald* columnist named Bill Cunningham)? They asked about the date of the *Nation* article. The Office of Naval Intelligence, they said, had no means of locating it except to go through the file, issue by issue. I restrained myself from mentioning the *Readers' Guide to Periodical Literature*.

They asked particularly about my association with that suspect organization American Defense–Harvard Group. Thinking to establish its respectability, I mentioned that Ralph Barton Perry was its moving spirit. One of the lieutenants said, "But isn't he a liberal?" in tones that mixed wonderment with perturbation. He added, "Isn't it odd to find liberals in favor of aid to Britain as early as 1940?" — a remark that made sense only if 'liberal' was equated with 'communist.'

A month later I received a communication from Admiral Louis Denfeld, the chief of naval personnel: "The Bureau regrets that it is impracticable to approve your application. In addition to the foregoing [there was no foregoing except the mysterious reference to impracticability], you do not meet the approved standards of physical qualification," by which they meant my "defective vision." In fact OSS, anticipating medical obstacles, had requested a waiver on the ground that nearsightedness would not interfere with my duties as an intelligence officer.

I immediately assumed that I had been blackballed on political grounds. OSS disagreed and, emphasizing that I was urgently needed for a job overseas, renewed the application. A week later the Navy threw it back. The OSS naval liaison officer, a Lieutenant Commander L. J. Cushing, tried to find out what the trouble was. ONI gave Cushing such an impression of my father's nefarious past that, when he got back, he said to Ev Gleason, "Is Schlesinger's father a Communist?"

The Navy investigators did not confuse me with my father (who was, of course, a stout anti-Communist); rather, they felt that the son was carrying on the father's dirty work. As I wrote to my father: "Those actions of yours (whatever they may be) which contributed to my rejection are only a source of pride to me, and it is only by accident that I have not committed them myself. And I gather from the navy point of view, your record only confirmed suspicions aroused by my own." The experience left me with a unnerving feeling of impotence. "There is no recourse," I told my parents; "no way to clear oneself; I have a complete sense of being tried and condemned without a chance to defend myself."

Drew Pearson, the "Washington Merry-Go-Round" columnist, picked up the tale somewhere, probably from Pat Jackson, and telephoned me. I asked him not to use the story, fearing that OSS repercussions might cancel my London assignment. Pearson in his usual style said that he was not calling to get the story — he already had it — but to inform me as a courtesy and to check the facts.

Drew broke the story on his weekly Sunday-evening broadcast on March 12, 1944. Admiral Denfeld must have heard, or heard of, the broadcast, for he promptly queried his underlings. A memorandum to Denfeld the next day said that "the report of [Schlesinger's] investigation had been unsatisfactory, and the applicant was not physically qualified." Pearson had not mentioned OSS, and there were no repercussions within the agency.

These were odd times, and the ONI investigators were an odd bunch. On the day I had applied for the commission I ran into an old friend from Massachusetts, an isolationist and admirer of Lindbergh and Bill Cunningham. He told me that he had not changed his mind and couldn't understand why we were fighting Germany. He got his commission.

*   *   *

London continued to send up signals. In April 1944 the economist Chandler Morse of Amherst, who had succeeded Brinton as R&A chief, told Colonel David K. E. Bruce, the director of OSS in London, of the pressing need for "assistance of the Schlesinger variety at an early date." In May: "The need for Schlesinger . . . increases with every new proliferation of our activities."

In May I finally received the permit to depart. I was assured a salary increase to $4600 and was given the 'assimilated' military rank of major. But the bureaucratic process was slow. D-day came, the sixth of June, that day of horror and hope, and the feeling of being out of things intensified. Nine days later an order at last arrived to report by 10:00 A.M. on June 19 at the Arsenal Building in Brooklyn. I paid a sad farewell to the twins, twenty-two months old and enchanting, and Marian and I took the train to New York.

I still have matchbooks preserved from our last night before embarkation, a night on 'jazz alley' — the Swing Club at 35 West Fifty-second Street, the Onyx at 57 West Fifty-second Street. At the Onyx we heard the matchless Billie Holiday with a gardenia in her hair, her voice floating huskily above the music, her rhythms and counter-rhythms dramatizing the lyrics, her "blue voice," as Carl Van Vechten called it, filled with heartbreak as she sang the song that lingered in my ears for the rest of the war:

> I'll be seeing you
> In all the old familiar places
> That this heart of mine embraces
> All day thru. . . .

*   *   *

I departed on the original *Queen Elizabeth*, the fastest large ship in the world, launched in 1940, converted in 1941 to a troop transport. At thirty knots, it was faster than German U-boats or American destroyer escorts. We crossed out of convoy in zigzag course from New York to Greenock, a Scottish port on the Clyde near Glasgow.

I sailed along with sixteen thousand others — Army, Red Cross, a smattering of civilians, the actor Broderick Crawford, now a sergeant, and Glenn Miller's Army Air Force Band. Twelve of us slept in standee bunks, stacked one on top of another, in a stateroom (M-104) built for two. We lined up for our two meals a day, breakfast and dinner, scanned the seas for enemy periscopes, and listened to Miller's band, led by the drummer Ray McKinley, play its stylish arrangements of "Tuxedo Junction," "In the Mood," "Moonlight Serenade." Captain Miller was already in England; the next December he died in a plane crash over the English Channel.

One of my cabin mates was a young man from Baltimore, Princeton and the Yale Law School, a week older than I, who, in addition to a passion for gin rummy, showed what seemed an inordinate and, in the circumstances, a rather disconcerting interest in the fate of the *Titanic.* The last thing we wanted to think about was the sinking of a mighty ocean liner, especially when the *Queen Elizabeth*'s lifeboats would accommodate fewer than a fifth of the people aboard. The *Titanic* man became a lifelong friend, a name to remember — Walter Lord.

We were in luck; there were no encounters with U-boats. On the fifth day we steamed safely into Greenock Harbor after solemnly filling out prewar Cunard landing cards asking whether we planned to disembark at Cherbourg before going on to Southampton. On the same day, the ship's news bulletin carried the headline AMERICANS BATTLING INTO CHERBOURG. Optimism was widespread. The war, we thought, would be over by late autumn.

*   *   *

As the OSS group debouched from the Glasgow train at London's Euston Station, we heard a loud buzzing sound and wondered why everyone else began to scurry from the platform. The buzz stopped; then thirty eerie seconds of silence; then a loud and terrifying blast. "A screaming comes across the sky," as Thomas Pynchon wrote in *Gravity's Rainbow.*

The German flying bomb assault on London had begun two weeks earlier. The infamous V-1 (*Vergeltungswaffe 1* — vengeance weapon) framed our lives for the rest of the summer, with a hundred and fifty bombs or so every day. One could never grow accustomed to the wail of the warning air-raid siren, the sinister scream growing ever louder overhead, the even more sinister silence when the motor cut off; finally the explosion, accompanied by an involuntary surge of relief that the bomb had landed somewhere else.

London by now was pitted with wrecked buildings and empty lots, mostly left over from the Battle of Britain four years before, a scene compounded and aggravated by the assault of the buzz bombs. The V-1 was not in a class with the blockbusters of 1940. It had limited power of penetration, and the blast, while respectable, was not cataclysmic. Unless you happened to be where the bomb fell or in a jerry-built house nearby, the chief danger came from flying glass. Still, these rudimentary cruise missiles killed eighty-eight hundred people in the next months. And had allied airplanes not delayed the V-1 assault by bombing research stations and launch sites, "if the German had succeeded in perfecting and using these new weapons six months earlier than he did," General Eisenhower later said, "our invasion of Europe would have proved exceedingly difficult, perhaps impossible."

Londoners were uncommonly agitated and angry. The 1940 Blitz had brought out their best. Now they faced a dismal and irritating replay. At night people had to seek refuge once again in the Underground stations. Coming home late, one picked one's way through families swathed in blankets trying to sleep. It was all too much. "They are tired as hell," I wrote to Marian, "their reserves of nervous energy are low; moreover, they felt that the war was nearly over, and there is considerable indignation that Hitler at this point, when he couldn't hope to win the war, should unleash this new weapon."

R&A by this time was established in a handsome Georgian mansion at 68 Brook Street, catercorner from Claridge's. I shared an office on the second floor with several analysts and secretaries. Large windows gave us an excellent view of incoming buzz bombs. My friend Richard Brown Baker, in later years a noted collector of contemporary art, recorded in his journal on July 17: "During the Section meeting this morning a bomb came so close that all the fifteen or twenty people, except Arthur Schlesinger, Jr., who boldly looked out the window, fell to the floor and crawled under the tables." Dick Baker, who had been injured by flying glass a few days earlier, did the sensible thing. I succumbed, as too often, to the fatal lure of curiosity.

One night Baker and I saw Jack Hulbert and Cicely Courtneidge, the popular musical comedy couple, in *Something for the Boys* at the

Palace. We could hear the flying bomb alerts in the theater, but the show went on. When Jack Hulbert, cued to begin a song-and-dance, came to his line "You'll have to get used to this," the all-clear sounded. The audience burst into hysterical laughter and applause out of sheer nervous relief.

As we left, according to Baker's journal, I predicted that "by the time the next war comes along the flying bombs will be so improved in range, accuracy, and explosive charge that they will make all cities unsafe." The V-1 was only the beginning. On September 9 I was sitting in Evangeline Bell's flat having a drink before we went out to dinner. Evangeline, my beloved friend from Radcliffe and Washington, was now Colonel Bruce's secretary. She had fallen in love, she said, and feared I would not approve. She declined to tell me his name. It did not occur to me that the fortunate fellow might be Colonel Bruce himself. (When I heard in December that it was indeed, I wrote to Marian, "He is an extremely winning, honest and pleasant person — a gentleman in the best Maryland sense of innate chivalry and good breeding." I was not yet aware of his keen diplomatic skills.)

At just this moment of revelation we heard a terrific explosion. There had been no foreplay — no siren, no screaming across the sky, no motor cutoff. Unlike the V-1, the explosion came without warning. It was the V-2, the first ballistic missile, far more destructive than the V-1 (and the personal contribution of Wernher von Braun to the Nazi war effort). The V-2 with its ton of explosives streaked down from the skies faster than the speed of sound. Before the war ended, over a thousand fell on England, half on Greater London.

We did regular night duty at 68 Brook Street as fireguards, sleeping on cots in the office and taking turns for a couple of hours on the roof. The barrage of bombs and rockets brought one's life to a higher pitch of tension than ever before. Surviving the blasts produced grim humor and constant exhilaration. We would say to one another, "I'm not worried till a bomb comes with my name on it." But, as a friend said to me while a V-1 roared overhead, "To hell with the bomb with my name on it. The bomb I'm worried about is the one marked: 'To whom it may concern.'"

*　　*　　*

Walter Lord and I found temporary lodgings in a drab but friendly hotel called the Principia. We looked at 2 Bedford Place, where the Schlesinger family had stayed ten years before, but it had now metamorphosed into the Czechoslovak National Home. Walter was a splendid roommate with delicious humor, sometimes turned against himself. He used to reproach me for the dilapidated condition of my hat. One day he passed on to me the opinion of the Army colonel who had shepherded us OSS civilians across the Atlantic. As someone had repeated it to Walter, the colonel was lamenting the decay of standards among civilians. "Take Schlesinger, for example," he had said. "He seems a nice enough young man, but no one with any sense of discipline could wear a hat like that." Immensely pleased, Walter told the story with gusto for several days. Then, walking down Brook Street, he encountered the colonel. "Good morning, Colonel Sutherland," Walter said politely. "Good morning, Schlesinger," the colonel replied. (Walter told that story with gusto too.)

After several frustrations in our search for better quarters, I decided in August to join a group of R&A economists — Paul Sweezy, Chandler Morse, Charles Kindleberger — in an elegant house at 33 Eaton Terrace, near Sloane Square. I owed this lucky invitation to my Marxist friend Sweezy, a man of great charm and humor, with whom I got along splendidly in every aspect except politics.

The new quarters came complete with cook and maid, family portraits, a Georgetown-style back garden and five newspapers every morning. For £25 a month, I had a bedroom (as the most recent arrival, however, I had the exposed room on the top floor), breakfast and three dinners a week. My housemates made it almost the equivalent of the New Deal's Hockley.

R&A/London's main impact came from its remarkable group of economists, including in addition Walt Rostow, Carl Kaysen and William Salant. Most, though not Sweezy, worked in the Enemy Objectives Unit, and their analyses had a decisive influence on allied bombing targets. Compared to the economists, with their brilliant fusion of analytical and quantitative techniques and their intimate involvement in military operations, the R&A historians and political scientists seemed a bunch of dilettantes. Economists dealt with the hard stuff, political analysts with the soft stuff.

Langer, in Washington, was increasingly dissatisfied with the political side of R&A/London. Crane Brinton's notable qualities as a historian, especially his skepticism about the capacity of human beings to change their character, made him a diffident administrator, inclined to give everyone a free hand. In February 1944 Chan Morse had succeeded him as R&A chief in tribute to both the primacy of economists in R&A work and Morse's own forceful and well-organized personality.

Morse was sympathetic to political analysis but, according to Walt Rostow's *R&A War Diary,* had to wean economists "away from the analytical and statistical studies of which they had been so proud, and to interest them in the larger but vaguer and more subjective type of analysis which was familiar to the political staff." The arrival in February of Harold Deutsch, an able historian of Germany from the University of Minnesota, greatly strengthened R&A's political analysis. Deutsch had described my job to Washington as "Chief Editor and Project Supervisor on the Political Staff . . . directly concerned with the servicing of psychological warfare operations." I imagine that he put in the business about psychological warfare as a selling point in Washington. His interest, like mine, lay in political analysis.

The British in the Political Warfare Executive (PWE) and the Special Operations Executive (SOE) were far more experienced in psychological warfare and all other aspects of the intelligence game than we were. "Ah, those first OSS arrivals in London!" recalled Malcolm Muggeridge of British intelligence. "How well I remember them — arriving like *jeunes filles en fleur* straight from finishing school, all fresh and innocent, to start work in our frowsty old intelligence brothel!" The British understood that psychological warfare was effective only when combined with a military offensive. It was in this connection that I first encountered R.H.S. Crossman, the resourceful chief of operations in the Psychological Warfare Division of SHAEF (Supreme Headquarters Allied Expeditionary Forces). R&A was too far removed from military operations to exert much influence on psychological warfare strategy.

* * *

In my capacity as editor of a classified weekly publication, the *European Political Report,* I found R&A in a state of administrative turmoil. New people were arriving every week. Strong personalities were competing to hold on to or to acquire domains of authority. The suspense of the invasion and the V-1 and V-2 bombardment stretched nerves and irascibilities. In mid-July Dick Baker noted in his journal: "We are supposed to be an assemblage of scholars and political analysts, but in fact we are a herd of baffled people under a barrage of silly orders from a top-heavy hierarchy of ambitious egotists."

Egotists no doubt were there. But the basic trouble was that political analysis simply did not fit into the operational urgencies of that tense and crucial summer. With one exception, our work had the glaring defect of irrelevance to immediate military needs. Political analysis did not, save for that single exception, contribute directly, as economic analysis did, to the goal topmost in all minds — victory over the Nazis.

The exception lay in R&A's assessment of European resistance movements. The FFI (Forces Françaises de l'Intérieur) were giving valuable assistance to the invasion, and the flow of underground military and political intelligence to London was steadily increasing. The question of the future of the anti-Nazi resistance led to serious debate. The issue, not often explicitly drawn, was the role of Communists in the resistance. After Hitler's attack on the Soviet Union, Communists turned overnight from collaborationists into freedom fighters, and very effective ones too. Some among us feared, and others among us hoped, that they might use the resistance as a way of vaulting into postwar power in France and Italy.

Most in R&A/London believed in the vital importance of preserving the Soviet alliance for the sake of world peace. Any premature suspicion of Communist purposes, we thought, would revive Moscow's mistrust of the Western democracies and undermine the hope of postwar amity. There were also those in Bill Donovan's ecumenical band who had a Marxist faith in the benevolence of the Soviet system and in the desirability of Communist revolution.

As a veteran anti-Stalinist, I was less hopeful about postwar felicities. The ensuing argument strained my friendship with Paul Sweezy. Unlike the EOU economists, Sweezy, as a Marxist, was less interested in picking bombing targets than in identifying the irreversible historical trends destined in the fullness of time to replace capitalism by communism. The United States' war aim, Paul thought, was to become the "hegemonic economic power." Russian aims were benign and elevated: full employment and military security. "Paul and I get along extremely well most of the time," I wrote to Marian, "— great correspondence in sense of humor, literary taste, political prejudice, etc., until Russia is mentioned, when I see black and he sees white."

London that summer still expected the war to be over in 1944. The shape of postwar Europe was under constant discussion. Parliament's radical firebrand Aneurin (Nye) Bevan and his wife, Jennie Lee, lived around the corner from Eaton Terrace at 23 Cliveden Place. Nye had no use for American capitalism but liked Americans for their spontaneity and irreverence. He was also appreciative of the whiskey OSS friends provided from the Navy wine mess. On August 16 they came to us for dinner. With his unruly hair, his melodious voice, his lilting Welsh intonations, his zest in argument and his command of invective, Nye fascinated us. So did Jennie, who, I wrote to Marian, "displayed her nice legs most of the evening" and seemed to me with her social passion to be what Eleanor Roosevelt might have been at the age of thirty if only Mrs. R. had been "small, pretty and vivacious."

Nye not only detested the United States as a reactionary capitalist state; he also detested the Soviet Union as a collectivist police state. He doubted that the alliance with Stalin would last. The struggle for postwar Europe, he predicted, would be between the democratic Socialists and the totalitarian Communists. "The Communist Party," Nye wrote in 1951, "is the sworn and inveterate enemy of the Socialist and Democratic Parties. When it associates with them it does so as a preliminary to destroying them." On that evening, as I told Marian, "Aneurin's cracks finally provoked Paul into a more frank avowal of his own position than I have ever before heard him make. After they left, the rest of us wrangled until about 2, and the discussion was continued this morning at breakfast."

We had a return engagement at the Bevans' house, recently restored from V-1 damage, on September 16. Nye, though a thoroughgoing egalitarian and Bohemian, believed in elegant living; he simply wanted it for everybody. "It was exceedingly pleasant, alcoholic and disputatious. Bevan is wonderful when he gets started. . . . They are very anti-Communist, very much upset over the sell-out at Warsaw [where the Red Army had paused outside the city while the Nazis wiped out the Polish resistance] and filled with the proper misgivings over any deals with the CP."

Nye and Jennie reinforced my conviction that the best hope for postwar Europe lay in the non-Communist left — in American terms, the extension of the New Deal, a *via media* between laissez-faire, the source of depression, and collectivism, the source of despotism. OSS in my view should do nothing that might strengthen the Communist position in Western Europe.

France was an object of special concern. We studied agents' messages, interrogations, manifestos, underground newspapers, to find out all we could about Combat, Liberation, the Front National, the Francs-Tireurs et Partisans, their composition, their politics and their relations with General de Gaulle in London and his tough intelligence chief, "Colonel Passy" (André Dewavrin). Most of us had disliked the chilly U.S. policy toward de Gaulle and the French Committee of National Liberation (FCNL), so FDR's decision in July to recognize the FCNL was greeted with heartfelt relief.

We also tried to size up resistance movements in Italy, the Low

Countries and Denmark. The internal R&A debate was subdued, but the unstated concern, papered over in bland R&A reports, was increasingly communism versus the non-Communist left.

* * *

In the meantime, private times in London oscillated between irritable exhaustion and manic merriment. Life under the flying bombs was more intense, more highly charged, for the fresh-faced Americans than anything most of us had experienced before. Paddy Chayefsky's exuberantly satiric script for Arthur Hiller's 1964 movie *The Americanization of Emily* does not unduly exaggerate the picture of the American military competing, conniving and disporting compulsively behind the lines in London while less fortunate Americans were killing and dying in France.

OSS civilians were less given to intraservice backstabbing and riotous behavior, but we too sought relief from flying bombs and sleepless nights. Drink was the great anodyne. Even Felix Gilbert, the model of a gentle scholar, wrote in his memoirs, "The amount of gin we absorbed staggers me now when I think of it." Whiskey was the therapy of choice at 33 Eaton Terrace.

Beyond the OSS circle, London was surprisingly filled with familiar faces from all layers of one's life. "I have a queer sense, as I meet these intermingled people," I wrote to my parents, "of my past having been churned up and suddenly spilled out." Charles Wintour, now a major, was with the Special Operations Executive in France. On one of his periodic returns to London he brought a bottle of cognac labeled (in German, of course) "reserved for the *Wehrmacht.*" When I produced it after one of our Eaton Terrace dinners, it gave us all splitting headaches. A French patriot must have spiked the *Wehrmacht*'s cognac with methylated spirits.

My old tutor Perry Miller was now an army captain attached in some drifting capacity to OSS. The austere scholar of Puritanism seemed bent on acting out adolescent fantasies. "When I come back," he had told his Harvard colleagues at a farewell dinner, "*if* I come back . . ." He appeared in London, where he had an attractive Irish mistress, then moved on to France. According to the *London Daily Herald,* dancing in the streets had begun slowly on Bastille Day in Cherbourg till Perry seized a tall Norman beauty around the waist and whirled her away. "I hear," I wrote to Marian, "via Paul [Sweezy] who got it from Harry Murray [the psychologist] who got it from Crane Brinton who got it from source, that Perry Miller has succeeded in killing a German. I suppose he will talk about it for the rest of his life."

Anne Whyte — "as ravissante as ever," I reported provocatively to my wife — was working for the Ministry of Information. Milton Mac-Kaye came through on a War Department mission. I had lunch with Eric Hobsbawm of Cambridge and dinner with Chadbourne Gilpatric of Harvard. Walking along the Strand, I ran into Mac Bundy, back from D-day, where he served as an aide to Admiral Alan Kirk. Harry St. John Philby came to dinner — "supposedly a Mohammedan, though not one who respects the Prophet on matters of alcohol. He has a beard and was charming." I cannot recall any mention of his son Kim.

The poet Dunstan Thompson and the novelist Harry Brown, author of one of the best Second World War novels, *A Walk in the Sun,* both working for the OWI film unit, gave a party — "like a transplanted *Harvard Advocate* party," I told Marian — in Harry's suite at the Ritz. Here I first met Stephen Spender, "a nice gangling guy." In later years he became a cherished friend.

One weekend I spent with Denis Brogan at Peterhouse. On another Dick Baker, who had been a Rhodes Scholar, took me to Oxford, and we called on Frank Pakenham, later Lord Longford; I somehow missed meeting his daughter Antonia, soon to become Antonia Fraser and another dear friend. At the end of September some of us were pressed by the English Speaking Union to take part in an "Anglo-American Youth Week-end" at Kirkburton, in Yorkshire. Between incompetent organizers, bad food, no drink and practically no audience, it was "a thoroughly macabre weekend," I wrote to Marian, "a combination of S. J. Perelman and *Cold Comfort Farm.*"

The London theater was, as ever, lively. Curtains rose that summer at six o'clock to enable people to start home before the city blacked out. I saw an intimate revue, *Sweeter and Lower,* in which Hermione Gingold got the absolute maximum of double-entendres out of what purported to be an air raid precautions song, "Is Your Stirrup Pump Still Working, Colonel Hough-Hough?" The rousing first-act curtain was a production number designed for the American invaders called "Thanks, Yanks." Yanks loved it.

Henry Pringle had given me an introduction to Constance Cummings, the beautiful actress whom I had admired in Harold Lloyd's *Movie Crazy.* I got up my nerve and invited her to lunch. She suggested meeting at the Ivy, then as now a leading theatrical restaurant. I reserved a table in my name. When I showed up, the maître d' looked at me with contempt and turned me over to a busboy, who sneered at me and grudgingly led me to a remote table by the kitchen door. A moment later the maître d' reappeared, asked if I were expecting Miss Cummings, bowed, scraped, and, overflowing with obsequiousness and apologies, observed how terrible it was that I had been given this table and took me to a premier table — an early lesson in the uses of celebrity.

Connie could not have been more lovely, amusing and welcoming. When she heard of my search for a place to live, she offered to call the actor Robert Donat (*The Thirty-Nine Steps, The Count of Monte Cristo, Goodbye, Mr. Chips*), who was about to leave town, and see whether his flat might be available. Hanson Baldwin, the respected military expert of the *New York Times,* dropped by our table and, after whispering, "Constance, how beautiful you look today," retired in some confusion. I had not imagined the author of his constricted columns to be capable of emotional excess. Connie became a good friend, as did her genial, bearded husband, the playwright, naval officer and Labour member of Parliament Benn W. Levy.

Anne Whyte took me to a party given by Norris Houghton of the American theater, where I had an odd run-in with the actor Michael Redgrave. He seemed, I wrote to Marian, "a taut and moody guy, who got very mad at me when I said that the Sunday *Times* had a letter from Donald Wolfit attacking John Gielgud." Redgrave called in a high-handed way for the paper, and "there was the letter, at which he retired discomfited." Actors should never argue with historians.

Dr., now Major, Douglas Bond, married to my sister-in-law Helen Cannon, was chief psychiatrist of the Eighth Air Force and came to London for long nights of alcoholic relaxation with stories of the intolerable tensions of bombing missions. In July my brother, Tom, wrote from the United States that his unit — the 358th Field Artillery — would be coming soon to England. "I don't want to leave," he said, "but I'll be glad to see what it's all about at first hand." He arrived in mid-August and came to London whenever he could wangle a pass. One night I took Tom and a soldier friend to dinner at a Sloane Square restaurant. A venerable British gentleman at the next table identified himself as an artillery officer in the Great War (he looked more as if it might have been the Crimean War) and, speaking with great dignity and feeling, arose and paid tribute to the courage of American soldiers on D-day and thereafter. It was a genuinely moving moment. Two weeks later Tom and his unit departed for France.

American politics sounded remotely across the Atlantic. The Democratic convention opened on July 19. FDR, running for his fourth term, dumped Henry Wallace, much to the disappointment of liberals like me (though not to tough-minded New Dealers like Harry Hopkins and Harold Ickes, but I did not know this till much later). Wallace's replacement was Senator Harry S. Truman of Missouri; my Missouri friend Irving Dilliard of the *St. Louis Post-Dispatch*, with whom I had drinks, dismissed him with contempt as a creature of the Pendergast machine in Kansas City. The president, Irving assured me, was headed for a smashing defeat.

I kept up with American news by reading periodicals in the American Embassy library. I remember particularly an article in the June 17 *New Yorker* by John Hersey. It was called "Survival" and told a story of heroism in the South Pacific. The leading figure was a young fellow I distantly remembered from Harvard named John F. Kennedy.

Friendship and drink filled the interstices of life as we hovered under the daily quota of flying bombs. One night, when I was walking home through the blacked-out city, the siren went off again, and a woman screamed despairingly as she ran down Regent Street. Her cries rang in my ears for hours. The all-clear that summer seemed the most beautiful sound in the world.

* * *

"My own job," I wrote to Marian in mid-August, "is exhausting, time-consuming and not altogether satisfactory. I am going stale on the matter of putting out a weekly magazine, which I have now done for about 75 weeks without much vacation; I feel, as each weekly rat race recommences, like the Chinese prisoner tortured by the implacable drop of water."

Moreover, as the summer wore on, I became increasingly concerned about the end-use of our R&A labors. No one knew whether OSS political analysis really made any difference to anything. "I sometimes feel," I told Marian, "as if we were all playing store together." In time of war, military and economic intelligence was far more important than political intelligence, even though political intelligence bore more vitally on the peace to come. As Churchill warned the House of Commons on Armistice Day in 1942, "The problems of victory are more agreeable than those of defeat, but they are no less difficult." Unfortunately, you have to win the war first.

My second conclusion was that intelligence is only as effective as its dissemination. And my third conclusion was that even the best-de-

signed dissemination system cannot persuade busy people to read political analysis unless it affects the decisions they are about to make.

In the winter of 1943–44, General Donovan had sent a young New
York lawyer named William J. Casey with vague instructions to help
Colonel Bruce by setting up a London secretariat. Bill Casey soon became London chief of the Secret Intelligence branch. He was in naval
uniform and spoke blunt words in an indistinct gravelly mumble. He
also had a sardonic sense of humor and a passion for American history. We became friends and, despite acute political disagreements in
later years, stayed friends of a sort till the end of his life.

Casey too was concerned about the end-use of OSS materials and
came up with the notion of a joint SI/R&A Reports Board to central-
ize the dissemination process. He was about to go to Paris to take
command of the OSS office and decided to bring SIRA along with
him. The chief of the SIRA Reports Board was to be an old friend,
Philip Horton, whom I had known as the biographer of Hart Crane
and curator of the poetry collection at Harvard. Horton, discreet, humorous and Machiavellian, showed an unexpected and uncommon
proficiency at intelligence collection. I was to be his deputy for political intelligence. The deputy for military intelligence was Major Harold Jefferson Coolidge, a descendant of Thomas Jefferson and, like
his illustrious ancestor, a naturalist and primatologist.

I looked forward to liberation from the weekly editorial grind, and,
like all good Americans, I especially looked forward to Paris. Since I
was now entering a military zone, I was ordered into an officer's uniform without insignia of rank — Eisenhower jacket, garrison cap,
khaki shirts, "a strange and wondrous sight," I told Marian.

On the fifteenth of October I had my twenty-seventh birthday. The
defeat in September of the British paratroops at Arnhem — a disaster predicted by the young intelligence officer Brian Urquhart — undercut expectations of victory in 1944. The Germans, driven out of
France, were digging in at the Siegfried Line and fiercely resisting a
strong American offensive at Aachen. Canadian forces were strug-
gling to liberate the vital supply port of Antwerp. The summer's optimism was now on hold. The war was far from over.

17

War's End

I LEFT LONDON, without great regret, on October 19, 1944, and flew through desultory gray clouds to Paris. As we approached the city, the skies abruptly cleared. The Eiffel Tower and the Arc de Triomphe gleamed in the sunlight below. There were also grimmer sights: railroad yards pitted by bomb craters. Driving in from the airport, we passed wrecked German tanks rusting by the side of the road. Pretty girls with absurd high hats rode by on bicycles, and I had an equally absurd feeling of excitement and delight.

We were billeted in a hotel on the rue François Premier, where I shared a room with an amiable R&A historian, John Christopher. Heat and hot water were intermittent, and electricity showed a tendency to falter. But Paris was Paris. Next door was a small, smart *boîte de nuit,* where a seductive blonde sang "I'll Be Seeing You." I thought of all the old familiar places.

The OSS offices at 79 Champs-Élysées were nearby. Phil Horton was already well established, with Walter Lord as his assistant. My job as SIRA's deputy for political intelligence was to disseminate relevant information to the intelligence officers of the American armies in the ETO (European Theater of Operations), the Psychological Warfare Division of SHAEF in Versailles and various OSS posts.

The far more vital job was deputy for military intelligence. Lives depended on the accuracy of reports on order-of-battle, troop movements and weaponry and on the speed with which information reached the appropriate commands. Ever the zoologist, Harold Coolidge seemed more interested in pursuing the Vosges wolf, apparently a rare species. He soon gave way to Lieutenant Harry Rositzke, a Harvard Ph.D. in Germanic philology and a keen, cool, resourceful, erudite and merry man. Horton, Rositzke, Lord and I got along exceptionally well.

* * *

Major Charles Wintour was now with the British Special Operations Executive at SHAEF, and we quickly established contact. Shortly after my arrival, he called to say that a problem had arisen over the SOE-OSS Jedburgh teams, parachuted at D-day to French resistance units in the *maquis*. The Jedburgh mission was to arrange air drops of weapons and to coordinate *maquis* actions with the allied invasion. The name derived from their training headquarters at Jedburgh in Roxburghshire, Scotland.

De Gaulle, Wintour told me, was insisting that the Jedburghs be pulled out. The general could never abide the idea of British and American agents inserting themselves between the Forces Françaises de l'Intérieur and himself. Some Gaullists affected to believe that it was all a plot to reestablish the old English kingdom of Aquitaine in France. Now that the invasion was well advanced, de Gaulle saw no further point in tolerating an Anglo-American presence. Joint SOE-OSS expeditions, Charles said, were now being laid on to tell the Jedburghs why their mission was over. SOE was sending him to the Bordeaux area, and he proposed that I get myself designated as his OSS partner.

I went to Bill Casey, who agreeably approved the trip. Charles and I drove south through ferocious rains to Blois, down the Loire to Tours and across to Châtellerault, where we spent the night. I remember how startled we were when the hotel barman casually broke eggs into a cocktail shaker for a very good brandy eggnog. It had been months since I had seen a fresh egg. Charles had not seen one for years.

We were heading toward FFI brigades surrounding the German "pockets" — that is, strongpoints near La Rochelle, Royan and Pointe de Grave, just north of Bordeaux. They were still in German hands because the war had swept by them and it seemed simpler to contain them than to root them out. Soon we arrived at the headquarters of Brigade Armagnac, an FFI unit engaged on the Royan front. The brigade officers had taken over a château where they served us a splendid dinner, roast beef with superb claret, followed by the finest armagnac, that velvety Gascon version of cognac.

We talked and drank till early in the morning. It all reminded one of a movie. The French officers were perfectly cast. Colonel Max Célerier was a Claude Rains type. His major was a saturnine character — Louis Jouvet? One of the leading saboteurs was a man with a paralyzed hand and the most singular gentleness of expression. The younger officers were handsome fellows in various cinematic styles.

The American Jedburgh attached to Brigade Armagnac was out of the movies too. Accompanied by a blonde mistress in FFI uniform, he regaled us with cynical and improbable tales of derring-do, the stories growing more extravagant the more armagnac he consumed. His name was Lucien Conein. I was not to hear that name again for nearly twenty years. One day in 1963, someone in the Kennedy White House told me that the CIA's liaison between Ambassador Henry Cabot Lodge in Saigon and the Vietnamese generals plotting to overthrow Diem was called Lucien Conein. When I heard that, my confidence in what we were doing in Saigon sank even more.

Conein died in 1998. According to the *New York Times* obituary, he used to claim that he had served in the French Foreign Legion, which may or may not have been true, and that he had lost two of his fingers on a dangerous secret mission. "In fact," the *Times* said, "he lost them fixing the engine of a car carrying him and his best friend's wife to an assignation, so the story had a basis in truth." Conein was a fabulist of the first order, and he did a lot of mischief in his time.

An American Jedburgh from a neighboring brigade was also there. I felt that for some reason I could not name him in my letter to Marian but described him discreetly as "a moody intellectual, whose brother you know of." It was Stewart Alsop. When I inevitably asked him whether he was by any chance related to the columnist Joseph Alsop, he muttered dourly, "Yes. My brother." Plainly, he was tired of the question.

But I felt in Stewart Alsop a kindred spirit. We had heard that afternoon over the Jedburgh radio that Franklin D. Roosevelt — Stewart's "Cousin Franklin" — had been elected to his fourth term, and we toasted him that evening in armagnac. And I learned a good deal more from Alsop about the politics of the *maquis* than I had from the egomaniacal Conein. When Charles and I explained why the Jedburgh mission was ending, Stewart expressed no surprise and told the following story.

On an inspection of the Royan front a few weeks before, de Gaulle had gone out of his way to insult a little British Jedburgh, much respected by the local *maquisards* for his courage in combat. Glaring down at him, de Gaulle said icily, "You will have left France in twenty-four hours." Later the general exhorted a small crowd: "*Ce sont vous mêmes, les Français, qui avez libéré la France.*" De Gaulle had humiliated the British major, Stewart said, because the Jedburgh was a living reminder that the French had not liberated France. The general was determined to rebuild French self-respect — and he did not like British agents roaming around *his* country.

The next morning Charles and I went on a tour of the Royan front. We raced along narrow, winding roads through the lovely countryside at 120 kilometers an hour in a small open car with a driver who, to our alarm, kept turning his head to chat with pals in the rumble seat. Finally we drew up about six hundred yards from the German lines. The night before, the Germans had planted a Nazi flag in French territory and laid mines around it in the hope that some hothead from the *maquis* would blow himself up trying to tear the flag down. When we arrived, FFI officers were conferring over the best way to grab the flag without losing any men.

The whole thing — this miniature war in the midst of the placid landscape of vineyards and salt marshes — was quite unreal. "The only factor which saved the whole business from having a Robin Hood quality," I wrote to Marian, "is the very grim consequences of capture. The Germans still treat the *maquis* as partisans, and the results — some of which I was shown in photographs — are far from pleasant."

On our drive back to Paris we stopped off in Chartres. Bombs had fallen on the town, but the great cathedral was unharmed. Its stained glass had long since been removed for safekeeping. Birds now flew in through rips in the fabric covering the tall windows and twittered wildly as they sought their bearings under the cavernous ceiling.

*   *   *

On the morning of Armistice Day 1944, OSS personnel watched the great parade from the roof of 79 Champs-Élysées. Churchill and de Gaulle drove to the Arc de Triomphe in an open car surrounded by a hollow square of grenadiers, and the crowd went wild. So did the OSS contingent on the roof. Then came the traditional moment of silence. This time the silence was overwhelming. The only sound one could hear across the immense throng was the faraway buzzing of planes overhead. What a salute to unknown soldiers! In the afternoon, delegations covered the Étoile with wreaths and fall flowers.

My job was both interesting and demanding. Appraisal of resistance groups was the priority — where were they located? which were doing enough fighting to deserve arms drops? and, a subordinate question but of interest to me, what were they politically? "It is absolutely essential to give the Commies no quarter," I wrote to my parents in November, "and the liberal movement in the USA will be injured by every form of collaboration with Communists. I cannot say too strongly how I feel about this."

One day in February 1945 a fellow named Noel Field arrived in Paris with a message from Allen Dulles, our man in Switzerland. I did not know Dulles personally then, but we had all been impressed by the flow of information about Germany coming from his operation in Bern. Field, Dulles said, was bringing a project for consideration by OSS/Paris.

I was one of those charged with discussing the project with Field. We found a tallish, stooped man, cultivated and courteous in appearance, soft-spoken but intense in manner. Hede Massing, who tried to recruit him for her espionage network, said in looks he was "a cross between Anthony Eden and André Gide." Field's notion, it developed, was that OSS subsidize a group of German "anti-fascist" refugees in France so that they could set up a Comité de l'Allemagne Libre Pour l'Ouest (CALPO), conduct political "reeducation" in prisoner-of-war camps and recruit agents to be dropped in Germany for espionage and sabotage.

Field's CALPO was obviously the extension to Western Europe of the Soviet-controlled Free Germany Committee set up in Moscow in 1943 behind a facade of captured German officers. His list of potential recruits had a strong Communist flavor. Giving them priority in the occupation of Germany seemed a poor idea. My impression in the course of several conversations was that Field's passion for the project and his studied evasiveness about its details and political implications exceeded the reasonable bounds of innocence or enthusiasm. Though Field had resumed a prewar job with the Unitarian Service Committee as cover, he acted, in my judgment, like a Soviet agent. Albert E. Jolis, the SI representative in the talks with Field, had the same reaction, and we both strongly recommended against the project.

Dulles, it turned out, had known Field for a long time. When he had first entered the intelligence game as a young diplomat in Switzerland during the First World War, he met Herbert Haviland Field, an American zoologist and Quaker living in Zurich. Dulles worked with him on intelligence matters and became acquainted with his family, including young Noel.

Born in 1904, Noel Field entered the Foreign Service in the Coolidge administration. The depression and the rise of fascism set his

Quaker idealism in a communist mold. In the mid-Thirties he probably joined the Communist party. Alger Hiss and Laurence Duggan
were particular State Department friends. Field wanted to help the
communist cause but had scruples about spying on his own government when he was in its service. He solved the ethical issue by leaving
State and joining the League of Nations secretariat. As an international civil servant, he presumably relinquished national allegiances.
When the war began, he left the League and caught on with the Unitarian Service Committee, where he did courageous work rescuing
anti-Nazi (especially Communist) refugees.

Then Dulles decided to use his old friend's Communist contacts.
An intelligence chief in Switzerland who failed to make use of Field
would have been delinquent. The Communists were an important
part of the anti-Nazi resistance. It was Dulles's job to collect intelligence from every source. CALPO, however, was another matter. Bert
Jolis and I thought we had stopped CALPO, but, as I learned later, we
hadn't.

CALPO was already in touch with SO and SI, two OSS branches in
urgent need of agents to drop into Germany. Like Donovan and
Dulles, they were ready to work with anybody who might help win
the war. At war's end, SO was even preparing to send a hundred
CALPO agents with machine guns and hand grenades into Germany. All Jolis and I succeeded in doing was to change unofficial
OSS "cooperation" with CALPO to a "hands-off" policy. The State Department, when it discovered in March 1945 that OSS/SO had been
subsidizing CALPO, was appalled.

Noel Field was a Quaker Communist, filled with idealism, smug-
ness and sacrifice. What struck me most was his self-righteous evasiveness. He had, as Flora Lewis wrote in her book about him, the "arrogance of humility." But he was not a formidable figure. He sought
nothing more than a life of pious devotion on the other side of the
Iron Curtain. His dedication to the Soviet Union did little damage to
the interests of the United States.

*　　*　　*

Paris was under wraps that winter. The weather was unwontedly cold
and dismal, and there was not much in the way of heat. In January
soft, wet snow blanketed the city. For a moment, Parisians engaged in
enthusiastic and incompetent snowfights. French girls, GIs and stray
passersby snowballed the MPs at the Arc de Triomphe. Then the snow

turned to slush; the slush froze; it snowed again; unheated rooms in-stitutionalized the cold. "It will take a long time," I wrote to Marian, "before I am used to atmosphere in which I cannot see my breath."

The cold was so intense that I drank cup after cup of coffee to keep warm. Then I began to suffer palpitations of the heart. Fearing an incipient heart attack, I went to the OSS doctor. He listened to my recital of symptoms and asked, "Do you drink much coffee?" I said, "A certain amount." "Why not give it up for a couple of weeks and see what happens?" I gave up coffee. The palpitations ceased. Un-American as it may sound, no coffee has passed my lips for over half a century.

There were diversions for the troops: movies at the Marignan the-ater on the Champs-Élysées; traveling troupes of performers. In No-vember the British brought in Noel Coward. After repeatedly stop-ping the show with his own songs, he announced that he wanted to sing a song from the best musical he had ever seen. With that, he sang the Rodgers and Hammerstein "Surrey with the Fringe on Top," com-plete with Oklahoma intonations. The GIs loved it.

Paris was filled with familiar faces. I had a drink with Evangeline Bell before she returned to London and Colonel Bruce. Captain Perry Miller was often around. He had shot one German, he told me, and had captured twenty-nine. His talk about his wife and his mistress reminded one of a high school senior discussing his girls, and his de-scription of his newly acquired "lust" for using his "BB gun" (carbine) seemed equally juvenile. Harvard friends arrived: Captain Chad-bourne Gilpatric was in OSS; Bob Wernick came in from Italy. Wash-ington friends: Helena Huntington Smith, now divorced from Henry Pringle, on assignment from the *Woman's Home Conpanion;* Henry himself on assignment from the War Department.

OSS people drifted in from Algiers. As a historian, I was particu-larly struck by an incongruous pair: Henry Hyde, a lawyer turned spymaster, and Stuart Hughes, a scholar turned political warfare spe-cialist. Forty years earlier, Stuart Hughes's grandfather Charles Evans Hughes had led the investigation of the Equitable Life Insurance Company scandals that drove James Hazen Hyde, the company's president and Henry's father, to live the rest of his life in France. Henry and Stuart never discussed the historic enmity between their families and, despite discordant political views, quite liked each other.

Born in Paris, Henry Hyde knew France and the French intimately and did a first-class job in putting together FFI networks. He was a man of the right, rumored to be a royalist and an advocate of the Comte de Paris; but I think he exaggerated his conservatism in order to *épater* the liberals. He was intelligent, witty, urbane and great fun, as I discovered in later years when we became good friends in New York.

One also saw French families. French restaurants were off-limits, but concerts at the Salle Pleyel, nightclubs at the Place Pigalle, were not. There was much talk of *épuration* — the purification of France through the punishment of those who had collaborated with the Nazis. I wrote home about "the hatred and contempt people have for the minority of genuine collaborationists, and on the other hand the overwhelming ambiguity of most people, so that no one who was outside the country is really entitled to pass judgment on the conduct of those who remained."

*   *   *

Behind the hard work and feverish gaiety of Paris always lay the horror of the war. For me this was personalized in my young brother. Three years before, when I was righteously agitating for American intervention, Tom, a Brown undergraduate, was happily listening to jazz in smoky backrooms. Now I was in comparative safety in Paris, and Tom was at the fighting front. I do not find much virtue in guilt, but this was one point in life when guilt was inescapable.

Tom was in the Headquarters Battery of the 358th Field Artillery, Third Army, 20 Corps. Knowing his mother's anxiety, he sent cheerful letters home, minimizing the danger he was in. Perhaps sensing my own guilty feelings, he wrote reassuringly to Paris. By early November he was in combat — "a strange thing and I'm not the first to be impressed by the impersonal aspects of a lonesome shell or distant explosion. . . . I've seen a few dead Germans and watched live ones through field glasses. The guns bang all the god damned time. . . . Doubt like Hell if I'll get to Paris. Meet you in Berlin though."

By the end of November his unit was in Germany. Two weeks later we were shocked by reports of a new German offensive careening through the Ardennes toward Antwerp. The war, it suddenly seemed, was far from over. Striking in bad weather, achieving both strategic and tactical surprise, Field Marshal von Rundstedt's Panzer divisions began the terrible Battle of the Bulge. Paris was filled with wild rumors. The day after Christmas we even had a German air raid.

I worried intensely about Tom and was relieved to hear that his unit was out of the main line of the offensive. He was a forward observer for the artillery — a dangerous job. But he survived, and in the

spring he finally got to Paris on a three-day pass. He brought me me-
mentoes, including a German revolver and a bayonet. Seeking a riotous alternative to life in the line, I took Tom on the first night to Bal
Tabarin in Montmartre.

In off moments that winter, I tried my hand at writing short stories,
destined for the *New Yorker* (but never accepted). "To Whom It May
Concern" was an attempt to deal with my guilt about Tom. The story
begins when Captain O'Neill in his cushy office in Paris receives a call
from an old friend, Lieutenant Wheeler, in town on a two-day pass after sixty rough days in the line. O'Neill decides to take Wheeler for an
evening in Montmartre.

"What's it like?" O'Neill says as they move along. "I don't know how
to say it," Wheeler replies. "Part of the time nothing happens, part of
the time all hell breaks loose. Some of our units had a pretty frightful
time when the Rundstedt offensive began. But you can get used to
hell — you can get used to anything. I really had it fairly easy, compared to what some of the boys went through."

After a moment Wheeler, the man from the front, reminds O'Neill
of a dinner they had at Harvey's in Washington in 1940. "It was right
after the fall of France. I guess I was still something of an isolationist. I
didn't realize until then what the war was about and what we were
fighting against. Boy, I realize now. You were so damn right."

The story continues: "O'Neill thought miserably about that evening. He remembered his glowing exposition of the current theme,
that this was no war but a world revolution, and he remembered beating down Wheeler's mild and uninformed doubts by the force of his
own rhetoric. It embarrassed him to discover that this amiable mind
still retained and still believed. 'I guess things haven't turned out
everywhere the way I expected,' he finally said."

Wheeler responds, "There's nothing like the front line for a good
practical education in democracy. If you boys at headquarters will
take care of the post-war world on the policy level, we fighting men
can do the operations." O'Neill looks at him sharply, but suddenly
perceives that the remark was without malice.

They walk back from Montmartre in the early morning down the silent boulevards. The frosty air slaps them like an icepack after the
smoke and heat of the cabaret. "You can't win," says O'Neill desperately. "The guilt comes in layers. The civilian feels inferior to the man
at the induction center. The inductee feels inferior to the man in basic training. The guy in basic feels lousy when he thinks of the soldier
at the port of embarkation, and they all feel inferior to the men in

England. Here in Paris I get irritated when I see a letter in *Yank* from someone in the UK claiming to speak for the Army; but everyone in Com Z feels inferior to you boys in the line."

"Look here," says Wheeler. His tone is curt, and O'Neill sees that his face is tight. "It gets no better when you're outside city limits. The Quartermaster Corps feels inferior to the Field Artilley, and the Artillery to the Infantry, and the man just come into the line to the man's been there for thirty days, and the man who is whole to the man who is wounded, and the man who has a shrapnel scratch to the man who has had his face blown off. There is no point short of death where you could not be a lot worse off. There is no point which can save you from the universal guilt." "No point short of death?" "And death you cannot escape."

Wheeler is returning to the line at seven in the morning. O'Neill glances at the somber sky. "I hope it doesn't snow," he says. "I don't envy you a trip back in a jeep." "I couldn't care less," Wheeler says.

*   *   *

There were odd interludes. My father-in-law, Dr. Cannon, sent me a letter of introduction to his friend Juan Negrín, a fellow physiologist and the last prime minister of the Spanish republic. Negrín had come to Paris in January, and that winter and on occasions thereafter I called on him in his suite at the Hotel Lancaster on the rue de Berri.

Urbane and rather courtly in manner, Negrín was determined to stay above refugee quarrels and build a united republican movement. He showed a certain embarrassment over the support he had recently received from the Communist-dominated Union Nacional Española but was confident of his ability to cope with the Communists, dismissing as a fraud the Communist claim that they had a central underground organization in Madrid called the Junta Suprema. I asked whether he thought Indalecio Prieto, a stalwart anti-Communist exile leader, could work with the Communists. Though Prieto was a man of "violent passions," Negrin said, he was essentially patriotic and would not obstruct the cause of republican unity.

As for the problem of *épuration,* the republic, Negrín said, had passed an amnesty law in 1937; that law had never been repealed and should not be. "The people of Spain," he said emphatically, "have had enough of bloodshed and civil war. There must be no campaign of reprisal." He would not even execute Franco, whom he described as an efficient staff officer accidentally projected into the dictator's chair.

"Send him to Fernando Po" — the Spanish island off the coast of Africa. "Once you begin to persecute people who collaborated with Franco, it is difficult to stop short of destroying the classes upon whom the future prosperity of Spain depends. But amnesty does not mean that people who committed crimes and are protected by the Franco regime can expect to escape."

With his philosophical grasp of politics, his general largeness of vision and his essential realism, Negrín was impressive. In later years Hugh Thomas, author of the classic history of the Spanish Civil War, introduced me to his son Juan Negrín, Jr., then a surgeon in New York City, married to the beautiful and delightful Spanish film star Rosita Diaz.

One day when my wife and I were lunching with the Negríns at Mortimer's in New York, I noticed that Diego Del Vayo had entered the restaurant. He was the son of Alvarez Del Vayo, the elder Negrin's foreign minister in the last days of the republic. Alvarez Del Vayo later became the éminence grise of the *Nation* magazine and steered it, many of us thought, pretty close to the party line. When I pointed young Del Vayo out and proposed an introduction, young Negrin said that he did not want to meet him. "His father," he explained, "caused much trouble for my father." I asked, "Do you suppose Alvarez Del Vayo was a party member?" "In a way," Juan said, "I think it was worse than that. He was a man who dwelt in the realm of fantasy — demagogic fantasy. He was easily manipulated by those around him. I would call him an innocent instrument."

*　　*　　*

One day a diffident GI, a short fellow in a corporal's uniform, came into our office in search of Philip Horton. Phil was off on some secret mission, and, as his deputy, I asked if the corporal cared to state his business. He said that it was not an official matter but had to do with the Harvard University Library; he had come to OSS because he understood that Mr. Horton had been curator of the Poetry Room in Widener. As he rose to go, I said that I was from Harvard too; perhaps I could help.

He inquired politely whether I had heard of Henry James. I assured him that I was a James fan. That very morning, the corporal said, he had come upon a cache of Morton Fullerton letters that had survived the Nazi occupation. He was looking for Horton in order to assure the safe delivery of the Fullerton letters to Widener. Fullerton of course was a great friend of James, the inspiration for Merton (= Morton) Densher in *The Wings of the Dove;* he was also the lover of Edith Wharton and, evidently, of young men too.

The corporal was Leon Edel, celebrated today as the author of the five-volume James biography. So zealous was Leon in pursuit of James that at times he seemed almost to identify with James, even wearing one of the Master's rings. The biography is indisputably a great work, wonderfully researched and written with style if marred a bit by psychoanalytic excess. Mary McCarthy once cruelly remarked that it read as if it had been co-authored by Dr. Rose Franzblau, the psychiatrist who delivered quasi-Freudian advice to the lovelorn in a *New York Post* column.

We saw something of Leon that winter and introduced him to an OSS WAC, Roberta Roberts, who herself became a psychiatrist after the war and married Leon in 1950; they were divorced in 1979. I saw much of Leon in later years at the American Academy of Arts and Letters. Not without vanity, he enjoyed controversy and put people down with relish. However, when not provoked, he was excellent company.

*   *   *

Leon and Roberta were not the only coupling of that long, cold winter. Several factors were at play: loneliness, pent-up sexuality, the warmth of another body in bed on freezing, heatless nights. Many of us succumbed. I was attracted to a charming girl in OSS who fascinated in part because of her multilinguality, speaking French, German and Spanish with idiomatic ease.

I wrote another of my unpublished sketches about such Paris affairs. It was entitled *"Je vous connais encore et c'est ce qui me tue."* A major and a girl are sitting in a café. She says, "I got another letter from him today." He asks, "What does he say this time?" "The same old thing. . . . It's like all the others. He says he loves me. He asks why haven't I written. He says that he understands how busy I am, but a V-mail would take so little time. I feel like such a heel."

They talk about Paris, about their first meeting. "It is a miraculous city," he says. "It is a great city. It is a great city to be in love in." "It is a fatal city," she says. "I love you more than I have ever loved any one in my life." He says, "Don't say that. Don't even think that. This is a pleasant interlude for both of us. I couldn't have done without you. But it's a blind alley."

"I know," she says. "It is the old story — love in the ETO. I get so tired of hearing about the plight of the girl back home. The girl overseas has her troubles too. The inevitable moment when the man pulls the pictures out of his wallet and shows you the wife and babies!"

They talk on. "Look, honey," he says, "these years don't count. They are not normal. They are unreal. Once you get home, the basic continuities will be restored — the pre-war continuities — and they will swallow up these years. It will be like a dream, and you will remember it like a dream. For God's sake, don't worry."

"You can talk," she says, her voice soft but almost savage. "You have a wife whom you love. You have children. All I have is someone in the States whom I don't love and whose letters I can't bear to read and who thinks I am going to marry him. . . . I hate you. I hate you for your happiness at home, and I hate you for your happiness here. You have everything."

He asks, "Do you want me never to speak to you again?" "No, Bill," she says. "I couldn't bear that. All right, I love you; you can take it from there. Perhaps after the war you will introduce me to your wife and your children." "Sure I will," he says, smiling warmly. "Sure I will. And I look forward to the time when you come up to me and say, 'Bill, I want you to meet my husband.'"

"I guess I can sweat it out," she says. They finish their drinks in silence. The automobiles are honking with pre-war vigor on the Champs-Élysées, and the GI line is beginning to form for the movies at the Marignan. "It's getting late," he says. "We had better hurry if we want to make mess."

*   *   *

Another matter complicated my life. Eyesight requirements for the draft had been lowered, and, before I left the United States, I had passed the pre-induction physical examination. The Cambridge draft board warned that I might be included in the October call, and Bill Langer sent the OSS Draft Deferment Committee a request for my deferment "because of the urgent need for his specialized services in the war effort and his growing responsibilities on the Continent."

The Draft Deferment Committee was unmoved. Soon after I reached Paris I received an "Order to Report for Induction" at the Cambridge City Hall. By the time the order arrived, the induction date had already passed, and I was, as the draft board tactfully put it, "technically delinquent." I wrote to my parents that I was at first rather jolted, but "this has been a soft war for me, and I have nothing at all to kick about." I informed the draft board that I was quite ready to be inducted, but, since I was already overseas, could not the Army induct me in France?

The Army, however, had other things on its mind. "The local authorities," I told my parents, "display no interest in inducting me and lack the facilities to induct any one, so, until that is bridged, I shall continue as I am." It took three months for the military to solve this momentous problem. On March 7, 1945, I finally made the Army. I was, I believe, the first man to be drafted into the American Army in France; perhaps the only man.

My Army career was absurd. As a civilian in a military zone, I wore a uniform. When I became a soldier, I was ordered into civilian clothes. The authorities deemed it inappropriate for someone dressed as a buck private to deal, as I had to do every day, with colonels and higher. They pointed out, however, that, as a soldier masquerading as a civilian, I was not, if captured by the enemy, entitled to the protection the Geneva Convention affords uniformed personnel. I accepted the risk.

The first night, no longer eligible for the officers' hotel, I slept in my office. My pay was drastically reduced, which meant a drastic reduction for Marian and the twins; luckily, grandparents were around to make up the deficit. The officers' mess was now closed to me; the enlisted men's mess was for men in uniform. With other enlisted men in civilian clothes, I had to climb dirty back stairs to eat with the cooks in a small, bare, hot room above the kitchen.

We had little in common beyond our complaints. My colleagues, I informed Marian, had a single subject — how much they hated the people responsible for putting them in this humiliating position. "The bitching is so continual, so inevitable, so obsessive and almost hysterical that it becomes amusing." One of the few genial topics was contemplation of the first meal we would have on our return to the States. I still recall my menu: an old-fashioned cocktail (bourbon with angostura bitters, sugar, orange slices and maraschino cherries — in retrospect, a horrid concoction), shrimp, rare porterhouse steak, vanilla ice cream with chocolate sauce. Half a century later I would replace the old-fashioned by more austere drinks, Knob Creek on the rocks or a Bombay martini, and reject shrimp for oysters, but the rest of the menu would remain the same.

One in our mess with whom I did have common interests (i.e., the future of the world) but minimal agreement was a jolly, voluble, truculent Stalinist named Carl Marzani. Our denunciations of each other considerably reduced the boredom quotient of our meals. Marzani was a talented graphic artist who, when OSS was disbanded, moved on to the State Department. Postwar loyalty investigations exposed Communist ties. He denied party membership, was convicted of lying and spent a couple of years in prison.

*　　*　　*

My urgent post-induction priority was the search for a bed. "I am trying desperately to find a permanent place," I wrote to Marian, "in a town where virtually everything except flophouses is requisitioned by somebody. . . . In the meantime, I sleep about." Lead after lead led nowhere. Finally, in the first week of April I found rooms in a flat on the avenue Junot, near the rue Caulaincourt, on the butte of Montmartre. The flat belonged to Madame Frankel, an artist, blonde and late thirtyish, with a fifteen-year-old son. Her husband, a physician, was, she gave me to understand, at the front; I was to occupy what had been his office.

Madame Frankel, an agreeable woman, invited me for tea one afternoon. Noticing the French translation of James M. Cain's *The Postman Always Rings Twice* in her bookcase, I offered some comment on it. "Oh, yes," she said, "they made that into a movie here, *Le Dernier Tournant.*" After a moment she added, "My niece was in it." That rang a bell, vaguely, and I asked her niece's name. She said, "Corinne Luchaire."

I gave a start of surprise. My hostess sighed and said sadly, "Yes. Yes. I am the sister of Jean Luchaire." Luchaire had been editor of the pro-Nazi Paris paper *Nouveaux Temps* and was notorious for his call to the Germans to exterminate the French resistance. He was now with other diehard collaborators in Sigmaringen Castle in Germany (about which Louis-Ferdinand Céline, who was there too, wrote his distraught novel *D'un château l'autre* — *Castle to Castle*). The lovely Corinne Luchaire had been the reputed mistress of Otto Abetz, the *Gauleiter* of Paris.

"My husband," Madame Frankel said, "is Jewish." During the first year of the Nazi occupation, her son was sick; food was scant; she felt the constant threat of having her furniture attached under the Jewish expropriation laws. Jean Luchaire had finally offered her a job on *Nouveaux Temps.* She took it for the little boy's sake. The employees, few of whom were pro-German, suspected her as her brother's spy. The Germans suspected her as the wife of a non-Aryan. Eventually she divorced her husband in order to safeguard her apartment and property. In the meantime, she tried to make herself as little beholden as possible to her brother. After Jean Luchaire fled to Germany, she spent a night in prison but was immediately released and had not been bothered since.

The name Luchaire struck another vague chord in my mind, but I couldn't quite identify it. I asked Madame Frankel about her father, Julien Luchaire, a novelist and playwright. "My father divorced my mother many years ago. He married twice subsequently, and his last wife was a Jewess. He thoroughly disapproved of Jean's politics and refused to come to Paris during the Occupation. When my other brother, André, joined the Milice [the French police force collaborating with the Gestapo], my father said he would never speak to him again. Now he can't get his books published because the name Luchaire is so hated everywhere in France."

"What happened to your mother?" I asked. "My father left her in Italy. She stayed on and married a professor of history at the University of Florence. The professor is now in the United States." I idly asked his name. "His name," she said, "is Gaetano Salvemini."

Suddenly it all clicked — the Salvemini-Luchaire connection. She had been brought up, Madame Frankel continued, in the Salvemini household. Though her mother would not go with him to the United States, "she is very much in love with him, and they have their own kind of happiness." I told her that my father was the one who brought her stepfather to America. The circularity of life!

"I have lived a strange life," said Madame Frankel, smiling wryly. "In Italy I suffered political persecution because my stepfather was an enemy of Mussolini. In France the Germans harassed me because I was married to a Jew. Now I am under suspicion because my brother is Jean Luchaire. I always have the wrong name: under the Occupation I was known as Frankel, which was bad; now I shall be known as Luchaire — an old family, an honorable name — and everywhere I see the expressions on people's faces when they hear the name."

My parents passed the news on to Salvemini in Cambridge. He must have thought that I was staying with his wife, not his stepdaughter, for soon he wrote me of "the good news that you are billeted with my good Ghita. She is a remarkable woman who has behaved magnificently during these years while her husband was a refugee. I am very glad that you are staying with such a person whom I love deeply."

Jean Luchaire was executed for treason after the war. His mother, Salvemini's wife, begged her husband to intervene with President

Roosevelt to save her son. A man of rigorous principle, Salvemini refused, though he had been fond of Jean as a child and flew to Paris to comfort Ghita. He said to my mother, "Jean will have to take his punishment." Corinne Luchaire was sentenced to ten years of "national degradation." She died soon after of tuberculosis.

*   *   *

Thursday, April 13, 1945, was a beautiful spring day. Walking to the Métro, I stopped by the newspaper kiosk and picked up, as I did every morning, a copy of *Combat*, the arresting new paper of the non-Communist left edited by a brilliant unknown named Albert Camus. My eyes passed casually over the headline — ROOSEVELT EST MORT. Then I did a complete double take and glanced wildly at the other papers. They all said the same crushing, incredible thing.

The news swept across the city. Parisians rushed to embrace Americans in uniform. Photographs of FDR, draped in black, appeared in shop windows. All places of amusement were closed, and at three in the afternoon there was a five-minute silence.

Americans in Paris were shaken and appalled. People my age hardly remembered any president before FDR. We unconsciously supposed that he would be president forever. He was only six weeks beyond his sixty-third birthday, but his buoyancy had been worn down by the depression, by the war, by the aftereffects of polio, by cigarette smoking. Now we discussed anxiously what would happen to our country and to the world. "It plunged me into a bad depression," I wrote to Marian. ". . . His death leaves a kind of awful vacancy." I speculated about the future: "Any others of the Big Three could have been much better spared. . . . What a shame Henry Wallace is not in there. Poor Harry Truman. As Paul Sweezy remarked, the Big Three will now have to be known as the Big Two and a Half."

My father wrote of the reaction in the United States: "It was as though a great light had suddenly gone out, and people were left groping in the dark." But my parents did not share my regret about Henry Wallace. "While we all are for him because he represents in a way the best of the New Deal," my mother had written in February, "he is a strange man and I gather he thinks that he is a man of destiny." When I wrote back, "I suppose Dad would prefer Truman," my father responded that the new president had always done better than people expected him to do. Dad was everlastingly right.

*   *   *

At times, an awful sense of permanence settled over the war. We began to feel that it would go on, year after year, for the rest of our lives. But the military news was now getting better. Soviet troops were advancing on Berlin. The allied forces, shocked by the horror, liberated Buchenwald and Belsen. On April 20 the defiant Germans at Royan, whom Charles Wintour and I had inspected from a distance in November, surrendered to Brigade Armagnac. On the twenty-eighth Mussolini and his mistress were shot by partisans and hung by the heels in the great square in Milan. The next day Hitler in his Berlin bunker married Eva Braun. Two days later they killed themselves. On May 7 the German military leadership signed the document of unconditional surrender.

That night I sat with Chadbourne Gilpatric and my Paris girl at a café on the Champs-Élysées. About nine-thirty low-flying planes began to drop white, red and green flares. One plane flew along the Champs at the fourth-story level, causing much excitement. Floodlights illuminated the Arc de Triomphe and the obelisk in the Place de la Concorde. Rockets soared into the sky.

We began to roam the streets. People were milling around, singing "La Marseillaise" or "It's a Long Way to Tipperary"; the latter, for some obscure reason, was popular with the French. Impromptu parades would start. Sometimes two parades going in opposite directions would meet, whereupon each would chant, *"Avec nous! Avec nous!"* until one dissolved and merged into the other. Trucks, jeeps, civilian cars, jammed with French and American soldiers and girls, whizzed around. An American soldier shouted from the top of a car, *"Chantez, chantez, la guerre est finie."* Late that night I walked back to my apartment and then on to Sacré-Coeur, where the lights of Paris stretched out before me and people danced in the streets of Montmartre below.

The war was over, at least in Europe. "The end of the war was a flop in Germany," Tom wrote. "Didn't have the benefit of a Paris setting and no one gave a damn. Too much of Japan left."

*　　*　　*

"I still want to see Germany," I wrote to Marian, "in order not to miss the last act." I was scheduled to go as chief political reports officer for SI, but my low rank continued to raise problems. My promotion from buck private to private first class did not change things. Then Chad Gilpatric came up with the ingenious idea of exempting an elite group of enlisted professionals in the OSS German mission from the Army's Jim Crow regulations.

This meant that noncommissioned analysts could associate socially with commissioned analysts rather than just cooks, truck drivers and guards — undemocratic, I fear, but not undesirable from an efficiency viewpoint. It also meant immunity from reveille, curfew, bed check, drill and other joys of GI existence. The emancipation proclamation read: "Your authorization to wear civilian clothes in non-military areas includes authority to wear para-military clothing in areas where this is required by military regulations." So I was now enabled to live as an officer in all respects except, alas, pay.

On June 20, 1945, I left Paris for Wiesbaden and thence to a suburb called Biebrich. The OSS offices were located, of all places, in the Henkel champagne factory, part of which was still producing champagne — available to us at, as I recall, a dime a glass. The champagne was not very good, but we had to drink it because the water was suspect. I was billeted in a pleasant house with a view of valleys and the Rhine in the distance.

Biebrich had been spared, but the devastation wrought by allied bombing in the Rhine Valley was inescapable. What was one to make of it? In June, before I left Paris, the historian Henry Steele Commager, fresh from the States on an Army educational mission, dropped by my office. As we were chatting, Perry Miller appeared by odd coincidence. Commager and Miller were old friends, but a painful scene ensued.

"Are you going on to Germany?" Perry asked. Henry said, "I hope not. Between German atrocities on the one hand and allied destruction on the other — it's nothing I want to see." Miller: "Do you mean that you don't like to see German cities in ruins?" Commager: "No." A brief silence followed. Then Miller said, very belligerently, "I *love* seeing German cities in ruins." There was a long, tense silence until someone changed the subject.

Driving around the countryside, I found myself midway between the two eminent scholars. In Ludwigshaven and Mannheim, block after block was reduced to rubble; only empty shells of buildings remained, their interiors burned out by phosphorus bombs. At the Deutsches Eck, the junction of the Rhine and the Moselle, an immense bronze equestrian statue of Wilhelm I bore a slogan celebrating the Reich and promising future greatness. Bombs had hit the memorial, and, in fine symbolism, the heads of the kaiser and his horse now hung down toward the base. The memorial's interior had been covered with feces by foreign workers and other displaced persons showing their contempt for the regime that enslaved them.

"I still tend to feel a certain satisfaction," I wrote to Marian, "in seeing how low the sons of bitches who talked so big a few years back have been laid. . . . I continue to hate their guts. Or at least the guts of everyone 14 years old and above. The people continue to appear sullen, smug and stubborn. They are god damn well getting what was coming to them."

The OSS work was not onerous, and friends were plentiful. There was the old crowd — Philip Horton, Harold Deutsch, Harry Rositzke, Paul Sweezy — and a perpetual poker game where some would win or lose a hundred bucks (= $1100 in 2000 money) in a night. (I abstained.) I visited Charles Wintour in the fantastic and hideous IG Farben building in Frankfurt, now SHAEF headquarters.

My new Washington friend Ken Galbraith, co-director of the United States Strategic Bombing Survey, was installed in baronial opulence in the Villa Grunewald in Bad Nauheim, an agreeable spa town near Frankfurt. On occasion some of us at Biebrich would be bid to a splendid USSBS dinner. Here I met Ken's co-director, George W. Ball, with whom I discovered a delightful and abiding affinity when it turned out that both of us, he at Northwestern, I at Harvard, had sat at the feet of Benny DeVoto.

"Only John O'Hara," I wrote home, "can adequately describe life in the U.S. Army of Occupation. . . . It is definitely a post-war life we are leading, and from certain points of view, such as ease of transportation, abundance of ice cream, lack of urgency in work, it is more like life in the USA than anything I have seen for a long time." I was struck by the strange contrast between our giddy existence and the background of desolation and rubble.

* * *

New OSS characters came into my life. The chief of mission arrived from Romania, where he had seen the Communist future at first hand and had not liked it at all. He was a New York lawyer from Mississippi, a sharp, intense, high-strung man named Frank Wisner. Though bruised by his Romanian experience, he was bright and approachable, and we got along. A couple of times there passed through an attractive young naval lieutenant, a cool and keen ex-journalist who had interviewed Hitler before the war. His name was Richard Helms. We got along too.

In mid-July Allan Evans, the chief of R&A/London, dissatisfied with the quality of OSS reporting on England, asked me to come back as chief of the Western European division. The idea appealed. I had had my fill of Germany, and I was also disturbed by the alacrity with which Frank Wisner seemed to be preparing for the Third World War. While I was vigorously anti-Stalinist, I thought we should do our best to get along with the Soviet Union if only to make sure that, when the break came, the world would have no doubt which side was to blame.

I was especially disturbed when I discovered that Wisner, in his anti-Soviet fixation, was beginning to draw on Nazi intelligence operatives and sources. No doubt I was naive, but I did not like the notion of American spooks cheerfully consorting with people like General Reinhard Gehlen, who until recently had been the Nazi intelligence chief on the Russian front. There was something aesthetically displeasing about Americans plotting with Nazis, who had recently been killing us, against Russians, whose sacrifices had made the allied victory possible.

The British security services regarded the Gehlen connection with professional distaste. My Cambridge friend Noel Annan asked someone in British intelligence what the Americans were up to in their cozy relations with Nazi intelligence officers. "You mean the OSS? They're a lot of cowboys," was the reply.

* * *

August 6, 1945: the United States dropped the atomic bomb on Hiroshima. The tricks of memory! My recollection has been that I heard the dreadful news with relief because it promised to bring the Pacific war to the speediest possible conclusion, thereby sparing Tom and me and a million others redeployment to the Far East.

My letters at the time strike a different note. "Think of the howl we would have set up" if the Nazis had used an atomic bomb, I wrote to Marian. ". . . I have a certain sympathy for the Vatican [antibomb] view, though it is to be noted that papal solicitude was very much lacking when the Germans were trotting out their weapons of devastation."

Ken Galbraith and George Ball held another dinner at Bad Nauheim just before I departed for London. "Everyone was somewhat depressed because the atomic bomb had necessarily rendered obsolete all the conclusions of the expensive and exhaustive investigations of the Strategic Bombing Survey." That judgment was in fact wrong. USSBS conclusions — that strategic bombing was considerably overrated as a decisive weapon — held for conventional bombing, and atomic bombs were not dropped again for the rest of the century.

I was slow in grasping the historical significance of our tumble into the nuclear age. Marian saw it at once; but when she sent a fat envelope filled with clippings about the bomb, I responded stupidly that it was too late to convert me to an interest in the internal workings of science, even if I were to be obliterated by the examples in question. It took time for me to understand that the world had now achieved the fatal capacity that Henry Adams had foreseen in 1862: "Some day science shall have the existence of mankind in its power, and the human race commit suicide by blowing up the planet."

The decision to drop the bomb was the most tragic decision in American history. Yet in retrospect I have come to believe that President Truman had no alternative but to bring the war to the speediest possible end.

The conventional attack on the decision suffers from grave deficiencies. There is neglect of the Japanese sources, which show that even after the bomb fell on Nagasaki, military opposition to surrender reached almost the point of revolt against the emperor. There is also astonishing indifference to the fate of the hundred thousand American and British prisoners of war rotting in Japanese prison camps whom the bomb saved from slow, miserable death by torture and starvation.

And suppose an invasion of the main island had brought fighting as bloody and desperate as that in Okinawa (twelve thousand Americans killed, thirty-six thousand wounded). Suppose Congress and the American people subsequently learned that Truman had at his command a weapon that would have ended the war overnight, a weapon developed at immense cost to the American taxpayer, and he had refused to use it. Truman would have been held personally accountable for the awful waste of American lives. And he would almost certainly have been impeached.

A younger generation of scholars may reject these points. I hope they might at least agree that, before final verdicts are rendered, Japanese sources must be consulted, the prisoners of war must be brought into the equation and the fate of a president who sent men to unnecessary death must be considered. ◆

On May 21, 1951, Reinhold Niebuhr, Francis Biddle, Joseph Rauh, Hubert Humphrey and I had a private meeting with President Truman. "The worst thing I ever did," he told us, "was to give the order which killed all those people over there [Hiroshima]. It was terrible;

but I had no alternative; and I would give such an order again if it ever became necessary. But [with great emphasis] we must not let it become necessary."

Charles E. Bohlen offered historians a useful concept in testimony before the Senate Foreign Relations Committee in 1953. After noting the advantages of "hindsight," Chip remarked that there was also such a thing as "hindmyopia" — refusal to see the specific circumstances, the particular pressures, the full context, that shaped decisions. "The terrific compulsions of the war," he said, "are absent when you look at it ten years afterward."

*   *   *

I arrived in London on August 13 and stayed with Allan Evans in a mews flat off Berkeley Square. Two days later came the Japanese surrender. That afternoon Allan and I went to a movie called *Blood on the Sun,* in which Jimmy Cagney anticipated General MacArthur in knocking the Japanese around. We walked out at twilight into an immense crowd gathered in Piccadilly Circus. We had a drink, met a WAC friend of Allan's, had more drinks and cooked dinner at the flat. Then we went into the night amid happy, milling throngs. We wandered along streets filled with cheering, weeping people, caught the ten-thirty performance of the king and queen at Buckingham Palace and ended drinking toasts at a bottle club.

The war was over. At last.

Of course the war was never over for my generation. We pretended it was, went home, picked up the broken threads of our lives. Many sought education under the GI Bill, married the girls they left behind, produced the baby boom and looked always to the future, not the past. The war seemed to slip away, almost as if we were in deliberate denial. Farley Mowat, the Canadian writer, spoke for the generation when he said about the war, "I kept the deeper agonies of it wrapped in the cotton wool of protective forgetfulness."

Silence went on for quite a time. Then, forty years later, in the Eighties, one noticed that veterans were beginning to unwrap their memories. Almost for the first time the war generation started telling one another what we had done in the war. By the Nineties we became shameless in reminiscence. At the turn of the century, Tom Brokaw's best seller celebrated *The Greatest Generation.*

We rejected the generous adjective. If any American generation deserved it, it was the generation that won the War for Independence and wrote the Constitution. The generation that fought the Second

World War consisted of ordinary folk who, confronted by mortal threats to their country, accepted their duty and performed it laconically, modestly, self-effacingly, without show, without flourish. A young naval lieutenant who saw action in the Solomon Islands registered the mood when asked how he had become a war hero. "It was involuntary," Jack Kennedy said. "They sank my boat."

It was, I suppose, a Good War. But like all wars, our war was accompanied by atrocity and sadism, by stupidities and lies, pomposity and chickenshit. War remains hell, but a few wars have been driven by decent purposes and produced beneficial results.

For my generation the Second World War was the supreme experience. And for many not killed or maimed, it was a liberating experience, annulling routine expectations, providing new contexts and challenges, testing abilities, widening horizons and opportunities, nourishing honesty, individuality, complexity, irony, stoicism.

Above all, war was a reminder of the savagery of life. Oliver Wendell Holmes, Jr., was thrice wounded in the Civil War. He had no romantic illusions about war. But he had a realistic understanding of war as an educator. "War when you are at it," Holmes wrote,

> is horrible and dull. It is only when time has passed that you see that its message is divine. I hope it may be long before we are called again to sit at that master's feet. But some teacher of that kind we all need. In this snug, over-safe corner of the world we need it, that we may realize that our comfortable routine is no eternal necessity of things, but merely a little space of calm in the midst of the untamed streaming of the world.

18

The Ages of Jackson

THE WAR WAS OVER, but the melody lingered on. My postwar promotion in London in September 1945 to the lofty rank of corporal wrought no visible change in status since I was soon enough disguised as a civilian. Leaving Germany, I could no longer wear a uniform. Arriving in England, I was sent to pick up a new kit of civilian clothes at the British demobilization center, where British servicemen of all ranks selected suits, shirts, shoes and overcoats. The process was egalitarian — everyone from a cockney costermonger to Major David Niven had the same choices. I specify Major Niven because he was next to me in line, an appearance that greatly excited the British WACs distributing the loot.

* * *

In the general election in July, the Labour party surprised everybody, or at least all the Americans, by sweeping Winston Churchill out of office. My supposed job was to report to Washington on Prime Minister Clement Attlee and the new Labour government. But this was more decisively the embassy's job, and with the war over and OSS rapidly fading away, there was little demand in Washington for my dispatches and consequently little for me to do.

I thoroughly enjoyed the new political climate, however. Nye Bevan was hard at work as the new minister of health. John Strachey was minister of food. And Labour's victory had brought in an impressive crop of younger MPs. I listed some in a report I wrote in October on the transport home: Major Woodrow Wyatt, a friend from before the war; R.H.S. Crossman, whom I had encountered in the Political Warfare Executive; Benn Levy, the playwright and Constance Cummings's husband; and two promising young men I had yet to meet, Hugh Gaitskell and Michael Foot.

Labour, my report predicted, would be more likely than the Tories to challenge the Soviet Union. Where fear of Labour opposition might have restrained a Conservative government, Ernest Bevin, the new foreign secretary, had no inhibitions about taking on the Russians. And a Socialist Britain, because it had greater appeal than a Tory Britain, would give Soviet communism far more serious competition on the left-leaning continent. Harold Laski, the Labour party chairman, was at that moment traveling about Western Europe, opposing Communist attempts to revive the popular front of the Thirties.

The atmosphere in London was markedly more anti-Soviet than it had been the year before. George Orwell, now the most influential writer on the left, came out with *Animal Farm* in mid-August. Though T. S. Eliot turned it down for Faber & Faber as politically inappropriate, Orwell's wonderful anti-Stalinist allegory sold out in a fortnight. I was enchanted by it and bought several copies to take back to the United States. Arthur Koestler's critique of Soviet communism in *The Yogi and the Commissar* had a far more sympathetic audience than it could have had two years earlier.

Revisionist historians in the United States have portrayed Harry Truman as an anti-Soviet crusader hustling a reluctant Europe into a needless Cold War. In fact, as British diplomatic papers show, the Foreign Office saw Truman until 1947 as an irresolute fellow appeasing Moscow under the delusion that the United States could serve as an honest broker between Britain and the USSR. James F. Byrnes, Truman's new secretary of state, reminded the Foreign Office of Neville Chamberlain going to Munich. "A new generation," Herbert Butterfield wrote in 1969, "does not know (and does not credit the fact when informed) that Western Europe once wondered whether the United States could ever be awakened to the danger from Russia."

Some in OSS agreed that we were going too far to appease Moscow, and not just Frank Wisner. Franz Neumann, with whom I dined one night on his way back from the Nuremberg trial, believed, as I reported to Marian, that allied policy "has handed over Germany to the USSR."

*   *   *

President Truman was intent on terminating the war agencies. He killed the Office of War Information a fortnight after the Japanese surrender. Robert Emmet Sherwood, the lanky playwright and FDR ghostwriter, came to town to watch over the dismantlement of OWI's Overseas Branch. He invited me to luncheon at the Connaught, which, he said, served "the best martinis in London; in fact, the only good martinis in London." We had several to test the validity of that proposition. Despite the weaker alcoholic content of British gin, the martinis were excellent, and we had a most congenial time.

Social life in London was never better than in those suddenly relaxed days after the war. Charles Wintour took me to a party where I met Harold Nicolson, older and more rotund than I expected. I saw dear Jennie Lee at a party given by an OSS friend, Louise Page Morris, a social Bostonian, clever and amusing. Pagey, who seemed to know everybody, went on to a picturesque career as a lover (allegedly) of General Donovan and later of a onetime Communist zealot turned anti-Communist zealot, Jay Lovestone.

I regularly stopped by the OWI library to catch up, rather testily, with American periodicals. The *New Republic* and *Nation,* I wrote to Marian, seemed "nauseating in the incredible naiveté and sentimentality of all their views on the Russian problem. . . . I shall be delighted to see how the Commie line press in the USA reacts to the Bevin speech and to Laski's careful sabotage of Socialist-Communist fusion." The scholarly journals afflicted me "with a different kind of horror. It is so hard to imagine returning to any of this truck."

What indeed to do now that the war was over? "The only possible career is the study of American civilization," I had noted in my journal toward the end of my undergraduate years. ". . . But the only institutions which would pay me to study American civilization are the universities; and, in sealing myself in them, I am cutting myself off from the only way of life that would give my work any particular depth."

This was set down well before the war, but the concerns expressed were still with me. I thought, then and later, that one learned from those who had more experience than oneself. Teaching less experienced students would, I feared, only encourage parochialism and complacency. As Henry Adams had put it, "No man, however strong, can serve ten years as schoolmaster, priest, or Senator, and remain fit for anything else. All the dogmatic stations in life have the effect of fixing a certain stiffness of attitude forever."

Such thoughts were much in mind as the time of departure for the United States grew near. "I find myself puzzled as hell," I wrote Benny DeVoto, "at what I should do if I ever get out of the army, not that I feel I have ever been in it. . . . Ideally I would like to connect with some magazine for a few years, then beat my way back to the universities."

At dinner with Ken Galbraith and George Ball as they passed through London on their way home, I learned that Henry Luce was preparing a new journal of opinion (it never came to pass) and that new weeklies were planned, as I wrote to Marian, by Marshall Field "and by (God save the mark) Gardner Cowles." Ken was now working contentedly for Luce's *Fortune,* and a magazine job seemed an attractive possibility.

A dinner with Henry H. (Joe) Fowler of the Board of Economic Warfare, later Lyndon Johnson's secretary of the treasury, persuaded me, I wrote to Marian, that "the first thing I want to do when I get back is a book on the New Deal." OSS had taught me that "I am not really an organization man. I have a certain unhappy knack at administration . . . but I probably will never be able to put my full energy into anything unless (a) it is a writing job, and (b) it is altogether my own. This is a conclusion I must remember."

*   *   *

While life spun along in London, OSS was dying in Washington. On September 20, 1945, Truman signed an executive order transferring R&A to the State Department and sending the other branches to the War Department for "salvage and liquidation." OSS personnel were to return to Washington for reassignment.

I was scheduled to depart in early October on a Liberty ship — one of those mass-produced freighters turned out by Henry J. Kaiser to carry men and supplies across the Atlantic. My ship had just arrived at Cardiff from Buenos Aires with a cargo of Argentine beef when a dockers' strike was called. Fearing that the strike would last indefinitely, the authorities ordered the ship to sail at once for Baltimore. So we steamed away before a full complement of GIs had come aboard and, happily, before the precious cargo was unloaded.

It took nearly three weeks to reach Baltimore. The Atlantic was placid. We ate steak for luncheon and steak for dinner and played bridge the rest of the time. Education trumped politics as the social dividing line. Those who had been to college gravitated to one another whatever their differences. My bridge partners were Bob Pickus, then a sort of Trotskyite, and a rich, anti–New Dealer from Long Island with one of those patrician reversible names. I forget our fourth, but he was a college man too, and we all genially suppressed political disagreements around the card table.

The reunion with my family in Cambridge after sixteen months was joyous, marred only by the sadness of Dr. Cannon's death a few weeks before. The twins, twenty-two months old when I left, were now more than three years old, walking and talking and apparently delighted to greet this stranger, their father. When I had to return to Washington, John Fairbank's mother kindly loaned Marian and me her Georgetown house. Next door, she said, lived a very nice young couple: the husband had just returned from the Pacific war; his wife was the daughter of Eugene Meyer, the proprietor of the *Washington Post.* Soon Philip and Katharine Graham stopped by for a drink, initiating a lifelong friendship.

Phil Graham was two years my senior, part of the Frankfurter diaspora. The first generation of New Dealers had so often been Felix's protégés from the Harvard Law School; the second generation were very often Felix's protégés from the Supreme Court. Joseph Rauh was his first law clerk; Adrian (Butch) Fisher his second; Ed Prichard and Phil Graham, his third and fourth. Prich, still yearning after Evangeline Bell Bruce, was also an admirer of Kay Meyer and had served as best man in the Graham wedding. Kay was quietly charming and welcoming, a little shy, transparently adoring of her irresistible husband.

Phil, who had just been persuaded by his father-in-law to become associate publisher of the *Post,* was a man of quite extraordinary vitality, audacity and charm. He was filled with life and wit, extremely bright, genially argumentative, charging everything he said or did with electric excitement. He joined an exceptional gift for intimacy with a restless desire to provoke and challenge his intimates. He knew everybody and was intimidated by nobody. He was fascinated by power and by other men who were fascinated by power.

Yet power for its own sake gave him only fleeting satisfaction. He wanted to *do* things. His sense of the general welfare was strong and usually sound. He was a forceful manager of people and situations in what he conceived as the public interest. Looking back, one can see flashes of psychological excess to come. But at the time they seemed the natural expressions of a vivid and exuberant personality. Joe Rauh told me in later years, "We all felt then that of all the young men in Washington the two most likely to become president were Ed Prichard and Phil Graham."

*   *   *

After the liquidation of OSS, I had been transferred to the State Department with the rest of R&A. But I was due for a forty-five-day leave. That completed, I received an honorable discharge from the Army. The State Department meanwhile had cut the R&A budget; R&A had to reduce staff; and on December 4, 1945, my resignation was gratefully accepted. Free at last.

I returned to the United States to find myself no longer an anonymous figure. Before going to London, I had finished the revision of the Jackson book, cutting fifty-eight chapters to thirty-seven and 330,000 words to 260,000. At DeVoto's suggestion, I submitted the manuscript to his Boston publisher, Little, Brown, in the spring of 1944. It was accepted. In my absence overseas, my father and Marian nobly undertook the tedious task of reading proofs.

An animated correspondence took place across the Atlantic over the title. My first thought — *Jackson and the American Democratic Tradition* — pleased nobody. How about *Democracy's Coming of Age: The Jacksonian Revolution* or *Democracy in Crisis: The Jacksonian Tradition* or *The Age of Jackson and the Democratic Tradition?* As press time neared, Roger Scaife of Little, Brown settled on *The Age of Jackson.* It was the right choice.

I was still in London when the book came out in September. A transatlantic phone call from Marian, rather a feat in those days, brought the exciting news that on September 16 *The Age of Jackson* commanded the front pages of both New York Sunday book sections. The two reviewers said everything an author could have wished for. It "gives the Jacksonian movement new meaning," Allan Nevins of Columbia wrote in the *Times*, ". . . a remarkable piece of analytical history, full of vitality, rich in insights and new facts, and casting a broad shaft of illumination over one of the more interesting periods in our national life." Benny DeVoto, a loyal friend, concluded in an equally generous *Herald Tribune* review that the book "overturns fundamental historical ideas." In the *New Republic* Richard Hofstadter of Columbia, a contemporary whom I had not met, later to become a good friend, called it "a work of mature insight marked by a fine feeling for the dialectic of ideas and events . . . and powered to such an unusual degree by a capacity for analytical thinking." Marquis James, the most recent Jackson biographer: "a landmark in American historical literature. The book has depth, clarity and ease — and its people live." "It is written with verve and is firm in judgment," said Charles Beard. "A real contribution to the history of the period" — a comment ill repaid by me when I later snottily attacked the books in which Beard accused a duplicitous FDR of maneuvering the republic into an unnecessary war.

Time had a curious but shrewd review. It began with a labored, allegedly humorous, retelling of the Jackson "legend" in what the writer fancied as redneck talk ("Once upon a time, when the Yew-nited States was just a little shaver among nations . . . there lived younder in Tennessee a lovable old man with a tongue like a rat-tailed file and a face so hard they called him Old Hickory," etc.). Then, with a shift of gears into standard English, the reviewer wrote that Schlesinger "in a brilliant justification of the New Deal disguised as a history of the age of Jackson, says that the legend and the facts do not jibe." The result "is an unusually readable history about one of the most opaque episodes in the American past." The reviewer noted my view that democracy "is a condition of tension, in which neither side has a permanent advantage. This theory of tension distingushes Historian Schlesinger from Revolutionist Karl Marx's theory of class struggle, which ends each bout in a sullen victory for one side or the other." Upon inquiry, I was told that the author of the review was a *Time* staffer unknown to me called Whittaker Chambers.

No reviewer then or later seems to have noticed a joke I proudly smuggled into the text, a comment about the unambitious but highly respected Senator Silas Wright of New York: "Of him it could be said with truth that he would rather be Wright than President." The *New Yorker* did pick up another joke for its "Words of One Syllable" department, a description of Thomas W. Dorr of Rhode Island as "a graduate of Exeter and Harvard but singularly high-principled and conscientious."

*   *   *

Frederick Jackson Turner had established the orthodox view of the origins of democracy, American style. The new democracy, Turner had written, "came, stark and strong and full of life, from the American forest. . . . It gained new strength each time it touched a new frontier. . . . American democracy is fundamentally the outcome of the experiences of the American people in dealing with the West."

In arguing that Jacksonian democracy was shaped by the east at least as much as by the west, by the city as much as by the forest, I was following my father in supplementing Turner's frontier hypothesis with an urban slant on American development. Class conflict, for example, was a favorite Jacksonian theme, but it was hardly a feature of the classless frontier. Where frontiers breed equality and individualism, class resentments arise in a developed and stratified economic order. It was the city, not the forest, that had the bitter experience of shrinking opportunity, growing inequality and hardening class lines.

I sought to prove the eastern impact by examining the ideas that produced, and were produced by, the Jacksonian revolution. *The Age of Jackson* thus aspired to be the intellectual history of a political movement. This seemed at that time a methodological hybrid. The history of ideas, as then practiced, tended to deal with ideas at a high level of abstraction from practical conflicts; and political history, as then practiced, rarely allowed that politicians, even if they weren't conscious of ideas, nonetheless acted them out. My view was that the twain should meet. My father saw the point at once. "It is a new kind of history," he wrote after reading the typescript, "joining intellectual and political history in what I hope may be permanent wedlock."

As Maynard Keynes had memorably put it in the last pages of his *General Theory*,

> The ideas of economists and political philosophers, both when they are right and when they are wrong, are more powerful than is commonly understood. Indeed the world is ruled by little else. Practical men, who believe themselves to be quite exempt from any intellectual influences, are usually the slaves of some defunct economist. Madmen in authority, who hear voices in the air, are distilling their frenzy from some academic scribbler of a few years back. I am sure that the power of vested interests is vastly exaggerated compared with the gradual encroachment of ideas.

*   *   *

Andrew Jackson had had a perilous historiographical career. At the start, respectable opinion — the men to whom Tocqueville, for example, talked during his American excursion — saw him as a rude and violent frontiersman who invented the spoils system, wrecked the banking system, brought the unwashed mob into the White House and speeded the degradation of the democratic dogma. This was somewhat the view expounded more tolerantly and genially by James Parton in his delightful and still valuable three-volume biography of Jackson (1859–60). It was reaffirmed more crisply during the long conservative interlude after the Civil War by the Yale sociologist William Graham Sumner in the incisive biography he wrote in 1882 for the American Statesmen series.

The Populist revolt in the 1890s, followed by the Progressive movement in the early twentieth century, generated new pressures and new perspectives. Progressive historians, seeking antecedents for presidents they admired, Theodore Roosevelt and Woodrow Wilson, found more to praise in Jackson than, ironically, TR and Wilson had done in their own days as historians. The pro-Jackson scholars did agree, however, with their anti-Jackson predecessors in seeing Jacksonian politics as a conflict of sections rather than of classes and the Jacksonian victory as a triumph of western ideals.

John Spencer Bassett in his excellent scholarly biography (1911), while reserved about some of Jackson's actions and policies, was unreserved in commending "his brave, frank, masterly leadershp of the democratic movement which then established itself in our life." Writing a quarter century later in the age of the second Roosevelt, Marquis James in his vivid and detailed biography (1933, 1937) saluted Jackson as a leader who "lived by valor" and who "saw for the people what they could not see for themselves."

In advancing my interpretation, I too was conditioned by the passions of my era. Conservatives in the angry Thirties used to fulminate against the New Deal as "un-American." I wanted to show that, far from importing foreign ideas, FDR was acting in a robust American spirit and tradition. Jackson's war against Nicholas Biddle and the Second Bank of the United States thus constituted a thoroughly American precedent for the battles FDR waged against the "economic royalists" of his (and my) day.

FDR saw it this way too. Years later, I came upon a letter he had written to Colonel Edward M. House, Woodrow Wilson's *homme de confiance*, in November 1933. "The real truth of the matter," Roosevelt told House, "is, as you and I know, that a financial element in the larger centers has owned the Government ever since the days of Andrew Jackson — and I am not wholly excepting the Administration of W. W. The country is going through a repetition of Jackson's fight with the Bank of the United States — only on a far bigger and broader basis."

Jackson and Roosevelt, it appeared, had much the same cast of supporters — farmers, workingmen, intellectuals and the poor — and much the same cast of adversaries — bankers, merchants, manufacturers and the rich. In seeking to legitimate the New Deal by finding precursors in the American past, I did not, I believed (and believe), impose an artificial schema on history. My belief was (and is) that I merely discerned patterns others had overlooked. As I put it in the *Book Find Review*, "You write history because you want to find out what actually went on in the past, not for purposes of propaganda, prediction or panacea."

Nevertheless several historians, adapting J. Franklin Jameson's crack about George Bancroft's histories voting for Jackson, have commented, not without a certain justice, that *The Age of Jackson* voted for Franklin Delano Roosevelt.

* * *

Within the historical guild *The Age of Jackson* has had its ups and downs. "The reaction to Schlesinger's work was immediate and dramatic," wrote Robert V. Remini, Jackson's most recent and best biographer. "It swept the historical profession like a tornado, eliciting both prodigious praise and, within a relatively short time, fierce denunciations." In the first thirty years, by Remini's calculation, "some 227 books and 353 articles (and an even more appalling number of doctoral dissertations) [on Jackson] tumbled from the minds and pens of scholars."

The book did indeed reawaken professional interest in a complex and abundant period of American history. It stirred controversy, and controversy is always fruitful for historians. Once again, changes in the political weather remolded historical interpretations. By the early Fifties the New Deal impulse was running its course. After two exhausting decades of depression and war, the nation was tired of wrangling and eager for healing. The onset of the Cold War increased the felt need to affirm national unity. President Eisenhower embodied the new mood. Progressive history, with its zest for conflict, began to give way to the delineation and, for some historians, celebration of the American consensus.

Consensus historians argued that the beliefs that united Americans — private property, free enterprise, individual opportunity, limited government — were far more significant than the disputes that occasionally divided them. The notorious confrontations beloved of the progressive historians — Jefferson versus Hamilton, Jackson versus Biddle, FDR versus Herbert Hoover — were dismissed as no more than family quarrels. Unlike the great revolutions of Europe, American political conflicts (the Civil War always excepted) were over nuances, not basic shifts in ideas and power.

Scrutinized through the lens of consensus history, the fierce political and ideological battles of the age of Jackson evaporated into inconsequence. The first shot against *The Age of Jackson* was fired by Bray Hammond, the assistant secretary of the Federal Reserve System's board of governors, in a scornful review in the May 1946 issue of the *Journal of Economic History*. His was a central banker's biting critique that he developed in subsequent articles and in his able but misleading Pulitzer Prize book of 1957, *Banks and Politics in America from the Revolution to the Civil War.* Dick Hofstadter, despite his generous notice of the book in 1945, joined in the deflation of Jackson in his brilliant work of 1947, *The American Political Tradition.*

Indeed, for a time *The Age of Jackson* became a designated target for Columbia faculty and graduate students, with Hofstadter, Richard B. Morris, Lee Benson, Edward Pessen and the historian of economic thought Joseph Dorfman organizing the attack. Columbia seminars, I was told, were devoted to meticulous exposures of Schlesinger's fallacies. (This did not prevent, I am glad to say, friendly personal relations with most of the Columbia critics.)

Jacksonian democrats and their Whig opponents, Hammond and Hofstadter contended, were all entrepreneurs together, all expectant capitalists, all committed to the acquisitive scramble, all men on the make fighting sham battles to advance individual fortunes. Or, in Lee Benson's version, ethnicity and religion were far more powerful determinants of voting than economic interests and political ideas. As for the take-no-prisoners tone of the debate between Jacksonians and Whigs, this, Benson declared in a major tract of the ethnocultural school, was no more than "campaign claptrap."

Benson's *The Concept of Jacksonian Democracy* oddly based its argument not on the elections of 1832 or 1836 but on the election of 1844, well after the ideological passions of the age of Jackson had subsided. It was as if someone had based a book called *The Concept of the New Deal* on the politics not of the 1930s but of the 1950s. For it is precisely when class and interest politics recedes that cultural politics — ethnicity, religion, morality, social status — comes to the fore.

In the age of Eisenhower, the consensus argument was eventually pressed to the point where it almost obliterated any differences between Jacksonians and Whigs and left the savage political temper of the age of Jackson a mystery. Of course *The Age of Jackson* had made it clear that there were entrepreneurial elements in the antiestablishment Jacksonian coalition of the 1830s — state banking interests, southern planters, western inflationists, eastern small merchants. As a movement, Jacksonian democracy included opportunists out for a fast buck as well as radical democrats faithful to pure doctrine. The same thing, *mutatis mutandis,* can be said of the Roosevelt coalition of the 1930s.

Yet it seems hard to conclude that the essence of Jacksonian de-

mocracy, or of the New Deal for that matter, was the theory and practice of acquisitive enterprise. To identify Jackson with Biddle (or FDR
with Hoover) would be to drain meaning from American politics.
Analysis depends on the capacity to draw distinctions.

If the Jacksonians were a rabble of grasping entrepreneurs, who
were the Whigs? If Jacksonian democracy served the interests of a
newly liberated capitalism, why were so many capitalists so ferociously
against it? If many of the self-styled "workingmen" of Jackson's day
were small proprietors fighting their way up, why should they define
themselves as members of the working class and carry on so about
those better off?

These were questions the entrepreneurial thesis failed to answer. I
have no doubt that historians writing, as I did, in the Thirties and
early Forties, with New Deal struggles reverberating in our minds,
tended to exaggerate conflict in the American past. But I have no
doubt either that historians writing in the Fifties, in a time of recoil
from controversy and craving for cohesion, tended to exaggerate
consensus in the American past. However much they may have had
in common, Jackson and Biddle and their respective followers disagreed furiously on *something*.

The consensus interpretation foundered eventually on its "campaign claptrap" assumptions. The Jacksonians and Whigs of the
1830s, the entrepreneurial thesis implied, did not mean what they
were talking about when they claimed that great differences divided
them. Their words misrepresented their real thoughts and motives,
and their testimony about why they were doing what they were doing
was either self-deceived or cynical — in any event, historically worthless.

Now the vanity of historians is to suppose that we understand better
than the people who were there what the shouting was all about. It is
true enough that scholars looking back can know some things better
than contemporary participants did. But 20–20 hindsight can be carried too far. There is always the risk of Chip Bohlen's 20–20 hindmyopia. Too often we suggest that those poor chaps in the past may
have thought they were acting for one set of reasons; but we, so much
wiser, *know* that they were acting for quite other reasons. This reductionism denies historical figures the validity of their own judgments
and thereby denies them their human dignity. And our arrogance invites future historians to practice the same reductionism on us. The
assertion that people in the past did not really know why they were do-

ing what they did leads to the conclusion that we do not really know why we are doing what we do today. When participants explain in urgent words why they lived, fought and bled, is it not hubris for historians to dismiss their testimony?

* * *

What, then, was the reason for the intensity of the Jacksonian conflict? My surmise is that it had to do with the basic question of a democratic polity: Who is to control the state? The clarity of this point is obscured, however, by confusing it with a separate question: What is the proper role of the state?

On the second question, Jackson regarded himself as a Jeffersonian who believed — or believed he believed — that that government was best which governed least. He sought to persuade his countrymen that they would find their happiness, "not in a splendid government supported by powerful monopolies and aristocratical establishments," but "in a plain system, void of pomp, protecting all and granting favors to none." That was what I termed "the Jeffersonian myth." In a time of wrenching economic change, the frugal virtues of the old republic had great appeal against the rising luxury and corruption associated with the concentrated money power.

In principle, the Jacksonians were indisputably antistatist. My critics had a point when they claimed the Whigs, and not the Jacksonians, as the real forerunners of the New Deal. The tradition of affirmative government was the tradition of Hamilton, not of Jefferson. Hamilton's enthusiasm over the dynamics of individual acquisition was always tempered by a belief in government regulation and control. Americans, he wrote, had "a certain activity of speculation and enterprise which, if properly directed, may be made subservient to useful purposes but which, if left entirely to itself, may be attended with pernicious effect." John Quincy Adams and Henry Clay elaborated the Hamiltonian vision into what Clay called the American System — a great dream of economic development under the leadership of the national state.

Looking back, I think I did Hamilton, Adams and Clay a good deal less than justice in *The Age of Jackson* (as Allan Nevins and others pointed out at the time). It is true that the American System, with its program of internal improvements, a protective tariff and Biddle's Bank of the United States, was designed to benefit the business classes; but this was not the whole truth. The Whig program was also designed to benefit the nation by accelerating economic growth. The Hamiltonians had a sounder conception of the role of government and a more constructive policy of economic development than the antistatist Jacksonians.

While I am confessing error, I must say a word too for Jackson's inadvertent allies in the war against the Bank, the wildcat bankers and their poorly secured paper notes. As Bray Hammond acidly pointed out, I knew very little about money when I wrote *The Age of Jackson*. My bias was in favor of Jackson's hard money policy — that is, the maintenance of a stable ratio between paper and specie — and against the unrestrained issue of paper notes by banks. As I now reflect on the Jacksonian period, having been enlightened in the years between by kindly instruction from Ken Galbraith and Seymour Harris, I am less distressed by wildcat banking. The hard money policy, systematically pursued, would have held back development. Wildcat banking enlarged the means of payment and stimulated growth. And as Peter Temin pointed out in his admirable *The Jacksonian Economy* (1969), the Panic of 1837 was caused, not by Jackson's veto of the Bank and consequent overissue of notes by local wildcat bankers, but by international monetary factors beyond Jackson's control.

* * *

Saying that Jacksonian doctrine was antistatist does not dispose of the question: Who is to control the state? It does not even dispose of the second question: What is the proper role of the state?

As Jackson said in his veto message denying recharter to the Second Bank of the United States, the resort to government "to make the rich richer and the potent more powerful" had to be halted in the interests of "the humble members of society — the farmers, mechanics, and laborers — who have neither the time or the means of securing like favors to themselves." The Jacksonians objected to the state because, as the radical editor William Leggett wrote during Jackson's presidency, the power of the state was "always" exercised "for the exclusive benefit of wealth. It was never wielded on behalf of the community."

But government intervention on behalf of "the community" would be another matter. Here the second question merged with the first: Who is to control the state? The Jacksonians were hostile to statism for the benefit of the rich and powerful, not necessarily to statism per se. Where the Jeffersonians had supposed that the state would inevitably abuse its power, Jackson in his 1837 Farewell Address relegated such abuse to the category of "extreme cases, which we have no reason to apprehend in a Government where the power is in the hands of a patriotic people."

Coming to the White House as a professed foe of strong national government, Jackson, for all his Jeffersonian nostalgia, left the national government stronger than ever before. He reinvented the presidency, changing the office from a rather passive and distant magistracy to an active source of energy, initiative and leadership. Executive deference to Congress was over, at least for a while. "The President," Jackson said, "is the direct representative of the American people" — more so, by implication, than the Congress. In this conviction he appealed over the heads of Congress to the people, as in his Bank veto message — "a manifesto of anarchy," Biddle said, "such as Marat or Robespierre might have issued to the mob of the Faubourg Saint-Antoine." Jackson vetoed more bills than all his half-dozen predecessors put together and did so on grounds of policy, not solely, as they had done, on presumptions of unconstitutionality. Though scholarship had shown that Jackson's exploits as a spoilsman were considerably exaggerated, he did establish the principle that the executive branch should be responsive to the purposes of the president. And he took control of national politics away from the congressional caucus and delivered it to the mass political party.

Even more important, Jackson defeated two basic challenges to the supremacy of the national government — one by a rebellious state; the other by the country's most powerful corporation. I refer, of course, to Jackson's proclamation condemning South Carolina's attempt to nullify the Tariff Act of 1832 and to his Bank veto. Had South Carolina got away with nullification, had Nicholas Biddle shown his Bank to be more powerful than the government, the implications for the future of the republic would have been considerable. "The Bank of the United States," Jackson told his cabinet in words that also applied to the state of South Carolina, "is in itself a Government which has gradually increased its strength from the day of its establishment. The question between itself and the people has become one of power." In turning back these two profound challenges to federal authority, Jackson established that authority more firmly than ever.

The Whig response confirms this proposition. "We are in the midst of a revolution, hitherto bloodless," cried Henry Clay, "but rapidly tending towards a total change of the pure republican character of the Government, and to the concentration of all power in the hands of one man."

*   *   *

In the years since *The Age of Jackson,* scholars have discerned competing visions of "republicanism" and "liberalism" in the early republic. "Republicanism," in the tradition of the Roman republic and of civic humanism, called on citizens to subordinate their individual interests to the common good. "Liberalism," in this usage, assumed that citizens promoted the common good by pursuing their individual interests.

Old Hickory once told "Young Hickory," James K. Polk, "My political creed was formed in the old republican school." The old republican school sanctioned public action to secure the common good. "The object and end of all government," wrote Roger B. Taney, whom Jackson made successively attorney general, secretary of the treasury and chief justice, "is to promote the happiness and prosperity of the community by which it is established; and it can never be assumed, that the government intended to diminish its power of accomplishing the end for which it was created."

Under the banner of antistatism, the Jacksonians carried on aggressive programs of public intervention and regulation. "A good deal of positive government," wrote John L. O'Sullivan, editor of the *Democratic Review,* "may be yet wanted to undo the manifold mischiefs of past government." Recent scholarship has demonstrated in detail how, after refusing to recharter Biddle's Bank, Jacksonians were determined to regulate and reform banking in the states. They called for governmental inspection and auditing of bank records, amendment of bank charters, elimination of small notes and of limited liability, requirements of a specie reserve for circulation and discount. "The relatively stable and more responsible conduct of the country's banks from the early 1840s to the Civil War," Professor James R. Sharp wrote in *The Jacksonians versus the Bank* (1970), "was due in large part to Democratic sponsored bank reform and the vigorous hard-money critique."

Even a Jacksonian like Orestes Brownson exclaimed with some dismay in 1837 at Jackson's "tendency to Centralization and his evident leaning to *Bureaucraticy.*" (Could Brownson have invented the word that was soon shortened to "bureaucracy"? The *Oxford English Dictionary*'s first citation of "bureaucracy" is to John Stuart Mill in 1848.) A young Jacksonian, that intelligent rogue Benjamin F. ("Beast") Butler of Massachusetts, wrote in his memoirs that, while he had been "dazzled with the brilliancy of Jackson's administration . . . I early had sense enough to see that it conflicted, in a very considerable degree, with the teachings of Jefferson." Ben Butler drew the obvious conclusion: "As to the powers and duties of the government of the United States, I am a Hamiltonian Federalist. As to the rights and privileges of the citizen, I am a Jeffersonian Democrat." The Jacksonians thus revised the democracy of Jefferson by their readiness to employ Hamiltonian means to attain Jeffersonian ends.

But Jacksonian democracy lacked a creative political philosopher who might have codified the Jacksonian revision of the Jeffersonian creed. Then the antislavery crusade diverted the ardor, drained off the energies and destroyed the party of Jacksonian democracy. The Jeffersonian myth survived, and Jacksonian revisionism was forgotten.

*   *   *

The ascendancy of the consensus school was the product of the placid Eisenhower Fifties. The angry divisions of the Sixties pricked the consensus bubble and restored conflict to the American past. Taking a fresh look back at the 1830s, historians decided that Jacksonians and Whigs were not peas in a pod, all jolly entrepreneurs together. They began to agree with the Jacksonians and Whigs themselves that the two parties represented very different attitudes toward business rule and represented, to a degree, different classes.

The entrepreneurial interpretation fell under severe attack. "The Democratic party," Professor Sharp observed, "did not engage in the battle over banks and currency as the party of the entrepreneur." "The entrepreneurial thesis, as it applies to Jacksonian democracy," John M. McFaul wrote in *The Politics of Jacksonian Finance* (1972), "requires severe modification if not abandonment." Hofstadter and the entrepreneurial school, Remini wrote in his Jackson biography, were "wrong about the Jacksonian movement and wrong about Jackson's place in American history." Bray Hammond was "totally wrong respecting Jackson's role and involvement in the Bank War."

The book by the English scholar John Ashworth *"Agrarians" and "Aristocrats": Party Ideology in the United States* (1983), in the judgment of the Jacksonian specialist Major L. Wilson, "virtually completes the process of overthrowing the entrepreneurial interpretation of Jacksonian Democracy." In his next book, *Slavery, Capitalism, and Politics in the Antebellum Republic* (1995), Ashworth wrote, "Schlesinger realized, as his critics did not, that there was an anticapitalist animus in the

Jacksonian movement. . . . Ironically, it was here, where Schlesinger had, if anything, understated his case, that the attacks came." Harry L. Watson, the author of *Liberty and Power: The Politics of Jacksonian America* (1990), improves over *The Age of Jackson* in his sophisticated analysis of class formation but concludes that despite vulnerability on many fronts, "it is clear that Schlesinger was on the right track."

It seems, half a century after *The Age of Jackson,* that there was after all a struggle in the 1830s between the business community and the rest of society over control of the state. As Charles Sellers said in his impressive overview of the period, *The Market Revolution: Jacksonian America, 1815–1846* (1991): "Schlesinger may yet be judged more nearly right than his critics." And Donald B. Cole in *The Presidency of Andrew Jackson* (1993): "The pendulum has now swung back toward Schlesinger."

Given the nature of pendulums, it will doubtless in due course swing away from *The Age of Jackson.* I well know the infirmities of the work. History reflects the age. I was preoccupied with the issues of economic power and the dilemmas of democratic capitalism made vivid for my generation by FDR and the New Deal. Responding to the felt pressures of my youth, I underplayed other aspects of the Jacksonian era. The predicament of women, of blacks, of Indians, given new salience by the felt pressures of later times, was shamefully out of mind. The perspective of 2000 is bound to be different from that of 1940. In this sense, the present persistently and inevitably re-creates the past.

The Jacksonian era, moreover, is filled with black holes that invite perpetual debate. As the business community was confusedly retreating from the Hamiltonian faith in affirmative government, so the opponents of rule by business were confusedly retreating from the Jeffersonian faith in negative government. This very complexity and obscurity, along with the brilliance of the protagonists and the ferocity of their polemics, make the age of Jackson so fascinating for the historian — and ensure that each new generation will reach back into this rich and exciting time to fashion its own image of Jacksonian democracy.

As the great Dutch historian Pieter Geyl so perfectly said, "History is indeed an argument without end."

* * *

The Age of Jackson appeared at a propitious time for a book about the American democratic tradition. Fascism had not turned out to be

Anne Morrow Lindbergh's wave of the future. Victory had vindicated the cause of liberal democracy. And the war, I wrote in the book's foreword, had given new urgency to the quest for the "meaning" of democracy: "If democracy is indeed to be the hope of the future, we know now that we must have its lineaments clearly in mind, so that we may the more surely recognize it and the more responsibly act upon it."

The key to democracy's meaning does not lie, I suggested, in the search for immutable moral abstractions of the democratic faith. It lies rather in the concrete record of what democracy had meant in the past. What range of possibilities has it in fact unfolded? What methods has it found legitimate? What have been its values and its resources?

The world after victory would contain perplexities of the utmost difficulty and importance. We could not know how in detail the American democracy would move to meet them; "but this we do know, that, if it is to remain a democracy, its moods, methods and purposes will bear a vital relation to its attack on similar (if less intense) crises of its past." History can contribute nothing in the way of panaceas. But it can assist vitally "in the formation of the sense of what is democratic, of what is in line with our republican traditions, which alone can save us."

Democracy in my view involved a struggle among competing groups for control of the state. "The business community has been ordinarily the most powerful of these groups, and liberalism in America has ordinarily been the movement on the part of the other sections of society to restrain the power of the business community." The book's last pages contrasted this view of liberalism with two active competitors: conservatism, rule by the business community; and socialism, rule by ideological planners.

Liberal democracy, I said, rejects both, and especially the second. "The Jacksonian attitude presumes a perpetual tension in society, a doubtful equilibrium, constantly breeding strife and struggle." I wondered whether a society that eliminated struggle would possess much liberty — or even much real stability. "World without conflict is the world of fantasy; and practical attempts to realize society without conflict by confiding power to a single authority have generally resulted . . . in producing a society where the means of suppressing conflict are rapid and efficient."

*　　*　　*

Though a book about the past, *The Age of Jackson* carried implications for the future. DeVoto called it "a study of the action of democracy in crisis to the end that we might foresee how it would act in crises to come." It is a book, wrote Merle Curti in the *Nation*, "which American liberals should welcome for the light it throws on the past, present, and future of democracy. . . . They should find their faith in democracy as an instrument for action today renewed, deepened and extended."

People sometimes sent the book to sons or husbands still overseas. Through the years I have run into men who told me how they read *The Age of Jackson* in the South Pacific or the Aleutians or on transports back to the United States. Eric Larrabee, whose book of 1987, *Commander in Chief*, remains the best account of the American military in the Second World War, once showed me a letter he had written home in December 1945: "The things Schlesinger has to say make *The Age of Jackson* an essential book about America *today*."

Coming out at this psychological moment, the book struck a nerve. By May 1946 it was in its eighth printing and had been on the bestseller list (at $5 a volume) for twenty-five weeks. It was adopted by George Braziller's liberal Book Find Club and underwent a thirty-thousand-word serialization in the *New Republic*, soon repented by the editors when the extent of my anticommunism became evident. That spring it received the Pulitzer Prize for history ($500). In its first year it sold ninety thousand copies. More than half a century later it is still in print. In 1989 the Book-of-the-Month Club, which had turned the book down in 1945, brought out a splendid illustrated edition with a new introduction (from parts of which I have drawn in this chapter).

In those early months after my return from overseas, the author had his fifteen minutes of demicelebrity. I enjoyed the fun but regarded it with a certain incredulity. I enjoyed, for example, appearing with Boris Karloff, Frankenstein's monster and a cultivated English gentleman, on the popular radio show "Information Please" (the critic Clifton Fadiman posing erudite questions to the regulars — the humorous columnist Franklin P. Adams, the sportswriter John Kieran and the musician and wit Oscar Levant — plus a couple of guests). When Bill Mauldin and I received the New York Newspaper Guild's Page One Awards, I particularly enjoyed meeting the man whose Willie and Joe cartoons in *Stars and Stripes* I inordinately admired. And others I admired, like S. J. Perelman, had become aware of me. "We're pulling out of here Saturday," wrote Perelman in a jokey letter of August 1946 from Martha's Vineyard to a *New Yorker* editor, "and I expect to be back in town pretty permanently for rehearsals of *Gang Aft Aglee* (that musical I wrote in collaboration with Schlesinger, author of *The Age of Jackson*)."

In January 1947 the U.S. Junior Chamber of Commerce picked me as one of "the nation's ten Outstanding Young Men of the Year" for "showing through history how the world of ideas and the world of action can profitably cooperate." Among others on the team were Bill Mauldin, Joe Louis, Charles Bolte of the liberal American Veterans Committee, the nuclear physicist Philip Morrison and, most presciently, Congressman John F. Kennedy of Massachusetts. But I didn't really believe any of it, and I was sure it wouldn't last.

19

Free Lance

I FELT NO URGENCY about returning to academia. The Schlesinger vogue in the larger world would soon pass, but I thought I might as well enjoy it while my star still flickered. Yale, the University of Chicago, Johns Hopkins and the University of Minnesota made proposals, but my thought was to try, at least for a while, the life of a writer. I could always in the end retreat to the cloisters.

Three possibilities attracted. Barry Bingham offered a job as editorial writer for his family newspaper, the *Louisville Courier-Journal.* The *Courier-Journal* was a brave and influential liberal paper with a national reputation. I had run into Barry Bingham several times during the war and liked him very much. Barry and his lustrous wife, Mary, had become warm friends of my parents. An interlude in another part of the country, Marian thought, would be a refreshing change. Henry Pringle agreed. Ed Prichard assured us that life in Louisville would be more than tolerable.

So I went out to Kentucky and visited at length with the Binghams and Mark Ethridge, the *Courier-Journal*'s publisher, and his breezy wife, Willie Snow. I departed with an abiding affection for a city in which I have spent many happy days since. But, as I reported to my parents, "I don't know whether I would be much good writing editorials, and I really don't care a hell of a lot about getting to be good at it."

Then Eugene Meyer, prompted no doubt by Phil Graham, invited me to lunch one day and asked whether I would be interested in writing a history of the *Washington Post.* I took personally at once to Butch, as Phil and Prich called Mr. Meyer (out of his hearing). He was a genial, shrewd, humorous man; he offered what seemed a lot of money; and I was far from averse to staying on in Washington. But to write the history of a newspaper?

Then Ralph Delahaye Paine, Jr., the editor of *Fortune,* prompted no doubt by Ken Galbraith, offered me a job for somewhat less money — $10,000 a year (about $120,000 in current dollars). I liked Del Paine too, and at *Fortune* I would write signed pieces rather than anonymous editorials. Also, I could live in Washington and work out of the *Time* bureau. My Harvard classmate Teddy White had just resigned from *Time* in protest over the mishandling (especially by Whittaker Chambers) of his dispatches from China, but he reassured me that at *Fortune* I would be exempt from such problems, at least so long as I didn't write about Chiang Kai-shek. My first assignment was to be the future of FDR's Good Neighbor policy toward Latin America, an idea that greatly appealed.

I decided to take a chance on *Fortune*. Writing editorials, I explained to Barry Bingham, was too much like the facile commentary I had been churning out for intelligence weeklies during the war. My book-writing priority, I explained to Mr. Meyer, was a history of the age of Roosevelt, and *Fortune* would enable me to write pieces bearing on the Roosevelt years.

As these negotiations went on, Harvard made an offer I could not refuse. So I accepted, and in April 1946 I was appointed an associate professor of history. The Harvard authorities benevolently agreed that I would not have to start teaching until September 1947. I had fifteen months to try the life of a free lance.

* * *

In March 1946 we settled in a house on the top of a hill at 4202 Curtis Road, just over the District line in Chevy Chase, Maryland. An ample backyard had swings and a sandbox for Katharine and Stephen. Georgetown was within easy striking distance. It was a cheerful time in Washington, a city filled with couples our age happily reunited after the war and now mingling carefree postwar gaiety with purposeful postwar ambitions.

One day, as I was strolling along Pennsylvania Avenue in front of the White House, I saw approaching a man with a vaguely familiar face. He too had an expression of incipient recognition. We stopped and quickly recalled each other. It was Stewart Alsop, whom I had met seventeen months earlier with the Brigade Armagnac. We chatted. After a moment he asked what I was doing on a certain date in a week or two. "My brother Joe is giving a stag dinner," Stewart said, "and I'm sure he would like you to come."

In due course an invitation arrived. I found myself seated at dinner next to Charles W. Thayer, a foreign service officer whom I had known a bit in the OSS. We discussed foreign policy. I ventured the thought that the postwar struggle for Europe would be between democratic socialism and communism. "Oh, so you're NCL," Charlie said. "NCL?" "Yes, non-Communist left." Then he said, "You must meet my brother-in-law Chip Bohlen. Come and bring your wife and have a drink with him," and he named a date. I knew of Bohlen as a Soviet expert in the State Department who had served as liaison between State and FDR and as FDR's interpreter at Yalta.

A few days later Marian and I went to the Thayer house in Georgetown. Charlie was then married to an Italian girl, pretty but selfish; perhaps she had married him in order to get to the United States. She welcomed us with rather strained politeness. Charlie was quiet and, it soon seemed, depressed. After a few moments, it occurred to me that they had been having a fight; maybe she had objected to unknown and unimpressive guests. Conversation proved difficult. Charlie, preoccupied and somber, answered monosyllabically. His wife, after her first (and not very convincing) welcome, grew indifferent and then bored.

I desperately tried to keep the conversation going. Charlie looked at his watch from time to time and said apologetically that Chip must have been detained at the department. The sun set, and the room fell dark. In the general apathy neither host nor hostess bestirred themselves to turn on a light. Conversation became stickier than ever. After what seemed an hour, I was about to propose our departure.

Just then the doorbell rang. Charlie disappeared to open the door. The drawing room was on the second floor, and one suddenly heard on the stairs the sound of voices — strong, vibrant voices — and laughter. In a moment, two new figures burst into the room. As they entered, Charlie snapped on the electric switch, and the sad, dark room was suddenly bathed in light and exhilaration.

Chip Bohlen was an exceptionally handsome man, St. Paul's and Harvard, easy, witty, a brilliant conversationalist. With him was another tall man with a great mop of tousled, snow-white hair. Nicolas Nabokov was a composer, son of a liberal aristocratic Russian family, first cousin of the novelist Vladimir Nabokov. He composed ballets for Diaghilev and collaborated with Archibald MacLeish in 1935 on *Union Pacific*, one of the first ballets with an American subject. He overflowed with vitality, was a notable raconteur in half a dozen languages, also a notable mimic, and had, what was rare in an artist, a penetrating and ironical political intelligence. Archie called Nicolas "an irresistible man," and indeed he was. He was presently back from Germany, where he was serving as cultural adviser for the United States Military Government.

Chip was then forty-two, Nicolas a year older. The two men were the closest of friends. Chip, Nicolas wrote in his memoir *Begazh*, "was always my model, my source of advice and often my comforter." Both were intimate friends of Isaiah Berlin. Like Isaiah, they combined political concern with immense joie de vivre. For the rest of their lives, Chip and Nicolas always had the same enlivening effect on me as at that first meeting — light and laughter in a dark age.

* * *

There were many dinners at Joe Alsop's house on the 2700 block of Dumbarton Avenue in Georgetown. He was thirty-six years old in 1946 and an ardent host. Reports to my parents about a series of evenings:

> Present were Averell Harriman, Paul Porter, Wilson Wyatt, Herbert Bayard Swope, Clark Clifford, Leslie Biffle [the secretary of the Senate], FDR Jr., Jimmy Wechsler, Stew Alsop. It was very entertaining. . . . I sat next to Harriman at dinner and was quite favorably impressed by him. Young Roosevelt looks astonishingly like his father and has adopted many of his mannerisms. He talked very sensibly and is certainly strongly anti-Communist.

> I had an entertaining evening at Joe Alsop's with Mrs. Alice Longworth and the Chip Bohlens. To my surprise Mrs. Longworth is really quite witty and entertaining.

> Saturday night we went to Joe Alsop's for dinner. The [Henry Cabot] Lodges, the Mike Monroneys and Jack Kennedy were there. We both liked Mrs. Lodge very much. She is exceedingly attractive and somewhat more liberal than her husband. . . . Kennedy seemed very sincere and not unintelligent, but kind of on the conservative side.

This was my first real meeting with the young congressman just elected from the Massachusetts district in which the Schlesingers would soon live.

Joe Alsop was the generous center of our social life. One found at his dinners Supreme Court justices, ambassadors, legislators, cabinet members, presidential aides, journalists. I renewed old friendships with Felix Frankfurter and Ed Prichard and met wise Ben Cohen, shrewd Fred Vinson, the chief justice, and Jimmy Byrnes, the secretary of state, who rather charmed me with his Irish brogue delivered in a southern drawl.

Joe's inner circle included Stewart and his lovely English wife, Tish, the Grahams, the Bohlens, the Bruces, Frank Wisner, my OSS chief in Germany, and his attractive wife, Polly, Robert Joyce of the State Department and his very pretty wife, Jane. Later this group crystalized in Sunday-evening suppers to which I was occasionally bid when in town.

Too many recall Joe only in his cranky old age as the hawk of hawks, the last-ditch defender of American intervention in Vietnam, the "doomed is what we are" Cold Warrior. All this is true enough, but it does not do him justice. Although the Cold War monopolized his columns toward the end and although he liked to tease friends as "liberals," to the accompaniment of his booming laugh, he began as a liberal himself.

His mother, Corinne Robinson Alsop, a frank and flavorsome lady, was a niece of Theodore Roosevelt, and his father was a Bull Moose Republican. Joe liked to recall his mother's attempt before he entered Groton to explain her son to the Reverend Endicott Peabody, Groton's renowned headmaster. She emphasized, perhaps overemphasized, Joe's joy in reading books. "That's all right, Corinne," the rector said. "We'll soon knock all that out of him."

He was a fat boy at school and college. Like many fat boys, he diverted attention from his physical appearance by noisiness and jokes. In Washington he sought a cure at the Johns Hopkins University Hospital, lost sixty-five pounds in three months and, with Yankee thriftiness, helped pay for it by selling a piece to the *Saturday Evening Post* entitled "How It Feels to Look Like Everybody Else." When I met him Joe was svelte, but he retained the diversionary reflexes of a fat boy.

Corinne Alsop, a stalwart Connecticut Republican, was fond of her cousin Eleanor Roosevelt but deeply opposed to Eleanor's husband. Joe, however, as a young reporter in the *New York Herald Tribune*'s Washington bureau, was a passionate admirer of FDR. He and Stewart used to say, half-humorously, that their mother, the Republican leader in Avon, Connecticut, burned their absentee ballots in presidential elections.

Joe's careful and well-informed books of the later Thirties — *The 168 Days* on FDR's fight with the Supreme Court (written with Turner Catledge), *The Men Around the President* (with Robert Kintner) and *American White Paper* (also with Kintner) on the coming of the war — remain indispensable for scholars. A third of a century later Joe produced perhaps the most enduring, and certainly the most endearing, of his books. His perceptive and affectionate *FDR: A Centenary Remembrance* saluted his kinsman for ending the WASP ascendancy in American politics and for "including the excluded" in American life. Joe was a liberal too in his unfailing commitment to freedoms of speech and expression.

He adored the children of his friends and was much adored in return. After we returned to Cambridge, he regularly spent the night with us when he came north for the annual dinner of the Porcellian Club. Our children looked forward to his visits, among other reasons for his ceremonious distribution of shiny quarters. In the Seventies, when I was rearing a new family in New York, Joe, bowing to inflation, raised the ante to a dollar, winning him the sobriquet among the new children of "Uncle Dollar."

Unlike most of Washington, Joe knew there was a world beyond politics. He was well and widely read and had an impressive personal library on art and architecture. He wrote a book on the Greek Bronze Age, *From the Silent Earth*, and after his retirement from journalism produced *The Rare Art Traditions*, a pioneer work on the modes of art collecting and their impact on culture.

It never occurred to me that Joe was homosexual. One day in the Sixties, Chip Bohlen, who had been ambassador to the Soviet Union when it all happened, told me how the KGB had set up Joe in 1957 and photographed him in bed with a male hooker. Joe had gone on to Leningrad, Chip said, leaving him a letter that he was not to open for ten days. Disturbed by Joe's manner, Chip opened it at once. Joe wrote (as I recall Chip's story) that he had brought disgrace on his family and his country and that there was only one way out. Chip, fearing suicide, summoned Joe back from Leningrad and talked him out of hasty action. If the KGB thought they could use the photographs to blackmail Joe, they were wrong. If anything, he became even more a foe of the Soviet Union.

One reason I never thought especially about Joe's sexuality was his evident delight in women. When I came to Washington from Cambridge, I ordinarily stayed at Joe's house. One morning as I prepared to depart, Joe said, "If you have no pressing reason to go back, why not stay over? The most beautiful woman in America is coming to dinner tonight." I was naturally curious to meet the most beautiful woman in America, so I stayed. Lily Cushing Emmet was indeed a beautiful woman — tall, Garboesque with high cheekbones and generous mouth, alert brown-green eyes, auburn hair, a low, warm voice and a charming laugh. The daughter of Howard Cushing, an early American impressionist, she was herself an accomplished painter whose vivid portraits and luxurious landscapes were acquired by New

York's Metropolitan Museum and the Museum of Modern Art and by the National Gallery in Washington.

Obviously the thought never crossed my mind that one day I would marry Lily Emmet's daughter. After Lily's death, Alexandra came upon a packet of letters from Joe that her mother had saved through the long years. He loved her, Joe wrote to Lily, and proposed marriage; it would be, he delicately indicated, companionship without sex, but their delight in each other would ensure happiness. Lily kindly turned Joe down and, having long since divorced Alexandra's father, William Temple Emmet, married a naval officer who turned out to be a morose right-wing fanatic.

Joe and I fell out over Vietnam in the late Sixties, but marriage to Lily's daughter restored me to his affections, and he once again became a vital part of our lives. Joe rejoiced in his friends, laughed and raged at human folly, cherished human courage, was a civilized man, a gentleman and a patriot.

*   *   *

Joe was one of three journalists who dominated the Washington scene in the Forties and for two decades thereafter. The other two were Walter Lippmann and James B. Reston.

Lippmann was a generation older. Fifty-seven in 1946, he lived in quiet elegance on Woodley Road near the Cathedral. He had known everyone in American politics from TR and Wilson, had been through the Great War and the Great Depression and saw the current rush of events with measuring and dispassionate eye. "This is not the last crisis in human affairs," he once wrote. "The world will go on somehow, and more crises will follow. It will go on best, however, if among us there are men who have stood apart, who refused to be anxious or too much concerned, who were cool and inquiring and had their eyes on a longer past and a longer future."

Yet for all that, he retained a lively interest in the twists and turns and gossip of policy and politics. Personally he was kind, courteous and correct. His wife, Helen Byrne Lippmann, Phyllis Cox's sister, was the more spontaneous and outspoken of the two, notoriously adoring of her husband, fiercely scornful of his critics. Their cocktail parties were great fun.

Scotty Reston, so called because he was born in Scotland, was thirty-seven in 1946, a year older than Joe Alsop. Brought to the United States and educated in Illinois, he began as a sportswriter, called the wrong winner in the Grand National, and, when war came, switched to international affairs. He was already the star of the *New York Times* Washington bureau, much to the chagrin of Arthur Krock, whose sometimes canny but more often pompous columns on the *Times* editorial page had long expressed the conventional wisdom of the day. (Ed Prichard used to refer to the politicos who sought Krock's favor as "Krock-suckers.")

Scotty was a great reporter with a trophy belt of scoops, and he infused his reporting with reflections and analysis. For all his stringent Scotch Presbyterian standards, he had the saving grace of humor and a tolerant acceptance of human vagaries, except for hypocrisy and deceit. He was excellent company, interested, interesting, unfailingly considerate. His wife, Sally Fulton Reston, was a lovely distillation of charm and practicality.

Joe Alsop was more flamboyant and outrageous than the impersonal Lippmann and the responsible Reston. His brother Stewart, his partner in the syndicated column "Matter of Fact," had his own qualities of independence, discernment and humor and served valuably to tone down Joe's extravaganzas. And there were other first-rate newspapermen around. Particular friends were Marquis Childs of the *St. Louis Post-Dispatch,* a nervy, incisive, scholarly man whose first wife had been a secretary of my father's in Iowa City and with whom I collaborated in choosing for *Look* in 1950 the twenty men and women who had most shaped the half century.

Lippmann's work will last longest. He had wider interests, saw things in greater analytical depth and longer historical perspective and was the best writer of the lot. The others wrote forcefully and well, but Walter combined lucidity and grace in a distinctive and distinguished way.

Relations among the big three were nominally friendly. Lippmann and Reston were really good friends, capable of serious discussion with each other. Reston and Mark Childs edited the book *Walter Lippmann and His Times* (1959), with essays by Reinhold Niebuhr, Raymond Aron, George Kennan, Allan Nevins and lesser lights (including me). Lippmann got along more or less with Alsop, at least until the Vietnam War, but at bottom each felt a bit uncomfortable with the other. Joe held Walter in respect but enjoyed making cracks about him. "A very brilliant man," Joe would say, "but even Walter's column was saved from constant repetition only by the simple fact that he changed his views roughly once every eight months."

Where Lippmann excelled in analysis, Reston and Alsop were both great reporters, rivals in a way, friendly but not really friends, with markedly contrasting styles. Both were happy to be on good social terms with politicians and diplomats — more the custom then for newspapermen than it became later. Lippmann too cultivated government officials, but one felt they mattered less to him; he had seen too many come and go. Alsop provoked and harangued his sources with a patrician imperiousness that Reston, with his Scottish and midwestern upbringing, suspected and disapproved. For his part, Alsop thought Reston a trifle provincial and was a little patronizing about him. He really liked and admired Sally Reston, though.

Whatever their flaws and foibles, these top journalists contributed a great deal to the education of the electorate and to the joy of life. They were terrific friends for a young historian.

* * *

Another center of Georgetown social life was Kay Halle's house on Avon Place. Kay was a beautiful, wealthy and hospitable woman, then in her early forties, with bright eyes, striking blonde hair and abundant if sometimes guileless enthusiasms. She came from Cleveland, the daughter of a German-Jewish department store owner and an Irish-Catholic working girl. She remained determinedly unmarried, despite close friendships at various times with George Gershwin, Joseph P. Kennedy, Averell Harriman, James V. Forrestal and especially Winston Churchill's son, Randolph. At Kay's cocktail hour one was likely to find a variety of movers and shakers — Harriman, Forrestal, Bohlen, Paul Porter, co-founder with Thurman Arnold and Abe Fortas of Washington's bustling new law firm (and soon to marry Kathleen Winsor, author of the scandalous success *Forever Amber*).

The Alsop set regarded Kay Halle with a certain disdain, but I liked her as a fellow Buckeye (i.e., native Ohioan) and as a generous-hearted and attractive woman. Under Kay's benevolent gaze I struck up an unlikely friendship with Jim Forrestal, soon to be the first secretary of defense.

Forrestal was a highly wound-up Wall Streeter with clenched jaw and mistrustful eyes who combined an abundance of caustic opinions with considerable intellectual curiosity and, it must be said, a certain magnetic charm. The son of an Irish contractor in upstate New York, he had risen by energy, intelligence and ambition through the dizzying Twenties and the chastening Thirties to end as president of Dillon, Read, the investment bank. On William O. Douglas's recommendation, FDR made him a special assistant in 1940. After Frank Knox's death, Jim became secretary of the Navy.

A serious reader of history, Forrestal would occasionally invite me over for a drink. His Prospect Street house was strewn with weekly magazines of political comment, British as well as American; he would talk freely of Bagehot, whom he admired, and Laski, whom he hated; he was fascinated by the clash of ideas. He would quiz me as if he were seizing the opportunity to find out what the liberal enemy was thinking.

Jim put me in mind of a character out of Scott Fitzgerald (he was two years ahead of Fitzgerald in Princeton). In his mad dash upward in life, one felt he had lost something he desperately wanted to recover — "the Great Gatsby in Washington," I called him in the *Partisan Review* in 1951. Like Gatsby, he was self-invented, a parvenu rising from obscurity to social acceptance. In the Twenties he had lived a West Egg life in Long Island's Old Westbury. His distraught wife, Jo, seemed almost a blurred Zelda. One felt Jim was forever yearning for a green light at the end of some dock. With his compressed lips and shortish, trim, erect figure, he looked rather like the Alan Ladd who played Gatsby in Elliott Nugent's film that came out the year Forrestal killed himself. Jim was all drive; there was no surcease in him. Lacking inner serenity, he came to find it harder and harder to make decisions. Indecision, in the end, tore him down and drove him on to the last decision, terrible and irrevocable.

The Fitzgerald novel in a sense foretold Forrestal, and his life and death tempted other novelists. John O'Hara was a good friend of Jim's (as well as one of Jo's lovers) and very likely used him as the model for the upwardly mobile protagonist in *From the Terrace*. Dos Passos (*The Great Days*) and George Backer (*Appearance of a Man*) also based novels on Forrestal-like characters.

*　　*　　*

Most interesting was Kay Halle's Churchill connection. Young Randolph had come to the United States in 1930–31 on a lecture tour. He met Kay in Cleveland, fell for her, proposed to her and informed his parents of his intentions. Winston and Clementine were horrified. Randolph was a kid of twenty; Kay was not only unknown to his parents but was eight years older. Luckily she turned him down, thereby gaining a lifelong devoted friend instead of an egotistical, irascible and short-term husband. The elder Churchills were relieved at the outcome and charmed by Kay when Randolph brought her to Chartwell in the autumn of 1931.

Kay later compiled three useful volumes of Churchilliana: *Irrepress-*

ible Churchill: A Treasury of Churchill's Wit (1966), *Winston Churchill on America and Britain* (with a foreword by Clementine Churchill and a preface by Averell Harriman, 1970) and *The Grand Original: Portraits of Randolph Churchill* (in England, *The Young Pretender,* 1971).

I saw Randolph from time to time, mostly with two people of whom he was genuinely fond — Kay, of course, with whom he always stayed in Washington, and Charles Wintour, who, as editor of the *Evening Standard* in London after the war, often used Randolph as a special correspondent. One has a montage of memories: Randolph arguing with a Georgetown cop who had dared stop a car he was driving rather drunkenly down Twenty-ninth Street sometime in the Fifties; Randolph red-faced and exultant at the Democratic convention in Los Angeles in 1960, rejoicing over the nomination of Jack Kennedy, whom he adored as extravagantly as he despised Jack's father; Randolph boasting of a Hollywood dinner given by Otto Preminger, the director, at which he successfully insulted so many guests that eight of them, he claimed, left the table; Randolph on a hilarious riff about the Munich crisis in which he gave leading characters Joycean names — Chamberpot and Holyfox and Mountbottom; Randolph drinking pint after pint of beer at Claridge's while holding forth on the way he planned to organize the writing of his father's biography.

I found him, most of the time, courteous, entertaining and no more disagreeable than the occasion demanded. Perhaps because I saw him so often in the company of people he really liked, I missed the historic explosions that adorned his cantankerous march through the social world. "Like the sirens in the blitz," wrote Malcolm Muggeridge, "his arrival at any social gathering sends everyone scampering for cover. . . . When the 'all clear' sounds and he departs, there is a corresponding sense of relief, but the intervening experience (as long as one has not been personally involved in the explosion) is exhilarating."

*　　*　　*

Having persuaded President-elect Kennedy in 1961 to celebrate the arts by inviting leading writers, composers and painters to his inauguration, Kay persuaded him in 1963 to make Winston Churchill an honorary citizen of the United States. Randolph came to Washington to receive the honorary citizenship on his father's behalf.

The night before the ceremony, Kay gave him a dinner party. I arrived late and found Randolph in a bad temper. After dinner he led me back into the dining room, slammed the door shut and complained about "gabby American women." We stayed there drinking for an hour or more while the party continued in the drawing room. Having separated himself from the gabby American women, Randolph became exceedingly charming and interesting. We talked about the American Winston Churchill, the author of the once popular novels *Coniston* and *Richard Carvel.* When the two Churchills met, the British Winston said to the American Winston, "Why don't you run for the presidency of the United States? Then I will become prime minister of Britain, and we will amaze everybody."

I asked Randolph about his impressions of FDR. He had only met the president a few times and saw him as rather a "feminine" figure, by which he meant that FDR exhibited prima donna traits of vanity and jealousy. Then he said, "But his voice — a great voice — instinct with courage." After a moment he added, "Even more so than my father's."

The citizenship ceremony took place the next afternoon in the Rose Garden. Randolph, resisting, as he later told me, the temptation to mimic his father (which he could do rather well), read Winston's letter of acceptance with great dignity. The crucial sentence was a majestic rejection of the theory that relegated Britain to a "tame and minor" position in the world. This was obviously aimed at Dean Acheson for his recent statement that Britain had lost an empire and not yet found a role. I was standing with Dean in the crowd, and he muttered to me, "Well, it hasn't taken Winston long to get used to American ways. He was not an American citizen for three minutes before he began attacking an ex–Secretary of State."

I remember too another dinner at Kay's with Randolph, Franklin D. Roosevelt, Jr., and Robert Kennedy. Bobby, though the youngest, somehow dominated the evening with his urgent vitality and teasing wit. One wondered about families. Winston Churchill and Franklin Roosevelt were incontestably greater men than Joseph P. Kennedy. Yet Randolph and Franklin Jr., both men of talent, charm and ambition, lived lives beneath their promise and ability, while the sons of Joe Kennedy, pursuing their capacities to the uttermost limits, rose far beyond their father and, no doubt, because of him.

*   *   *

Daisy Harriman — formally, Mrs. J. Borden Harriman — was in 1946 an engaging dowager of seventy-six. She had been a patrician feminist, a social reformer, a Democratic party stalwart and FDR's minister to Norway at the time of the Nazi invasion. Now she held supper parties on Sunday nights where, with imperious charm, she set up debates on hot issues.

Marian and I were often invited. On one occasion Mrs. Harriman directed me to take on General Patrick J. Hurley, Hoover's secretary of war and a roving diplomat for FDR during the Second World War, ending as ambassador to China. A third of a century my elder, he had a lavish mustache, a large ego, a short temper, flashy rhetoric and a hatred of persons whom he thought to be Communists, especially foreign service officers who had warned (correctly) of a probable victory for Mao Tse-tung over Chiang Kai-shek. (Marian's old beau John Paton Davies was a particular villain in Hurley's eyes.) My ego, I suppose, was large too and my temper short, and we had a slam-bang altercation. I guess I lost because Daisy Harriman's guests felt that a cocky ex-corporal should show more respect for an aged ex-general.

Our Chevy Chase house was too far out for easy entertaining, but resolute friends were prepared to make the trip. Samuel Eliot Morison, now a rear admiral writing his fifteen-volume history of American naval operations during the war — an astonishing tour de force — was often in Washington and kindly accepted an invitation to dinner. After due consideration, we decided that David and Evangeline Bruce would be the most appropriate company. The evening was not a success. One concluded that the difference between patrician Virginians and patrician Bay Staters was that the first were equally courteous to everyone and the second were equally frosty to everyone.

* * *

Evangeline's old admirer Ed Prichard had decided to return to Kentucky. His Washington reputation was high. After a brief stint in the Army, he was invalided out and returned to the White House, working for Jimmy Byrnes in the Office of War Mobilization. With a small, crack staff, including Ben Cohen, Paul Porter and Sam Lubell as well, Byrnes did an effective job of bringing a measure of coherence to the domestic front. Prich was a star. "He was, I think," Ken Galbraith said, "the most brilliant lawyer I ever knew."

But there was a dangerous carelessness about Prich in those days. The young men of FDR's Washington were not deficient in willfulness and presumption. Judge Learned Hand, who liked the New Deal but not necessarily the New Dealers, confided to Justice Harlan Stone, "The Filii Aurorae make me actively sick at my stomach; they are so conceited, so insensitive, so arrogant." Prich was notably spoiled. He could be irresponsible and outrageous. His friends were constantly protecting him, forgiving him and picking up the pieces after him.

He planned in time to run for governor of Kentucky, but his return was not unanimously welcomed by the state political establishment. Some resented his Washington success, his highhandedness and his vaulting expectations. They felt he had not paid his local political dues. Others saw him as the most promising man to come out of Kentucky since Henry Clay.

In 1948 Virgil Chapman, a hack congressman, won the Democratic nomination for senator. His Republican opponent was the intelligent, highminded and liberal John Sherman Cooper. On election day in Paris, Prich's home town, inspectors found ballot boxes already stuffed with 254 ballots. All but one were marked for Chapman. When the news appeared on the ticker, Joe Alsop, knowing of Prich's contempt for Chapman and affection for Cooper, sent off a jocular telegram saying he assumed Prich was responsible for the single Cooper ballot.

Alas, it was no joke. Prich was responsible for all the stuffed ballots. The next year he was brought to trial, convicted and sentenced to two years in the federal penitentiary. Why had he stuffed the ballots? It was partly out of an impulse to show that, despite his association with big shots in Washington, he was still one of the boys in Bourbon County. Ballot-stuffing, he told a reporter years later, "was as common in Bourbon County as chicken-fighting, and no more serious. I . . . thought of it as something you did for fun." It was partly the "heady wine" of his New Deal days. "I got to feeling, perhaps, that I was bigger than I was, that the rules didn't always apply to me. . . . It was wrong, and I know it was wrong, and I think you may grant that I paid for it."

President Truman pardoned Prich on Christmas Day 1949, but a brilliant career seemed irretrievably shattered. Prich sank into deep depression. The story, however, does not end there.

*   *   *

Denis Brogan showed up in Washington and one day brought over the new correspondent of the *Daily Telegraph* of London, Malcolm Muggeridge. Muggeridge and I hit it off at once. With snapping blue eyes and a seductive laugh, Malcolm, whose talent for making friends was exceeded only (as I one day discovered) by his talent for breaking with them, was an extremely funny man, given to saturnine, not to say satanic, rants. Across long years I remember few people who made me laugh so much. The novelist Anthony Powell, his closest friend (till Muggeridge turned against him in 1967), splendidly described his "anarcho-anti-Left-anti-Churchill-anti-intellectual-nihilistic-sex is fun/sex is sinful-diatribes against everything and everybody, expressed in a copious flow of political paradox and four-letter-word imagery."

I was an admirer of Muggeridge's *Winter in Moscow* (1934), an early specimen of what came to be called a nonfiction novel. Malcolm had gone to the Soviet Union in 1932 as an idealistic young correspondent for the *Manchester Guardian*. His wife, Kitty, was the niece of Beatrice Webb and shared the Webbs' illusions about Stalin's "new civilization." The Muggeridges were quickly disenchanted. *Winter in Moscow* revealed the ghastliness of Stalinism, especially the terrible famine of 1933, in a series of vivid episodes. The gullibility of foreign pilgrims come to worship at the Soviet shrine provoked Muggeridge to passages of wondrous acidity.

Henry Wallace was just then emerging as the Truman administration's champion of a soft policy toward the Soviet Union. Malcolm was delighted when I came upon letters Wallace sent to FDR in 1933 opposing diplomatic recognition of the Soviet Union and enclosing a series of Muggeridge's Moscow dispatches to buttress his case.

Malcolm had a deeply cynical view of life. "I'm a voyeur as far as politics is concerned," he wrote to Hugh Kingsmill from Washington, "peeping with fascinated disgust at the obscenities of power." He could not recall an election, he once said, in which he had not hoped for the defeat of the incumbent. Like Mencken, he regarded great leaders like Churchill and Roosevelt as great charlatans. Nevertheless he prided himself on his professionalism as a journalist, and he was so much at ease with cynicism that one only discovered much later that it masked a hunger for spiritual certitudes.

* * *

I especially owe Malcolm my introduction to Anthony Powell's novels and later to Tony himself, who lived up to expectations; not always the case with writers one admires. His wife, Lady Violet Pakenham, was a witty woman. Arthur Mizener of Cornell, an even earlier American admirer of Powell's novels, once told me that he had sent her a copy of *The Age of Jackson*. "She thanked me by saying she had always wondered why the Biddles all had that guilty look, and that now she knew."

Powell's elegant and glittering twelve-volume sequence, *A Dance to the Music of Time*, so delighted me that I ventured into literary criticism and wrote about it for the *New Republic*. His work also clarified for me one of the great mysteries. I have been recurrently struck by the role of coincidence in my life. *The Music of Time* illustrates the way coincidence seems interwoven into the very fabric of contemporary society.

Powell took his title from Poussin's painting in the Wallace Collection in London. Interpretations of the painting vary, but Tony saw it as the ritualistic dance of the Four Seasons while Time, an "extraordinarily sinister" figure, plays on a lyre. The Seasons break "into seemingly meaningless gyrations, while partners disappear only to reappear again . . . unable to control the melody, unable, perhaps, to control the steps of the dance."

His subject was the plight of the old governing class in England, undermined by the Great War and then by the Great Depression and at last beginning to sense its extreme vulnerability. His own generation found itself bemused by new ideas and new guilts, tempted by Bohemia, threatened by coarse new energies and unscrupulous new men, haunted by the fear that in some sense the game was up.

In a style of beautiful, ironical felicity halfway between Marcel Proust and Evelyn Waugh, Powell shows the ebb and flow within social configurations, the transient and shifting friendships, quarrels, parties, jobs, marriages, affairs, divorces. Because his characters are sensitive to the barometric pressure of events, they reflect the larger world beyond. The great historical happenings — war, depression, Nazism, communism, war again — are persistent offstage presences. Characters appear and disappear and then reappear in vividly different settings and circumstances, the rhythm of life sooner or later bringing them together again "as in the performance of one or another sequences of a ritual dance."

The circularity of life — this is a salient feature of one's own experience and memory. How to explain Powell's Law — "the inexorable law of coincidence"? How is the historian to account for life's weird circularity? I derive some consolation from Henry James's remark in "Pandora," the story he wrote about Mrs. Henry Adams: "There are some things that even the most philosophical historian isn't bound to account for."

*   *   *

Writing about the age of Roosevelt was my long-term objective. My approach was greatly influenced by James Parton's search for Andrew Jackson.

Setting to work a dozen years after Jackson's death, Parton began by reading everything he could find about Jackson. He read, he said, "endless newspapers, pamphlets, books, without arriving at any conclusion whatsoever." If anyone asked what he had discovered,

> I might have answered thus: 'Andrew Jackson, I am given to understand, was a patriot and a traitor. He was one of the greatest of generals, and wholly ignorant of the art of war. . . . The first of statesmen, he never devised, he never framed a measure. He was the most candid of men, and was capable of the profoundest dissimulation. A most law-defying, law-abiding citizen. . . . A democratic autocrat. An urbane savage. An atrocious saint.'

In his perplexity, Parton resorted to what we now call oral history: "At Washington I conversed with politicians of the last generation, who have no longer an interest in concealing the truth." He visited a third of the states, receiving the recollections of men and women, bond and free, who knew Jackson well, knew him at all periods of his life, lived near him and with him, served him and were served by him. "I listened, also, to many who were always opposed to the man, and still like him not. . . . And thus it was that contradictions were reconciled, that mysteries were revealed, and that the truth was made apparent."

One can only admire the diligence with which Parton preserved for future historians testimony that witnesses would otherwise have carried to their graves. Of course, oral history is subject to the treachery of memory. Also, Parton inevitably asked the questions of his own time, and these were not always the questions later historians wish he had asked. Still, every scholar of the age of Jackson remains in debt to James Parton.

*   *   *

My first *Fortune* assignment — the fate of the Good Neighbor policy — combined my search for Franklin Roosevelt with a growing interest in the past and future of Latin America.

In formulating the Good Neighbor policy, FDR had sought to change the relationship of the United States to the rest of the Americas. Instead of the traditional role as master of the hemisphere ("practically sovereign on this continent," as Secretary of State Richard Olney put it forty years earlier, "and its fiat is law"), Roosevelt proposed a new role as cooperative friend. The first step was the renunciation of the right claimed by TR and others to intervene when Latin American countries misbehaved. Secretary of State Cordell Hull and the top man on Latin America, FDR's family friend Assistant Secretary (later Undersecretary) Sumner Welles, agreed enthusiastically on that. But during the Second World War Hull and Welles fell out, not only about policy toward what Hull called the "bad neighbor," Argentina, but more fundamentally over Welles's superior access to the president; Hull finally forced Welles's resignation in 1943 after allegations of homosexuality.

Argentina was still an issue. The Buenos Aires government, long accustomed to playing off Europe against the United States and not without an ill-concealed weakness for fascism, had resisted Washington's pressure to break relations with the Axis powers. Hull favored the unilateral coercion of Argentina; Welles favored multilateral action through the inter-American community. Nelson Rockefeller, coordinator of inter-American affairs and in December 1944 assistant secretary of state for Latin America, agreed with Welles. Spruille Braden, ambassador to Argentina and then Rockefeller's successor at State, agreed with Hull.

I interviewed them all. Welles greatly impressed me — his intelligence, candor, lucidity of mind, distinction of manner; also, very likely, his unqualified praise for *The Age of Jackson*. He seemed not at all a cold and unfeeling man as advertised; rather, I wrote to my parents, "a man whose strong passions are under exquisite control." He had, I thought, a "curiously abstract but intense vision of the imperative need for raising living standards in South America and in meeting the desire for greater popular control."

As for Braden, I thought him "a big, fat dope, with a certain charm of which he is not unaware, a shrewd instinct for publicity and probably some capacity for dealing with South Americans." He showed little interest in raising living standards, "apparently because he has done so much business down there that he despairs of doing anything moneywise which would not be wasted in graft and inefficiency." His Buenos Aires act as the two-fisted fighter for democracy against Colonel Juan Perón had failed to stop Perón's election as president or to gain the support of leftist Latin regimes like those of Mexico and Chile.

Nelson Rockefeller, I wrote for *Fortune*, showed "the natural mistrust with which a thoughtful rich boy must always view the world, wondering whether people like him for himself or for his money. . . . a successful bureaucratic infighter, concealing a curious deviousness and even ruthlessness beneath a winning manner. His face is ordinarily lighted by a friendly smile, but in repose it becomes suspicious, almost sullen." But Rockefeller understood the crucial role of economic questions, he pioneered development assistance as coordinator of inter-American affairs, and his earnest advocacy of the inter-American system at the founding conference of the United Nations in San Francisco helped bring about the U.N. Charter's endorsement of regional organizations.

I talked to Henry Morgenthau, Jr., FDR's secretary of the treasury, who supported Braden, and to Larry Duggan, who supported Welles. Especially helpful was Adolf Berle, a member of FDR's original brain trust, a man of acute intelligence, sharp tongue and diverse expertise who got along better with young people than with his own generation. As I reported to my parents, "He was more modest and less cocky than I had been led [by the Frankfurter-Acheson crowd, who disliked Berle] to expect; and he made a lot of sense."

Berle, who had tried in vain to mediate between Hull and Welles, thought that Braden was right that we should stand up for democracy in the Americas, but that his particular tactics were ill conceived. The flounderings of Bradenism, Berle suggested, should be seen as a first attempt to work out the democratic implications of the Good Neighbor system. Welles, Berle said, was right in calling for the support of economic development and human rights within a multilateral framework.

"Good Fences Make Good Neighbors" came out in the August 1946 issue of *Fortune*. "I only wish your article had appeared some eighteen months ago," Welles wrote. "Had it been published then, it might have done much to prevent the further deterioration in inter-American relations which has since taken place." "Frankly," wrote to Nelson Rockefeller, "it is the most penetrating and constructive analysis of the subject I have seen anywhere. You certainly did a job," and he concluded with an invitation to luncheon. This was nice on Nelson's part, considering what I had written about him. Braden fumed in the State Department and dictated a blast that he decided in the end not to send. This crusader for democracy in Latin America curiously ended thirty years later as a right-wing extremist in the United States.

The *Fortune* piece led to lasting friendships with Welles, Berle, Morgenthau and Rockefeller, and it nourished my understanding of the tragic problems of the southern half of the Western Hemisphere. Rereading the piece more than half a century later, I find it sensible enough in content but uneasily journalistic and cliché-ridden in style — several steps down from *The Age of Jackson*. I had yet to get my bearings as a free-lance writer.

20

CPUSA vs. ADA

THE GOOD NEIGHBOR PIECE was my initiation into Henry R. Luce's journalistic empire. *Fortune,* a monthly given to quasi-scholarly articles and located off by itself in New York City's Empire State Building, had its own leisured tempo and was somewhat apart and aloof from Luce's other magazines. My next assignment — a text piece for the great picture magazine, *Life* — plunged me into the heart of Luce's high-pressure, self-contained, all-devouring world.

Life and *Time* were headquartered sixteen blocks uptown, at 9 Rockefeller Center. Time Inc. in those frenetic days was a cult to which all else was to be sacrificed. Luce was of course the high priest. Exigent weekly deadlines filled staff writers and researchers on both magazines with a mixture of anxiety and zeal that made the next issue seem far more important than wives, husbands and children. The atmosphere was one of chronic crisis, periodically relieved by dry martinis.

Bid to luncheon with Luce two or three times, I was struck by his combination of genuine intellectual curiosity about everything with stubborn resistance to changing his mind about anything. Yet he tolerated liberals (Archie MacLeish, Ken Galbraith, John Hersey, Dwight Macdonald, Teddy White, me, etc., etc.) on his magazines, only explaining grumpily, "For some goddamn reason Republicans can't write."

I was struck by his impact on any editors present at the luncheon table. Luce's speech was sometimes halting and stammering, and his editors, fluent of voice on all other occasions, would suddenly begin to halt and stammer too. For all his righteous Presbyterian certitude and bleak lack of small talk, Harry Luce was not without humor, and I found him an oddly likable man.

Relationships between *Time* and *Life* writers and researchers were particularly close and tense. The writers, almost all men in those misbegotten days, put down their words in careless and confident masculinity; the researchers, all women, edited and 'checked' with dedicated exactitude, defiantly imprinting their arsenal of dots over each word — red dots (OK), black dots (probable), no dots (up to the writer to prove). The researchers were often brighter than the writers and certainly more principled. Though barred by their sex from advancement on the masthead, they took their lowly jobs with extreme seriousness and held writers and editors to higher standards than the men would have imposed on themselves. I had become accustomed to the system in Henry Pringle's Writers Division in OWI, and I was lucky to have the acute and merciless Barbara Wendell Kerr, now returned to Time Inc. as my meticulous researcher and editor on the Good Neighbor piece and on several pieces thereafter.

*　　*　　*

I forget now how I happened to write the article about the American Communist party for *Life* rather than *Fortune,* nor do I remember whose idea the article was. Certainly I found an investigation of the CPUSA a congenial theme; perhaps I proposed it at one of the Luce luncheons.

Barbara Kerr and I began our inquiry in the spring of 1946. (I draw on her notes in describing the interviews.) No top Communist would see me, but we spoke to Earl Browder, the fallen party chief. Browder had been the idolized leader of the CPUSA for fifteen years. Then his effort to Americanize and broaden the party provoked an attack in April 1945 by the French Communist Jacques Duclos. It was assumed that Duclos, in condemning Browder's arguments for class collaboration, was speaking for Moscow. In June the CPUSA, in an orgy of repentance, dismissed Browder as the party leader; in February 1946 the party expelled him.

Browder then left for Moscow, where he still retained ties and hoped to be restored to Stalin's favor. He came back with a five-year contract to represent Soviet publishing houses in the United States. We saw him at the end of June with his brother William, the former business manager of the *Daily Worker.* It was the only interview Browder granted after his return; the reason for the exception, he explained, was his high regard for *The Age of Jackson.* This did not stop him from putting the interview off the record.

Browder looked at first glance like the average suburban commuter — nondescript grayish tropical worsted suit, matching gray tie, white shirt, white socks, new brown shoes. Iron gray hair and mustache gave him an air of old-fashioned respectability. The benign exterior was marred by a pair of shifty eyes and a trick of twisting a match packet in his left hand when questions were too direct. At such times there was a hesitancy in replying, each word carefully planned and followed by a crafty smile. His face had an overcrowded look — not enough room between forehead and chin for eyes and nose.

His issue with William Z. Foster, his successor as party leader, he told us, was whether the CPUSA would work with other progressive groups on an attainable program of social reform or whether it would become once again a narrow, sectarian, conspiratorial group calling for unattainable goals. One felt that, where Foster identified proudly with his Marxist notion of the working class, Browder was a white-collar man who had started on class collaboration as a tactic but soon grew to like it as a passport to respectability.

Browder was not without self-esteem. "If it hadn't been for us," he said, "Roosevelt would never have been elected in 1944. Our little band of 80,000 got in there and worked as hard as they could. They provided the leaven which held the whole Roosevelt coalition together. We are the people who did it." In the last half of 1944, he continued, "we were really making great strides in breaking down the prejudice against communism. It was melting away. Now Foster is alienating all our former allies. The united liberal front is broken." Foster's idea of a third party, Browder said, would benefit only the Republicans. "It is perfectly clear," I wrote to my parents, "that he is sore as hell at the American Party and also that he was exceedingly well treated in Moscow; but he became very cagey at all tricky questions and did not talk very freely."

I saw Browder a couple of times in later years. He soon abandoned hope of reinstatement and ended by living quietly with his son, a Princeton professor. A few weeks before his death in 1973, he offered his verdict on communism. "Stalin needed the Cold War," he told the *Philadelphia Inquirer*. ". . . To keep up the sharp international tensions by which he alone could maintain such a regime in Russia, Stalin had to pick a quarrel with the United States, the leading capitalist country. And I was the victim of it."

* * *

We talked to a number of CPUSA sympathizers. Leo Huberman, who in 1949 would found the Marxist *Monthly Review* with Paul Sweezy, praised the CPUSA for its "magnificent" work, especially in the unions. But he had refused to join the party because of "the inept leadership that overdoes everything," particularly internal ideological discipline and external worship of the Soviet Union.

Corliss Lamont, a credulous rich man of the no-enemy-to-the-left school, praised the party's work in the Thirties, dismissed the current leadership as "ignorant" of American realities and "slavish" toward the Soviet Union but spent a good deal more time denouncing what he deemed the far worse sin of red-baiting.

Ella Winter, widow of the muckraker Lincoln Steffens and wife of the gentle satirist Donald Ogden Stewart, had been a secretary of Felix Frankfurter's and a friend of my parents; but she refused to see me, castigating me over the telephone for joining the Luce plot to organize a worldwide crusade against the Soviet Union. Some years later I met the Stewarts, now Joe McCarthy exiles in London, at a dinner given by Constance Cummings and Benn Levy. Don Stewart, the author of *A Parody Outline of History* and the model for Bill Gorton in *The Sun Also Rises*, was a wry wit and a most incongruous fellow traveler, and I got along with him. Ella Winter fixed me with a beady eye throughout the evening.

We interviewed anti-Stalinist liberals like Pat Jackson, Dave Niles, Jim Loeb of the Union for Democratic Action, Charles Bolte of the American Veterans Committee and Jimmy Wechsler of the *New York Post*. We interviewed anti-Stalinist radicals like Dwight Macdonald, James T. Farrell and the ex-Trotskyite Herbert Solow of *Fortune*.

And we interviewed anti-Communist zealots. Ray Murphy of the State Department, a florid, expansive man, seemed to exist solely for the purpose of running an FBI of his own. After twenty-five years in the department, he had accumulated considerable information and considerable misinformation about the communist movement. The CPUSA, he told us, "controlled" (including trade unions) eight hundred thousand to a million Americans. Two thousand party members, he said, had penetrated the federal government; "a conservative estimate," he added. His pal Ben Mandel, a former party member, now research director for the House Un-American Activities Committee, agreed that the estimate was conservative. We were in touch too with the red-hunters of the *New York World-Telegram*, Fred Woltman and his sidekick, the amiable Nelson Frank, who informed us that *Life* itself was "heavily infiltrated."

*　　*　　*

Herbert Solow urged me to talk to Whittaker Chambers of *Time*. An appointment was arranged with some difficulty. Barbara Kerr and I were eventually ushered into Chambers's small, untidy office. He was a squat, dour, unprepossessing man, and for a time he responded laconically and unhelpfully to our questions. Then he filibustered, giving us a potted history of the CPUSA — the fall of Jay Lovestone, the rise and fall of Earl Browder, the fall and rise of William Z. Foster, etc. Barbara nearly went to sleep. It was history at a distance; Chambers claimed no personal acquaintance with the leadership. He did say that none of the top leaders was capable except possibly for Louis Budenz, a *Daily Worker* editor who had just resigned from the party, and Sam Darcy, a veteran organizer, recently expelled.

The party, he went on, was financed by Moscow, but up to a certain point. Funds had been reduced during the Five Year Plan. However, if the party really needed money, Moscow would be forthcoming. The leaders were honest according to their lights. Rarely if ever did Communists steal, but from other viewpoints they were impossible.

They organized the party along parallel lines, Chambers told us — an open party and "a much larger underground." Intellectual discussion had pretty well gone out of the movement, perhaps because the time had come for revolutionary action. "The end of the war has seen the two large capitalistic powers licking mortal wounds. Where the prewar schedule for world revolution ran from two to three generations, it has now been shortened to one generation." Current objectives, Chambers continued, were the dismemberment of the British Empire, the domination of Central Europe and the obstruction of the U.S. recovery through strikes.

I tried to elicit personal testimony, but Chambers was not illuminating about himself nor about his motives for joining the party. I was surprised, however, by the pride this latter-day anti-Communist seemed to take in the CPUSA's achievements of the Thirties. The party, he said, appealed to the unemployed, the unions, the intellectuals, and was well on its way to popular influence when the Moscow trials brought disillusion. He described with melodramatic relish his own break with the party, how he moved furtively around the city, how he slept in a different bed every night and always with a gun by his side.

After a while I raised the question of Communist penetration of the government. Recalling conversations with Pat Jackson and Dave Niles, I dropped the names of Harry Dexter White and Alger Hiss. Later Chambers told me, "When you called for an appointment, I checked with a friend who said you were close to the party. That is why I was so guarded at first. Then you started naming Communists in Washington, and I decided that it was all right to talk to you." The underground, he claimed, contained such people as Hiss and his brother Donald; also Alger Hiss's wife, "blonde, blue-eyed, baby-faced Priscilla." The Hiss assignment, he said vaguely, was to provide information when needed. He made no allusion to Soviet espionage.

He told us that we could not use the Hiss story; he had communicated the facts, he said, to responsible authorities in Washington; beyond that, he had tacitly agreed with the Communists to leave them alone if they would leave him alone.

*   *   *

"The U.S. Communist Party" appeared in the July 29, 1946, issue of *Life* (Vivien Leigh was on the cover). "To understand the Communists," I wrote, "you must think of them in terms, not of a normal political party, but in terms of the Jesuits, the Mormons or Jehovah's Witnesses." Though there was considerable turnover in membership, the threat of expulsion appalled hard-core communicants as the threat of excommunication appalled devout Catholics. The fear of being cast out kept many in line even after they began to doubt the infallibility of the Soviet Union. "The appeal is essentially the appeal of a religious sect — small, persecuted, dedicated, stubbornly convinced that it alone knows the path to salvation."

From the start, I wrote, CPUSA operations were conspiratorial, its activities largely clandestine. I discussed the Communist penetration of the government, of trade unions, of liberal organizations like the Independent Citizens Committee of the Arts, Sciences and Professions. Communists carry "their infection of intrigue and deceit wherever they go." Their methods are "irreconcilable with honest cooperation." With their systematic mendacity and duplicity, "Communists are engaged in a massive attack on the moral fabric of the American left."

I rejected the idea, noisily asserted by congressmen like Martin Dies of Texas, the less talented Joe McCarthy of the day, and John Rankin, a racist demagogue from Mississippi, that Communist infiltration constituted a threat to the republic. "The Communist party is no menace to the right in the U.S. It is a great help to the right because of its success in dividing and neutralizing the left. It is to the American left that Communism presents the most serious danger."

The CPUSA, I concluded, was looking forward to the next depression as its great opportunity. The way to defeat the Communists was "to prevent that depression and to correct the faults and injustices in our present system which make even freedom-loving Americans look wistfully at Russia." Fulfilling the promise of American life would return the CPUSA "to its proper place beside the Buchmanites and Holy Rollers."

*   *   *

I was belabored by conservatives, then and later, for the bit about freedom-loving Americans looking wistfully at the Soviet Union. I also attracted the attention of Westbrook Pegler, a columnist who presented wildly reactionary attitudes in wonderfully entertaining phrases. Searching the index of the Dies Committee reports, he joyfully uncovered damning references to my father in connection with the Spanish Civil War and the National Citizens Political Action Committee. "How young Schlesinger could have overlooked the National Citizens Political Action Committee and his father's implication in it, in his review of the Red menace for *Life*," Pegler exulted, "I cannot, for the life of me, see. Just an absent-minded son of the traditional absent-minded professor."

The Communists lost no time in striking back. On July 30 the *Daily Worker* began a series of anti-Schlesinger columns by Milton Howard. In August the *New Masses* ran articles by John Stuart endearingly titled "Schlesinger: Rankin Historian" and "Schlesinger: Luce Liberal." The *Worker* returned to the attack in September with a series by Samuel Sillen.

The anti-Stalinist left naturally approved. A letter from Dwight Macdonald called the piece "very knowledgeable. A couple of ex-Trotskyites were wondering how in the world you were able to give such an 'inside' picture." Randall Jarrell, the poet and critic, now literary editor of the *Nation*, found it "extremely, *extremely* good." The *Progressive*, the La Follette magazine in Wisconsin, applauded. "The traitors and knaves within the walls," Young Bob La Follette, the stalwart progressive son of the third party candidate in 1924, observed of the Communists, "are always much more dangerous than those without." (In 1946 Wisconsin Communists opposed La Follette's reelection and helped send to the Senate a young Republican named Joe McCarthy.)

But many liberals rested their hope for peace on continuation of the wartime alliance with the Soviet Union. Some, still thinking of Communists as liberals in a hurry, had grown so beguiled by the united front hocus-pocus that they had fallen into the habit of defending in the Soviet Union things they would condemn in any other country. Some liberals even felt tremors of guilt that they lacked the party's ruthless dedication to the cause of humanity. Some felt that anticommunism put one in such distasteful company — Martin Dies, William Randolph Hearst, Mrs. Dilling of *The Red Network.*

Even among old and good friends I sensed disappointment and reproach. My admired teacher F. O. Matthiessen cut me for a while at the Harvard Faculty Club. Premature anti-Communists in the Forties received as much censure from the left as premature antifascists in the Thirties had received from the right.

My paragraph on the Independent Citizens Committee of the Arts, Sciences and Professions embroiled me in an argument with that redoubtable New Deal polemicist, FDR's secretary of the interior, now ICCASP's executive chairman, Harold Ickes. I had written that, while most ICCASP chapters were free from Communist control, the national organization took the Soviet line on foreign policy or else kept quiet. Ickes's response was characteristically rough. He derided my case against ICCASP and concluded: "If Mr. Schlesinger had restricted himself to a philosophical discussion of the Communistic policy in America he might have made a very real contribution but he discredits his whole article by loose and unjustified statements."

In retrospect, I must agree that the article did not cite substantial evidence against ICCASP. But I was essentially right, as Ickes himself soon learned. In September, addressing an ICCASP conference in Chicago, he criticized "the steady and rapid expansion of Russian territory and influence" — and then was surprised to discover, as he later wrote, that "certain persons in charge of the meeting . . . chose not to make copies of the text available to the press." In a few weeks he resigned from ICCASP and thereafter denounced the idea that liberals should work with Communists.

Ickes was a great secretary of the interior, the best ever, and I was sorry never to have met him, though I became friendly with Jane Ickes, his widow, in the Seventies and with his son Harold in the Nineties.

* * *

There were other incidents. I felt that my cause was righteous and that only knaves or fools could defend Stalinism; my temper was not under reliable control; and in those careless days I enjoyed taking the offensive.

I had come back from the war bearing copies of Orwell's *Animal Farm.* When Little, Brown, the publisher of *The Age of Jackson,* gave me a luncheon after my return, I urged the editors to publish this wonderful satiric fable about the Soviet Union. As I talked on, I felt a chill arising, especially from an editor I had not previously met named Angus Cameron. Little, Brown quickly turned *Animal Farm* down.

Upon inquiry I was told that Cameron was a faithful follower of the party line. He was not a party member, but he was in the party's orbit, joining the John Reed Club in Indianapolis, justifying the Stalin-Hitler Pact and so on. "I suppose you could have called me a fellow traveler," he said in his Columbia University oral history (1979). He was also, I gathered, a good editor, if with a weakness for party-line books.

Thinking it over, I decided that I did not wish to be published by a house that had a fellow traveler as editor-in-chief. In December 1947 I sent a rather pompous letter to Alfred McIntyre, the head of Little, Brown: "I would never have signed up in 1939 if one of your leading members had been an active pro-Nazi; and I have no more intention of being published by Little, Brown today when one of your leading members is taking an active part in opposing the democratic effort to check the spread of Soviet totalitarianism." According to Cameron, McIntyre, a nonpolitical soul, told him, "I will not dignify this letter by answering it," and he didn't.

Was I justified in doing this? If Cameron had indeed been a Nazi fellow traveler, I don't suppose anybody would have objected. In retrospect, Stalin probably killed more innocent people than Hitler did, but the defenders of Stalin, unlike the defenders of Hitler, were somehow deemed within the circle of civilized people. This was, I guess, because they were really defending not Stalin's deeds (which they mostly denied) but their own illusions, and those illusions were often generous and hopeful.

Still I have no doubt that I would have been personally unhappy to have a defender of Stalinism as my editor-in-chief, so I did the necessary thing. I only wish I had written McIntyre a less pompous letter. As for Cameron, his continued left-wing activities led half a dozen years later to a forced resignation from Little, Brown. He went into independent publishing, for a while with my Paris antagonist Carl Marzani; then he became an editor with Knopf. He was, as I noted, a good editor, and he no longer imposed his politics, though, according to his oral history, he never changed his conclusion of 1932 "that the contradictions in the system were such that it couldn't be reformed."

About the same time Benny DeVoto, fed up with Little, Brown for other reasons (because, as he wrote to a friend, "nobody in the firm has ever been interested in my books"), was moving over to another

Boston publisher, Houghton Mifflin. He persuaded me to follow him, and I have never regretted it.

* * *

My antipathy toward Communists was increased by a curious situation involving my father-in-law. After Dr. Cannon's death in 1945, the Joint Anti-Fascist Refugee Committee proposed to Mrs. Cannon that a hospital for Spanish republican refugees in Toulouse be renamed in memory of her husband. The Unitarian Service Committee was to supervise its operation. Cornelia Cannon gratefully consented to the use of Dr. Cannon's name.

It soon became evident that the "Dr. Walter B. Cannon Memorial Hospital" was a name adopted by the Varsovie (Warsaw) Hospital in Toulouse purely to raise funds in the United States. Socialist and trade union sources among Toulouse refugees testified that the Varsovie Hospital was Communist-controlled and discriminated against non-Communists as both doctors and patients. In 1948 the Unitarian Service Committee withdrew its support.

Mrs. Cannon then asked the refugee committee to stop using Dr. Cannon's name. The JAFRC ignored her request and continued to invoke Dr. Cannon. Howard Fast, the Communist novelist, in a letter to a protestor, the wife of Percy W. Bridgman, the Nobel Prize physicist, denied that the hospital discriminated against non-Communists, adding: "What if it were Communist-dominated? . . . Isn't it time that intelligent people here in America began to understand that there is no movement so devoted to human life itself as the Communist movement?" (Fast changed his mind in 1956.)

* * *

There were other flare-ups. Agnes Smedley, an American radical who had long supported the Chinese Communists, appeared in Boston. She later reported to a Chinese friend, "I had a fierce and ugly fight with Arthur Schlesinger . . . who told me with fierce anger: 'You whitewash everything the Chinese Communists do — such as the attack on the American Marines at Anping. They lied about that incident, yet you whitewash them.'"

Agnes Smedley responded (still her account) that the Marines had no right to be at Anping or anywhere in China. "If foreign troops were on the soil of the United States, I also would ambush them and kill as many as possible." Schlesinger: "The Communists denied attacking. They lied. There is such a thing as *truth*." Smedley: "You are taking a small truth and putting it above a major truth, which was that the Marines had no right to be there. . . . The guerrillas had as much right to ambush that convoy as the French underground had to ambush German Nazis in France." Schlesinger: "The Communists lied." Smedley, referring to General Marshall's mission to China: "Marshall has lied, by commission and by omission." And so on — a typical conversation of the day.

One incident I recall with genuine regret. In 1946 or 1947 I spoke at a banquet given by some organization in Boston. Another speaker was W.E.B. Du Bois, the eminent black scholar and activist. Du Bois, a strong anti-Communist in the Thirties, had now become a defender of Stalin and the Soviet Union; before his death in 1963, he even joined the Communist party. In my remarks, I seized the occasion to rebuke people who propagated illusions about Stalin and his Russia.

I did not mention Du Bois by name, but he looked both bemused and offended at this implied attack by a smartass kid of twenty-eight on a distinguished man half a century older. I have no doubt that I was right on the substance, but my manners were deplorable. As Gibbon said of Bishop Warburton, "I cannot forgive myself the contemptuous treatment of a man who, with all his faults, was entitled to my esteem."

*   *   *

The 'Cold War' had begun. Herbert Bayard Swope, the once famed journalist and editor, originated the phrase and passed it on to his patron Bernard Baruch in the summer of 1946. Baruch used it in a speech in the spring of 1947. When Walter Lippmann made it the title of a book later that year, it became the ordained name for the rivalry that grimly shadowed the planet for the next forty years.

Looking back from the twenty-first century, recalling the ramshackle and dilapidated Soviet society, new generations may well wonder what all the shouting was about. Now that communism has fallen, in Trotsky's old phrase, into the dustbin of history, why were we so agitated about the Communist threat? Why should the Western democracies ever have been scared by such a paper tiger and patent fraud as the Soviet Union?

Things looked very different in the Forties. The Red Army had played the largest role in the defeat of Nazism. Joseph Stalin was a powerful world leader in command not only of the Soviet Union but of a network of Communist parties around the globe. Victory had given communism an ideological recharge. People forgot Stalin's pact with Hitler. With the Axis states vanquished, the European allies battered and exhausted, the colonial empires in dissolution and the underdeveloped world in tumult, great gaping holes appeared in the structure of world power. War had left the Soviet Union and the United States as the only nations with the military strength, ideological conviction and political will to fill these vacuums of power.

Still, new generations may well wonder why this geopolitical rivalry billowed into a holy war so fanatic and obsessive as to threaten the very survival of life on the planet. This came about, I would suggest, because the two powers were constructed on opposite and profoundly antagonistic principles. They were divided by fundamental disagreements over human rights, individual liberties, the direction of history, the destiny of man.

Roosevelt and Churchill had hoped nonetheless to live at peace with the Soviet Union; but for Stalin, democratic capitalism was by Leninist definition the mortal foe, its continued existence an intolerable threat. With ideological conflict thus piled upon geopolitical rivalry, no one should be surprised by what ensued. The real historical surprise would have been if there had been no Cold War.

*　　*　　*

In the glory days of the Cold War, the two powers, as Henry Kissinger well put it, "behaved like two heavily armed blind men feeling their way around the room, each believing himself in mortal peril from the other whom he assumes to have perfect vision." Each side saw the other as an evil empire. Each attributed to the other a master plan for world domination and diabolical efficiency in the plan's execution.

The master plans were fantasies. Soviet leaders certainly believed that the dialectic of history would one day assure the triumph of communism, just as Western leaders believed that the nature of man and markets would one day assure the triumph of free society. But such pie-in-the-sky hopes were far removed from operational plans. Each side should have known that uncertainty, ignorance, guesswork, are the sidekicks of policy. Yet each ascribed to the other a consistency, foresight and coherence that it should have seen from its own experience was impossible. On each side the military exaggerated the danger from the other in order to increase its own power and budget. As President Kennedy said to Norman Cousins in 1963, "The hard-liners in the Soviet Union and the United States feed on one another."

The two blind men were spurred on by authentic differences in principle, by real and supposed clashes of interest and by a wide range of misperception, misunderstanding and demagoguery. Each undertook for what it honestly saw as defensive reasons actions that the other honestly saw as unacceptably threatening and requiring countermeasures. Each succumbed to the propensity to perceive local conflicts in global terms, political conflicts in moral terms and relative differences in absolute terms. Together, in lockstep, they deepened the Cold War.

This inadvertent collusion implied no moral equivalence. Whatever the parallelism in misconceptions, there remained the profound, the impassable, difference in conceptions between a police tyranny and a free society.

* * *

As we anti-Stalinist liberals saw it, communism was a threat *to* America, not a threat *in* America. In the course of 1946, Stalin, breaking his Yalta declarations on liberated Europe and on Poland, proceeded to consolidate the Soviet grip on Eastern Europe. At the same time, Western Europe was nearing economic collapse, with strong Communist parties in Italy and France waiting in the wings and hoping to be voted into power.

One wondered whether Harry Truman was adequate to the challenge. My first attempt at presidential speechwriting had not improved my view of the new president. Someone at the White House — I now forget who — was a fan of *The Age of Jackson* and asked me to prepare a draft for the new president's Jackson Day address in March. I suffered the ghostwriter's chronic chagrin when only five sentences of my immortal words appeared in the final text. Henry Wallace, the secretary of commerce, the last Roosevelt appointee still in Truman's cabinet, also spoke. "Wallace's speech was better," I wrote to my parents, "except for that wretched passage praising Truman."

Like many liberals (not my parents, however), I regarded Wallace as FDR's heir. If only he were president, I wrote in a special FDR issue of the *New Republic* in April 1946, "the collapse of the New Deal might not have been so complete or so pathetic as it has been under Truman." But Wallace seemed now to be moving in strange directions.

In 1946 the American attitude toward the Soviet Union, heretofore regarded by our British friends as dangerously soft, began to harden. In September Wallace publicly attacked the growing anti-Soviet tendency. Truman, after first appearing to condone Wallace's speech, was soon forced by Secretary of State Byrnes to fire him.

I switched to a plague on both houses. "Truman has put on a performance of incompetence unsurpassed in my memory of U.S. presidents," I wrote to my parents hyperbolically. "Wallace acted pretty foolishly too, but Truman's was the responsibility. As Ed Lahey [of the *Chicago Daily News*] says, 'Government by chowderheads.' God knows what fatuities Wallace will not commit now that he is out. He is a fool. But so is the president."

*   *   *

In the summer Edward Weeks, the editor of the *Atlantic Monthly*, asked me to write a piece about the impending midterm elections. I thought it would be a good idea to visit the important states and test the political atmosphere. Illinois, a pivotal state, was high on my itinerary. The day I was to leave Washington on the overnight train to Chicago (people still traveled on sleepers) I happened to lunch with George Ball. When I told him my assignment, he said, "You must talk to my old friend Adlai Stevenson — he's been staying with us, and he will be on your train tonight. Give me your seat number."

Soon after I settled in my seat and the train was chugging away from Union Station, an agreeable man of medium height, balding head and beguiling smile introduced himself. He suggested a drink. We had more than one, then went to the dining car (no plastic prepared meals then), then adjourned to the club car and talked till well after midnight.

Stevenson had recently returned from London where he was a U.S. delegate to the United Nations Preparatory Commission. In the early Thirties he had joined the mass migration of bright young men to Washington to work for FDR and the New Deal. Returning to law practice in Chicago, the nation's capital of militant isolationism, he became chairman of the Chicago branch of the Committee to Defend America by Aiding the Allies. His cool nerve in defying isolationist thunderbolts hurled by Colonel Robert R. McCormick from the *Tribune* tower impressed Frank Knox of the *Daily News*. When FDR called Knox to Washington to serve as secretary of the Navy, Knox brought Stevenson with him as his special assistant. From there Adlai went to the State Department to assist at the founding conference of the U.N. in San Francisco.

He was forty-six years old. I was utterly delighted by him, his wit, his wide range of reference, his shrewd, slightly cynical insight into people, his belief in high standards of public service. We talked with the easy candor of old friends, and I felt that I had never in my life got to know anyone so well so quickly. Very odd: in subsequent years of close association, I never felt that I had got to know him much better than on that first night. His engaging openness masked a mysterious privacy.

*   *   *

"How We Will Vote" appeared in the *Atlantic*'s October issue. This was the first national election since the death of Roosevelt, the first since the atomic bomb, the first since the end of the war, the first since the increasing sense of irrepressible conflict between East and West. The most grave and consequential issues were posed for judgment. And how were the voters responding? With, I thought, "deep and widespread apathy."

After all, the American people had been through exhausting emotional experiences: the Great Depression, the New Deal, the war. Their generous instincts had had a thorough workout, and those instincts were flagging. "War has always tended to produce the Grants and the Hardings — the administrations characterized by moral indolence and indulged by a people undone by compulsions toward taking it easy." Conservative businessmen and politicians, I thought, were now running both parties, and the party of Franklin D. Roosevelt was heading toward "that no-man's land where in the flickering half-light the donkey is indistinguishable from the elephant."

I was less literary when I spoke at the Frances Sweeney dinner in October. "The Truman Administration," I said, freely plagiarizing a line from British politics, "has all the attributes of a jelly-fish except the sting." Jimmy Byrnes was pursuing "a negative, niggardly policy, principally of checking Russia and doing nothing else." As for Henry Wallace, he "thinks of Russia as a sort of Brook Farm community." One stood for "blind and sterile firmness," the other for "blind and sterile appeasement." To a *New York Post* interviewer in October I called it "a hopeless, feeble administration."

It is hard to remember, now that Harry Truman is (correctly) enshrined as a fighting liberal leader, how despairing liberals were about his first two years in the White House. "Not only is he himself a man of mediocre and limited capacity," I wrote in the *Atlantic* in November, "but, after considerable hiring and firing, he has managed to surround himslf with his intellectual equals."

The political wisecrack of 1946 was: "To err is Truman." In October the Republicans cried, "Had enough?" The voters said yes and in November gave the Republicans both houses of the Eightieth Congress.

*   *   *

In October I had a long talk with Mrs. Roosevelt, now in a state of personal transition. Her husband's death, I believe, had altered her sense of herself and of her obligations. When FDR was alive, she saw her duty as that of advocating principled idealism in the court of the unprincipled idealist who was a master realist. Now that she no longer had FDR to play off against, she began to incorporate within herself the things she had learned from him. Striking a balance between idealism and realism, once reached by compromise between partners, was now the responsibility of the surviving partner alone. Mrs. R. was becoming in these postwar years less and less a visionary, more and more an old pro; a tough old bird indeed. With Henry Wallace and later with Adlai Stevenson, she found herself playing the realist, assuming with them the cautionary role that FDR had so often assumed with her.

"She is quite upset over Wallace," I wrote to my parents, "and feels that he has been misled by bad advisers, particularly Lee Pressman." Pressman had worked for Wallace in the Agricultural Adjustment Administration; he had long been associated with the CPUSA and was now general counsel for the CIO. Mrs. Roosevelt had gone on to describe the ICCASP as "Communist-dominated" and the National Citizens Political Action Committee as "badly infiltrated."

In 1945 the labor leader Sidney Hillman had asked her to head the NCPAC. She investigated, was repelled by the Communist role and declined. "I did not feel I could control the Committee's policies," she explained. She preferred the Union for Democratic Action, now headed by Reinhold Niebuhr, and urged it to maintain its resistance to the united front embrace. The united front, as James Loeb, UDA's national director, used to say, was always more front than united.

But the UDA membership was small and its budget meager. In May 1946 Loeb argued in a letter to the *New Republic* that liberals should not work with Communists in the same political organizations. In a follow-up letter, Roger Baldwin of the American Civil Liberties Union, whose initial sympathy for the communist experiment in Russia had long since been eroded by his dealings with Communists in America, observed that collaboration with secret Communists was "a morally indefensible alliance. It rests on deception. Yet it is the common pattern of Communist operations in liberal circles." As Niebuhr said, "I don't believe in the slogan, 'My country, right or wrong' — particularly when it isn't even my country."

The response encouraged Loeb to wonder whether there might be enough anti-Communist liberals to build a strong national organization with two objectives: to infuse the Truman administration with the spirit of the New Deal, and to liberate the democratic left from Communist manipulation. Mrs. Roosevelt was ready to help. The Republican capture of Congress gave urgent importance to the first objective, the deepening of the Cold War to the second.

*   *   *

I remembered Jim Loeb and the UDA from the great debate in the months before Pearl Harbor, and the *Life* article now led him to ask whether I would join a group planning a conference of the non-Communist left. The group included David Ginsburg, an astute lawyer who had clerked for Justice William O. Douglas and served as the OPA's general counsel; John Edelman of the Textile Workers; the old Schlesinger friend Gardner Jackson; George Weaver, a forceful black organizer from the CIO; and two men destined to make a real difference in my life, Joseph L. Rauh, Jr., and James A. Wechsler.

Joe Rauh was thirty-five years old, a graduate of Harvard College and the Harvard Law School, law clerk to Justice Cardozo and then to Justice Frankfurter, best friends with Phil Graham and Ed Prichard, a lieutenant-colonel on General MacArthur's staff in the Pacific War and, after the liberation of the Philippines, the de facto mayor of Manila. His military service won him the Legion of Merit. A robust, hearty man, he had played basketball at Harvard (Jimmy Wechsler used to say that Joe's experience on losing Harvard basketball teams explained his subsequent sympathy for the underdog) and loved martinis and Kentucky bourbon and the Washington Redskins and steaks and a good time.

He was high-spirited and greathearted and tough-minded and brave and funny and wise. He was a great American patriot who believed profoundly and stubbornly in American democracy, in the Constitution and in the Bill of Rights. He dedicated his life to making the promises of America real for all Americans. He fought for his country in wartime, and he fought for it in peacetime. He enjoyed a good fight and much preferred winning to losing. He laughed a great deal, mostly at himself. *Who's Who in America* invites people to sum up their philosophy of life, and Joe's entry concluded: "Do your best and don't take yourself too seriously." He was antidogmatic and antisentimental, and he was not wobbled by the thought of power. An unrepentant New Dealer, he embodied the old, realistic, exuberant American liberal tradition — liberalism without mawkishness, without self-pity, without guilt, without illusion, but with zest in the struggle and unquenchable hope for all humanity.

Jimmy Wechsler was a stocky, lively man of twenty-nine. He had edited the *Spectator* at Columbia and after college was briefly a member of the Young Communist League. His had been the articles that impressed me a decade earlier as the only literate feature of the American Student Union's *Student Advocate.* Jimmy had long since broken with the Communists to work first on *PM* and then, in revolt against its communist leanings, on the *New York Post,* a very different paper under Dorothy Schiff from Rupert Murdoch's paper of the same name at the end of the century.

Jimmy was first of all a newspaperman. His style in the profession was a happy mingling of modes of the Twenties and the Thirties. There was more than a little in him of *The Front Page* — the hard-drinking, hard-smoking (alas, cigarettes were to kill him), jaunty, iconoclastic scribe who revels in the comedy of life and views authority with sardonic skepticism. One recalls Jimmy at his desk, writing nonstop, a bottle of bourbon by his side and the radio blaring out the baseball game. But, while we were all fascinated by the cynical Twenties, we had grown up in the ardent Thirties. FDR and the New Deal had endowed us as young men with a commitment to social justice that in Jimmy's case never faltered or faded. His combination of the irreverence of the Twenties with the passion of the Thirties made him not only a brilliant journalist but an adorable man.

Liberalism often tends to be a solemn creed, or, when not solemn, sentimental, or, too often, both. Jimmy was mistrustful of sentimentality and incapable of solemnity. He argued the liberal case not only with lucid intelligence and rushing eloquence but with sparkling wit.

I don't want to overdo the importance of humor. Still, merry liberals are a good deal more palatable than righteous liberals. Joe and Jimmy both had an irrepressible sense of the absurdities of life, and humor eased the tensions of politics without cutting the nerve of responsibility. Working with them was the greatest fun. I loved them both. And both, it should be added, had, and kept, bright and delightful wives, Olie Westheimer Rauh and Nancy Frankel Wechsler. And both were inveterate wearers of bow ties.

* * *

The liberal split was crystalizing. In the last week of 1946, the two popular front organizations ICCASP and NCPAC merged to create the

Progressive Citizens of America. Henry Wallace, now editor of the *New Republic*, spoke at the convention and was plainly PCA's choice for the presidency in 1948.

His fellow New Dealer Harold Ickes was not impressed. As he wrote me early in January 1947, "I have felt for some time that Henry Wallace should not be permitted to range all over the universe plucking and sticking, in halo-like form, the bright flowers that he preferred and which he seemed to think adorned him in particular." In his newspaper column, Ickes informed the PCA that "the cornerstone of the organization should have been a stern injunction that no Communist or sympathizer with Communism would be admitted to membership."

A week after the birth of the PCA, Jim Loeb's troops met at the Willard Hotel in Washington. The turnout was impressive — Eleanor Roosevelt, Reinhold Niebuhr, Elmer Davis, Leon Henderson, Wilson Wyatt, a former mayor of Louisville and more recently Truman's housing expediter, Hubert Humphrey, the eloquent young mayor of Minneapolis, John Kenneth Galbraith, Chester Bowles, FDR Jr., Walter White of the National Association for the Advancement of Colored People. From the press came Barry Bingham, Marquis Childs, Stewart Alsop and Jimmy Wechsler and from the labor movement Walter Reuther of the United Auto Workers, David Dubinsky of the Ladies Garment Workers, James B. Carey of the Electrical Workers, Emil Rieve of the Textile Workers. Elmer Davis, chairing the conference, surveyed the room and said, "This crowd looks very much like the United States government-in-exile." The new organization was christened Americans for Democratic Action. Leon Henderson and Wilson Wyatt were elected co-chairmen.

I was particularly impressed by two men I had not met before. One was Reinhold Niebuhr. The impassioned preacher in the pulpit turned out to be direct, unassuming and approachable in the corridors — wise, trenchant, erudite, yet disarmingly open to the views of others and full of humor and humanity. He was unaffected, high-minded and generous-hearted, spontaneous in his enthusiasm and in his (occasional) wrath, endlessly curious about ideas and people, never pompous or overbearing. An unforced humility always underlay his polemical vigor.

The other was Walter Reuther, thirty-nine years old, the new president of the Auto Workers. He was a trim, compact man, neatly dressed, impersonal in manner but with an engaging smile, easy affability, vast self-confidence and a wonderful fluency of speech. He combined first-class organizing ability with evangelical idealism. He had a taste for power and relish in using it. He had a taste for rhetoric as well and a relish in using that. "Our watchword," he told the conference in a generally electrifying speech, "must not be back to the New Deal but forward from the New Deal." His social vision, while rooted in the labor movement, embraced ideas that would benefit all Americans.

ADA and PCA were in substantial agreement on domestic issues, but they disagreed on qualifications for membership. ADA rejected "any association with Communism or sympathizers with communism as completely as we rejected any association with fascists or their sympathizers. Both are hostile to the principles of freedom and democracy on which this Republic has grown great." PCA, on the other hand, welcomed "all progressive men and women in our nation, regardless of . . . political affiliation." The real difference between the two organizations, commented Ickes, "is that the PCA lacked the courage and vision to draw a sharp line as to Communism." And the admission of Communists moved PCA toward the Soviet side in the Cold War.

Squeamish liberals charged ADA with 'red-baiting.' Max Lerner wrote to Mrs. Roosevelt in that vein. "The American Communists," she stoutly replied, "seem to have succeeded very well in jeopardizing whatever the liberals work for. Therefore, to keep them out of policy-making and staff positions seems to be very essential even at the price of being called red-baiters."

Leon Henderson gave a party for new Democratic members of Congress. At one point a young fellow who appeared to Jim Loeb about fifteen years old came in the door. No one seemed to know him, and he had to introduce himself: "I'm Congressman Kennedy of Massachusetts." Though he maintained friendly relations with ADA, Kennedy did not join then or later. A Hollywood actor did join, however, and on October 25, 1947, Loeb wrote him, "It was an encouraging experience to have had a chance to talk to you and to know there are people in your position who share so completely a liberal point of view." The letter began "Dear Ronnie."

*　　*　　*

On February 13, 1947, the associate publisher of the *New Republic* sent me an invitation "to lunch here at the office, with Mr. Wallace and some of the other editors, the next time you are in New York." We agreed on a date, but when I arrived at the *New Republic* office the next week, I was told that Wallace had an engagement and would join us later. Present at the lunch were Michael Straight, the magazine's owner, and several editors — the veteran journalist Bruce Bliven (his autobiography was entitled *Five Million Words Later*), my Harvard classmate Teddy White, my OWI colleague Hank Brennan and the writers William Harlan Hale and Penn Kimball.

I had hardly sat down when Teddy White said, "What we want to find out is what ADA has against the *New Republic*." The conversation rapidly turned to the question of collaboration with Communists. I reiterated my views that all the Communists did was to corrupt and immobilize the American left. Bliven, White and Kimball responded that the Communist question was not just an American issue; it had to be considered in light of the total world situation. "From everything we can gather," Kimball said, "ADA is obsessed with the Communist problem to the neglect of all the great fascist and war-making forces which are the real enemy of liberals."

Teddy White then formulated the *New Republic*'s position. "We believe," he said, "that the present U.S. policy toward the U.S.S.R. menaces the U.S.S.R. more and is more provocative than the present U.S.S.R. policy toward the U.S." (It occurred to me that Teddy was unduly extrapolating from his Chinese experience.) "The most important thing in the world," said Bruce Bliven, "is to avoid war. What is more important?" I remarked that in 1941 he had thought other things more important than avoiding war. "If you really mean that," Bliven said, furious, "you must be in favor of a preventive war." I said rather angrily that it was a hell of a note if a liberal could not question Soviet policy without being accused of favoring preventive war.

Henry Wallace arrived in the midst of this discussion. He was fifty-nine years old, and very gray, had a potbelly and was inarticulate and uncommunicative. The imminence of the Third World War seemed to prey on his mind to the exclusion of everything else. "His comments were ignorant and doctrinaire," I wrote in a memorandum to Wilson Wyatt and Leon Henderson. "His emotions, however, were compelling, and his bashful charm remains." I came away feeling that Wallace's emotions so dominated the *New Republic* staff that any meeting of minds with ADA would be very difficult.

The *New Republic*'s position, as I summed it up, was that the "war party" (as Bliven and the others kept calling the administration) was trying to whip up public opinion in favor of the Third World War. Attacks on American Communists or talk about the "Communist problem" (which wasn't in their view much of a problem) only strengthened the war party. If you expressed concern about Soviet suppression of political and intellectual freedom, you were helping the war party. Anti-Stalinism was per se warmongering. ADA was thus accelerating the drift toward war. (Commenting on a person who thought, if war came, those who criticized communism would be responsible, Eleanor Roosevelt observed, "Letting the Communists do whatever they wish to do in this country doesn't seem to me to be the way to avoid war.")

Michael Straight took curiously little part, sitting through the discussion, as I reported to Wyatt and Henderson, with a look of "profound dejection" on his face. I thought him "obviously unhappy" about the magazine's political tendencies. I did not know then about his own Communist background at Cambridge, but his firsthand knowledge of Soviet espionage might well have persuaded him that the ADA attitude had its points.

*　　*　　*

On March 12, 1947, President Truman forced the foreign policy issue when he called for emergency aid to help a Greek government besieged by Communist guerrillas and to strengthen Turkish resistance to Soviet pressure. Senator Arthur Vandenberg of Michigan, an indispensable Republican ally, advised him that the only way to get a Greek-Turkish aid bill through Congress was to scare the hell out of the country.

This Truman proceeded to do. His picture of the crisis was, in the words of Dean Acheson, his undersecretary of state, "clearer than truth" and resulted in what was immediately christened the Truman Doctrine: "It must be the policy of the United States to support free peoples who are resisting attempted subjugation by armed minorities or outside pressures."

While ADA supported aid to Greece and Turkey, many of us flinched at the global rhetoric that seemed to commit us far beyond the immediate issue. Truman's brave but vague language could be read as pledging the republic to an unlimited crusade in which it would welcome as allies all anti-Soviet states, no matter how corrupt or dictatorial. Some in the administration, notably the Soviet experts George Kennan and Chip Bohlen, tried in vain to tone down the message. Walter Lippmann worried influentially about the vista of unlimited and worldwide commitment.

Henry Wallace predictably denounced the whole idea and soon carried his denunciations on a speaking tour of Western Europe.

Kingsley Martin and Richard Crossman of the *New Statesman* had issued the invitation to England, and Martha Dodd Stern, the fellow-traveling daughter of the historian William E. Dodd, FDR's ambassador to Nazi Germany, had secretly arranged with French leftists like Pierre Cot to welcome Wallace to Paris.

The trip caused one of those foolish Washington agitations. Congressmen fulminated about the Logan Act, never applied since its passage in 1798. Senator J. William Fulbright thought Wallace's speeches sounded as if they had been written in the Kremlin. Jim Forrestal proposed that his passport be lifted. The administration ignored these helpful suggestions.

Joe Alsop and I sent a joint letter to the *Times* of London affirming Wallace's right to travel and to orate but rejecting any thought that he was carrying out FDR's foreign policy. Wallace, we said, has become "a lay figure, very useful by reason of his past titles and present undeniable charm" to "the small but active and well-organized group of American Soviet sympathizers."

Someone showed the letter to Mrs. Roosevelt, who, without mentioning that one of the signers was her cousin, gently spanked us in her "My Day" column, remarking that even "these two brilliant young journalists" could not be sure what her husband's policies would be today. She was ready, however, to speak for herself. After watching Soviet attempts to tie up the United Nations, she concluded, in another "My Day," that the Kremlin wanted to bring about a mood in this country "which will force our government to abandon all interest in Europe." Once the Americans withdraw, the Soviets feel sure that "they can, in one way or another, control the whole of Europe."

Charles Wintour kept me informed about Wallace's British tour. One of the *New Statesman* circle replied to a criticism that Wallace didn't think very clearly, "Ah, but he feels so clearly." Charles was not impressed: "I can't conceive why you are so worked up about Wallace, an obviously incompetent politician." Dick Crossman, a sponsor of the trip, told me in London in September 1948, "I can't make up my mind whether Wallace is a crook or a fool — probably something of both."

*　　*　　*

The rhetorical ambiguity of the Truman Doctrine remained disturbing, and ADA had its quota of doubters. But doubts were laid to rest with General Marshall's call on June 5, 1947, at the Harvard commencement, for American aid in the economic reconstruction of Europe.

The CPUSA promptly condemned the Marshall Plan as a "cold-blooded scheme of American monopolists to establish their ruthless domination over harassed world humanity." Four days after Marshall's speech, Wallace said in Newark that the United States had become "the center of world reaction" and that "at the present rate of progress it will be less than a decade before Americans start praising Hitler and Mussolini as heroes who prepared the way for us to fight Russia."

But to most of us the Marshall Plan seemed precisely the kind of affirmative policy required for both the revival of Europe and the containment of Soviet power. Battle lines were drawn ever more tightly in the liberals' civil war.

21

Alarums and Excursions

I DO NOT WANT to leave the impression that I spent all my time in Washington trying to rescue American liberalism from the Red menace. This was a worthy enterprise, and I quite enjoyed the accompanying controversies. But there were other things in life.

The Schlesinger family was growing. On November 19, 1946, flying back from New York to take Marian to the hospital in Washington, I became a father for the third time. We named our second daughter Christina, in fond memory of the Garbo movie. And my period as a free lance in Washington was drawing to an end. In September 1947 I was due to take up the appointment at Harvard. Meanwhile I rejoiced in the opportunity to write about a variety of issues and people (and also, with a growing family, to make more money in 1947 than Harvard would pay me in 1948).

My next assignment for *Fortune*— the Supreme Court of the United States — attracted as a way of expediting my James Parton quest to talk to significant New Dealers. And of course an American historian found it fascinating for its own sake. "Scarcely any political question arises in the United States," said Tocqueville, "that is not resolved, sooner or later, into a judicial question." The history of the United States has been bound up in the Constitution, and the Constitution, as Chief Justice Charles Evans Hughes had put it, "is what the judges say it is." Yet judges say contradictory things and argue furiously among themselves. Every great justice has put his own interpretation on the Constitution — and has been attacked for it. The Supreme Court has been the stage for great central dramas of American history.

And what a cast the Court presented in 1946! The Nine Old Men who had tried to outlaw the New Deal in the Thirties had long since gone. It was now a Roosevelt Court. Four of the FDR justices — Hugo Black, Felix Frankfurter, William O. Douglas and Robert H. Jackson — were brilliant and histrionic figures. Frank Murphy was less brilliant but amply histrionic. Stanley Reed and Wiley Rutledge were capable and colorless moderates; so was Harold Burton, the single Republican and Truman's first appointment.

Roosevelt's justices agreed on the New Deal, but they now sharply disagreed on judicial questions. Moreover, Chief Justice Harlan Stone had died in April, and an unseemly quarrel had broken out over the succession. FDR had given Justice Jackson to understand that he would be next in line for chief. But FDR was dead. When Truman named Fred Vinson as chief justice in June, Jackson, absent as chief prosecutor in the Nuremberg war crimes trial, attributed his rejection to Justice Black's opposition and issued a bitter public statement criticizing Black's participation in a case involving a former law partner. Truman commented, "The Supreme Court has really made a mess of itself."

*   *   *

The Court had begun to settle down by the time I began my round of interviews three months later. The interviews were off the record, but the justices were discreet anyway, as they should have been.

Frankfurter was of course the justice I knew best — in fact, the only one I knew at all, save for casual meetings with Douglas and Vinson at Joe Alsop's dinners. Felix was a pal of my parents; he had been kind to me in Washington and was fond of Marian. My sense of what he was about was increased by close friendship with three favorite pupils at Harvard Law School who had become three of his first four law clerks at the Court, Joe Rauh, Ed Prichard and Phil Graham. Felix was effervescent, erudite, challenging and affectionate, given to gusts of enthusiasm or outrage. Isaiah Berlin spoke of "the golden shower of intellectual and emotional generosity that was poured forth before his friends." As a teacher, he delighted in irreverent young men. The early Frankfurter clerks, a high-spirited and iconoclastic bunch, took full advantage of their license to challenge their master.

Without children of his own, Felix found surrogates in his protégés. On the Court, he became more conservative, more possessive, more insistent on agreement. Some among his bright young men came to feel that they had to break with him in order to live their own lives. In 1975, after the publication of the Frankfurter diaries, Prich recalled in a letter to me Mrs. Mark Howe's opinion that Felix was an intellectual and spiritual vampire sucking the blood of his disciples. "While I must agree that there is some truth in this contention," Prich wrote, "it is also true that he, at the same time, pumped their blood full of life, giving oxygen, so that it was really Felix's giving and Felix's taking away." Though nothing ever interrupted their affection for him, Prich and Joe Rauh felt, as did Ben Cohen, that Frankfurter's reputation would have been higher had he never gone on the Court.

When I interviewed Felix, he talked about the functions of the Court and the dangers of judicial lawmaking. He refused to speak about personalities, but he did call my attention to a letter written by Morrison R. Waite, a late-nineteenth-century chief justice, animadverting on a fellow justice who hankered after the White House. The unspoken application was to Bill Douglas.

The other interview I particularly remember was with Hugo Black. He was most urbane and cordial, but he was the only justice who could not be inveigled into discussing the Court at all. He had made it his practice, he said, never to talk to anyone about the Court. (When I told this to Frankfurter, he noted in his diary, "I did not tell Arthur Schlesinger that that, of course, is not true, that in the case of partisans of his, he talked with considerable freedom to get his self-righteous interpretation of his actions into circulation.")

Instead of holding forth on judicial questions, Black said disarmingly that he had so much enjoyed *The Age of Jackson* that he had sent copies to several friends. The only thing he had not liked in the book, he added, was my portrayal of Andrew Johnson. Black considered Johnson "a great man," had read everything he could about him and had even made a pilgrimage to his grave in Greeneville, Tennessee. I had praised Johnson's concern for farmers and workingmen, his hostility to the planter aristocracy, his determination to rise in life and his personal courage. But I had also emphasized Johnson's implacability and his "combination of envy, suspicion and brutality."

As he talked, it suddenly occurred to me that similar criticisms had been made of Black and that on some level he identified with Andrew Johnson. "Black has come far from humble beginnings," I wrote in *Fortune.* "He has had to fight hard for everything he has got — in politics, in education, and in life — and the experience has left its mark, not at all on his manners, but on his ideas and his will." I also said that "his clear, driving intelligence hits legal fundamentals. He is an honorable person, not given to petty politicking."

Bill Douglas, I remember, was wary and not very helpful, and I don't recall much about the others. Chief Justice Vinson was too busy to see me. I did, however, call on the only living ex–chief justice. Charles Evans Hughes, now eighty-five years old, was, I wrote to my father, "very friendly and nice," an erect, well-preserved, affable and cagey old man. "He can spot a leading question a mile off," and, though Hughes would make no comment about the present Court, he did talk a bit about FDR's fight with his own Court.

I also interviewed legal scholars who covered each decision day as avidly as drama critics covered openings: Reed Powell, Paul Freund and Henry Hart of the Harvard Law School, Fred Rodell of the Yale Law School, ex-clerks like Tom Corcoran who had clerked for Holmes and David Ginsburg who had clerked for Douglas as well as Rauh, Prichard and Graham.

* * *

"The Supreme Court: 1947" came out in the January 1947 issue of *Fortune.* My thesis was that the argument dividing the New Deal justices — Black and Douglas versus Frankfurter and Jackson — was at bottom an argument between two theories of the way judges should decide cases. Black and Douglas, I said, stood for "judicial activism," Frankfurter and Jackson for "judicial self-restraint." I got the idea, and perhaps the terms too, from Reed Powell, but I believe that the *Fortune* piece first put the terms into general circulation.

The salient distinction was the activists' addiction to results, based on the philosophy of 'legal realism,' and the self-restrainers' more traditional addiction to process. The Black-Douglas group, I wrote, saw the Court as an instrument to achieve social justice, especially for the otherwise unprotected in society; the Frankfurter-Jackson group saw it as an instrument to permit legislatures to achieve the results, for better or worse, that a majority might wish (except when statutes blocked the channels of self-correction).

As a historian, I traced the contrast back to Brandeis, who was inclined to read his social views into the Constitution, and Holmes, who believed that if his fellow citizens wanted to go to hell, he saw nothing in the Constitution to stop them. It was also, I suggested, an argument between the Yale and Harvard Law schools — an oversimplified point, perhaps a parochial one, but there was a little something to it.

A half century later the article seems to me analytical, measured and quite well written. I tried to state each side as fairly as I could, though I came out in the end for judicial self-restraint. The memory of the judicial activism practiced in favor of business by the Nine Old Men only a decade before was still vivid in mind, and one did not want to make activism the routine philosophy of the Court.

* * *

I was surprised by the ferocity of the ensuing controversy. Part of it came from my personal characterizations of the justices. Phil Graham, who had clerked for Stanley Reed before he went on to Frankfurter, told me that Reed was much hurt by a picture caption describing him as "nice, dull, friendly." I don't remember that I wrote the captions; in any event, I must have cleared them. By "dull" I meant "boring"; Reed evidently thought I meant "dull-witted."

Frank Murphy was particularly irritated. "His peculiarities of temperament," I had written, "give him a semi-mystical urge toward isolated positions. . . . His egotism is vast and somewhat messianic." While applauding "his devoted concern for individual rights," I noted that his legal competence was questioned more often than that of any other justice. When *Fortune* sent Murphy an enlarged print of his photograph, he indignantly returned it, saying that it "would serve only as an unwanted reminder of the highly distorted and inaccurate article." The author, he said, had seen fit to attack his character after a very brief interview. "I am left with the impression that the attack was conceived beforehand or was inspired by others."

The last phrase doubtless referred to Frankfurter, who now took action in self-defense. "Young Arthur Schlesinger's article in *Fortune* has apparently greatly disturbed Brother Murphy," Frankfurter said in a note to his fellow justices. ". . . I should like all the brethren to see the letter I have written him."

Murphy had told Frankfurter that "a member of this Court" had said that Frankfurter had seen the article in manuscript. Felix stoutly, and altogether correctly, denied this. "Young Arthur's father," he explained, "is one of my close friends at Harvard." When young Arthur asked to see him about the *Fortune* piece, he had made it clear that he would not speak about the Court's work or about its members. At no stage of the writing had he ever seen a draft. Later, Felix wrote me and others, implausibly, that he had not even read the published article.

When I first saw him after publication, Felix was entirely friendly, though he said to my Marian (his wife was also a Marion) that the article, which he insisted to me as late as March he still had not read, was filled with inaccuracies. A few weeks later he invited me to lunch at the Court. His remarks about the article, I wrote to my father, "indicate that he will be upset by anything which suggests that he and Jackson are not perfect; but he got the bile out of his system and became very genial."

As for Murphy, I was even told (unreliably) that he wanted to sue me for libel, though I can't imagine what I wrote that was libelous, nor can I imagine that such a doughty champion of the First Amendment would try to prevent the free expression of opinion. My unreliable informant was Eliot Janeway, a brilliant busybody, close to Bill Douglas. Constituting himself a one-man protection gang for Douglas, Janeway fell upon me one day in the *Fortune* office, charged that I was probably a Frankfurter stooge and, if I was, I must be prepared for war to the death. He was melodramatic and threatening.

I tried conciliation, which Janeway unscrupulously spread about as capitulation. "Young Schlesinger and I have had what at Yale is called a manly talk," he wrote to Herbert Solow. It would be interesting after the talk, he continued, to find in the piece "a paragraph Schlesinger would now defend with any degree of confidence." Schlesinger is "willing to admit that the complexities his piece has wandered into are too much for him."

I was willing to admit no such thing. Del Paine sent the correspondence to me, saying that Janeway was "broadcasting the insulting sentiments herein disclosed" and that I had better "set the record straight and get Janeway to cease his character assassination." I replied that it was all the consequence of my misguided effort to be pleasant. "Of course I never disowned the piece. We never even talked about the main thesis." To Solow I wrote, "In our whole god damn conversation we never discussed the legal issues." Paine replied, "You say you are 'somewhat fed up'; I don't blame you. Write it off as the cost of some graduate work in certain tired New Deal political tactics."

All things, or at least many things, blow over. Later Eliot Janeway, an entertaining fellow, and I became pretty good friends, and his wife, Elizabeth, an excellent novelist, and his son Michael, a thoughtful journalist, really good friends.

*   *   *

An infinitely more impressive dissent was filed by Judge Jerome Frank of the Second Circuit Court. Frank, who had worked with Douglas on the Securities and Exchange Commission, was an influential legal philosopher. His *Law and the Modern Mind* is a classic of legal realism. The *Fortune* article, he wrote, "contains much that is excellent," but the desire to depict a sharp ideological antithesis had resulted in grave distortions.

Frank challenged the antithesis, citing a number of cases in which self-restrainers took activist positions and activists invoked self-restraint. On one level he was quite right. 'Activism' and 'self-restraint' were ideal types. The distinction between them sometimes became murky when applied to concrete cases. He also objected to my suggestion that the debate was between the Harvard and Yale Law schools, pointing out quite correctly that, well before Yale had succumbed to legal realism, Holmes, Frankfurter (while a professor) and Reed Powell had propagated the view that Supreme Court justices were largely guided by their social and economic predilections. He took strong objection to my notion that his friend Douglas had a "disruptive personality." His tone throughout was courteous.

I had meant, I responded, that Douglas had the reputation of a "disruptive personality." I noted that Reed Powell of Harvard and Fred Rodell of Yale had read the piece in manuscript without rejecting the Harvard-Yale contrast. I dealt with other points that Frank had raised and concluded that I sometimes looked back nostalgically to the comfort of writing about the age of Jackson, with all the characters dead and all emotions spent.

Frank replied in a six-page, single-spaced letter reiterating his difficulty with my too-sharp demarcation between activism and self-restraint. His own feeling, he said, was that, while there were real differences in intellectual positions among the justices, needless disturbances had been caused by personality clashes. He had feared my article would only aggravate these personal tensions. "If you would bother to investigate," he concluded, "you would find that my fears were justified."

After the letter was written, he added in a postscript that he had just spent an evening with Justice Black.

> He likes you and admires your Jackson book. You would, he thought, by your writings contribute much to the desirable development of this country. Your point of view in your article on the Court was "naive," and probably ascribable to your inexperience in this field, with a consequent inability to appraise accurately misinformation coming to you from prejudiced sources. He had become so accustomed to adverse, unfair criticism that he ceased to resent it. . . . He did, however, regret your unfair criticism of Douglas.

Jerry Frank was an accomplished, voluble and goodhearted man with far-ranging intellectual interests. We later became good friends.

"I feel badly about the Supreme Court repercussions," I wrote to my parents. "Everyone is apparently mad at me — Douglas very hurt and very mad, because he thought I was on his side; Black, resigned; Murphy, furious and wanting to sue me for libel; Jackson, mad; Frankfurter, annoyed because he is credited with having inspired the piece; Reed, annoyed because of the way he was brushed off; etc. It is much simpler to write about dead people."

I wrote to Jerry Frank that the "fantastic over-reaction" was "the best evidence I know of the steam-heated and semi-neurotic atmosphere on the Court."

*   *   *

Others thought better of the piece. Soon after it came out Phil and Kay Graham had us to dinner. The Vinsons and the Frankfurters were among the guests. The chief justice was most amiable and thanked me for being so "generous" toward a newcomer to the Court. In a broadly favorable, or at least hopeful, sketch of Vinson, I had, however, written that it would be hard for him to cope intellectually with men like Black and Frankfurter; "his mind does not move fast in the same way." In the course of the evening, Felix made a verbal slip. Vinson corrected him and turning to me, quick as a flash, said with good humor, "I guess his mind wasn't moving so fast that time."

Reed Powell wrote of the piece, "I was delighted with it beyond words." Judge Herbert Goodrich of the Third Circuit: "a beautful piece of work." Fred Rodell of Yale, a Douglas man: "By and large it is an excellent and perceptive job." Dean Louis Jaffe of the University of Buffalo Law School, a Brandeis law clerk: "Your *Fortune* article was splendid. . . . You do a real service I think in attempting to bridge the differences in the Court." (When I showed Jaffe's letter to Frankfurter, he underlined that last sentence and scrawled in the margin: "How silly that is!")

In 1958 Professor Sam Krislov of the University of Oklahoma made a study of the way political science textbooks were handling the Supreme Court. "In book after book," he wrote, "the discussion . . . was a rather close paraphrase of an article by Arthur Schlesinger, Jr., which had appeared in *Fortune* magazine some time ago. . . . Fully half of the textbooks had been treating the Court in the terms set by Schlesinger's article."

Looking back from the twenty-first century, one sees the same old issues at play on the Supreme Court stage today — but with a considerably less stellar cast.

*   *   *

While *Fortune* was setting the cat among the pigeons on the Supreme Court, I was engaged in a different venture. *Collier's,* the rival of the *Saturday Evening Post* as the weekly general-interest magazine for middle-class families, asked me to do a piece on Senator Robert A. Taft of Ohio. The notion appealed. Bob Taft — "Mr. Republican" — was the dominating Republican intellect in Congress, at least in domestic policy. As the son of the former president and chief justice, he was the living representative of an honorable conservative dynasty. He was also the favorite target of the New Dealers, who had made him the symbol of archreaction. Exploring the Taft personality and tradition seemed a fine way to discover what American conservatism was all about.

Taft was indeed deeply conservative by instinct and temperament. He had a Donald Duck reaction to new ideas. "Dumb" and "stupid" were favorite adjectives when he was confronted by New Dealish proposals. All this was accompanied by a lawyer's intelligence, hard and logical, and by a lawyer's facility at constructing or tearing down a case. "He has the best mind in Washington," said Paul Porter, "until he makes it up."

I talked to senators, reporters and Republicans about Taft and then in early November went out to Cincinnati, where I spent two mornings and an afternoon with Taft himself and the rest of the time with veterans of the city's political wars like my father's friend Murray Seasongood, a two-term mayor. Taft was then fifty-seven years old, straightforward and prosaic, neatly dressed with rimless glasses and receding hairline. Determination, obstinacy and a sense of rectitude that stopped just short of self-righteousness were stamped on his face. His manner in conversation was without guile. He jingled coins or keys in his hand, smiled in an oddly boyish way and said what he thought. His comfortable house on Indian Hill had big, airy rooms, a superb view and a stubborn lack of distinction.

To my surprise, I found that I liked him. "Taft talked very freely and honestly about practically everything," I told my parents. "He is a shy, graceless man, but has no front at all and has many winning qualities." I also found that underneath a dogmatic facade he was, up to a point, what later generations would call a compassionate conservative. Though his faith in organized business and his abhorrence of organized labor were indestructible, and though he deeply believed that the function of the opposition was to oppose, he had come to acknowledge in certain circumstances an affirmative role for government. "If the free enterprise system does not do its best to prevent hardship and poverty," he said, ". . . it will find itself superseded by a less progressive system that does. Our policy is to maintain a floor under subsistence, education, medical care, and housing. . . . to give to all a minimum standard of decent living." His theory was to bring this about through federally financed, state-managed programs. It all sounded to me a lot like a conservative version of the welfare state.

How had he got that way? "When someone proposes the appropriation of fifty million dollars for some worthy cause," Bob La Follette told me, "Taft's snap reaction is, 'Outrageous. Nonsense. It can't be done.' But get him tied up in a subcommittee and rub his nose in the facts. His automatic negative reaction melts away under the pressure of evidence." As I wrote in *Collier's*, "His saving grace is a clear-cut logical intelligence and a basic respect for facts, which undercut his own impulses toward dogmatism."

He had demonstrated this by changing his mind about federal aid for housing and for education. Initially hostile, he looked into the housing problem and concluded, "You don't get decent housing from the free-enterprise system." The federal government must therefore step in and do the job, and he joined Senator Robert Wagner, the great New York liberal, in proposing a public housing bill. He went through a similar double take on education, finally deciding that the federal government must underwrite the school system in order to guarantee every child an indispensable minimum of education. John W. Bricker, Ohio's other senator, was reported to have said, "I hear that the Socialists have gotten to Bob Taft."

He felt, Taft told me, that he had to steer the Republican party on a middle path between Harold Stassen, "basically a New Dealer," and Bricker, "or rather the people around Bricker, who are reactionaries." Bricker was central casting's idea of a senator. Alice Longworth called him "an honest Harding." John Gunther memorably wrote of him that year in *Inside U.S.A.*, "Intellectually, he is a nothingness, like interstellar space — a vast vacuum occasionally crossed by homeless wandering clichés."

Bricker had been the Republican vice-presidential candidate in 1944, and some spoke of him for the top of the ticket in 1948. Taft seemed not yet to have decided whether to try for the nomination himself or to back Bricker, who he thought had more popular appeal and whom he was confident he could control. However, Taft's entourage assured me that by 1948 Bricker would have eliminated himself by a woeful performance in the Senate.

Taft was still an unregenerate isolationist. Before Pearl Harbor, he had opposed neutrality act repeal, selective service, the 1940 transfer of destroyers to beleaguered Britain, lend-lease and draft extension. In 1941 he had even advocated a negotiated peace "with Hitler domination on the continent." When I talked to him, he was still not sure that we would have been worse off had we stayed out. Since the war's end, he had voted against the Bretton Woods agreements and the 1946 British loan. But I did not make much of his foreign policy in the article. I took Taft as the Republican voice on domestic affairs; Arthur Vandenberg would set the Republican course abroad. In his talks to me, Taft's references to Vandenberg were uniformly friendly.

The article appeared in *Collier's* on February 22, 1947, under the title "His Eyes Have Seen the Glory" (a *Collier's* title; mine was "Old Sobersides"). For a change, my piece provoked no controversy beyond a feeling on the part of some New Dealers that I had exaggerated the extent of Taft's evolution. "Sure, Taft has progressed," muttered one Washingtonian, "but the progress is only from James A. Garfield to William McKinley."

*   *   *

The Taft article led to a new proposal from *Collier's*. Henry Morgenthau, Jr., had accumulated a "diary" of more than eight hundred bound volumes during his service as Roosevelt's secretary of the treasury. It was not a diary in the usual sense of the word — that is, a personal record of the day's or week's experiences. There was some of this, but it was mostly a grab bag from the secretary's daily In and Out boxes: letters, memoranda, minutes of meetings, transcripts of telephone conversations, government documents, press cuttings. Of all the cabinet members, Morgenthau had been the closest personally to Roosevelt. A separate series called the "Presidential Diary" contained invaluable reports of FDR's table talk as set down by Morgenthau immediately after their frequent meetings.

The Morgenthau diaries constituted both a rich resource and a puzzling challenge. How to shape this chaos of raw material into a continuous narrative? *Collier's* had contracted with the former secretary for a series of articles derived from the diaries; Allan Nevins had tried his hand at reducing the hodgepodge into a rational sequence of pieces, but the result had satisfied neither Morgenthau nor the peppery editor of *Collier's*, Walter Davenport. The series had been advertised; the deadline was approaching; and I was brought in at the last moment in the hope that something could be put together.

I specified that the articles were to be signed only by Morgenthau; "in this way I can devote myself more equably to expressing his viewpoint." I asked them to take on Barbara Kerr as a research assistant. And: "there should be an escape clause, of course, so that Mr. Morgenthau can lay me off if I begin to drive him nuts, and vice versa." I was to be paid $2000 an article — a most appetizing sum (about $20,000 in the depreciated dollar of the early twenty-first century). I wanted to do this not just to build the family exchequer but to advance my Parton-like quest into the inner history of the New Deal.

Morgenthau was then only fifty-six years old, but he seemed much older. It never occurred to me throughout our acquaintance to trade on New Deal informalities and call him anything but "Mr. Morgenthau." He was a tall, heavyset, nearsighted, partly bald man of grave courtesy, slow in speech, often hesitant and wary in reaction, always apprehensive and not seldom gloomy but possessed of great stubbornness and drive. His inarticulateness caused people to underrate his intelligence. He had been a capable and effective secretary of the treasury, but in public he tended toward worry and suspicion, and his government career had mingled insecurity and aggression. In private relations, he was decent, kindly and quizzical. Once he had given his confidence, he was a person of much delicacy and warmth.

Ours was an intensive collaboration, lasting three or four months. He would go over my drafts with anxious concern not just line by line but word by word. On occasion my formulations troubled him, but he generally had trouble explaining why. It would sometimes take a while before one understood the nature of his objection. Almost always he had a point.

Another problem was that each draft had to run a gauntlet of approval, with vetoes wielded by Mrs. Morgenthau, Mrs. Roosevelt, General Edward Greenbaum, his lawyer, and Henrietta Klotz, his secretary. Once the procedure seemed to take so much out of the text that in July *Collier's* threatened to cancel the series.

But we persevered, and beginning in September 1947 the half-dozen articles appeared; a seventh on the Morgenthau Plan for the semipastoralization of Germany came out later in the *New York Post*. These articles did not come near to doing justice to Morgenthau and his diaries, and I later proposed that the historian Professor John Morton Blum be invited to write a biography. The result was Blum's splendid three-volume *From the Morgenthau Diaries,* one of the fundamental works of the age of Roosevelt.

The project left me with an abiding affection for Henry Morgenthau, Jr., and strong friendships with his two sons, Robert Morgenthau, the famed Manhattan district attorney, and Henry III, a television producer and author of the charming and informative family history, *Mostly Morgenthaus.*

* * *

One incident from the collaboration remains vividly in mind. We were talking about the Morgenthau Plan. The secretary had discussed it with the president at Warm Springs on April 11, 1945, the night before FDR died. I asked him to describe the evening. He was shocked, he said, when he saw the president. FDR had aged terrifically and looked frail and haggard. After a couple of cocktails he seemed more himself, but his memory was bad and he was constantly confusing names. At dinner, Morgenthau said, the two men sat at the two ends of the table with two ladies on each side. After dinner the ladies went upstairs, and FDR and Morgenthau discussed the future of Germany. Later, the ladies returned and, when Morgenthau departed, they were sitting around, laughing and chatting, "and I must say the President seemed to be happy and enjoying himself."

Morgenthau's mention of ladies set off a flash of recollection. A short time before I had lunched with Chip Bohlen. It was just two years after FDR's death. Chip told me that his mother, a friend of Lucy Mercer Rutherfurd, FDR's onetime love, had said something to him suggesting that Mrs. Rutherfurd had been at Warm Springs the day FDR died.

I now asked Morgenthau, "Who were the ladies?" He named Margaret Suckley and Laura Delano, amiable spinster ladies who often accompanied FDR on trips of relaxation, and Madame Elizabeth Shoumatoff, who was painting his portrait when the ultimate stroke felled him the next day. Remembering Chip's conjecture, I asked, "Was Mrs. Rutherfurd one of the ladies?"

I don't think I have ever said anything with such an immediate impact. The color drained from Morgenthau's face, and he said in a strangled voice something like: "I told Eleanor she shouldn't try to hide it." After a moment, he recovered and, without answering my question, he fumbled on to recount FDR's last comments on the Morgenthau Plan.

Years later, a letter from Mrs. Rutherfurd turned up in Eleanor Roosevelt's papers in the Roosevelt Library in Hyde Park. It was written three weeks after FDR's death.

Dear Eleanor —

Margaret Suckley has written that you gave the little water color of Franklin by Mme. Shoumatoff to send me. Thank you so very much — you must know that it will be treasured always.

I have wanted to write you for a long time to tell you that I had seen Franklin and of his great kindness about my husband when he was desperately ill in Washington, & how helpful he was too to his boys — and that I hoped very much that I might see you again.

I can't tell you how deeply I feel for you and how constantly I think of your sorrow — You, whom I have always felt to be the most blessed & privileged of women, must now feel immeasurable grief and pain and they must be almost unbearable.

The whole universe finds it difficult to readjust itself to a world without Franklin — and to you and to his family the emptiness must be appalling.

I send you — as I find it impossible not to — my love and my deep deep sympathy.

As always affectionately
Lucy Rutherfurd

✶ ✶ ✶

One winter day my OSS friend Bill Casey came to town. He was now running the Research Institute of America, one of those outfits advising businessmen about taxes, investments and the state of the economy. The Institute, Bill said, had decided to put out a fortnightly Foreign Report. Our OSS friend Walter Lord was to be its editor. Would I serve as their Washington correspondent sending two letters a month reporting on political developments abroad?

Given the different paths we subsequently took, a partnership between Casey and Schlesinger seems improbable. But we were good friends and remained so through the vicissitudes of argument and age. Rereading my fortnightly letters, I am rather impressed by the range of contacts and information. The file, running from December 1946 to September 1947, when I left Washington for Cambridge, might be of mild interest to historians curious about Washington's interpretation of international events during those agitated times; no interest, however, for memoirs.

While I was thus doing my bit for the business community, I was also engaged in contributing to a series, "The Future of Socialism," for the *Partisan Review*. *PR*, an interesting and often original combination of radicalism in politics and modernism in the arts, was the house organ of what came to be known as the 'New York intellectuals.' I was never a New York intellectual, but I had friendly relations with them through Mary McCarthy, Dwight Macdonald and Lionel and Diana Trilling. I liked the *PR* editors, William Phillips and Philip Rahv, and thought they were putting out the most stimulating magazine of the day.

The Soviet experience had obviously discredited socialism, and the editors wanted to know what could be salvaged from the wreckage. I joined George Orwell, Sidney Hook and Granville Hicks in speculating whether socialism had a future. In my contribution I repeated my by now familiar views about the Soviet Union. Accepting Stalinism as a form of socialism, which system, I asked, capitalism or socialism, had "more successfully dehumanized the worker, fettered the working class, and extinguished personal and political liberty?"

But might socialism take other forms? I thought democratic socialism would be possible if "brought about step by step in a way which will not disrupt the fabric of custom, law, and mutual confidence upon which personal rights depend." I had in mind the Labour government in Great Britain and the social democratic governments of Scandinavia. I added, imprudently, "There seems no inherent obstacle to the gradual advance of socialism in the United States through a series of New Deals."

Fifteeen years later, when I was a special assistant to President Kennedy, some diligent researcher dug up this last sentence. The disclosure gave right-wingers a new weapon with which to belabor the Kennedy administration. Representative Bruce Alger (R., Texas) denounced me. "Schlesinger Should Go" wrote Henry J. Taylor, the columnist, and Senator Hugh Scott (R., Pennsylvania) inserted the column in the *Congressional Record.* "I ask President Kennedy," said Representative Charles Goodell (R., New York), "to take cognizance of this article and to give serious consideration to replacing Mr. Schlesinger in his inner circle of advisers."

I protested that the article was an exercise in analysis, not in advocacy, and that participation in a symposium on the future of socialism no more turned me into a socialist than participation in a symposium on the future of the steel industry would turn me into Roger Blough (then president of U.S. Steel). Those points were true enough, but the article did not emphasize, as it should have done, the implications of state ownership of the means of production for the freedoms of speech and opposition. In any case the uproar, such as it was, soon died down. If President Kennedy ever followed Charlie Goodell's advice and took cognizance of the *PR* article, he never mentioned it to me.

We ADA types held the British experiment in socialism to be of far greater value to Americans than the Russian experiment in communism. I tried to make this point in lectures, but I guess democratic socialism, at least in its British version, lacked high drama. It was altogether too bourgeois.

I learned this myself when on a visit to London I interviewed Prime Minister Attlee. Philip Jordan, his press secretary, told me that I would have a half hour. I arrived at 10 Downing Street armed with an hour or more of questions. Attlee was entirely courteous, but he answered every question monosyllabically, ventured no remarks on his own and reduced me in fifteen minutes to despairing silence. It was not one of my more productive interviews.

*   *   *

Pursuing my Parton quest, I wrote a piece for *Life* in April 1947, "The Roosevelt Family." I talked to Mrs. R. and all the children — Elliott, Franklin and John in New York, Anna in Arizona, Jimmy in California. I talked to family friends: Henry Morgenthau, Archie MacLeish, Sam Rosenman, Jim Farley (an ex-friend), Adolf Berle, Dave Niles, Pat Jackson. "I know a great deal more," I informed my parents after the round of interviews, "about the inner history of the Roosevelt family."

I was particularly taken with Anna, who with her husband, John Boettiger, appeared happily engaged in trying to establish a newspaper in Phoenix. A tall, handsome, breezy, free-swinging woman of forty, her golden hair turning gray, her language vivid and untethered, her judgments shrewd and realistic, she struck me as the most intelligent, balanced and candid of the children.

During the last year of her father's life, with her mother often away, Anna served as White House hostess. Much later I learned that, knowing how desperately FDR needed diversion from the relentless pressures of war, she received Lucy Rutherfurd several times at the White House for tea or dinner. Conscious both of her father's need and her mother's vulnerability, she wrote to her husband overseas, "I pray I don't get caught in a crossfire between those two. Human nature is so damn ticklish to deal with!"

Human nature turned out to be damn ticklish to deal with in her own marriage. John Boettiger was subject to periodic onslaughts of clinical depression. The eventual failure of the Phoenix paper deepened his melancholy, and in a while the marriage collapsed. Unable to shake the demons, John Boettiger killed himself in 1950. (In 1978 their son John R. Boettiger published an honest and poignant account of his parents' life together called *A Love in Shadow*.) Anna later married James Halsted, a rangy, agreeable doctor; it was then that I came to know her well. One more illustration of the circularity of life: some time after Anna's death in 1975, Jim Halsted married the daughter of Harry Hopkins.

*   *   *

Directly from Anna, more obliquely from her brothers, I began to have a new understanding of their mother. She emerged, I told my parents, "as an increasingly complicated person. It will be hard to put the full psychological story down on paper." I tried my best in the *Life* piece. Eleanor Roosevelt's airtight facade of graciousness and poise, I proposed, was the product of a long and difficult personal history. Obstacles and frustrations that would have driven a lesser woman into corrosive self-pity had driven her into greatness.

The awkward, gawky daughter of a beautiful and remote mother, she acquired as a child indelible feelings of personal insecurity. These she sought to quench by doing things for people who needed her — for her charming, weak, alcoholic father and for her young brother. "The feeling that I was useful," she recalled, "was perhaps the greatest joy I experienced."

Marriage confirmed her need for stern self-control. She had to school herself to sharing her husband — with his mother, with Josephus Daniels and Woodrow Wilson, with Louis Howe, with Albany, with the New Deal. The conquest of Eleanor Roosevelt's private insecurities was, it seemed to me, a triumph of character, a sheer and terrifying act of will. It had produced her strength and serenity and invincible charm.

But the conquest of self, I wrote, also kept her at a pitch of inner tension. Her faultless courtesy contained a barely perceptible tautness of its own. Her hands trembled ever so slightly. She would twine her fingers, shift her feet. Years of self-discipline had numbed her capacity for intimacy. People interested her mostly when they needed her and appealed to her hoard of protective love. Self-discipline also made her indifferent to the amenities of life. Her capacity for humor, a friend of hers told me, was "blank." Mrs. Roosevelt, with her faith in the efficacy of willpower, used to say she had built up a sense of humor through the years. She really hadn't.

One noticed a division among the intimate Roosevelt circles between the friends of FDR and the friends of Mrs. R. In the war years especially, Mrs. Roosevelt seemed oblivious to FDR's manifold burdens. Although doctors told her that her husband should have a half hour of unalloyed relaxation at the end of the day, she would bustle in, Anna recalled, with an enormous bundle of letters that she wanted to discuss immediately and have a decision about. One day, "Father blew his top. He took the bundle of letters and pushed it over to me. 'Sis, you handle this.'"

Mrs. R. was equally oblivious to the decline in her husband's health. Anna was increasingly worried about her father, but her mother, saying she was not interested in "physiology," paid little attention to FDR's physical condition. Anna finally insisted on bringing in specialists, who diagnosed advanced cardiovascular disease and recommended such remedial action as was available at the time. ●

*   *   *

As for the male side, all four Roosevelt boys had splendid war records — Franklin Jr. and John in the Navy, Elliott in the Army Air Corps, Jimmy in the Marines. Franklin, whom I had known slightly in college, was most like his father. He was an exceptionally handsome young man, quick, intelligent and magnetic, but his face was harder than his father's, his voice more rasping, his manner sometimes arrogant when his father would have been urbane. Where polio resolved his father's conflict between a social conscience and the bright lights, for Franklin Jr. the conflict still went on. In the end he must have been disappointed with his life, but he was a gallant man who kept on going, and he found much personal happiness with his last wife, Tobie Stevenson Weicker. I was very fond of him and spoke at his memorial service in 1988.

Elliott was at this time something of a mystery. His book of 1946, *As He Saw It*, portrayed his father as systematically pro-Soviet and anti-British. The drift of the book and especially the tone of the last chapter closely followed the Communist line. There was an extra twist of the literary knife every time Winston Churchill came on the scene. In a guarded maternal foreword, Mrs. Roosevelt wrote, "I am quite sure that many of the people who heard many of the conversations recorded herein, interpreted them differently."

Elliott's siblings were unanimous in disliking the book and in doubting that he had written it. He told me that he had done two drafts, but, finding them documentary and dull, he had called on editorial assistance to "sharpen up" the language. Indirect conversation, for example, was converted into dialogue. His collaborator must have given the book its fellow-traveling spin. I once asked Franklin whether he could find out who Elliott's collaborator was. He tried and got nowhere.

While Franklin and Anna were all for ADA, Elliott made a dramatic appearance at the PCA's rally against the Truman Doctrine at Madison Square Garden on March 31, 1947. The high point of the evening came when a spotlight focused on an actor saying: "I've been wondering what FDR would think of all this business, Greece, red-baiting, and so on. Wonder what he'd say about it if he were alive." An actress: "I wonder too. Be interesting to know."

Then the spot blacked out and in the darkness a voice cried: "I can tell you." Four converging spots switched on, and there was . . . Elliott Roosevelt. In the moment of awed silence inspired by this WPA theater technique, Elliott had time to say: "My name is Elliott Roosevelt. I am a liberal, but I am not a scared liberal." The Garden burst into an uproar of applause.

But Elliott was no Communist or fellow traveler. He wasn't even very political. He was just an agreeable fellow, not too bright or quick, who wanted very much for people to like him. One feels, I wrote in the *Life* piece, "that his sales resistance is low, that he can be induced to buy almost anything, whether a doubtful business proposition or a doubtful political idea."

Jimmy Roosevelt, the oldest son, was a charmer, but shallow, opportunistic and unprincipled (I did not write this in the *Life* piece). After the war, he was for six months involved with ICCASP but departed because of Communist infiltration. Now he was the Democratic state chairman in Calfornia. He and Anna had disagreed over a 1946 Democratic primary in the state of Washington, with Jimmy endorsing Hugh De Lacy, a fellow-traveling congressman, while Anna endorsed Howard Costigan, a stalwart anti-Communist radical. (De Lacy won the primary, lost the election.) Jimmy later served six terms in Congress. John, the youngest son and my Harvard classmate, was the odd man out, the only Republican, a businessman, nice and conventional.

The Roosevelts, well inured to a critical press, took the piece in their diverse strides. Robert Watson, a Harvard dean and Franklin's classmate, wrote me that Franklin considered it a fair presentation and was extremely pleased. (Franklin later told me that he liked it all except the part about his brother Jimmy, which he thought too favorable.) "Elliott is annoyed," Bob Watson added, "and Mrs. R. pretty upset." But Mrs. Henry Morgenthau and Grace Tully, FDR's secretary, told me it was the best explanation they had ever read of Mrs. Roosevelt.

I concluded the piece lamely, wondering whether the American people would yearn again "for the limitless energy, limitless confidence and limitless dash which the Roosevelts have periodically injected into American history." In time the American people did so yearn; but, with the cunning of history, the limitless energy, confidence and dash were to be provided by another family.

*   *   *

It had been a fairly frantic spring and summer. My last hurrah was an article for the *Saturday Evening Post* in July 1947 on a subject of less interest then than in years to come — the fate of presidential papers.

I began "Washington's Missing-Papers Mystery" by reviewing the record. Through most of American history, I pointed out, no one had questioned the right of presidents to carry off their papers and dispose of them as they wished. The Adams papers were still under the absolute control of the Adams family. Robert Todd Lincoln had directed that his father's papers be withheld till twenty-one years after his own death — and, if Nicholas Murray Butler's memory can be relied on, it was only by chance and by the president of Columbia's eloquence that the younger Lincoln was dissuaded from burning them all up.

FDR was the first president to deposit his papers in the National Archives in trust for the American people. But questions remained: What about the distinction between official and personal papers? Homer Ferguson of Michigan, a senator who appeared on the floor mostly to call for new congressional investigations, attempted to spell out the distinction. Letters addressed to FDR's dog, Fala, he said, should not be considered public papers because Fala was not a public official. "Fala may not have been a public official," Alben Barkley of Kentucky interposed, "but he was treated by some of the critics and opponents of the late President Roosevelt as though he were a high-ranking officer." Sorting out the personal from the official is not always easy. In which category to place a president's political correspondence?

Ferguson's insistence on the congressional power to investigate raised another question: What about the investigators' interest in immediate disclosure as against the scholars' interest in a rich and full record? Judge Alexander Holtzoff, a federal district judge, had just handed down a decision that appeared to vindicate unrestricted right of access by Congress "if the subject matter under scrutiny may have any possible relevancy and materiality no matter how remote, to some possible legislation."

Would John Quincy Adams, James K. Polk and Rutherford B. Hayes have labored over their presidential diaries, night after night, if they knew that deposit in the Archives and possible disclosure to political enemies would be the reward for their pains? Should the Holtzoff standard prevail (it didn't quite), the *Washington Post* anticipated "a general burning of historical documents such as has scarcely occurred since the destruction of the Alexandrian library."

Obviously the government must retain all records essential to the conduct of public business. But, as a historian, I wanted this to be achieved without destroying the incentive for public officials to maintain the personal records on which future scholars must rely for the color, the conflict, the intimate detail, that breathe life into history.

Fifteen years later, during the Kennedy administration, I kept a diary. In the Nineties, when friends joined the White House staff, I urged them to do the same. They owed it, I would say, to history. They replied in effect, "Are you kidding? A diary today means a subpoena tomorrow." Clio has become the loser.

*   *   *

As autumn 1947 approached, we completed plans for a return to Cambridge. My parents had found a large Victorian frame house for sale at 109 Irving Street, and, after inspection, we grabbed it for $17,000. Irving Street was in a most agreeable neighborhood, eight minutes from Harvard Yard. William James had built the house at 95 Irving, and his courteous, diffident, amused painter son Billy now lived there with his redoubtable wife, Alice. In due course, our beloved friends Ken and Kitty Galbraith bought the house over our back fence, and soon Julia and Paul Child bought a house midway between the Jameses and the Schlesingers. We left Washington with regret, arrived in Cambridge with anticipation.

22

Back to Harvard

WE WERE SOON cheerfully at home in our commodious house on Irving Street. Marian, a painter, had a studio on the first floor; my study was on the second floor; the three children had their own rooms. There were plenty of bookshelves and a spacious backyard. Faithful to the Cannon-Schlesinger tradition, Katharine and Stephen went off to public school.

I set to work on my lectures. My father had for many years given a course on American social and intellectual history. He now generously retitled his famed History 63 (later 163) to make it American Social and Cultural History and surrendered intellectual history to me. Intellectual history was coming into its own in these postwar years as an independent subject, and History 169, American Intellectual History, was my account of the way ideas shaped American politics, religion, literature and life. I also offered seminars for graduate students and had my quota of undergraduate tutees.

By now I was a relatively hardened performer at the podium; in a few years History 169 was the largest course in the department. I was conscientious too, revising my lectures every year to incorporate second thoughts, new slants and new scholarship. The subject absorbed me, and I have always regretted that I never made a book out of it.

Although I now rather enjoyed lecturing, I never quite escaped the impostor complex, the fear that I would one day be found out. My knowledge was by some standards considerable, but it was outweighed by my awareness of my ignorance. I always saw myself skating over thin ice. The impostor complex had its value. It created a great reluctance, for example, to impose my views on students. I could never have founded a school. Pupils who adopted my techniques or arguments produced more guilt than satisfaction. Was I misleading them? Would I thereafter assume a certain responsibility for their careers and lives? But the discovery that, no matter how little I knew, I probably knew more than the students helped contain the impostor complex. If by any chance any of them knew more than I did about one or another point, I could generally talk my way out of it or, better, confess ignorance and seek correction without undue loss of status.

Many years later, I read with recognition a poem by Geoffrey Strickland called "The Dying Scholar's Confession":

> Now I am about to die and the secret
> Of my ignorance dies with me.
> That I put it over them the more discerning
> Guessed, their eyes told me, but how much I fooled them
> None will ever know. My secret dies with me. . . .
> Fortunately they thought of me only as a good show,
> One of the more *stimulating* lecturers. . . .
> Now that I am dying, I can lapse back into my ignorance,
> It will be expected of me even, I shall be honoured for it.
> They will say: 'Once he knew many things, now he knows nothing,
> Which is why we mourn for him.'
> What have I ever known?

If recurring anxiety dreams constitute evidence, what really worried me was far less consequential. Just as students for years after college still dream about the panic of taking exams — oversleeping, forgetting to do the reading, forgetting where the exam is taking place, struck dumb by the questions — so for many years I was dogged by a dream about *setting* exams. I hated making up examinations; and in my dream examination day would arrive, I would have neglected to prepare the exam, would rush to have it printed, could not locate the printing office, could not locate the examination room, and so on.

Harvard mercifully provided teaching assistants to grade examinations. My first assistant was Bernard Bailyn, beginning his distinguished career as a colonial historian and eventually to be Sam Morison's successor. I did, however, faithfully read and grade term papers myself. I found this both enjoyable and instructive. Occasionally I would learn things, and always I would get a better sense of undergraduate concerns and apprehensions.

Students, undergraduates as well as graduates, were probably never more serious, intelligent and self-reliant than in these years after the war. Many were veterans, coming to Harvard under that great creative piece of legislation the Servicemen's Readjustment Act of 1944, better known as the GI Bill of Rights. The formal atmosphere of the Thirties gave way to khaki pants, heavy boots, flannel shirts, Eisenhower jackets, arctic parkas. Students who had seen combat in Europe or the Pacific were mature, determined to learn and unimpressed by authority. It was an exciting time for their teachers.

* * *

The Harvard history department was then unsurpassed in the country. Sam Morison, John Fairbank, Bill Langer, Crane Brinton, Charles H. Taylor, Donald McKay, Myron Gilmore, Dick Leopold, Edwin Reischauer, Sterling Dow, were back from the wars; my father, Fred Merk, Paul Buck, David Owen, Mason Hammond, had held the fort during their absence. All welcomed the newcomer with open arms and without nepotistic resentments. It was an admirable department staffed by admirable men.

There were other old friends on the faculty — Ken Galbraith; Perry Miller; F. O. Matthiessen, rather hostile because of my aggressive anti-Stalinism; former Junior Fellows now tenured professors, Harry Levin and George Homans. And there were new friends. I especially took to the economist Seymour Harris, a most engaging and generous-hearted man, an ardent Keynesian, a prolific writer and a spirited liberal. Sam Beer and Louis Hartz of the government department became good friends and allies.

In 1948 there arrived from the University of Pennsylvania a philosopher of my own age commended to me by Lionel Trilling. Morton White was a lively, witty, serious man who talked lucidly and entertainingly about the history of ideas and the vicissitudes of radical politics and with whom I formed an immediate attachment. Morton soon began to apply the skills of an analytic philosopher to a study of ideas in America. Later we edited *Paths of American Thought*, a collection of essays by such hands as Daniel Bell, Paul Samuelson, Richard Hofstadter, Alfred Kazin, Irving Howe, James B. Conant, McGeorge Bundy and others of equal distinction. Morton was also, it turned out, a cousin of Jimmy Wechsler's, one more expression of the circularity of life.

I often attended the Monday night dinners of the Society of Fellows. Crane Brinton had succeeded L. J. Henderson as chairman. His touch was lighter, and his deft skepticism produced a certain intellectual gaiety in the table talk. The Junior Fellows were an exceptionally strong group: Mac Bundy, resuming his fellowship; John E. Sawyer, a close friend of mine from OSS and an able economic historian, later a great reform president of Williams; Richard Wilbur, the graceful poet and superb translator of Molière; Carl Kaysen and James Tobin, brilliant, inventive economists (Jim a Nobel Prize winner), with whom I was to work in the Kennedy administration; John V. Kelleher, a charming, stuttering specialist in Irish history and literature.

Then there was Cord Meyer. Cord had enlisted in the Marine Corps and lost an eye on Guam. His twin brother was killed in Okinawa. He had earned the right to apocalyptic visions, and he had become an impassioned proselytizer for world government. Soon he took leave from the Society to serve as president of the United World Federalists, explaining to me that, if we did not have world government by 1950, we would have world war. (I replied that by 1950 we would have neither world government nor world war.)

By 1951, disappointed in the hope of world government, Cord swung from the extremes of idealism to the extremes of realism and joined the Central Intelligence Agency. He soon became an *apparatchik* of formidable rigidity. I rather liked Cord and liked especially his lovely wife, Mary Pinchot, who divorced him in 1958. Cord and I maintained a mild social friendship through the years. In 1976, when I was working on a biography of Robert Kennedy, I noted that Cord had been the CIA representative on an interagency youth committee formed by Kennedy. The next time I was in Washington I had a drink with him in order to get impressions of the committee and RFK's role. Later, when I obtained my CIA file under the Freedom of Information Act, I was startled to find a meticulous report by Cord Meyer to the Director of Central Intelligence on his conversation with me! I had thought we were just a couple of old friends having a drink.

*   *   *

And there were always the DeVotos. Benny and Avis were now comfortably settled at 8 Berkeley Street in the ample house built by the historian and biographer William Roscoe Thayer. *The Year of Decision,* for which Benny had recruited me in our 1940 trip along the Santa Fe Trail, had been a considerable success; *Across the Wide Missouri* was to win the Pulitzer Prize in 1948; and *The Course of Empire,* the third volume in his splendid trilogy of westward expansion, was already in mind. He subsidized his historical labors by his monthly "Easy Chair" in *Harper's* and by popular serials for *Collier's* written under the pseudonym of John August. These were later published as books that, to his chagrin, outsold the novels he wrote under his own name.

Benny was as rebellious, pugnacious, scathing, affectionate and deeply, mutely, vulnerable as ever. His interludes of relaxation came in the Sunday-afternoon ritual that he celebrated in the most lyrical treatise ever written on booze. *The Hour* was a social and spiritual history of drink in America. "In the heroic age," he wrote, "our forefathers invented self-government, the Constitution, and bourbon. . . . Our political institutions were shaped by our whiskeys, would be inconceivable without them, and share their nature." And, as Benny saw it, the culmination, the ultimate vindication of the American way of life, the "supreme American gift to world culture," was the dry martini.

The dry martini, originating in the years after the Civil War, had a mixed history. The recipe was standardized around the turn of the century, and it became the drink of elite choice in the Twenties and Thirties. Who can forget William Powell and Myrna Loy lining up martini glasses along the bar in *The Thin Man?* FDR was an aficionado of the martini, though he and his coevals poured in far too much vermouth for the taste of later generations.

After the war, FDR's 2:1 ratio gave way to 5, or 6, or 7:1. Dean Acheson was the new classicist of martinis. Once scheduled to give a late-afternoon lecture at the Brookings Institution, he was offered a glass of white wine. Rejecting this with appropriate contempt, he called for a dry martini. The Brookings people politely said that spirits were not available. "No martini," said Acheson, "no lecture." (He got the martini.)

In the Seventies the martini fell out of favor, with Jimmy Carter denouncing the "three-martini lunch." People turned incomprehensibly, to my generation at least, to white wine. This could not last. By the Nineties there was a martini revival, but it took bizarre forms. DeVoto would have regarded such latter-day heresies as a martini on the rocks or a vodka martini as abominations.

Bourbon, *The Hour* pointed out, may be drunk at any hour of day or night, but the dry martini is the sacred drink for six o'clock in the evening. (I have lapsed. The martini has been for many years my luncheon indulgence; bourbon is my pre-dinner drink; nothing after dinner.) Martinis, Benny emphasized, should *never* be mixed in advance; "you can no more keep a martini in the refrigerator than you can keep a kiss there." The union of gin and vermouth is a great and sudden glory, and the fragile tie of ecstasy is quickly broken.

Six o'clock, he wrote, "is the violet hour, the hour of hush and wonder, when the affections glow and valor is reborn, when the shadows deepen magically along the edge of the forest and we believe that, if we watch carefully, at any moment we may see the unicorn. . . . It is the healer, the weaver of forgiveness and reconciliation, the justifier of us to ourselves and one another." So at six on Sundays we would forgather at the DeVotos — the Galbraiths, the Paul Bucks, the Sargent Kennedys, when in town the Elmer Davises and the Wallace Stegners — none among us alcoholics, but, at the end of a hard week's work, cherishing the dry martini shimmering beautifully in its elegant, long-stemmed glass.

Benny on *The Hour:* "May six o'clock never find you alone."

* * *

Benny was an ally in my next contribution to the endless argument of history. In December 1945, during a post-demobilization holiday in Florida, I reviewed the first two volumes of James G. Randall's *Lincoln the President* for the *Nation.* Randall, a professor at the University of Illinois, was a meticulous scholar. Collating documents, weighing witnesses, analyzing divergent testimonies constituted his forte. This was a process from which most historians would print only the conclusions, but in Randall's case the cross-examination of evidence formed a substantial part of his narrative. Unfortunately, his relentless caution about the details of Lincoln's life did not extend to his account of the causes of the Civil War.

William H. Seward, a Republican leader in the 1850s and later Lincoln's secretary of state, had called the rising tension between the free and slave states "an irrepressible conflict." Lincoln in his Second Inaugural named slavery as "the cause of the war." Up to the late Thirties, historians had mostly agreed in seeing slavery as the single factor without which there would have been no Civil War. And they mostly agreed that, given slavery, the Civil War was more or less inevitable.

Then in 1939 Professor Avery Craven of the University of Chicago published a book called *The Repressible Conflict.* Randall now joined Craven in denying both that the war was inevitable and that slavery was its cause. The issues arising over slavery were in Randall's judgment "highly artificial, almost fabricated. . . . They produced quarrels out of things that would have settled themselves were it not for political agitation." Slavery was in any case, Craven thought, a much overrated problem. It is "perfectly clear," he wrote, "that slavery played a rather minor part in the life of the South and of the Negro."

The real cause of the war, Randall and Craven said, was fanaticism, especially the fanaticism of the abolitionists. Phrases like "whipped-up crisis" and "psychopathic case" adorned Randall's explanation. Craven called the growing sectional antagonism "an artificial creation of inflamed minds. . . . Distortion led a people into bloody war."

There was in the Randall-Craven view no legitimate moral power in the slavery argument, no profound conflict in values, for which men might kill and die. Rather, a "blundering generation" had transformed a "repressible conflict" into a "needless war."

I had touched a bit on this question in *The Age of Jackson*. "In essence," I had written, "the emotion which moved the North to battlefield and bloodshed was moral disgust" against the horrible fact of human bondage. So I objected to these dismissals of the significance of slavery in American history. "I finished the Randall Lincoln with great disgust," I wrote my father. "It is a very useful book if you care whether or not Lincoln was playing handball on the day when he received news of his nomination."

To DeVoto I expressed the wish that he would read Randall, read Craven's *The Coming of the Civil War* "and do an Easy Chair on the doughface interpretation of history." 'Doughface' was the antebellum term for northern legislators who voted with the south, northern men with southern principles. Doughface, Randall wrote, was "said opprobriously . . . as if it were a base thing for a Northern man to work with Southern fellows."

A few days later I dispatched a second letter to DeVoto, three pages, single-spaced: "There seem to me to be two broad implications of the Craven-Randall thesis: a) that the agitation, propaganda, etc., against slavery were unnecessary; in other words, that the agitators deliberately made a choice and decided to go in for some gratuitous hell-raising; and b) that the slavery problem would have been solved without war." The antislavery agitation, I argued, was not the work of what Randall had called "vicious forces." Its mainspring was something more than warmongering and motiveless malice. Abolitionism arose from authentic outrage against a system in which one man could own another as private property. "Randall does just not feel any moral urgency in the slavery issue; his moral sympathies are with Stephen A. Douglas and the people, who because they felt no moral urgency, were always in favor of compromise; and, because he is a bad historian, he refuses to allow other people a sense of widespread and honest moral urgency."

The refusal to see the Civil War as emerging from legitimate moral outrage led Randall, I continued, to distort and diminish Lincoln. "I don't know a hell of a lot about Lincoln; but I suspect that he was a guy not unlike FDR, who could be sordid and conservative enough to keep the Jesse Joneses in the party while still being moral and idealistic enough to keep the Henry Wallaces." Part of Lincoln's greatness was that the antislavery people — rightly — never lost faith in him. It was odd, I thought, to see the struggle in the book between Randall's formal commitment to Lincoln as his hero and his unconscious private conviction that Stephen A. Douglas, President Buchanan and General McClellan were right in their disagreements with Lincoln and that Lincoln was right only so far as he approached their positions.

Benny responded by writing devastating critiques of Civil War revisionism in the February and March 1946 *Harper's*. Revisionism, he wrote, "has no position but only a vague sentiment: that if the South had been left quite alone, somehow the slaves would eventually have been freed, an equitable system established, and the evils of war and reconstruction prevented." Revisionism refused to face the economic fact that slavery was obsolete or the moral fact that it was an evil thing. Surely we expect more from historians. Surely history, he concluded, should understand the vast difference between a man who is legally a slave and one who is legally free.

* * *

The Civil War was our great national trauma, a savage fraternal conflict leaving wounds that had hardly healed a century later. Did the war so tragically inflicted on the American democracy result from the impact of unbridled emotion on incompetent leaders? Did 620,000 Americans die in an unnecessary conflict?

Revisionism in the Forties was the new orthodoxy. DeVoto's powerful indictment had small impact on the historical profession. After all, he was a literary man. Randall and Craven were respected professionals. In 1948 an exasperated DeVoto observed sarcastically to a publisher wondering whether to bring out one more neo-Confederate tract, "It is now an established principle of American history that the War of the Rebellion was . . . a hideous by-product of a conspiracy of hireling, maniacal abolitionists and owners of heavy industry." The last phrase referred to Charles and Mary Beard, who saw an irrepressible conflict between northern industrial capitalism and southern plantation agriculture but agreed with the revisionists in minimizing slavery as the cause of the war. "The institution of slavery as a question of ethics," the Beards had written in *The Rise of American Civilization,* "was not the fundamental issue in the years preceding the bombardment of Fort Sumter."

Sharing Benny's exasperation, I fired some tentative shots against revisionism in the *Saturday Review of Literature* and then decided to try a systematic examination of the unarticulated premises of the revisionist case. The result was "The Causes of the Civil War: A Note on Historical Sentimentalism" in the *Partisan Review* of October 1949.

What, I asked, was the revisionist alternative to the Civil War? Were there policies with which a nonblundering generation would have resolved the slavery crisis? and were these policies so obvious that the failure to adopt them indicated blundering of an exceptionally horrendous nature? If no such policies could be produced even by hindsight, it would seem excessive to condemn the politicians of the 1850s for failing to discover them at the time.

The revisionists, I thought, had made only perfunctory stabs at this problem. "Any kind of sane policy in Washington in 1860 might have saved the day," remarked Craven; but he did not vouchsafe the details of even one kind of sane policy. Randall declared that there were few policies he would wish repeated if the 1850s were to be lived over again; but he was not communicative about the policies he would wish pursued. Allan Nevins, though not a true revisionist, blamed the war in *Ordeal of the Union*, his very able history of the 1850s, on the "collapse of American statesmanship" but refrained from expounding what noncollapsible statesmanship should have done.

In view of this reticence on a point so crucial to their argument, I tried to figure out how revisionists, if pressed, might say the slavery question could have been solved without war. The nonviolent abolition of slavery could conceivably have come about, I suggested, in three ways: through internal reform in the south, through economic exhaustion of the slavery system in the south, or through some federal plan of gradual and compensated emancipation of the slaves.

The revisionists seemed to think that the south might have ended the slavery system on its own, if only the vociferous abolitionists had not spoiled everything by causing southern ranks to close in self-defense. This assumed the existence of a southern reform movement. But southerners had done nothing to end slavery in the long years before William Lloyd Garrison and Harriet Beecher Stowe came down the pike to harass them. Quite the contrary: slaveholders had effectively suppressed all opposition to their system, affirming slavery as a positive good and converting the south into a closed society on this question.

The revisionist argument also assumed that northerners should have denied themselves expressions of disapproval over slavery. "To say there 'should' have been no abolitionists in America before the Civil War," I wrote, "is about as sensible as to say that there 'should' have been no anti-Nazis in the nineteen-thirties or that there 'should' be no anti-Communists today."

If the internal reform argument failed to persuade, how about the economic exhaustion argument — that southern planters would recognize slavery as increasingly uneconomic and would, of their own volition, end it. Slavery, Craven claimed, "may have been almost ready to break down of its own weight." But the south always blamed its economic troubles not on its own system but on northern exploitation and domination. Hard times in the 1850s led not to southern doubts about the economic future of slavery but to blasts against the north for the high price of manufactured goods and demands for the reopening of the slave trade.

As for compensated emancipation, the south had rejected Lincoln's repeated proposals to this effect. In the end, all the revisionists had to offer was a nebulous hope that the invincible march of progress would somehow, some day, free the slaves. "To suppose," Randall weakly said, "that the Union could not have been continued or slavery outmoded without the war and without the corrupt concomitants of war is hardly an enlightened assumption."

*   *   *

What the revisionists did not understand was that abolition was basically a moral issue, even though it required a configuration of nonmoral factors — economic, political, social, military — before moral protest could gather the strength to change history. The Civil War seemed to present almost as stark a clash of irreconcilable ideologies as the war against Nazism.

Comparisons were inescapable. I quoted Allan Nevins on the 1850s: "The primary task of statesmanship in this era was to furnish a workable adjustment between the two sections, while offering strong inducements to the southern people to regard their labor system not as static but evolutionary, and equal persuasions to the northern people to assume a helpful rather than scolding attitude." Would some future historian, I wondered, write about our own time: "The primary task of statesmanship in the 1930s was to furnish a workable adjustment between the United States and Germany, while offering strong inducements to the German people to abandon the police state and equal persuasions to the Americans to help the Nazis rather than scold them"? Would some future historian adapt the Randall formula and write that the word "appeaser" was used "opprobriously," as if it were a "base" thing for an American to work with his Nazi fellow?

All this raised the question of the place of moral judgment in the work of the historian. Historians, I thought, have no license to roam through the past, handing down moral verdicts on individuals. All persons, including historians, are trapped in a web of circumstance that should curtail moral pontification.

But there seem certain profound issues that demand moral recognition by historians if they are to understand the great movements of history. Such issues are relatively few because there aren't many historical phenomena that we can confidently identify as evil. These few basic issues appear, moreover, not in pure form but compromised by the infernal complexity and ambiguity of human motivation. Their advocates may often be neurotics and fanatics, like the abolitionists. Yet the nature neither of the context nor of the advocates alters the character of the issue. And human slavery is assuredly one of the few issues of whose evil we can be certain.

The revisionists seemed to me to misconceive and sentimentalize the nature of history by supposing that evil would be "outmoded" by the invincible march of progress. Life does occasionally impose on us the necessity for disagreeable action. If any problem in American history does force such decisions, it is the Civil War. I wrote:

> History is not a redeemer, promising to solve all human problems in time; nor is man capable of transcending the limitations of his being. Man generally is entangled in insoluble problems; history is consequently a tragedy in which we are all involved, whose keynote is anxiety and frustration, not progress and fulfillment. Nothing exists in history to assure us that the great moral dilemmas can be resolved without pain; we cannot therefore be relieved from the duty of moral judgment on issues so appalling and inescapable as those involved in human slavery. . . .
>
> One must emphasize, however, that this duty of judgment applies to issues. Because we are all implicated in the same tragedy, we must judge the men of the past with the same forbearance and charity which we hope the future will apply toward us.

I offered a gloomy conclusion: "The unhappy fact is that man occasionally works himself into a log-jam; and that the log-jam must be burst by violence."

*   *   *

Historians, I have noted, are (like everybody else) prisoners of their own experience. Disillusion following the First World War doubtless led historians of the Randall-Craven generation to reject war as a solution to anything. The Second World War led historians of my generation to the reluctant conclusion, founded on our own experience, that there were some problems — some logjams — that only war could solve.

Fred Merk well expressed the older generation's view in a letter about the article. "Wars seem to me merely to alter the character of problems, not solve them," he wrote me.

> The slavery evil was changed in character by the Civil War. The southern Negro ceased to be the slave of the planter, to become the slave of Southern society. The change amounted to something, but not much. . . . If the evil of slavery could really have been solved by the war, I would be reconciled to the cost of the war. But since the underlying problem remained, I am not sure that the horrid cost of the war in lives, maiming, hate, debt, Grand Army of the Republic and the Republican Party hegemony for generations, was worth it. If I had lived in 1860 I would have voted for Douglas.

Randall made no direct reply to the *PR* piece, but his 1953 presidential address to the American Historical Association warned that "the slanting of history may go so far as to become startlingly dangerous" in its impact on foreign policy. "Arguments for the alleged 'inevitability' of war, together with its 'log jam' corollary" could lead on, he claimed, to preventive war.

The logjam corollary also troubled some nonrevisionist historians. Henry Commager said he agreed with ninety percent of my piece and pointed out (correctly) that he had long since made clear his own rejection of revisionism in his reviews of the Craven and Randall books. But he was worried by the words "must be burst by violence" in the logjam sentence: "let us hope that somehow we can figure out some other way than violence to break our present log-jams." Harvey Wish of Western Reserve made the same point. Commager and Wish were right, though in writing the sentence I actually had the Second World War, not the Cold War, in mind.

Avery Craven did respond to the critique. He simply denied what I had read as the plain meaning of his words. In February 1948 he sent a cease-and-desist letter, asking me "not to repeat the absolutely false statement which you have twice made in recent months to the effect that I 'blame' the Civil War 'on the gratuitous agitation of meddling propogandists' [sic]. I do not, and never have, thought anything of the kind. . . . Please stop it." After the *PR* article, he wrote more temperately, "Neither Randall nor I think any of the perfectly silly things with which you charge us, but I don't mind and I don't think Randall does either. . . . I think your general criticism of historians is sound, but I do wish that both you and DeVoto would stop distorting other people's views in order to make your own points." But he did beat a certain substantive retreat. By 1952 he called it "probably true" that "Negro slavery was the fundamental factor in producing the American Civil War."

Agnostic letters about the piece came from Merle Curti of Wisconsin ("very stimulating") and George Pierson of Yale ("most interesting") and less cautious letters from Leonard Labaree of Yale ("you have made a bull's eye"), Ralph Gabriel of Yale ("a first-class job"), Harry Jaffa of Chicago ("brilliant") and Selig Adler of Buffalo ("a job which was much in the need of doing"). Paul Buck, Harvard's specialist in southern history, said, "No one can upset you on your main position." John Dos Passos wrote, however, that both revisionists and critics missed the point: the Civil War was simply "a consolidation within this continent of the big North American power unit," and slavery, "like Hitler's atrocities," was useful as propaganda.

At least the revisionist enthusiasm had now been challenged, if not yet checked. Others joined the fray. The Dutch historian Pieter Geyl, the scholar who described history as an argument without end, took on the revisionists in an 1951 article in the *New England Quarterly*. But Geyl was not, like Randall and Craven, a Civil War specialist, nor certainly was I; and the profession could ignore our dissents. In 1954 Thomas J. Pressly of the University of Washington published a perceptive examination of the controversy since Appomattox in his thorough and valuable *Americans Interpret Their Civil War*. Though he was himself judiciously critical of Randall and Craven, he concluded that revisionism was still widely held among American historians.

Nineteen sixty-one marked the centennial of the attack on Fort Sumter, and there were still revisionists about. "The American Civil War was not the 'irrepressible conflict,'" Bruce Catton, the author of a series of vivid and knowledgeable Civil War histories, said that year. "It need not have taken place. It settled nothing that reasonable men of good will could not have settled if they had been willing to make the effort." "Who won the Civil War, anyway?" asked an exasperated Fawn Brodie the next year in the *New York Times*, pointing out that the southern viewpoint — minimizing the horrors of slavery and exposing abolitionists as the true villains, with the implication that the Civil War had not been worth fighting — now permeated the writings of historians from every section of the country.

The Civil War did indeed exact terrible costs. But in the centennial year, one amateur historian of impeccable Confederate ancestry justified the war in a comment on MacKinlay Kantor's article in *Look* "If the South Had Won the Civil War." Had Lee won at Gettysburg, the writer said,

> England would have recognized the Confederacy, and France would have stayed in Mexico with a French Empire from Panama to the Rio Grande. . . . The Northwest would have seceded from the Northeast and taken over 54/40. Russia would have kept Alaska and in all probability have taken all Northwest Canada.
>
> There would have been the Northwest Republic, the Northeast Republic, the Confederate Republic, the Mexican Empire in the Southwest, with California, Utah, Arizona and New Mexico as part of that Empire.
>
> And the Bolsheviks would have had the whole Northwest, and what then? Maybe the Northeast and the Southeast could have created an alliance and held the Russians at the Mississippi. Isn't it great to contemplate?
>
> My sympathies and all my family were on the side of the South. But I think the organization of the greatest republic in the history of the world was worth all the sacrifices made to save it.
>
> Harry S. Truman
> Independence, Mo.

*　*　*

Civil War revisionism flourished in the Forties and Fifties. In the Sixties it was swept away by the freshening moral winds of the civil rights movement. The struggle to assure black Americans the rights due them as American citizens, rights so long and so brutally denied, placed slavery where it belonged — in the center of the national experience — and sealed the fate of Civil War revisionism.

At the end of the Nineties appeared the book *Writing the Civil War*, edited by James M. McPherson and William J. Cooper, Jr., and praised by David Donald, a Randall student himself, as a superb summary of "the vast literature on disputed points concerning the Civil War." An interesting feature of *Writing the Civil War* is that it contains no discussion at all of the war's causes. That disputed point seems now settled. As Jim McPherson, our leading Civil War scholar, has put it, no one can doubt any more "the salience of slavery as the root of secession." We are finally back to Lincoln on the causes of the Civil War.

And we are instructed once again how history is forever haunted by the preoccupations and crises of the age in which it is written.

Historiographical quarrels about the past often reflect, and disguise, debates about the future. As Croce said, all history is contemporary history. Hence the inevitability of revisionism.

Every war in American history has been followed in due course by skeptical reassessments of supposedly sacred assumptions. So the War of 1812, fought at the time for the freedom of the seas, was in later years blamed on the expansionist ambitions of congressional war hawks; so the Mexican War was blamed on a slaveholders' conspiracy; so the First World War was blamed on munitions makers and international bankers.

In the Forties, while scholars were revising the Civil War, the Second World War was itself undergoing the inevitable postwar scrutiny. Isolationists like Charles Beard contended that Franklin Roosevelt had deceived the nation into another needless war. Anti-Soviet zealots like William C. Bullitt contended that everything that had gone wrong since the end of the war was due to Roosevelt's feebleness or folly at Yalta. This outburst of revisionism led me to write a piece, "Roosevelt and His Detractors," in the June 1950 *Harper's*.

Yalta was a particular focus of the revisionist gospel. I pointed out that Stalin, in order to work his will, had to break the Yalta declarations on liberated Europe and on Poland. This would suggest that those agreements were in our interest, not in his. Beyond that, no one has been able to show convincingly how diplomatic methods alone could have prevented the Soviet domination of Eastern Europe.

I added that no one in charge of foreign policy in a democracy could have assumed the responsibility for initiating an anti-Soviet policy in advance of demonstrated Soviet purposes of systematic hostility. We had, I thought, to make the attempt to get along. "If we had refused even the attempt," I quoted André Malraux, "I do not think that anyone could have stayed in power in France, or even in the United States, if he had brought about a break with Russia, which at that time would have seemed to have no justification."

I was thrilled to receive a note from Walter Lippmann: "Hearty congratulations. . . . You have answered the arguments better than anyone else has ever done." That generous letter from a mighty figure to an uncertain young man meant so much to me that I resolved that, whenever I read something I particularly admired, I would let the author know — a resolution that I have tried to keep, but with, I fear, imperfect success.

As a moderately successful revisionist myself (*The Age of Jackson*), I have no objection in principle to revisionism. It should be noted, though, that many past exercises in revisionism have failed to stick. Second opinions are not necessarily wiser than first. Few historians believe that the war hawks caused the War of 1812 or the slaveholders the Mexican War, or that the Civil War was needless, or that the House of Morgan brought America into the First World War, or that Yalta gave Stalin Eastern Europe. Time often revises the revisionists.

Nevertheless, revisionism is an essential part of the process by which history, through the disclosure of new sources, the posing of new problems and the investigation of new possibilities, enlarges its perspectives and enriches its insights. History is indeed an argument without end. That is why it is so much fun. "The one duty we owe to history," said Oscar Wilde, "is to rewrite it."

23

1948

THE INCREASINGLY ANGRY ARGUMENT about Franklin Roosevelt reflected the intensification of the Cold War. Political lines were drawn ever tighter, not only between left and right but perhaps even more bitterly within the left itself. If it came to a choice between Harry Truman and Robert A. Taft, Henry Wallace said in December 1947, he would vote for Taft as the man more likely to keep the peace. Soon Wallace predicted that Truman's "bipartisan reactionary war policy" would end with American soldiers "lying in their Arctic suits in the Russian snow." The United States, Wallace said, was heading into fascism: "we recognize Hitlerite methods when we see them in our own land." Brandishing such sentiments, he announced on December 30, 1947, his own candidacy for president in 1948.

When Wallace declared his candidacy, he resigned as the *New Republic*'s editor. Several of the participants in my *New Republic* luncheon a year earlier had changed their minds rather drastically. Teddy White had come to find Wallace a "bitter man; eccentric, ambitious, self-righteous," who, among other things, "literally loathed" FDR and was counseled by, flattered by and, in his innocence and vanity, acquiescent to Communists. Michael Straight and Bruce Bliven had been worrying about mysterious callers parading through Wallace's office. "What had happened," Bliven wrote later, "was that the American Communist Party had closed in on him. . . . They planned the Progressive Party, and found in Henry an ideal man to be its titular head."

Indeed, two years before, the top CPUSA leadership had resolved "to establish in time for the 1948 elections a national third party — a broad people's anti-monopoly, anti-imperialist party." The mass base, Eugene Dennis, the general secretary, said, lay in the National Citizens Political Action Committee and the Independent Citizens Committee for the Arts, Sciences and Professions — the two groups that merged later that year to form the Progressive Citizens of America. Lee Pressman and John Abt, both secret Communists, were prominent in Wallace's new Progressive party. The verdict of the radical journalist I. F. Stone, rendered in the *New York Compass* on February 28, 1950, seems fair enough: "The Communists have been the dominant influence in the Progressive Party. . . . If it had not been for the Communists, there would have been no Progressive Party." Fellow travelers joined in abundance. I noticed with interest that Angus Cameron of Little, Brown was chairman of the party in Massachusetts and treasurer of the national Wallace for President Committee.

Many non-Communists and some non–fellow travelers, it should be emphasized, also favored the third party at the start. Rexford G. Tugwell, a member of FDR's original brain trust, later a creative official in Wallace's Department of Agriculture, still later a good friend of mine, had been a member of both ADA and PCA. In January 1948 Tugwell resigned from ADA. He was the single notable New Dealer to back Wallace, but many grass-roots liberals around the country turned for a season to the Progressive party.

*   *   *

Eleanor Roosevelt had held Wallace in high regard. On the day in 1945 that she moved out of the White House, she had written him, "You are peculiarly fitted to carry on the ideals which were close to my husband's heart." She now led in the liberal repudiation of Wallace.

"What strange things the desire to be president makes men do!" she wrote the day after Wallace announced. ". . . He never has been a good politician, he never has been able to gauge public opinion, and he never has picked his advisers wisely. . . . As a leader of a third party he will accomplish nothing. He will merely destroy the very things he wishes to achieve. I am sorry that he has listened to people as inept politically as he is himself."

On January 2, 1948, she wrote, "The American Communists will be the nucleus of Mr. Wallace's third party." On January 3: "Oh, Mr. Wallace, if you were president you would not have such pat sentences to offer us!" On January 5: "My conclusion is that Mr. Wallace has done both his own country and the world a great disservice." Talk about a public spanking!

In one "My Day" she even compared Wallace to Neville Chamberlain. Wallace replied harshly by saying that those who likened him to Chamberlain reminded him of the anti-Communists of the Thirties: "The anti-Comintern bloc of those days produced war and misery. Its spiritual descendants of today will produce a greater war and a greater misery." Mrs. R. was unrelenting. On February 26 she was reminded of occasions during the New Deal when Wallace was "more on the conservative side than on the courageous, liberal side." Soon she told the Oregon ADA, "Any use of my husband's name in connection with that party is from my point of view entirely dishonest."

In the meantime, the Progressive party won a congressional by-election in the Bronx. (Soon I debated the victor, Leo Isacson, before the Harvard Law School Forum.) Wallace began his national campaign in the spring, well before the major party conventions. By April he had made nearly thirty speeches in nine states, addressing seventy-five thousand or so cheering people. Asked about his Communist supporters, he would say, "If they want to help us out on some of these problems, why God bless them, let them come along." Newspapers estimated that he might well poll five million votes in November. ADA, following his campaign with concern, issued two long mimeographed analyses, prepared by Elizabeth Donahue and William Dufty of the staff — documents devastating for Wallace, useful for historians.

Even more devastating were the contributions of Dwight Macdonald. Trained on Harry Luce's *Fortune*, Macdonald had moved on to *Partisan Review* before establishing his anarchopacifist magazine *Politics* in 1944. Dwight was a great natural journalist, as Ted Williams was a great natural baseball player. His curiosity was insatiable; his irreverence was boundless; he was enthusiastically and remorselessly iconoclastic; and he could make the most boring subjects compulsively readable. We became friends in this period, a somewhat precarious status, since Dwight's polemical zest could be directed against friends almost as easily as against enemies. Tall, rambunctious, bearded, sartorially audacious, he had a quick and penetrating wit, loved argument and was excellent company except when overstimulated by booze.

He regarded Wallace as an unmitigated and self-deluded phony and took great pleasure in documenting this case in a couple of long *Politics* articles in 1947, elaborated the next year in a joyous book, *Henry Wallace: The Man and the Myth.* Inspired no doubt by Mencken's famed "Gamalielese" on the rhetoric of Warren G. Harding, Dwight had a comparable riff on "Wallese," a debased provincial dialect spoken by the natives of Wallaceland, "a region of perpetual fog caused by the warm winds of the liberal Gulf Stream coming in contact with the Soviet glacier."

I made more modest contributions to the cause. Wallace's opposition to the Marshall Plan, I told students at Middlebury, at Brown, at

Tufts, served the interests of the Soviet Union. The Progressive party, I wrote in the *Nation,* clarified the split in the liberal movement between the doers and the wailers, between those for whom liberalism was a program to be put into action and those for whom liberalism was an outlet for frustrations and grievances, between supporters of liberal democracy and defenders of a police state. Let us, I urged, do our job of devising policies that will take into account the world as it is. "Politics will not do right by us unless we do right by it."

*   *   *

But we doers had problems of our own. We were stuck with the Democratic party and with a president who had no chance at all to win the election. The Marshall Plan had made us think better of Truman than we had thought in 1946, and in January 1948 he moved materially to the left in his State of the Union address. This was the result of a small group of Truman insiders who, unknown to us (or at least to me), had been meeting on Monday nights at the Wardman Park apartment of Oscar Ewing and plotting to point the administration in a more liberal direction.

Ewing was the head of the Federal Security Agency. Security in those guileless days meant 'economic security,' not 'national security'; FSA was the predecessor of the Department of Health, Education and Welfare, and Ewing was the particular advocate of national health insurance. David Morse, assistant secretary of labor, stressed the importance of organized labor. Leon Keyserling of the Council of Economic Advisers showed how social spending would strengthen the economy. Clark Clifford conveyed the Monday night group's recommendations to the White House. Jim Rowe gave the group a memorandum arguing that a swing to the left was the only way to win in 1948. Clifford, fearing that Truman's dislike of Rowe's law partner, Tom Corcoran, would disqualify anything signed by Rowe, retouched the memorandum, signed it himself and sent it on to Truman.

Actually, Truman had been a loyal New Dealer in the Senate, and his annual messages had taken the New Deal line. But the influence of right-wing Democrats like John Snyder, the Missouri chum he had made secretary of the treasury, and the oil man Ed Pauley had given his administration a conservative cast. "He knows the words," I said in the *Nation* in March, "rather than the tune." "Why in hell doesn't ADA come out for a liberal candidate to put up against Truman?" Dwight Macdonald wrote me. ". . . If ADA is just part of the Truman forces, what's the use of it? No wonder Henry steals all your thunder." Dwight was still sounding the alarm in April. "I'm worried," he wrote to Jim Loeb, "when I see the Commies and Wallace putting on such a vigorous and bold campaign."

But who was the alternative to Truman? Bill Douglas of the Supreme Court was a perennial suggestion, but, as usual, he was playing hard to get. Then, toward the end of March, Franklin D. Roosevelt, Jr., urged Democrats to draft General Eisenhower. Leon Henderson endorsed the idea. Others followed. No one knew how Eisenhower stood on the issues or whether he was even a Democrat; but his war-hero stature, his popularity and his genial bearing were thought sufficient to assure a Democratic victory in November. Hardened political bosses — Jake Arvey in Chicago, Frank Hague in Jersey City, Harry Byrd of Virginia — joined the cry for Ike.

Organized labor, however, showed limited enthusiasm, and influential ADA members were opposed. "I am dead set against this Eisenhower boom among liberals," Reinhold Niebuhr told Jim Loeb. Though Jimmy and Elliott Roosevelt had joined Franklin in backing Ike, their mother kept a skeptical silence. I regret to say that Jimmy Wechsler and I rather dubiously joined the boom. Truman's record, we thought, was not bad, and his intentions were good, but he was, Jimmy said, like the baseball player: "good field, no hit." Ike would at least assure the election of a Democratic Congress and help liberal Democratic candidates like Adlai Stevenson and Paul Douglas in Illinois, Hubert Humphrey in Minnesota, Chester Bowles in Connecticut, Estes Kefauver in Tennessee, Lyndon Johnson in Texas, G. Mennen Williams in Michigan. So we went along with Ike.

I learned a lesson from the Eisenhower boom of 1948: never back a presidential candidate whose views are top secret.

*   *   *

On April 21, 1948, Joe Rauh, Washington counsel for the United Auto Workers, phoned with frightening news. Walter Reuther, he said, had been shot the night before at home in Detroit. Returning from a UAW board meeting, Walter ate a late supper in the kitchen, then went to the refrigerator to get a bowl of peaches for dessert. As he turned to say a word to his wife, a shotgun blast shattered the kitchen window and hit him on the right arm and shoulder. Had he not turned away just at that moment, the buckshot would have hit him full in the chest, and he would have died instantly. Instead he fell bleeding to the floor, conscious enough to say "Those dirty bastards! They have to shoot a fellow in the back. They won't come out in the open and fight." He was rushed to the hospital and given blood transfusions as doctors labored to save his arm.

The immediate prognosis was unclear. I still remember the shock and foreboding that swept over me after Joe's call. As Niebuhr was ADA's intellectual leader, Reuther was its political mainstay. Where most of us in ADA were unaffiliated intellectuals, Walter was a man of ideas in command of a powerful union, skilled in organizing and ready to assume responsibility. His death would have been a bitter blow to the non-Communist left.

Walter did not die, but it took eighteen months before he was active again, and he never recovered the full use of his right arm. A year later his brother Victor was shot in much the same way. He too escaped death but was blinded in one eye.

Who was responsible for these attacks? Reuther himself told his daughter Elisabeth that diverse groups were united by a common desire to eliminate him — gangsters trying to manipulate UAW locals; Communists losing in the struggle for control of the union; diehard employers hoping to weaken the UAW. The local police showed little enthusiasm for the investigation; some cops may have been complicit.

Joe Rauh went to Truman's attorney general, Tom Clark, and asked that the FBI take on the case. Eight years before, when Reuther was proposed for a federal commission, Hoover had stopped the appointment, charging that he was a Communist. Hoover refused now to involve the FBI, saying the attempted assassination was a local responsibility. "Fellows," Clark reluctantly told Joe and his UAW associates, "Edgar says no. He says he's not going to send the FBI in every time some nigger woman gets raped."

The Reuther assassination plots remain to this day unsolved; no one was ever brought to justice. And the acute concern one felt about the possible loss of Walter Reuther suggests the precarious status of American liberalism in the spring of 1948.

It was a gloomy time. Constantine Gazulis, who had kept the Frances Sweeney Committee going after Fran's death, died. I went to his Greek Orthodox funeral. Mourners, I among them, filed by the open casket. There lay my old raffish friend Gus, now improbably clad in a tuxedo. I had never seen a dead man before, and I was shaken by the sight.

I then caught a plane to New York, where I had an appointment with General Donovan. Somehow in our conversation I mentioned my shock of the morning. "You're a Unitarian," Bill Donovan said. "That's the trouble with your liberal faiths. They hide the dead. They don't prepare you to face death."

* * *

That spring, the author of *Darkness at Noon* arrived on his first visit to America. Arthur Koestler came to raise money for the International Rescue and Relief Committee by giving talks about the plight of European intellectuals needing relief and rescue.

I met him at a cocktail party in Washington at the house of Kenneth Crawford of *Newsweek*. Koestler was a short, intense, nervous man, forty-two years old, a chain smoker and a chain drinker, but with a captivating smile, unmistakable magnetism and, when he cared to apply it, compelling charm. At Ken Crawford's he was evidently not in a cocktail party mood, "very distant and snotty," I noted, spending his time talking in the corner with Martin Agronsky, a radio commentator, warming up only when a pretty girl hove in sight. He had come from an unproductive meeting with Felix Frankfurter, whom he described dismissively as a "Jewish Truman." As for the United States, "Five times a day I am telling myself that this is the country where I want to be forever and five times a day that I would rather be dead than live here" — or so he wrote to the lovely Mamaine Paget, soon to become his second wife.

His speaking tour ended in Boston toward the end of April, and one day we gave him a luncheon. The other guests were Gaetano Salvemini, I. A. Richards, Crane Brinton and Jack Sawyer. Koestler was in an unusually affable mood, and the luncheon was a great success. His opening remark — "What I would like to know is why you Americans aren't all isolationists?" — carried the implication that Europe was hardly worth saving.

Koestler, who had spent ninety-five days in a Franco prison expecting to be executed each morning, exchanged personal anecdotes with Salvemini, comparing Franco's prisons with Mussolini's. As Salvemini left, they embraced in a rather touching way. Koestler's farewell to the elderly Italian antifascist: "See you in the concentration camp."

Arthur stayed after the others. He was playing with the idea, he said, of coming to America for a year or so to work on a book, "The Psychology of Artistic Creation." As a graduate of the Vienna Technische Hochschule (and as a man who would spend his last years as an amateur neurologist), he was excited to learn that W. B. Cannon, the author of *Bodily Changes in Pain, Hunger, Fear, and Rage,* was Marian's father. He pronounced the name Can-yon with a Spanish twist.

Taking our copy of *Darkness at Noon* from the shelves to be autographed, I discovered that it had "W. B. Cannon" inscribed in front, with annotations and underlinings throughout the text. Koestler was very pleased, asked whether he could have the book and promised to send another copy in exchange, which he eventually did. We did not have the heart to tell him that the pencilings were all in Mrs. Cannon's handwriting.

Back in New York, Arthur sent a letter thanking us for the luncheon, adding, "I shall cherish Cannon's copy of *Darkness at Noon* as a very precious gift." He also mentioned his dinner with the Nieman Fellows, newspapermen spending a year at Harvard, where he had tangled with Justin McCarthy of the *Chicago Sun-Times,* a Wallaceite. Koestler, whose book *The Yogi and the Commissar* had come out a few years before, said contemptuously that Wallace was a yogi in the hands of the commissars. "I am very sorry I lost my temper with McCarthy," he wrote, "and have ever since reproached myself for my discourtesy," but he had enjoyed drinks at the railroad station with Robert Shaplen and George Weller (the author of the Harvard novel I so much admired, *Not to Eat, Not for Love*). He invited us for a weekend on his farm in North Wales.

* * *

The Republicans met in Philadelphia on June 21. On the third ballot they nominated, once again, Thomas E. Dewey. The delegates dispersed with cheerful confidence in the certainty of victory. Three weeks later the Democrats went to the same convention hall, looking, according to the Associated Press, as if they had accepted "an invitation to a funeral."

ADA took over a University of Pennsylvania fraternity house a few blocks away. We were a particularly dispirited lot. The Eisenhower bubble had been (fortunately) pricked by the general's own Shermanoid statement four days earlier. There was no alternative to Harry Truman. That evening, we gathered gloomily in the convention hall for Senator Alben Barkley's keynote address.

To my surprise and delight, I heard one of the rousing orations of my life — comparable among the century's keynotes only to Mario Cuomo's in 1984. A robust old pro, now seventy years old, Barkley thrilled the audience for an hour and eight minutes. It was an old-style Kentucky stemwinder delivered with such wit, such passion, such dramatic instinct and such fervent New Deal emotion that it impressed even the skeptics of ADA. For a moment Barkley dispelled the prevailing defeatism and sent delegates away filled with pride and optimism. The speech, among other things, made Barkley the vice-presidential nominee.

Going back to the fraternity house, I felt indisposed; more so the next morning. Something in my neck was troubling: swollen glands, perhaps? I consulted an ADA member who was an M.D. from Baltimore. He took one look and said, "You have the mumps. Go to bed at once." The fraternity house was not inviting, so I took the first plane back to Boston, thereby missing the critical fight over the civil rights plank in the platform — the issue on which ADA, lacking a candidate, had decided to take its stand.

The fiery young mayor of Minneapolis, Hubert Humphrey, was to be ADA's point man. The resolutions committee had adopted an innocuous plank blessing equal rights in terms so general and so restricted that southern Democrats would be hard put to object. The ADA minority plank, written by Joe Rauh and Andrew Biemiller, a Wisconsin congressman who had lost his seat in the Republican sweep of 1946 (and would regain it in 1948), called for specific civil rights actions in terms likely to alienate the south and thereby, some thought, to destroy any chance of a Democratic victory in November.

The party establishment brought intense pressure on Humphrey not to fight the majority plank. Hubert was a man of high intelligence, boundless energy and generous heart but not always of great personal strength. He was concerned about his race for the Senate against Joe Ball, a popular incumbent, who, though a Republican, had endorsed Roosevelt in 1944. He was concerned too about the effect an act of mutiny might have on his future in the Democratic party. Dave Niles, now the White House specialist on minorities, warned Joe Rauh, "You won't get fifty votes on your minority plank; all you'll do is ruin the chances of the number one prospect for liberalism in this country."

The argument in the fraternity house continued all night. At one point Leon Henderson said, "Hubert, I'll tell you this. If you don't speak for the minority plank, I promise you that you won't get a dime of Jew money out of New York" (or so Bill Dufty, who was there, told Murray Kempton the next day, and so Murray later told me). Finally, around five in the morning, Eugenie Anderson, Minnesota's national committeewoman, suggested adding to the minority plank a sentence commending President Truman for his courageous stand on civil rights. As Joe Rauh said, this took the "anti-Truman sting" out of the plank, and Hubert said OK; he would lead the fight.

I was in my bed on Irving Street when Hubert gave the great (and for Hubert exceptionally short) speech the next afternoon — a speech mostly written, I believe, by Milton Stewart and Joe Rauh, with additions by Humphrey himself. "There are those who say to you," he concluded, "we are rushing this issue of civil rights. I say we are one hundred and seventy-two years late. There are those who say — this issue of civil rights is an infringement on states' rights. The time has arrived for the Democratic party to get out of the shadow of states' rights and walk forthrightly into the bright sunshine of human rights."

Even for someone lying miserably in bed with the mumps, it was an exciting moment. The ADA minority plank, backed also by northern city bosses eager for the black vote — Ed Flynn in New York, David Lawrence in Pennsylvania, Jake Arvey in Illinois — carried a majority of delegates. The next day the Mississippi delegation and half the delegates from Alabama walked out of the convention, vowing never to cast their votes for Harry Truman.

Later that night — actually, at two the next morning — Truman accepted the nomination in a confident, derisive, militant speech. It appeared that Harry might be good hit as well as good field after all. The delegates departed on a high, but few among them believed that their nominee had even a fighting chance.

*   *   *

With the mumps gone, I departed too, for France. Nineteen forty-eight was the year the Marshall Plan began. I had not been present at the 1947 Harvard commencement, when Secretary of State Marshall called for a collective effort by the nations of Europe to work together for economic recovery and to combat those ancient enemies "hunger, poverty, desperation and chaos." The speech was written by Chip Bohlen, Harvard '27. The British Embassy, considering it one more commencement address, mailed the text to London instead of cabling it, but Malcolm Muggeridge of the *Daily Telegraph* and Leonard Miall of the BBC saw the implications and gave the speech stop-press treatment. "When the Marshall proposals were announced," Ernest

Bevin, the British foreign secretary, said, "I grabbed them with both hands."

The European response and a vigorous campaign of public education led to the passage of enabling legislation early in April 1948. The operating agency was called the Economic Cooperation Administration, and President Truman named as its head Paul Hoffman, a liberal Republican, president of the Studebaker Company and chairman of the Committee for Economic Development, an enlightened business group. Hoffman's assistant administrator was a proficient and forceful economist whom I had often met at Joe Alsop's, Richard M. Bissell, Jr. For chief of the Marshall Plan in Europe, Truman chose Averell Harriman.

I had run into Harriman on a number of social occasions in Washington and liked him very much. What struck me was that, despite the formidable gap in age, experience, status, knowledge and savoir-faire, not to mention wealth, he wasted no time on ceremony, treated me as a contemporary, instructed me to call him by his first name and placed our relations on a basis of ease and candor. Before he left for Paris to run ECA in Europe, he quite surprised me by proposing that I come over for a few months as his special assistant. Liking Harriman and loving Paris, on top of a historian's natural interest in watching history in the making, I said yes at once.

Harriman, a tall, handsome man who slouched slightly when he walked, with distinguished manners except when confronted by incompetence or stupidity, was fifty-six years old, with a varied career behind him in business, government and sports (polo, skiing). No American then living had, it seemed, been more identified with the rise of the United States as a force in world affairs. When he was born, in 1891, Benjamin Harrison was president, and the republic was still on the periphery of international politics. "There was no talk then," Harrison himself later recalled of the years after the Civil War, "of being a world power."

But the era of Little America was drawing to a close. When Averell was seven, he watched the great parade along Fifth Avenue welcoming Admiral Dewey, who had just won the Battle of Manila Bay on the other side of the planet. His father, the railroad magnate E. H. Harriman, with his dream of a round-the-world transportation system, had a global vision of the American future. He took young Averell with him to Alaska in 1899 on the celebrated Harriman scientific expedition starring the naturalists John Muir and John Burroughs. The ship put in for a day at Plover Bay in Siberia. Averell thus first set foot in Russia without a passport, as nearly half a century later he took delight in telling Stalin. (Stalin replied, "Well, you couldn't do that now.")

In 1905 E.H. took his son to Japan. Averell never quite forgave Endicott Peabody of Groton for refusing his father's request that he be permitted to go on with his father to Manchuria and China. Instead, the rector threatened expulsion if Averell did not return to school by the beginning of term. The elder Harriman rerouted a Pacific Mail liner to get Averell to the school on time. Nor did Averell ever forget his father's admonition: "Wealth is a responsibility; use it constructively and creatively."

In the Twenties, besides his international career as a polo player, he was an investment banker with worldwide interests, including a manganese concession in the Soviet Union. In the Thirties he was one of the very rare American capitalists with the historical insight to back FDR and the New Deal. Harry Hopkins was his New Deal patron; FDR welcomed a fellow Grotonian; and, as war approached, Harriman moved out of domestic affairs to serve successively as lend-lease expediter in Great Britain, Roosevelt's ambassador to the Soviet Union and Truman's ambassador to Britain.

Harriman had a long background in Soviet-American relations, longer perhaps in 1948 than any official on either side of the Cold War. He had negotiated with Trotsky in 1927 about the manganese concession; he knew Stalin well (as he would later know Khrushchev, Brezhnev and Andropov). In 1945 his press briefings sounded so anti-Soviet that Walter Lippmann and Raymond Swing walked out of one in indignant protest during the U.N. conference in San Francisco. Forty years later, the Soviet government conferred on him the Order of the Patriotic War, First Degree, "for his profound personal contribution to the establishment and consolidation of Soviet-American cooperation."

Averell had not changed his views. He always believed that the United States and the USSR had irreconcilable political objectives but must somehow find ways to live peacefully together. This made him appear a hardliner in the time of illusions about communism and an anti-hardliner in the black-and-white days of the Cold War. He was a charter member of the NCL group and could not abide Republicans like Harold Stassen, who wanted to cut off aid to any democratic Socialist government of Western Europe that insisted on nationalizing anything.

When Truman fired Wallace, he brought Averell back from London to take over the Commerce Department. Wallace said of his successor that Harriman "gives the superficial appearance of being dumb and hesitating. That impression is incorrect. . . . He may find it very difficult to express himself but he has a very strong will and when he eventually makes up his mind, he pursues his course relentlessly." Averell's manner — patrician, reserved, discreet, single-minded, dogged, laconic — concealed a bold and imaginative temperament. He was curious and questing, devoid of complacency, fond of experiment, exhilarated by new ideas. "I find," he once said, "I am an adventurer at heart." And he had a delightful and irreverent wife, Marie Norton, who had run an influential art gallery in New York in the Thirties and who dropped witty remarks out of the side of her mouth in a fashionable, mock-tough Long Island drawl.

*   *   *

Averell and Marie left for Paris in April. I filled out the ECA forms and awaited the completion of my appointment. Days passed without word, messages from Harriman inquired about the delay, and telephone calls to Dick Bissell produced evasive responses. Finally, recalling my experience with the Navy, I wondered whether someone had got it into his head that I was a subversive. I put the question directly to Bissell. He answered uncomfortably that this was indeed the case, but that everything would be OK in a few days. A few days passed, and everything was not OK.

Messages continued from Paris. The summer was wasting away. I had to return to teaching by late September. I told Phil Graham about my plight. Phil, a man of action, promptly called J. Edgar Hoover and asked what the delay was all about. Hoover told him to talk to Louis B. Nichols, the FBI's assistant director. Years later, I obtained through the Freedom of Information Act an (expurgated) copy of Lou Nichols's report on the Schlesinger case, so I may as well turn the story over to him:

> [Name blacked out but obviously Phil Graham] called this morning and wanted to see me. I saw him at noon. He outlined that one of his very close friends over a period of time was Arthur Schlesinger, Jr., who had worked for OWI and OSS and whom Averill [sic] Harriman wanted to take to Paris in the middle of June to aid in setting up the information services in connection with the Marshall Plan. He said that Schlesinger could not be cleared by ECA as the Bureau [FBI] was alleged to have reported unfavor-

ably on him. . . . He was calling on the Bureau to give testimony on behalf of Schlesinger.

Nichols told Graham that the Bureau would look into the matter immediately. The trouble, it developed, could not be blamed directly on the FBI. Somewhere in my government files rested the zany statement by the Army's Military Intelligence Division that one Arthur Schlesinger had been a Communist in New England in 1941. "Identity with Subject has not been established," MID had said, claiming, however, that the unidentified source was reliable. This undocumented accusation had not troubled OWI, OSS or the Civil Service Commission during the war, though it doubtless contributed to my rejection by the Navy. However, it now upset the ECA security director, an ex–FBI agent named J. W. Yeagley, and he refused clearance until he could pursue me into the FBI files.

What evidently bothered the FBI more even than the MID accusation was a statement submitted by some local patriot to the Boston FBI office that at a dinner in honor of Dr. George Coleman, the founder of the Ford Hall Forum, with speakers delivering two-minute tributes,

> Schlesinger broke the rule of the evening by talking ten minutes making two points — namely, praising Ford Hall Forum for their willingness to allow liberal and progressive speakers to appear and, secondly, an attack on the FBI and the Un-American Activities Committee for unwarranted interference with our democratic way of life; and that Schlesinger also stated that there was no difference between the Director and John Rankin [the right-wing racist congressman from Mississippi], if anything the Director represented a more destructive force in public life today than any Fascist who might be named including Rankin.

Nichols told Phil Graham that he would be "very happy to talk to Mr. Schlesinger if he so desired." I so desired, and Nichols and I soon had a point-by-point discussion of the allegations against me. Asked about the Coleman dinner, I said that I had indeed attacked the House Un-American Activities Committee and its chairman, J. Parnell Thomas, but had not attacked Hoover, that I did not use the term "fascist" in this loose manner but in its correct context and that I considered Hoover an antidote to Rankin. The FBI, reinterviewing the informant a few days later, reported that he "could offer nothing additional and, in fact, his then recollections of what Schlesinger said did not include the above statement [the Hoover denunciation] he previously attributed to Schlesinger."

I wish now that I had said all the things the informant attributed to me, but at the time I had the idea that the FBI was a professional agency and much to be preferred to the demagogic red-hunting lynch mobs of press and politics. I learned more about J. Edgar Hoover in due course. Asked in 1999 to nominate the best and worst Americans of the twentieth century, I named Hoover as the worst because, by legitimating and encouraging the more despicable aspects of our national behavior, he brought out the worst in my fellow countrymen. (My candidate for the best was FDR, because he most effectively appealed to what the best American of the nineteenth century called "the better angels of our nature.")

Phil Graham's intervention led Hoover to put on an urgent field investigation, to be completed by July 12. I have seen the sanitized result, and the FBI censor, while blacking out names, sometimes failed to black out addresses, so I am able to identify some of the witnesses. Chip Bohlen described me as "very definitely anti-Communist, but intelligently so"; the FBI man editing the document for submission to Hoover circled "but" and scrawled in the margin "omit." Scotty Reston said I was "100 per cent loyal" and of the highest character and reputation.

Phil's intervention also led Hoover to decide to do no more name checks for ECA. On July 12 Yeagley wrote to Hoover, regretting the trouble caused the Bureau by Schlesinger because ECA had denied him immediate employment. "Even considering the make-up of the man involved and the rather typical tactics that he resorted to . . . his action in making unjust accusations against the FBI, and in attempting to bring pressure to bear, was to my mind in bad taste. . . . I have heard that he also attempted to bring some pressure to bear on Military Intelligence, and the Department of State as well." (He heard wrong.) Yeagley implored Hoover to resume name checks for ECA, but Hoover said no.

In the meantime, I was cleared by ECA and speeded on my way to Paris. I could not but reflect, however, on the fate of innocent persons falsely accused who did not have the good luck to have a powerful newspaper publisher as a friend. The incident increased doubts about the entire loyalty program. "The suspicion arises," wrote Joe and Stewart Alsop in August, "that a good many investigating officials must be singularly ignorant and stupid, when the temporary Government appointment of a man like Arthur Schlesinger, Jr., is held up for weeks on security. . . . Any one capable of charging him with actual membership in the Communist Party, as he was recently charged, must believe that all us citizens except the friends of Representative [J. Parnell] Thomas, carry concealed party cards."

* * *

In Paris, Harriman had installed ECA in the Hôtel de Talleyrand, an elegant eighteenth-century mansion (not a hotel with rooms to rent) across from the American Embassy and next to the Hôtel Crillon (a hotel with rooms to rent) on the Place de la Concorde. Apparently Stalin had once expressed interest in acquiring the Hôtel de Talleyrand for Soviet diplomats. Averell rejoiced in his preemptive strike.

I arrived in mid-July, found a room in the Élysée Park at the Rond Point, a hotel I knew from the war, and presented myself at ECA headquarters. I was to assist a Washington friend, Alfred Friendly of the *Washington Post*, now Harriman's public affairs officer, and a new friend, Waldemar Nielsen, later to become an expert on foundations, in figuring out an information policy for the Marshall Plan.

Working for Averell was not always easy. He was a no-frills chief, single-minded in his concentration on the job. One evening he took me to a dinner given by a fashionable French hostess. Busy at the office, we arrived late, and after dinner Averell rose to return to our labors. "Averell," his hostess said, "just because you were last to arrive doesn't mean that you can be the first to leave." We left anyway.

He rarely slept and expected his associates to be on call at any hour of day or night. He had the rich man's bad habit of never carrying much cash on his person. Impecunious subordinates accompanying him sometimes had to dig into their own pockets to pay bills. His finicky insistence on getting small points exactly right earned him the sobriquet of Honest Ave the Hairsplitter. "He recognized no interest outside his work," wrote George Kennan, his deputy in Moscow. "Personal life did not exist for him." Averell never brought up with Kennan the odd coincidence that another George Kennan, the cousin of George's grandfather and an earlier Russian expert, had written the standard two-volume biography of E. H. Harriman. "A hundred times," wrote the younger Kennan, "I came away from our common labors asking myself, without finding an answer: 'Why do I still like this man?'"

Exasperating and even crusty as Harriman could sometimes be, he won extraordinary devotion from his associates. "The United States never had a more faithful public servant," Kennan said, answering his own question. "He never invited our affection, nor gave the impression that he would have reciprocated it; but in a curious way I think he had it, at least from those of us who were thrown together constantly with him." I do not know anyone who worked for Harriman, then or later, who failed to emerge not alone with admiration for his boldness of mind and intensity of purpose but with affection for his straightness, decency and occasional bursts of charm.

Al Friendly and I had special responsibility for his public appearances. Averell later became a rather effective speaker, but in those days he was an inveterate mumbler. After he had mumbled away at a speech before an increasingly bored audience at a luncheon of the American Chamber of Commerce in Paris, Al and I, unable to face him, sought fortification at a convenient café and did not reappear in the office till late in the afternoon. Averell glared at us and said, "All right, what did I do wrong?" We told him. He grunted, dismissed us brusquely and returned to work. Still later he came by and, without further word about the speech, invited us to dinner at Maxim's.

His political adviser was Philip Bonsal, an intelligent, urbane and liberal-minded foreign service officer who became a good friend. One day Bonsal's old associate Larry Duggan passed through Paris, and the three of us had a jolly lunch; this was four months before Duggan's mysterious death. My Belgian friend Robert Triffin was in Paris, working on what would crystalize in 1950 as the European Payments Union.

Another friend from this period was Jim Forrestal's son Michael, who, because of his mother's alcoholism and his father's preoccupation, had been largely reared by the Harrimans. A close friend in later years, Mike was a man of amused wit and infectious good cheer with a strong character, a great love of opera and sailing and sound views on public policy, as he later demonstrated on President Kennedy's National Security Council staff in his doubts about the Vietnam War.

Then there was a fellow named Howard Hunt who had gone to Brown with my brother, Tom. He attracted attention in ECA as a certified published novelist. His first book, *Limit of Darkness,* had had pretty good reviews, and he was to write modestly successful spy novels in years to come. I did not much like him; he seemed on the sneaky side. In the Fifties Hunt joined the CIA; in the Seventies he moved on to Richard Nixon's Watergate Plumbers, from which in due course he went to prison. I can't remember what he was supposed to be doing for the Marshall Plan.

*   *   *

Europe was still reeling under the shock of war. Churchill had described the continent in 1947 as "a rubble heap, a charnel house, a breeding ground for pestilence and hate." Though production was beginning to revive, European governments were hobbled by the dollar shortage, self-confidence was low, Communists were banging at the gates, and pessimism colored the future. The Marshall Plan confronted political and psychological as well as economic problems.

Harriman took me along on his visits to Marshall Plan countries. One of our first trips was to Vienna, the city whose darkly ambiguous atmosphere was caught with precision the next year in Carol Reed's film of Graham Greene's *The Third Man*. (I cannot refrain from adding that, when the sheet music of the *Third Man* theme came out in the United States, Walter Lord provided the English lyrics.) We went to Stockholm, Oslo, Brussels, Rome. In international affairs, Averell had what Max Weber called a "trained intuition, something like a musical ear." His sure political instincts lapsed only when, in the Fifties, he confronted the incomprehensible politics of his native state of New York.

I was impressed by the linguistic skills of his military aide and interpreter Major Vernon Walters. Whatever capital we visited, Dick Walters spoke the language with fluency and flair. He also showed zest as a raconteur, but there he had one signal defect: his stories were not necessarily true, as I learned to my sorrow thirty years later.

We had encountered each other again in the Kennedy years when, as military attaché at the Rome embassy, he served as my interpreter in a meeting with President Antonio Segni. According to Walters in his 1978 autobiography, *Silent Missions,* I bullied a most reluctant Segni to comment in total confidence on Italian political personalities and then published his remarks in a book, causing "great furor" in Italy and "widespread demands for Segni's resignation," as a result of which Segni had a stroke, resigned and died. This was total fiction. I never published any remarks Segni made to me, and I was not responsible for his unfortunate stroke, resignation and death. When I pointed this out to Walters, he apologized, saying that he had instructed the publishers to delete the story in future printings, adding that he had been misinformed "by sources I considered reliable." Since Walters had served four years as deputy director of the CIA, I wondered what sort of critical eye he could have cast on the intelligence reports that passed over his desk.

*   *   *

Life in Paris was, as always, delightful. David Bruce was chief of the ECA mission to France, and I lunched regularly with my adored Evangeline in Left Bank bistros. The Bruces gave stylish dinner parties. At one of them, for friends just over from England, I was staggered when a stunning tall blonde girl in a smashing red dress swept into the room, walking in beauty and radiating gaiety and delight as she walked. I fell in love with her the first second I saw her.

She turned out to be an American girl, Marietta Peabody, from Massachusetts, the granddaughter of the rector of Groton. She was married to a former British MP, Ronald Tree, whose house at Ditchley provided Churchill with a weekend refuge during the war when the moon was high and Chequers lay exposed to Nazi bombers. Ronnie was half-American; his grandfather was Marshall Field. He had lost his seat in the Labour landslide of 1945.

With her beauty, intelligence and charm, Marietta could have coasted through life. But her Massachusetts ancestors had been ministers, abolitionists, educators, reformers, and the blood had not run thin. Marietta had the old New England passion to improve the world. She did not, it must be said, dedicate herself in the Boston manner to plain living as well as to high thinking. She beautifully united two contrasting American traditions — a New Yorker in her style, a New Englander in her soul. Far from being immobilized by the conflict between worldliness and public service, she serenely transcended it. She once told me that her ideal was to be a combination of Carole Lombard and Eleanor Roosevelt.

With her first husband, Desmond FitzGerald, later of the CIA, overseas during the war, Marietta went to work for *Life* magazine and was radicalized by membership in the Newspaper Guild, at least to the extent of abandoning her ancestral Republicanism for the New Deal. She also fascinated the film director John Huston, a man of wit and magnetism, who wanted to marry her. When FitzGerald returned from the war, he and Marietta met as strangers, and the marriage collapsed. But the undependable Huston seemed too heavy a dose, as he himself demonstrated by eloping in a drunken moment with the actress Evelyn Keyes. In later years Marietta felt that marriage to Huston would have been a disaster. Instead, they remained dear friends for the rest of their lives. Huston cast her in a couple of his movies: in *The Misfits* (1961) she is the divorcée who tries to tempt Clark Gable with a laundry in Kansas City; in *Mr. North* (1988) she is cast, more appropriately, as Mrs. Vanderbilt.

Ronald Tree seemed rich, reliable and manageable. But Marietta was not very happy in England. Her political earnestness did not play well, and champions of Ronnie's first wife were systematically mean to her. She was starved for American political talk and fell on me as a recent arrival from the States who could fill her in on everything. We got along famously, then and later.

*   *   *

On a trip to London I made two new friends — Thomas K. Finletter, chief of the ECA mission, and his wife, Gretchen, known to all as Gay. She was a daughter of the conductor Walter Damrosch and a granddaughter of James G. Blaine, the silver-tongued orator (or, as his opponents said, the continental liar) from the state of Maine who dominated Republican politics in the latter nineteenth century.

Tom Finletter was a staunch liberal Democrat, an advocate of world government and, paradoxically, until this nirvana could be achieved, an advocate of air-atomic power as the center of our military strategy — a case made in the 1948 report of the Finletter Commission on Air Policy. His book of 1945, *Can Representative Government Do the Job?*, is still the most ingenious argument for a merger of presidential and parliamentary systems. In manner Tom was laconic, incisive and ironic, Gay was a sublimely witty lady and a successful light novelist, and I liked them both at once.

I renewed friendships with Labour friends, especially Aneurin Bevan. Nye was in exuberant form, less anti-American than before, more anti-Soviet than before. He propounded the dangerous line that a drawn-out Cold War would be to our disadvantage. The democracies, he said, would be forced to devote an ever-increasing share of resources to rearmament. This would lead to inflation followed by a crash; and, if that happened, the democracies would find it hard to preserve a united will to resist communism. In the meantime, the Soviet Union, tormented by spreading Titoism, would turn increasingly to foreign aggression as a means of escaping communism's internal contradictions. If the period of tension lasted long enough, Nye predicted, war would come when the democracies were weary and divided and the Soviet Union would have had time to overcome critical deficiencies in atomic weapons and steel production.

At this point I said, "That sounds almost like an argument for a preventive war." Bevan replied, "But a democracy, of course, cannot fight a preventive war." Schlesinger: "What policy do you propose then?" Bevan: "A policy of inviting the Soviets to make a mistake." Schlesinger: "Do you mean that we should stick out our chin and let the

Russians take a swing at it?" Bevan: "Something like that." (I take this dialogue from a memorandum to Harriman of September 20, 1948.)

Two months earlier, the Soviet Union had imposed a blockade on land traffic to Berlin. The allied response was the famous airlift. Obviously, Nye said, we can't withdraw from Berlin, nor can we expect a negotiated settlement. Maintaining the airlift through the winter will be extremely difficult and, if it works, only defers a solution. The thing to do is "to force a crisis now" — to secure land routes to Berlin, first through ultimatums and appeals to world opinion; then, if necessary, by force. The Russians would probably not go to war because they must know how weak they are. Their retreat will mean an immense loss in prestige. And if they do go to war, would it not be better to get it over with at once than to wait while they build their military power? Nye appeared convinced that a war with the Soviet Union in 1948 would be short and simple.

I doubt that he would have talked this way if he had been foreign secretary rather than minister of health, but his attitude was indicative of the rather desperate mood of the year. So too was a memorandum I gave Harriman about ECA information policies. One point was the great advantage the Soviet Union had enjoyed in political warfare. Since the end of the war, the Communists, with the field pretty much to themselves, had implanted two basic stereotypes in the European mind: the U.S.S.R. as a powerful and dynamic nation, ruthless no doubt, but ruthlessly dedicated to the interests of the masses; and the U.S.A. as a powerful and regressive nation ruthlessly dedicated to enslavement of the masses by capitalist monopolies.

The European Recovery Program, I suggested, created the opportunity to combat these stereotypes. The Marshall Plan had put the Communists on the defensive politically, but they still retained the propaganda initiative. My proposal, not very realistic in retrospect, was to overcome this propaganda advantage by tapping the moral energy supposedly coming from what I thought to be a profound popular desire for European unity.

This was a major hope I brought back when I returned to the United States in late September. In two pieces the *New Republic* published in November, I argued the virtues of a European federation and the need for the United States to underwrite such a federation through military guarantees. The great obstacle among the democracies to a united Europe, I discerned, was Great Britain. Alas, half a century later, economic integration has progressed admirably, but political unification is still a distant and, in the eyes of some Europeans and many Britishers, a dubious objective. The notion of a United States of Europe naturally appealed to citizens of the United States of America. But I should have reflected that the American states had a common language, common currency, common legal traditions, common political experience, common national interests — and yet, with all those advantages, it took a bitter and bloody civil war to create the American nation.

The Marshall Plan itself remains an extraordinary act of imaginative statesmanship. Over four years the United States contributed more than $13 billion, 6 to 9 percent of the federal budget — over $90 billion in the currency of 2000 — to European recovery. I am aware of the revisionist view, ably argued by the British economic historian Alan Milward, that recovery was already beginning before Marshall aid arrived and would have taken place in due course had there been no Marshall aid at all.

From a historian's viewpoint, this narrowly economic argument omits the political and psychological context. The Marshall Plan was under relentless attack from Communist parties, newspapers, labor unions and demonstrations. By speeding recovery and increasing employment, income and productivity, Marshall aid reduced communism's appeal to the working classes. By formally committing the United States to European recovery, Marshall aid infused Western Europe with new confidence in the future. By its reliance on European initiatives and its insistence on regional cooperation, the Marshall approach allowed Europe to define its own interests, helping to revitalize European morale and to instill a sense of common European purpose. As Helmut Schmidt said in 1997, "The United States ought not to forget that the emerging European Union is one of its own greatest achievements: it would never have happened without the Marshall Plan."

For a historian, it was thrilling to take part in the first months of one of the most successful and beneficial projects in the history of the twentieth century.

* * *

While I was away saving Europe, politics rolled on at home. The two breakaway factions of the Democratic party had complicated the impending election by setting themselves up as parties in their own right.

The southern secessionists met in Birmingham in mid-July, the hall decked with Confederate battle flags, to form the States' Rights party, known to the rest of the country as the Dixiecrats. They adopted a platform denouncing the "infamous and iniquitous" civil rights program as a "totalitarian" effort to impose a "police state" and nominated Governor Strom Thurmond of South Carolina for president. Thurmond intended to base his campaign on states' rights, not on race, but soon he was Claghorning around the south, crying: "There's not enough troops in the Army to break down segregation and admit the Negro into our homes, our eating places, our swimming pools and our theaters." (Forty years later, Thurmond, now a Republican senator, had black Americans working as professionals in his office.)

A week later, the Progressive party held its convention in Philadelphia. I noticed in the Paris *Herald Tribune* that Harvard's F. O. Matthiessen seconded Wallace's nomination and that ADA's Jim Loeb challenged the party's pro-Soviet slant in hard-hitting testimony before the resolutions committee. The delegates thereafter confirmed Jim's point by shouting down the so-called Vermont resolution declaring that the Progressive party refused "to give blanket endorsement to the foreign policy of any nation." There was no doubt about the nation whose foreign policy in Progressive eyes was entitled to blanket endorsement.

Wallace campaigned energetically and courageously, even insisting on unsegregated audiences and lodgings in the south. Jimmy Wechsler, who covered him for most of the year, noted that in informal talks with small groups or on college campuses he appeared reasonable and unhysterical, expressing his awareness of the magnitude of the problems Truman had inherited, but by the evening of the same day he would change into God's angry man, sanctimoniously blessing the Communist worldview.

He handled the Communist issue maladroitly. He insisted repeatedly that he knew very little about communism. "Probably there are just as many kinds of Communists," he would say, "as there are kinds of Republicans and Democrats." Surely, Wechsler noted, a man who took so many dogmatic stands on issues involving world communism weakened his authority when he boasted in the next paragraph that he didn't know what he was talking about.

The Communist hand was less and less hidden. Herbert Aptheker, the Communist historian, came out with a pamphlet, "Task Force ADA," attacking Niebuhr and me at some length, saying that all we were up to was "to prolong the life of an obsolete social order" and "hide its decay with euphonious lies." Liberals felt increasingly uneasy in the Wallace camp. The poet John Ciardi, a lecturer in the Harvard English Department, had thrown himself into the campaign, traveling with Wallace and speaking every night of the week (and speaking well). The closer he became to Wallace, the more his doubts grew. As he said, "I began to feel he would have made a great professor for a course in Thoreau and Emerson, but that as President of the United States he would be a disaster."

By October Ciardi was beginning to see that the Progressive party was a tool of the Communist party. Wallace, he concluded, was, at best, a good man duped by ambition, which was to say, finally, a small man. But John had already committed himself to public appearances for Wallace and could not bring himself to cancel them. "It was only in the confessional of the voting booth with the curtains drawn behind me that I pushed the lever for Truman."

Many early supporters finished the same way. Even Rex Tugwell was disturbed by the Communist role. In August he told the *Baltimore Sun*, "I certainly don't know whether they are Communists, but they act as though they were." With that, Tugwell dropped quietly out of the campaign.

On the brink of his ninetieth birthday, John Dewey said, "There can be no compromise, no matter how temporary, with totalitarianism. . . . In the Wallace candidacy, I see no hope for progressives." In mid-October Harold Ickes, objecting to the Wallace people's effort to "wrap themselves in the glory of Franklin Roosevelt," sent prominent New Dealers a statement calling on "every American who takes pride in our liberal past and who wishes to enlist in the fight for a liberal future" to reject the Progressive party — a party that repudiated "the methods and purposes of Franklin D. Roosevelt" and was "the most serious attempt in the history of our nation by a totalitarian group to capture and destroy American liberalism." Forty leading New Dealers signed, including such figures as Francis Biddle, Thurman Arnold, Ben Cohen, Mary McLeod Bethune, Aubrey Williams, Herbert Lehman, Chester Bowles, Maury Maverick, Archie MacLeish, Bob Sherwood, Elmer Davis, Isador Lubin. (The turndowns, Libby Donahue told me four days before ADA released the statement, were an odd group: Cordell Hull, Henry Morgenthau, Steve Early, FDR's press secretary, and Milo Perkins, a close friend of Wallace.)

*   *   *

When I returned from Paris, it was hardly as a Truman enthusiast. I have no memory of this, but a Rochester newspaper reports me as telling the City Club that historians would have to go back to the contest in 1872 between Ulysses S. Grant and Horace Greeley "to find so bleak an alternative" as Truman versus Dewey. "Truman makes friends without influencing people," I continued, "and Dewey influences people without making friends." Truman "says everything in the book" while Dewey, "who says nothing," is like the winning football team "freezing the ball until the last whistle is blown."

But I must have been swept along by Harry Truman's rollicking whistle-stop campaigning as against what seemed the cataleptic complacency of Tom Dewey. Stiff and formal when reading from a script, Truman was amusing and rousing when speaking from notes. The crowds clustered around the railroad tracks would shout: "Give 'em hell, Harry," and Truman would respond: "I'll tell 'em the truth and they'll think it's hell" and plunge into his free-wheeling castigation of the "do-nothing, good-for-nothing Eightieth Congress."

There was something about his lonely gallantry as well as his increasingly liberal message that was hard to resist. "Travelling with him," Richard Rovere wrote in the *New Yorker,* "you get the feeling that the American people . . . would be willing to give him just about anything he wants except the presidency." By October I was saying enthusiastically, according to the *Harvard Crimson,* "I would rather vote for the haberdasher than the dummy in his window." (This excellent crack was, I fear, not original with me.)

In early October my OWI friend W. McNeil Lowry paid a call on Clark Clifford at the White House. Mac, now a political correspondent for James M. Cox's newspapers in Dayton and Atlanta, pointed out that a reduction in grain storage bins passed by the Eightieth Congress in June had forced farmers to sell their surplus grain at less than the support price. His series of articles under such headlines as CONGRESS ACTS TO FORCE DOWN FARMERS' PRICE AT BEHEST OF GRAIN LOBBY galvanized the farm vote. Lowry even secretly contributed language to Truman's farm speeches. Truman himself accused the Republican Congress of sticking "a pitchfork in the farmer's back." But the urban press had little interest in grain storage bins, and the simmering agrarian discontent went largely unnoticed.

As election day approached, pollsters, scientifically assured of the outcome, stopped polling. Professor Samuel Stouffer, an eminent Harvard sociologist, recalled to the Nieman Fellows the failure of the *Literary Digest* poll in 1936 when, contrary to the forecast of a Landon victory, FDR carried all but two states. "This can't happen now," Sam Stouffer, a nice man, said. "We have developed polling methods into an exact science. If any of you think there is a chance that this election will be close, you are deceiving yourself." Joe and Stewart Alsop wrote in the *Saturday Evening Post* that Dewey was "the most important American political leader of the year 1948 and perhaps for a good many years to come." *Newsweek* canvassed fifty journalistic know-it-alls; each one predicted a GOP sweep. When Truman read the *Newsweek* story, he told Clark Clifford not to worry: "I know every one of those fifty fellows, and not one of them has enough sense to pound sand into a rathole" (a mysterious Missouri putdown).

In mid-October Clifford called from the White House to ask whether I would draft a speech for President Truman to deliver in Boston. I of course said yes. David Noyes of the presidential staff, later a co-author of Truman's memoirs, followed up. The president, he said, felt very strongly about the mounting racial and religious tensions here and abroad and would like to devote at least part of the speech to the problems of intolerance. Noyes enclosed a copy of the speech Dewey had given in Boston at the end of his 1944 campaign; "Mr. Dewey should be confronted with the extreme position then taken by him."

Dewey had indeed made a mean-spirited speech in Boston on November 1, 1944. "With the aid of Sidney Hillman," he had said, "the Communists are seizing control of the New Deal, through which they hope to control the government of the United States," and his spotlighting of Hillman and David Dubinsky seemed to savor of anti-Semitism. FDR came to detest Dewey and told Harry Hopkins it was the meanest campaign of his life.

Dewey was after all a prosecutor; still, the Boston speech was probably out of character, but it was all too characteristic of tired candidates in the last desperate days before the final countdown (look at Alf Landon's attacks on social security in 1936 or Adlai Stevenson's speech about Eisenhower's health in 1956). The memory of his 1944 excesses was undoubtedly a factor in Dewey's 1948 strategy of renouncing the prosecutorial style and settling for solemn banalities.

In later years I got to know Dewey a bit when he was courting Kitty Carlisle Hart. Since Kitty's guests were predominantly from the theater, Dewey recognized me as from the political world and therefore someone he could talk to. I found him a humane, agreeable and civilized man, surely one of the more enlightened members of what never struck me in a long life as a notably enlightened party.

My draft for Truman? I was still a novice ghostwriter, and my speech, though perhaps adequate for stately speakers, was of no use for a staccato president.

* * *

On election night we called in friends to mourn the anticipated result. The Galbraiths came and the Perry Millers and the Gardner Coxes. Two former New Deal congressmen were there with their wives: Tom and Lois Eliot and Joe and Constance Casey (whose son John Casey became a significant novelist).

We were surprised early on by the doughty fight Truman seemed to be putting on and by apparent Democratic successes in the Congress. The thought never occurred to me that Truman might actually win. Barbara Kerr, who, though a good liberal Democrat, was now writing editorials for the strictly Republican *Boston Traveler,* evidently had a premonition. In the midst of it all, she put on her coat and prepared to leave. Ken Galbraith asked her where she was going. "That editorial on 'Return to Sanity' isn't going to run," she replied. "I've got to substitute my alternative editorial, 'No Mandate for Socialism.'"

When the party finally broke up at four-thirty in the morning, it looked as if there might well be a Democratic Congress. I still had no expectation that Truman himself could make it. The Wallace vote had already delivered New York to Dewey. But when we awoke the next morning, Truman was leading in the electoral college. I then began to think that the Progressives and Dixiecrats might siphon off enough electoral votes to send the decision to the House of Representatives. This would have happened if Dewey, who eventually lost California, Illinois and Ohio by less than 1 percent of the popular vote, had carried two of those states.

Suddenly, at 11:15 A.M., Dewey conceded. When I met my twelve o'clock class, I was greeted with resounding applause. Democrats were in a state of shock and exultation, and even Republicans seemed not to mind all that much. Rather, they appeared reluctantly delighted by the triumph of homely virtue over the city slicker.

What had happened? The Republican defeat could be attributed partly to the complacency of Dewey's campaign and partly to the two breakaway Democratic factions that, contrary to expectation, helped Truman more than they hurt him. The Progressives saved Truman from charges of leftism, thereby reassuring the Catholic vote, and the Dixiecrats brought out the black vote, thereby providing the winning margin in California, Illinois and Ohio. Then there was the grain storage bin issue. "You can analyze figures from now to kingdom come," Dewey himself said to Herbert Brownell, his campaign manager, "and all they will show is that we lost the farm vote which we had in 1944 and that lost the election." And there was the union vote. "Labor did it," Truman himself was reported to have said.

As for Henry Wallace, he claimed credit for Truman's victory. The Progressive party, he said, had "forced the Democrats to don the mantle of Roosevelt and to promise the American people a return to the New Deal." But in 1950, when North Korea invaded South Korea, Wallace broke with the Progressives and backed the United States and the United Nations. The scales belatedly fell from his eyes. In 1951 he told Ed Lahey, "I didn't actually realize how strong the Communists were in the Progressive party." In 1952 he told Herbert Philbrick, the FBI informant who penetrated the Communist party and thereafter wrote *I Led Three Lives,* that the Communists had made "a shambles out of a party which could have served a very useful function."

*   *   *

In the meantime, the Schlesinger family grew. A fortnight after the vindication of Harry Truman, our fourth child, a son, was born. My parents were in the Netherlands for a year at the University of Leyden, and my father suggested, I think humorously, that we might want to call the new baby Harry T. Schlesinger. Remembering his own narrow escape from Grover Cleveland, we resisted that thought. Instead, we named the new baby Andrew after the age of Jackson — Andrew Bancroft Schlesinger.

24

Deals Fair and Unfair

NINETEEN FORTY-NINE OPENED in a mood of exhilaration, at least for Roosevelt's children. Despite the do-nothing, good-for-nothing Eightieth Congress, the New Deal was evidently not a spent force. The *Economist* talked of FDR's "Fifth Term." On January 5, in his State of the Union address, President Truman extended the New Deal in a broad and bracing program and christened it the Fair Deal.

Though the Democrats had regained nominal control of Congress, the president faced a de facto conservative majority — Republicans plus southern Democrats. Truman fought valiantly for his Fair Deal but mostly in vain. In November he confided to his diary, "Trying to make the Eighty-first Congress perform is and has been worse than cussing the 80th." But he kept on fighting, and it was increasingly plain that he really cared.

I considerably revised my initially scornful assessment of Truman. So did much of the country. His inauguration in 1949 even produced a burst of comparisons with Andrew Jackson. This seemed to me excessive. Jackson, I wrote in April in Max Ascoli's new magazine, the *Reporter,* was one of those half-dozen presidents who had supplied "the nation, for better or for worse, with new political premises. These men, in a sense, worked transformations." Truman was obviously not in the transformative class. The more appropriate comparison, I suggested, would be with a lesser president in the Jacksonian tradition, "the unspectacular, unimpressive and underrated James K. Polk."

"Of all our array of Presidents," my father's student Jim Thurber had rashly written in 1937, "there was none less memorable than James K. Polk." On the other hand, George Bancroft, who was Polk's secretary of the Navy and minister to Britain, had said in 1888: "His Administration, viewed from the standpoint of results, was perhaps the greatest in our national history, certainly one of the greatest." The historical verdict is closer to Bancroft than to Thurber. My father's 1962 poll of historians and political scientists and other more recent polls invariably place Polk along with Truman in the 'near great' category.

Neither Polk nor Truman was one of those creative presidents who make the nation look at things in a new way. Neither had the greatness to anticipate and master history. But both had the intelligence and the courage to accept the challenge of history. History might have broken them, as it broke Buchanan and Hoover. Instead it forced them, not into personal greatness, but into the performance of great things.

Polk, like Truman, had had a serious and respectable career in Congress; he was indeed the only Speaker of the House of Representatives ever to make the White House. Both Polk and Truman came to power in the shadow of presidents they greatly admired, but both rather quickly divested themselves of old Jacksonians and old Rooseveltians and built their own administrations. In this respect they were bolder than Lyndon Johnson, who retained most of John Kennedy's cabinet and advisers.

Neither Polk nor Truman had a high sense of what George Bush, who also lacked it, called "the vision thing." But both grasped historic opportunities with unassuming precision. The president who comes to terms with history, I concluded in the *Reporter,* is less great than the president who transforms history; but he is enormously to be preferred to the president who is run over by history.

* * *

Truman's history-making accomplishments were mostly in foreign affairs. At home he aspired to the consolidation and completion of the New Deal. His Fair Deal proposed to employ federal power to underwrite personal security to a degree unprecedented in American history. The destination was called in the Forties the 'welfare state' — a proud term then. By the Reaganite Eighties, the word 'welfare,' originally a reference to the Constitution's high command to "promote the general welfare," had been trivialized into an alleged subsidy for alleged welfare queens. 'Welfare state' ended as a term of abuse.

In 1949 I adopted the phrase with enthusiasm, lectured in support of the welfare state and hoped to persuade *Fortune* to run a defense of the concept. The welfare state, I observed, did not at all mean direct government control over the economy. It was perfectly compatible with the free market. It meant simply the establishment of basic national standards of living for all citizens. I summoned impeccably conservative witnesses, quoting Bob Taft on the need "to put a floor

under the necessities of life" and Winston Churchill on the "maintenance of a basic standard of life and labor below which a man or
woman, however old or weak, shall not be allowed to fall." This, Churchill said, "must be the first care of the state and must have priority
over all other peacetime needs."

I still don't see what's so wrong with all this — with putting a floor
under the necessities of life or, as a later generation would put it, with
providing a firm social safety net. "A decent provision for the poor,"
said Dr. Johnson, "is the true test of civilization." For the richest country in the world it is surely a moral obligation.

The attack on the welfare state began almost at once. "The slogan of a 'welfare state,'" said the obdurate Herbert Hoover, "has
emerged as a disguise for the totalitarian state by the route of spending." Friedrich Hayek's *The Road to Serfdom* (1944) endorsed the thesis
that countries go totalitarian when governments acquire power under the pretext of doing good for their citizens.

The Hoover-Hayek thesis was, and is, historical nonsense. As I
wrote to my friend John Chamberlain in 1949, there is no example
on record of progressive social legislation leading to totalitarianism.
Chamberlain himself was an interesting case. In 1932 he published
Farewell to Reform, a radical essay that lived brilliantly up to its title. In
the early Thirties he was a sharp and influential daily book reviewer
for the *New York Times.* In 1940 he published *The American Stakes,* a
shrewd and original analysis of the New Deal. But this intelligent
book turned out to be a midstation in John's passage from the left to
the right. By the late Forties, he had become an ardent apostle of laissez-faire.

Chamberlain was an extremely nice, if increasingly wrong-headed,
man. We lunched together fairly regularly for years before his death
in 1995. He is remembered today mostly as the inspiration for Mary
McCarthy's famous short story "Portrait of the Intellectual as a Yale
Man" in *The Company She Keeps.* John, a good sport as befits a Yale
man, gave the book a favorable review, saying that "its satire is administered as gently and as murderously as a cat administers death to a
mouse."

"Impotent democratic government, and not potent democratic
government," I wrote to Chamberlain, "lays the foundation for totalitarianism." The New Deal did not put the republic on the road to
serfdom; it liberated the serfs to become producers and consumers.
The menacing dictatorships of the Thirties and Forties — the Soviet
Union, Germany, Italy, Spain — arose not because democratic gov-

ernment was too powerful but because it was too weak. "Every dictatorship which we now know," said Thurman Arnold in 1936, "flowed
into power like air into a vacuum because the central government, in
the face of a real difficulty, declined to exercise authority."

One wondered too why Hoover and other enemies of the welfare
state believed that government aid to business was wise and virtuous
while government aid to farmers or workers or the unemployed or
the elderly was vicious and led to collectivism. Hoover himself had
signed the Smoot-Hawley tariff, the highest in American history, and
protectionism is of course a subsidy to business.

And it seemed to us equally odd that so many of those who denounced "statism" when it meant government assurance of social
protection or government regulation of anti-social business practices
were also the most zealous advocates of statism in the really sinister
sense of calling on the government to crack down on citizens thinking unpopular thoughts. "You have the curious paradox," I wrote to
Chamberlain, "that those who most loudly denounce statism on the
economic front are the ones who advocate it most vociferously on
the intellectual front — who demand loyalty tests, witch-hunts, expulsion of liberal professors from colleges, and so on. The government
agency which contains the greatest statist potential is, of course,
the FBI."

What really led to totalitarianism, I told the Student League for Industrial Democracy in March 1950, was total state ownership of the
means of production and distribution. It was not just that centralized
planning created a disastrous inflexibility. "The planners tend to have
a vested interest in their plans, covering every mistake with more regulations until the economy is held in rigid control." It was above all
that total state ownership of the economy undermined political freedom. "Political opposition can only exist," I said, "when resources for
that opposition are outside the reach of those in power."

But total state ownership was a very different animal from the
welfare state. And the discussion in any case was entirely theoretical.
No democratic socialist government has ever nationalized all the
means of production and distribution. Enemies of the welfare state
were combatting fantasies concocted by their own inflamed imagination.

Rereading the welfare state article, I find it a reasonable enough
statement of the case. *Fortune* thought otherwise and declined to publish a document so contrary to Harry Luce's general line.

*   *   *

Both as a historian and as a liberal, I was much interested in the relationship between the Fair Deal and the New Deal. *Life* thought the contrast might make a good piece, and in 1949 I conducted a round of interviews with New Dealers and Fair Dealers. Some put their thoughts off the record; but a half century has passed, and I doubt that any of them, wherever they are, would now reject the claims of history.

"FDR and the New Dealers," Clark Clifford told me, "were like General Patton and the Third Army. They made a brilliant breakthrough, but they were beginning to outrun their lines of communication. Now it is time for mopping-up operations and for a steady advance along a broad front. In a time of prosperity there is less scope and demand for drastic action. Still, things can and must be done to shore up the system."

In fact, the Fair Deal, building as it did on the New Deal, was programmatically the more radical of the two. President Truman integrated the armed forces, sought a permanent Fair Employment Practices Commission and even advocated the government operation of steel plants. Secretary of Agriculture Charles Brannan's farm plan called for a shift from price to income maintenance and imposed limits on federal payments to rich farmers. Leon Keyserling's Employment Act of 1946 committed the federal government to maximum employment, production and purchasing power.

Oscar Ewing's national health plan envisaged universal coverage — an objective still unachieved at the end of the century. "Sickness comes to everybody," Clifford said, "so why shouldn't a man anticipate it? Why shouldn't the government, or organized medicine, let him pay for his care and the care of his family in advance, a little each month, and share the risk with his compatriots? Organized medicine won't do it, so the government must do it. And the plan the President proposes is nothing more than an insurance plan. I haven't yet heard life insurance called socialistic. Have you?"

President Truman thus wished to move beyond the New Deal. On the other hand, he never cared much for ideological New Dealers. In embracing more of the welfare state than Roosevelt ever was able to do, Truman did so without benefit of the breed he scorned as "professional liberals."

"FDR," Clifford told me, "liked a world of ideas. When people came in bubbling over with ideas, FDR could pick out the one good from the six bad. All this makes President Truman uncomfortable. He is suspicious of what he calls the 'crackpot' and 'do-good' people in the New Deal. He is out of his element in an atmosphere of intellectual combat. He likes issues to be carefully worked out, prepared, documented. Then, when pros and cons are clearly presented, he makes his decisions — and always," Clifford added, "on the liberal side."

Charlie Ross, Truman's old newspaper friend and now his press secretary, similarly emphasized to me the "temperamental incompatibility" between his president and the New Dealers. They operated on different wavelengths — the one placing a premium on personal loyalty, party regularity, teamwork; the other on principles, programs, ideas. Truman thought people who resigned over principles — Harold Ickes, Henry Wallace, Wilson Wyatt, Chester Bowles, Paul Porter — were unreliable and egotistical. Yet Ross agreed with Clifford that the president's Missouri populism, with its suspicion of "the interests," led him to come down in the end on the liberal side.

* * *

New Dealers and Fair Dealers were indeed distinct psychological types. New Dealers did exist in the world of ideas. They were lawyers, professors, social workers, precipitated into political life by the Great Depression, and they were less concerned with politics than with policy. They sought power avidly, and some were corrupted by it; but most wanted power not for personal gratification but to achieve social goals. They ate, drank and slept national issues, they labored, theorized and schemed without rest, and their commitment united them in a crusade of social reform. They were sophisticated in their talk and cosmopolitan in their orientation.

The Fair Dealers were cut from a different pattern. Harry Truman was the first president from west of the Mississippi (except for Hoover, whose connection with Iowa and California was mostly historical), and his administration had a strong midwestern flavor. He liked practical-minded, middlebrow, nontheoretical people. The atmosphere of the Fair Deal was anticleverness and anticrusade.

New Dealers were typically people extruded from American life, too highly charged for the towns that produced them and to which so few of them ever returned. Fair Dealers seemed to spring straight from the common life of the country. Most could sink back into it without leaving a ripple on the surface. With their pink cheeks and bland, unlined faces, their healthy, handsome daughters and their warm family lives, their affable extroversions and their boisterous practical jokes, they were part of the American landscape.

"Every midwestern community," I wrote for *Life,*

has its Clark Clifford, resplendent in tails at its country club dances, its Tom Clark around the courthouse stove, its Harry Vaughan [a Truman pal from the First World War] in the American Legion post, its Bill Boyle [Democratic National Committee] on the local ward committee, its Mon Wallgren [Truman senatorial pal, now on the Federal Power Commission] behind the counter of the local jewelry store, its paper match covers marked with snappy sentiments like: "I swiped this from Harry S. Truman."

The New Deal had been an improvised, somewhat helter-skelter, response to the economic and political breakdown of American capitalism. The Fair Deal, coming at a time of general prosperity, represented the normalization, rationalization, bureaucratization, of the New Deal, an assimilation of the New Deal by old-line elements of the Democratic party and an absorption of the New Deal into the structure of American politics and folkways.

The New Deal was once a revolution. Now, under the name of the Fair Deal, it had become an orthodoxy. As an orthodoxy, it lacked the fire of a crusade. The very name — Fair Deal — suggested a deliberate shading of meaning, an emphasis less on audacity and change than on reconciliation and stability.

I thought it a pretty good piece for *Life;* John Shaw Billings, the editorial director of the Luce publications, thought otherwise. "He's such a rampant 'liberal,'" Billings wrote of me in his diary, "that it colors and contradicts all his conclusions. When I told Thorndike [*Life*'s editor] I disliked it, he agreed to kill it."

*   *   *

In the next years there emerged one more salient difference between New and Fair Dealers. New Dealers as a class were incorruptible. The Roosevelt years were notable for the absence of money scandals. For all the government spending in the Thirties, there was a minimum of graft and malfeasance. This was no doubt a felicitous by-product of the instinctive New Deal mistrust of businessmen. Truman's crowd was a good deal less immunized against temptation.

"There are two Trumans," Elmer Davis said, "— the White House Truman and the courthouse Truman. He does the big things right, and the little things wrong." Revelations of corruption in Truman's second term revived the image of the courthouse Truman. Scandals centered in parts of the government that, above all others, had to be above suspicion — the Bureau of Internal Revenue, the tax desks of Justice and the Reconstruction Finance Corporation.

These disclosures called attention to the general decline in the federal service brought about in part by Truman's preference for deserving Democrats — that is, party hacks — over "professional liberals." What became known as the "mess in Washington" helped persuade much of the electorate that the Democrats had been in power too long. That, along with the unpopular Korean War, drove Truman's approval rating at the end of his term down to the mid-twenties.

* * *

Of course, the major problem the Fair Deal faced was that it was in the end a sideshow. The main event was the Cold War. In the Thirties lights had burned late in government buildings where New Dealers drafted memoranda and plotted strategy on domestic policy. In the Forties lights burned late in the State Department, the Economic Cooperation Administration and the Pentagon. That was where the action was. When Averell Harriman returned to the United States in 1950, he used to summon me to Washington to help draft speeches and messages on mutual security issues. One found in foreign affairs the sense of urgency, the crusading fervor, that the Fair Deal lacked.

The Cold War affected the New Deal in another way. Charlie Brannan, a fine Colorado liberal, said to me that "anti-Communist hysteria" was discouraging venturesome thinking in Washington. Only a successful Wall Street lawyer like Oscar Ewing, he said, would dare propose anything as radical as national health insurance. Pat Jackson, when he wasn't doing his damnedest in March 1948 to defeat Henry Wallace, worried (in a letter to Libby Donahue) about "the atmosphere of hysteria that is gripping our land these days" and found it "more terrifying than the terror in fear of which the hysteria is being manufactured."

Concern spread far beyond Communist espionage into the influence, vastly exaggerated, of Communist ideas. In 1947 the House Un-American Activities Committee staged a ridiculous investigation of communism in Hollywood. "It reaches the height of imbecility," I wrote in the *New York Times Magazine* in November of that year, "in such episodes as the attack on the film 'The Best Years of Our Lives' as Communist-minded because it makes fun of the American businessman." In any case, "The private political views of a Hollywood writer . . . hardly seem to be the proper consideration of the United States Government or a committee of Congress."

But panic was spreading. In Massachusetts the Republican attorney general called for a bill barring people who advocated "Communist doctrines" (undefined) from teaching in the state's schools. In February 1948 I testified before the legislature's committee on education. The Barnes bill, I said, was absurd and ambiguous; it would lead every school to run its private witch-hunt; there was no "clear and present danger" to justify so repressive a measure. "We required no such bill during the war. We do not require it now." I pointed out that Vaclav Kopecky, the minister of information in Czechoslovakia, had recently announced, according to the *New York Times,* that Czech "universities must be purged of professors who are too opposed to communism." It would comfort Kopecky, I noted, to know that in Clarence Barnes he had a soulmate in Massachusetts.

The Barnes bill got nowhere, and Barnes himself was defeated in the next election. But his bill represented a spreading national idiocy, a fear of ideas curious in a country presumably dedicated to freedom of speech and expression.

*　　*　　*

Education was an area of special sensitivity. Sidney Hook of New York University, an able philosopher and all-out anti-Communist crusader, was making a powerful argument against permitting Communists to teach. Alexander Meiklejohn, a brilliant educator and all-out civil libertarian, was making a powerful argument for unlimited academic freedom.

My view was closer to Meiklejohn's than to Hook's. We recognize, I wrote in the *Saturday Review of Literature* in May 1949, that the right of political opposition is the heart of free society. Those who wished to curtail free speech must demonstrate that such speech created a clear and present danger. That did not mean a clear and present danger of changing the nation's mind by argument. It did not mean a clear and present danger of offending someone's principles or prejudices. It meant something quite specific: a clear and present danger of inciting overt acts in violation of law. The finding of clear and present danger was a delicate decision, to be taken by the courts on the basis of overwhelming evidence. "If there be time to expose through discussion the falsehood and fallacies, to avert the evil by the processes of education," Justice Brandeis had said in *Whitney v. California,* "the remedy to be applied is more speech, not enforced silence. Only an emergency can justify repression."

Did Communist teachers create an emergency that warranted extreme measures to ferret them out and discharge them? I did not think so. The University of Washington in 1949 put three professors on academic trial on the single charge that they were members of the CPUSA. The unfortunate professors were not accused of inciting students to illegal acts nor even of propagating Communist doctrine in the classroom. Their only offense was their party membership. "If the existence of three Party-line teachers on the University of Washington campus did, indeed, create a grave threat to the intellectual chastity of the undergraduates," I wrote, "it would be a devastating commentary on the effectiveness of the 700 non-Communist members of the faculty, not to mention on the strength of the democratic idea itself."

Harry Gideonse, the president of Brooklyn College, accepted the Hook line that party members were Soviet agents and therefore should be fired on the ground of party membership alone. To him I wrote in one of my many officious letters of the period that this argument, if it meant anything, would require a system of detection, and "the cost our educational system would pay for the machinery of detection would far outweigh the advantages the system would gain from the exclusion of the few Communist teachers. . . . Only demonstrable dangers arising from the presence of CP teachers on university faculties would seem to me to justify the administrative program which the logic of your argument renders necessary." And no one ever produced serious evidence of "demonstrable dangers" from Communist teachers.

The Bill of Rights, I argued in the *Saturday Review,* included the right to loathsome ideas. The principle of free thought, Justice Holmes had said in *U.S. v. Schwimmer,* meant not just "free thought for those who agree with us but freedom for the thought that we hate." So long as unbounded debate prevailed, no one need worry about the intellectual health of the students. The world was full of dangerous ideas, and, if we set out to protect young people against them, we would produce, in the words of my father's student, Dean Wilbur J. Bender of Harvard, "gullible innocents, not tough-minded realists who know what they believe because they have faced the enemies of their beliefs." My *Saturday Review* piece concluded, "If democratic ideas are as good as we believe them to be, this is the testing which will prove it."

This meant freedom for Communist ideas too, even if Communists did not believe in free speech except as a means of gaining power for themselves, after which they had always proceeded in all Communist countries to deny free speech to everybody else. At a so-called Bill of Rights conference in New York on July 17, 1949, Paul Robeson led the fight against a resolution calling for the restoration of civil rights to eighteen members of the Trotskyite Socialist Workers party convicted under the Smith Act. "Would you give civil rights to the Ku Klux Klan?" the sainted Robeson asked the conference. "These men are the allies of fascism who want to destroy the new democracies of the world. . . . They are the enemies of the working class." The delegates applauded Robeson, voted down the resolution — and then went on to protest the application of the Smith Act to the CPUSA. Where liberal organizations like ADA and the ACLU opposed the Smith Act for everybody, American Communists had little regard for the Bill of Rights except as a means of self-protection.

*   *   *

Debate was the means of dealing with communism in the national arena. The employment of Communists in the federal government, especially in national security agencies, raised different questions. The presence of Communists in the State Department during a cold war with communism would certainly create a clear and present danger of overt acts against the nation's interests. As Roger Baldwin, Mr. Civil Liberties himself, put it, "A superior loyalty to a foreign government disqualifies a citizen for service to ours." And the United States government was obviously the world's number-one target for Soviet espionage.

The disclosure of a Soviet spy ring in Canada in 1946 stimulated congressional cries for investigations of possible Communists in our own government. Truman at first ignored the clamor, but confronted in 1947 by a Republican Congress, he was forced to act. In March he issued an executive order establishing a loyalty program under which federal employees could be fired if "reasonable grounds" existed for questioning their loyalty. The order also sought to provide procedural protections for the persons accused.

These protections were hopelessly inadequate. The accused were denied the elementary right to confront their accusers or to know the sources of the evidence used against them on the ground that this would expose our counterespionage methodology. The enforcers of the executive order, the FBI and the departmental security people, were too often crude and ignorant. By the autumn of 1947, the loyalty program was already a botch. Truman's Fair Deal was matched by a spectacularly unfair deal.

This is why the *Times Magazine* asked me to do a piece on the general subject. "What Is Loyalty? A Difficult Question" appeared on November 2, 1947. "The most shocking actions of the Administration," I wrote, "— the President's executive order, the State Department's loyalty code, and some of the recent firings — have doubtless been motivated in great part by a desire to head off more extreme action by Congress. Yet this very process of appeasing the worst element in Congress has led to the compromise of principles which cannot be properly compromised in a democracy."

Still, a real espionage danger existed, and government must be conceded the right of self-protection. But how to identify agents of the Kremlin? One side proclaimed that the American way of life was in imminent danger from anyone who doubted the eternal rightness of the capitalist system. The other side proclaimed that an unbridled witch-hunt was already transforming the United States into a totalitarian police state. The situation, I thought, called for a little less hysteria and a little more calm sense.

The solution, I wrote, too facilely, was to construct some means of ridding the security agencies of questionable characters while retaining enough safeguards to ensure against indiscriminate purges. Discharge in advance of overt acts would seem a rough policy. Yet in 1938 liberals would not have objected if Nazis and fascist fellow travelers were summarily dismissed from the State Department. I proposed that accused persons should have the right to appeal to a government review board that, if sources had to be protected for security reasons, would itself have the power to interrogate the accusers.

I also said that those liberals who complained that the Communist hunters failed to distinguish between liberals and Communists "should remember that too often they have failed to make that distinction themselves." And I might have added that some liberals had thrown around the word 'fascist' with the same abandon that some conservatives were now throwing around the word 'communist.' The *Times Magazine* had run an article in April 1944 entitled "The Danger of American Fascism." The author opined, "If we define an American fascist as one who in the case of conflict puts money and power ahead of human beings, then there are undoubtedly several million fascists in the United States." The author? Henry A. Wallace.

Get Communists out of the government, and for the rest let free discussion and debate handle the communist problem. Traditional methods had worked pretty well so far. In 1947 Communists still had a certain influence in the labor movement and the liberal community.

By 1949 communism was a negligible political and intellectual force in the United States.

* * *

In August 1948 the question of Soviet penetration of the government was brought vividly before the American people. Whittaker Chambers, in testimony before the House Un-American Activities Committee, accused Alger Hiss, a former State Department official, of secret membership in the Communist party.

In 1946, when I was working on the *Life* article about the CPUSA, both Pat Jackson and Dave Niles had mentioned their suspicions about Hiss. Pat, who had witnessed Hiss's close friendship with Lee Pressman in the Agricultural Adjustment Administration, had little doubt that he had been a party member. When *Life* printed the article, Hiss was still in the State Department. I had not mentioned his name, but I felt obliged to tell Philip Graham in the strictest confidence of the doubts about him, asking Phil to communicate the story to his friend Dean Acheson, then undersecretary of state. This in due course Phil did. Acheson then talked to Secretary Byrnes. Byrnes said that he had heard the same thing from J. Edgar Hoover, that he had informed Hiss that he was under suspicion and that Hiss had denied everything. At Hoover's specific request, Byrnes had not mentioned to Hiss the name of the man who fingered him to the FBI, Whittaker Chambers.

This last fact assumed importance as a result of an odd set of circumstances. On New Year's Day 1948 Barbara Kerr, my researcher, dined with Yale friends of her husband, Chester Kerr. There were a dozen people around the table, and much liquor was consumed. In the course of the discussion Barbara let slide the remark "Loyalty tests are absolutely worthless. They would never catch any of the really important Communists like the Hiss brothers." She was sitting next to Edward T. Miller, a former assistant of Acheson's and later assistant secretary of state for inter-American affairs. Eddie Miller had had a good deal to drink, and Barbara's remark sent him into a rage. He accused her of malicious slander and said that such a suspicion was absolutely impossible. The whole table stopped talking to listen to the argument and occasionally to join in denouncing Barbara's remarks.

Forced to the wall, Barbara denied that she was repeating idle gossip. Finally she mentioned the name of Whittaker Chambers. "I did not elaborate on our whole interview with Chambers," she told me later, "being painfully conscious that we were not supposed to reveal it. Unfortunately, after a year and a half, the stringency of that injunction had worn off." Miller announced that he would inform Alger Hiss of the whole thing and suggest that he sue Barbara Kerr for libel. The evening broke up on a less than cordial note.

Barbara, alarmed by Eddie Miller's belligerence, called me up the next day. I advised her to tell Miller that in the general excitement she had said more than she intended and that she would do her best to let the matter drop. She also called Herbert Solow, an intimate friend of Chambers, to ask whether Chambers might back her up in case Hiss brought suit. Solow said that Chambers most probably would not testify; the last thing he wanted was publicity. Solow added cryptically that she need not worry about Hiss suing her for libel. Miller himself called in a few days to say that Hiss was a kindhearted man and would not sue. He then said, "Let's just agree that we were all tight." Barbara said, "If that makes you and Mr. Hiss happy, that's all right with me. I can guarantee that I will not make the statement again."

John Ferguson, another former Acheson assistant, had been present at the ill-starred dinner. When he next saw Barbara, he asked why she was so firmly persuaded of the validity of her views. She showed him the memorandum of our conversation with Chambers. Ferg then asked her permission to discuss the matter with Acheson. Barbara said, "Yes, it is time that Acheson should know about it." Soon Ferg reported that Acheson had discounted the story and thought that Chambers was probably a crackpot.

Hiss himself alluded to these events in his testimony before the House Un-American Activities Committee, where Richard M. Nixon was making his first lunge at a national reputation. Early in 1948, Hiss told the committee, a friend called from New York to say that someone was making accusations against him. Hiss asked his friend to find out more about the source of the accusations. Subsequently his friend called back to say that the person who had made the charges had apparently been passing things on in an exaggerated or garbled form.

Hearing this, Hiss testified that he had paid no more attention to the incident. Though Miller must have named names, Hiss made no effort to reach Barbara Kerr or Whittaker Chambers and ask them what the hell they were up to. As Barbara said to me, "Had those remarks been made about me and the matter called to my attention, I think I would have made direct inquiries as to the nature of my accuser."

In October 1948 William Marbury, Hiss's lawyer, came to see me in Cambridge. We discussed the date when Hiss could first have learned that Chambers was his accuser. Marbury quoted Acheson as saying, "Everyone knew the name of Chambers. Arthur Schlesinger was mentioning it at every cocktail party in Washington." I sent a letter of protest to Acheson, who promptly replied: "I did not intend to give him [Marbury] such an impression and certainly did not have it myself. In fact, I knew only of your talks with the two people mentioned in your letter — Phil Graham and John Ferguson."

*　　*　　*

My own sense of things was that Hiss had been a party member in the Thirties and did give Soviet agents documents, most of which, judging by the famous pumpkin papers, were of small consequence. Whether he was still involved in the Forties was to my mind less certain. Maybe he had left the party soon after Chambers did. Chip Bohlen told me that he had observed no fellow-traveling signs in Hiss when they worked together in the State Department. Jerome Frank, who had felt betrayed by Hiss in the AAA troubles, told me that Hiss was an upwardly mobile opportunist of low character who would not have had the guts or principle to persist in anything that might impede his career. Frank refused to appear as a character witness for Hiss but privately doubted that he could have been a traitor.

The Venona documents, messages exchanged between Soviet intelligence offices in Washington and Moscow and decrypted by American codebreakers, were released in 1996. One cable seems to suggest that Hiss continued a relationship with Soviet intelligence into the Forties. This message deals with an agent in the State Department cover named Ales. The FBI identified Ales as "probably" Hiss. What appeared to be the clincher was an interpretation of the message that had Ales at the Yalta conference and then proceeding to Moscow to receive congratulations from Andrei Vyshinskii.

Hiss was indeed at Yalta (where in fact he had opposed the inclusion of Soviet republics as members of the projected United Nations organization), and he did proceed to Moscow as part of a State Department delegation. But Vyshinskii was at Yalta too, and a strict grammarian's reading of the Venona message would make the man who went from Yalta to Moscow not Ales but Vyshinskii: "After the Yalta conference, when he had gone on to Moscow, a Soviet personage in a very responsible position (Ales gave us to understand that it was Comrade Vyshinskii) allegedly got in touch with Ales and at the behest of the Military Neighbors [GRU, Soviet military intelligence] passed on to him their gratitude." Moreover, the message also described Ales as working "on obtaining military information only." But Hiss, in the State Department, was not in a position to provide much in the way of military information.

Perhaps further disclosures from GRU archives may one day clear up the mystery. As for Hiss, his protestations of total innocence to Byrnes and Acheson left him no room for nuance, retreat or maneuver. He had to stick by his original denials lest changing his story would disillusion friends like Acheson and Frankfurter, who had gone to bat for him.

I did not meet Hiss for another quarter century. Alexandra Emmet, my second wife, had a charming and talented English friend named Sally Belfrage. Sally was the daughter of Cedric Belfrage, an English journalist who had settled in America. He was probably a party member, certainly a close associate of party members. During the war Belfrage served in the New York office of British intelligence and, according to the Venona cables, passed secret British and American documents to the KGB.

Sally Belfrage adored her father and sympathized with his causes. Alexandra had shared an apartment in New York with her before Sally returned to London and began to write books. One day Sally called to say that she was coming to New York to launch a new book. Alexandra said that we must give her a party. At our request, Sally cabled a list of prospective invitees. The name of Alger Hiss was near the top of the list.

"By all means invite him," I said. "There isn't a chance in the world that he'll come. He must know that I believe him to be guilty. I've written it often enough." But because the list contained a number of fellow travelers whom I had no particular desire to see and who had no desire to see me, I suggested that we hold the party on a Tuesday, my seminar day, when I would have a solid excuse for arriving toward the end.

We then lived on East Sixty-fourth Street in New York, and Richard M. Nixon had a house on East Sixty-fifth Street, over our back fence. The last sight I had from our bedroom window before departing for the university was Nixon prowling restlessly around his garden. The first sight that greeted me on my return to a bustling party was Alger Hiss. The circularity of life!

I thought, "What the hell — if Hiss comes to my house, I'll certainly welcome him," so I immediately went to him. We shook hands and had a moment's agreeable conversation about his brother Donald, whom I had known pleasantly in Washington.

Little would rejoice me more than incontrovertible proof that Alger Hiss had been framed by J. Edgar Hoover. But I fear this will not be the case.

* * *

In January 1948, lecturing in Cleveland, I stayed with Helen Cannon, my sister-in-law, and her husband and my dear Eighth Air Force friend, Douglas Bond, now head of the department of psychiatry at the Western Reserve Medical School. At dinner I met a couple named Field, who had recently returned from a trip to Poland. Hermann Field, a Harvard graduate and an architect, had lived in Europe before the war, working with the Czech Refugee Trust Fund. In 1940 he returned to the United States with his attractive English wife, Kate Thornycroft. In his late thirties, he was slated to become dean of the Western Reserve School of Architecture.

Henry Wallace had just announced his presidential candidacy, and I found myself embroiled in an increasingly angry argument with the Fields. Hermann was glowingly and naively enthusiastic about the "people's democracies" of Eastern Europe and bitterly critical of "pro-fascists" in the State Department. Identifying communism with city planning and land reform, he was cheerfully oblivious of any machinery of repression and terror. Hermann Field was no Communist himself but a hopeful liberal whose Quakerism would not permit him to see evil in people who, like Communists, professed good. A vague echo stirred in my mind. I said to him, "Are you by any chance related to a man called Noel Field?" He said, "Yes. He's my brother."

In 1948 Noel Field and his wife, Herta, were still living in Switzerland. In May 1949, Noel went to Prague with the idea of getting an appointment at Charles University. A few days later he walked out of his hotel accompanied by two unidentified men, leaving papers, suitcases and traveler's cheques in his room, as if he expected to return. Instead, he simply disappeared.

Herta Field, back in Switzerland, increasingly concerned about the lack of word from her husband, eventually went herself to Prague in the hope of extracting information from the Czech authorities. Hermann was again in Europe that summer, and she asked him to help in the search. Invited by Polish architectural friends to Warsaw, Hermann planned to see Herta in Prague on his way back to London, where Kate was staying with their two small sons.

In late August 1949 his Polish friends took Hermann to the airport to put him on the plane to Prague. When the plane arrived, Hermann was not on it. Like Noel, he had mysteriously disappeared. Three days later Herta herself disappeared. And in August 1950 Erica Wallach, Noel Field's foster daughter, who had worked during the war for the OSS and had briefly joined the Communist party after the war, went to East Berlin in the hope of finding out what had happened to her foster parents. Then she disappeared too.

Four members of the Field family thus vanished behind the Iron Curtain. Soon, however, the names of the two brothers began to appear in connection with the purge of leading Communists in Hungary and Czechoslovakia. Stalin, rattled by Tito's defection in 1948, was determined in some mad spasm of paranoia to destroy all the leaders of the "people's democracies" who could be suspected of Titoist or Zionist tendencies. Any Communist who had fought in Spain, spent the Second World War in Europe or was otherwise contaminated by the West was under suspicion as a Western agent. Obviously no one could be more suspect than a man like Noel Field, who had actually worked with Allen Dulles and OSS.

The show trials of Laszlo Rajk and company in Budapest in September 1949 and of Rudolf Slansky and company in Prague in November 1952 put on parade Communist leaders who, after torture, confessed to any plot the KGB script demanded. Prosecutors made much, in the words of the Czech minister of information, of "how the whole international network of Anglo-American espionage was unmasked in connection with the well-known Field."

Hermann Field, who had no role at all in espionage or any other form of subversion, was in Stalinist eyes a British agent who had worked under the cover of the Czech Refugee Trust Fund. After his arrest, an interrogator asked him sarcastically, "Who is Allen Dulles?" Hermann, who knew nothing of Allen Dulles, said he had heard of John Foster Dulles; perhaps Allen was John Foster's son or brother? The inquisitor took this as evidence that Hermann was playing games with him. In fact, Hermann was a political innocent.

So was Erica Wallach. This did not save them from five years of inextinguishable suffering. Hermann was confined to dark underground cells, an ordeal grimly remembered in the remarkable memoir *Trapped in the Cold War*, with alternating chapters by Kate Field, describing her anguished efforts to discover his fate. Erica was condemned to death by a Soviet military court in Berlin; her sentence was later commuted to fifteen years in a slave labor camp, and she was sent to Vorkuta, north of the Arctic Circle, all graphically recalled in her memoir, *Light at Midnight.*

In 1954 and 1955, after Stalin's death in 1953, they were all released and exonerated. The political innocents, Hermann and Kate Field and Erica Wallach, saw the horror of the system and lost any illusions about the Soviet utopia. Noel and Herta Field, committed Communists, remained true to the faith. On their release they surprised their family by asking to remain in Hungary. "My accusers," Noel Field wrote, "essentially have the same convictions that I do, they hate the same things and the same people I hate — the conscious enemies of socialism, the fascists, the renegades, the traitors. Given their belief in my guilt, I cannot blame them, I cannot but approve their detestation. That is the real horror of it all." It certainly was.

I had followed the Field saga with personal interest. I saw something of Kate Field in London in 1950 and later that year sent her a series of articles about Noel that Jimmy Wechsler had commissioned for the *New York Post.* I wrote the concluding article myself, reporting that Americans regarded Noel Field as a faithful Communist; I said this in the hope that it would undercut the Soviet assumption that he was an American spy. Kate wrote me that she was "puzzled that you say you think your article might conceivably help Noel. How?" I was sorry that the article distressed her because I thought her such an admirable woman.

After their release, Hermann and Kate returned to the United States, settling on a farm in Shirley, Massachusetts. Hermann became a professor at Tufts and an early environmentalist. Kate served in an administrative position at Harvard. Erica Wallach, reunited with her husband, lived in Warrenton, Virginia, surrounded by children, dogs and horses. When she died in 1994, Harry Rositzke spoke at her memorial service. Noel Field died in Hungary in 1970, Herta in 1980.

Early in 1994, Hermann Field came to see me one day in New York. He had recently returned from Budapest and Warsaw, where he had looked for documents in the Ministry of Interior archives that might throw light on what had happened to his brother and himself. Could the Soviet leaders have *really* believed that the Fields were spies for the CIA? He thought that the Poles must have decided after a time that he was not involved. Erica had been an OSS secretary and later a party member; they may have been more suspicious of her. Noel's association with Allen Dulles made him a prime object of suspicion.

His investigation of Noel's dossier, Hermann said, was a very disturbing, shocking experience. After his capture in Prague, Noel had been drugged and driven to a villa in Hungary. There he was put down a coal chute and subjected to a variety of tortures. Soon he agreed to anything his interrogators wanted him to say. He was, he confessed, an American agent.

According to documents said by two not entirely convincing sources to exist in Hungarian and Czech archives, Noel also named Alger Hiss as a Soviet agent. Hermann had no knowledge of this. Noel later repudiated the forced confessions and drafted a long, self-justifying autobiographical statement. Hermann had read it — more than a hundred pages in Noel's own handwriting. There were two problems with the document, Hermann said: it had many factual errors; and Noel, in trying to prove his loyalty to communism, exaggerated what he had done for the Soviet Union.

Actually, Hermann said, Noel had been of little use to the Kremlin. His last contact with a Soviet control, the dossier showed, had been in 1939. There had been a feeler in 1940, when he was working for the Unitarian Service Committee in Marseilles, but it had not been followed up. "They had become suspicious of him," Hermann said, "and the more he tried to show his loyalty to them, the more suspect he became." Perhaps the CALPO project he had brought to OSS/Paris was not something he was pushing under Soviet orders but rather another attempt on his part to ingratiate himself with Moscow.

Noel's dominating motive, Hermann said, was a desire for world peace. After the First World War their father ordered an automobile from the United States — an Overland — and took young Noel, thirteen years old, on a tour of battlefields where the carnage of war was still all too visible. "This had terrific impact on Noel," Hermann said. "He decided to devote his life to the prevention of war." He came to feel that communism offered the surest road to lasting peace. The tragedy, Hermann said, was that people like Noel, who had dedicated their lives to the Communist party, had to choose between holding fast to the faith or admitting that they had wasted their lives in the service of a cruel illusion.

"After his release," Hermann said, "he would never talk to me about his years in prison. He dismissed the episode as a Stalinist aberration. He was a true believer." "To the end of his life?" I asked. "I think so," Hermann said. "Yes, to the end of his life."

I had not seen Hermann for nearly half a century. He talked slowly and precisely, with considerable perception and occasional eloquence. After all the savagery of life, he had achieved a kind of serenity. "My experience taught me a great deal," he said. "It taught me that human beings can be destructive as well as constructive. It taught me that one can survive if one preserves the will to survive. It taught me that a negative experience can have positive effects."

25

The Vital Center

STALIN'S EXCOMMUNICATION of Tito in the spring of 1948 threw an ominous light on Soviet policy. To many of us it seemed to prove the utter absurdity of the argument that a different American attitude — as, for example, Henry Wallace's — might have allayed the fears of the Kremlin, averted the Cold War and ushered in a time of peace and tranquility. If Stalin so categorically distrusted another Communist country, why in the world would he ever bring himself to trust the United States? For America was the stronghold of world capitalism and therefore by Leninist definition the mortal enemy of communism.

Nothing short of conversion to communism could have cleansed America of its original sin; and now the denunciation of Tito showed that even this, alas, would not suffice, that even communist states must be entirely subservient to Moscow before they ceased to be threats to Soviet security. "There is only one road," cried Vyshinskii in his farewell appearance in Belgrade, "and that is the Stalin road." And the Stalin road evidently led into a paranoia that saw enemies everywhere, not only in capitalist America, but among non-Russian Communists like the Hungarian Rajk, the Czech Slansky, the Bulgarian Traicho Kostov, the Pole Wladyslaw Gomulka and the American Noel Field.

My friend Max Lerner, writing in the *New York Star,* a successor to the now extinct *PM,* still held to a belief in a nonaggressive Stalin. "I detect in the *Star,*" I wrote to Max in December 1948, "a constant implication that the U.S. by a change of its own policy could end the Cold War. I cannot state too emphatically what a wildly wrong analysis of the European situation this seems to me to be. Soviet policy is *not* primarily a response to U.S. policy. It would be carrying on the identical policy in Europe if Socialist Britain were its only opponent."

Max had argued that the Soviet Union wanted to reach a serious agreement with the West. "If I thought for a moment," I wrote, "that there was any chance of Russia's making and keeping a European agreement, I would be all for getting it." But did Max seriously believe that "any conceivable paper agreement with the USSR would deter it from pressing its disruptive activities in Western Europe so long as conditions in Western Europe give Communist disruption the slightest hope of success?" The time for a workable agreement would come only after solid foundations were created in the economic, political and military recovery of democratic Europe.

Tito's defection was the first dividend, I thought, of the policy of peaceful containment. It showed that, even for Communists, nationalism was more potent than ideology, at least when a choice was possible — and, unlike the unfortunate countries along the Soviet frontier, Tito was remote from the USSR, had come to power on his own, not on the shoulders of the Red Army, and had his own army and police securely behind him.

Titoism, I suggested in a lecture in November 1949, might even foreshadow the possible breakup of the Soviet empire: "Of all internal Soviet contradictions, the most acute is the contradiction between Moscow-orientation and nationalism." And, though the bonds of ideology were still strong, polycentrism had the potential, if peaceful containment were pursued, of altering the character of the Soviet threat. I nominated Mao Tse-tung and Ho Chi Minh as future Titos.

*   *   *

On the cultural front the Cold War was getting hotter, or was it colder? Grammarians could never decide which metaphorical direction would signify an increase in tension. New York intellectuals were increasingly concerned about their European counterparts. In 1948 Mary McCarthy had the idea of forming Europe-America Groups, to promote communication between American and European writers. Her brother, the actor Kevin McCarthy, Dwight Macdonald, Elizabeth Hardwick, Alfred Kazin, Richard Rovere, Montgomery Clift, Nicolas Nabokov, Saul Steinberg, Sidney Hook and I supported Mary in this effort. The Europe-America Groups manifesto stated bluntly: "We regard Stalinism as the main enemy in Europe."

In the end, the EAG came to little. This was because the Yugoslav heresy, with its intimations of polycentrism, was creating a division among American anti-Communist intellectuals. On the one hand, obsessive anti-Communists continued, despite Tito, to see an unbreakable Soviet monolith, unchanged, unchanging and unchangeable. On the other, rational anti-Communists saw a top-heavy despotism subject to internal contradictions and to the vicissitudes of history. The obsessive anti-Communists clustered around Hook and included for a moment the *Partisan Review* group. "Mary, the [EAG] sparkplug," Dwight Macdonald said, "has been mostly sparkless and lethargic (partly because of the dreary tension with the PR get-Russia-at-all-costs attitude)." Nonetheless, the objective of supporting European intellectuals remained much in our minds.

Mary's idea had been to buck up anti-Communist European writers, not to engage in personal attacks on Soviet writers. There was no reciprocity. As Alexander Fadeyev, a very minor writer but a major literary bureaucrat, now general secretary of the Union of Soviet Writers, delicately put it at a Soviet-sponsored World Congress of Intellectuals in Wroclaw (once Breslau), Poland, in August 1948, "If hyenas could type and jackals could use a fountain pen," they would write like T. S. Eliot, John Dos Passos, Jean-Paul Sartre and André Malraux.

A follow-up to the Wroclaw conference was scheduled at the Waldorf-Astoria in New York in March 1949 under the formidable name "The Scientific and Cultural Conference for World Peace." Fadeyev led the Soviet delegation, which included a pale, tense and apparently coerced Dmitri Shostakovich. To Dwight Macdonald, Fadeyev looked "more like a plain-clothes detective than a writer," and Shostakovich was "a tragic and heart-rending figure." Harlow Shapley was the conference chairman, and the American sponsors included the usual suspects — Paul Robeson, Lillian Hellman, Ella Winter, Dalton Trumbo, Corliss Lamont, Angus Cameron, Agnes Smedley, Herbert Aptheker, along with some eminent political innocents — Albert Einstein, Thomas Mann, Jo Davidson, Rockwell Kent, Aaron Copland, Leonard Bernstein.

The Waldorf conference seemed to demand an antidote, and the energetic Sidney Hook proceeded to organize what Nicolas Nabokov termed "an agitprop apparatus of our own." Nicolas added, "Many of us objected to the way Sidney Hook ordered, or at least tried to order, some of us around." Macdonald, Mary McCarthy and Nabokov, largely evading Hook's orders, got delegate's passes to the conference. They succeeded in asking the Russian delegation searching questions but received uniformly dusty answers.

I was detained in Cambridge and could not join them until the last day, and I regretted to hear that old friends had uttered what seemed to me nonsense — F. O. Matthiessen describing Emerson, Thoreau, Whitman and Melville as the Henry Wallaces of their day, Paul Sweezy attacking the Marshall Plan as designed to "block a real revolution in the economic institutions of Western Europe," I. F. Stone claiming that "the machinery of American government is set for war." On the other hand, Norman Mailer, whom I did not yet know, came, he said, as a Trojan horse and, expressing, Dwight Macdonald thought, a "profound and even disagreeable (to him, as well as to his hearers) change of mind and heart," roundly rejected the party line, for which he was roundly booed by the faithful.

The Waldorf conference stimulated the tireless and combative Hook to organize on the last day a countermeeting at Freedom House, on West Fortieth Street, in the name of an ad hoc group called Americans for Intellectual Freedom. I was among the speakers, along with Hook himself (inevitably), Nicolas Nabokov, the painter George Biddle, the geneticist H. J. Muller, among others. It was standing room only in Freedom House, and more than a thousand people listened to the proceedings in Bryant Park, across the way, via loudspeakers on the Freedom House balcony.

*　　*　　*

Sidney Hook deserves a word. A short, stocky, angry man with a mustache and spectacles and a weakness for New Yorkish sarcastic humor, he applied a lucid and efficient logical mind to a wide range of problems in education, culture, politics and philosophy. I cannot judge his work in technical philosophy, but *The Hero in History* remains a first-rate essay in the philosophy of history. He was an illuminating analyst and clarifier of Marxism and, though he supported the Communist ticket in the 1932 election, he soon became a trenchant anti-Stalinist at a time when the going was rough. I was at Hook's side in some of those battles after the war, and I rejoiced with him as he doughtily struck down the infidel.

Hook's great error, in my view, was in letting anticommunism take over his life. His memoir of 1987, *Out of Step: An Unquiet Life in the 20th Century,* considerably exaggerates the power of American Communists — an overestimate that, ironically, Hook shared with the New Left historians of the Sixties and Seventies. Communist influence in the Thirties, he wrote, was "so strong that it amounted to domination of key areas of American cultural life, in literature, art, and movies." And again: "The climate of opinion in American liberal and literary circles with respect to the [Moscow] Trials, until the Nazi-Soviet pact of August 1939, remained overwhelmingly favorable to the Soviet Union." His own evidence — the distinguished list of signers of the antitotalitarian manifesto of his Committee for Cultural Freedom, three months before the Nazi-Soviet pact — refutes such rash generalizations.

It was Hook's obsessive anticommunism that explained his steady movement to the right. He soon became too much for his allies at the *Partisan Review*. William Barrett, another NYU philosopher and a *PR* editor, recalls Philip Rahv's crude dismissal when someone proposed Hook for an article: "No. Sidney will only tell you once again that Stalin stinks." And, while still describing himself as a socialist in *Out of Step*, Hook was at the same time an unabashed supporter of Richard Nixon and Ronald Reagan. He found more sustenance in right-wing anticommunist fundamentalism than in what seemed to him the dangerous softness of liberals who detected changes in the Soviet Union or who worried about nuclear war.

One could understand Hook's resentment against the Stalinists. It was harder to understand his resentment against the anti-Stalinists who declined to make anticommunism the permanent center of their lives. One wonders why this sturdy logic-chopper with so much to his credit ended such a bitter man. *Out of Step* bristles with barely controlled rancor and rage. Thus: Irving Howe's autobiography was "replete with bare-faced inventions"; Norman Mailer "would forgive murder"; Mary McCarthy had "an almost infinite capacity for self-destruction"; Nicolas Nabokov had "the morals of an alley cat"; Alfred Kazin "reconstructed his political past to make it fit the prejudices of the current literary Establishment."

I was not on the hit list. Sidney and I remained on good terms — I spoke at his sixty-fifth birthday dinner — until I expressed my concern about his obsessiveness in a review of *Out of Step*. I was then consigned to the doghouse too.

Some ex-Communists are transfixed by anticommunism for the rest of their lives. Others decide that they have other lives to live and refuse to let their Communist episodes dominate the remainder of their years. After their Communist flings, Richard Hofstadter, James Wechsler, Richard Rovere, Murray Kempton, Theodore Draper, kept their political and intellectual balance, concluding that there were more things in heaven and earth than were dreamt of in the anti-Communist philosophy.

Sidney Hook was a highly intelligent man who permitted anticommunism to consume his life to the point that his obsession, like Aaron's rod, swallowed up nearly everything else. In the end he put me in mind of Hawthorne's Hollingsworth, one of those men "who have surrendered themselves to an overruling purpose. . . . They will keep no friend unless he makes himself the mirror of his purposes; they will smite and slay you, and trample your dead corpse under foot, if you take the first step with them, and cannot take the second, and the third, and every other step of their terribly strait path."

* * *

In April 1948 the *New York Times Magazine* published a piece of mine under the title "Not Left, Not Right, But a Vital Center." The article began by arguing that the traditional linear division into right and left, adequate to the political simplicities of the nineteenth century, did not fit the complexities of the twentieth. On the linear conception fascism and communism were polar opposites, one on the far right, the other on the far left. Yet in basic structural respects — a single leader, a single infallible ideology, a single party, a single mass of disciplined followers, a merciless secret police, a fear and hatred of political and intellectual freedom — fascism and communism clearly resembled each other more than they resembled anything on the line between them. Similarly the constitutional Right and the democratic Left had more in common than either had with fascism or communism.

This dilemma drove DeWitt C. Poole, who had been American chargé d'affaires in Moscow during the Bolshevik Revolution and whom I had known as chief of the Foreign Nationalities Branch of OSS, to an inspired suggestion. Right and left, he said, should be conceived in terms not of a line but of a circle, with the extremes — fascism and communism — meeting at the bottom. You can then look at the circle in two ways: with respect to property, fascism and the constitutional right were side by side against communism and the demo-

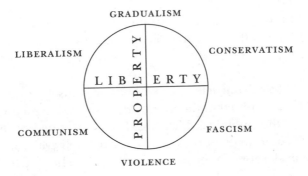

cratic left; with respect to liberty, the constitutional right and the democratic left were side by side against fascism and communism.

The times, I argued, called for an alliance between the non-Communist left and the non-fascist right. "Hope for the future surely lies in the revival of the Center — in the triumph of those who believe deeply in civil liberties, in constitutional processes and in the democratic determination of political and economic policies." The epigraph was from Yeats's "The Second Coming" (less of a cliché in 1948 than it became later):

> Things fall apart; the centre cannot hold;
> Mere anarchy is loosed upon the world,
> The blood-dimmed tide is loosed, and everywhere
> The ceremony of innocence is drowned;
> The best lack all conviction, while the worst
> Are full of passionate intensity. . . .
> And what rough beast, its hour come round at last,
> Slouches towards Bethlehem to be born?

The "vital center" was thus liberal democracy standing on the global stage against the totalitarian twins, communism and fascism. "The best must recover a sense of principle; and, on the basis of principle, they may develop a passionate intensity. We cannot afford to loose the blood-dimmed tide ever again."

How did "center" acquire "vital"? Many years later someone called my attention to the Epilogue in *Moby-Dick*. Ishmael, the last survivor, is drawn into the vortex of the sinking *Pequod*. Round and round he floats, ever revolving about the buttonlike black bubble at the axis of the slowly wheeling circle, "till, gaining that vital centre, the black bubble upward burst; and now, liberated by reason of its cunning spring, and, owing to its great buoyancy, rising with great force, the coffin life-buoy shot length-wise from the sea, fell over, and floated by my side." Did Melville's "vital center" lodge in my unconscious? Probably not; but the phrase encapsulated my point in locating liberal democracy between the extremes of communism and fascism.

*   *   *

The *Times Magazine* article led to a book and also provided its title. *The Vital Center,* I noted in the foreword, was not designed to set forth novel or startling political doctrines. It was intended rather as a report on the enterprise of reexamination and self-criticism that liberalism had undergone in the preceding decade. The leaders in this enterprise, I noted, had been the wise men of an older generation. But its chief beneficiaries were my own contemporaries, and its main consequence, I thought, was to create a new and distinct political generation.

The moment seemed ripe for a redefinition of liberal democracy. Mid-century liberalism, I thought, had been "fundamentally reshaped by the hope of the New Deal, by the exposure of the Soviet Union and by the deepening of our knowledge of man." (My consciousness not having been sufficiently raised in 1949, I used the word 'man,' according to the custom of the time, as shorthand for 'human being.' My apologies.)

My generation had been brought up to regard human nature as benign and human society as perfectible. Evil was a theological superstition. Educational and institutional reforms would do the job of social salvation. These were the premises of goodhearted, hopeful American liberalism in the style of John Dewey. But these premises, seen in the baleful light of Hitler and Stalin, appeared shallow and shaky. Obviously human nature had dark depths beyond the reach of conventional liberalism.

*　　*　　*

The Augustinian tradition, as rendered by Perry Miller and most profoundly and passionately by Reinhold Niebuhr, was far more successful in accounting for the horrors of the twentieth century and therefore offered liberalism, it seemed to me, a much more solid foundation. I immersed myself in Niebuhr, particularly his Gifford Lectures at the University of Edinburgh in 1939, published in two volumes, *The Nature and Destiny of Man* (1941, 1942). He cast his argument in religious terms. Yet even nonreligious readers found two themes especially powerful — or at least I did.

One was Niebuhr's presentation of the mixed nature of man. "The plight of the self," he wrote, "is that it cannot do the good it intends." For man's pretensions to reason and virtue, he argued, are ineradicably tainted by self-interest and self-love. Original sin lies in man's illusion that he can overcome his inherent finiteness and weakness. Overweening self-pride vitiates all human endeavor and brings evil into history.

The second theme was the relationship between history and eternity. The modern fallacy, Niebuhr thought, was the idea that redemption is possible within history. But man must understand the incompleteness of all historic good as well as the corruption of all historic achievement. Wisdom, Niebuhr wrote, "is dependent upon a humble recognition of the limits of our knowledge and our power."

"Nothing worth doing is completed in our lifetime," Niebuhr wrote in a later book. "Therefore, we must be saved by hope. . . . Nothing we do, however virtuous, can be accomplished alone; therefore, we are saved by love. No virtuous act is quite as virtuous from the standpoint of our friend or foe as from our standpoint. Therefore, we must be saved by the final form of love which is forgiveness."

Niebuhr's skepticism about human nature made some wonder how he reconciled his theological conservatism with his political radicalism. Throughout history the doctrine of original sin had given despots the pretext to establish governments absolute enough to restrain man's wicked impulses. But Niebuhr had no trouble with that. Why should anyone suppose, he asked in his 1944 book, *The Children of Light and the Children of Darkness,* that despots themselves are immune to original sin? Quite the contrary: the greater the power, the more certain the corruption. Recognition of the frailty of man requires the democratization of authority. He summed up his argument in a single mighty sentence: "Man's capacity for justice makes democracy possible; but man's inclination to injustice makes democracy necessary."

I came to understand that original sin, a proposition I was prepared to accept not as revealed truth but as powerful metaphor, undermined absolutist pretensions and set sharp limits on human wisdom and aspiration. Nor did recognition of sinfulness enjoin passivity or withdrawal: this was the point I had first heard at Harvard's Memorial Church. Man is at once free and unfree, creator as well as creature of history; he has the obligation to act or suffer the consequences of inaction. His knowledge is fragmentary, his righteousness is illusory, his motives are tainted, but, aware of the precariousness of human striving, he must strive nevertheless. He acts best when he understands his own fallibility and his puniness in the face of eternity. Lincoln was Niebuhr's model of the statesman who combines "resoluteness about the immediate issues with a religious awareness of another dimension of meaning or judgment." Humility must temper, not sever, the nerve of action.

Niebuhr's personality reinforced his philosophy. An occasional sadness in life is the discovery that people may be less than the books they write. Niebuhr never disappointed. It was in these years that I became friends with Niebuhr and his wife, the former Ursula Keppel-Compton, a brilliant and lovely Englishwoman who had been at Oxford with Isaiah Berlin and Wystan Auden. Theirs was a welcoming household, whether at their apartment in Morningside Heights or at their summer retreat in the Berkshires.

At the center was Reinie, so overflowing with restless vitality that he could not sit still for long and strode the room to make his points. For all his robust ego, he was a man of endearing humility. Once denouncing the Christian pacifism of E. Stanley Jones, he stopped in midstream and said, "But who am I to pass judgment on Stanley Jones? He's one of the great Christian saints of our time."

"I doubt," said George Kennan, "that any less sanctimonious man ever wore clerical cloth." Though the truest of believers himself, Niebuhr had unlimited tolerance, at times perhaps even a distinct preference, for unbelievers. There was his famous exchange with Felix Frankfurter after a sermon: "I like what you said, Reinie, and I speak as a believing unbeliever." "I'm glad you did," said Niebuhr. "For I spoke as an unbelieving believer." My friend the philosopher Morton White said there ought to be an organization called Atheists for Niebuhr. Perry Miller would have been president. One felt the irony — did Reinie also? — that unbelievers, appropriating so much of his thought, left off when the part that mattered most to him — the ineffable mystery and grace of God — came in.

"I had a few thoughts and a tremendous urge to express myself," he once wrote to his friend Bishop Will Scarlett. "I spoke and wrote all over the place and now when the stuff is reviewed most of it turns out to be slightly cockeyed and partly askew." Let us all hope to be as cockeyed and askew as Reinhold Niebuhr.

*　　*　　*

The theology of Niebuhr could deal with the angst that seemed to characterize the postwar West. People, their nerves strung out after grim years of depression and war, confronted now by unexpected and unsolicited threats, were in a volatile and vulnerable mood. Hot war had been followed too quickly by cold war. What Auden called in his 1947 baroque eclogue "the age of anxiety" did not, it seemed to me, bode well for the future of democracy. "Anxiety," said Kierkegaard, "is the dizziness of freedom." I was much influenced by the contention of Dostoievski's Grand Inquisitor that the burden of free choice imposes unanswerable anxieties and therefore drives people to flee from liberty to authority — an argument ably developed in Erich Fromm's provocative 1941 book, *Escape from Freedom*. Neither conservatives nor progressives, I argued, were able to contain or alleviate the terrific repercussions of industrial society which calls on man to "organize beyond his moral and emotional means."

With Nazism and Stalinism so long extinct, it is hard in the twenty-first century to remember how potent the totalitarian appeal was in the Thirties and Forties to men and women drifting helplessly amid the economic and military wreckage of the day. The attraction to frightened and forgotten people of discipline and dogma, of solidarity in struggle, was palpable during the Great Depression. In the immediate confusions after the war, the indispensable Soviet contribution to victory erased past sins and returned American Communists to a certain influence in the labor movement and the intellectual community — an influence they devoted, as always, to the unconditional defense of Stalin.

This explains *The Vital Center*'s preoccupation with the frustrations of freedom and its slightly pessimistic evaluation of the counter-appeal of democracy. It also explains the incredulity with which one looked on those who, after the famine and the trials and the pact, excused Stalinism and thought Trumanism worse. Looking for historical analogues, I tried to revive the term 'Doughface,' as applicable to democratic men with totalitarian principles. Doughface did not, however, stick, or click, a century later.

*　　*　　*

If I were writing *The Vital Center* today, I would tone down the rhetoric. From time to time there is too much hortatory lushness.

I would not greatly modify the analysis of the grounds of the totalitarian appeal. I would, however, disown my flirtation with the mystical theory of totalitarianism popularized by George Orwell and Hannah Arendt. This theory must have been much in the air in the late Forties because *The Vital Center* came out before *1984* (published later in 1949) and *The Origins of Totalitarianism* (1951).

Orwell's vision was of a society absolutely controlled by absolute power using absolute terror to remake the human soul. His *1984* was not about incremental evolution à la Herbert Hoover and Hayek, from the welfare state into the total state. It was about a shattering discontinuity, a qualitative transformation, an ultimate change of phase. Orwell carried the inner logic of Nazism and Stalinism to the end of night. In so doing, he encouraged the theory of totalitarianism as unitary and irreversible, obliterating all autonomous institutions in society and reconstructing the human personality itself.

In a distinction once made by Arthur Koestler, *1984* belongs to the literature of warning, not to the literature of prophecy. Orwell was telling us in 1949 that a nightmare lay in wait if we did not recognize the danger and act to avert it. But the nightmare gained new authority with Hannah Arendt's *Origins of Totalitarianism;* for Arendt claimed as historical actuality what Orwell conceived as admonitory fantasy.

Now that we know far more about the inner workings of Hitlerism and Stalinism, it seems clear that the totalitarian states, while quite as cruel as Orwell and Arendt (and I) supposed, were far less effectively monolithic than we believed; that the totalitarian project of remaking human nature was far less feasible than we thought; that totalitarianism in the pure and complete sense was inherently unattainable; and in consequence that totalitarian states were not unchanging and unchangeable.

I should have learned this when in 1947 I reviewed Hugh Trevor-Roper's *The Last Days of Hitler,* with its brilliant argument about the impossibility of pure totalitarianism; but somehow I was carried away by melodramatic social theory. The perseverance of normality under totalitarianism did not really register for me until Czeslaw Milosz's *The Captive Mind* (1953) unveiled the subterfuges by which people in totalitarian states managed, against all odds, to maintain a saving minimum of privacy and sanity. The totalitarian state can indeed persecute, torture and kill. But "human nature" proved too stubborn, devious, recalcitrant and — dare one say? — courageous to surrender to total transformation.

Totalitarian states were simply not the foolproof, leakproof tyrannies of *1984* and *The Origins of Totalitarianism.* They were vicious but chaotic despotisms riven by internal feuds and hatreds. They were inefficient in their use of labor and in their allocation of resources. They practiced systematic and appalling barbarities; but so have despots done through the ages, if never on so large a scale. Totalitarian states, far from achieving, as I thought in 1949, a radical break in social organization, were hardly more than Tartar courts equipped with modern technology and ideology. They were Tartar courts too in their tribalism. I had the sense in *The Vital Center* to detect the rising conflict between Russian hegemony and the varieties of national communism and to foresee the Sino-Soviet split. And I also had the sense to warn against obsessive anticommunism: we must not permit ourselves "to become the slaves of Stalinism, as any man may become the slave of the things he hates."

*   *   *

The Vital Center overestimated the stagnation of capitalism. Here I was misled by Joseph A. Schumpeter and his exciting book of 1942, *Capitalism, Socialism, and Democracy*. Schumpeter, whom I got to know a bit at Harvard after the war, was a fascinating man, the minister of finance in Austria's first republican government, a Harvard professor from 1932, an original and stimulating economic theorist, a dramatic preceptor who donned and doffed his cloak with operatic flourish. He was a conservative who had no use for FDR and the New Deal, but he enjoyed, even seemed to prefer, the company of New Dealers like Seymour Harris and Marxists like Paul Sweezy. He once remarked, "When I see those who espouse my cause, I begin to wonder about the validity of my position."

The two grand themes of *Capitalism, Socialism, and Democracy* were an expansive celebration of the entrepreneur as the mainspring of capitalism and a gloomy prediction that capitalism was in inevitable decline and would be displaced by some form of socialism. The very success of capitalism, Schumpeter argued, was undermining the institutions that protected it and subsidizing the criticism that would ultimately do it in.

As it has turned out, his celebration of the dynamism of capitalism and of the heroic entrepreneurs with their gales of "creative destruction" was far more accurate than his prediction of capitalism as its own gravedigger. But I was captivated by Schumpeter's aristocratic scorn for merchants, as I had been by Georges Sorel's contempt for the cowardice of the bourgeoisie in his *Reflections on Violence*. So, without predicting its demise, I underrated the vitality of capitalism. The movement into the age of the computer is a triumphant vindication of the other half of Schumpeter's argument — his theory of economic development as propelled by technological breakthroughs and entrepreneurial adventurers.

Another thing saving capitalism was to my mind the very New Deal that Schumpeter abhorred. Karl Marx, whom Schumpeter rather admired, rested his case for the inevitability of communism on the theory that capitalism contained the seeds of its own destruction. Captalism, he argued, generated inexorable inner tendencies — "contradictions" — that would infallibly bring about its downfall. One inexorable tendency was the increasing wealth of the rich and the increasing poverty of the poor. Another was the increasing frequency and severity of economic crisis. All this would intensify class conflict to the point of revolutionary "ripeness," when the proletariat would rise in its wrath, overthrow the possessing classes and establish a classless society.

Marx's prediction rested on the assumption that capitalism was incapable of reform. "The executive of the modern state," he wrote in *The Communist Manifesto*, "is but a committee for managing the common affairs of the bourgeoisie." The theory of the state as the faithful servant of the capitalist class was Marx's fatal error.

Political democracy put the state up for grabs. The electoral process offered the means by which noncapitalists — farmers, workers, intellectuals, minorities — could invoke the state to defend themselves against capitalist exploitation. The affirmative democratic state brought about a relative redistribution of wealth that defeated Marx's prediction of the immiseration of the poor; and it brought about a relative economic stability that defeated Marx's prediction of ever-worsening economic crisis. "The more we condemn unadulterated Marxian Socialism," said Theodore Roosevelt, "the stouter should be our insistence on thoroughgoing social reforms." Democracy thus summoned the state to humanize the industrial order, to mitigate the impact of unrestrained competition, to put a floor under the necessities of life, to combine individual opportunity with social responsibility.

To carry out this program, advocates of the affirmative state had to fight conservatism at every step along the way. The liberals persevered, however, and the revolutionary fires within capitalism, lit by the great freebooters of the nineteenth century, were put out in the twentieth by the combination of consumer goods and social reform. In the end, capitalism defeated the apocalyptic Marxist prophecy because of the long campaign mounted by liberals to reduce the suffering, and thereby the rebel passions, of those to whom accidents of birth denied an equal chance in life.

* * *

In foreign affairs I repent not a word of the anti-Stalinism that is one of the book's major themes. By the end of the century Russian historians and Soviet archives showed that, if anything, the West understated the excesses of Stalin and his brutal regime. I should have written more about the dangers of nuclear war, but the Soviet Union did not explode its first nuclear device until after the book was published. The control and abolition of nuclear weapons I regard as one of the supreme problems passed on to the twenty-first century. Later critics say that I should have noted the growing militarization of American foreign policy; but that did not take place until the Korean War reversed Truman's policy of military retrenchment.

In domestic affairs, I should have paid more attention to the question of racial justice. I do call the treatment of black America "the most basic challenge to the American conscience," but I wish I had devoted more space to the battle for civil rights. I should have made more than a passing reference to the ecological challenge. The discussion of economic policy is only of historical interest, if that. I followed the lead of *Saving American Capitalism,* a post–New Deal liberal compendium edited in 1948 by Seymour Harris, to which I was one of the contributors. *The Vital Center* advocates an activist but limited state, one that would define the ground rules of the free market and would use fiscal and monetary levers to assure maximum employment but would not try to be a play-by-play economic planner. "Total planners do not have the information or the wisdom to plan successfully."

* * *

Heinemann brought out *The Vital Center* in Great Britain the next year under the title *The Politics of Freedom,* with a generous introduction by Malcolm Muggeridge. The question the book addressed, Malcolm wrote, was how to counter totalitarianism without adopting totalitarianism's methods. Schlesinger, he said, was "one of the most acute minds in contemporary America," a judgment he would later repent. Charles Wintour wrote me that he feared the Muggeridge introduction might discourage readers whose views were closer to my own; "he seems too anxious to make the point that an individual of right-wing views may read the book without committing a sin."

The American reviewers were mostly tolerant. Some were comfortingly enthusiastic. Jerome Frank in the *New York Post* called *The Vital Center* "a profoundly searching book. . . . Every decent American owes it to himself and to our democratic society to read this book." Jonathan Daniels, the liberal North Carolina editor, a son of FDR's old boss in Wilson's cabinet and himself a veteran of both FDR's and Truman's White House, wrote in the *Saturday Review,* "It seemed to me one of those books which may suddenly and clearly announce the spirit of the age to itself." Henry Steele Commager in the *New York Herald Tribune,* August Heckscher in the *Reporter,* Robert Bendiner in the *Nation,* Mary McGrory in the *Washington Star,* were comparably friendly. Joe Rauh in the *Harvard Law Review* was warmly sympathetic, but thought (correctly) that I conceded too much to the Truman loyalty program.

Some reviewers were angry. The ever reliable Herbert Aptheker denounced "The Schlesinger Fraud" in the Communist monthly *Masses & Mainstream* as "a program groomed to the needs of a ruling class seeking war and fascism." In December 1949 Aptheker and I held a debate. Neither of us persuaded the other of anything.

According to Ben Bagdikian in the *Providence Journal,* I denied "the Left a legitimate existence in American politics." The philosopher Abraham Edel in the *New York Compass* accused me of "abandoning liberalism" and underwriting "the present state of capitalism." Sebastian Barr in the *National Guardian:* "*The Vital Center* might be defined as a small island of opportunism entirely surrounded by hot air." Dr. Melchior Palyi in the *Chicago Tribune:* "Supercilious and sofisticated [Colonel McCormick's reformed spelling] but platitudinous editorializing takes the place of logical and historical analysis." Clinton Rossiter, the Cornell political scientist (and later a good friend), regretted in the *Review of Politics* that I had written "a book as unoriginal, loose, and glib as *The Vital Center*" and predicted that I would end up as the American Harold Laski.

The book was a mild success. It has been reprinted in 1962, 1988 and 1998.

*   *   *

A rum moment in the afterlife of *The Vital Center* came when the work was charged with contributing to the triumph of Abstract Expressionism in painting. In his book of 1983, *How New York Stole the Idea of Modern Art,* Serge Gilbaut, a French art historian at the University of British Columbia, exposed the dastardly plot by which Vital Center liberalism and the Truman administration conspired to use Abstract Expressionism as a weapon in the Cold War.

The New York school of painting became, Gilbaut wrote, "a symbol of the fragility of freedom in the battle waged by the liberals to protect the vital center." Against the boring Soviet 'socialist realism,' abstract expressionism "offered the exuberant Jackson Pollock, the very image of exaltation and spontaneity. His psychological problems were but cruel tokens of the hardships of freedom. In his 'extremism' and violence Pollock represented the man possessed, the rebel, transformed for the sake of the cause into nothing less than a liberal warrior in the Cold War." By refuting European myths of American philistinism, the New York school appealed to European elites and served American purposes in the struggle with the Soviet Union.

Gilbaut's argument seems a very long stretch. Abstract Expressionism is a style for which the author of *The Vital Center* had (and has) minimal sympathy. As for President Truman, he dismissed avantgarde painting as "ham and eggs art." The painters themselves were in the main studiously apolitical and nonideological, dedicated to art for art's sake. Nonetheless, according to David Lehman in 1995, *How New York Stole the Idea of Modern Art* was in wide use as a college textbook.

* * *

In the Nineties, after nearly half a century, *The Vital Center,* or at least the phrase, had an unexpected revival. "What this nation really needs," President Bill Clinton said in August 1993, "is a vital center, one committed to fundamental and profound and relentless and continuing change." "We proclaim," he said on the night of his reelection in 1996, "that the vital American center is alive and well." In a press conference two days later: "Our people voted for the ideas of the vital American center." August 1997: "In these past months, we have seen how the politics of the vital center can work to make progress on many of our most difficult problems." January 2000: "We restored the vital center, replacing outmoded ideologies with a new vision."

The revival, moreover, had a bipartisan tinge. In 1996 Newt Gingrich, then Speaker of the House of Representatives, author of the briefly famous Contract with America and an all-purpose Republican firebrand, startled R. W. Apple, Jr., of the *New York Times,* not to mention *The Vital Center*'s author, by quoting with approval the following sentence from the book: "The conservative must not identify a particular status quo with the survival of civilization, and the radical equally must recognize that his protests are likely to be as much the expressions of his own self-interest as they are of some infallible dogma" — a plea for humility that neither Gingrich nor I have always observed.

President Clinton evidently added "American" to place his vital center in a domestic context. My vital center had been in a global context — liberal democracy against its mortal international enemies, fascism to the right, communism to the left. It was not immediately clear what Clinton meant by the "vital American center." Conservatives hoped that he meant the "middle of the road" — the position preferred by cautious politicians who want to alienate as few voters as possible. In my view, the middle of the road is definitely not the vital center. It is the dead center.

President Clinton's view? He certainly adopted a middle-of-the-road strategy: "triangulation," as his onetime strategist Dick Morris called it. But I think he was also saying that the United States faces novel problems that the American people must meet without reference to the shibboleths of the past. He had tried variations on the phrase before. "This is a time of such profound change," he said in April 1995, "that we need a dynamic center that is not in the middle of what is left and right but is way beyond it. . . . I want us [Democrats and Republicans] to surprise everybody in America by rolling up our sleeves and working together."

What was the "profound change" remolding American life? In a December 1996 press conference, Clinton recalled the time a century before when "we moved from the farm to the factory" and "became primarily an urban manufacturing country." Today, he suggested, we were undergoing a parallel mutation compelled by the shock of a "new basis of economic activity, knowledge and information and technology."

Clinton understood that America, and indeed the whole developed world, was undergoing a structural transformation as profound as the shift two centuries ago from a farm-based to a factory-based economy. Americans at the end of the twentieth century were experiencing an even more traumatic shift, from a factory-based to a computer-based economy. This shift was more traumatic because the Industrial Revolution extended over generations, allowing time for human and institutional adjustment. The Computer Revolution is far more dynamic, far more compressed, far more drastic, in its impact. Because no one can foresee its consequences for human society and the human mind — so Clinton seems to feel — the digital challenge renders the familiar division between left and right obsolescent. His vital center, if it means more than political phrase-making, presumably aims to establish a new framework for the computer age.

*   *   *

The Vital Center concluded like *The Age of Jackson,* by affirming the reality of struggle. So long as society stays free, so long will it continue in a state of tension, breeding contradiction, breeding strife. But conflict is also the guarantee of freedom; it is the instrument of change; it is, above all, the source of discovery, the source of art, the source of love. If free society is to survive and prosper, freedom must become, in Holmes's phrase, a "fighting faith." What Walt Whitman called "the exercise of Democracy" may yet save us.

Whitman, the grand poet of democracy, grew obsessed in his later years with the moral indolence of the citizenry. He looked about and saw people "with hearts of rag and souls of chalk." As he pondered "the shallowness and miserable selfism of these crowds of men, with all their minds so blank of high humanity and aspiration," there came "the terrible query. . . . Is not Democracy of human rights humbug after all?" The query has not been definitively answered to this day.

The hope for free society lies, in the last resort, in the people it creates. "Tyranny may always enter," said Whitman, "— there is no charm, no bar against it — the only bar against it is a large resolute breed of men." In times past, when freedom has been a fighting faith producing that "large resolute breed of men," it acquired its dynamism from communion in action. "The exercise of Democracy" has quickened the sense of the value of the individual; and, in that exercise, the individual has found a just and fruitful relation to the community.

We required then, and I believe we require today, exactly such a rededication to concrete democratic ends; so that the exercise of democracy can bring about a revival of democratic *élan* and a resurgence of faith in government by the people. The best, and not the worst, must be full of passionate intensity if that rough beast is to be stopped before Bethlehem.

It is, I suppose, evidence of lack of imagination or of some other infirmity of character, but I am somewhat embarrassed to confess that I have not radically altered my general outlook in the more than half century since *The Vital Center*'s publication. Perhaps I should apologize for not being able to claim disillusions, revelations, conversions. But in fact I have not been born again, and there it is.

*   *   *

I wrote *The Vital Center* in the second-floor study of our Irving Street house in Cambridge. I have always written at home (except for my memoir of the Kennedy administration, *A Thousand Days*). Poets, novelists, playwrights, drawing their art out of their unconscious, can write anywhere. Historians require their notes, their files, their books, their familiar surroundings.

Having perhaps the soul of a hack, I have never been bothered by writer's block, nor am I unduly distracted by noise. Asked years later to describe her father, my daughter Christina wrote, "My father's self-confidence and power of concentration have always impressed me. When we kids were little, he wrote his books with all of us screaming around him. I used to play in the wastebasket while he typed." True: before Christina, I stowed the twins in a wastebasket by my desk and wrote my pieces for *Life* and *Fortune*. I did not mind the clamor of children and never closed my study door to the life of the household.

Approaching 1950, the halfway mark of the twentieth century, and soon to confront my own first third of a century, I rejoiced in our four children, rather enjoyed my new life at Harvard, intermittently contemplated the inevitable tensions of marriage, pursued my investigations of the age of Roosevelt, wondered how to balance academic respectability and political activism, viewed the decade to come with mingled foreboding and hope.

The Cold War was now under way. As 1949 drew to a close, the Soviet Union exploded its own atomic bomb, thereby creating the awful possibility of nuclear war. Communism, I thought, was a threat *to* America and obsessive anticommunism a threat *in* America. But, after the New Deal and the war, one had buoyant expectations about the vitality of American democratic traditions and pride in the ability of the American people to rise to new challenges.

More than ever, however, I was persuaded of the unknowability of the future. As I later put it, someone trying in the spring of 1940 to forecast the next three American presidents would hardly have named as the first president after FDR a little-known senator from Missouri anticipating defeat by the governor of his state in the Democratic primaries; as the second, a lieutenant-colonel in the U.S. Army; and, as the third, a kid still in college.

History has a marvelous capacity to outwit all our certitudes. "Providence," wrote Tocqueville in the concluding words of *Democracy in America*, "has not created mankind entirely independent or entirely free. It is true that around every man a fatal circle is traced beyond which he cannot pass; but within the wide verge of that circle he is powerful and free; as it is with man, so with communities." The very inscrutability of history refutes theories of determinism and leaves a margin in which people are free to make their own future. Or so I believed then, and still believe now.

Index

476; Wallace on, 477; in New Deal (Dewey), 480; and anti-Communism of Truman administration, 490–95; and free speech, 492; in government, 493–94; as negligible influence in U.S. (1949), 494–95; and Alger Hiss, 495–99; and ordeal of Noel and Hermann Field, 499–503; vs. nationalism, 505, 515; and fascism, 509; influence of heightened by WWII, 514. *See also* Stalinism

Communitarianism, 48

Compassionate conservative, Robert A. Taft as, 426

Computer age, 516, 521

Comstock, Ada, 121

Conant, James B., 171; and Buck, 43; Al Smith supported by, 56; and democratization of Harvard, 120; and DeVoto, 171; Cox portrait of, 237; isolationist reasoning expressed to, 243; as interventionist, 244–45; as colleague, 441

Concepts of Jacksonian Democracy, The (Benson), 364

Conein, Lucien, 332

Conlan, Jim, 56

Consensus historians, 363–65, 370

Conservative(s): AMS Sr. on, 34, 40; ancient arguments of, 127; on Mussolini dictatorship, 173; intelligent representatives of, 223; vs. liberals, 372, 517; and CPUSA article, 400; as controlling both parties (1946), 408; Taft as, 426; and vital center, 520

Conspiracy of Pontiac (Parkman), 62

Constitution, U.S., and Supreme Court, 418

Containment policy, 505

Cooke, Elwood, 215

Coolidge, Calvin, 47, 48, 90

Coolidge, Harold Jefferson, 329, 330

Cooper, John Sherman, 388

Cooper, William J., Jr., 452

Copland, Aaron, 506

Corcoran, Tom, 295, 421, 458

Cornford, F. M., 208

Cornford, John, 208

Corwin, Norman, 290

Costigan, Howard, 436

Cot, Pierre, 416

Coughlin, Father Charles, 98, 244, 249, 253

Course of Empire, The (DeVoto), 442

Courtneidge, Cicely, 319

Cousins, Norman, 405

Cowan, Lou, 308

Coward, Noel, 87, 103, 336

Cowles, Gardner, Jr. (Mike), 265, 269, 288, 289–91, 292–93, 357

Cowley, Malcolm, 133, 278, 290

Cowling, Maurice, 193

Cox, Gardner, 61, 237, 481

Cox, James M., 17, 47, 479

Cox, Phyllis Byrne, 237, 280, 481

Craig, Hardin, 28

Craven, Avery, 444, 445, 447, 448, 450

Cravens, Hamilton, 24

Crawford, Kenneth, 461

Crèvecoeur, Hector St. John de, 31

Cripps, Sir Stafford, 211

Croce, Benedetto, 174, 453

Croly, Herbert, 198

Croly, Jane Cunningham, 61

Cromwell, John, 69

Crossman, R.H.S., 322, 354

Crossman, Richard, 416

Crouch, Stanley, 36

Cruze, James, 141

Cultural politics, 364

Cultural warfare of 1920s, 47–53; and Sacco-Vanzetti case, 55; Yankees vs. Irish, 55–56; as seen in Thirties, 86–87

Cummings, Constance, 106, 326–27, 397

Cummings, E. E., 78, 86, 119, 238

Cunningham, Bill, 315, 317

Cunningham, Robert, 83

Cuomo, Mario, 462

Curley, James, 40

Curti, Merle, 159, 373, 451

Curtis, Charles P., 112, 170

Curwen, Henry Darcy, 84, 91

Cushing, Harvey, 184

Cushing, Mrs. Harvey, 184–85

Cushing, Howard, 380

Cushing, L. J., 316

Cutting, Bronson, 91

Cycles of American History, The (AMS Jr.), 32

Cyclical theory of American politics, 32, 39, 247

Czechoslovakia, Nazi takeover of, 211

Czech Refugee Trust Fund, 499, 500

Czolgosz, Leon, 4, 12

Daily Worker, 130, 400

Damrong, Prince, 100

Dance to the Music of Time, A (Powell), 389–90

Daniels, Bebe, 112

Daniels, Jonathan, 518

Daniels, Josephus, 434